629.2

AUTOMOTIVE
engines MAINTENANCE AND REPAIR

AUTOMOTIVE engines

MAINTENANCE AND REPAIR

FOURTH EDITION

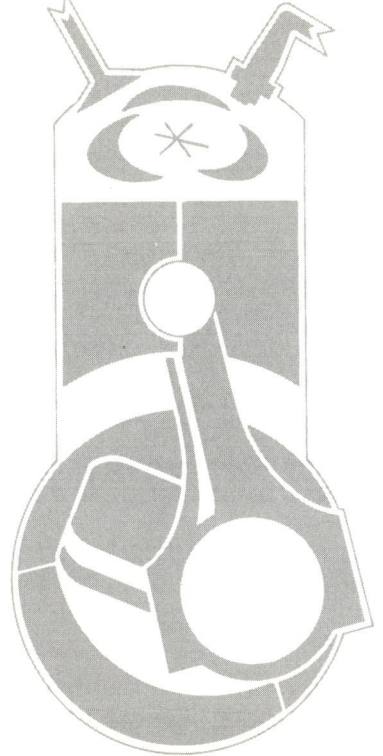

WALTER BILLIET
M. Ed.

New Jersey Director, Office of Area Vocational Technical Schools. Formerly Coordinator of Automotive Training, Henry Ford Community College, Dearborn, Michigan

AMERICAN TECHNICAL SOCIETY
CHICAGO, 60637

COPYRIGHT © 1951, 1957, 1964, 1973
BY AMERICAN TECHNICAL SOCIETY

Library of Congress Catalog Number: 72-88611

First Edition
1st Printing January, 1951
2d Printing October, 1951
3d Printing 1953
4th Printing 1955

Second Edition
5th Printing 1957
6th Printing 1958
7th Printing 1960
8th Printing 1962
9th Printing 1963
10th Printing 1963
11th Printing 1963

Third Edition
12th Printing 1964
13th Printing 1965
14th Printing 1967
15th Printing 1970

Fourth Edition
16th Printing 1973

No portion of this book may be reproduced by the mimeograph process or by any other process without permission from the publishers.

ISBN 0-8269-0062-3
PRINTED IN THE UNITED STATES OF AMERICA

Preface To the Fourth Edition

The automotive industry is the largest single industry in the United States. Hundreds of thousands of people are employed in automotive design, assembly and service. A large number of these people will work in the area of engine maintenance and repair. Therefore, the automotive industry constantly needs thousands of technically qualified men.

If you have comprehensive training in automotive engines and equipment, your knowledge and special skills can help you to a wide selection of jobs. Automotive specialists are needed in every area of the United States, therefore the skilled mechanic can usually choose his work location. Wages, working conditions, and opportunities for further study and advancement are all good.

The automotive specialist is and will remain in great demand and he will also be in a strong position for promotion if he keeps abreast of the ever-changing industry. *Automotive Engines—Maintenance and Repair,* Fourth Edition, can help you to attain this goal.

Automotive engines and ignition systems have changed and will continue to change. Fuel injection and transistorized ignition systems are now in use and may be considered standard equipment in the future. Emission control systems are federally mandated as standard equipment. A high degree of training will be needed to service these units. Throughout the text new up-to-date information and illustrations have been added to cover these and other new technical developments. In addition, a new section has been added covering the operating principles of the Wankel engine.

A complete new chapter has been added covering emission systems including tune-up, service, and trouble-shooting information which is an absolute "must" for the mechanic who will service late-model cars. Each system, along with the complex interrelationships between the components of each system is illustrated and discussed for complete understanding.

The material in each chapter is arranged so that the mechanic can follow through the operational information and the service procedures in a simple step-by-step learning sequence.

The *Appendix* has four illustrated units: comparisons and conversions of English and metric measuring systems, angular measurements, micrometer instructions, and engine power measurements. These appendices give needed background material and help to make *Automotive Engines —Maintenance and Repair* a reference tool worthy of a prominent position on the qualified mechanic's bookshelf.

The text material of the revised Fourth Edition has been reviewed by Leslie Goings, M. Ed., Instructor in Automotive Technology, Henry Ford Community College, Dearborn, Michigan. His comments have been most helpful.

The author, Walter Billiet, Ed. D., is the New Jersey Director of Technical Education, State Department of Education; he was formerly Coordinator of Automotive Training, Henry Ford Community College, Dearborn, Michigan. He has worked as an automobile mechanic and now has 32 years of experience in training mechanics.

THE PUBLISHERS

Contents

	PAGE
Chapter 1. The Automotive Mechanic and His Tools	**1**
Automotive Service	1
Safety in the Shop	6
The Mechanic's Tools	14
Cleaning of Automotive Parts	37
Chapter 2. Engine Operation and Design	**43**
Basic Engine Operation	49
Major Differences in Engine Design	55
Chapter 3. Cylinder Blocks, Crankshafts, and Flywheels	**75**
Cylinder Blocks	75
Crankshafts	85
Main Bearings	93
Flywheels	95
Vibration Dampers	97
Inspection and Repair of Cylinder Block	99
Inspection and Repair of Crankshaft	106
Inspection of Main Bearings	109
Inspection of Flywheel	116
Inspection of Vibration Damper	117
Chapter 4. Pistons and Connecting Rods	**119**
Types, Materials, and Design	119
Disassembly and Cleaning	140
Inspection and Repair	142
Assembly	163
Chapter 5. Cylinder Heads, Valves, and Valve Operating Mechanisms	**169**
Cylinder Head Construction	169
Valves and Valve Operating Mechanism	174
Cleaning, Inspection, and Repair of Cylinder Heads	195
Inspection and Repair of Valves	198
Valve Seats	200
Valve Springs	204
Valve Guides	206
Camshaft	208
Timing Gears	211
Timing Chain	213
Valve Lifters	216
Pushrods and Rocker Arms	219
Valve Stem Clearance Adjustment	221

Chapter 6. Engine Cooling Systems 226
    Types of Cooling Systems 226
    Parts of a Liquid Cooling System 229
    Pressure Type Cooling System 245
    Antifreeze Solutions 247
    Cooling System Service 248

Chapter 7. Engine Lubrication 258
    Engine Oils 259
    Lubricating Systems 265
    Parts of an Engine Lubricating System 266
    Inspection and Repair 275

Chapter 8. Emissions Systems 279
    Crankcase Ventilation Systems 282
    Exhaust Emission Control Systems 288
    Vapor Emission Control Systems 321

Chapter 9. Fuel and Fuel Systems 326
    Automotive Fuels 326
    Components of the Fuel System 340

Chapter 10. Carburetors and Carburetion 362
    Carburetor Fundamentals 362
    Air-Fuel Mixture Requirements 364
    Carburetor Systems 365
    Auxiliary Carburetor Features 383
    Multiple Barrel Carburetors 388
    Compound (Multiple) Carburetion 401
    Gasoline Fuel Injection 403
    Superchargers 404

Chapter 11. Fuel System and Carburetor Servicing . . . 406
    Repairing a Fuel Tank 406
    Fuel Filter Service 407
    Repairing and Replacing Fuel Lines 409
    Fuel Pump Troubleshooting 410
    Air Cleaner Service 412
    Fuel System Troubleshooting 413
    Diagnosing Carburetor Troubles 419
    Carburetor Service 421
    Carburetor Repair 423
    Carburetor Adjustments 428

Chapter 12. Ignition Systems 445
    The Primary Circuit and the Secondary Circuit . . 447
    Operation of the Conventional Ignition System . . 458
    Transistorized Battery-Coil Ignition Systems . . . 461
    Types of Transistorized Ignition Systems 465

Chapter 13. Ignition System Service 470
    Ignition Troubleshooting 472
    Ignition Service 476
    Ignition Timing 481

Appendix **484**

Index **501**

A man who works with his hands is a Laborer.

*A man who works with his hands
and his head is a Craftsman.*

*A man who works with his hands,
his head, and his heart is an Artist.*

JOB OPPORTUNITIES

Service Manager
Parts Manager
Auto Mechanic
Automotive Technician
Alignment Specialist
Carburetor and Ignition Specialist
Auto Electrical Specialist
Brake Specialist
Radiator Specialist
Transmission Specialist
Auto Air Conditioning Specialist
Power System Specialist
Body and Fender Straightener
Auto Tune-Up Specialist
Auto Testing Specialist
Garage Manager
New and Used Car Dealer
Automobile Sales Manager
Used Car Manager
Salesman
Automotive Instructor
Auto Parts Dealer
Automotive Machinist
Service Station Operator
Truck Line Maintenance Supervisor
Automotive Claim Adjuster
Auto Painting Expert
Tool Engineer

The Automotive Mechanic and His Tools

Chapter

1

Since the development of the first automobile in the United States, more than 200 million motor vehicles have been built. Of this number, some 104,500,000 registered cars, trucks, and buses are in use today. It is estimated that by 1975 there will be 118 million cars, trucks, and buses on the road. This is more than twice the total number of motor vehicles found in the rest of the world.

The modern automobile is a complex machine that plays a vital role in our daily lives. The transition of the automobile from a luxury to a necessity has caused a tremendous growth in the automobile industry, resulting in its present important position in our economy. It is estimated that one out of seven persons in this country is directly or indirectly employed in this industry.

Automotive Service

The business of maintaining motor vehicles has also grown in size and importance. Throughout America, in community after community, many vehicles are in constant need of service. Each year, more and more cars and trucks are appearing on our streets and highways, and they are being driven longer distances. Refinements such as automatic transmissions, power steering, power brakes, air conditioning, and high compression engines, while making cars more com-

Automotive Engines

Fig. 1-1. Electronic Engine Tester. (Sun Electric Corp.)

fortable, safer, and easier to drive, have further increased the owner's dependence upon trained personnel who can utilize modern test equipment such as that shown in Fig. 1-1. It is, therefore, no exaggeration that our automotive system of transportation would soon collapse without men properly trained for motor vehicle service.

The service field offers a challenging and rewarding career to the young man interested in automobiles. This field also demands that he have an alert mind, a sense of responsibility, and the desire to learn. Upon completion of a training period, a wide range of job opportunities awaits him.

The Automotive Mechanic

Any auto service business must stand or fall on the merit of the work done by the mechanics. The auto mechanic is, in a sense, a "jack of all trades." He must be able to perform correctly and efficiently almost any work needed on an automobile. Because of the shortage of trained mechanics, a person entering the field can be sure that he will receive high wages and have job security. While the duties of a mechanic are demanding, the man who fulfills them can look forward to advancement, both as a mechanic and within the automotive industry.

Duties of an Automotive Mechanic. In a broad sense, the duty of the mechanic is to restore an automobile so that it can perform as it did when it was new. This involves diagnosing and repairing automobiles in poor condition and performing maintenance on those in good condition.

Maintenance. For a car to stay in good running condition, it must have check-ups frequently and maintenance work regularly. Regular maintenance work will include such things as oil changes, chassis lubrication, tire service, tune-ups, etc. The vast majority of automotive service involves maintenance. No great skill is needed in carrying out most maintenance, but it enables the skilled mechanic to find a potential trouble spot and inform the customer before it can develop into something serious.

Diagnosis. When a customer has a complaint about his car, he has only a hazy idea of what the trouble is. He might tell the mechanic: "it is running noisy" or "it has no pick-up". A good mechanic will diagnose the trouble by using a logical system of checks and tests, so that he will know how to complete the repair with a minimum expenditure of time and effort. After diagnosis, the mechanic must tell the customer what the possible causes of trouble are and, barring the unexpected, what it will cost to make the repair.

Repair. After the trouble is diagnosed, repair begins. Usually this involves measurement, disassembly, replacement or machining, and reassembly. One of the major parts of repair work is deciding whether to repair or to replace some part. For instance, usually it is cheaper to replace the ignition points than to repair them, but carburetor work might include anything from simple adjustments to a complete disassembly, cleaning, parts replacement, reassembly, and adjustments.

Characteristics of a Good Mechanic. A successful career in automotive service today involves much more than mechanical skill or ability to replace parts. The modern service man who gets ahead must know not only about cars and trucks but also the retail business as well. He should also develop correct working habits and possess a well-balanced personality. Some of the characteristics of a good auto mechanic are listed as follows:

Competence. A good mechanic is judged according to the quality of his work. His know-how is a result of years of experience and learning. Yet, he is never satisfied; even though he is kept busy, he still finds time to keep up with the technological improvements in the automotive industry.

Efficiency. An auto mechanic realizes the importance of time both to the customer and to his own employer. He also knows that labor is an important cost factor in this highly competitive industry. He seeks to finish his job as quickly as possible to ensure the customer's satisfaction and make himself more valuable to his employer. A good mechanic develops a certain amount of business ability.

Attention. A good automotive mechanic must give his undivided attention to his work at all times. He knows that his personal problems have no place in his work. He does not become distracted while doing his own work, nor does he divert the attention of other mechanics.

Orderliness. Another desirable quality of an auto mechanic is his methodical approach. The good mechanic lays out his tools neatly so that he can quickly select any tool he needs without wasting time to search frantically for it at the last moment. He disassembles parts in an orderly manner and places bolts and nuts in right places to avoid errors in assembly. He does not clutter up his pockets or his tool box unnecessarily.

Cleanliness. A mechanic must wear suitable work clothes. He keeps his work area clean. He uses soap and other cleaners frequently so as not to work with dirty or greasy hands or to present an untidy appearance.

Courtesy. A polite and cheerful worker is well liked not only by his fellow workers but also by his customers. While he may disagree with others, he does not lose his patience. He shows his respect for his customer's pocketbook by explaining the services required on a car.

Safety. The most efficient worker is the careful one. He never endangers himself or his fellow workers. An auto mechanic should be familiar with all of the safe practices which apply to auto work.

Opportunities for the Mechanic. A mechanic can advance himself in his trade or, if he so desires, in some other phase of the automotive industry. The following are just a few of the jobs open to the mechanic:

Specialty Mechanic. A specialty mechanic is a service man whose job is restricted to one phase of repair work only, Fig. 1-2. One can specialize in diagnosis and tune-up, electrical repair, body work, automatic transmission, front-end suspension and steering, or any other line in the vast field of automotive service. The prerequisites for this job are: interest, special training or skill, experience, and proven ability.

The line between an auto mechanic and a specialty mechanic is not always clear cut. Sometimes one doubles as the other, depending on the employer.

Shop Foreman. He is the man in charge of mechanics in an automotive dealership, an independent service garage, or the private ga-

The Auto Mechanic and His Tools

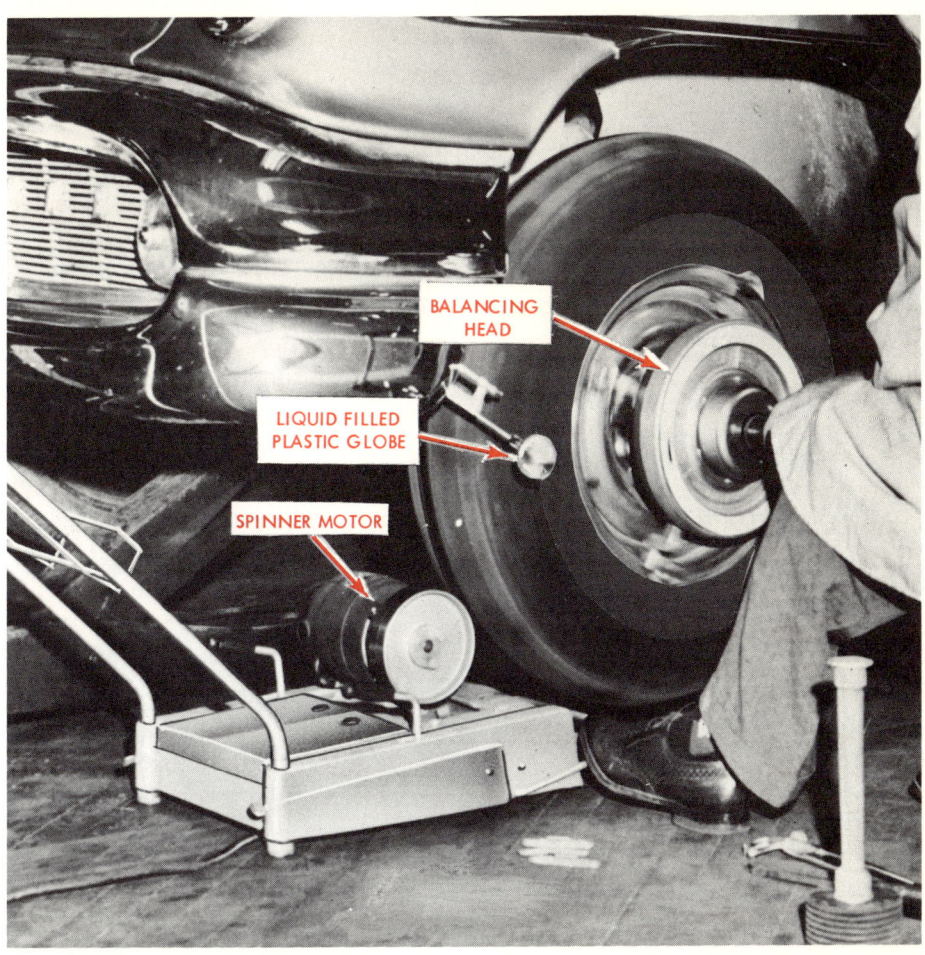

Fig. 1-2. On-the-car type of wheel balancer being used to statically balance the front wheel of a vehicle. Notice that the vehicle is supported by a floor jack placed at the center of the front suspension cross member. The small, round object attached to the bumper (above the spinner motor) is a liquid filled plastic globe. When the wheel is revolving smoothly, the liquid in the globe will not ripple. A balancer of this type may be used on wheel diameters which range from 12 to 16 inches without special adaptors. (John Bean Corp.)

rage of a transportation company. Usually, he is an expert mechanic who has been promoted to foreman after years of service. His job involves scheduling and routing repair work as it comes into the shop, supervising and instructing mechanics, inspecting finished repairs, and accepting responsibility for the quality of work, costs of operation, and shop safety.

Service Manager. He is the department head, supervising all service employees and responsible for customer satisfaction. He should be a good manager who knows his business and should, in addition, have the ability to get along with employees and customers. Besides supervisory work, he should also try to build up business for his employer. Estimates indicate that each year there are openings for over 19,600 trained auto mechanics for automotive service work.

Other Opportunities in the Automotive Industry. Often the mechanic's job is a stepping stone to other opportunities in the automotive industry. If he is hard working and conscientious, the door is open for even higher-paying positions suited to his interest and ability.

Opportunities exist as a parts manager, factory inspector, auto test technician, engineer, instructor, or repair shop owner. In the sales field, the mechanic may become a jobber salesman, a car, truck, or parts salesman, a sales manager, or even a car dealer.

Mechanic's Responsibilities. A mechanic assumes certain liability when servicing an automobile. Federal legislation states that emission control systems must not be removed or redesigned. All adjustments to the system must be kept within established limits.

The mechanic is held liable for all maintenance which he performs on a vehicle if an accident occurs as a result of faulty workmanship. The mechanic is also obligated to report to the vehicle owner any obvious defect he may discover when servicing a vehicle if the defect involves safety.

Safety in the Shop

Safety is a matter of common sense and good work habits. The worker who learns the proper way to use a tool learns the safe way to use it. Good work habits should be learned at the beginning. The auto mechanic works with such a diversity of tools and equipment that he is exposed to more hazards than the shop worker in general. Within minutes, the mechanic may work with hand tools, power tools, and then, perhaps, have to move some very heavy piece of machinery, such as an engine or an entire automobile, with a lifting device.

It is common sense, for example, to say that people shouldn't smoke

The Auto Mechanic and His Tools

around open containers of gasoline. The man busy with a job may think that it's all right to permit gasoline to stand in an open container "for a few minutes" while he finishes a job. He feels that the risk is slight. If the shop burns down, it makes little difference that the risk was slight. A mechanic is not paid to take chances, and no employer will want him to risk his life to save a few pennies on a job, Fig. 1-3. The man who takes the little short cuts and gets away with them is the one who eventually ends up with a serious injury.

Remember that your shop is not a playground. A little joke can become a large accident. Moving machinery has no sense of humor. It performs its job in the same way every time whether it is working on a piece of metal or a bit of flesh. Some general rules to follow are:

1. Be neat and clean in your work, and keep your work area clean.
2. Learn the proper way to use equipment and stick to it.
3. Look where you are going and at what you are doing.
4. Be deliberate in your work. It doesn't pay to make sudden moves around equipment.
5. Never use any "short cuts" that involve taking a risk, no matter how small.
6. Be wary of the man who is a careless worker and takes risks. He causes as many accidents for others as he does for himself.

Engineers have shown that the efficient worker is the one who is safety conscious. He turns out good work and, just as important, stays healthy to continue working. Remember that an accident can cost many days of lost pay in addition to any injury suffered. Since the auto shop involves special hazards, you must know the safe procedures for auto repair work.

Most of the dangers for an auto mechanic involve a running engine, chemicals, or lifting and moving heavy parts. Road tests also involve some hazards.

Working Around the Engine

Whenever you work on a running engine or one that has just been

Fig. 1-3.

shut off, move carefully and deliberately. Be careful around all moving parts, and remember that there are many hot parts on a running engine or one that has been running recently. Some of the things to be on the alert for are:

The Fan and Fan Belt. The fan itself can cause severe injury if it hits you. If the engine is running fast, the fan can strike you with great force. *Never stand over or around the fan when an engine is being raced,* Fig. 1-4. A cracked blade can leave its hub and cause a fatal injury! *Keep fingers, rags, and clothing away from the moving fan belt.*

Carburetor and Fuel Lines. Few people think of the carburetor as potentially dangerous, but if an engine backfires while the air cleaner is off the carburetor, a flame two or three feet long can shoot out of the carburetor throat. *Never look into the carburetor throat when starting or running an engine. Never use an open can of gas to prime a carburetor.* Use a "squirt" type oil can when priming the carburetor. This keeps your hands away from the carburetor throat. It also removes the danger of a can of gas catching fire and being thrown in panic.

If you replace any part of the fuel system, crank the engine a few times with a remote starter switch and check for any leaks. This is particularly important if the engine should have an electric fuel pump. Electric fuel pumps will keep pumping so long as they have current and encounter no back pressure.

Ignition High-Voltage Circuit. *Don't grab the spark plug wires or the coil-to-distributor wire with your bare hand when the engine is running.* The voltage in the system could be fatal to someone with a weak heart. A healthy person probably would not be harmed by the voltage produced, but the shock would probably make him jerk his hand back. He could then injure himself by contacting a hot manifold, a hot radiator, the fan or fan belt.

When testing ignition spark, in-

Fig. 1-4.

sulate yourself from the floor by standing on a good insulator and from the auto by using a clean fender pad. Grasp the spark plug wire itself with insulated pliers or by using several folds of a clean dry cloth to insulate your hand.

Radiator. *When the engine is hot, exercise extreme caution when removing the radiator cap.* It is best to drape a heavy cloth over the cap when removing it. This protects you from pressurized steam when the cap is turned. Turn the cap only one quarter of a turn so that it cannot pop off.

If an engine is overheated, it is best to let it cool off before trying to remove the radiator cap. Most caps have a pressure release device. Turn the cap a small amount until all the pressure is released. It is then safe to remove the cap. Always treat the radiator as if it were hot.

Manifolds and Exhausts. *Always treat the manifolds and exhaust system as if they were hot.* This is a good point to remember when working under a car just brought in off of the road.

Exhaust fumes are poisonous. Even a small amount of exhaust fumes in the air can cause severe headaches. *Always be sure that the work area is well ventilated. Be sure to connect an exhaust tube, if available, to the engine exhaust before running the engine in the shop.*

The Hood. *Always prop the hood open with a stick when working on an engine.* When doing major work with the engine in the car, it is safer and more convenient to take a few minutes to remove the hood.

Working With Chemicals

The two most common chemicals in the auto industry are gasoline and oil. Most accidents with chemicals in the industry are related to the obvious fact that gasoline burns and lubricants are slippery. The rest have to do with toxic and corrosive effects of chemicals.

Fire. Some of the dangers of working with gasoline near a running engine have been covered in the previous section. A common cause of fires is the draining of a gas tank or fuel lines into an open pan and then leaving it uncovered. *Always store gasoline and other flammable liquids in a closed container.* Never use gasoline or any other flammable liquid as a cleaner.

Follow all safety procedures when working with welding equipment. Remember that pure oxygen can cause a fire to spread with explosive force. Always wear goggles when welding. *Never look directly into a welding flame with the naked eye.*

If welding repairs are required on or near the gas tank, *drain it and either fill it with water or blow it out with compressed air.* An empty tank full of fumes is much

Automotive Engines

Fig. 1-5.

more flammable and explosive than one containing flammable liquids. Usually the gas tank is removed from the car before being welded.

Know where the fire extinguishers and the fire exits are. Do not try to be heroic in fighting a fire. It is safe to put out a small fire with dry chemical and/or CO_2 hand extinguishers, but larger fires have a way of spreading with amazing speed and leading to explosions.

All flammable liquids must be stored in a designated ventilated area in closed containers. Rags which have been soaked in flammable liquids should be stored in closed containers or put in outside trash containers. Spontaneous combustion of greasy rags is still the most common cause of fires.

Never smoke while you are work-

ing, and smoke only in designated areas, Fig. 1-5.

Oil and Other Lubricants. *Always keep your work area clean.* Oil and grease on the floor can cause someone to slip and fall. Fig. 1-6. Tools that are oily can cause you to lose your grip. When working under a car, wear goggles to keep oil and dirt from your eyes.

If you should have occasion to work with oxyacetylene welding equipment, *make sure that there are no oil products on you or the work area.* Oil and oxygen make an explosive mixture.

Battery Acid. *Battery acid, if it gets in your eyes, can cause immediate damage.* If you get acid on yourself, wash it away with plenty of clean water. The material which builds up on battery terminals will

Fig. 1-6.

The Auto Mechanic and His Tools

re-form as acid when dissolved and should be neutralized by washing with a baking soda and water solution. *Don't smoke around a battery being charged; it gives off hydrogen which is extremely explosive.*

Solvents and Fumes. Always work in well ventilated areas when working with cleaning solutions, glues, gasoline, or any other chemicals which give off strong fumes.

Many compounds, such as tetraethyl lead, found in anti-knock gasoline are cumulative poisons. Taking them into your system in small amounts over a period of years can result in liver damage and other harmful effects. Keep this in mind when siphoning gasoline.

Paints. *Work out of doors or in a spray booth when spraying paint. Always wear goggles and a mask.* Paint is, of course, very harmful to the eyes. Many paints contain lead and other compounds which are poisonous if they enter your system. Paints and thinners are generally flammable and should be mixed only in safe areas. Paint as a spray can explode.

Hydraulic Fluid. *Hydraulic fluid can be blinding.* Exercise care when bleeding brakes and working around hydraulic lines. *Never disconnect a power accessory hydraulic line while the engine is running.*

Refrigerant-12. Exercise caution when servicing vehicles equipped with air conditioning because of the possible danger of Refrigerant-12 under pressure being discharged from a broken line.

When servicing the air conditioning system remember that Refrigerant-12 must always be handled with caution. Therefore:

1. Keep the work area well ventilated, because the refrigerant tends to vaporize and can suffocate if it is discharged in a closed room.

2. Always wear protective goggles. Refrigerant-12 vaporizes so rapidly that it may freeze anything it contacts. If the vapor contacts your eye, severe damage may result. Your skin should also be protected from contact.

3. Keep all refrigerants away from open flames. If the vapor contacts a flame, it can form a poisonous gas.

4. Keep heat away from the air conditioning system. Heated Refrigerant-12 in a closed system will build up high pressure which may cause the system to rupture.

Road Tests

Perhaps you have heard of what the Air Force calls "target fixation". This sometimes happens when, while strafing or firing rockets, the pilot concentrates so heavily on the target mentally, that he mistakenly flies into the target. A mechanic can have a similar problem when road testing a car. He may become so mentally involved in testing the car that he forgets he is on the road and has a collision.

Automotive Engines

It is best to have two men in the car during a road test. One man can test the car while the other can watch the road.

Another place to test a car is on a race track or drag strip. A large vacant parking lot can sometimes serve the purpose. If you must use the public roads, make your tests when there is little or no traffic. If a customer wants to know how his car performs at top speed, and the test must be made on public roads, let him test it himself to avoid the possibility of your having an accident or receiving a traffic citation.

Sometimes a vehicle can be tested utilizing a *chassis dynamometer* which simulates all road and load conditions while the vehicle is in the shop.

Heavy Lifting

Never get under an auto which is supported by a jack. The car should be supported with car stands, Fig. 1-7, or be on blocks. Always chock the wheels, Fig. 1-8, to keep the car from rolling.

Always use the safety pins in a hydraulic lift or a chain hoist. A car dropping from six feet in the air will crush almost anything in its way. Be sure that the car is properly centered and supported when using a lift. *Never operate the engine of a car on a lift.*

Always use your legs and not your back when lifting anything heavy, Fig. 1-9. Use the lifting de-

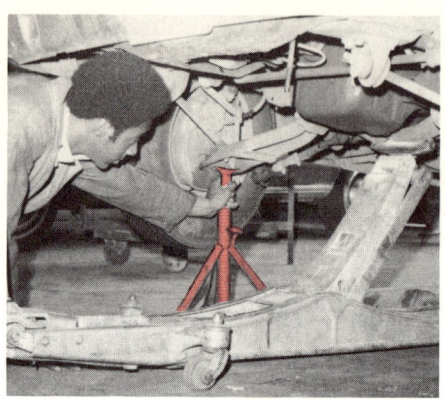

Fig. 1-7. Always support the car on something firm, such as a car stand, before working under it. (Paul Lawrence Dunbar Vocational High School, Chicago, Illinois)

Fig. 1-8. Always chock the wheels of any car you are working on to prevent it from rolling. (Paul Lawrence Dunbar Vocational High School, Chicago, Illinois)

vices available in an auto shop when moving very heavy objects.

No matter how careful a worker is, he will sometimes drop tools or other objects. The man who is

The Auto Mechanic and His Tools

Fig. 1-9.

wearing steel-toed shoes is protected if he drops something.

Tools and Power Equipment

As mentioned previously, you should know how to use tools in the correct and the safe manner. If you learn correct work habits, you will have little trouble with accidents. Specific things to remember about various tools will be mentioned in the next section. The major thing to remember is to use the proper tool at all times. A wrench is not a hammer, and an adjustable wrench is no substitute for a socket wrench. Improper use of tools invariably leads to their damage and often causes accidents.

Always know the danger spots on power tools. Know when you should be wearing goggles and where you should have your hands. Power tools should be kept clean and dry. An accumulation of dirt and grease could lead to a short circuit or a shock.

Portable power tools should always be grounded to avoid any chance of electrical shock, Fig. 1-10. When using power tools, let the tool do the work. Do not try to speed up the tool by applying a great amount of force. Often this leads to breakage and flying pieces of metal. Keep in mind that electrical power tools often have internal sparks which you cannot see but which can easily ignite the vapors from an inflammable liquid. The same is true of electrical switches of all types.

Always make use of the protective shields and other safety devices that come with power equip-

Fig. 1-10.

Automotive Engines

ment. *Never try to remove a safety device*, Fig. 1-11.

Clean all tools and equipment before putting them away. Any tool or piece of equipment not in use should be put away and not left lying about.

Fig. 1-11.

First Aid

Treat all injuries, major and minor, as soon as possible. A mechanic should never overlook a minor cut or burn because his work offers so many sources of infection. Remember that any dirt is a source of infection.

Such things as battery acid and lime should be washed off immediately on contact. Any solution which is acid or caustic should be removed by rinsing liberally with water.

Do not use grease or butter on burns. If a burn blisters, the blisters will eventually break. When this happens, the grease or butter will be a source of infection. If salted butter is used, there will be extreme pain. In general, if any injury requires more than minor attention, see a nurse or a doctor.

The Mechanic's Tools

The auto mechanic's tools are his means of earning a livelihood. Without them, he cannot perform his job. Skill in the use of hand tools comes only with experience. A skilled mechanic need not announce his skill; he demonstrates it in the way he selects, uses, and cares for his tools.

Good tools cost more money but are better in the long run because they will outlast cheaper ones.

There is also something about the feel of a good tool that inspires a mechanic to turn out better work. The mechanic should always use the proper tool for the job to be done, because using the wrong one may cause breakage or an injury.

The mechanic's tools fall into three general categories: hand tools, power tools, and measuring tools. Metal fastening devices are not tools in any strict sense, because

The Auto Mechanic and His Tools

they are, or become, part of the car. They are, however, included here because you should be familiar with them, and they are all used in conjunction with tools.

Basic Hand Tools

There are so many kinds of hand tools available today that it would take several catalogs to list all of them. Some of the more common ones are described below. Be familiar with as many of them as possible, since there is a tool for almost every job you do.

Hammers and Mallets. Consist of shaped heads attached to handles. Hammers are used to drive tools (usually for cutting purposes), to bend metals, to join or to separate close fit or force fit parts, and for other purposes.

Always be sure that the hammer head is firmly attached to the handle. If the head begins to flatten or mushroom, dress it to its original shape with a grinder. When holding a tool to be driven, such as a chisel, hold the tool near its head. Make sure the hammer head strikes its target squarely, Fig. 1-12.

If a job requires a great hammering force, select a heavy hammer rather than a light one so you will not have to use a fast or hard swing. When you want to hammer

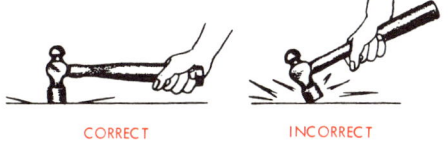

Fig. 1-12. The hammer should be held near the end of the handle and it should strike the object squarely.

BALL PEEN

(1) The Ball Peen Hammer. This is the general purpose hammer. The ball peen hammer is used mostly for driving chisels and punches and other general work. It is also called the machinists' hammer.

MALLET

(2) The Mallet. Mallets have soft faces and are properly used only when a steel hammer would mar the work. Mallet faces can be plastic, rawhide, brass, lead, wood or any other soft, durable material. Mallets will last a very long time if used on the proper materials.

MECHANIC'S

(3) The Mechanics' Hammer. The mechanics' hammer is used when a great striking force is needed. Very often a piece of wood is put over the object to be hammered to prevent marring and breakage.

Fig. 1-13. These are the three most common hammers used in an auto repair shop.

lightly, or if the surface to be hammered should be protected, use a mallet.

There are many special purpose hammers, such as those used by body men, but you will use three, Fig. 1-13 for most engine work; the ball peen hammer, the mallet, and the heavy duty or mechanic's hammer. All of these hammers come in many sizes and weights.

Pliers. Pincer-like instruments with jaws that are longer than pincers and which have teeth for gripping. Pliers, Fig. 1-14 are used for cutting, bending, tightening small nuts or bolts which need be only a little more than hand tight, and holding small parts. In general, pliers should not be used to tighten or loosen bolts or nuts since they often slip and damage the corners of the nut or bolt head.

Pliers should not be used on hardened surfaces, because this dulls the teeth and impairs their gripping ability.

Screwdrivers. For loosening and tightening slotted screws. Blades are available in various lengths and diameters to fit different types and sizes of screws. The most commonly used types are shown in Fig. 1-15. In selecting a screwdriver, make certain that the blade fits snugly in the screw slot and that the screwdriver is the proper size to give the desired leverage.

Keep the blade tips properly ground, Fig. 1-15 with the sides of the blade almost parallel at the end. Do not hammer on the end of a screwdriver or use a screwdriver as a pry bar. Never hold screwdriver in one hand and your work in the other, because the screwdriver may slip and gouge your hand.

Punches. Rod-like tools with a tapered or straight shank at one

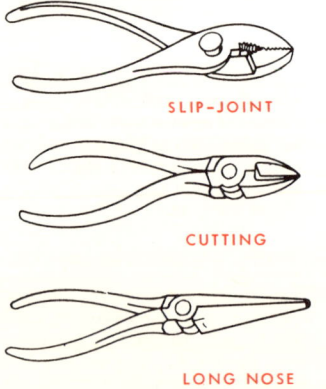

SLIP-JOINT

CUTTING

LONG NOSE

(1) Slip-Joint or Combination Pliers. Mostly used for gripping. This type is put to all-round use.

(2) Cutting Pliers. Sometimes called Diagonal Pliers. Used mostly for cutting off small rivets, pins, cotter pins and sometimes for gripping.

(3) Long Nose Pliers. Also called needle nose pliers. Used mostly for handling small parts and for bending and forming. Also useful in soldering and usually has a wire cutter. Handy for retrieving articles from hard to reach places.

Fig. 1-14. These are some of the pliers a mechanic uses.

The Auto Mechanic and His Tools

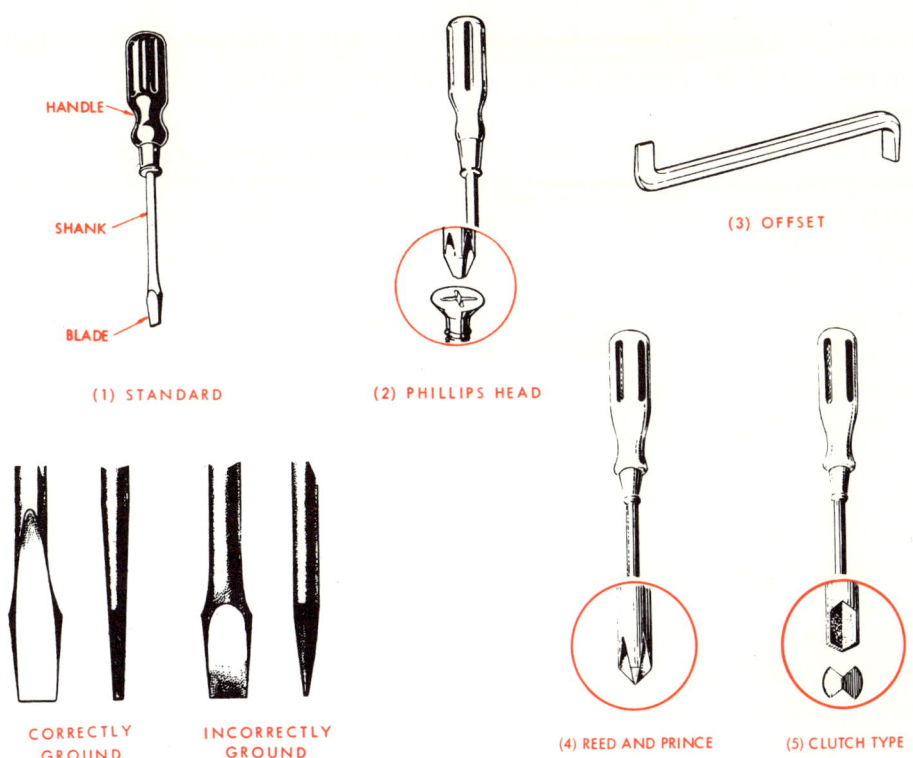

(1) Standard Screwdriver. Should be selected so that the blade is a close fit and as wide as the screw. When the blade becomes worn or chipped, the screwdriver should be reground on a grinding wheel.

(2) Phillips Screwdriver. Phillips head screws have specially formed crossed slots and require a screwdriver with a blade shaped to fit the slot. Phillips screwdrivers can be reshaped with a three-cornered saw file. File it to the pattern of a new screwdriver.

(3) Offset Screwdriver. Used to remove screws when there is insufficient space to use a regular screwdriver. The blades at opposite ends are at right angles to each other. When swinging space for the screwdriver is limited, the end can be changed after each swing to work the screw in or out of the threaded hole.

(4) Reed and Prince Screwdriver. Similar to the Phillips screwdriver except that the end is pointed. The screw head is deeper.

(5) Clutch Type Screwdriver. Must be used on screws with a clutch type head.

Fig. 1-15. Types of screwdrivers. When grinding a screwdriver, do not grind the blade too thin and be sure the tip is not rounded.

Automotive Engines

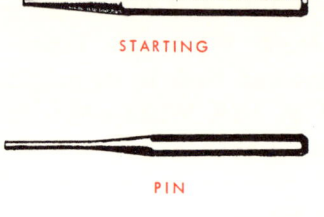

STARTING

(1) Starting Punch. Sometimes called a drift, is tapered to start and partially drive out bolts and pins that are tight in their holes.

PIN

(2) Pin Punch. If the starting punch is too large for the hole, a pin punch (which has a straight shank) can finish driving out the bolt or pin. Always use the largest drift or pin punch that can fit the hole.

CENTER

(3) Center Punch. The point at which a hole is to be drilled is usually marked with a center punch. This mark usually prevents the drill from wandering, permitting the hole to be drilled where you want it. Center punches are also used for marking two or more parts before disassembly, permitting reassembly in original position.

ALIGNING

(4) Aligning Punch. Very often when it is difficult to reassemble some mechanism because of problems of aligning holes for bolts or pins, one or two taps on the aligning punch will solve the problem.

Fig. 1-16. Typical punches. Be sure to select the proper punch for the job.

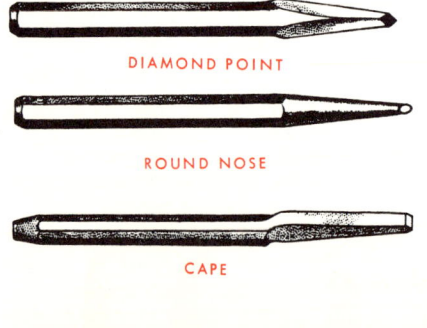

DIAMOND POINT

(1) Diamond Point Chisel. Used for drawing holes, making grooves, and cutting holes in flat plates.

ROUND NOSE

(2) Round Nose Chisel. Sometimes used to start holes for drilling, as is the center punch. Also used for cutting channels or grooves.

CAPE

(3) Cape Chisel. Used for cutting keyways, channels, etc. It can also be used to rough up a surface which is too wide for a cold chisel to chip.

FLAT

(4) Cold or Flat Chisel. The one most used by auto mechanics. Used for cutting and chipping. When grinding this chisel, the cutting edge should be 70 degrees and slightly rounded to give a better cutting action.

Fig. 1-17. Chisels.

The Auto Mechanic and His Tools

end, Fig. 1-16. Used for aligning, removing pins and bolts, starting holes to be drilled, and for marking. The head should be reground if it begins to flatten. Wear goggles when working with punches.

Chisels. Rod-like tools with a cutting edge at one end. A chisel is driven by a hammer and is used for cutting or chipping metal. Chisels are available in various shapes and sizes as shown in Fig. 1-17.

When cutting metal, hold the chisel in your left hand with the finger muscles relaxed. It is best to watch the edge, not the head, of the chisel when working. Oil the cutting edge of the chisel frequently with an oil-soaked rag. Do not try to work to close limits with a chisel, but finish the work with a file. All work should be solidly anchored in a vise. Use sharp, quick blows, taking care that the hammer does not slip off the end of the chisel and injure your hand. When chipping with a chisel, always wear goggles.

Repeated hammering will mushroom (flatten) the blunt end of the chisel. When this happens, grind the end back to its original shape, Fig. 1-18. When regrinding a tool such as a chisel, screwdriver, or punch, dip the tool in water when it becomes hot so the temper is not removed.

It is dangerous to use a chisel with a mushroomed head because pieces of metal may fly off and cause injury. A chip can fly off with the force of a bullet. In one case, a mechanic had to have a chip removed from his liver.

Taps and Dies. For cutting external and internal threads. The auto mechanic uses taps, Fig. 1-19, and dies, Fig. 1-20, chiefly to restore bolt or bolt hole threads which have been "stripped." When installing nonstandard or special equipment, a mechanic must occasionally drill a hole and then thread it. An internal thread cutter is called a tap and an external thread cutter a die.

To cut threads, mount the die in a die stock or the tap in a tap

  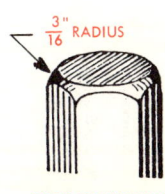

DRESS IT NOW   DON'T WAIT FOR THIS   DRESS IT THIS WAY

Fig. 1-18. Always dress the head of a punch or a chisel that begins to mushroom. Flying chips from a punch or a chisel have been known to penetrate deeply into the mechanic's body. (National Safety Council)

Automotive Engines

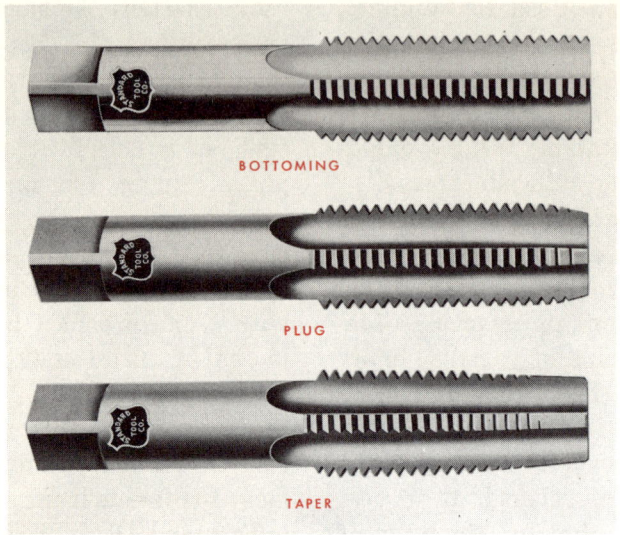

Fig. 1-19. Types of taps. Taps are brittle and damaged easily if not used carefully. Usually they are tapered so no one thread does all of the cutting and each succeeding thread cuts away a little more metal. The taper also eases entry and starting. (The Standard Tool Co.)

Fig. 1-20. When using a die to cut threads on bolts and screws, always mount the work in a vise and be certain that the die (left) is held firmly in the die holder (right). (The Standard Tool Co.)

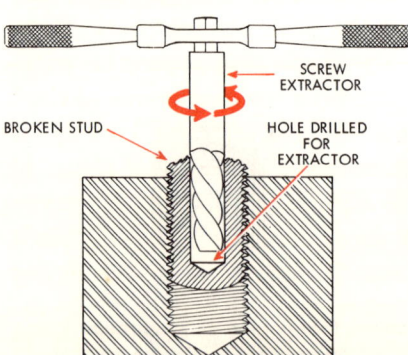

Fig. 1-21. A Screw Extractor. Usually it is wise to put penetrating oil on any screw which is to be removed with an extractor.

wrench. Hold the tap or die square with the hole or stock, and turn smoothly in the proper direction with both hands on the handle. Turn until the tap or die binds. Then turn backwards to break off the chips. Do not force the tap or die or you will break the tap or threads of the die. Repeat the above operations until the desired thread is cut. To cut smooth threads, lubricate steel with lard oil and aluminum with kerosene. Lubricate liberally to prevent the threads from tearing.

Screw Extractors. For extracting broken studs where wrenches or screw-drivers cannot remove them, Fig. 1-21. To use, first center-punch the stud and drill a hole ¾ of the stud's diameter to near the bottom of the stud. Insert the extractor, and tap lightly in position. With a wrench, gently turn the extractor counter-clockwise to remove the stud. If the stud fails to come out, apply penetrating oil, hammer the broken stud lightly to help loosen it, and then remove it with the extractor.

Hacksaw. Consists of a metal frame and a special saw blade that can cut metal or other hard surfaces, Fig. 1-22. The frame is usually adjustable for blades of various lengths, and has provisions for mounting the blade in several positions. When installing the blade, it should be placed upon the frame pins with the teeth pointing toward

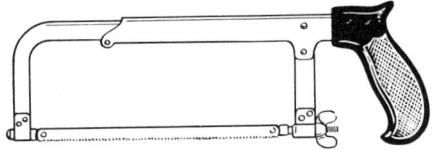

Fig. 1-22. A Hacksaw. Several types of blades can be installed in the frame of the saw. The frame is also adjustable to take different length blades.

the front of the frame. Tighten the blade to the proper tension so the blade is rigid without receiving too much strain.

The selection of a proper blade for the job is very important, Fig. 1-23. Hacksaw blades have from 14 to 32 teeth per inch. Using a blade with the wrong number of teeth may lead to breakage of teeth or blade.

When using a hacksaw, start cutting on the widest surface of the workpiece. Hold the hacksaw vertically, and move it forward with a light, steady stroke. At the end of the stroke, relieve the pressure and draw the blade straight back. Make the strokes as long as possible without striking the saw frame against the work. For efficient cutting of metals, saw at the rate of about 40 to 50 strokes per minute. When you put the saw away, protect the blade so that its teeth will not be dulled by other tools. Wipe the blade occasionally with an oily cloth to prevent rusting.

Automotive Engines

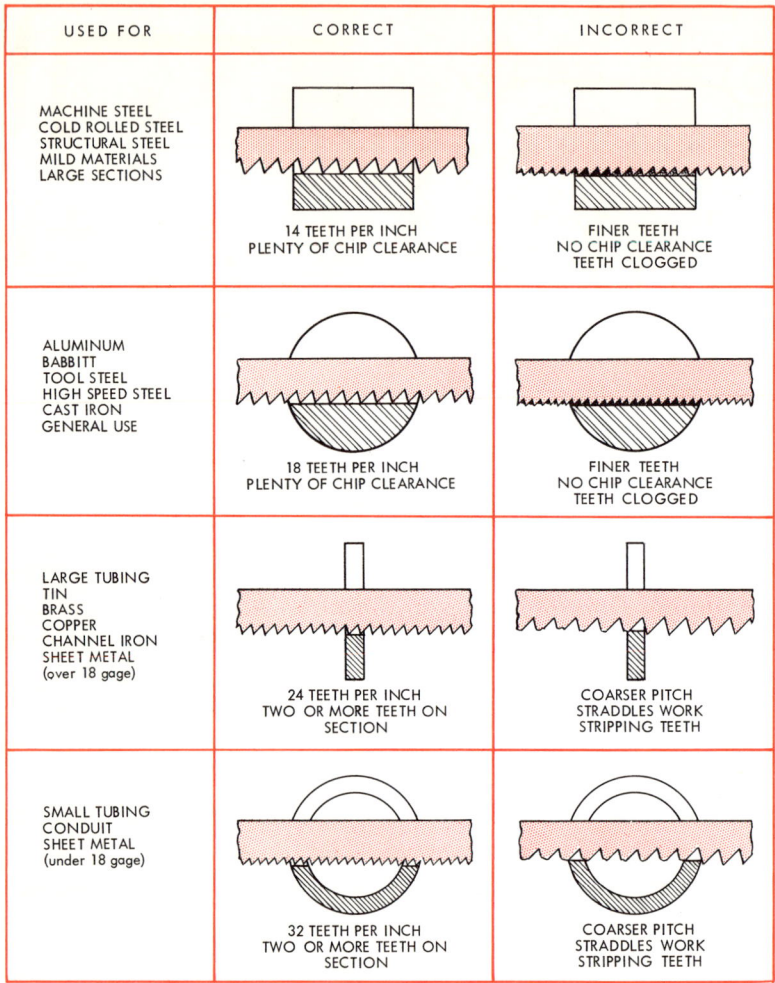

Fig. 1-23. Hacksaw blades should be selected according to the material to be cut and the size of the section. The saw teeth are not drawn to scale.

Wrenches. For loosening or tightening nuts and bolts, Fig. 1-24. Common types are open-end, box, adjustable, socket, pipe, and Allen wrenches. Always be sure that the wrench fits the nut or bolt. If a wrong size is used, it will damage the nut or bolt and may spread or break the jaws of the wrench. Always *pull* a wrench—don't *push*. If you must push, do it with the open palm, keeping your fingers out

The Auto Mechanic and His Tools

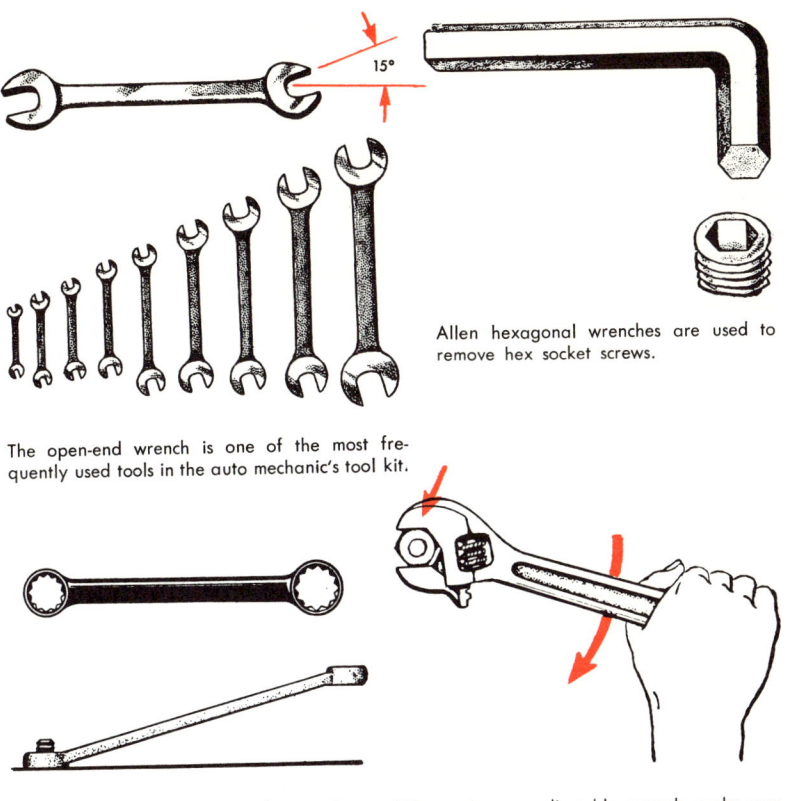

Allen hexagonal wrenches are used to remove hex socket screws.

The open-end wrench is one of the most frequently used tools in the auto mechanic's tool kit.

Box wrenches are ideal for working in close quarters.

When using an adjustable wrench, make sure that the load is imposed on the stationary jaw.

Fig. 1-24. Common types of wrenches. All are used to adjust nuts and bolts.

of the way to avoid injuries. *Never apply a wrench to moving machinery.*

Open-End Wrenches. Have openings of various sizes at each end to accommodate nuts and bolts, Fig. 1-24. The openings are set at 15° to the body to permit working in close quarters. By turning the wrench 180° so the other face is down after each stroke, the angle of the head is reversed and it is possible to turn the nut or bolt continuously even if the swing of the wrench is limited to 30°.

Box Wrenches. They completely surround the bolt head or nut; will not slip, Fig. 1-24. Suited for nuts that are hard to get at with an open-end wrench. Also known as 12-point wrenches; have 12 notches within the wrench opening, Fig. 1-

23

24. Can loosen or tighten a nut with only a 15° swing of the handle.

Adjustable Wrench. Shaped like an open-end wrench but with an adjustable jaw. Not for heavy-duty service but good as any emergency tool, since one adjustable wrench can serve as several open-end wrenches. When using, make sure that the wrench fits the nut snugly, Fig. 1-24.

Socket Wrenches. Indispensable in repair work. Usually has a 12-point opening for the nut on one end and a ⅜″ or ½″ square opening on the other for the handle. Socket sets usually contain sufficient sockets, Fig. 1-25, to fit all sizes of hexagonal nuts and bolt heads encountered in a normal repair job. Larger and smaller sizes are available.

Six-point sockets are also available which usually are more serviceable for heavy use. Generally heavy duty six-point sockets are used with an impact wrench. Most sockets can also be obtained in a deep design which permits additional applications.

Torque Wrenches. Used to tighten nuts and screws to manufacturer's specifications. The wrench, Fig. 1-26, uses a socket at one end for tightening. The amount of torque exerted registers on a calibrated gage near the handle.

Drills. Tools with pointed centers

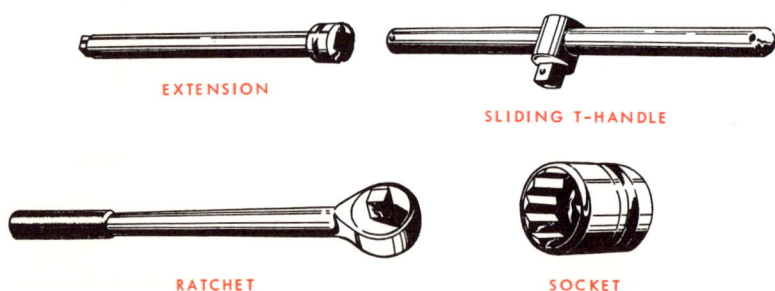

Fig. 1-25. Here are some of the elements found in a socket wrench set.

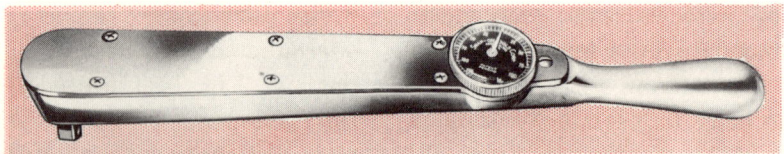

Fig. 1-26. Torque wrenches are used to set bolts to a specified tension. Lubricate the threads to obtain an accurate torque reading. (Snap-on Tool Corp.)

The Auto Mechanic and His Tools

for making holes. Twist drills are used for cutting metal by rotation. Such drills are made from carbon steel and high-speed steels. Drills of high-speed steels are more expensive, but with proper use they give lasting cutting effectiveness. Drills are available with straight aluminum, both lips of the drill should be of the same length and ground to an angle of 59°. The heel of the drill (surface back of cutting edges) should be ground away from the cutting edges at an angle of from 12° to 15°. Improperly ground drills may bind in the hole and

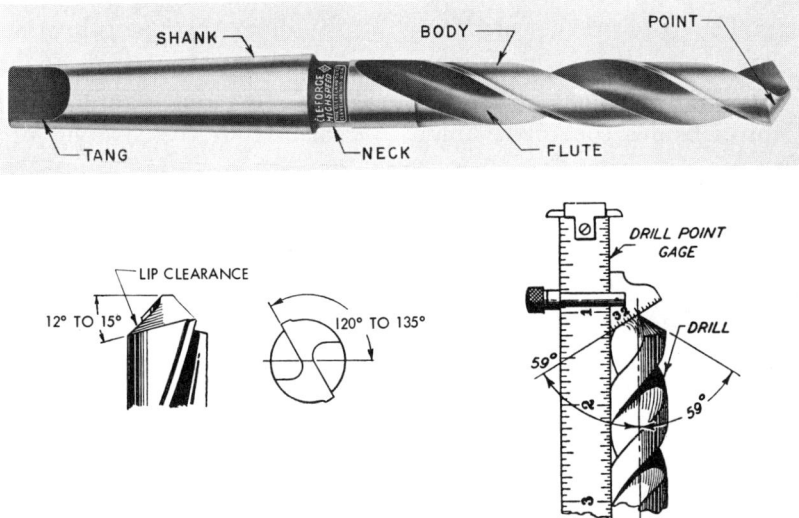

Fig. 1-27. A drill must be ground properly if it is to cut effectively. (Cleveland Twist Drill Co.)

or tapered shanks. Drill sizes are numbered from #80 to #1 (0.0135″ to 0.228″), in alphabetical lettering from A to Z (0.234 to 0.413 in.), or in fractions from $\frac{1}{64}$″ to over 1″.

A drill must be properly ground. Figure 1-27 shows the angles of a twist drill point. For general purpose drilling in steel, cast iron, or overheat, drill the hole oversize, or if the lip clearance is too great chip off at the cutting edges.

Reamers. Cutting tools to fit parts closely by enlarging and truing (bringing to exact form) a hole. Made of carbon and high speed steels. Available as solid reamers or expansion-type reamers, Fig. 1-28. Solid reamers are available in standard sizes as well as in variations of 0.001″ for special work. Expansion reamers of the one-piece type can be expanded only a few thousandths of an inch, while the adjustable-flute type can be expanded $\frac{1}{32}$″.

When reaming a hole, the reamer should be turned in the cutting direction only with an even, steady turning. This is to prevent chattering—rapid vibration which may mark or score the hole. Reamers with spiral blades cost more than those with straight flutes but are less likely to chatter.

Files. Hardened steel tools for removing, smoothing, or polishing metal, Fig. 1-29. The cutting edges or teeth on a file are made of diagonal rows of chisel cuts.

Files may be classified according to cross section as *flat, half round, square, round,* or *triangular* and may be straight or tapered throughout their length. Also classified as *single cut* or *double cut files.* They may again be graded according to the spacing of their

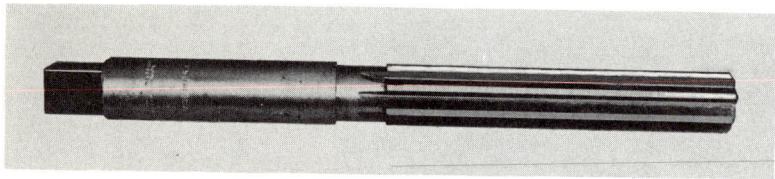

SQUARE

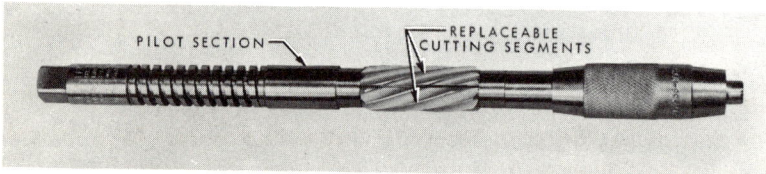

HELICAL

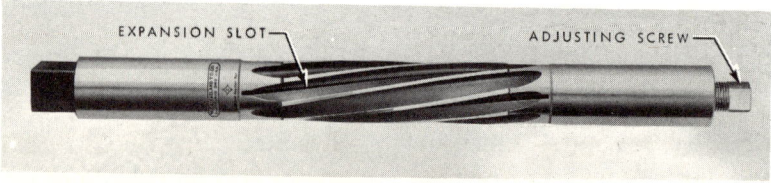

EXPANSION

Fig. 1-28. Solid and expansion type reamers. Reamers with spiral blades are more expensive, but they cut better. (Keystone Reamer and Tool Co., top; Lempco Products, Inc., middle; Cleveland Twist Drill Co., bottom)

The Auto Mechanic and His Tools

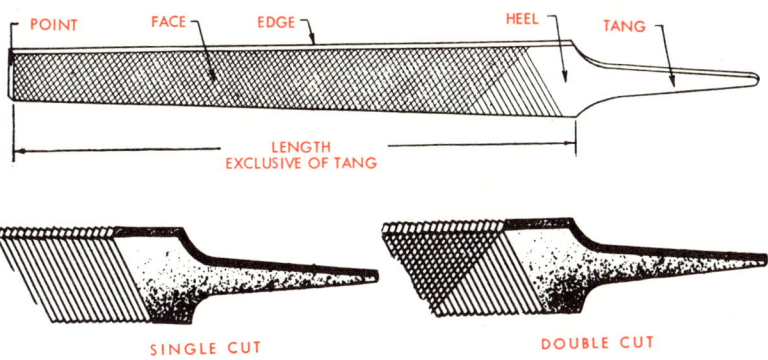

Fig. 1-29. Files are used for cutting, removing, smoothing, and polishing metal.

cutting teeth as *rough, coarse, bastard, second cut, smooth,* or *dead-smooth.* Coarse files have large teeth, and smooth files have small teeth. The coarser the teeth the more the metal removed at each stroke of the file.

Never use a file without a handle, since the tang is sharp and might cut your hand. To install a handle, select one of the right size, and place it on the tang. Tap the back end of the handle on a bench to make sure that it is on straight. Use the file in the forward direction only. On the back stroke, lift it from the workpiece to prevent dulling the file teeth, unless used on soft metals such as aluminum or lead.

Bench Vise. When performing bench work operations such as filing, sawing, and chipping, a mechanic employs a holding device to grip the work securely. The bench vise is commonly used to hold the workpiece. All vises consist of a fixed and a movable jaw, a screw, and a handle by which the screw is turned to bring the movable jaw into the desired position. The jaw faces are usually serrated to provide a firm grip for heavy work but may be of smooth finish to prevent marring of the workpiece. Marring can also be avoided by putting pieces of wood or rubber over the jaws. Some vises have swivel bases for easy adjustment.

Power Tools

Power or machine tools save much hand labor. Usually driven by electric motors, they are used where the volume of work performed is great enough or the labor saved is sufficient to warrant the cost. The auto mechanic should know what they are and what they can do, because they usually can

27

be adapted to his special field. The basic machine tools include the drill press, the engine lathe, the shaper, the planer, the milling machine, and the grinding machine.

The revolving cutters of milling machines cut gears and slots, saw stock, finish flat surfaces, etc. Lathes usually turn the work while it is being machined. Shapers and planers use a reciprocating—back and forth—motion to machine the work. Grinding machines remove metal with an abrasive wheel. Other machine tools, such as turret lathes, boring mills, and automatic screw machines, are modifications of the basic machine tools.

Power tools are usually complex, and you should not attempt to use one until you have been properly instructed in its operation. Wear goggles when working with any power tool that throws off chips or sparks; especially grinding wheels. When using a power drill, always start the hole with a center punch so the drill will not wander or slip. Never hold the work in your hands.

Remember that power tools are used as a substitute for your effort. Do not try to force a power tool against the work because the tool or work may slip or break and you might be injured. Common portable power tools used in automotive work include electric drills and electric air impact tools.

An impact wrench operated by electricity or air is a necessary tool for the mechanic. The impact wrench reduces greatly the time and effort required for removing and installing bolts, nuts, and studs.

Measuring Tools

When a particular section of the engine is disassembled for repairs, its parts must be measured carefully. Only by so doing can we accurately determine the clearance between parts, the condition of wear, and the need for service or repair. Different types of measuring tools are used for automotive needs. The tools most often used are the steel rule, micrometer caliper, telescoping gage, dial indicator, and thickness gage.

Steel Rule. Used for securing dimensions and measurements and as a straightedge. Sometimes referred to as a scale, it is made in various lengths, widths, thicknesses, and graduations. Commonly used for making semi-precise measurements—not having to be accurate to more than $\frac{1}{64}''$, Fig. 1-30 (See Appendix A.)

In lengths of 18" or more, the steel rule can be used as a straightedge to check such things as the amount of warp in cylinder heads and the distortion of the cylinder block.

Micrometer Caliper. Devices which measure accurately to one-thousandth (0.001) of an inch, Fig. 1-31. Some have vernier scales and

The Auto Mechanic and His Tools

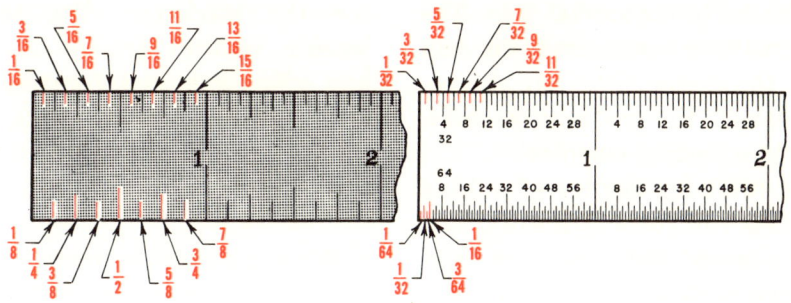

Fig. 1-30. Steel rules are used where measurements need be no more accurate than 1/64 inch.

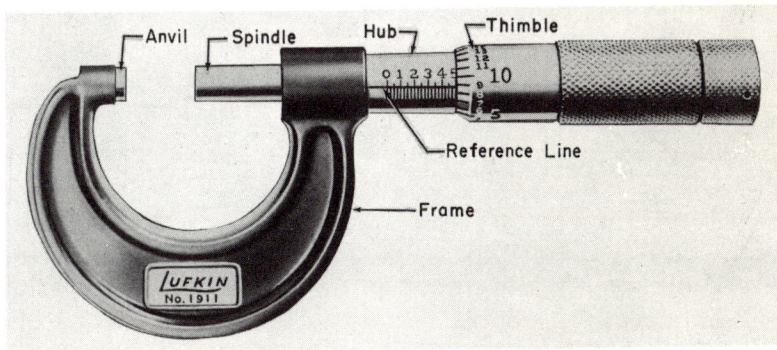

Fig. 1-31. The micrometer caliper is accurate to 1/1000 inch.

are capable of measuring accurately to one ten-thousandth of an inch (0.0001″).

Used chiefly for measuring the size of engine parts to determine the amount of wear or clearance between parts. The object to be measured is placed between the anvil and the spindle, and the thimble is turned until the spindle tightens slightly on the object. The size of the object is read from the scales on both the hub (also known as "sleeve") and the thimble. (Detailed instructions on the use of the micrometer caliper can be found in Appendix C of this book.)

Most micrometer calipers have an adjustable measuring range of only one inch. Special micrometer

29

Automotive Engines

calipers with larger ranges are used for measurements of more than one inch.

Inside micrometers, Fig. 1-32, are, as the name suggests, for measuring hole diameters, such as the bore of an engine cylinder, a main bearing, connecting rod, or a camshaft bearing.

Telescoping Gage. Measures the inside diameter of a hole or bore, Fig. 1-33. Made in various sizes to measure holes as small as $5/16''$ diameter. Consists of two spring-loaded telescoping members and a locking handle. In use, the gage is placed in the hole or bore with the handle parallel to the sides of the

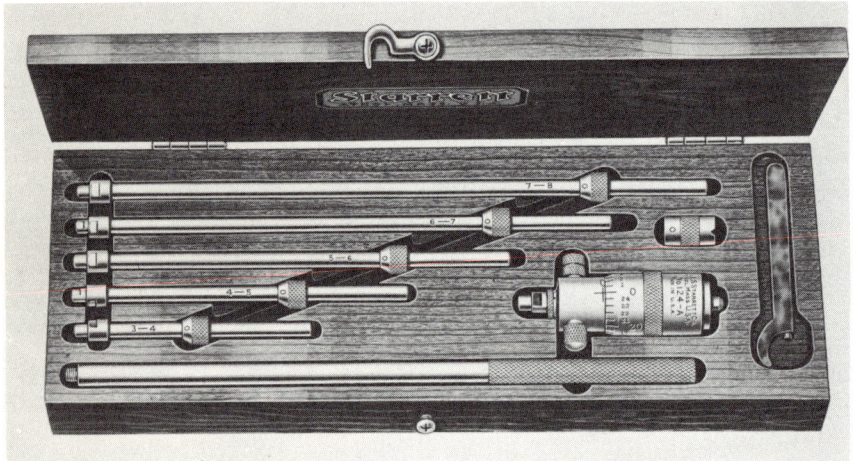

Fig. 1-32. Inside micrometer with extension rods to permit measurement of various diameters.

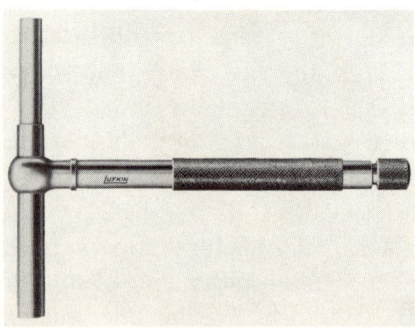

Fig. 1-33. A telescoping gage is used to measure small diameters. It is expanded to the size of the hole and removed; then the distance across the telescoping members is measured with a micrometer caliper. (Lufkin Rule Co.)

The Auto Mechanic and His Tools

bore. The gage is moved up and down several times to center it in the bore. An inner coil spring holds the telescoping members against the sides of the hole. The handle is then turned to lock the gage. Upon removal, the distance—hole diameter—across telescoping members is measured with a micrometer caliper. (See Appendix C.)

Dial Indicator. For checking the out-of-round and taper condition of the cylinder walls in an engine. With proper attachments, also used for checking the amount of lost motion—backlash—between two gears, the amount of runout of a flywheel, Fig. 1-34, or a sprung shaft, and numerous other measurements.

Consists of a movable dial which can be adjusted to zero and a pointer connected by means of gears to a plunger or shaft. The plunger moves inward against the tension of a light spring. As the plunger moves inward, the pointer moves to the plus (+) side of the dial. Outward movement of the plunger due to spring tension pushes the pointer toward the minus (−) side of the dial. On most indicators, the dial is graduated in thousandths, each space indicating a plunger movement of .001".

Thickness Gage. Used on such adjustments as valves, ignition contacts, piston clearance, or brakes.

One type of thickness gage consists of one or more accurately

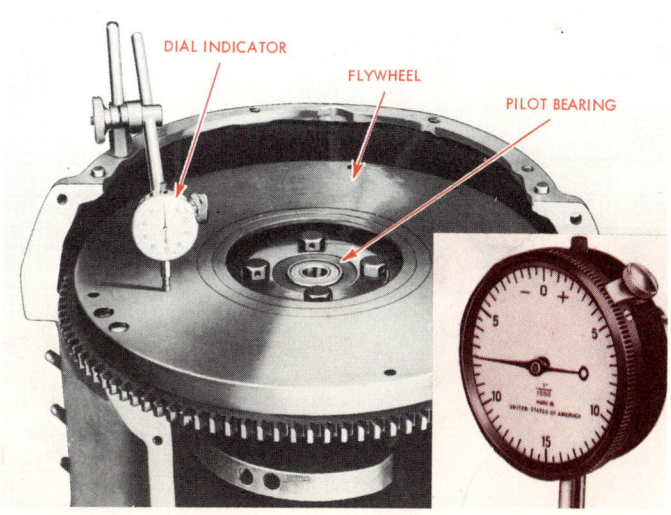

Fig. 1-34. Checking flywheel runout with a dial indicator. (Ford Motor Co., Brown and Sharpe Mfg. Co.)

Automotive Engines

ground blades, Fig. 1-35. The flexible blades can be used individually or in combinations to obtain almost any desired thickness within the limits of the gage.

To insure accurate measurements, the blades should be clean and flat. Clearances are measured by selecting the blade or combination of blades that will just pass between two surfaces with a light drag on the gage. Thin blades should be pushed into the gap with a sliding motion to prevent bending.

Another type of thickness gage consists of one or more accurately drawn pieces of wire, Fig. 1-35. Each wire is used singly and not in combination to measure clearances. The wire gage is preferred for measuring spark plug gap and ignition contact clearance because it gives a more accurate measurement between uneven surfaces than the blade type gage.

Fastening Devices

The automobile mechanic, in the performance of his work, is con-

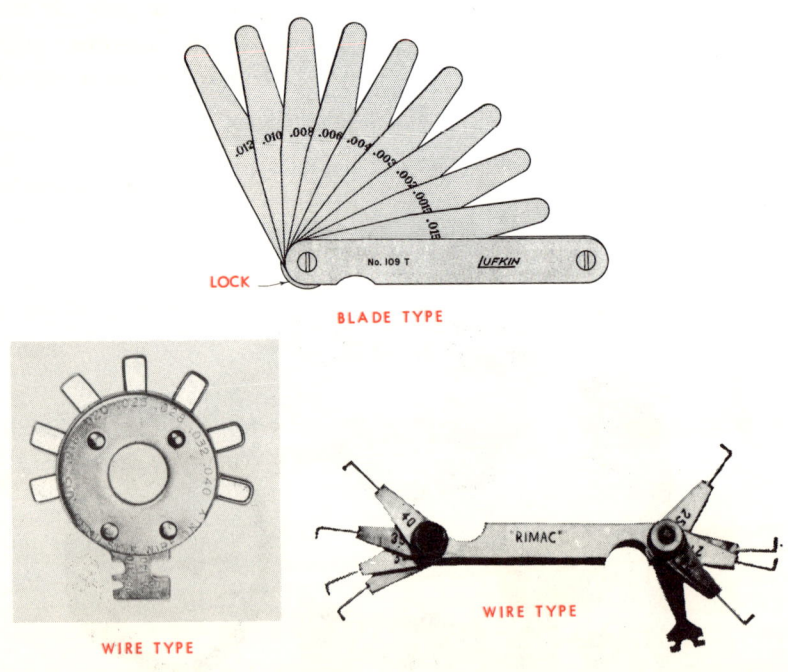

Fig. 1-35. When measuring ignition contact clearance, use a wire thickness gage rather than the blade type. Slight build-ups on the contacts will give a less accurate reading if the blade type is used. (Lufkin Rule Co., top; and Rinck-McIlwaine, Inc., bottom)

cerned with the removal and replacement of parts. The automobile is assembled with various types of metal fastening devices which attach and hold parts together securely, maintain adjustment, and hold parts in proper alignment.

Threaded Fasteners. Nuts, bolts, studs, and screws are the most common fastening devices used in the auto shop. They are all threaded.

Nuts. Square or hexagonal blocks, Fig. 1-36, with an internal or female screw thread. Nuts are used on bolts, Fig. 1-37, or screws for tightening or holding. Some have a self-locking feature which keeps them from becoming loose.

Bolts. Threaded rods with a square or hexagonal head at one end for loosening or tightening, Fig. 1-37.

Studs. Made from round rods in the same diameters as bolt sizes, Fig. 1-38.

Screws. In smaller diameters, some threaded fasteners are called

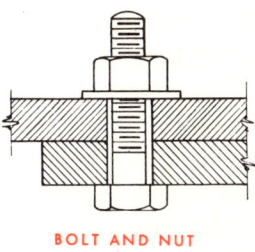

BOLT AND NUT

Fig. 1-37. Bolts are used in conjunction with nuts to hold two or more parts together securely between the bolt head and the nut.

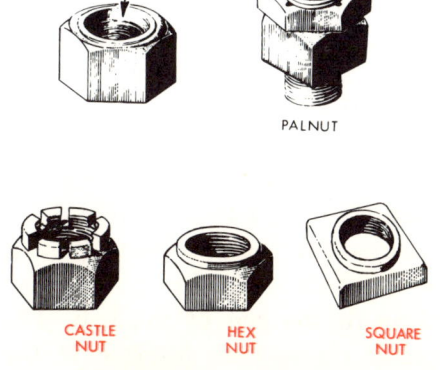

Fig. 1-36. Common types of nuts used in the automotive shop. Self-locking nuts are designed to remain tight in spite of vibration.

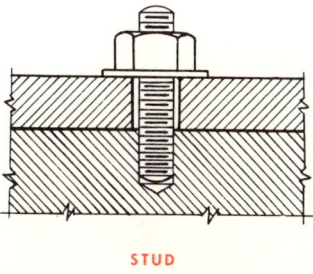

STUD

Fig. 1-38. A stud is threaded at both ends. One end screws into a threaded hole and, when the mating part is placed over the stud, the nut is tightened onto the other end, holding the parts securely.

machine screws or stove bolts, Fig. 1-39.

Threads. Projecting helical or spiral ribs of screws, bolts, or other fastening devices are called threads. Screws, bolts, and nuts have external threads, but nuts and machined holes have internal threads. Threads are designated by size, pitch, and series.

Thread Sizes. The diameter of a bolt or a screw determines the thread size. Sizes having less than a ¼ in. diameter are indicated by standard numbers running from zero to 12 plus a thread designation number. The first number indicates the diameter, and the second figure indicates the number of threads per inch. Sizes of ¼ in. diameter and larger are indicated in inch fractions: ¼-20 would indicate a ¼ in. bolt with twenty threads per inch.

Thread Pitch. The distance from a point on a screw thread to a corresponding point on the adjacent thread measured parallel to the axis is called pitch. Pitch can be determined by counting the number of threads per inch, Fig. 1-40A. A fast method is to use a thread pitch gage, Fig. 1-40B. Each blade of the gage has a different number of teeth per inch. The blade that fits the threads indicates the pitch and the number of threads per inch.

Thread Series. Two standard screw threads are in use in the United States that are commonly employed for automotive fasteners. One is the *United National Coarse*, UNC thread series, and the other is the *United National Fine*, UNF series.

The UNC series is used where rapid and easy assembly is desired since a coarse bolt thread requires fewer turns to install or remove. The UNF series is used on automobiles and airplanes, where minimum weight and maximum bolt strength are desired.

Cotter Pins. Used to prevent the nut from becoming loose on the bolt. A slotted nut is securely tightened so the slots are in alignment with a hole which has been drilled through the end of the bolt. The cotter pin is then inserted in the hole and the two arms of the pin bent. Fig. 1-41.

Lock Washers. Used between the nut or head of a bolt or screw and the machined part. The edges of a lock washer grip the part and the nut or bolt head to prevent them from becoming loose, Fig. 1-42.

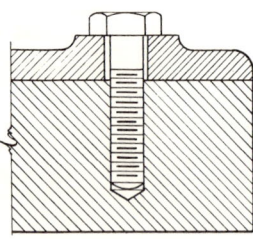

Fig. 1-39. Usually, parts held together by machine screws have threaded holes in one of the parts to receive the screws.

The Auto Mechanic and His Tools

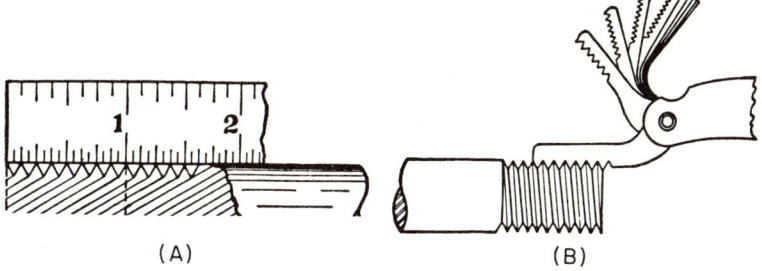

Fig. 1-40. (A) Counting threads per inch. (B) The pitch gage indicates threads per inch.

Fig. 1-41. Often, a cotter pin is used to lock a nut which is subject to loosening through vibration.

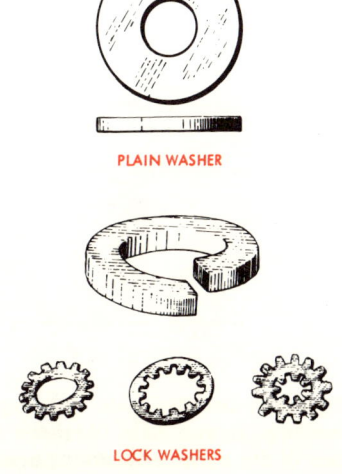

Fig. 1-42. Use a lock washer to prevent a nut, bolt, or screw from becoming loose due to vibration.

Automotive Engines

Fig. 1-43. Keys align pulleys, gears, and sleeves and lock them from twisting against their shafts.

Keys. A straight or half-moon shaped piece of metal that fits into slots in the shaft and hub on a pulley or gear, Fig. 1-43. The key locks the pulley or gear to the shaft.

Splines. Splines are formed by machining evenly spaced grooves around a shaft (external splines) or hole (internal splines) leaving a certain amount of metal between the grooves, Fig. 1-44. When a splined gear or part is placed on a splined shaft, the metal between the grooves acts like keys, locking the parts so they are forced to rotate together. In some cases, the splined parts are designed to form a tight fit while in others the splines fit loosely permitting the parts to slide on the splined shaft.

Snap Rings. Snap rings are round, metal rings that fit in grooves cut in shafts, pistons, housings, or other parts to hold the parts assembled to them, Fig. 1-45.

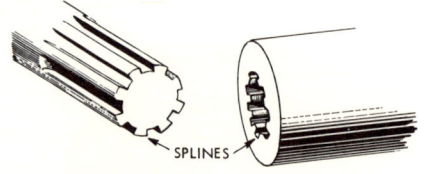

Fig. 1-44. Splines are used to lock two parts so they will rotate together.

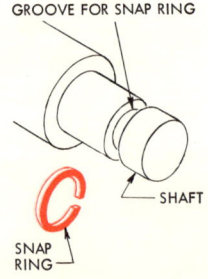
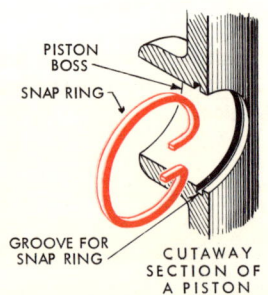

Fig. 1-45. Snap rings are also used as easy disconnect devices.

The Auto Mechanic and His Tools

Cleaning of Automotive Parts

In time, automotive engines and other components become coated with a layer of oil, grease, and dirt. This grime must be removed before an efficient job of disassembly, inspection, and repair can be performed. Hand cleaning can be one of the most expensive steps in the entire repair operation. If a skilled mechanic spends his time scraping, scrubbing, and wiping, he is not using his specialized skills. No matter what size the repair shop, the selection of efficient cleaning methods will conserve the mechanic's time and shorten time spent on repair jobs.

The speed, thoroughness, and economy of the cleaning operation depends upon the cleaner selected and the method of application. The accumulations on engines and their parts are so varied that no one cleaner or method will remove them all.

Some cleaners are used at room temperatures; others are heated. Some are sprayed; others are used as tank or immersion cleaners. A few cleaners can be used in more than one way. The most common methods of cleaning auto parts are steam cleaning, water pressure cleaning, and solution cleaning.

Fig. 1-46. One of the fastest methods of cleaning an engine is with a steam cleaner. (Homestead Valve Manufacturing Co.)

Steam Cleaning

Modern steam cleaners, Fig. 1-46, furnish a compact, mobile source of high-pressure vapor spray that quickly removes oil, grease, and dirt from the engine exterior and the chassis. Steam makes an excellent cleaner because of its high temperature and impact when directed from a pressure nozzle.

When the steam nozzle is directed at the parts to be cleaned, the heat melts or softens the grease and oil. Then the steam pressure can carry the grease, oil and dirt away leaving the cleaned parts to cool off. Evaporation dries them quickly. The steam never heats the parts enough to damage them, but steps should be taken to protect electrical parts from damage due to the moisture.

The use of detergents in steam cleaners greatly accelerates the cleaning action. Generally, the detergent contains a wetting agent that assures speedier penetration of the dirt deposits. The detergent also breaks up and detaches masses of oil, grease, and solid dirt by its emulsifying action. Generally, steam cleaning is performed outdoors because steam forms a great deal of vapor.

Water Pressure Cleaning

Pressure washing is accomplished by mechanically pumping water and cleaning compound at several hundred pounds pressure through a restricted opening in a gun nozzle. Usually, the cleaning unit is designed to fit on top of a 55 gallon drum in which the cleaning solution is mixed. It can also be a self-contained unit provided with a tank of concentrated cleaning solution that is automatically mixed with the water as the solution enters the cleaning gun. The unit has a built-in electrical heating unit which speeds up the cleaning action.

Solution Cleaning

Cleaning solutions in automotive work are usually emulsions, solvents, or a combination of the two. These solutions are used at room temperature or may require heating and are either sprayed on the work or the work is immersed in the solutions. Such cleaners soften and dissolve the binders that hold the dirt deposits together and to the parts. These solution cleaners remove dirt entirely or leave it softened to such an extent that it can be flushed off with a pressure rinse.

Cleaning solutions are available with various degrees of alkalinity. Cleaning solutions high in alkalinity remove grease and dirt more rapidly than those of low alkalinity. Cleansers with a high degree of alkalinity are excellent in removing dirt and grease from steel or iron

The Auto Mechanic and His Tools

parts, but they will damage parts made of aluminum.

When a combination of steel, iron, and aluminum parts is to be cleaned, a material should be used that will have no harmful effect on the most sensitive metal or alloy. Specially prepared cleaning compounds are available which will provide a rapid cleaning action with complete protection to the parts being cleaned. Babbitt bearings are subject to damage in some cleaning solutions and should be removed from the assembly being cleaned if the particular cleaning solution being used attacks such bearings.

Emulsion Cleaners. Emulsion type cleaners consist of a concentrated liquid soap that has the property of taking the "cling" or adhesive quality out of oil or grease. Emulsion type cleaners have little effect on the carbonized deposits found on pistons, connecting rods, etc., or on the gasoline residues found in carburetors and fuel pumps. Emulsion type cleaners can be used in two ways: they can be sprayed on in concentrated form for cleaning large parts such as the engine itself. In the diluted form, they are used to clean smaller parts by soaking.

Spray Cleaning. Protect the distributor, coil, and generator or alternator with a rubber hood before starting to clean an engine. The solution is sprayed or brushed on all surfaces of the engine or chassis and allowed to soak for 10 to 15 minutes to permit thorough penetration. During the soak-in period, the cleaning solution penetrates into the dirt deposits down to the metal surface, loosening the bond between them and the metal surfaces. When cleaning a dirty engine, quicker results will be obtained if the engine is run until dry and warm before spraying.

The next operation is to flush the engine or chassis with cold water under pressure. When the water hits the cleaner and dirt deposits, an emulsion is formed in which the dirt is suspended. The water pressure removes the loosened dirt which is carried away in the emulsion as the flushing continues. All grease, oil, and dirt will be removed, leaving the engine or chassis clean without injury to the paint.

Tank Cleaning. After disassembly, it is generally more economical to clean smaller parts by allowing them to soak clean in a tank. This permits the mechanic to perform other work while the parts are cleaning. Most shops use emulsion type cleaners for this sort of cleaning when the volume of parts to be cleaned is not too great and when there is no great hurry. Another saving with this sort of cleaning is that the solutions can be used cold with no heating cost.

The parts to be cleaned are submerged in the solution for one to six hours, depending on the amount of grease and dirt to be removed. For faster cleaning, the parts may be agitated in the solution circulated through the tank, Fig. 1-47. Heating also speeds up the cleaning action. After removal from the tank, the parts are flushed with a pressure stream of water.

Solvent Cleaning. Oil and gasoline leave a light deposit or residue wherever they come in contact with engine parts, particularly when heat is present. After many hours of engine operation, these deposits and residues have built up enough to reduce engine efficiency considerably. These heat-bonded deposits in the form of carbon and engine varnish are found on pistons and connecting rods and in the combustion chamber. Gasoline residues also build up in the carburetor and fuel pump. Therefore, a powerful solvent mixture must be used to clean the parts quickly with a minimum of effort.

Emulsion-solvent cleaners capable of removing baked-on engine deposits are a blend of several energetic synthetic solvents. Through their combined action, they are capable of loosening and removing the accumulations.

Parts made of aluminum, brass, steel, and copper should not be placed in contact with each other

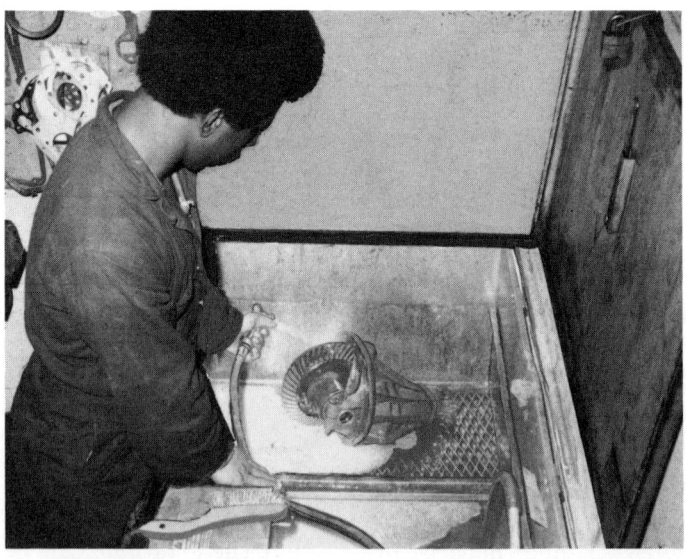

Fig. 1-47. Tank cleaning of parts. Circulation of the solution speeds up the cleaning process considerably. (Gray Mills Corp.)

The Auto Mechanic and His Tools

while in the cleaning solution in order to avoid the problem of electrolytic action. While emulsion-solvent cleaning solutions are safe to use on reactive metals, it is generally considered good practice to avoid cleaning dissimilar metals in one tank.

To clean the parts, place them in a rack and immerse them in the tank of cleaning solution, Fig. 1-48. The time required to loosen and soften the accumulations depends largely upon the thickness and hardness of the deposits. Twenty to thirty minutes of soaking usually is sufficient to clean most parts. Soaking time can be reduced considerably if the parts are agitated while in the solution or if the solution is heated. The recommendations of the various manufacturers should be followed carefully as the temperatures recommended vary from 100 to 180°F. Due to the high volatility of the solvents, such cleaning solutions should never be heated over an open flame but by means of steam or hot water coils controlled by a thermostat.

The cleaning action of the solution is basically a physical one. The solution acts by penetrating through the carbon, engine varnish, and baked on dirt, destroying their adhesion to the metal. It dissolves the gums and resinous binders that hold the carbon and varnish to the surface, releasing the solid dirt so it either settles to the bottom of the tank or remains on the parts as fine, nonadhesive particles. As soon as

Fig. 1-48. Cleaning carburetor parts with a cold immersion carbon solvent cleaner. (Gunk Chicago Co.)

the deposits have been thoroughly loosened, the parts should be removed from the tank and subjected to a pressure-spray water rinse to flush off the softened deposits. Very hard deposits may require brushing with a stiff brush for their complete removal.

Checking On Your Knowledge

The following questions give you the opportunity to check up on yourself. If you have read the chapter carefully, you should be able to answer the questions. If you have any difficulty, read the chapter over once more so that you have the information well in mind before you go on with your reading.

DO YOU KNOW

1. What are some of the characteristics of a good automobile mechanic?
2. What type of hammer should be used to preventing marring surfaces?
3. What are the different uses of taps and dies?
4. What is a common safety precaution that one should follow when using wrenches?
5. What is the function of the torque wrench?
6. What is the difference between single-cut and double-cut files?
7. What measuring tools are used in measuring hole diameters?
8. What is the difference between a bolt, a screw, and a stud?
9. What is the difference between the UNC and the UNF thread series?
10. What are the differences between pressure and steam cleaning?
11. What effect does alkalinity have on the cleaning power of a cleaning solution?
12. What are some of the advantages of tank cleaning of parts?
13. What type of cleaner should be used to clean carburetor parts?
14. What advantage do spiral blade reamers usually have over straight blade reamers?

Engine Operation and Design

Chapter
2

Although modern automotive engines vary greatly in size and design, the operating principles are essentially the same as those of the first models developed over 75 years ago. Despite the fact that these basic principles have not changed, many mechanics do not clearly understand why the engine operates as it does.

Expansion of Gases

Gasoline is a liquid fuel which will change to a gas and expand if it is heated or burned. This expansion is a force which can be harnessed to drive the automobile engine. All matter, whether a solid, a liquid, or a gas, is made up of molecules which are moving and colliding at high speed. When the molecules collide, they bounce apart and cause the matter to expand.

Increasing the temperature of gasoline molecules increases their speed, causing more collisions and expansion if there is sufficient room for expansion.

If a mixture of air and gasoline vapor is confined under pressure within a cylinder, the pressure will generate heat. The heat will cause the air and gasoline vapor mixture to expand and exert a much greater pressure within the cylinder. If this confined mixture of air and gasoline is ignited and burned, the heat, pressure, and the tendency to expand are multiplied many times. This tendency to expand provides the force which drives the automobile engine.

Atmospheric Pressure

Not only is the engine's power dependent upon the expansion of

Automotive Engines

gases but it is also influenced by the layer of air surrounding the earth. This air is a mixture of gases known as the *atmosphere*, Fig. 2-1.

The atmosphere extends all around us and thins gradually into outer space. At sea level, the pressure of the atmosphere is 14.7 psi (pounds pressure per square inch), while on a mountain at 10,000 feet

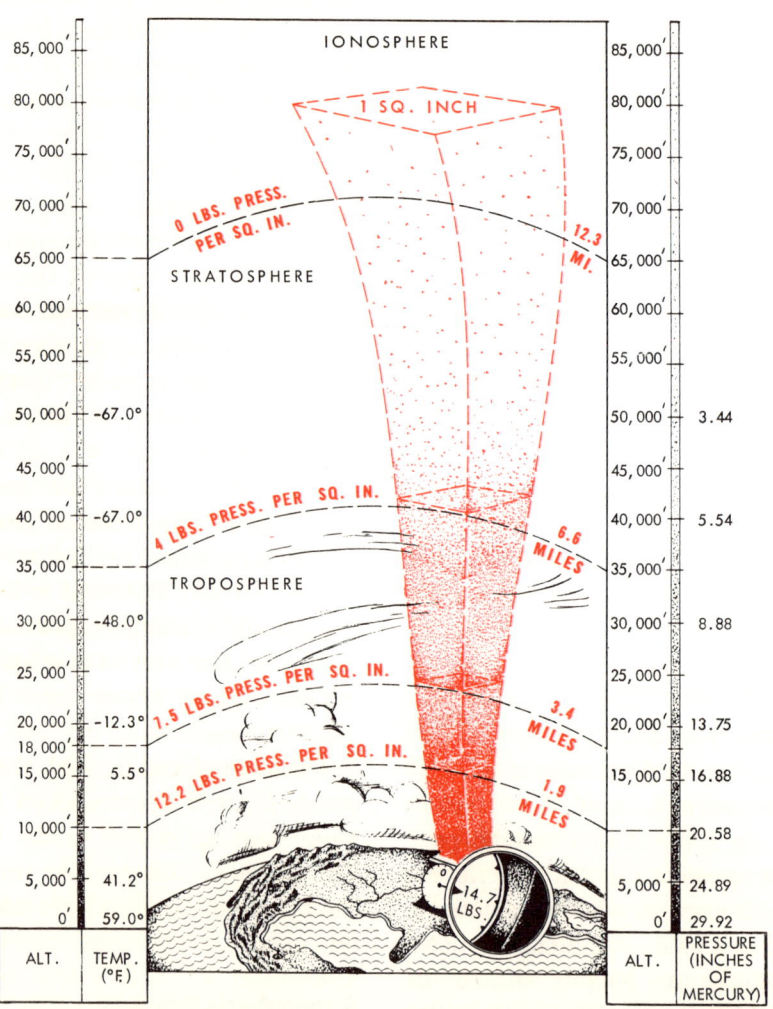

Fig. 2-1. We live in an "ocean of air" that exerts a pressure on the earth's surface. The pressure decreases as altitude increases. Because air has weight and is compressible, the density of the air is greater at sea level than at higher altitudes.

Engine Operation and Design

above sea level the pressure is only 12.2 psi.

When the pressure in a sealed container, such as an engine cylinder, is less than the atmospheric pressure, a partial vacuum exists in the cylinder. If an opening is made in the container, the outside air will rush into the container until the pressure inside the container is equal to the atmospheric pressure. This fact plays an important part in the operation of an engine.

Transforming Energy

Energy is the ability to do work. There is a great deal of energy stored in liquid gasoline. We call this potential energy because it will not do any work until it is transformed into a gas, burned, or compressed.

In an automobile engine, liquid gasoline is not only transformed into a gas, but it is also compressed and burned. Burning, or combustion, releases the energy in the gasoline so that it can perform work. This working energy is called *kinetic* energy, and it serves to move the pistons in the engine.

The gasoline engine and the diesel engine are classified as *internal-combustion* engines because their fuels are burned within the engine. A steam engine is classified as an *external-combustion* engine because the actual burning of the fuel takes place outside of the engine.

Engine Parts

Engines vary greatly in size, horsepower developed, and design. All engines, however, are made up of parts which perform similar functions. We will now briefly describe these parts and their functions. We will not discuss fuel or ignition systems. They will be covered separately later.

Cylinder Block. The cylinder block, together with the crankcase, forms the main body of the engine. The block and crankcase are cast *en bloc* to form a single casting, Fig. 2-2. The cylinder block provides the smooth cylinders which guide the pistons, Fig. 2-3. The crankcase supports the crankshaft and camshaft by means of bearings. It also supports many other engine parts. An oil pan bolted to the bottom of the crankcase forms a tight covering for the crankshaft and serves as a reservoir for lubricating oil.

Cylinder Head. The cylinder head, Figs. 2-2 and 2-3, is a one-piece casting bolted to the top of the cylinder block. The cylinder head covers the end of the cylinders to form a combustion chamber, or container, where burning and expansion of gases take place.

Pistons. Pistons receive the force from the combustion within the

45

Automotive Engines

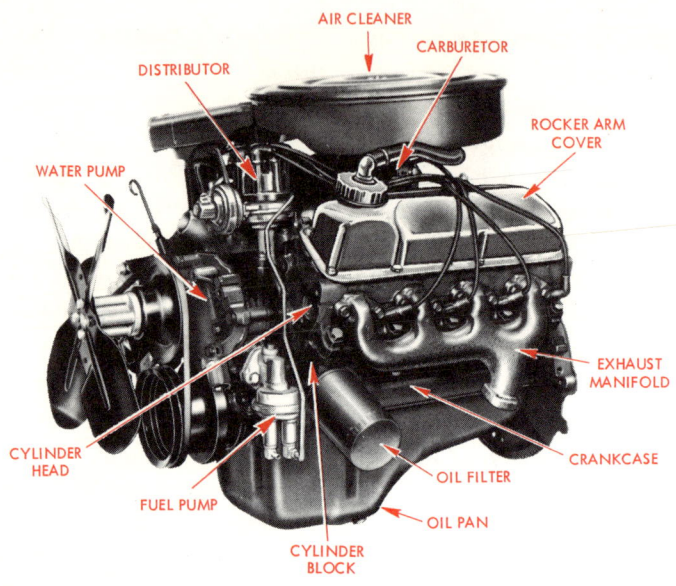

Fig. 2-2. In this V-type engine, the cylinder block and the crankcase are cast together in one piece (en bloc) known as the cylinder block. The crankcase section is in the lower part of the cylinder block. (Ford Div., Ford Motor Co.)

cylinders. When the piston is forced downward, it transmits the motion through a connecting rod to the crankshaft, Fig. 2-3.

Piston Rings. Piston rings are used to maintain a pressure-tight seal between the moving piston and the cylinder wall, Fig. 2-3. Piston rings conduct heat away from the piston head and prevent oil from entering the combustion chamber.

Piston Pins. A piston pin, sometimes called the wrist pin, connects the piston to the upper end of a connecting rod, Fig. 2-3. Each end of the piston pin fits into holes bored in the piston bosses. The center of the pin fits through the upper end of the connecting rod. This arrangement allows the rod to swing back and forth on the piston pin.

Connecting Rod. A connecting rod, Figs. 2-3 and 2-4, attached to the piston by the piston pin, converts the up and down motion of the piston to a rotary motion of the crankshaft. The lower end of the connecting rod contains a journal bearing and is split to permit assembly to the crankshaft.

Crankshaft. The crankshaft receives power from the piston and connecting rod and transmits this power to the drive train of the automobile. It uses some of the power to return the piston to the top of the cylinder. The crankshaft has large journals which

46

Engine Operation and Design

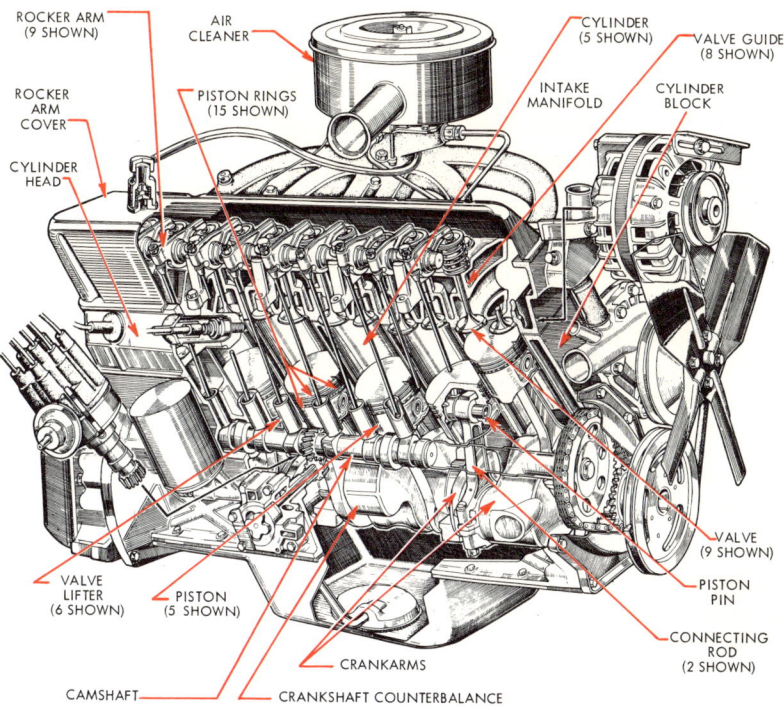

Fig. 2-3. This six-cylinder engine has been cut away so you can see the basic parts of the engine in relation to one another. In this design, cylinders are cast on a slant in the cylinder block to save space in the engine compartment. (Plymouth Div., Chrysler Corp.)

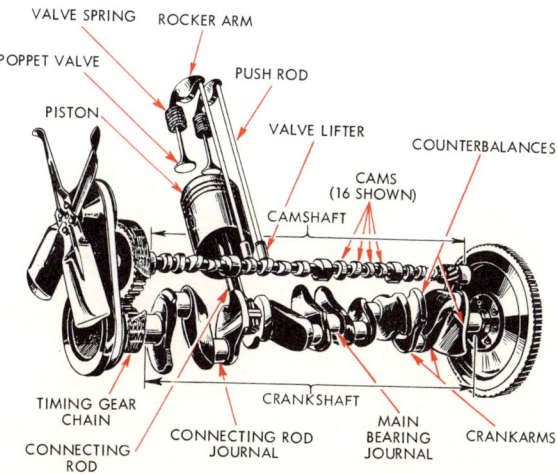

Fig. 2-4. These moving parts of a V-type engine are all in operating position. For simplicity, the basic valve operating mechanism for only one cylinder is shown. Both valves are closed.

Automotive Engines

rotate in the bearings supported in the crankcase. Crankarms with connecting rod journals provide bearing surfaces for the attached large ends of the connecting rods, Figs. 2-3 and 2-4. Counterbalances on the crankshaft and a flywheel bolted to the end of the crankshaft serve the purpose of improving engine smoothness.

Engine Bearings. The rotating crankshaft and camshaft journals turn in plain bearings made of anti-friction metal, Figs. 2-3 and 2-4. This metal is an alloy such as babbitt, copper-lead, cadmium silver, and others. These bearings must withstand heavy loads and high speeds and temperatures.

Valves. Most engines employ intake and exhaust valves, Figs. 2-3 and 2-4, to open and close the passages through which the gases enter and leave the cylinders. The valves are mounted in the cylinder block or the cylinder head.

Camshaft. A camshaft, Figs. 2-3 and 2-4, opens each valve against the tension of a valve spring for the required interval, then releases the valve, and a valve spring closes it. There is a separate cam to operate each valve. The crankshaft drives the camshaft through gears, a chain and sprockets, or a belt and sprockets, depending on the design of the particular engine.

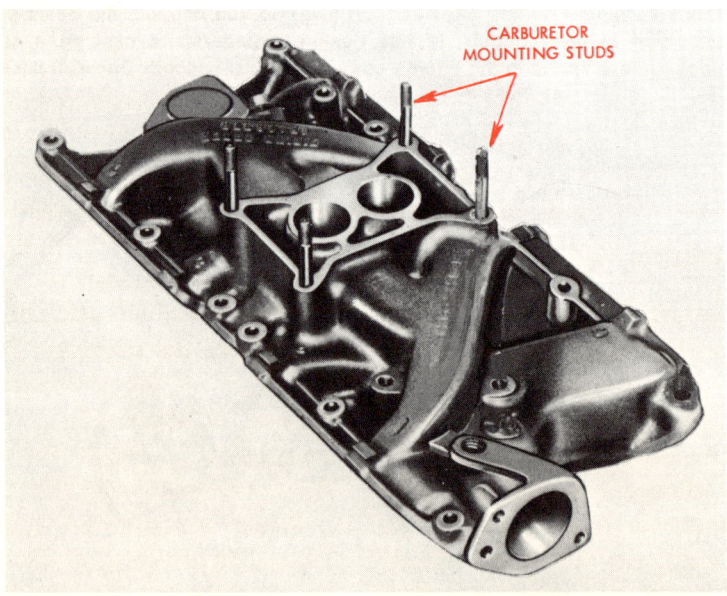

Fig. 2-5. This intake manifold for a V-type engine is mounted separately from the exhaust manifolds. (Ford Div., Ford Motor Co.)

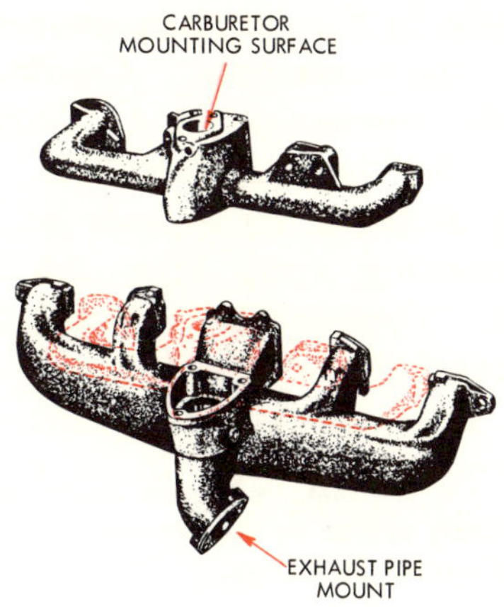

Engine Operation and Design

Fig. 2-6. This intake manifold (top) and exhaust manifold (bottom) are for a six-cylinder engine. They are bolted together when mounted on the engine. Both are designed for efficient transport of gases. (Ford Div., Ford Motor Co.)

Valve Lifters. Valve lifters, sometimes called valve push rods or tappets, are pushed by the camshaft to open the valves.

Manifolds. Manifolds conduct gases to and from the cylinders. The intake manifold, Figs. 2-5 and 2-6 (top), conducts the air-fuel mixture to the cylinders. An exhaust manifold provides a passage for the burned gases leaving the cylinders, Fig. 2-6 (bottom).

Basic Engine Operation

The internal combustion engine does work by converting the potential energy in gasoline into kinetic energy. This conversion takes place within the engine cylinder.

The Cylinder. A cylinder is a metal container that is shaped like a tube with the upper end closed and the lower end open. A piston fits inside the cylinder as snugly as possible. As the piston moves up, it decreases the amount of space in the top of the cylinder. When the piston moves down, it increases the amount of space, Fig. 2-7. A connecting rod connects the piston to the crankshaft below the cylinder.

When an air-fuel mixture is burned in the top of the cylinder, the combustion releases expanding gases with great force against the piston and drives the piston down.

Automotive Engines

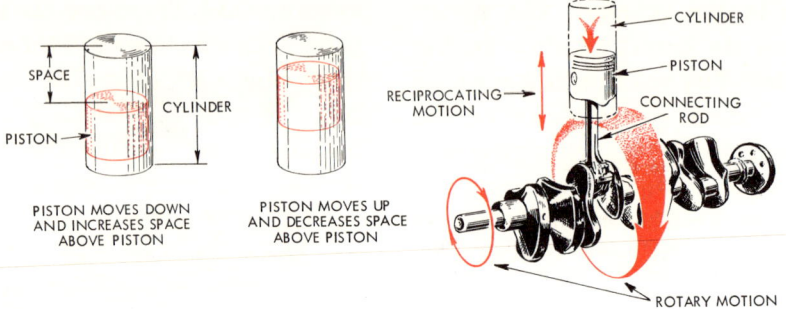

Fig. 2-7. The piston's up and down (reciprocating) movement in the cylinder is converted to rotary motion by the crankshaft.

The connecting rod is free to swing back and forth on a piston pin so the piston's up and down movement causes the rotary movement of the crankshaft, Fig. 2-7.

Valves. Most gasoline engines use two valves at the top of each cylinder. A valve is an accurately machined plug that opens or closes a passageway which conducts gases to or from the cylinder. The intake valve opens the passageway which conducts air-fuel mixture into the cylinder. The exhaust valve must open to allow the burned gases to leave the cylinder. The valve operating mechanism, Fig. 2-4, opens and closes the valves at the correct moment.

The Four-Stroke Cycle

An upward stroke is a piston movement from its lowest position in the cylinder to its highest position. A downward stroke moves from highest to lowest position. When burning gases force the piston downward in the cylinder, a power stroke is completed, but not every stroke of the piston is a power stroke. The engine must complete a set order or cycle of strokes, and only one of these strokes in the cycle is a power stroke. Most gasoline engines operate on a four-stroke cycle. The order of these strokes is: (1) the intake stroke; (2) the compression stroke; (3) the power stroke; (4) the exhaust stroke.

All four strokes are completed during two revolutions of the crankshaft—one half of a revolution for each stroke.

Intake. The stroke begins when the piston is at its highest position in the cylinder. The position is known as *top dead center* (TDC).

The exhaust valve remains closed and the intake valve opens. The piston moves downward enlarging the space at the top of the cylinder, Fig. 2-8. Atmospheric pressure pushes air-fuel mixture in to fill the

Engine Operation and Design

space in the cylinder. The piston reaches its lowest position in the cylinder. The position is known as *bottom dead center* (BDC). The pressure inside the cylinder is still somewhat less than atmospheric pressure. This means that the air-fuel mixture can enter the cylinder—even after the piston begins to move upward. Therefore, the intake valve does not close until the crankshaft arm is 44° past BDC, in Fig. 2-8.

Compression. After the intake stroke, both valves remain closed and the piston moves upward, Fig. 2-9. The piston compresses the air-fuel mixture by pushing it upward

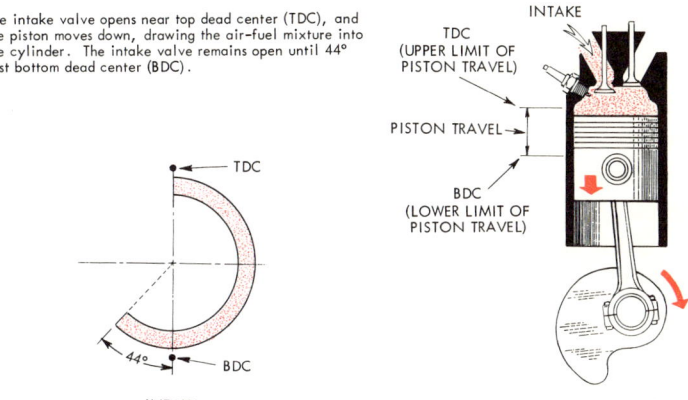

Fig. 2-8. The intake stroke of the four-stroke cycle is the first stroke occurring in the cycle.

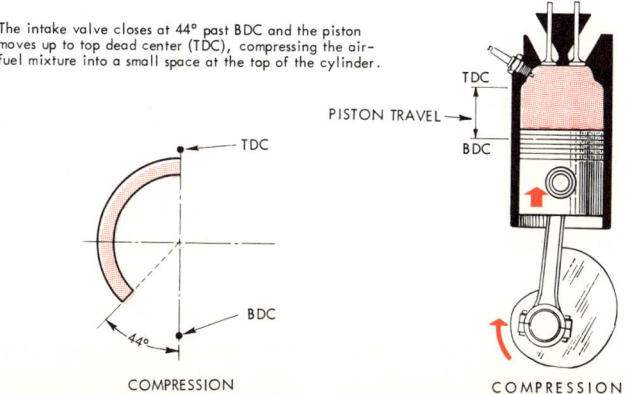

Fig. 2-9. The compression stroke is the second stroke to occur in the four-stroke cycle.

51

Automotive Engines

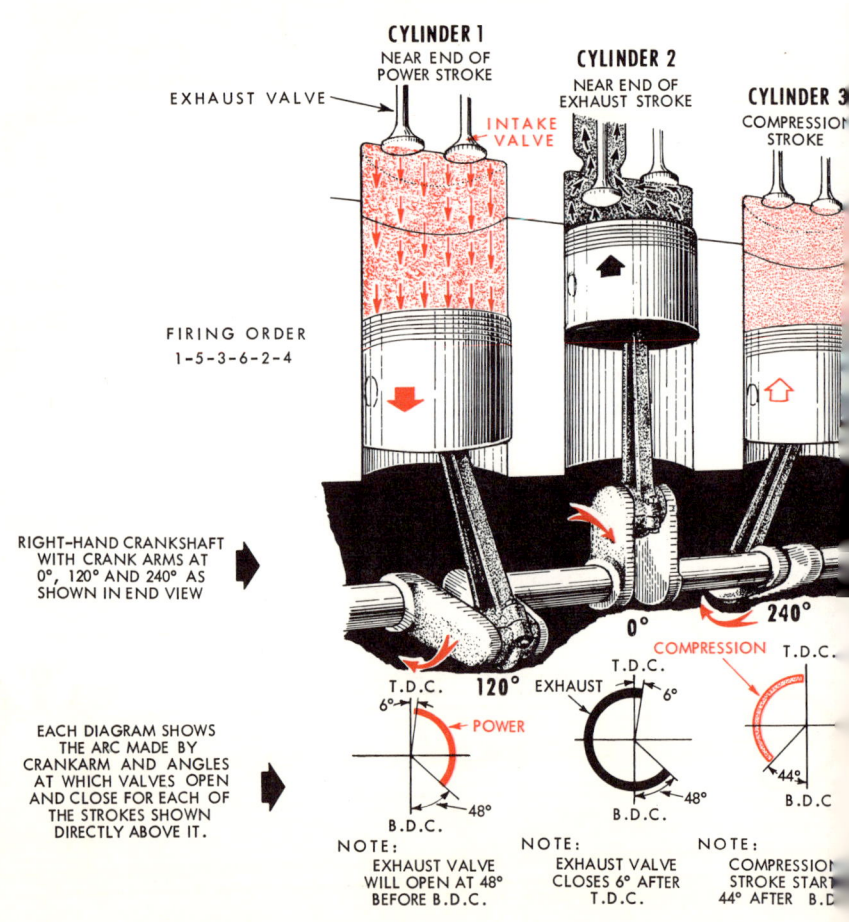

Engine Operation and Design

Four—Stroke—Cycle   6-Cylinder Engine

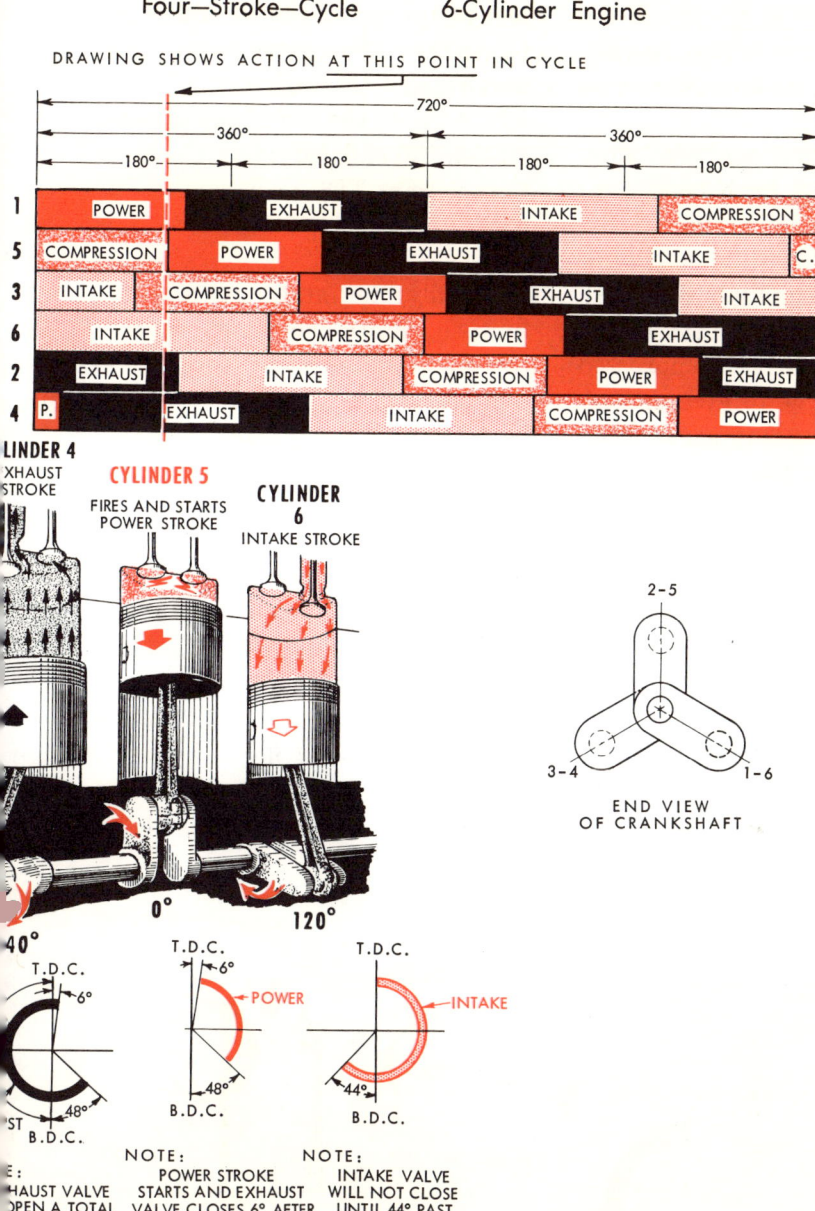

into a small space at the top of the cylinder. When the piston reaches TDC, the compression stroke is complete.

Two strokes and one revolution of the crankshaft have been completed since the beginning of the cycle.

Power. This stroke begins with the piston at TDC and both valves closed. The piston has compressed the air-fuel charge to give greater force to the expanding gases when combustion takes place.

At this point, a spark ignites the fuel and it burns with explosive force driving the piston down, Fig. 2-10. The connecting rod transmits this force to the crankarm which then turns the crankshaft.

Exhaust. The exhaust stroke begins when the piston reaches BDC at the end of the power stroke. The exhaust valve opens. The piston moves upward in the cylinder and forces the burned gases out through the exhaust passageway or port, Fig. 2-11. At the end of the exhaust stroke, the exhaust valve closes. It may close at TDC or as late as 10° past TDC. The exhaust stroke is complete.

Usually, the intake valve begins to open before the piston reaches the top of the exhaust stroke so it will be opening as the piston again begins the intake stroke.

The crankshaft has now made two revolutions to complete the four-stroke cycle. The piston has made four strokes through the cylinder: (1) a downward intake stroke; (2) an upward compression stroke; (3) a downward power stroke; (4) an upward exhaust stroke. At cruising speed, the average automobile engine crankshaft turns at about 3600 revolutions per

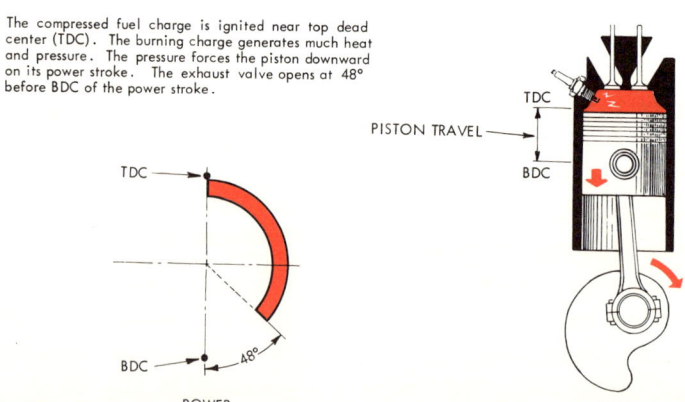

Fig. 2-10. The power stroke is the third stroke to occur in the four-stroke cycle.

Engine Operation and Design

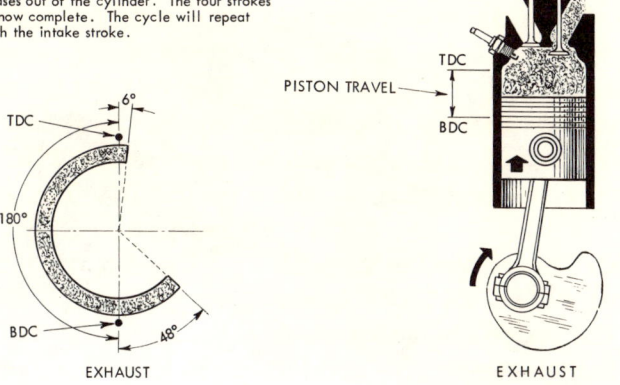

The piston reaches BDC after completing its power stroke. The exhaust valve is open and the piston moves up, pushing the burned gases out of the cylinder. The four strokes of the cycle are now complete. The cycle will repeat itself starting with the intake stroke.

Fig. 2-11. The exhaust stroke is the fourth and last stroke of the four-stroke cycle.

minute, and the full cycle (these four strokes) is repeated 30 times per second in each cylinder.

The fuel and ignition systems are crucially important to engine operation, but we have mentioned them only briefly here. We will discuss them in detail later in this book. At present, it is most important that you understand very thoroughly each one of the strokes and their interrelationship in the four-stroke cycle. (Also see pp. 52-53.)

Major Differences in Engine Design

The great variety of engines in use today can be very confusing. All of these engines are basically alike in that they all require air, fuel, and a method of igniting the air-fuel charge. We have discussed the features and operating principles that are common to most engines. Now we shall see that there are also some differences.

We shall discuss only the major differences. Engines may differ in number and arrangement of cylinders, valve arrangement, method of operation, fuels used, and method of cooling.

Cylinder Number and Arrangement

Usually, automotive engines are classified according to the number and physical arrangement of the cylinders in the block. The most commonly used engine designs are

55

Automotive Engines

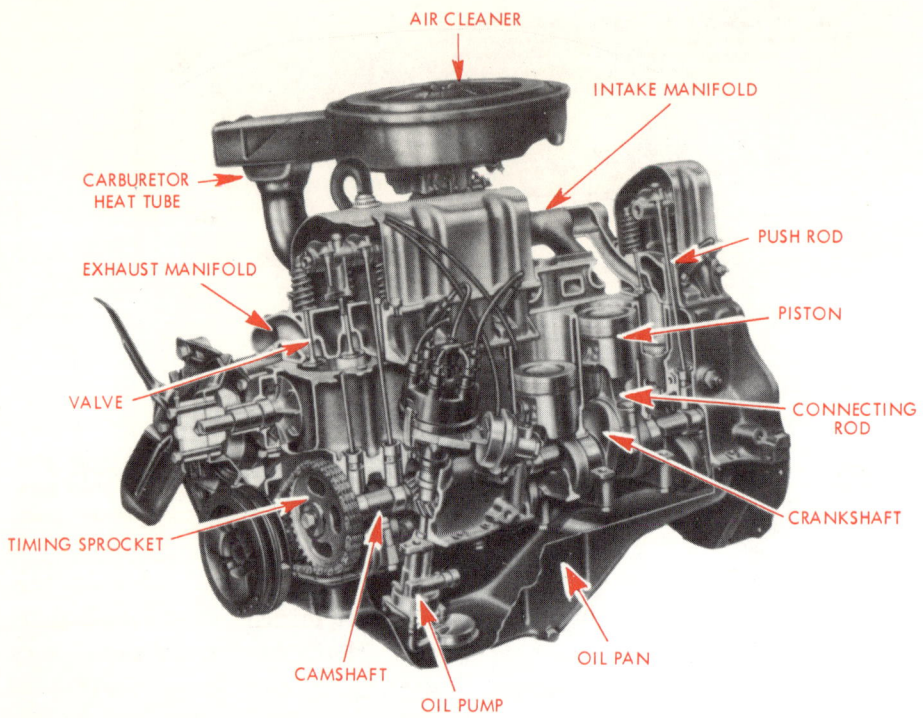

Fig. 2-12. This in-line engine has six vertical cylinders above a common crankshaft. The cylinders are numbered from the front to the rear of the engine. (Ford Div., Ford Motor Co.)

the in-line, the V-type, and the horizontally opposed type.

In-line. Usually in-line engines have four, six, or eight cylinders mounted in a straight line, one after the other. Usually, the cylinders are vertical above a common crankshaft, Fig. 2-12. On some engines, the cylinders are inclined 30 degrees from the vertical so the block is on a slant which conserves space in the engine compartment, Fig. 2-13. In-line engines are cast en bloc, and the cylinders are numbered from front to rear.

V-type. Two or more cylinders are mounted above a common crankshaft to form the letter V (as the engine is viewed from either end). Today, most V-type engines have eight cylinders cast en bloc in two rows or banks. Each bank contains one half of the cylinders. Usually, the banks form a 90° angle although other angular spacings have been used. The V design gives a shorter and more rigid engine with less tendency toward torsional vibration (twisting of the crankshaft). Fig. 2-14 shows a

Engine Operation and Design

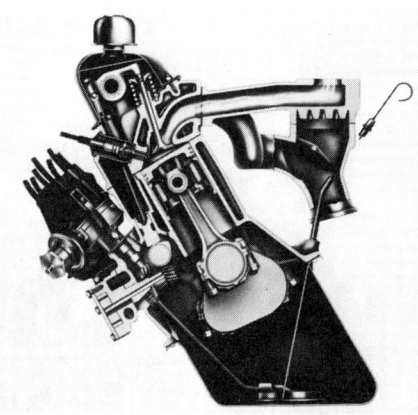

Fig. 2-13. On this in-line engine, the cylinders are inclined at an angle of 30 degrees from the vertical. It is similar to the engine shown in Fig. 2-3, but this is a cross sectioned view from the front. Look at the parts labeled in Fig. 2-3 and see if you can identify them here. (Plymouth Div., Chrysler Corp.)

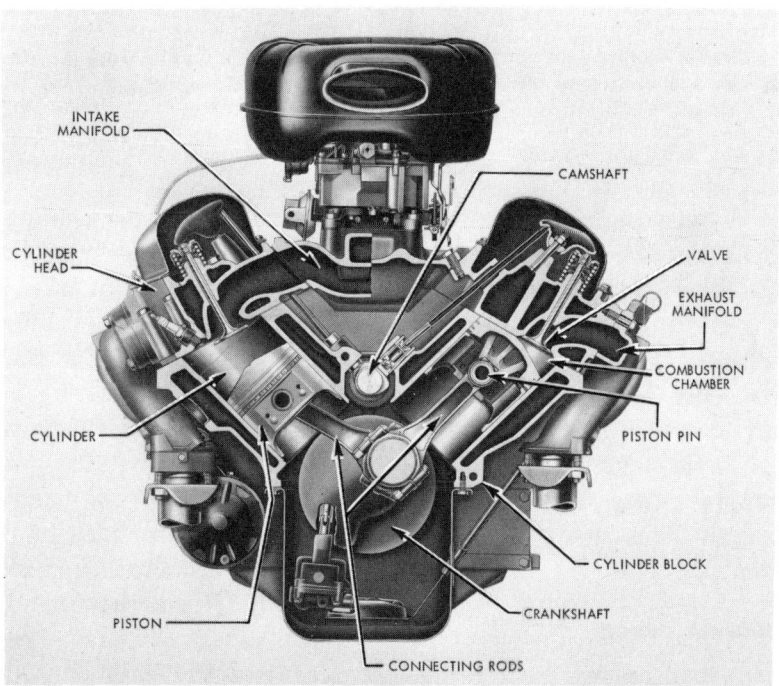

Fig. 2-14. Cross sectioned end view of a V-8 engine. (Chevrolet Motor Div., General Motors Corp.)

Automotive Engines

Fig. 2-15. This is a cross sectioned six-cylinder V-type engine viewed from the side. It has three cylinders in each bank. (Buick Div., General Motors Corp.)

typical V-type eight-cylinder engine, commonly known as a V-8 engine. A six cylinder V-type engine with three cylinders in each bank is shown in Fig. 2-15.

Horizontally Opposed. The cylinders are arranged in two banks lying in a single plane with the crankshaft between them, Fig. 2-16. This design also saves space in the engine compartment.

Valve Arrangement

There are three common arrangements: The L-head, the I-head, and the F-head.

L-head. The cross sectional view is shaped like a reversed letter L, Fig. 2-17. Both the intake and the exhaust valves are located in the block along one side of the cylinders. The valve operating mechanism is located below the valves, and a camshaft operates the valve lifters which operate the valves. This arrangement simplifies lubrication of the valve operating mechanism.

I-head. This arrangement is also known as *valve-in-head*. The intake valve and the exhaust valve are mounted in an inverted position in the cylinder head directly above the

Engine Operation and Design

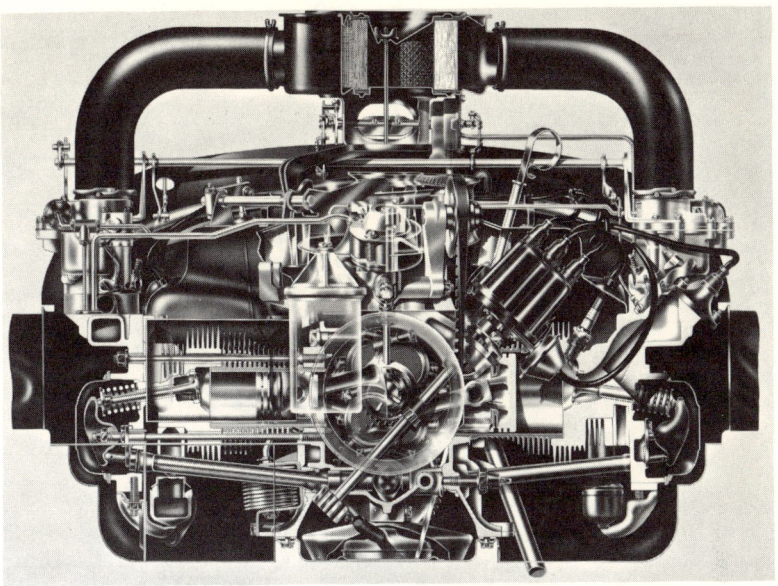

Fig. 2-16. This horizontally opposed six-cylinder engine is air cooled. You can see the cooling fins in this cross sectioned end view. The crankshaft halves and each of the cylinders are cast separately and then bolted together. (Chevrolet Motor Div., General Motors Corp.)

Fig. 2-17. In this L-head engine, the intake and exhaust valves both are located to one side of the cylinders (to the left of the cylinder in this illustration).

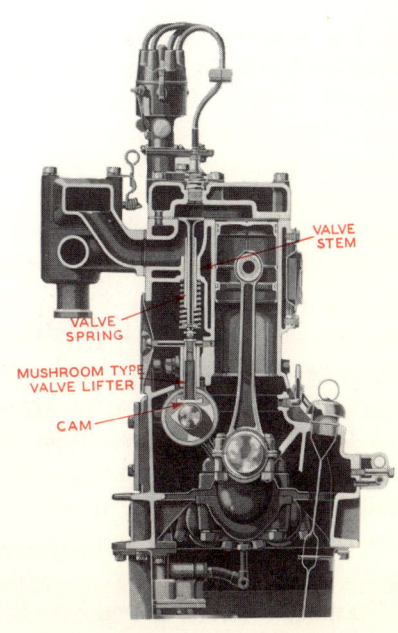

Automotive Engines

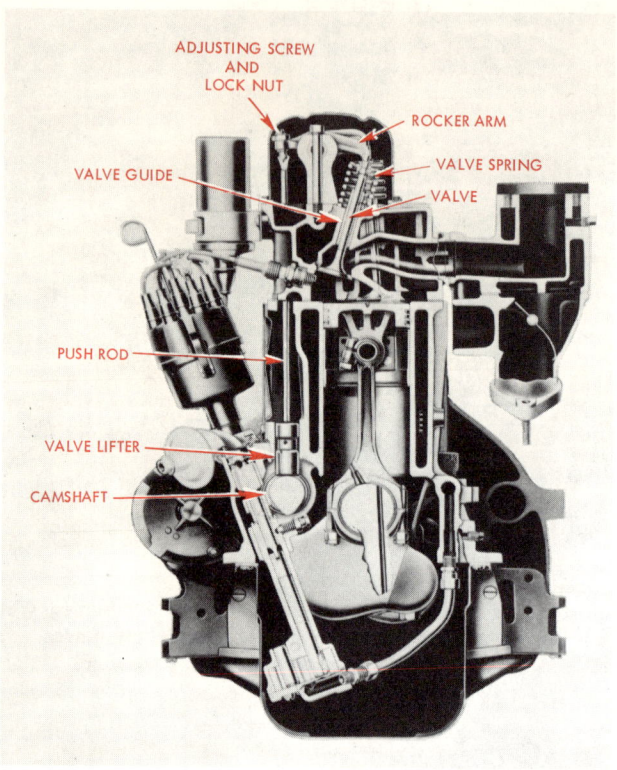

Fig. 2-18. In the I-head or valve-in-head type of valve arrangement, the intake and exhaust valves are located in the cylinder head. (Chevrolet Motor Div., General Motors Corp.)

cylinder, Figs. 2-16 and 2-18. The cross sectioned view is like the letter I. The valves are far away from the camshaft which is below in the crankcase. Therefore, valve lifters, pushrods, and rocker arms transmit the camshaft's motion to the valves in the cylinder head above. Oil must be pumped upward to lubricate the valves and rocker arms.

On most engines, the camshaft is located in the crankcase, but some camshafts are located on the cylinder head and driven by a silent chain or a belt, Fig. 2-19. This arrangement gives a more direct valve action.

F-head. One valve in the cylinder head, and one valve is in the cylinder block, Fig. 2-20. A single camshaft operates both valves. A rocker arm arrangement operates the valve in the head.

Engine Operation and Design

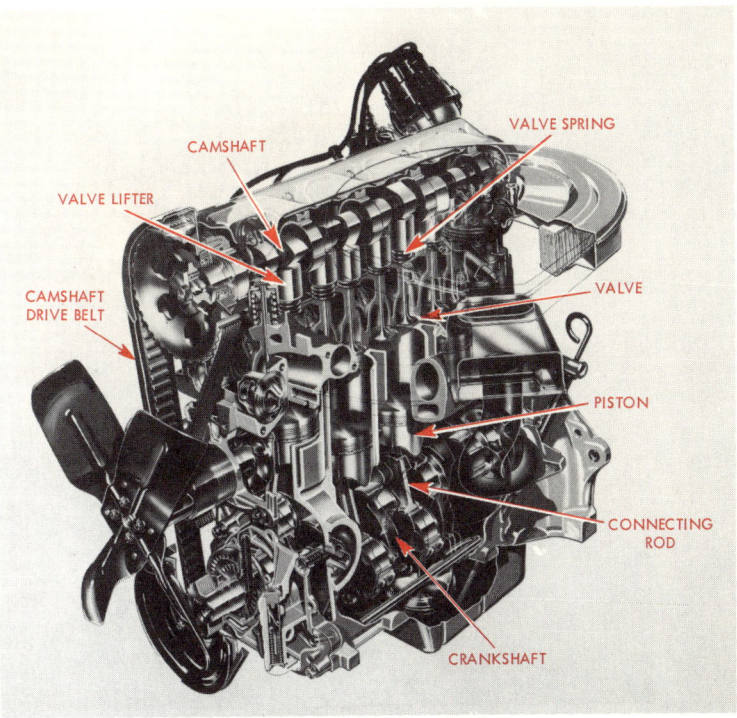

Fig. 2-19. The camshaft is located on the cylinder head and is driven by a belt to give a direct valve action. (Chevrolet Motor Div., General Motors Corp.)

Engine Operation

Engines also differ in their manner of operation. We shall discuss operating differences in terms of (1) the number of strokes in a cycle, (2) the firing order, and (3) piston movement.

Number of Strokes in a Cycle. In addition to four-stroke-cycle engines, there are some engines which operate on a cycle of only two strokes. Two-stroke-cycle engines burn either gasoline or diesel oil. The gasoline-types power motorbikes, lawn mowers, boats, and small cars. Some are used as light stationary engines, and some drive portable electric generators and chainsaws. The diesel types are used in ships, buses, trucks, tractors, and other conveyances.

The two-stroke cycle differs from the four-stroke cycle in two ways: (a) the method of transmitting the gases into and out of the cylinders, and (b) the same cycle of events—intake, compression, power, and exhaust—is completed in only two strokes of the piston instead of four. This results in a power stroke being developed on each downward stroke of the piston or once every revolution.

Automotive Engines

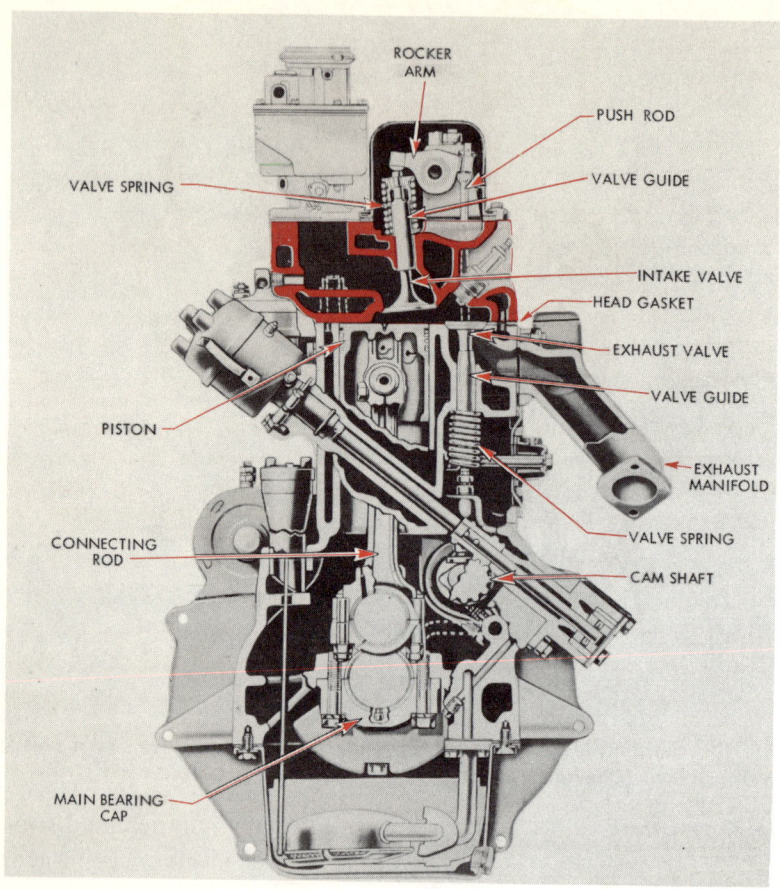

Fig. 2-20. An F-head four cylinder in-line engine. One valve is located at the side of the cylinder in the engine block as in an L-head engine. The other valve is inverted and in the cylinder head as in the I-head design. A single camshaft operates all of the valves in the engine.

Two-stroke-cycle gasoline engines have no valve mechanism. Intake and exhaust port openings are on each side of the cylinders. The intake port is connected to the engine crankcase. The crankcase receives the air-fuel mixture from the carburetor.

On the first upward stroke of the piston, a partial vacuum, or reduced pressure, is created in the engine crankcase. As the piston moves upward and nears the top of its stroke, the intake port connected with the carburetor opens so that the air-fuel mixture flows from the carburetor into the engine crankcase, Fig. 2-21A.

Engine Operation and Design

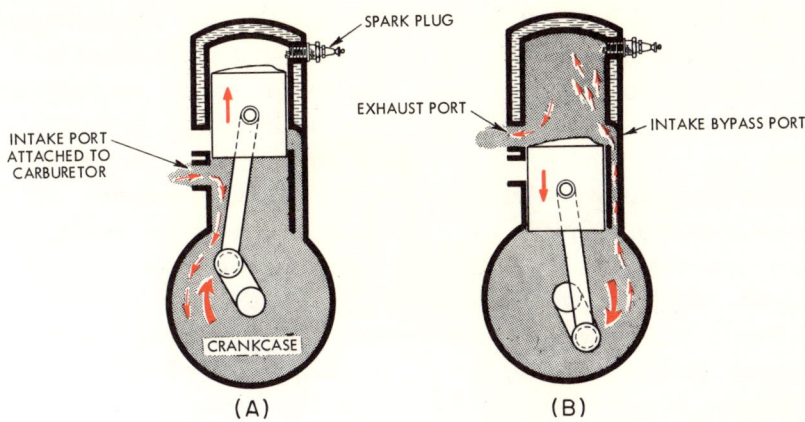

Fig. 2-21. This is the two-stroke-cycle principle of gasoline engine operation. (A) The upward movement of the piston is permitting air-fuel mixture to flow into the crankcase. Compression is also taking place and ignition will occur near top dead center. (B) Both intake and exhaust are occurring. The incoming air-fuel mixture forces out the exhaust gases.

At the top of the first stroke, the piston reverses its direction and begins a downward movement, covering or closing the intake port, Fig. 2-21B. The piston continues downward compressing the fuel in the crankcase. Near the bottom of the stroke, the piston uncovers the intake bypass port that connects the combustion chamber with the crankcase. This releases the compressed fuel charge in the crankcase so it flows through the bypass port into the cylinder. A deflector in the top of the piston directs the gases upward in the cylinder.

The piston reaches bottom and moves upward on its stroke, compressing the air-fuel mixture in the cylinder, Fig. 2-21A. (Meanwhile, a new fuel charge is drawn into the engine crankcase.) As the piston nears the top of the compression stroke, a spark at the spark plug ignites the air-fuel mixture. An explosion results and forces the piston downward on the power stroke.

As the piston nears the bottom of the power stroke, it uncovers the exhaust port opening slightly before the intake bypass port. Because the pressure of the exhaust gases in the cylinder is still comparatively high, the early opening of the exhaust port permits the exhaust gases to start escaping. Further downward travel of the piston uncovers the intake bypass port. This enables the compressed fuel charge in the crankcase to enter the cylinder. The incoming charge assists in forcing the exhaust gases out of the cylinder to complete the cycle. The engine has now produced a full cycle in only two piston strokes.

Since at any given speed a two-stroke-cycle engine delivers twice as many power strokes as a four-stroke-cycle engine, it would seem that it should deliver twice as much horsepower. This is not true, however, because two-stroke-cycle engines lose considerable power due to lower compression ratios which reduces efficiency both in introducing fuel into the cylinders and in expelling the exhaust gases.

Firing Order

The sequence or order in which the air-fuel mixture in each cylinder is ignited in an engine is called the *firing order*. The arrangement of crankpins on the crankshaft and the design of the camshaft determine firing order.

Four Cylinders. Crankshafts used in four-cylinder engines may have three or five main bearings. Two inner and two outer crankpins in a single plane are spaced 180° apart, Fig. 2-22. The firing order of such engines is 1-3-4-2 or 1-2-4-3. Note that the cylinders are numbered consecutively from front to rear, starting with the one nearest the radiator.

Six Cylinders. Crankshafts for six-cylinder engines have three, four, or seven main bearings with the crankpins paired in planes spaced 120° apart, Fig. 2-23. The common firing order of such engines is 1-5-3-6-2-4.

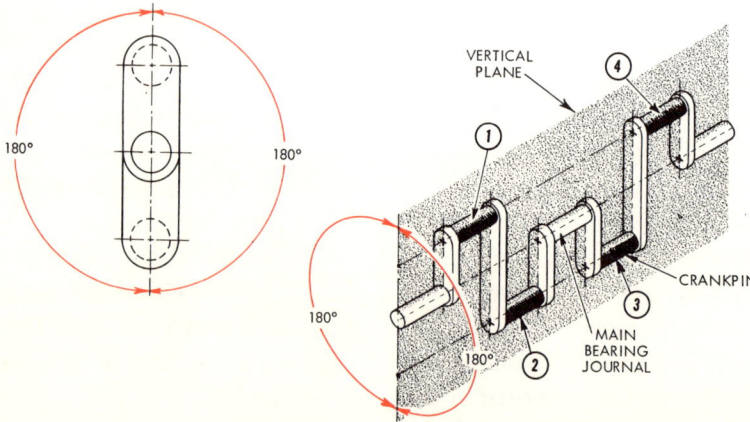

Fig. 2-22. This is a crankarm arrangement for a four-cylinder engine. Notice the consecutive numbering of crankpins from front to rear.

Engine Operation and Design

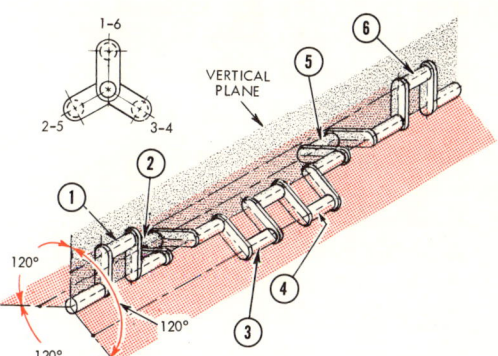

Fig. 2-23. Crankarm arrangement used in six-cylinder engines.

Eight Cylinders. In the past, the eight-cylinder in-line engine was very popular, but it has been replaced by the V-8 engine. In V-8 engines, the crankshaft is supported by three or five main bearings. The crankshaft has four crankpins spaced 90° apart with the connecting rods from opposite cylinders attached to the same crankpin, Fig. 2-24. A typical firing order is 1-8-4-3-6-5-7-2. The method of numbering the cylinders in a V-8 engine may vary according to the different

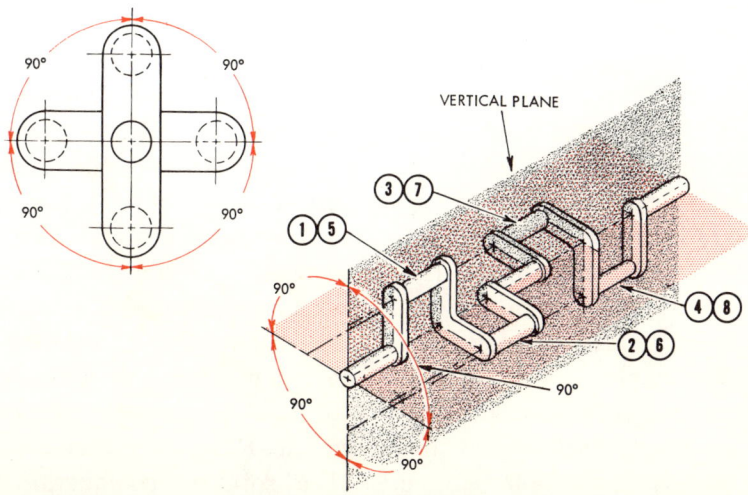

Fig. 2-24. This V-8 crankarm arrangement features three main bearing journals. Some V-8 crankshafts use five.

65

manufacturers. This is one of the reasons for the different firing orders.

Rotating Combustion Engine

All of the engines discussed so far have been reciprocating engines. That is, to produce power, the pistons move up and down in the cylinders, driving a crankshaft which changes the up-and-down movement to rotary motion. Recently, however, an engine has been developed in which power is produced by the action of a rotor turning inside an oval shaped combustion chamber. A German engineer, Felix Wankel, first designed the rotating combustion engine; therefore, the name *Wankel*. Several companies have been licensed to adopt the use of the engine to the many different types of installations which require power. While, as yet, production for automobile usage has been limited to vehicles produced in Europe and Asia, Curtiss-Wright Corporation and some automobile manufacturers in the United States have been doing a considerable amount of developmental work with this engine. Because of its simple design, the reduced number of moving parts, and its high horsepower to low weight ratio, many engineers feel this engine holds much promise for the future. Another important feature is that, although the Wankel engine's emission level is about equal to that of the reciprocating engine, it readily lends itself to the use of an exhaust reactor. With an exhaust reactor, the emission level can be greatly reduced.

The engine operates on gasoline and is adaptable to either liquid or air cooling. The rotating combustion principle is a different concept of the four-stroke cycle of engine operation. The term "four-stroke cycle" cannot be used because the mode of operation eliminates reciprocating motion (stroke) from the cycle. The conventional piston is replaced with a three-sided rotor. Rotor combustion chamber pockets are rotated past an intake port, a spark plug and an exhaust port; hence the term "rotating combustion." In one complete revolution of the rotor, there are three firing impulses which produce constant rotary motion. The combustion cycle follows the familiar pattern of the conventional four-stroke-cycle internal combustion engine in the sequence of events—intake, compression, power and exhaust. It should be noted that the rotating combustion engine provides torque output for about two-thirds of one shaft revolution as compared to only one-quarter of the two crankshaft revolutions of a single cylinder four-stroke-cycle reciprocating engine. Fig. 2-25 is a cutaway view of a rotating combustion engine with two rotors. Each rotor has three lobes and is connected to

Engine Operation and Design

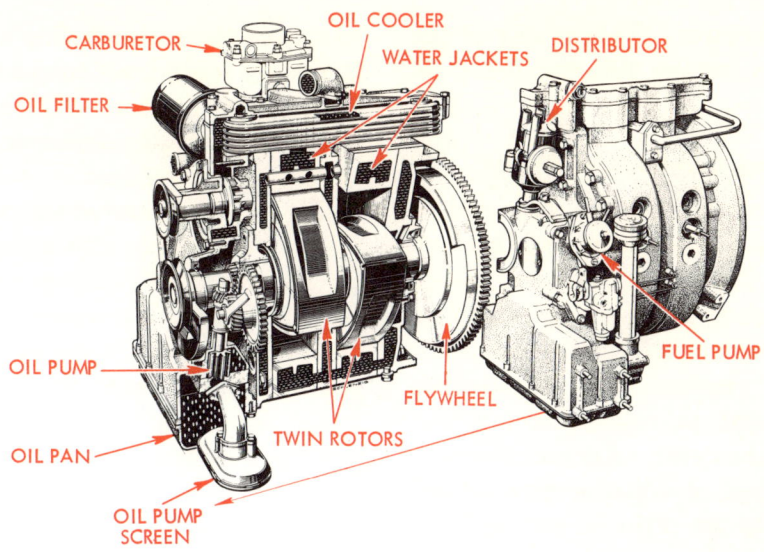

Fig. 2-25. Twin rotor rotating combustion engine. The two rotors are connected to a single crankshaft like the pistons of a conventional engine are connected to one crankshaft. (NSU Motorenwerke)

the shaft through internal and external gears.

In operation, the rotor revolves around its own geometric center; at the same time, the internal gears, within the rotor, move its center in an eccentric path. The result of this action is that all three corners of the rotor are in constant contact with the housing walls. Notice the depressions in the rotors; they form part of the combustion chamber.

As the rotor revolves, the three rotor lobes form three moving combustion chambers within the housing. Because of the shape of the rotor and housing walls, the combustion chamber is constantly changing in size as the rotor revolves. This action occurs in each of the three combustion chambers and brings about the intake, compression, power and exhaust effect that is similar to the four-stroke cycle of the reciprocating engine except that it delivers three power phases for each revolution of the rotor.

Fig. 2-26 illustrates the action that takes place as one lobe of the rotor passes through the intake, compression, power and exhaust phases. In Fig. 2-26A, the intake port has been uncovered by the moving rotor and the combustion

Automotive Engines

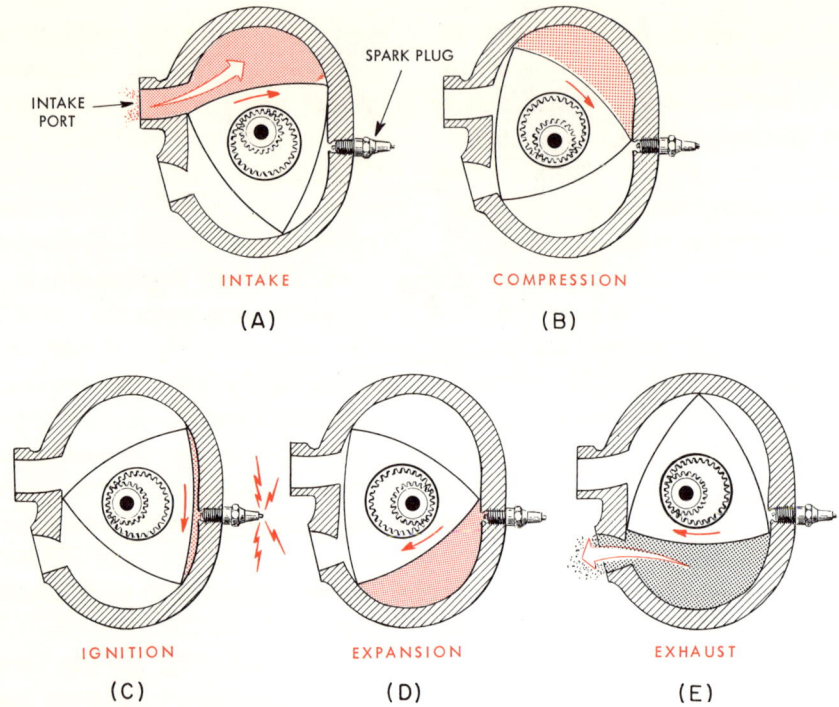

Fig. 2-26. Operating Principles of a Rotating Combustion Engine (NSU Motorenwerke)

chamber begins to fill with air-fuel mixture. In Fig. 2-26B the rotor has closed the intake port and the combustion chamber contains a maximum air-fuel mixture. As the rotor continues to revolve, the combustion chamber decreases in volume and the air-fuel mixture is compressed. In Fig. 2-26C maximum compression has been reached and the spark plug ignites the air-fuel mixture. In Fig. 2-26D, the burning gases expand forcing the rotor around. In Fig. 2-26E, the rotor has moved to a point where it uncovers the exhaust port and further rotation forces the exhaust gases out of the chamber.

While this has been taking place each of the other two combustion chambers has also been moving through the stages of the cycle. One chamber follows so closely upon the other that firing is almost continuous and produces a smooth flow of power. The engine is available in a one- or two-rotor design.

Turbine Engine

Another type of engine which

Engine Operation and Design

has been given consideration by various manufacturers relative to the reduction of undesirable emission factors is the turbine engine.

All turbine engines contain three common components, a compressor, a combustion section (combustor), and a turbine. Fig. 2-27 is a sketch of the components of a turbine engine. Air is drawn into the engine through the intake. The compressor squeezes the air to many times atmospheric pressure and forces it into the combustion section. Here, fuel is sprayed into the compressed air, ignited, and then burns continuously like a torch. The burning gases expand rapidly and blast rearward where they pass through a wheel-with-blades called a *turbine*. The turbine converts the force of the rapidly expanding gases to rotational energy. This energy is transmitted by a shaft to the compressor which packs in more fresh air. The gases then pass through another turbine called a power turbine. This turbine shaft is connected to a power transmission system which is used to drive the vehicle in the conventional manner.

The gas turbine has reached a point of commercial application for trucks, buses, and other heavy-duty operations but for passenger car use some developmental problems must be overcome. In city traffic, fuel economy and acceleration are unsatisfactory. The engine requires costly metals and is expensive to produce. Although hydrocarbons and carbon monoxide emissions are extremely low, nitrogen oxides are higher than proposed emission standards. Various manufacturers do see potential for the gas turbine engine for passenger vehicle installations in the future.

Engine Fuels

The type of fuel to be used can have a great effect on the design of an engine. Although most automotive engines use gasoline for

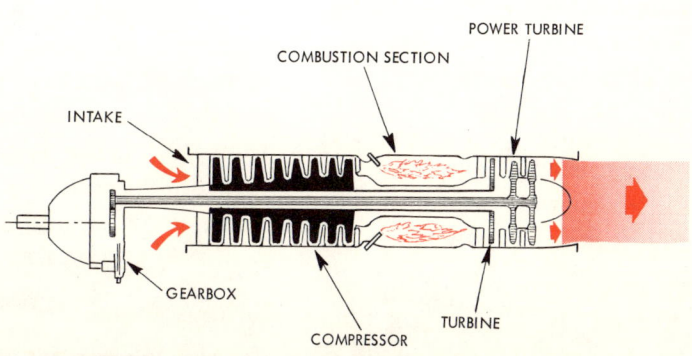

Fig. 2-27. Turbine engine components (Curtis-Wright Corp.)

Automotive Engines

fuel, some bus, truck, and stationary engines use a liquified petroleum gas (LPG). Such engines are basically the same as gasoline engines except they have special carbureting devices for mixing air and LPG in the proper proportions.

Vehicles using diesel oil as a fuel are equipped with diesel engines, Fig. 2-28. There are features in the diesel engine design which are quite different from the gasoline engine.

The Diesel Engine

Because diesel fuel is cheaper than gasoline, diesel engines have been adapted to almost every use for which other engines have been employed. They are used in central power stations, industrial apparatus, ships, launches, trains, tractors and motor vehicles.

Diesel and gasoline engines use different methods of supplying and igniting the fuel charge. Since this book is based primarily on gasoline engines, we will point out certain operating characteristics of diesel engines.

The diesel engine generates extreme heat in the combustion chamber through high compression. It utilizes this heat to ignite the fuel during the power stroke. When cold, diesel engines present certain starting problems due to insufficient heat being generated. To offset this condition, a glow plug is built into the combustion chamber. For starting, the glow plug is heated by a battery to provide the additional heat needed.

Various other types of starting systems are employed. Some of these are electric starters, air-operated starters, and auxiliary gasoline engines attached to the diesel engine. Some diesel engines are designed to operate on gasoline for starting purposes, switching over to diesel fuel after the engine is warm. Others, classed as low-compression engines, employ a fuel-injection system in connection with electric spark ignition.

Diesel engines operate on both the two- and four-stroke-cycle principles. Fig. 2-28 illustrates a four-stroke-cycle diesel engine.

Fig. 2-28. This is a four-stroke-cycle diesel engine. (International Harvester Co.)

Engine Operation and Design

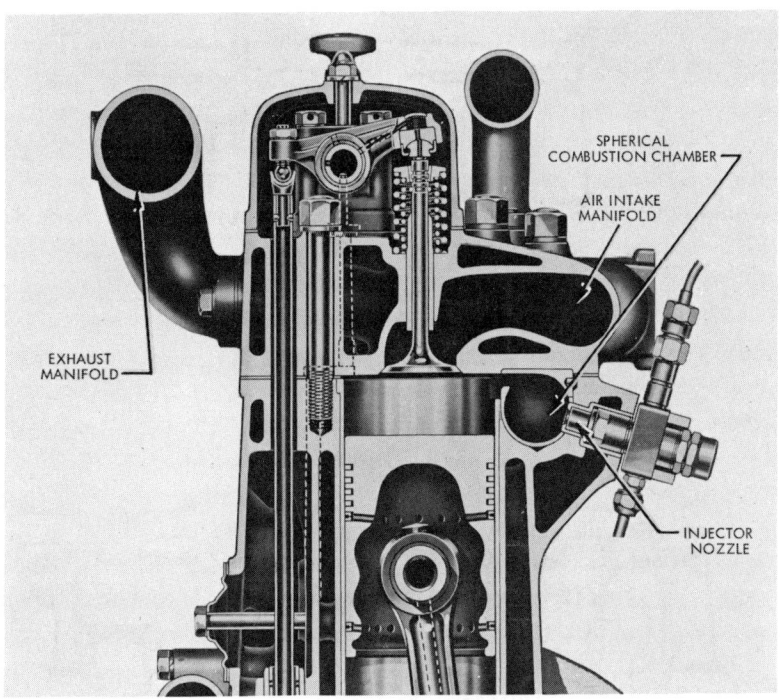

Fig. 2-29. In this cross sectioned view of a four-stroke-cycle diesel engine, you can see the similarity to a gasoline engine. (Hercules Motor Corp.)

A cross-sectional view of a four-stroke-cycle diesel engine is shown in Fig. 2-29. It must be pointed out that although the engine is similar in construction to a gasoline engine the various parts are made heavier to withstand greater loads.

Four-Stroke-Cycle Diesel Engine. The operation of the four-stroke-cycle diesel engine is shown in Fig. 2-30. On the intake stroke, the intake valve is opened and air alone enters the cylinder. This air is compressed on the compression stroke into a space $\frac{1}{15}$ to $\frac{1}{20}$ of its original volume.

The engine contains a spherical combustion chamber located at the side of each cylinder. Air compressed into the cylinder is given a high-speed, whirling motion by the piston as it moves to the end of its compression stroke. The extreme compression raises the pressure in the cylinder to about 550 to 650 psi. Since heat is generated during compression, the temperature of the air is raised to about 1200° F.

71

Automotive Engines

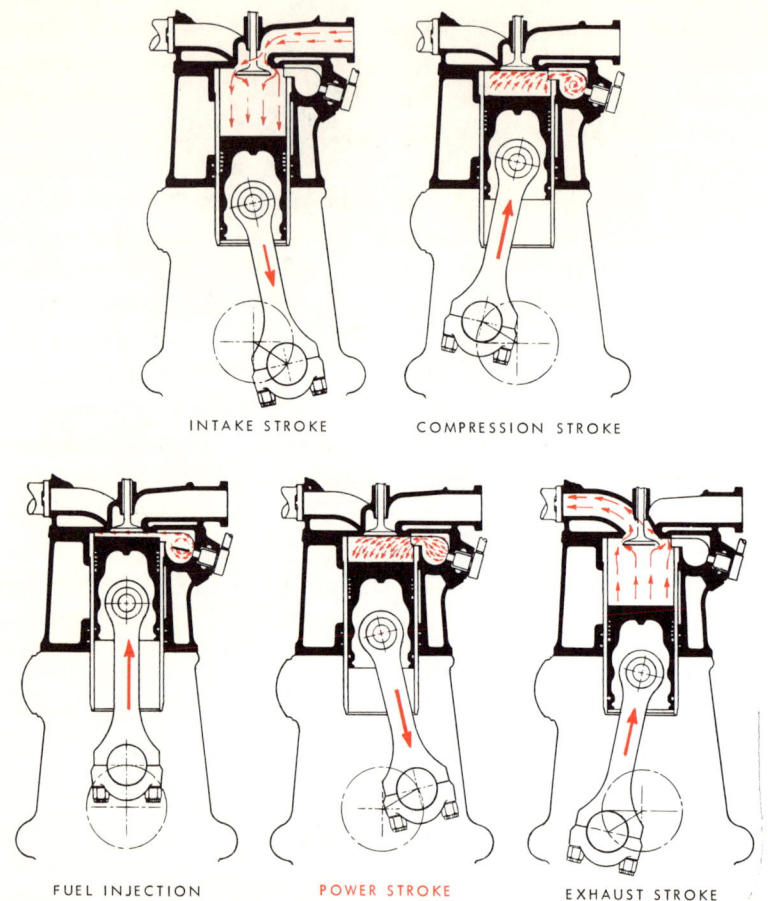

Fig. 2-30. You can compare the four-stroke-cycle diesel principle above to the four-stroke-cycle gasoline principle shown earlier in this chapter. (Hercules Motor Corp.)

As the piston nears top dead center, fuel is sprayed into the turbulent air in the spherical combustion chamber by an injection nozzle which projects into this area. The amount of fuel varies with the speed and load requirements of the engine. The high temperature of the compressed air ignites the fuel, and the expanding gases pass out of the opening in the combustion chamber and into the cylinder. These gases push down on the piston, causing it to move downward on its power stroke.

At the end of the power stroke, an exhaust valve is opened, and the burned fuel charge is expelled

Engine Operation and Design

from the cylinder. This cycle is repeated every two revolutions of the crankshaft in each cylinder.

Two-Stroke-Cycle Diesel Engine. The two-stroke-cycle diesel engine requires only two strokes, or one revolution of the crankshaft, to complete its cycle. Such engines require a supply of air to blow out the exhaust gases and to refill the cylinder with clean air. Usually, this is accomplished by means of an engine-driven blower or air compressor. Fig. 2-31 shows a two-stroke-cycle diesel engine employing a Roots-type blower.

In operation, air under pressure enters the cylinder through port openings—located in the side of the cylinder—when the piston is at the bottom of its stroke. The upward movement of the piston compresses the air, so its pressure and temperature are raised. Near the end of the compression stroke, fuel oil is sprayed into the cylinder by an injector. The heat of compression is sufficient to ignite the fuel charge. The resulting explosion then forces the piston downward on its power stroke. At the end of the power stroke, the exhaust valve is opened, followed shortly by the opening of the intake port as the piston continues its downward movement. The air entering the intake port not only assists in removing exhaust gases but also fills the cylin-

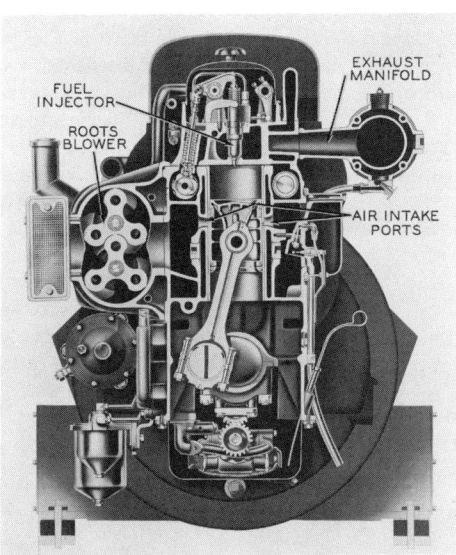

Fig. 2-31. This two-stroke-cycle diesel engine uses a Roots blower to blow out exhaust gases and to refill the cylinder with clean air. (Detroit Diesel Div., General Motors Corp.)

der with a new supply of air in preparation for the next cycle. Some designs permit the air to enter the cylinder through a cam-actuated intake valve, and the exhaust gases leave through a port opening in the side of the cylinder.

Methods of Cooling

Internal combustion engines may be classified as air cooled or liquid cooled. Although some early American and some present-day European cars have air-cooled engines, present-day engines in American automobiles are, except in the case of Corvair, liquid cooled.

Air Cooled. In air-cooled engines, the cylinders are mounted separately on the engine crankcase and have integral horizontal and vertical fins on the outside surfaces. Air passing through the fins cools the cylinders by radiation.

Liquid Cooled. In today's modern liquid-cooled engines, a solution of ethylene glycol and water is the recommended cooling medium. The solution is circulated throughout the water jackets.

Checking On Your Knowledge

The following questions give you the opportunity to check up on yourself. If you have read the chapter carefully, you should be able to answer the questions. If you have any difficulty, read the chapter over once more so that you have the information well in mind before you go on with your reading.

DO YOU KNOW

1. How do modern engines differ from early type engines?
2. How does a change in temperature affect molecular activity?
3. What is the purpose of compressing the fuel mixture contained within the cylinders?
4. What is the difference between potential and kinetic energy?
5. What is meant by a cast *en bloc* type of cylinder block?
6. What is the purpose of the piston rings?
7. What characteristics should a bearing metal possess to make it suitable for use in engine bearings?
8. What is the function of the connecting rods?
9. What purpose do the intake and exhaust valves serve?
10. What are the four strokes of a four-stroke-cycle gasoline engine?
11. Why is the intake valve held open to a point after bottom dead center?
12. What pressures are developed during combustion to force the piston downward on its power stroke?
13. What cylinder arrangements are employed on modern automobile engines?
14. How does the L-head engine differ in construction from the I-head engine?
15. Can you explain how the two-stroke-cycle gasoline engine operates?
16. What parts of the engine determine the firing order of an engine?
17. How does the four-stroke-cycle diesel differ from the four-stroke-cycle principle employed on gasoline engines?
18. What purpose does the blower or air compressor serve on two-stroke-cycle diesel engines?
19. How many firing impulses are produced in one revolution of the rotor of the rotating combustion engine?

Cylinder Blocks, Crankshafts, and Flywheels

Chapter **3**

The cylinder block houses the reciprocating and revolving engine parts and provides for the cooling of the engine cylinders. The functions of the cylinder block are described in this chapter.

The crankshaft, the flywheel, and the vibration damper are the main rotating parts of the engine. The crankshaft is supported by and rotates in the main bearings in alignment with the cylinder bores. There are various types of crankshafts, main bearings, flywheels, and vibration dampers. They vary both in construction and operation. The procedures used in cleaning, inspecting and measuring clearances and wear allowances are also discussed in this chapter.

Cylinder Block

The cylinder block forms the main body of the engine. The other parts are assembled in and on the cylinder block to form the complete engine. In addition to this structural function, the cylinder block provides the smooth, cylindrical bores which guide the motion of the pistons. The cylinders and the cylinder head form the combustion chambers in which the burning of fuel and expansion of gases take place. This process changes the heat energy in the fuel into mechanical energy.

Construction and Design

The design and construction of

cylinders and cylinder blocks are dependent upon several factors. Some of these are the number and arrangement of the cylinders, bore and stroke, compression ratio, valve arrangement, method of cooling, materials used in the construction of the block, and methods of casting and machining.

Materials. Usually the cylinder block of automotive engines is made of cast gray iron. Gray iron contains approximately three per cent carbon which exists mainly as free graphite. The graphitic carbon gives the iron its characteristic gray appearance when fractured. Only a small percentage of the total carbon in the metal is in chemical combination with the iron.

Cast gray iron is low in cost and has many properties that make it a valuable industrial metal. It will not warp under the high temperatures and pressures within the cylinders. For its strength, it is not exceptionally heavy. The metal is soft enough for machining, can be readily finished to a smooth surface, wears well, absorbs vibrations, and has good corrosion resistance. Gray iron can be cast readily in sand molds into the intricate shapes required when the water jackets, valve ports, etc., are cast integrally with the cylinder block.

Some gray iron cylinder blocks are cast with small percentages of the more common alloying elements added, such as nickel, molybdenum, and chromium. The alloys are used to improve the strength and hardness of the castings without decreasing their machinability. The addition of such alloys affects the amount of combined carbon in the metal and the size of the graphite flakes. The addition of nickel forms strong, machinable castings. Molybdenum and chromium increase the amount of combined carbon, therefore increasing hardness and wear resistance.

Some engines use a cast aluminum cylinder block. Aluminum reduces the weight of the engine. Since aluminum has a higher heat conductivity than cast iron, it dissipates heat more rapidly.

Casting Methods. The two basic methods of casting automotive engines are the *en bloc* casting for water-cooled engines and individual cylinder castings for air-cooled engines.

En Bloc Castings. All water-cooled auto engines are cast "en bloc." This means that the cylinder block and the upper half of the crankcase are cast together in a single unit. Note: Sometimes the lower portion of the cylinder block which supports the crankshaft and the oilpan is referred to as the crankcase. In a few very large engines, such as those used in trucks or buses, the cylinder block and crankcase may be cast separately and then bolted together. There are still some diesel engines built which

Blocks, Crankshafts, and Flywheels

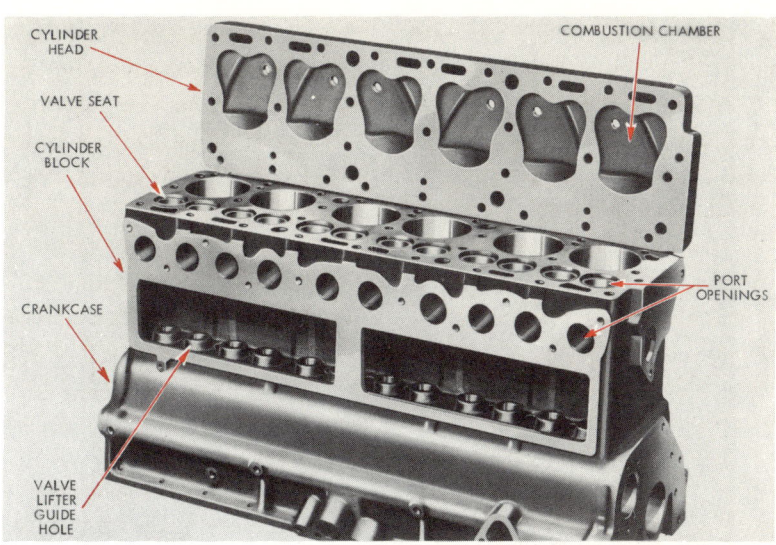

Fig. 3-1. Cylinder block for an L-head in-line engine. In this design, the valves are located in the block and not in the head. The valve parts are cast integrally with the block. (Pontiac Motor Div., General Motors Corp.)

have individually cast cylinders which are bolted to the crankcase. Casting the cylinders "en bloc" makes possible a shorter, more compact, and more rigid form of construction. Casting "en bloc" is also cheaper than separate castings; assembly is simplified and it is easier to enclose the valve operating mechanism.

Whether an engine is cast "en bloc" or made of separate castings, cylinder heads are always cast separately and attached to the cylinder block with bolts or with studs and nuts.

The design of cylinder blocks for L-head engines, Fig. 3-1, differs from that of I-head engines, Figs. 3-2 and 3-3. On L-head engines, the valve ports are cast integrally with the block.

The valve seats may be machined directly in the block or may consist of alloy steel inserts pressed into a recess machined in the block. The valve lifters are guided by guide holes machined in the block casting or by valve lifter guide brackets that bolt to the block.

Cylinder blocks for I-head engines, Figs. 3-2 and 3-3, have no valve ports or valve seats in the cylinder block. On such engines,

77

Automotive Engines

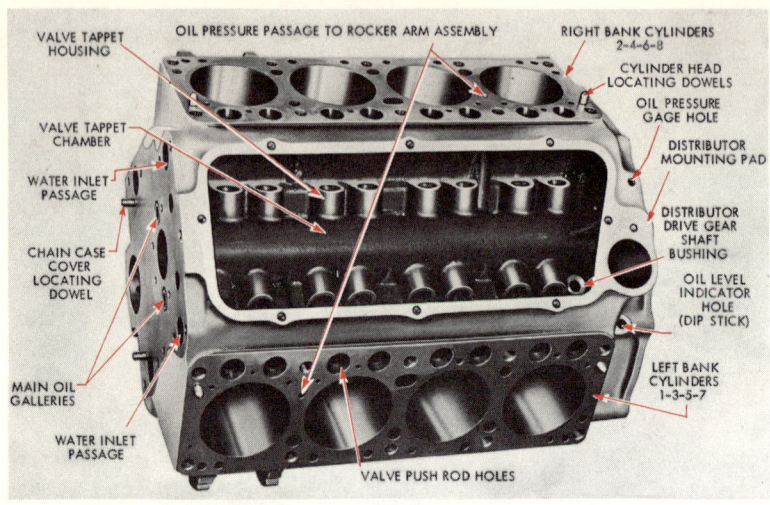

Fig. 3-2. Cylinder block for an I-head, V-8 engine. This type of casting is very compact and sturdy. Valve seats and parts are located in separate heads that are attached to each cylinder block by bolts or studs and nuts. (Chrysler Corp.)

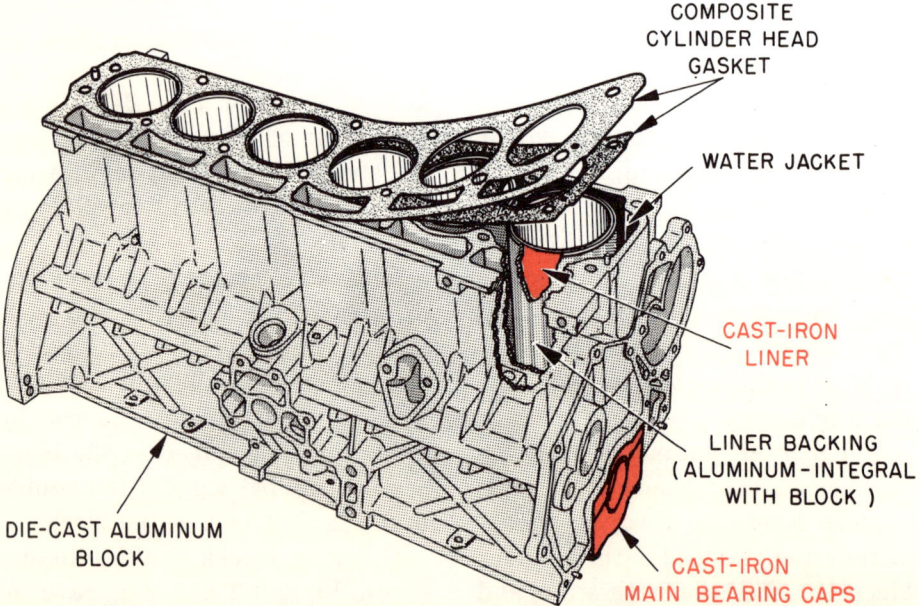

Fig. 3-3. Aluminum cylinder block for an I-head, in-line, six-cylinder engine. Threaded holes in the aluminum block are lined with iron for durability. (Plymouth Div., Chrysler Corp.)

Blocks, Crankshafts, and Flywheels

the valve ports and seats are contained in the removable cylinder head. The valve lifters in I-head engines are guided by guide holes machined in the block.

Cylinder blocks employed on V-type engines consist of two banks of cylinders located at an angle to each other and cast as an integral single unit with the crankcase, Fig. 3-2.

The main engine parts consisting of the crankshaft, connecting rods and pistons, and camshaft (and in L-head engines the valves and valve operating mechanism) are contained in the block, simplifying the assembly and disassembly of the engine.

Water jackets extending to the bottom of the cylinder are cast integrally with the cylinder block to provide for cooling of the engine. The outer walls of the jackets are made quite thin, because their main function is to retain the water in the engine. The water passages are formed during casting by means of sand cores supported by wires. After the casting has cooled, the sand and wires are removed through the water connections and through special openings provided for this purpose. These openings are later closed with metal plugs.

In many respects, the die-cast aluminum cylinder block and crankcase assembly is quite similar in design and construction to that made of cast gray iron, Fig. 3-3. Usually it has cast gray iron main bearing caps to withstand the forces imposed by the crankshaft and nonreplaceable cast gray iron cylinder liners that are placed in the mold before the block assembly is cast.

Individual Cylinder Castings. Air-cooled engines dissipate their heat to the air from fins on each cylinder. It would be extremely complicated to form an engine with fins on each cylinder from a single casting. Therefore, the cylinders, Fig. 3-4, are cast individually and bolted to the crankcase.

The cooling fins are cast integrally with the cylinders. Aluminum is used for these castings as it does a better job of dissipating heat than iron.

Machining. The cylinder block, as it comes from the mold, has internal strains within the metal due to uneven cooling between the thin and thick sections of the casting. The removal of the hard surface layer of iron by machining relieves only part of the strains in the casting. Machined castings tend to warp, producing slight changes in the shape of the casting. To prevent such an occurrence, it was a common practice to allow the castings to season after the initial machining operations by storing them in the open for a time. This method has been supplanted by a heat-treating operation, reducing the time for seasoning.

Automotive Engines

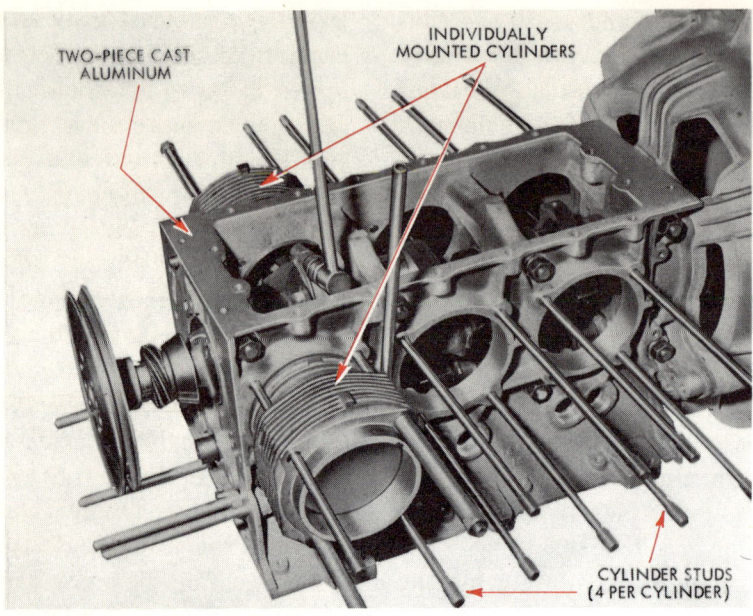

Fig. 3-4. Cylinders for an air-cooled engine are mounted individually on the crankcase. This is a six-cylinder opposed engine. Aluminum is used as often as possible because of its superior heat dissipating qualities. (Chevrolet Motor Div., General Motors Corp.)

In a completed cylinder block, the cylinders must be round and true and must be finished to a smooth surface if efficient engine performance is to be obtained. This is accomplished by boring, grinding, and/or honing (in that order). The precision finish which results offers little friction, and there is a uniform seal formed by the cylinder wall and the piston rings. The out-of-round and taper of the cylinder bore are held to an accuracy not to exceed 0.0005 inch. Generally the cylinder bores are finished to standard sizes, the allowance for clearance being made on the piston.

The cylinder bores are machined so they form an angle of 90 degrees with the crankshaft. The top and bottom surfaces of the cylinder block are machined parallel to each other, and the cylinder bores should be at right angles (90 degrees) to these surfaces.

Sleeves. Replaceable cylinder sleeves or liners are used in some gasoline and diesel engines. Engines with aluminum blocks have nonreplaceable cylinder liners. When wear conditions require reboring, such cylinders can be rebored to a maximum of 0.040 in. oversize.

Blocks, Crankshafts, and Flywheels

The use of replaceable cylinder sleeves makes possible a rapid and economical replacement of cylinder bores when excess wear makes such replacement necessary. The sleeves are made of cast gray iron, steel, or other alloyed metals, and are sometimes heat treated to give them improved wearing qualities.

Wet Type. Replaceable cylinder sleeves in use today are of the wet type. The wet type sleeve comes in contact with the coolant. There are gaskets at the bottom and sometimes at the top of the sleeves. The sleeve forms the entire cylinder wall, Fig. 3-5. The sleeve is a press fit in the cylinder block and usually requires the use of gaskets to prevent cooling system leaks. The use of wet sleeves is confined primarily to tractors and heavy truck engines.

Dry Type. A dry type of cylinder sleeve was used on some automobile engines in the past. Dry type sleeves did not come in contact with the engine coolant. Usually the dry type of sleeve was made of steel accurately machined on both inner and outer surfaces. The cylinder sleeve was pressed or driven into the cylinder bore, becoming an inner lining to the cylinder. Sometimes a dry cast-iron

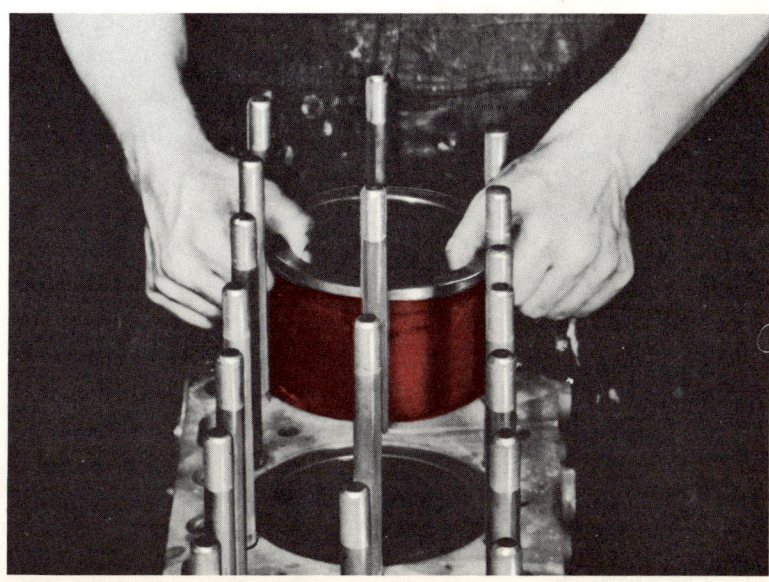

Fig. 3-5. Replaceable wet type cylinder sleeve. The inner surface of the sleeve has the same dimensions as the original cylinder sleeve so that standard size piston rings may be used. (International Harvester Co.)

sleeve is used when a cylinder wall has been deeply scored or cracked.

Cylinder Wear. The wear that occurs in the cylinders is due mainly to the side thrust of the pistons and the pressure of the piston rings against the cylinder walls. This wear results in the cylinders becoming worn out-of-round and tapered, Fig. 3-6.

The side thrust of the pistons against the cylinder walls is due to the angular relationship between the connecting rod and crankshaft and the pressures developed within the cylinders on the compression and power strokes, Fig. 3-7. As the pressures exerted on the piston are much greater on the power stroke than on the compression stroke, a greater side thrust is developed when the piston moves downward on its power stroke than when it is moving upward on the compression stroke. As a result, the cylinder wears more on the power thrust side of the cylinder than on the compression thrust side. In addi-

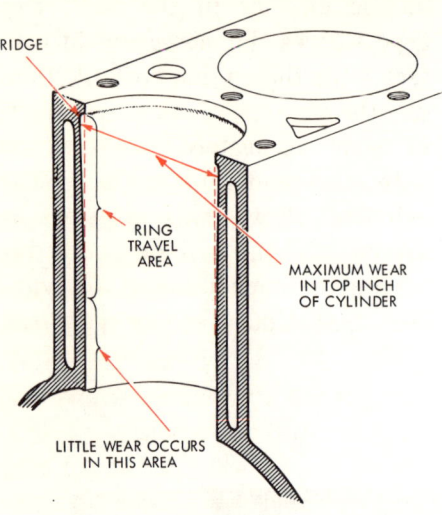

Fig. 3-6. Areas of wear in a cylinder.

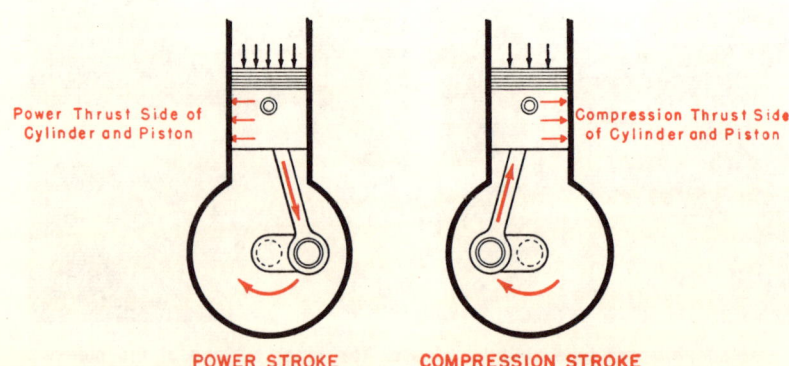

Fig. 3-7. Thrust forces which cause wear in an engine cylinder.

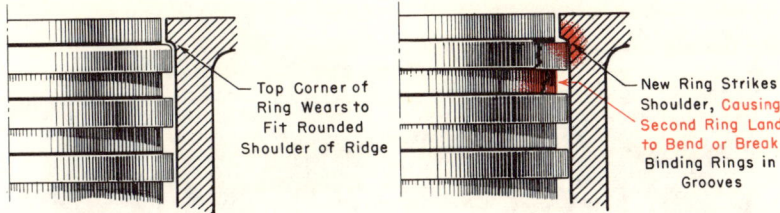

Fig. 3-8. The cylinder ridge must be removed to avoid possible ring or land breakage.

tion, because the greatest pressures are developed when the piston is at the top of its stroke and decrease as it moves downward, a greater amount of wear occurs at the top of the cylinder than at the bottom.

The pressure the piston rings exert against the cylinder walls is also responsible for cylinder wear in the area of ring travel. This area extends from just below the top of the cylinder to within several inches from the bottom of the cylinder. In addition to the above factors, the difficulty encountered in lubricating the upper portions of the cylinder walls and the high temperatures at the top of the cylinder which tend to burn the oil off the cylinders are also responsible for cylinder wear.

Most of the wear, therefore, occurs at the top of the cylinder, resulting in the formation of a ridge or shoulder around the top of the cylinder. As the cylinder wears, the upper, outer corner of the top piston rings wears to fit the rounded shoulder, Fig. 3-8. If a new, square-cornered ring is installed in a cylinder in which the ridge has not been removed, the sharp corner of the ring will strike the rounded surface of the ridge at the top of the piston stroke. During engine operation, this causes a knocking sound and may result in the bending or breakage of the top ring or second ring land on the piston. This action may bind the top and second piston rings in their grooves, preventing their effective action in the cylinder.

An excessive amount of out-of-round or taper in the cylinder walls makes it difficult to maintain a tight seal between the pistons and cylinder walls. Such cylinders should be restored to a round condition with the walls parallel.

Lower Cylinder Block. The lower part of the cylinder block has, in the past, been referred to as the crankcase. This supports the crankshaft and camshaft in bearings, and acts as a support for the oil pump, oil lines, starting motor, and

Automotive Engines

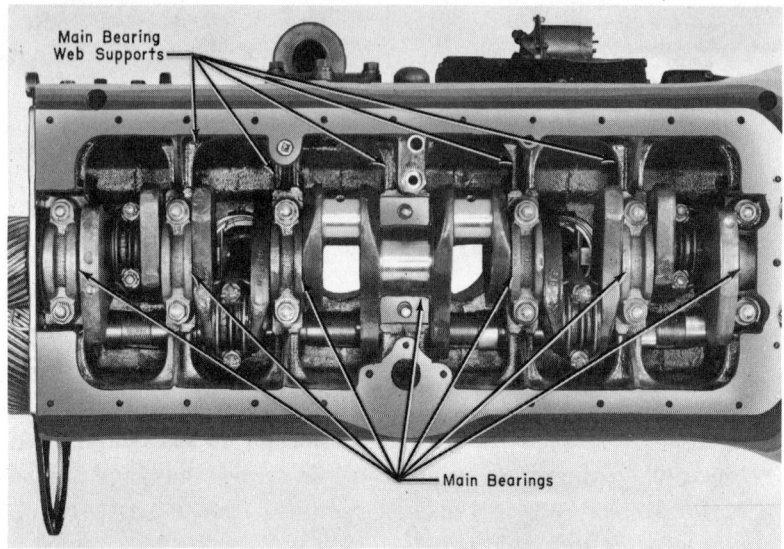

Fig. 3-9. Main bearing placement in the crankcase of an in-line engine. The center main bearing cap has been removed. (Chrysler Div., Chrysler Corp.)

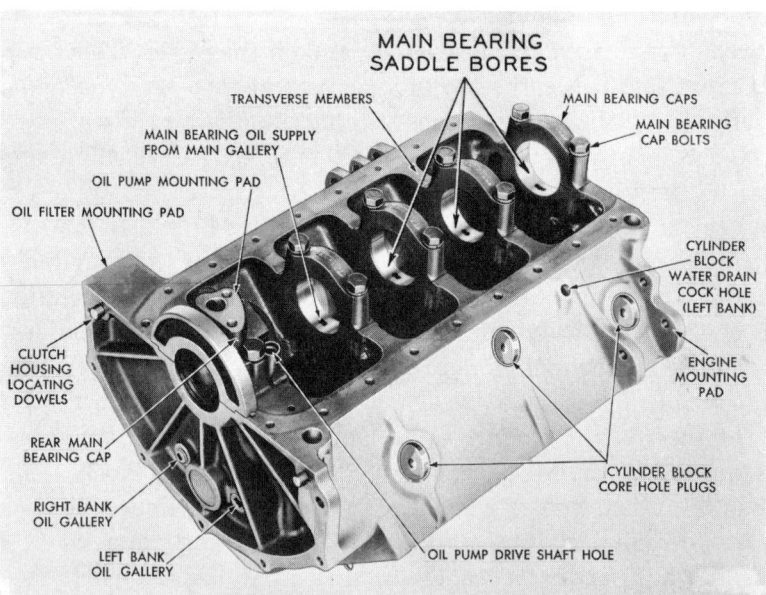

Fig. 3-10. Block of a V-8 engine turned over to show construction and main bearing placement. V-type engines require fewer main bearings than in-line engines because the crankshaft is shorter. (Chrysler Div., Chrysler Corp.)

numerous other engine parts. Figs. 3-9 and 3-10 illustrate the crankcase construction of typical in-line and V-type engines.

The lower part of the block, together with the oil pan, forms an enclosure for the revolving crankshaft that is airtight except at points where ventilation is provided.

The camshaft and crankshaft are supported in the block in sliding friction type bearings. Usually, the camshaft is supported in three to five one-piece tubular bearings. Camshaft bearings have no provisions for adjustment and must be replaced when excessive clearances occur.

The crankshaft is supported in main bearings in the cylinder block, the shaft being held in place by bearing caps bolted to the block. The number of main bearings employed in an engine varies with the design. In-line four-cylinder and V-type eight-cylinder engines are designed with three or five main bearings. Six-cylinder in-line engines may have three, four, or seven main bearings. The V-type six-cylinder engine has its crankshaft supported in four main bearings.

The cylinder block must be made rigid and strong to withstand the forces developed by the engine and the distortion imposed by road conditions. The main bearings are mounted in the saddle bores machined in the webs which are cast integrally with the block, Fig. 3-10. The webs add rigidity and lessen crankshaft distortion and vibration.

The block of a horizontally opposed type six-cylinder engine was illustrated in Fig. 3-4. The cylinder block is cast of aluminum and is divided vertically into two halves. The crankshaft and camshaft are mounted in bearings between the two halves. The halves are held together at the parting line by means of bolts. Each block-half has three openings which position the individual cast iron cylinders. The cylinders and the removable cylinder heads are secured to the block by means of long studs and nuts.

Crankshafts

The crankshaft receives the power from the pistons and connecting rods and transmits it to the flywheel and clutch. Depending upon the design, a crankshaft has one or more crankarms (throws), and the connecting rods are attached to crankpins located be-

Automotive Engines

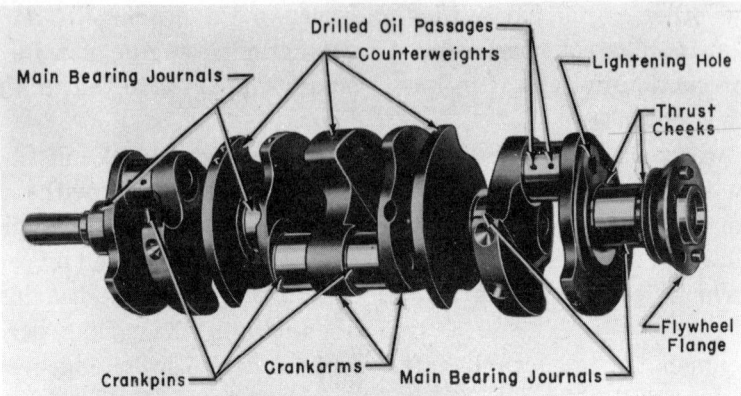

Fig. 3-11. Crankshaft construction. (Ford Motor Co.)

tween the crankarms, Fig. 3-11. The number, grouping and spacing of the crankarms and crankpins depend upon the number of cylinders and the design of the engine.

Counterweights are employed opposite the crankpins to balance the rotating forces developed by the crankarm, crankpin, and connecting rod. Some crankshafts have hollow crankpins, thus reducing their weight and the rotating forces developed. The crankshaft journals rotate in main bearings located in the engine crankcase. The crankshaft must be supported strongly in the crankcase. Therefore, crankshafts have a main bearing journal at each end of the crankshaft and at one or more points between the crankpins.

As the crankshaft turns, a tendency to move endwise often occurs. This tendency is known as *thrust*.

Thrust bearings or surfaces limit this end play. The crankshaft has thrust cheeks at both ends of one main bearing journal to take the thrust imposed on the crankshaft.

Usually, crankshafts are forged or cast of alloy steels and heat treated to resist wear, bending, and twisting. The crankshaft is forged or cast to approximate dimensions and then is heat treated and machined. Generally, machining consists of turning and grinding the main and connecting rod bearing journals to proper dimensions and finish. On some crankshafts, the crankarms, or throws, are also machined. The counterweights located opposite the crankpins are forged or cast integrally with the crankshaft.

Oil passages are drilled from the main bearing journals to the crankpins, Fig. 3-12, so as oil is supplied

Blocks, Crankshafts, and Flywheels

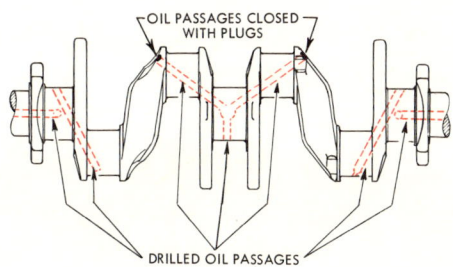

Fig. 3-12. Oil holes must be cleaned during engine overhaul to insure adequate lubrication for connecting rod bearings.

under pressure to the main bearings it also flows through the oil passages to lubricate the connecting rod bearings.

Variations in Crankshaft Design

While numerous factors enter into design of the crankshaft, the length, the number, and arrangement of crankarms around the shaft are determined by the number and arrangement of cylinders in the engine. The firing order of the engine is established by the crankarm arrangement in conjunction with the camshaft.

Four-Cylinder In-Line Crankshafts. All of the crankarms are arranged in one plane. The two end crankarms are spaced 180 degrees apart from the two center crankarms, Fig. 3-13. The crankshaft may rotate in three main bearings. However in many engines, five main bearings are provided. When the crankshaft is rotating at high speeds, the crankarms develop forces due to centrifugal action of the crankpins. These forces tend to distort the shaft, causing vibration and severe stress on the shaft. Counterweights reduce these forces, and smoother engine operation results.

The four-stroke-cycle, four-cylinder engine produces four power strokes every two revolutions of the crankshaft or one every 180 degrees. The average power stroke is 140 degrees in length. Therefore there is approximately a 40-degree lapse between power strokes, Fig. 3-14.

Six-Cylinder In-line Crankshafts. The crankarms are arranged in three planes spaced 120 degrees apart. There are two crankarms in each plane, Fig. 3-15. Six-cylinder in-line engine crankshafts rotate in either three, four, or seven main bearings.

Power overlap. A six-cylinder in-line engine produces a power stroke every 120 degrees of crank-

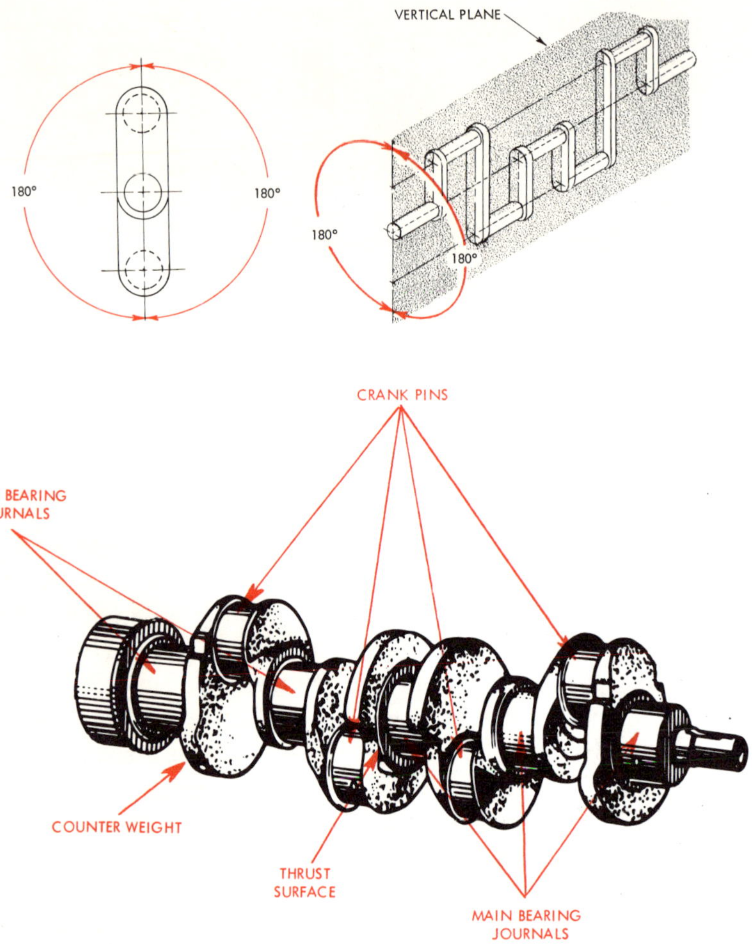

Automotive Engines

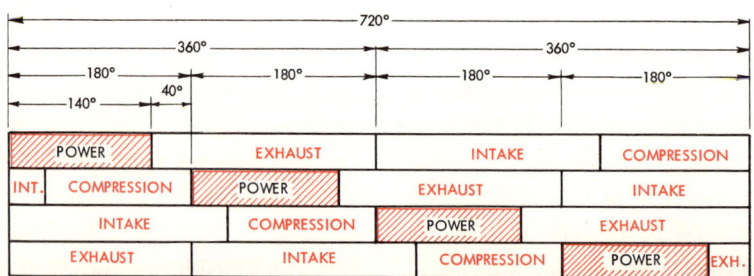

Fig. 3-13. Four-cylinder engine crankarms are arranged 180 degrees apart.

Fig. 3-14. There is a lapse or interruption of power in four-cylinder engines.

Blocks, Crankshafts, and Flywheels

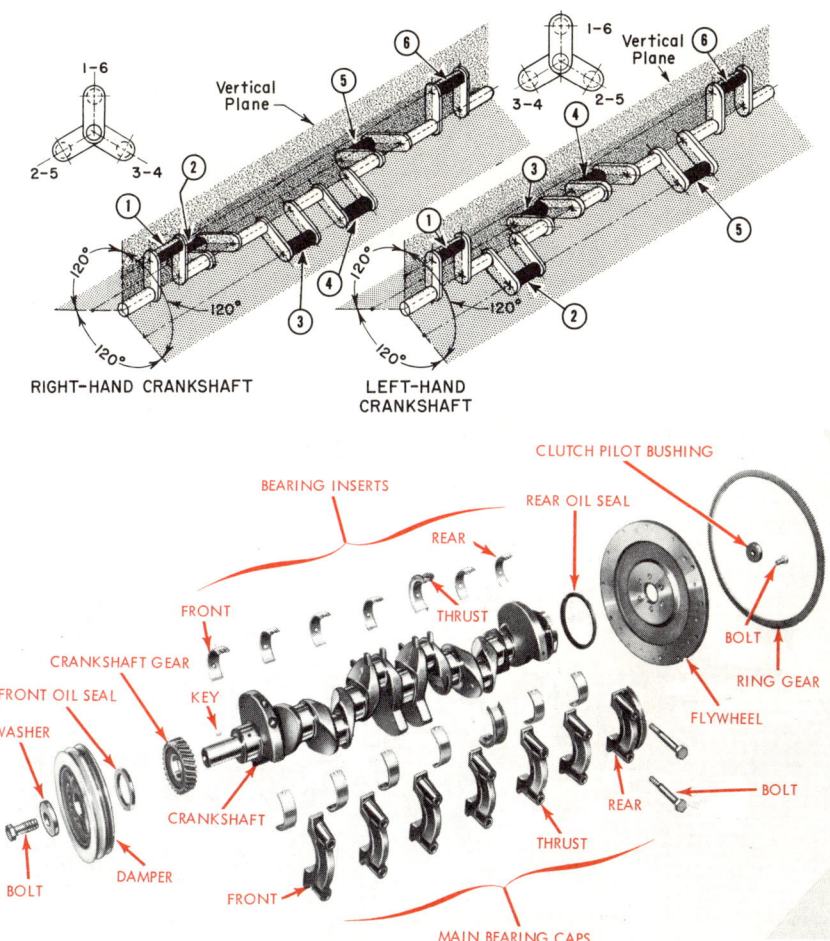

Fig. 3-15. Six-cylinder in-line engine crankarms are arranged in three planes 120 degrees apart. (Ford Motor Co.)

shaft rotation. There are approximately 20 degrees of "power overlap." Power overlap occurs when a piston starts on the power stroke before the power stroke in the preceding cylinder in the firing order is completed, Fig. 3-16. Power overlap smooths the power flow.

V-Type Six-Cylinder Crankshafts. There are two banks of cylinders with three cylinders in each bank. The banks are at a 90-degree angle to one another. The crankshaft has only three crankarms spaced 120 degrees apart. Connecting rods from opposing cylinders attach to the same crankpin. Therefore, connecting rods from cylinders No. 1 and No. 2 are connected to the front crankpin, No. 3 and No. 4 to the

Automotive Engines

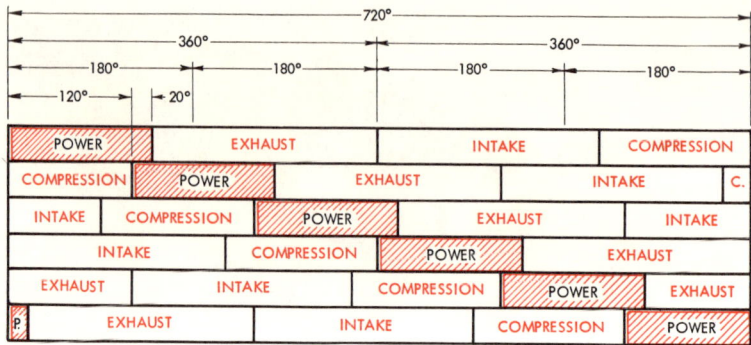

Fig. 3-16. The six-cylinder in-line engine has 20 degrees of power overlap.

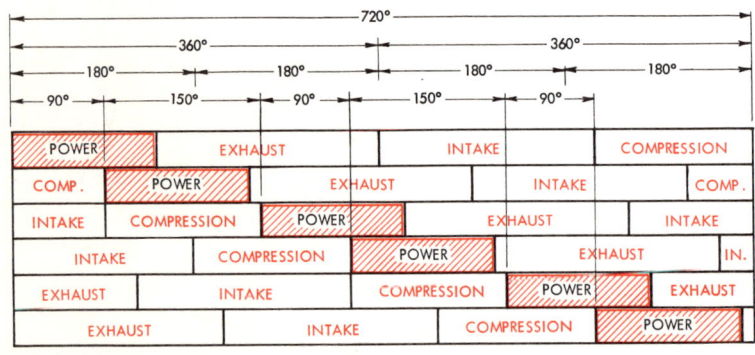

Fig. 3-17. The six-cylinder V-type engine has both power overlap and power lapse.

next, and No. 5 and No. 6 to the rear crankpin. The crankshaft rotates in four main bearings.

A six-cylinder V-type engine produces power strokes at 90-degree and 150-degree intervals, Fig. 3-17. The uneven spacing between power strokes is a result of the 90-degree V-type engine design and the crankshaft design.

V-Type Eight-Cylinder Crankshafts. Crankshafts used in V-type eight-cylinder engines have only four crankpins, and the connecting rods from opposing cylinders are attached to the same crankpin. The crankshaft rotates in either three or five main bearings.

Two types of crankshafts are used in V-8 engines. The main difference between the two types is the crankpin spacing around the shaft. One type has all its crankpins in one plane and spaced 180

Blocks, Crankshafts, and Flywheels

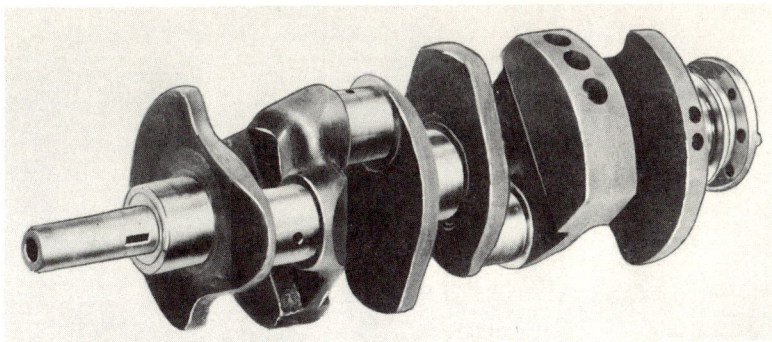

Fig. 3-18. This V-type eight-cylinder crankshaft design provides evenly spaced power overlap. (Ford Motor Co.)

degrees apart. It is very similar to the four-cylinder in-line engine crankshaft, Fig. 3-13. A second type of V-8 crankshaft has each crankpin in a separate plane with a 90-degree spacing between them, Fig. 3-18. This second type provides better engine balance and, therefore, smoother operation.

Usually V-8 engines have the crankshaft centrally located in the engine and a 90-degree angle between cylinder banks. The power strokes are equally spaced at 90-degree intervals throughout the cycle, Fig. 3-19.

Some V-8 engines have an uneven overlap of power strokes to reduce or eliminate the rhythmic vibration induced by evenly spaced power impulses. Uneven overlap is accomplished by locating the crank-

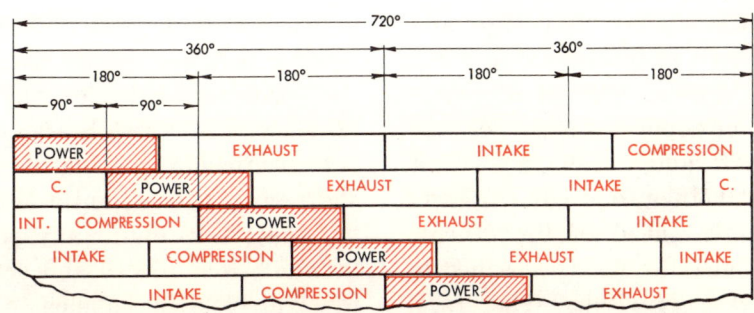

Fig. 3-19. Power overlap in an eight-cylinder, V-type engine.

91

Automotive Engines

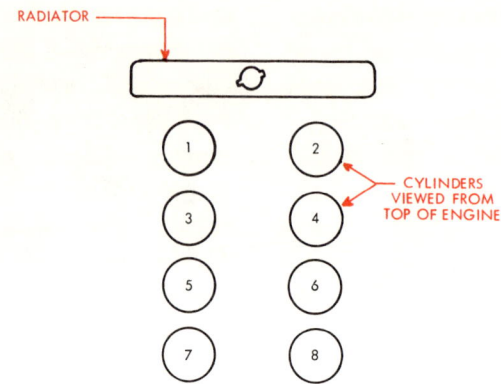

Fig. 3-20. Usual method of numbering cylinders in a V-type engine.

shaft slightly to one side of the engine center line or by having an angle other than 90 degrees between the cylinder blocks.

Fig. 3-20 illustrates a common method of numbering V-type engine cylinders. According to this numbering system, the odd numbered cylinders are in the left cylinder bank and the even numbered cylinders are in the right bank. The forward cylinder in the left bank is No. 1.

Opposed Engine Crankshafts. These are similar in design and construction to those used in other types of engines. The cylinders are located on opposite sides of the crankshaft and usually are offset from each other (one cylinder bank set slightly ahead of the other). Each connecting rod is attached to a separate crankpin. Therefore, most six-cylinder opposed engines would employ a conventional six throw, six-cylinder crankshaft similar to that shown in Fig. 3-15.

Crankshaft Balance

A crankshaft is said to be in balance if no unbalanced forces are developed during rotation that tend to bend or distort the shaft. The unbalanced forces cause vibration, high main bearing pressures, and excessive strains on the shaft. The crankshaft must be in both static and dynamic balance if smooth engine operation is to be obtained.

Static Balance. Static balance is the state of balance when the crankshaft is at rest. Static balance is determined by placing the crankshaft on a pair of knife edges. If the shaft remains at any position in which it is placed and does not revolve, it is in balance. An unbalanced crankshaft will rotate as

Blocks, Crankshafts, and Flywheels

gravity pulls the heavy side downward. Therefore, metal must be removed from the heavy side until perfect balance is obtained.

Dynamic Balance. A special machine is used to balance a crankshaft dynamically. A test is made while the shaft is revolving at different speeds. Indicators show exactly where and how much the shaft is out of balance. Metal is removed from the sections that are out of balance until the machine indicates that the shaft is free from vibration. The machine performs both the static and dynamic tests at the same time.

Other Balance Factors. Smooth engine operation involves several other factors besides crankshaft balance. We already know that crankshaft balancing problems consist mainly of compensating for the centrifugal forces affecting rotation. In an operating engine, however, inertia forces develop that are more difficult to balance; the up-and-down movement of the piston and connecting rod assemblies must be stopped at the end of each stroke and their direction of travel reversed. In addition, the crankshaft is subjected to load deflections (bending) induced by power impulses. The load deflections produce a torsional (twisting) vibration in the crankshaft which must be absorbed to obtain smooth engine operation.

Manufacturers balance these other factors by using weights, Figs. 3-15 and 3-18. The weights, or counterbalances, are made as part of the crankshaft.

Although manufacturers exercise extreme care to secure the best possible balance, all crankshafts have one or more critical speeds at which a vibration period develops. Often this critical speed vibration causes nearby parts to vibrate. By careful design and balancing, manufacturers locate the critical vibration periods at infrequently used speeds or entirely out of the speed range of the engine.

Main Bearings

The number of main bearings employed in an engine varies with the number of cylinders and the engine design. The journals on the crankshaft turn within bearings of antifriction metal such as cadmium-silver, copper alloy, babbitt, copper-lead, etc. Such alloys develop little friction and withstand the heavy bearing loads, high speeds, and high temperatures encountered during engine operation.

The main bearings are designed to take the *radial* loads (perpendicular to the crankshaft) imposed on the crankshaft during engine operation. However, when the clutch is engaged, it imposes a thrust load on the crankshaft (parallel to the crankshaft). The timing gears also impose a thrust load during engine operation. This thrust is taken by one of the main bearings designed for the purpose. The bearing has an antifriction surface on each side which bears against a thrust cheek or collar on the crankshaft. The thrust bearing may be located toward the front or rear of the engine and limits the endplay of the crankshaft.

Clearances

Main bearings are fitted with a clearance to provide space for a film of oil to lubricate the bearing. As a rule, pressure lubricated bearings on crankshafts with journals up to $2\frac{3}{4}$ in. diameter are fitted to a total clearance of 0.0005 to 0.0015 inch. Crankshafts with journals from $2\frac{13}{16}$ to $3\frac{1}{2}$ in. in diameter are fitted to a clearance of 0.0015 to 0.0025 inch. The crankshaft must also have end clearance at the thrust bearing to prevent the shaft from binding when operating at high temperatures. This end clearance varies from 0.004 to 0.010 in., depending on the diameter of the thrust bearing journal. The thrust bearing has much less end clearance than the other main bearings to permit it to take the thrust load.

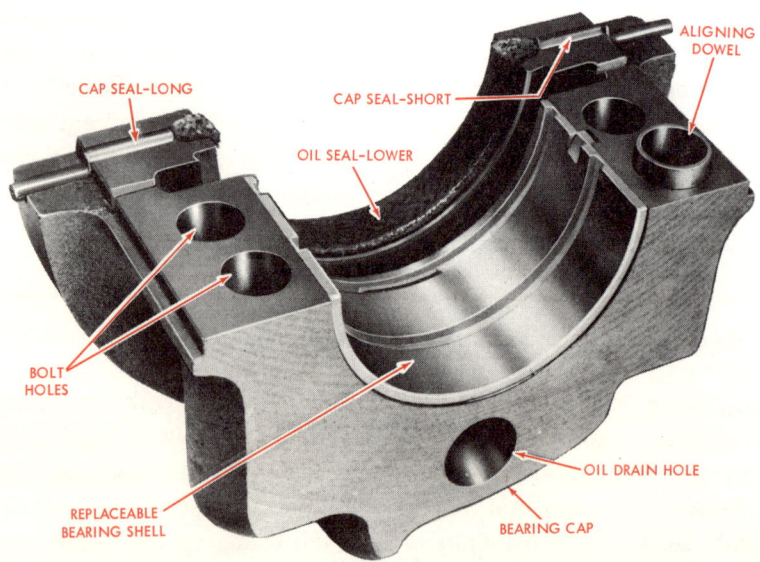

Fig. 3-21. Lower main bearing cap with replaceable insert bearing. (Plymouth Div., Chrysler Corp.)

Blocks, Crankshafts, and Flywheels

The greater clearance of the bearings allows the crankshaft to expand. The connecting rod bearing on the crankpin and the small end of the connecting rod on the piston pin are provided with a side clearance to prevent binding due to expansion.

The main bearings in general use are the precision type replaceable insert bearing, Fig. 3-21.

Insert Main Bearings

Precision type insert bearings consist of a steel or bronze backing, lined with a thin layer of alloy bearing material. The bearing consists of two halves. The upper half is in the engine block. The lower half is in the bearing cap. A projection on the bearing, or a dowel pin, positions the bearing in the crankcase and prevents it from turning. Such bearings are replaced easily and quickly when they become worn. Insert bearings are made accurately to size and are also available for boring to the exact size required. Such bearings are bored to fit worn or reground crankshafts when the available standard undersize bearings will not establish the desired clearances. Provided that the crankshaft journals are within the allowable limits of out-of-round, taper, and wear, or have been reground to standard undersize dimensions, the replaceable bearings establish correct clearances without fitting.

Flywheels

The flywheel is bolted to the crankshaft and is balanced accurately to assure smooth engine operation at all speeds. Two or more dowels on the crankshaft flange position the flywheel.

The flywheel rotates with the crankshaft and tends to distribute the power impulses evenly throughout the engine cycle. Thus, the rotation of the crankshaft is continued from one power stroke to the next.

The flexibility and pickup of an engine are dependent to some extent upon the flywheel design. A light flywheel tends to permit rapid acceleration, but its light weight causes an engine with no power overlap to run unevenly at low speeds. A heavy flywheel gives smooth, low speed operation for engines with no power overlap (four cylinders or less). Engines with more than four cylinders can use lighter flywheels because they have power overlap.

On some of the older engines, ignition and valve timing marks were stamped on the front face of

Automotive Engines

the flywheel. On some engines, a steel ball was imbedded in the flywheel for ignition timing purposes.

Flywheels differ somewhat in their construction, depending upon whether they are used with the conventional clutch or with a fluid coupling or with a torque converter.

Fig. 3-22. This type of flywheel is used with a friction type clutch. (Oldsmobile Div., General Motors Corp.)

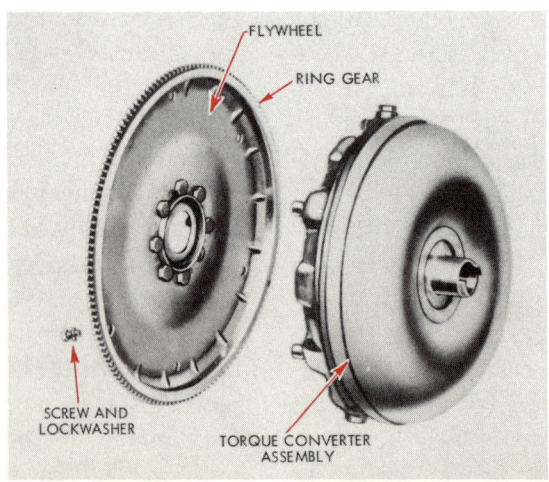

Fig. 3-23. The torque converter performs all the functions of the flywheel.

Blocks, Crankshafts, and Flywheels

Flywheel with Friction Clutch

The flywheel is made of cast gray iron and has a steel ring gear shrunk onto its outer diameter. The starter drive pinion meshes with the ring gear when cranking the engine, Fig. 3-22. The rear face of the flywheel is machined to a smooth surface and acts as one of the clutch pressure surfaces.

Flywheel With Fluid Coupling or Torque Converter

Fluid couplings and torque converters transmit engine torque from the engine to the rest of the vehicle. They are similar in that they both serve as hydraulic couplings and perform all the functions of the conventional friction clutch. They are bolted to the flywheel, Fig. 3-23.

A steel ring gear is welded to the perimeter of the flywheel. The starter pinion gear meshes with the flywheel ring gear to crank the engine when the ignition key switch is turned to the starting position.

Vibration Dampers

On most engines, vibration dampers are used to damp out crankshaft torsional vibration. The vibration damper is mounted on the front end of the crankshaft and usually is combined with the crankshaft fan drive pulley.

Most vibration dampers have timing marks stamped on the rim of the balancer weight with a pointer mounted on the timing gear cover. The timing marks are used when timing the engine.

Torsional Vibration

Torsional vibration is a twisting action in a crankshaft due to sudden application of power. The flywheel at the rear of the crankshaft has sufficient mass so it resists sudden changes in speed. As a result, when a power impulse occurs in one of the cylinders, the sudden high pressure on the crankpin twists the crankshaft between the cylinder and the flywheel in a manner similar to twisting a coil spring. Near the end of the power stroke, the crankshaft tends to unwind, just as a coil spring will unwind when released. Because the sudden application of power stores energy in the crankshaft, the shaft tends to twist back and forth. The amount and speed of the twisting action are lessened somewhat by the stiffness of the crankshaft and the spacing between power impulses.

The time interval between power impulses, depending on the engine

97

speed, may increase or decrease the torsional vibration. If the impulses which follow occur at the time the crankshaft begins to uncoil from the backward spring, the impulses tend to increase the amount of twisting action. Continued operation under such conditions would result in a constantly increasing torsional vibration until the crankshaft broke. When the power impulses and the direction of crankshaft twist oppose each other, the two forces tend to neutralize each other, reducing or eliminating the torsional vibration in the shaft.

Usually, crankshafts have several speeds at which such vibration occurs. Long crankshafts tend to develop greater torsional vibration than short crankshafts. Therefore, vibration dampers vary somewhat in their design.

Rubber Damping. Three types of vibration dampers have been used in the past—a rubber friction type damper, a spring friction type, and a viscous type. All dampers used today are of the rubber friction type.

A flywheel, or balance weight, is connected by rubber to a hub, Fig. 3-24. Due to the rubber connection, the flywheel floats on the hub with a slight back-and-forth movement.

When torsional vibration occurs in a crankshaft, the crankshaft actually rotates faster during the time that the twist is in the direction of rotation. Because the bal-

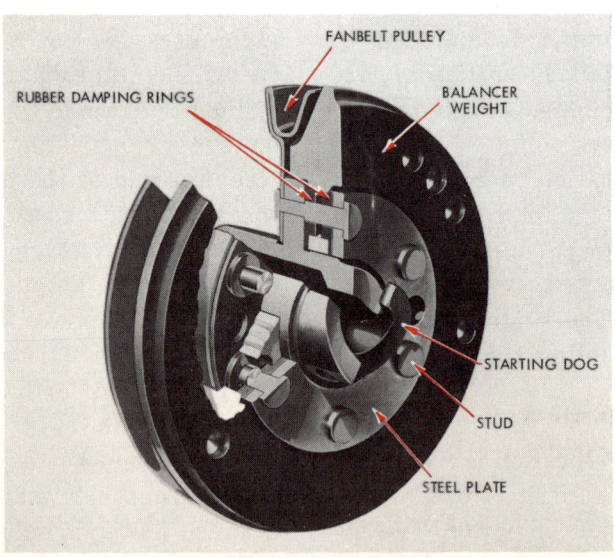

Fig. 3-24. This damper uses rubber to counteract vibration. (Chevrolet Motor Div., General Motors Corp.)

Blocks, Crankshafts, and Flywheels

ancer floats on its hub, any sudden changes in the speed of crankshaft rotation is carried to the damper through the hub and the rubber ring. The balancer has sufficient weight to resist any such sudden changes in speed. Therefore, the balancer exerts a force in a direction opposite to that of twist. This force counteracts the twisting action and absorbs vibration.

Some engines do not have a vibration damper. Instead, a heavier crankshaft pulley is used. Usually small engines do not develop so great a twisting force and, therefore, can operate effectively without the need for a vibration damper.

Inspection and Repair of Cylinder Block

The cylinder block should be inspected to determine condition and state of wear. The inspections performed should be made carefully, as they are the basis upon which the type of repairs to be performed are determined.

After disassembly, the cylinder block should be cleaned thoroughly to remove all carbon, oil, dirt, and sludge. The water jackets should be cleaned to remove rust and lime deposits. All the old gaskets, and the oil passage plugs should be removed before cleaning. A small diameter rod or stiff copper bristle brush should be run through the oil passages to loosen any carbon or sludge that may have collected in the passages. The assembly can be cleaned with petroleum-type solvents and a stiff brush or an emulsifying liquid cleaner, steam, or by soaking in a cleaning tank containing either a hot or cold cleaning solution. Additional flushing with a stream of water may be necessary with some types of cleaning solutions. During the cleaning operation, the oil passages should be flushed and blown out with compressed air. When the block is thoroughly clean, the oil passage plugs can be installed. Aluminum cylinder blocks require a special cleaning solution that will not attack the aluminum.

While the main bearings, camshaft bearings, and (in L-head engines) the valves are also located in the cylinder block, their inspection and repair are dealt with in later chapters of this book.

Inspection

The inspection of the cylinder block should be performed both visually and with precision measuring tools. Visual inspection indicates the general condition of the casting and related parts. Measurement with precision tools indicates the amount of wear that has taken place and determines whether the cylinders are within serviceable limits or in need of reconditioning.

Visual Inspection. The cylinder block should be given a thorough visual inspection to determine whether the water jackets are free of rust and lime deposits. See that the block is clean. Look for broken studs or bolts, cracks, or other defects in the casting, a ridge or shoulder worn into the top of the cylinders, and scored cylinders.

All broken or damaged studs or bolts should be replaced. Cracks may occur in the water jackets, around the valve seats, in the valve chambers, cylinder bores, and the engine support brackets. Depending upon the location of the crack and the design of the casting, sometimes a crack can be repaired by the electric arc welding method. A cylinder block with a crack in the cylinder bore should be replaced. Occasionally it is necessary to subject the cylinder block to a water pressure test to locate the leaks in the block. Check the top surface of the cylinder block with a straight-edge and thickness gage, and if it is warped 0.020 in. or more the top of the block should be resurfaced.

Precision Measurement. After the ridge has been removed from the top of the cylinder and the piston pulled, the size of the cylinder and the amount of out-of-round and taper can be measured accurately with a telescoping gage and micrometer, Fig. 3-25. The cylinder bore should be cleaned thoroughly, after which its diameter should be measured with the telescoping gage at the top of the cylinder, both parallel and at right angles to the long dimension of the cylinder block. The measurements should be taken just below the shoulder or ridge worn into the top of the cylinder (point of greatest wear). A comparison of the two readings obtained by measuring the gage with the outside micrometer gives the amount that the cylinder is worn out-of-round at the top. The cylinder bore also should be measured about two inches up from the bottom of the cylinder, both parallel and at right angles to the long dimension of the cylinder block. The difference between the two readings indicates the amount of out-of-round at the bottom of the cylinder. An inside micrometer may also be used for measurement. (Detailed instructions on the use of the micrometer caliper can be found in Appendix C of this book.)

To determine the amount of taper in the cylinder, a comparison is made between the measurements at right angles to the cylinder block at both the top and bottom of the cylinder. The greatest amount of wear in the cylinder occurs in this direction due to the thrust imposed by the piston. The difference between the two measurements indi-

Blocks, Crankshafts, and Flywheels

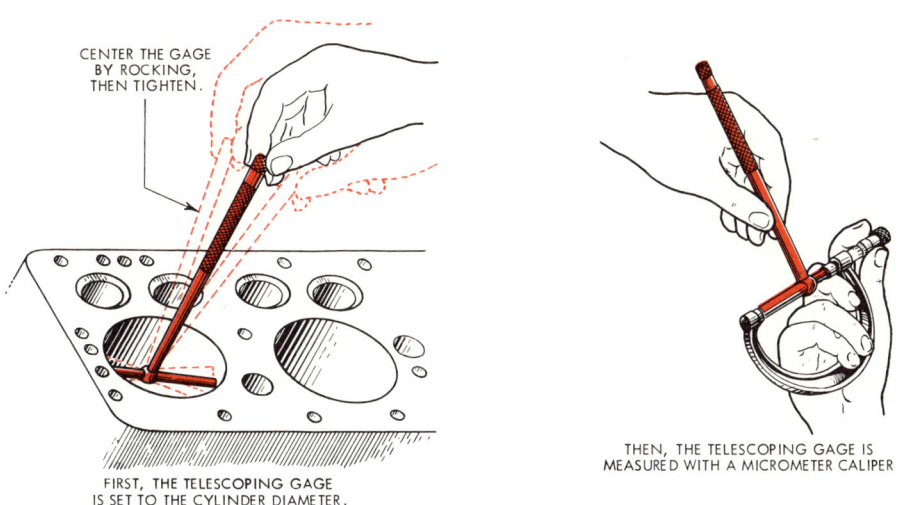

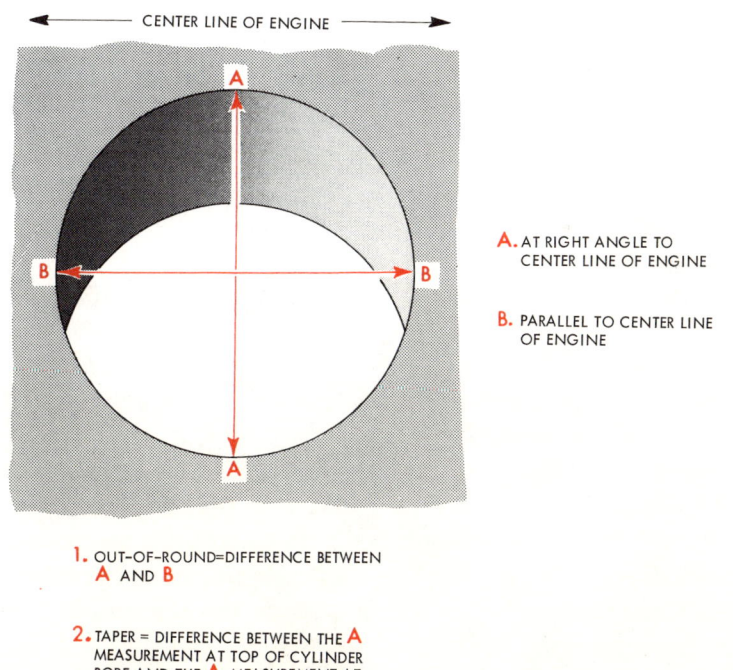

Fig. 3-25. Checking cylinder out-of-round and taper with a telescoping gage. Measurements should be taken at several places in the cylinder, both parallel and at right angles to the long dimension of the cylinder block. (Ford Motor Co.)

cates the amount of taper in the cylinder. The maximum amount of taper and out-of-round in a cylinder should not exceed 0.010 in. taper and 0.005 in. out-of-round. When the amount of out-of-round or taper equals or exceeds this amount, the cylinders should be honed, rebored, or ground to the next oversize for which pistons are available. Usually cylinders are rebored to fit standard oversize pistons of 0.020, 0.030, 0.040, or 0.060 in. oversize.

To determine the amount of wear in a cylinder, the maximum diameter at the top of the cylinder should be compared with the original diameter of the cylinder. The oversize to which a cylinder should be rebored is determined by adding to the original diameter of the cylinder the amount of metal that must be removed to produce a round and true cylinder.

The amount of out-of-round and taper in cylinders can also be determined by the use of a dial gage, Fig. 3-26, which reads in thousandths of an inch. The gage hand indicates instantly the slightest variation in cylinder bores. To check the cylinder, insert the gage in the cylinder bore and move from top to bottom the full length of the cylinder to determine the amount of taper. Turn or completely rotate the gage in the cylinder at several points, taking a reading at each point to determine out-of-round.

Fig. 3-26. Checking cylinder out-of-round and taper with a dial gage. The gage gives a positive or negative reading from the point of initial setting. (Chevrolet Motor Div., General Motors Corp.)

Blocks, Crankshafts, and Flywheels

Sometimes engines with standard or rebored cylinders that are worn less than the maximum limits are overhauled without reconditioning the cylinder bores. In such engines, the shoulder or ridge at the top of the cylinders must be removed before new piston rings are installed.

When cylinders are worn excessively, or are badly scored, and a true cylinder cannot be obtained to accommodate the largest oversize piston available, the cylinders can be rebored to accommodate a cast-iron sleeve. This method makes it possible to obtain additional service from a cylinder block which would otherwise have to be scrapped.

Repair

To restore the engine to an efficient operating condition, certain repair operations must be performed on the engine cylinders when the wear exceeds the maximum limits. The operations consist of removing the cylinder ridge at the top of the cylinder, honing or reboring the cylinders oversize to restore them to a round and straight condition, and replacement of damaged or broken studs or bolts.

Ridge Removal. The shoulder or ridge that is formed at the top of the cylinder due to wear can be removed with a cylinder ridge reamer, Fig. 3-27, in cylinder

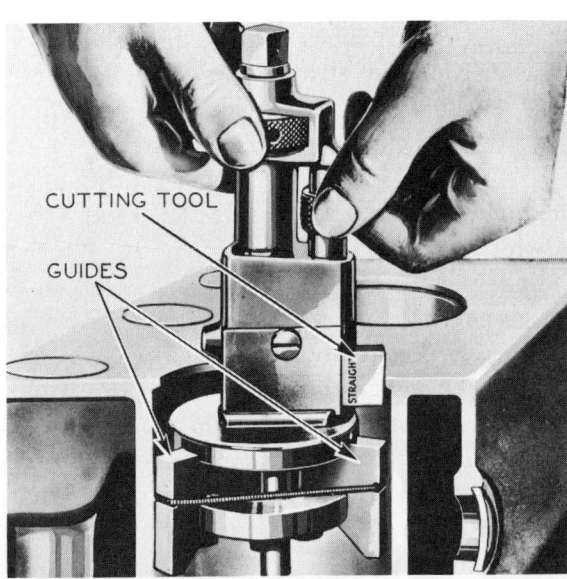

Fig. 3-27. Adjusting the cutting tool on a ridge reamer. Do not cut away too much metal. (Plymouth Div., Chrysler Corp.)

blocks having cylinders of cast gray iron. Ridge reamers are adjustable to accommodate various sizes of cylinders and generally have a single cutting blade. The adjustable features of the ridge reamer permit it to be firmly supported in the cylinder while the ridge is being removed. Care must be taken not to cut more than $\frac{1}{64}$ in. below the bottom of the ridge.

Reconditioning Cylinders. Cylinder walls that are moderately rough or scored and which are less than 0.005 in. out-of-round or .010 inch taper require only partial refinishing. This can be accomplished by honing the cylinder walls. Hones are abrasive stones, and honing resizes the cylinders by grinding them.

When cylinder walls are badly scored, scuffed, or are worn more than 0.005 in. out-of-round or .010 inch taper, they should be refinished completely by being rebored.

Honing. The hone is used to remove the glaze which forms on the walls of the cylinders and to true up the cylinders as much as possible without enlarging them too much. Often, honing permits the use of standard size piston rings since standard size rings usually measure to the upper tolerance for production rings. Standard size rings are, therefore, the size of the largest production rings.

Ordinarily, the cylinder should not be enlarged by honing more than 0.002 in. unless the pistons are to be expanded or replaced. In such cases, up to 0.005 in. can be removed. Generally, the removal of 0.001 to 0.002 in. will clean up a cylinder bore so the surface is sufficiently improved.

When honing such cylinders, grinding is started at the lower end of the cylinder, using a medium pressure on the stones. The hone is moved up and down rapidly, with about 1 to 1½ in. strokes. When the glaze is cut and the bore begins to enlarge, the length of the stroke is increased until the hone touches the entire cylinder wall except for an area just below the upper limit of ring travel.

When used for deglazing the cylinder walls, the cylinder hone is moved up and down rapidly in long strokes while being revolved by the electric drill. This action leaves a cross-hatched pattern and permits proper seating of new piston rings. Always clean the cylinder wall thoroughly after honing. If any abrasive is left in the engine it will cause excessive ring wear and may even ruin the overhaul job.

Reboring. Cylinders that are 0.005 in. or more out-of-round or taper should be rebored by means of a boring bar that attaches to the top of the cylinder block, Fig. 3-28. Boring bars are cutting tools that resize cylinders by cutting metal from the cylinder walls. Rebored

Blocks, Crankshafts, and Flywheels

Fig. 3-28. Cylinder boring machine. Once the machine is set, the boring operation is automatic. (Cedar Rapids Engineering Co.)

cylinders should all be resized to take the same diameter oversize piston. This means they must all be rebored to the size required for the most worn cylinder.

Before attaching the boring bar, the top of the cylinder block should be filed lightly to remove all burrs that could interfere with alignment of the bar. The crankshaft bearing caps should also be in place and tightened to the proper torque value to prevent distortion of the bores in final assembly of the engine.

To rebore the cylinders, the boring bar is centered and clamped over one of the cylinders. With the cutter adjusted to bore the cylinder 0.002 in. under the desired oversize, the motor is started and the automatic feed is engaged. The revolving cutter progresses throughout the length of the cylinder, and the machine shuts off automatically when the boring operation is complete. The cylinder is finish honed to establish the desired piston clearance. Unless the boring bar was sharpened perfectly and aligned, honing must follow reboring. The wall will look perfectly smooth, but a microscopic examination would show "hills" in the finish. These "hills" will prevent the rings from sealing properly.

After honing, clean the bores thoroughly with a scrub brush and soap and water. Do not use a wire brush. Scrub until the soap-suds stay white. Dry the cylinders, and apply a light coat of oil to prevent rusting.

Usually, new sleeves are manufactured with a finished cylinder bore to accommodate a standard size piston and do not require additional finishing. With the sleeve installed, check the fit of the piston in the cylinder with a new piston without rings. If the piston binds as it is moved up and down in the cylinder, it indicates the cylinder has closed in due to the press fit. To restore the proper piston clearance, the cylinder should be honed with a cylinder hone. When a cast-iron sleeve is installed in a cylinder block in which the other cylinders are oversize, the sleeve should be rebored and honed to match the size of the other cylinders.

Stud Replacement. All studs with stripped or damaged threads should be removed from the cylinder block with a stud puller. Broken studs or bolts should be drilled down their exact centers to a depth of approximately two-thirds the length of the portion remaining in the cylinder block. A drill should be used that will leave a wall thicker than the depth of the thread. A screw extractor of the proper size should be placed in the hole and the remaining portion of the broken stud or bolt turned out. After removing the stud, clean the threads in the cylinder block with a bottoming tap, and blow out any chips or dirt in the threaded hole with compressed air, protecting other engine parts from dirt or chips. New studs should be installed with a stud driver and should be tightened in the cylinder block until no threads show above the surface of the block.

Inspection and Repair of Crankshaft

After crankshafts have been in service for a long time, their oil passages may be clogged. The crankshaft, crankshaft bearings, flywheel, and vibration damper should be cleaned. Oil passages should be cleaned with a rifle brush or a wire and solvent.

Blocks, Crankshafts, and Flywheels

A careful inspection of the crankshaft, crankshaft bearings, flywheel, and vibration damper will indicate whether they are serviceable, whether repairs must be made, or if they must be replaced.

The main bearing journals and crankpins on the crankshaft are subject to wear during engine operation. Pressures imposed on the journals and crankpins, misalignment of parts, and abrasive materials in the oil cause the bearing journals to become scored, grooved, worn out-of-round, tapered, or worn undersize. All of these conditions cause excessive bearing clearances.

Out-of-round. The out-of-round wear on the main bearing journals and crankpins is due to greater pressure imposed on the bearings and journals during the power and compression strokes than is imposed during the intake and exhaust strokes. Since the crankpins usually are smaller in diameter and have less bearing area, they tend to wear out-of-round more than the main bearing journals.

Taper. Usually the taper wear that occurs on main bearing journals is due to warpage of the bearing caps, or of the webs, which support the main bearings in the crankcase. The taper wear in a crankpin may be caused by a bent connecting rod, misaligned piston pin, or abrasive materials in the oil.

On crankshafts with drilled oil passages, abrasive materials in the oil tend to wear one side of the crankpin more than the other, Fig. 3-29. This is because the oil hole in the crankcase is drilled at an angle which causes the oil and abrasive material to flow more readily to the side of the crankpin in the direction of flow.

Straightness. In addition to the wear on the journal surfaces, the loads imposed on the crankshaft may cause it to spring or bend at some point and whip as it revolves, imposing greater than normal loads on the main bearings.

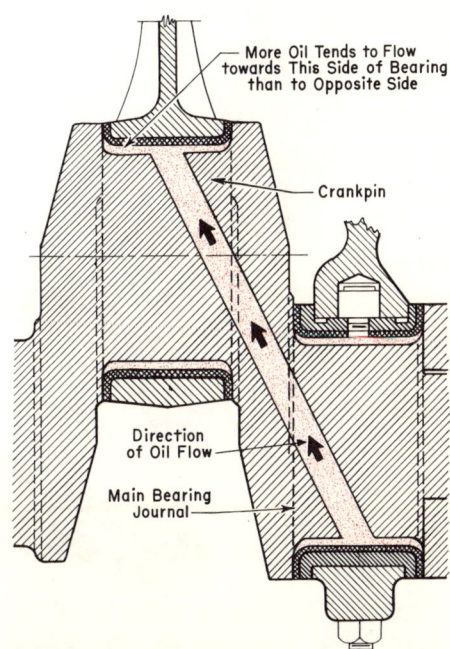

Fig. 3-29. Uneven oil flow to crankpin bearings can cause taper wear.

107

Automotive Engines

Checking Crankshaft for Straightness

The shaft should be supported on the front and rear main bearing journals in V blocks, Fig. 3-30. A dial indicator mounted on a pedestal base is used to check the amount of runout at each main bearing journal. Crankshafts should run true within 0.003 in. Any bend in excess of this amount should be corrected by straightening the shaft in an arbor press. The crankshaft is straightened by supporting the shaft on V blocks and applying pressure against the high side of the shaft.

The crankshaft can be checked for straightness by placing the shaft between centers in a lathe and checking the runout at the main bearings with a dial indicator. Care must be taken to see that the centers in each end of the crankshaft are not marred or the indications obtained will not be correct.

Fig. 3-30. A straight crankshaft is essential to avoid excessive bearing wear.

Blocks, Crankshafts, and Flywheels

Inspecting Crankshaft Journals

If the main bearing journals or the crankpin journals are scored or grooved, the crankshaft should be remachined to fit the available undersize bearing or replaced. Light scores or scratches on the journals can be honed with an oilstone; then polished with #320 grit polishing paper.

With a micrometer caliper, measure each journal at a minimum of four places to determine its size and the amount of out-of-round. Measure each journal at both ends to determine the amount of taper wear in the journal. Remachine any journals that are out-of-round more than 0.0015 in. or tapered more than 0.001 inch.

Journals need not be reground if:
1. Journals are worn evenly.
2. Journals are worn less than 0.001 in. taper and less than 0.0015 in. out-of-round.
3. The available undersize bearings provide a clearance that does not exceed the manufacturer's specifications by more than 0.001 inch.

If the thrust collars on the crankshaft are grooved or worn, they should be machined to fit available bearings of oversize width. If this is not possible, the crankshaft should be replaced.

Inspection of Main Bearings

The crankshaft main bearings should be inspected and then measured with precision measuring tools to determine their condition and the amount of clearance that exists between the bearing and the crankshaft journal. A careful inspection will indicate whether the bearings are serviceable or must be replaced. Whenever the crankshaft is removed from the cylinder block during overhaul, the main bearing saddle bores in the block should be checked for a warped or out-of-round condition.

Checking Main Bearing Saddle Bores in the Cylinder Block

Over a period of operation, the main bearing saddles in the cylinder block and the bearing caps may become warped or out-of-round due to the effects of heating and cooling of the engine and the forces imposed on the crankshaft and main bearings. Usually, the out-of-round condition of the bearing caps or saddles is caused by the closing in of the caps or the webs in which the saddles are machined. The di-

109

ameter at right angles to the parting surfaces becomes greater than the diameter across the parting surfaces. If this condition is not corrected and new precision insert bearings are installed, the bearing shells take the form of the saddles into which they are placed, resulting in an out-of-round bearing hole. An out-of-round condition of 0.003 in. or more seriously affects the oil clearance and may result in heavy pressures at the parting surfaces of the bearing, leading to early bearing failure.

With the bearing caps in place and the nuts tightened to the correct torque value, the bearing saddles should be checked at several points with a telescoping gage and micrometer caliper to determine the amount of out-of-round. (See Appendix C if you want micrometer instructions.) If the saddle bores are less than 0.002 in. out-of-round, standard undersize insert bearings can be installed providing the crankpin dimensions are within recommended tolerances. Saddle bores out-of-round 0.002 in., or more, must be line-bored. The bearing cap mating surfaces should be milled slightly more than the amount of out-of-round and bolted back in place at the recommended torque value. Then the saddles are line-bored to the original diameter and center line to establish round and true bearing saddles. Care must be taken not to remove any metal from the block portion of the saddle as this would change the distance between the center lines of the crankshaft and camshaft, affecting the mesh of the timing gears.

After line-boring the bearing saddles, semifinished replacement bearings should be installed. The inner diameter of the semifinished bearings should be small enough so there will be enough metal to allow for line-boring again, which will compensate for any out-of-roundness or deviation from true alignment of the saddle bores. With the semifinished bearings in place, the caps are again tightened to the correct torque value. Then the semifinished bearings are line-bored to the desired diameter.

Inspecting Main Bearings

Main bearings that are worn, scored, pitted, cracked, or show signs of corrosion or fatigue should be replaced. Replace all damaged main bearing bolts, studs, or nuts. Examine all oil passages that lead to the main bearings to make certain that they are clean.

Checking Main Bearing Clearances. Main bearing clearances are determined by measuring the diameter of the main bearings with a telescoping gage and micrometer caliper. Then, measure the diameter of the main journals on the crankshaft with a micrometer cali-

Blocks, Crankshafts, and Flywheels

TABLE 3-1 RECOMMENDED MAIN BEARING OIL CLEARANCES

Diameter of Crankshaft Journal in Inches	Recommended Oil Clearances in Inches	Maximum Allowable Clearances in Inches (Wear Limit)
2 to 2 3/4	0.0005 to 0.00015	0.0045
2 13/16 to 3 1/2	0.0015 to 0.0025	0.0055

per. (See Appendix C if you want micrometer instructions.)

To check the diameter of the main bearings, the bearing caps and bearings should be assembled on the crankcase in their proper order and tightened to the proper torque value. Each bearing should be measured at several points with the telescoping gage and micrometer caliper to determine the greatest diameter. The main bearing journals on the crankshaft should be measured with the micrometer caliper at several points to determine their size and the amount of out-of-round and taper. The difference between the greatest diameter of the worn main bearing and the greatest diameter of the worn bearing journal is the clearance of the bearing to be checked against the maximum allowable clearance. (See Appendix C if you want micrometer reading instructions.)

If the main bearing clearance equals or exceeds the maximum allowable clearances (Table 3-1) for crankshafts with main bearing journals of different diameters, replace the main bearings to restore the recommended clearance.

Main bearing clearances can also be checked with the crankshaft assembled in the crankcase. To check the clearance of a main bearing, the bearing cap is removed and a piece of feeler gage stock 0.0015 in. thick, ¾ in. long, and ¼ in. wide, with the edges slightly rounded on an oilstone, is coated with oil and placed between the bearing surface and the bearing journal, Fig. 3-31. The bearing cap is installed and the bolts or nuts tightened to the proper torque value. If the bearing clearance is correct, there will be a slight increase in the amount of drag felt when the crankshaft is turned. If the clearance is greater than the thickness of the feeler gage stock, no additional drag will be felt. Various thicknesses of feeler gage stock can be tried until one is found that creates a drag on the bearing. The thickness of the feeler gage stock indicates the clearance in the bearing. Each of the main bearings is checked in a similar manner to determine the clearance. The main bearings can be checked in this manner with the piston and connecting rod assemblies either in or out of the engine.

Crankshaft bearing clearances can also be determined with Plasti-

Automotive Engines

Fig. 3-31. Checking main bearing clearance with feeler gage stock. (Plymouth Div., Chrysler Corp.)

gage, a plastic thread which flattens when placed between the crankshaft and bearing. Since Plastigage is soluble in oil, be sure the crankshaft oil hole is up to avoid oil contacting the Plastigage. Place paper shims in the lower halves of adjacent main bearings and tighten the bearing caps to raise the crankshaft in the main bearing being checked. To measure bearing clearance, place a piece of Plastigage along the width of the bearing cap. Install the bear-

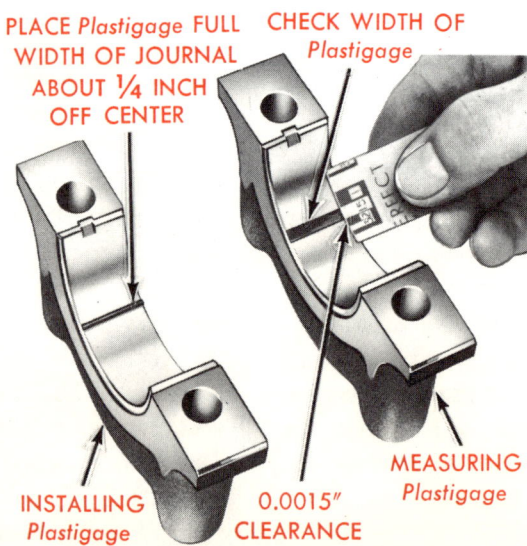

Fig. 3-32. Checking main bearing clearance with Plastigage. (Ford Div., Ford Motor Co.)

Blocks, Crankshafts, and Flywheels

ing cap with the Plastigage between the bearing and the journal and tighten the cap to the correct torque value. *Do not turn the crankshaft while the Plastigage is in place.*

Remove the bearing cap and, with the gage provided, check the width of the flattened Plastigage. The gage has a number of different width graduations which are marked to indicate bearing clearance in thousandths of an inch. Match the width of the flattened Plastigage with one of the gage marks of equal width to determine the clearance in the bearing, Fig. 3-32.

Checking Crankshaft End Play. The amount of crankshaft end play or clearance is determined with the crankshaft installed in the crankcase and the bearing caps securely tightened in place. The clearance is measured on one side of the thrust bearing, between the thrust surface of the bearing and the thrust collar on the crankshaft. The crankshaft should be pried to the extreme forward or rear position and the clearance measured with a thickness gage as shown in Fig. 3-33.

If the crankshaft end clearance exceeds the maximum allowable end clearance shown in Table 3-2, the thrust bearing should be re-

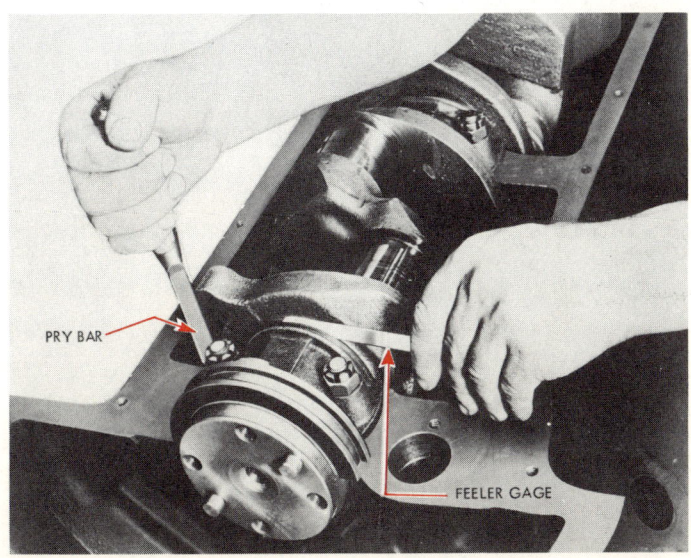

Fig. 3-33. Checking crankshaft end play with a feeler gage. (Ford Motor. Co.)

Automotive Engines

TABLE 3-2 RECOMMENDED CRANKSHAFT END CLEARANCE AT THRUST BEARING

Diameter of Crankshaft Journal in Inches	Recommended Crankshaft End Clearance in Inches	Maximum Allowable End Clearance in Inches (wear Limit)
2 to 2 3/4	0.004 to 0.006	0.010
2 13/16 to 3 1/2	0.006 to 0.008	0.012
Over 3 1/2	0.008 to 0.010	0.014

Fig. 3-34. Checking crankshaft end play with dial indicator. (American Motors Corp.)

placed and the new bearing fitted to the clearances recommended. When available, manufacturer's specifications should be followed.

The amount of end play in the crankshaft can also be checked with a dial indicator, Fig. 3-34. The dial indicator is attached to the cylinder block so the plunger of the gage bears against the end of the crankshaft. As the shaft is pried forward, the dial indicator indicates the number of thousandths of an inch of end play in the crankshaft.

Adjusting Main Bearing Clearance

Bearing inserts are available in a standard size, in 0.001, 0.002, 0.010, 0.020, 0.030, and 0.060 in. undersizes and as semifinished bearings. The semifinished bearings and the large undersizes can be bored to the correct undersize when the proper clearances cannot be estab-

Blocks, Crankshafts, and Flywheels

lished with the available standard undersize bearings.

The proper size of insert bearing to be installed in an engine is determined by the size and condition of the main bearing journals. Measure the main bearing journals at several points to determine the greatest diameter and the amount of out-of-round and taper. If the out-of-round does not exceed 0.0015 in. and the taper 0.001 in. and the journal surfaces are free of grooves or ridges, the crankshaft is satisfactory and replacement bearings of the correct undersize can be installed. If the out-of-round and taper exceeds the allowable limits, the journals should be reground to a standard undersize and replacement bearings of the correct undersize installed.

To determine the correct undersize insert bearings to install when the wear is within the allowable limits, compare the greatest diameter of the journal with the original standard diameter. The difference in the two dimensions is the amount the journal is worn and is the size of the undersize bearing that should be installed. Thus, a main bearing journal with a large diameter that is 0.002 in. smaller than the original standard diameter would require a 0.002 in. undersize replacement bearing to establish the desired clearance.

Standard size bearings should be installed if the main bearing journals are worn less than 0.001 in. and are within the allowable limits of out-of-round and taper. If the journals are worn 0.001 or more, standard undersize bearings of the correct size should be installed if such bearings will establish the desired clearance. When the amount of wear on the journals is such that the desired clearance cannot be obtained with the standard undersize bearings available, semifinished insert bearings bored to the correct undersize should be installed. To determine the diameter to which semifinished bearings should be bored, the desired oil clearance should be added to the greatest journal diameter and the bearing inserts bored to that diameter on a connecting rod reboring machine.

When the crankshaft thrust surfaces are worn to the extent that a replacement thrust bearing of standard width will not restore the crankshaft to the end clearance recommended, semifinished thrust bearings should be used and the bearing bored and refaced to establish the desired oil clearance and crankshaft end play.

Some of the older engines had main bearings which were cast into the block and bearing cap. The correct clearance was obtained on these bearings by filling the cap and/or using shims. When the bearings were worn beyond allowable limits, they had to be recast and then sized to fit the crankshaft.

Automotive Engines

Inspection of Flywheel

On automobiles with a cast-iron flywheel, the rear face of the flywheel is used as one of the friction surfaces of the clutch. Through normal use, the slippage which occurs because of improper clutch use or adjustment, this face may become scored, grooved, or roughened by heat cracks. In addition, the meshing of the starter drive pinion with the flywheel ring gear subjects the teeth on the ring gear to wear at several points on its circumference. Such conditions must be corrected if the clutch and starting motor are to operate satisfactorily.

Replace or reface a flywheel on which the friction face is excessively worn, scored, or cracked. Replace a flywheel ring gear that is cracked or has chipped or excessively worn gear teeth. Replace the clutch pilot bearing if it is worn excessively. If a ball bearing is used, the ball bearing should revolve freely and smoothly. On automobiles equipped with a fluid type drive, it may be necessary to replace the entire fluid coupling unit if it leaks oil or if the ring gear teeth are worn.

Replacing Flywheel Ring Gear

Drill a hole slightly smaller than the solid portion of the ring gear nearly through the gear and on the same side of the flywheel from which the ring gear is installed. Split the ring gear at the drilled hole with a hammer and chisel and lift the ring gear off the flywheel. It may be necessary to grind or chisel off the welds if the ring gear has been spot tacked. Clean the ring gear recess on the flywheel. Heat the new ring gear evenly to 360°F (a straw yellow color) on a gas heater designed to heat the entire ring at once. Place the hot ring gear on the cold flywheel, making certain that the side with the beveled gear teeth is facing in the proper direction and that the gear is fully seated in the recess of the flywheel. The gear will cool and contract to a tight fit on the flywheel.

Refacing Flywheel

The flywheel should be aligned carefully in a lathe or in a machine designed to reface flywheels. Then, remove just enough material from the friction surface to obtain a smooth, flat surface parallel with the mounting flange. The same amount of material must be removed from the portion of the flywheel to which the clutch pressure plate is attached. If more than $1/16$ in. must be removed from the friction surface to obtain a smooth flat surface, the flywheel should be re-

Blocks, Crankshafts, and Flywheels

placed. Removing more than 1/16 in. from the face of the flywheel may change the relative position of the clutch throwout lever to the extent that the clutch cannot be adjusted properly.

Replacing Clutch Pilot Bearing

Drive the clutch pilot bearing out of the flywheel. Install the new pilot bearing with the open side of the bearing toward the engine side of the flywheel. Use a driver that applies pressure to the outer race of the bearing, because pressure on the inner race of the bearing may damage the races or balls.

On some engines, the pilot bearing consists of a bushing located in the end of the crankshaft. To remove the bushing, split it using the blade of a hacksaw and remove it from its bore in the crankshaft. Install the new bushing in the crankshaft using the correct size driver.

Inspection of Vibration Damper

The vibration damper parts are not serviced separately. Replace the vibration damper if the fan drive pulley is cracked or broken. Replace the vibration damper if the rubber bushings or seals have become softened from prolonged contact with oil.

Checking On Your Knowledge

The following questions give you the opportunity to check up on yourself. If you have read the chapter carefully, you should be able to answer the questions.

If you have any difficulty, read the chapter over once more so that you have the information well in mind before you go on with your reading.

DO YOU KNOW

1. What are some of the effects obtained by adding nickel, molybdenum, or chromium to cast gray iron?
2. What form of cylinder block is used on most internal combustion engines?
3. How do cylinder blocks used on L-head engines differ in construction from those used on I-head engines?
4. What is the purpose of heat treating cylinder blocks before machining?
5. What differences are there between the dry and the wet types of cylinder sleeves?

Automotive Engines

6. At what point in the cylinder does the greatest wear occur?

7. What are some of the causes of cylinder wear?

8. What may happen in an engine of new position rings are installed without removing the ridge at the top of the cylinders?

9. How many main bearings may a six-cylinder in-line engine have?

10. What is the purpose of the webs in a cylinder block?

11. What factors determine the number and arrangement of crankarms on the crankshaft?

12. How is the crankshaft supported in the crankcase?

13. Of what materials are crankshafts usually made?

14. What is the purpose of the drilled passages in the crankshaft?

15. What determines the firing order of an engine?

16. What is the average lapse between power strokes in a four-cylinder in-line engine?

17. In what way is the six-cylinder, V-type crankshaft similar to a six-cylinder in-line crankshaft?

18. What is the spacing in degrees between crankpins on crankshafts employed in modern V-type eight-cylinder engines?

19. What effect does locating the crankshaft to one side of the engine center line have on the spacing between power strokes?

20. What are the effects of unbalanced forces on a crankshaft?

21. What is meant by static balance? Dynamic balance?

22. What is the purpose of the counterbalances employed on most crankshafts?

23. How do insert-type bearings differ in construction from cast bearings?

24. What provisions are incorporated into the engine bearings to take care of the thrust load imposed on the crankshaft when the clutch is engaged?

25. To what clearance per inch in diameter are pressure-lubricated main bearings fitted?

26. What is the purpose of the flywheel?

27. How is the flywheel ring gear attached to the flywheel?

28. What serves as the clutch in vehicles equipped with a liquid type of coupling?

29. What is meant by torsional vibration in a crankshaft?

30. What means are employed to absorb torsional vibration?

31. What is the maximum permissible runout at the crankshaft main bearings?

32. What is the maximum amount of out-of-round or taper to which the main or connecting rod bearing journals can be worn before they should be remachined?

33. What is the maximum amount of out-of-round permissible in main bearing saddle bores?

34. What is the recommended oil clearance for a 2½ in. main bearing journal?

Pistons and Connecting Rods

Chapter

4

The piston and connecting rod assembly transmits the power to the crankshaft. This assembly operates under such severe conditions that at some point in the life of the engine, repairs must be made to restore engine efficiency.

In this chapter the types, construction, and operation of piston and connecting rod assemblies will be discussed. The chapter will also cover cleaning, inspection, measurement of clearances, and the final rebuilding of the piston and connecting rod assemblies to a "like new" condition.

Types, Materials, and Design

Modern automotive engines employ varying types of pistons, piston rings, piston pins, and connecting rods. These units form the piston and connecting rod assembly. Fig. 4-1 illustrates a typical piston and connecting rod assembly.

Pistons

The pistons must be strong enough to withstand the high temperatures and pressures developed within the cylinders. Pistons must be as light in weight as possible to lessen "inertia forces" (the tendency of each piston to keep moving in the same direction) developed by starting and stopping them at the end of each stroke. The pistons are manufactured within close limits of weight and size so that they are interchangeable, well balanced, and free from vibration.

Automotive Engines

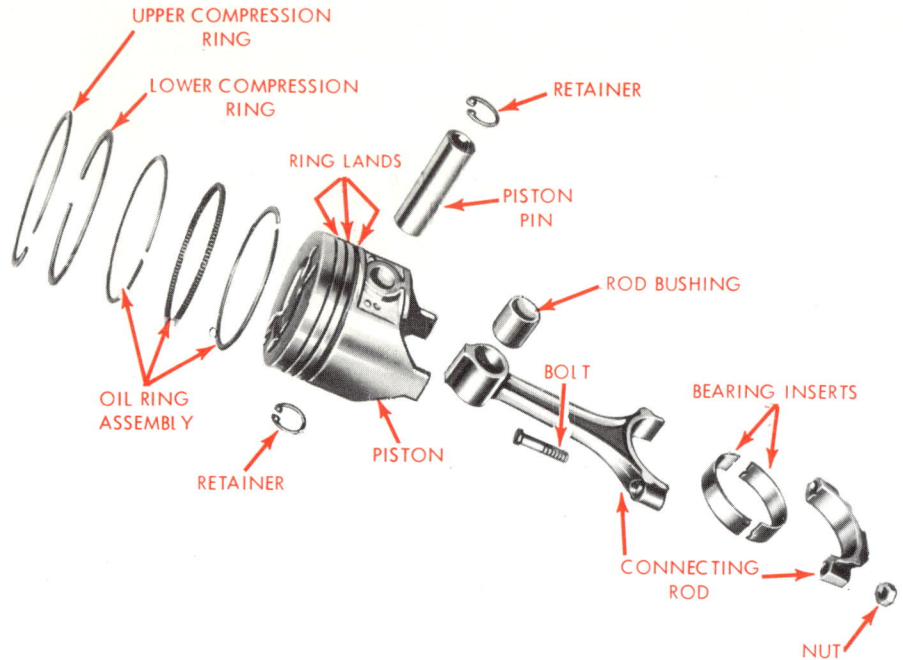

Fig. 4-1. Typical piston and connecting rod assembly. (Ford Div., Ford Motor Co.)

Design. Fig. 4-2 illustrates the design of a typical automotive piston.

The head of the piston is usually flat although some diesel engines use a dished or concave type of head. Notches may be cast in some piston heads to provide clearance for the valve head.

Ribs are often employed to rein-

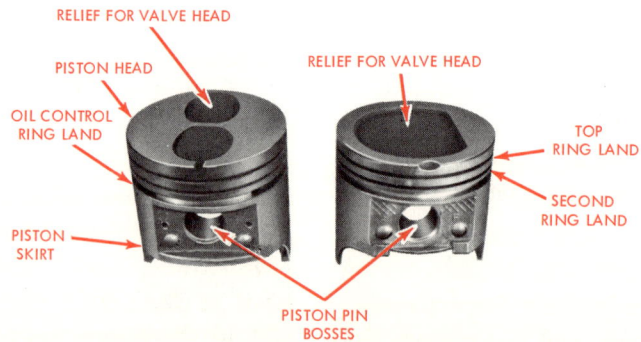

Fig. 4-2. Piston design and nomenclature.

Pistons, Connecting Rods

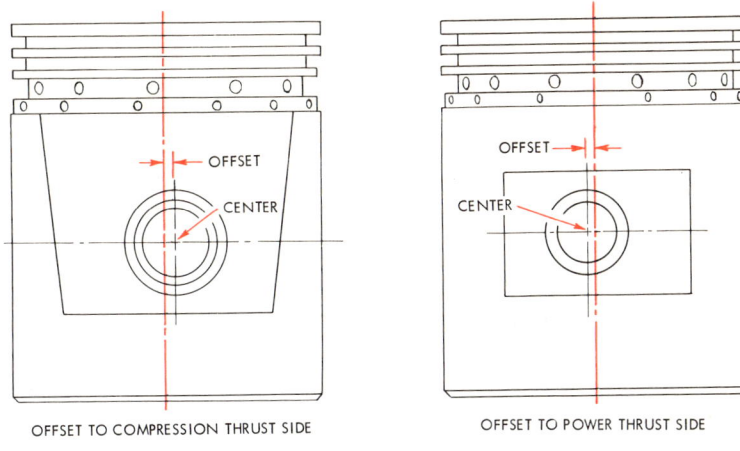

OFFSET TO COMPRESSION THRUST SIDE   OFFSET TO POWER THRUST SIDE

Fig. 4-3. Some pistons have offset bosses.

force the underside of the piston head. The ribs also assist in carrying the heat away from the head of the piston to the piston rings and piston skirt, where it is dissipated to the cylinder walls and cooling system. On some pistons, the piston skirt is reinforced by means of a rib located on the inside of the piston near the bottom of the piston skirt. Such ribs are also used for balancing purposes, metal being removed from the lower edge of the rib to bring the piston within the desired weight limits.

The piston bosses support and provide bearing surfaces for the piston pin. On most pistons, the piston wall around the piston pin opening is relieved (undercut) to provide an allowance for expansion of the bosses and to reduce the weight of the piston. While most engines have the piston bosses centered in the piston, some engines have the piston bosses offset approximately $\frac{1}{16}$ in. toward either the compression or power thrust side of the piston, Fig. 4-3. Piston bosses are offset in the piston to reduce the tendency of the piston to slap (rock) in the cylinders.

When the piston is at top dead center, a line drawn through the center of the spark plug electrode and the center of the piston head indicates the direction of the thrust imposed on the head of the piston by the pressure developed during combustion of fuel mixture in the cylinder, Fig. 4-4. On engines with offset piston pins and bosses, the thrust is applied on the head of the piston slightly to one side of the piston pin and tends to hold the piston skirt flat against

Automotive Engines

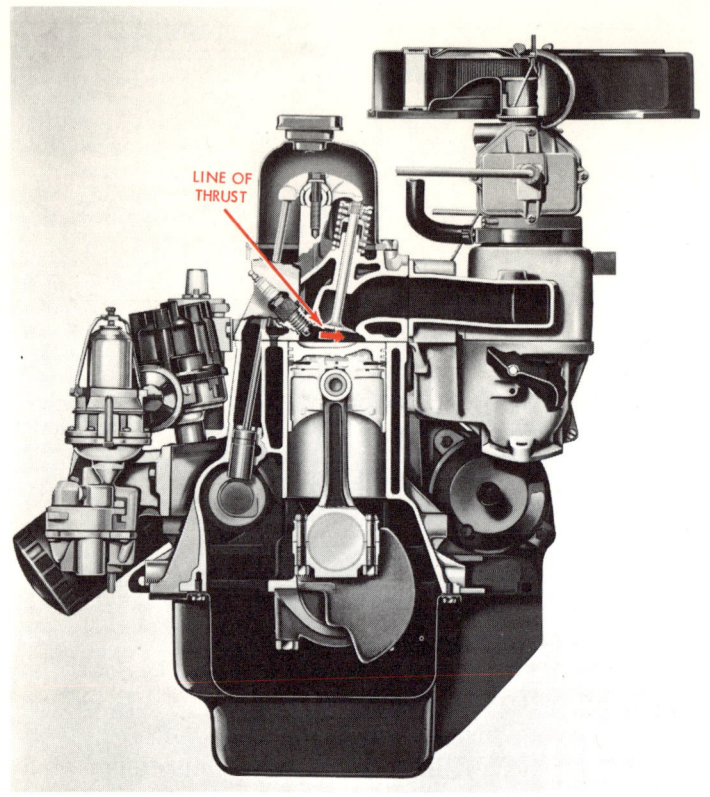

Fig. 4-4. Line of explosive thrust in cylinder due to location of spark plug. (American Motors Corp.)

the cylinder wall. As the piston moves up and down in the cylinder, the angle of the connecting rod and the pressure exerted on the head of the piston tend to keep the skirt of the piston in contact with the cylinder wall, preventing piston slap by keeping the piston from rocking in the cylinder. Piston ring grooves are provided at the top of the piston.

Several different skirt designs are used to permit expansion of the piston without excessively increasing the diameter across the thrust faces. Most pistons are designed with an interrupted skirt to permit closer fitting of pistons.

In the process of manufacture, the piston skirt is ground to finished size in either a round or an elliptical shape. Round pistons have a uniform diameter at all points on the skirt. Elliptical pistons, the most common type, are the result of cam grinding and are

Pistons, Connecting Rods

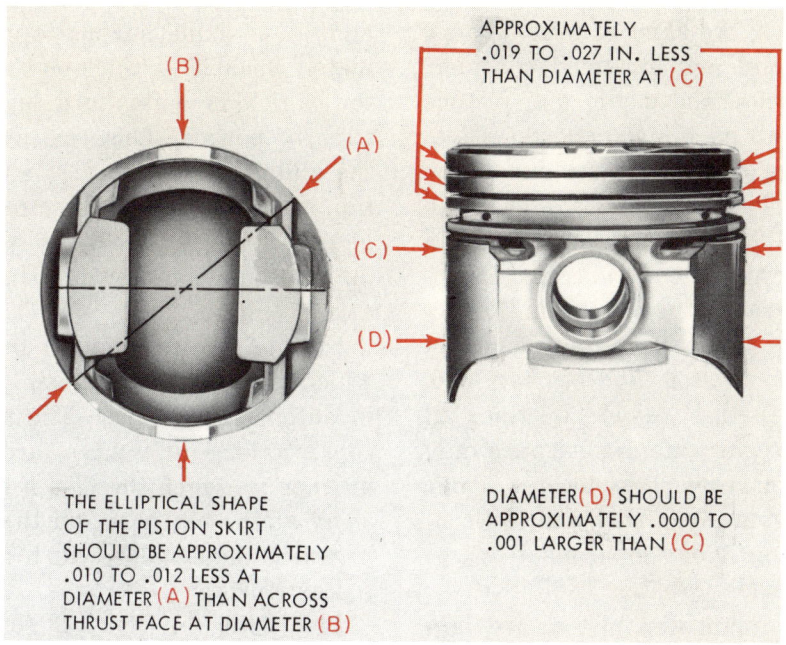

Fig. 4-5. Elliptical shaped piston skirt (Plymouth Div., Chrysler Corp.)

not round but have varying diameters; the diameter of the skirt in line with the piston pin is from 0.005 to 0.016 in. less than the diameter at right angles to the pin, Fig. 4-5.

In addition to cam grinding, the piston skirt usually is tapered. The diameter at the bottom of the skirt is ground about 0.0015 in. greater in diameter than the diameter just below the piston rings.

A greater clearance is needed at the top of the piston than at the skirt, because the head of the piston is directly exposed to the flame of the burning gases and expands more. To provide this clearance, the ring lands, Fig. 4-1, are made several thousandths of an inch smaller in diameter than the piston skirt.

Materials. Todays automotive pistons are commonly made of aluminum alloys.

Some manufacturers electroplate the pistons with a soft material such as tin. Such plating acts as a lubricant and shortens the break-in period.

Over the years, pistons that have been used in engines were made of cast iron, cast steel, aluminum, and aluminum alloy. All engines being manufactured now use an aluminum alloy type of piston. While formerly the skirt of most pistons was solid and extended considerably below the piston pin, pistons today all have much shorter skirts and are cut away to the extent that primarily they act as a guide to hold the head of the piston in proper alignment and transmit motion through the piston pin. Reducing the piston skirt reduces piston weight, friction, and bearing load.

To further reduce friction, all automotive pistons now have only three narrow rings located above the piston pin. Usually the oil control ring is of the segmented type to provide greater flexibility.

Aluminum alloy pistons are light in weight. Because of the high heat conductivity of aluminum, such pistons dissipate heat rapidly and, therefore, operate at lower temperatures. Aluminum alloys have a high coefficient of expansion and ordinarily require greater clearance between the piston and cylinder wall than either iron or steel. However, various piston designs have been developed that permit the piston to expand at high temperatures without materially changing the piston clearances. As a result, such pistons can be fitted with small clearances without danger of seizing at high temperatures.

Aluminum alloy pistons are sometimes heat treated and given an electrolytic (anodic) treatment. The anodic treatment produces an aluminum oxide surface approximately 0.00025 in. thick on the piston which is quite hard and yet slightly porous. This coating has the ability to resist water and retain oil in its pores, protecting the piston during periods of sparse lubrication, such as when starting a cold engine.

Fig. 4-6 shows different pistons which have been or are being used in automotive engines. The major construction differences are the manner in which the piston is cut away at the pin boss and the way in which the slots are cut to allow for expansion.

The piston in Fig. 4-6 (bottom right) is the type generally used in today's engines. The skirt is solid, but a considerable amount of material has been removed from under the bosses to reduce weight, friction, and expansion. Spaces between the piston head and skirt reduce heat transfer from the head of the piston to the skirt.

These pistons are cam ground (ground out-of-round) so that they can be fitted in the cylinders with a small amount of clearance. The out-of-round design of the piston skirt compensates for heat expansion along the line of the piston pin bosses. The expansion that takes place in the cam ground skirt causes the skirt to assume a rounded shape without seriously reducing the operating clearances.

Piston Clearance. Since the pis-

Pistons, Connecting Rods

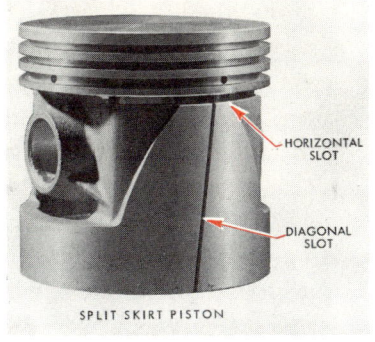
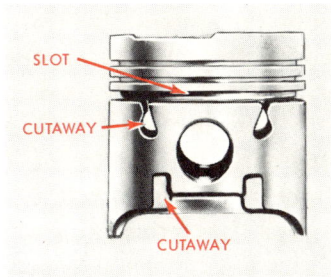

Fig. 4-6. Various types of pistons.

tons are subjected to high operating temperatures, a clearance must be provided between the piston and cylinder wall to allow for expansion. The amount of clearance required is dependent upon the material from which the piston is made, the diameter, and the design.

Because the head of the piston is exposed to higher temperatures than the piston skirt, greater clearances must be provided at this point. To provide this clearance, the ring lands are machined 0.020 in. to 0.030 in. smaller in diameter than the skirt. While clearance requirements vary somewhat among the different types of aluminum alloy pistons, the total clearance at the thrust surfaces of the skirt (widest diameter) is often as low as 0.0005 to 0.0015 in.

Piston Pins

The piston is connected to the upper end of the connecting rod by a piston pin or, as it is sometimes called, the "wrist pin." The pin passes through the piston at the piston bosses and through the upper end of the connecting rod, which rides on the central portion of the pin. Piston pins are made of alloy steel and are casehardened, ground, and lapped to provide a smooth, durable wearing surface. They are made hollow to remove unnecessary weight, thus reducing the inertia forces developed at the end of each stroke.

Different methods have been used to retain the piston pins in the piston. In some cases the pin was clamped in the connecting rod by a bolt; in other installations, a bolt was threaded into the piston pin boss and extended into a hole in the pin.

In today's engines, retainers (lock rings) may be inserted in grooves in each end of the piston pin boss to permit the pin to "float" in the pin boss and connecting rod but prevents the pin from coming out and contacting the cylinder wall. When the floating type of piston pin is used, a bushing is pressed in the connecting rod. When excessive wear occurs, the piston bosses and the piston pin bushing in the end of the connecting rod can be reamed and/or honed and an oversized piston pin installed.

Many of today's engines depend upon the friction between the piston pin and the connecting rod to retain the piston pin in its proper place. A special tool is needed to remove, install, and position the pin properly. Oversize piston pins cannot be used. Therefore, when there is excessive wear, both the piston and pin must be replaced as a set. Fig. 4-7 shows a piston, piston pin, and connecting rod assembly using lock rings to retain the pin in the piston. Also shown is the assembly which depends upon the friction between the pin and connecting rod to retain the pin in the proper position in the piston.

Piston Rings

The purpose of the piston rings is to maintain a pressure-tight seal between the piston and cylinder wall, to aid in controlling oil, to permit proper lubrication of the cylinders, and to assist in cooling the pistons.

Although most piston rings are made of cast gray iron, alloy steels are also used in the construction of some types of piston rings. Both cast iron and alloy steel form a good wearing surface, are capable of withstanding the heat imposed upon them, and retain a large percentage of their original elasticity after considerable use.

Some piston rings are plated

Pistons, Connecting Rods

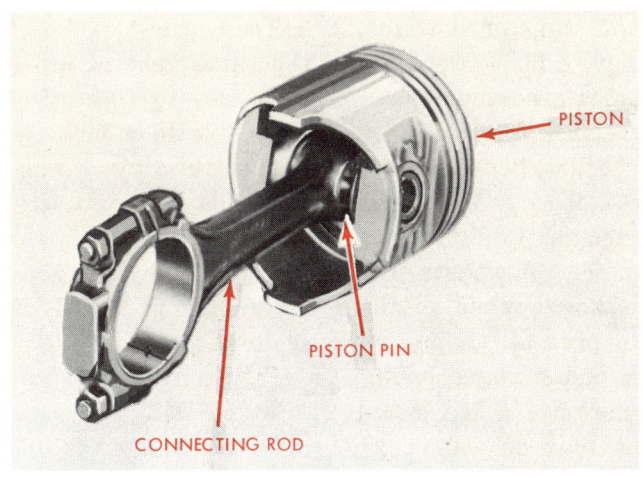

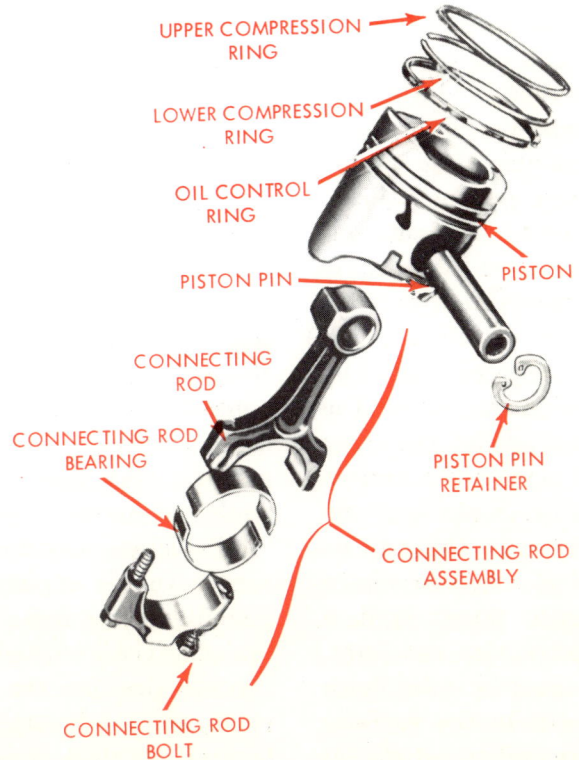

Fig. 4-7. Common methods of retaining piston pins. (Plymouth Div., Chrysler Corp.)

with cadmium, tin, or chrome, while others have a black magnetic oxide or phosphate coating on all surfaces of the piston ring. Since scuffing or scoring between two metal surfaces can occur only if the two surfaces are absolutely free of plated, oxide, or phosphate deposits, the coating applied to the rings tends to prevent scuffing or scoring of the piston rings during the break-in period. NOTE: Scoring or scuffing may be defined as a scraping or dragging movement which makes scratches, ridges, and/or grooves, thereby marring an otherwise smooth surface.

Design. Various designs of piston rings have been used over the years. All pistons presently being used have concentric rings, while some of the older pistons utilized an eccentric ring to help compensate for piston thrust. Rings having a tapered cross section were installed on pistons specifically designed for this type of ring. The taper feature helped to prevent the ring from binding in the ring groove. Pinned rings had a limited usage at one time. A pin kept the ring from turning in the groove. Different types of ring joints have been used, such as a butt joint, a miter joint, and a step cut joint. Oil control rings cast solid with holes or slots cut in the surface, which permit the oil to return inside the piston, have been used quite extensively.

Today most piston rings have the same general design: concentric, free to rotate in the piston groove, with a butt joint, and an oil control ring of the segmented type. To reduce friction and increase flexibility, rings being used in today's engines are much narrower than previously, and are also segmented for the same reason.

Piston rings are split at the ring joint so that they can be passed over the ring lands and placed in the ring grooves on the piston. The rings must fit freely in the ring grooves with a small amount of side clearance. The rings must be compressed when the piston is placed in the cylinder and, when in the cylinder, must have sufficient end clearance at the joint to allow for expansion without the ends meeting as the temperature of the ring increases.

When an engine is assembled, the gaps on adjacent rings are staggered so that ring gaps are on opposite sides of the piston. Because the rings are free in their grooves, they may rotate slightly while the engine is in operation.

All pistons used in today's passenger vehicle engines have three piston rings located above the piston pin. The first and second ring grooves are for the compression rings, and the lowest groove is for the oil control ring. Fig. 4-8 illustrates a typical installation.

When installed in the cylinder,

Pistons, Connecting Rods

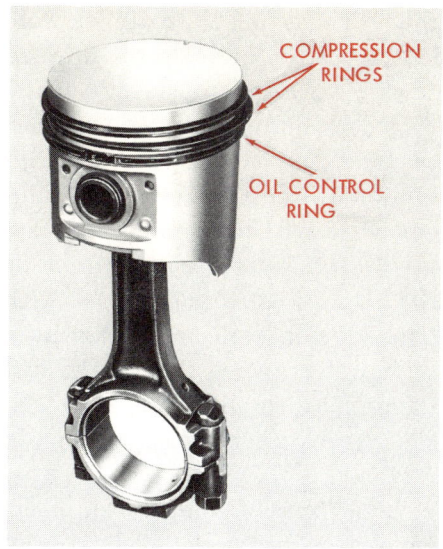

Fig. 4-8. Arrangement of piston rings. (Plymouth Div., Chrysler Corp.)

the piston ring must exert a pressure against the cylinder wall if a gastight seal is to be maintained. The total pressure exerted by piston rings against the cylinder wall varies according to the type of ring. High ring pressures, besides causing a drag on the engine, result in excessive wear on the cylinder walls and piston rings, and are often responsible for the scuffing or scoring (scratches) which may occur on the face of the ring.

The unit pressure (pressure per square inch) that a ring exerts on the cylinder wall varies with the amount of ring face that is in contact with the cylinder wall. Fig. 4-9A illustrates a ring with a rectangular cross section. The full face of the ring is in contact with the cylinder wall and the outward pressure of the ring is distributed over the entire width of the ring. In Fig. 4-9B, the face of the ring is narrower, and if the outward force exerted by the ring remains the same, the entire pressure exerted by the ring is concentrated on the narrow face. This results in a higher unit pressure against the

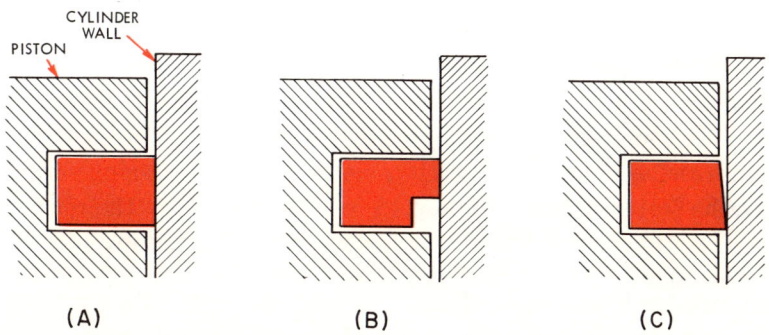

Fig. 4-9. If the face of the above piston ring is made narrower, its pressure per unit of area against the cylinder wall increases.

cylinder wall. Fig. 4-9C shows a ring with a much narrower face. Because the outward force is concentrated on the narrow face, the unit pressure is much higher for the small area of the face in contact with the cylinder wall. Piston rings are designed with faces of different widths to satisfactorily maintain compression and reduce oil consumption.

Compression Rings. The purpose of compression rings is to prevent the blow-by (leakage) of gases from the combustion chamber, and to assist the oil rings in controlling the amount of oil on the cylinder wall. Compression rings cannot control blow-by unless a thin film of oil is left on the cylinder wall. The oil acts as a seal between the cylinder wall and the faces of the compression ring.

Most compression rings installed as original equipment are of one-piece construction and are rectangular in cross section. In a worn cylinder, a ring with a grooved beveled edge on the upper outer corner to assure lower edge contact or a ring with a tapered face, may be used as a replacement. Tapered face compression rings are slightly wider at the bottom than at the top, resulting in the face of the ring being tapered way from the cylinder wall about 0.001 in. On the downward stroke of the piston, the sharp lower edge of the ring tends to scrape the excess oil left by the oil ring from the cylinder wall, leaving a thin film. On the upward stroke, since the upper edge of the ring does not contact the cylinder, the ring tends to slide over the thin film of oil remaining on the cylinder wall without scraping it upward. The tapered construction of the ring gives a line contact with the cylinder wall, resulting in a high unit pressure. Such rings seat themselves rapidly and give efficient service early in the break-in period.

Some types of compression rings have a right angle groove or a bevel machined in the upper inside edge of the ring or a groove in the bottom, outside edge, Figs. 4-10D and 4-10E. When such rings are compressed and placed in the cylinder, the groove or bevel causes the internal forces (which cause the ring to exert an outward pressure) to become unbalanced. The unbalanced condition causes the ring to tip or twist in its groove; the top outer edge of the ring is tipped away from the cylinder wall.

When the piston moves downward on either the power stroke or the intake stroke, the bottom outer edge of the ring scrapes most of the oil left by the oil ring from the cylinder, leaving a thin film on the cylinder wall, Fig. 4-11.

On the compression and power strokes, the pressures developed within the cylinders exert a force on the compression rings which

Pistons, Connecting Rods

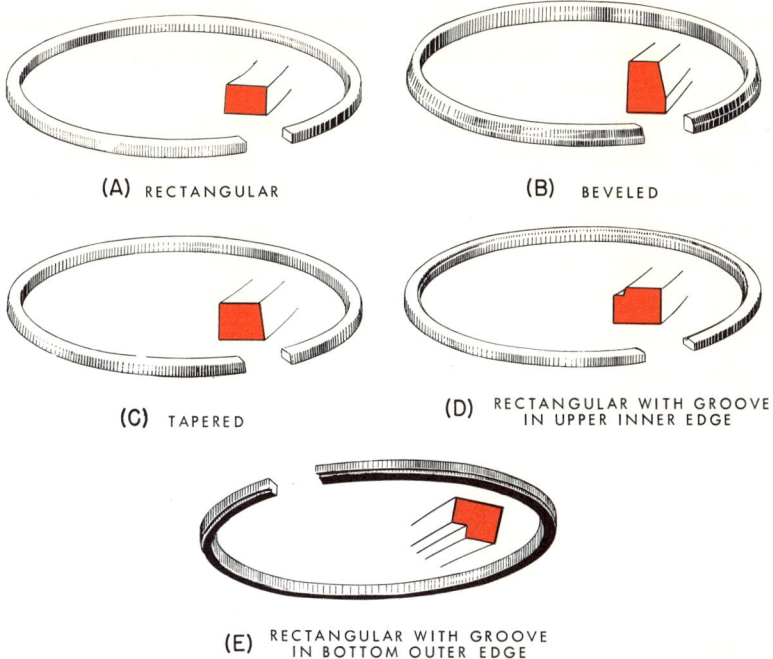

Fig. 4-10. Compression rings not only seal combustion chambers to provide good compression, but they also help to control the oil film on the cylinder walls. Each one of these compression rings does this by becoming unbalanced and exerting different unit pressures against the cylinder walls during engine operation.

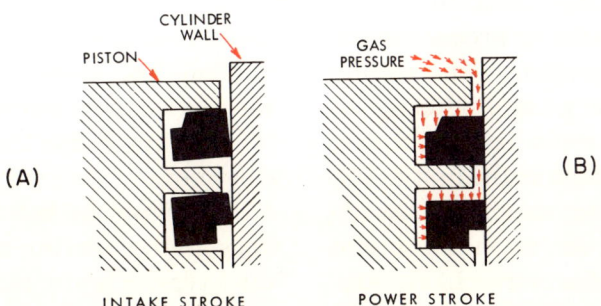

Fig. 4-11. These grooved compression rings seal compression during some engine strokes. During other strokes, the rings help to control oil film on the cylinder wall.

131

overcomes the force which twists the ring in its groove. This causes the ring to flatten out in its groove so that it has a full face contact against the cylinder wall and against the lower side of the ring groove, Fig. 4-11B. This seals the cylinder effectively against blow-by on both the compression and power strokes.

On the exhaust stroke, the reduced pressure within the cylinder permits the internal forces of the ring to tip the top outer edge away from the cylinder wall. As the piston moves upward, the ring slides over the thin film of oil on the cylinder wall without scraping the oil upward, Fig. 4-11A.

Installation. Tapered and grooved or beveled rings must be installed correctly if they are to function properly in the cylinder. Generally such rings are marked, and the rings should be installed with the side marked *top* upward. Compression rings with a tapered face are usually installed in the first and second ring grooves at the top of the piston. Compression rings with the groove or bevel on the upper inside edge of the ring are usually placed in the first or top ring groove on the piston, while rings with the groove in the bottom outside edge are placed in the second ring groove, Fig. 4-11. The top ring has a wider face than the ring in the second groove and, as a result, exerts a lower unit pressure against the cylinder wall. This tends to decrease the wear on the top inch of the cylinder, which normally is difficult to lubricate.

Oil Control Rings. The function of oil control rings is to minimize oil consumption. The oil rings must meter sufficient oil to the upper part of the cylinder to lubricate the cylinder wall and the compression rings. When the pistons have the proper cylinder clearance, the bottom edge of the piston removes most of the oil from the cylinder wall on each downward stroke, permitting the rings to control cylinder lubrication properly. When piston clearances are excessive, the pistons cannot scrape their share of oil from the cylinder wall, with the result that the rings are forced to control much more than the normal amount of oil. This often results in excessive cylinder lubrication and oil consumption.

Over the years various designs of oil control rings have been used. In each case, the oil control ring has had openings in the face of the ring so that oil could drain back into the oil pan through the slots or holes provided in the piston ring groove.

Until recently, most oil control rings were cast iron of the ventilated type. The ventilated type of oil control ring is a one-piece ring having a continuous channel cut in the face of the ring and has slots cut completely through the ring at

Pistons, Connecting Rods

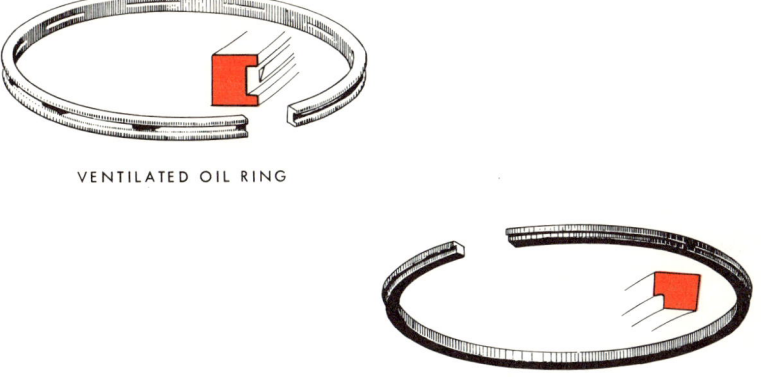

Fig. 4-12. Oil control rings scrape excess oil from the cylinder walls to help prevent oil from being burned during combustion.

equal intervals around the channel, Fig. 4-12. The narrow faces of the ring above and below the channel bear against the cylinder wall and collect oil in the channel and slots between the faces as the piston moves up and down in the cylinder. The oil in the channel and slots drains back into the crankcase through holes drilled in the ring groove.

To provide greater flexibility so the ring will better follow the cylinder wall, some types of compression and oil control rings have been designed for use with spring expanders, Fig. 4-13. Spring expanders are made of spring steel with a number of "humps" or "crimps" spaced equally around its circumference. Generally the outer ring of such piston rings exerts about 50 percent of the outward pressure exerted on one-piece rings. These rings use the additional outward pressure exerted by the spring ex-

Fig. 4-13. Two-piece spring expander piston ring. Usually expander type rings are used in rebuilding engines with excess cylinder wear.

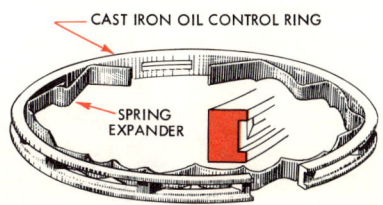

133

pander to exert the total required pressure against the cylinder wall.

Generally spring expander rings are used to control the amount of oil in cylinders having an excessive amount of taper and out-of-round condition in the cylinder walls. Because the expanders also tend to support the piston centrally in the cylinder bore, they assist in reducing or eliminating piston slap.

Some four-piece oil control rings are made in several designs to accommodate the various cylinder conditions.

The spring expanders are usually notched out, and the oil that collects in the channel and slots of the ring drains back into the crankcase through holes drilled in the back of the piston ring grooves.

Some expander rings employ four pieces to form the complete ring, Fig. 4-14. The central portion of the ring consists of a cast center channel with slots cut through to the back of the ring. Steel side rails made of a single turn of thin, flat steel are located above and below the center portion of the ring.

Depending on the design of the ring, the expander spring exerts a pressure against both the steel side rails and center section, or only the steel rails, holding them in contact with the cylinder wall. The narrow faces of the steel rails provide an effective scraping action that collects the excess oil in the center channel of the ring. The oil drains back into the crankcase through the holes in the back of the ring groove.

Some four-piece oil control rings have a steel expander between the steel rails in place of a cast-iron spacer. An expander spring is also

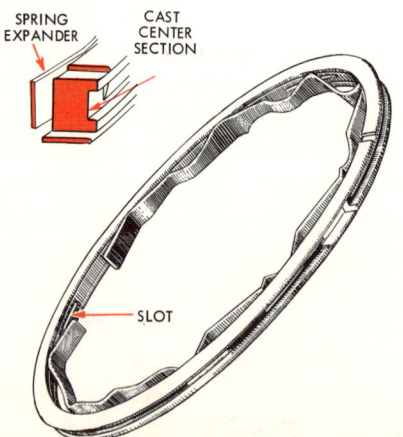

Fig. 4-14. Four-piece ring with cast-iron center section.

Pistons, Connecting Rods

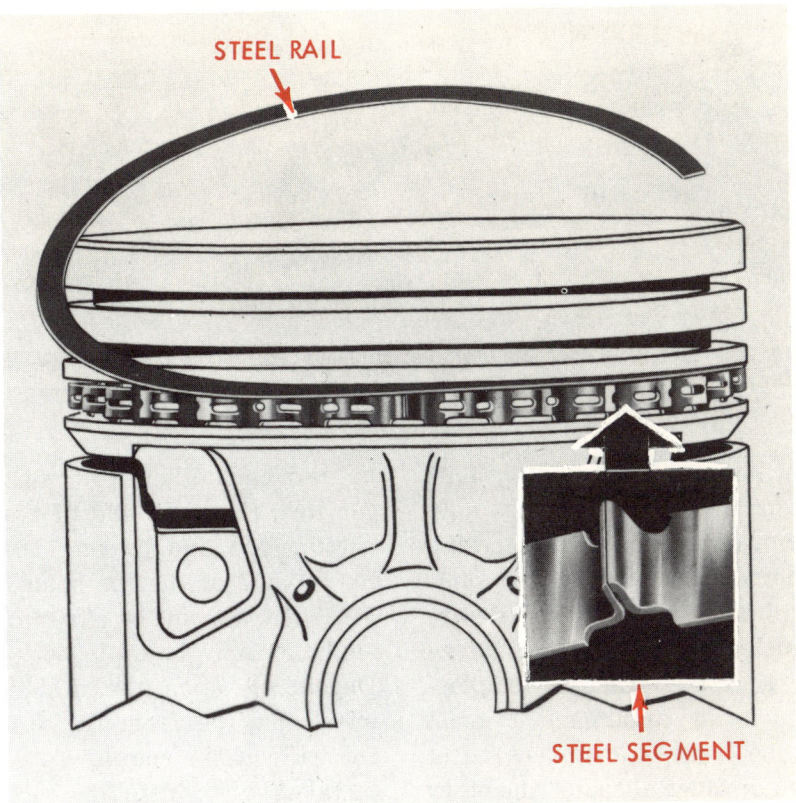

Fig. 4-15. Segmented oil control ring. (American Motors Corp.)

used behind the ring. The steel expander provides for greater flexibility and reduces the possibility of the openings in the ring plugging up with carbon and sludge.

The most common type of oil control ring installed as original equipment in today's engines consists of two steel rails with a steel segment in between the rails. The steel segment holds the rails in place and permits oil to flow to the openings in the ring grooves, Fig. 4-15.

Connecting Rods

The connecting rod must be strong enough to transmit the thrust of the piston to the crankshaft without deflection (bending of the rod). To assure a better balance of reciprocating parts and to permit interchangeability, the connecting rods are held to very close weight limits at the time of manufacture.

Design and Construction. Connecting rods may differ from the

Automotive Engines

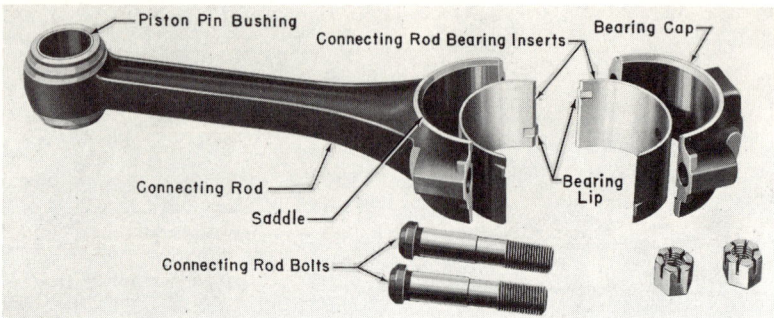

Fig. 4-16. This is a typical connecting rod design using replaceable type bearings. (Pontiac Motor Div., General Motors Corp.)

typical design shown in Fig. 4-16.

V-type automotive engines have the connecting rods from opposing cylinders attached to the same crankpin. The connecting rods are mounted in a side-by-side arrangement, Fig. 4-17. Engines employing such an arrangement must have one bank of cylinders offset a small distance ahead of the other to allow the two connecting rods to clear each other. To compensate for this, the large end of the connecting rod and bearing is offset to one side of the rod shank, Fig. 4-18. The amount of offset may be slight or may be quite noticeable. Depending upon the design, the offset may be from the front or the back of the engine. Care must be taken when installing such connecting rods to make certain the

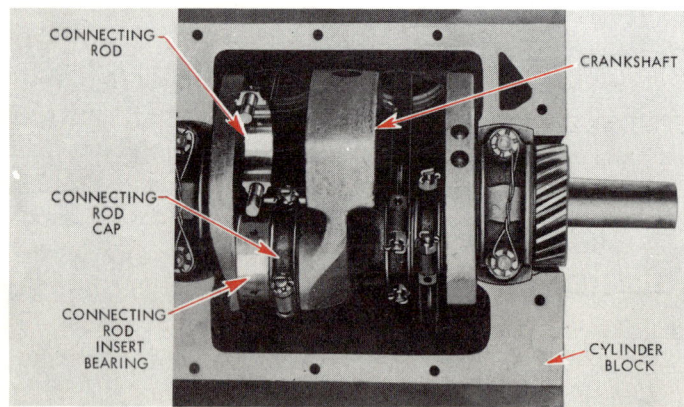

Fig. 4-17. You can see why the cylinder banks in this V-type engine must be offset to accommodate the side-by-side connecting rods. (Ford Motor Co.)

136

Pistons, Connecting Rods

Fig. 4-18. Offset connecting rods must be installed carefully.

rod is installed with the offset to the proper end of the engine.

Connecting rods are usually drop-forged from alloy steels and are made with an I-beam cross section to provide strength with a minimum of weight.

Rod Bushings. The upper or small end of the connecting rod is connected to the piston by the piston pin. When the piston pin is free to turn in the connecting rod, the upper end of the connecting rod is equipped with a bronze bushing pressed into the rod.

As the crankshaft revolves, the crankpin revolves within the bearing in the large end of the connecting rod, while the upper end of the rod oscillates on the piston pin. Although the movement of the piston pin in the bushing is small, the pressures and temperatures under which it operates are great. This makes lubrication of the piston pin bearings extremely difficult. Generally, piston pins are lubricated through a hole in the top of the connecting rod and bushing by oil sprayed from an oil spray hole drilled in the saddle of the upper half of the connecting rod and bearing as well as oil thrown off by the connecting rod bearings, Fig. 4-19. This also provides lubrication for the thrust side of the exposed cylinder wall.

In some older engines, lubricating oil was forced under pressure to the bushing in the connecting rod through an oil hole drilled the entire length of the connecting rod.

Rod Bearings. The lower end of the connecting rod is split to permit assembly and contains a bearing which bears on the crankpin, Fig. 4-19. The bottom bearing cap is attached to the rod by means of bolts and nuts. The bearing is made of an antifriction metal.

Materials. Bearing metals com-

Automotive Engines

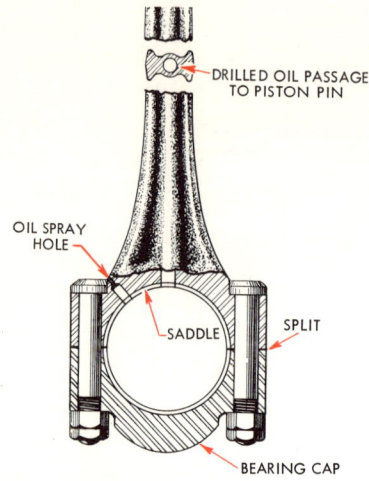

Fig. 4-19. Connecting rod with spray hole. When installing, be sure that the oil hole in the rod and in the bearing points toward the thrust side of the cylinder.

monly used are babbitt (composed of lead, tin, and antimony), copper-lead, cadmium-silver, etc. Such bearing metals, when used against steel surfaces, have a low coefficient of friction and are capable of withstanding heavy loads.

Some copper-lead bearings have a 0.001 in. thick layer of lead-tin alloy chemically deposited on the surface of the bearing. The lead-tin layer improves the load-carrying capacity of the bearing and reduces the possibility of scoring during the breaking-in period. Often a lead-bronze bearing material high in lead content is employed in some makes of diesel engines.

Bearings employed for connecting rods are of the replaceable type. Replaceable bearings consist of steel or bronze inserts lined with a thin layer of bearing material.

The bearing consists of two halves; the upper half is assembled in the rod, and the lower half, in the bearing cap. A lip or projection on each half of the bearing prevents the bearing from shifting or turning in the connecting rod, Figs. 4-16 and 4-17.

The insert bearings must fit closely in the bore of the connecting rod when the cap is installed and the nuts tightened to the proper torque value. To assure this, the diameter of the two inserts when placed together is from 0.001 to 0.002 in. greater than the diameter of the bore in the connecting rod, Fig. 4-20. Thus, when installed in the connecting rod, the ends of the bearings extend slightly beyond the parting surfaces of the rod and cap, and this amount must be compressed when the bearing is drawn up tight. This

Pistons, Connecting Rods

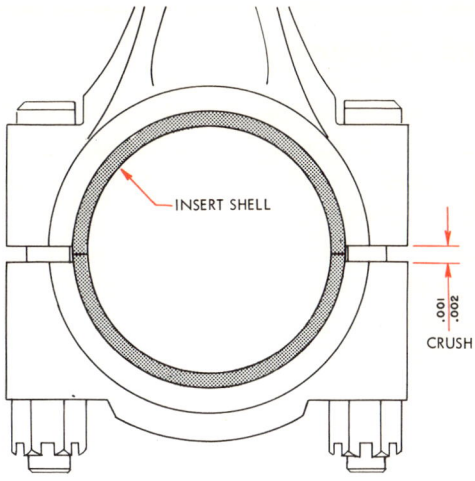

Fig. 4-20. Bearing "crush" assures a tight fit of the insert bearing in the connecting rod bore. This drawing shows the rod before the nuts have been tightened to the correct torque value.

excess is called the bearing "crush," and its purpose is to permit the bearing inserts to be seated solidly in the bore of the connecting rod, thus promoting rapid heat conduction away from the bearing surface.

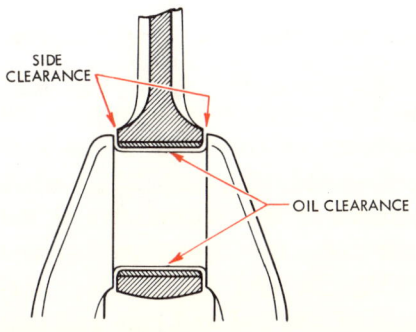

Fig. 4-21. Two types of clearance are needed for the rod bearing.

Bearing Oil Clearance. Connecting rod bearings are fitted to the crankpin with an oil clearance space between the crankpin and the bearing, Fig. 4-21. For pressure lubricated bearings, this clearance is approximately 0.001 in. for each inch of crankpin diameter. The total bearing clearance is influenced by the type of bearing metal alloy used and may vary slightly on the different makes of engines.

Rod and Bearing Side Clearance. When assembled on the crankpin, connecting rods and bearings must also have sufficient side clearance, Fig. 4-21, to assure that the sides of the connecting rod bearings do not bind on the fillets at the end of the crankpins.

Disassembly and Cleaning

The troubles that occur in the piston and connecting rod assembly usually are the result of wear that takes place in the piston, piston rings, piston pin, or connecting rod bearing. Such wear often results in noise, loss of power, and oil consumption. The individual parts of the assembly must be inspected to determine their condition, the repairs required, and whether further disassembly is required to make the repairs. The required inspections can be made on the assembled unit, but it is best to disassemble the piston from the connecting rod if:

(1) The piston pin shows any looseness in the piston or connecting rod bushing.

(2) A visual inspection shows that the piston rings are loose in their grooves.

(3) The piston skirt is scuffed, scored, or collapsed.

Disassembly

In disassembling the piston and connecting rod assembly, Fig. 4-22, the piston rings should be removed

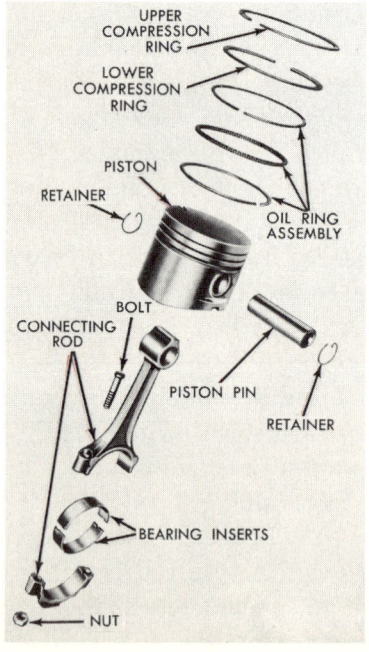

Fig. 4-22. This is a completely disassembled piston and connecting rod assembly. (Lincoln-Mercury Div., Ford Motor Co.)

Pistons, Connecting Rods

Fig. 4-23. Removing piston pin. (Plymouth Div., Chrysler Corp.)

from the piston with a piston ring expander tool. This tool expands the rings to permit their removal without damaging the rings or the ring lands.

Remove the piston pin retaining device. Push the piston pin out of the piston, or force it out with a soft metal drift and a hammer. Some piston pins are not held in place by retainers; instead, friction between the piston pin and connecting rod holds the pin in place. A special tool is required to remove the pin from the piston, Fig. 4-23.

Cleaning

To determine the condition of the parts of the piston and connecting rod assembly, they must be cleaned to remove all traces of carbon, varnish, and other accumulations.

Every part should be cleaned in a cleaning solution capable of dissolving the bond that holds the particles of accumulations together and to the part. Care must be taken not to clean the pistons and connecting rod bearings in solutions which attack aluminum or the metals used in the bearings. The pistons should be soaked in the cleaning solution until the carbon becomes softened. Then remove the carbon with a fairly stiff bristle

141

Automotive Engines

brush. If necessary, the carbon in the piston ring grooves can be removed by means of a ring groove cleaning tool. Any of the oil drain holes in the piston skirt or in the piston ring grooves should be carefully cleaned without enlarging the holes.

Inspection and Repair

The piston and connecting rod assembly parts should be carefully inspected visually to determine their condition and should be checked with precision measuring tools to determine their size and the clearances between the moving parts. A thorough inspection will determine whether the parts can be used again as they are, whether repairs will make them serviceable, or whether they must be replaced. If efficient and quiet engine operation is to be obtained, the repair operations on the various parts must be carefully performed to restore the clearances to the specifications recommended by the manufacturer.

Pistons

Piston wear causes excessive clearances, excessive oil consumption, and engine knocks.

Inspection. When the pistons have been thoroughly cleaned, inspect them for scuffing or scoring, collapsed skirts, worn ring grooves, bent or broken ring lands, cracks in the head or skirt, burned spots,

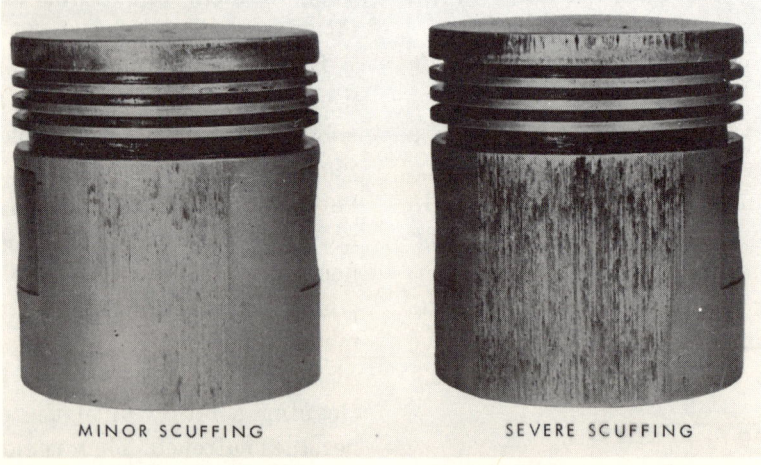

Fig. 4-24. The piston on the right must be replaced.

Pistons, Connecting Rods

and fit in the cylinder bore. Any pistons which are scored, cracked, or damaged, have burned spots, or are worn beyond repair should be discarded. Depending upon their condition, repairs can be made to some types of pistons to make them serviceable again.

Scuffed Piston. Scuffing is usually apparent on the thrust faces of the piston skirt, Fig. 4-24. Scuffing generally occurs during the first few moments after an engine is started, when there is little oil film on the cylinder walls, or in an overheated engine where it is difficult to maintain an oil film.

Minor cases of scuffing usually can be polished out and the piston can be made serviceable. Severe cases of scuffing require that a new piston be installed.

Worn Ring Grooves. The ring grooves should be free of carbon when determining the amount of ring side clearance. Use a new piston ring to check the amount of wear in each groove. The amount is determined by checking with a thickness gage the clearance between the piston ring and the side of the groove, Fig. 4-25. If the clearance is 0.006 in. or more, the piston can be regrooved for wider

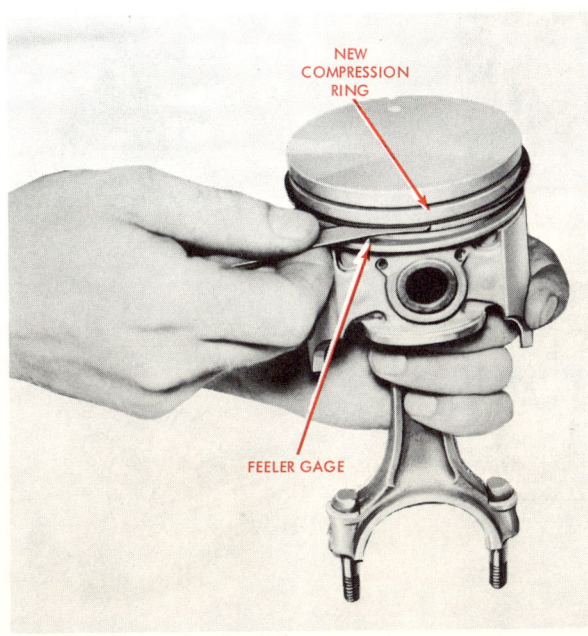

Fig. 4-25. Checking ring groove clearance. (Chevrolet Div., General Motors Corp.)

Automotive Engines

rings if the piston is satisfactory otherwise. On engines where the expense of replacing or regrooving the pistons is not justifiable, special rings are available which are designed to take up the side clearance of the piston rings.

Collapsed Skirt. Pistons with split skirts should be examined to determine whether the skirt has collapsed. The forces that cause collapse exert their pressure at right angles to the axis of the piston pin, causing the skirt to collapse at the thrust surfaces of the skirt, Fig. 4-26. Collapsed skirts cause the piston ring faces to wear to an oval (due to rocking of the piston), which causes the rings to lose their ability to scrape oil from the cylinder surfaces.

Extreme cases of skirt collapse cause a taper in the slot of the skirt, indicating that the skirt is smaller in diameter at the bottom (across the thrust surfaces) than at the top, Fig. 4-26.

A collapsed skirt also can be determined by measuring with a micrometer caliper, Fig. 4-26. Generally on new pistons the skirt is made about 0.0015 in. smaller in

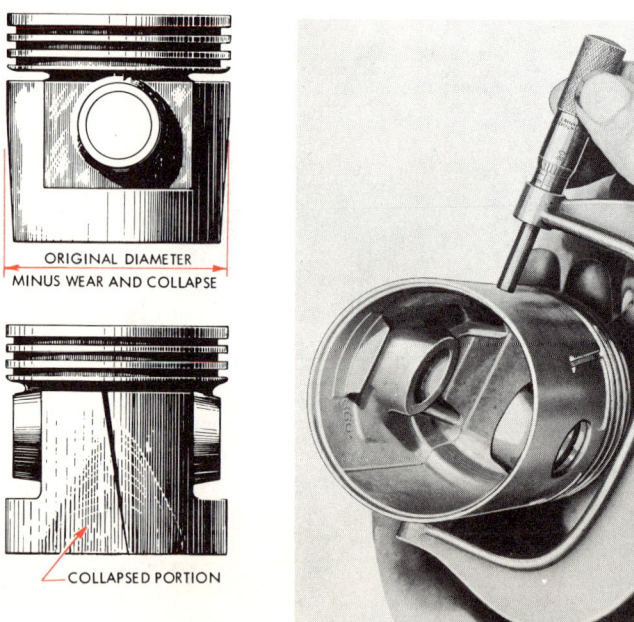

Fig. 4-26. Skirt collapse occurs along the thrust surface of the piston skirt. The amount of skirt collapse can be measured with a micrometer caliper.

Pistons, Connecting Rods

diameter at the top than at the bottom. Take care when determining the amount of collapse on cam ground pistons since they are larger in diameter across the thrust surfaces than at points 90 degrees from the thrust surfaces.

If the piston skirt is collapsed, the condition can be corrected by expanding the skirt diameter through a mechanical process or by replacing the piston.

Piston and Cylinder Clearance.

The piston clearance in the cylinder should be checked with the pistons and cylinder block at normal room temperatures (70°F) with the piston pin removed. In a worn cylinder bore, the piston clearance should be checked in the upper worn portion of the cylinder.

To check the piston clearance, place a thickness gage ½ in. wide against the side of the cylinder. Insert the piston upside down in the cylinder bore, Fig. 4-27. The thick-

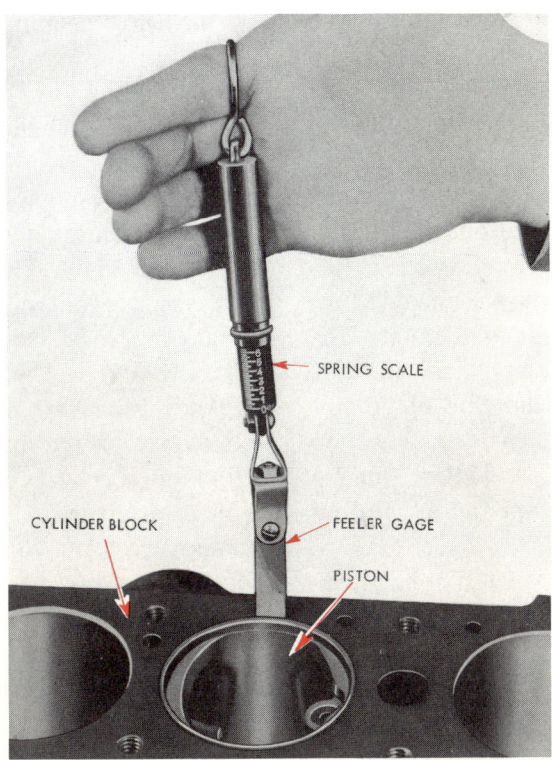

Fig. 4-27. Use a thickness gage and spring scale to check piston fit. (Oldsmobile Div., General Motors Corp.)

ness gage should be exactly 90 degrees from the piston pin hole and in line with the thrust surface on the power thrust side of the piston. This thrust surface is opposite the split or slots in the skirt in split skirt, T-slot, and U-slot pistons. Withdraw the thickness gage by pulling on the spring scale and observe the pounds of pull required while the gage is being removed. Check the piston with various size gages until the pull required to remove the gage is from six to ten pounds. The thickness of the gage indicates the fit of the piston in the cylinder. When available, the pounds pull the piston fitting specifications recommended by the manufacturer should be followed.

Repair. Various processes have been developed by which pistons can be expanded to obtain the desired piston fit, providing the cylinders are within the serviceable limits of out-of-round and taper. The piston fit must be 0.002 in. (or more) greater than the fit recommended for new pistons. The pistons can be expanded by means of one of the piston-expanding processes.

If the engine is to give satisfactory service with the expanded pistons, the cylinders should be "trued up" by honing. The amount to which the pistons can be expanded is determined by the amount of out-of-round and taper wear in the cylinder. If the amount of cylinder wear is such that the removal of up to 0.005 in. will straighten or partially straighten the cylinder bore, the cylinder should be honed.

In most mass-produced engines, pistons are not costly. Sometimes the cost of new pistons is less than the labor cost involved in attempting to "resize" old pistons. Likewise, if the piston skirt has collapsed, probably some wear has occurred in the ring grooves, and the useful life of the resized piston might be shortened by excessive side clearance of the rings. A couple of methods of resizing pistons are in use: "peening" and "knurlizing". In the peening process the piston skirts are expanded by means of a mechanically operated peening hammer. The peening hammer is spring-loaded and is operated at high speed by a double cam mechanism. The force of the hammer is controlled by a foot pedal, Fig. 4-28.

Knurlizing is the most common expanding process. Pistons can be expanded on a knurlizing machine, a specially designed lathe which produces several knurled bands across the thrust surface of the piston. The knurling operation raises the metal on the two thrust faces of the piston. The metal is permanently displaced, the displacement resulting in an increase in the piston diameter. The knurled pattern provides an "interrupted surface" on the piston skirt which

Pistons, Connecting Rods

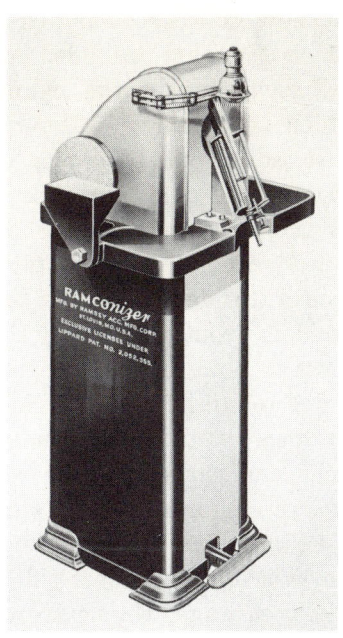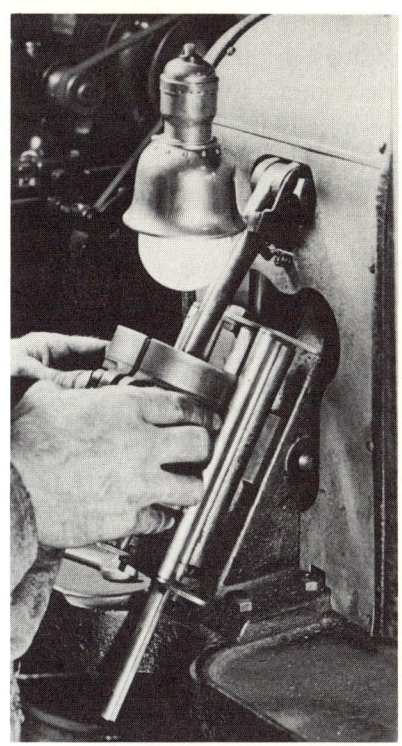

Fig. 4-28. The piston peening machine expands the piston by peening the inside of the skirt. (Ramsey Corp.)

has a high load-carrying capacity and permits a close piston fit with minimum danger of scuffing or scoring.

Remachining Ring Grooves. Sometimes pistons with worn ring grooves are regrooved to take the next oversize piston rings if the piston is otherwise satisfactory for reuse. Usually the replacement rings are $\frac{1}{32}$ in. wider than the original rings. Pistons should be regrooved only if the ring lands are of such width that remachining will not weaken the lands seriously. To increase the width of the ring grooves, the piston is centered accurately in a lathe or piston-turning machine and a light cut taken off both sides of the ring lands. The depth of the ring groove should not be increased.

After remachining, the width of the ring grooves (except for the top ring) should be from the same as the fractional size of the replacement ring to 0.001 in. greater than the fractional size. Thus, if the original rings were $\frac{1}{8}$ in. wide and the new rings are $\frac{5}{32}$ in. wide, the minimum width would be $\frac{5}{32}$ in. and the maximum width $\frac{5}{32}$ in. plus 0.001 in. The rings will have the proper side clearance since they are made slightly smaller than the fractional size of the rings.

Since the top rings operate at a higher temperature than the other rings, a worn top ring groove should be machined so as to accept a new standard ring plus a steel spacer inserted in the groove on top of the ring.

Piston Rings

When an engine is being overhauled, usually the old piston rings are replaced with new rings. When the pistons are removed from an engine with low mileage, the piston rings should not be removed from the pistons if they are to be used again. The piston rings should be examined to see that they are free in their grooves, that the slots in the oil control rings are not clogged with carbon, and that the rings are not scuffed or scored. Rings that are not satisfactory should be replaced. When installing new rings, care should be taken to make certain that the replacement rings are of the correct size. In addition to the standard size diameters, piston rings are available in 0.005, 0.010, 0.015, 0.020, 0.030, 0.040, and 0.060 in. oversizes.

When new piston rings are to be installed in the engine, the rings should be checked for side clearance in the piston ring grooves of the new or regrooved pistons for which they are intended and for end clearance in the cylinder in which they will operate.

Measuring Side Clearance. To determine the side clearance of piston rings, a new ring should be rolled around the piston ring groove to determine if there is freedom from binding. If the ring tends to bind in spots, generally it is due to slight nicks or carbon in the face of the ring lands. Such nicks and carbon can be removed by scraping or by using a small file. The ring should roll freely around the groove. When checked with a thickness gage, Fig. 4-25, new or regrooved pistons should have a side clearance of not less than the minimum or more than the maximum shown in Table 4-1. Pistons. with worn grooves can be reused if the side clearance does not exceed the maximum wear limit and if there is no shoulder worn in the groove. Each piston ring should be checked in the ring groove in which it is to be installed. The side clearance of a piston ring is extremely important because the rings must not rock on the cylinder bore.

Measuring End Clearance. To check the end clearance of a new piston ring in cylinders within the serviceable limits of out-of-round

Pistons, Connecting Rods

TABLE 4-1. RECOMMENDED PISTON RING SIDE CLEARANCE IN RING GROOVES (IN INCHES)

Type of Piston	Top Groove		Other Grooves	
	Recommended Clearance	Wear Limit	Recommended Clearance	Wear Limit
Aluminum	0.0015 to 0.002	0.006	0.001 to 0.0015	0.004
All trucks and tractors	0.003 to 0.004	0.006	0.003 to 0.004	0.006

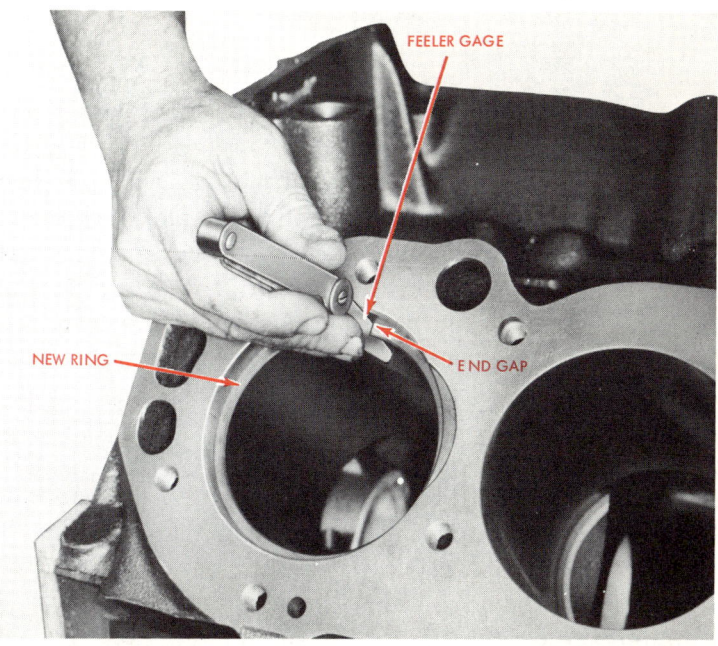

Fig. 4-29. Measuring ring gap with a feeler gage. (Chevrolet Div., General Motors Corp.)

and taper, the ring should be placed in the bottom of the cylinder bore near the lowest point of ring travel. The ring should then be moved with an inverted piston (so the ring will be square with the cylinder wall) to the lowest point to which the rings travel. The gap or clearance between the ends of the ring is measured with a thickness gage. In newly reconditioned cylinders known to be straight and round, the piston rings can be checked for end clearance at any convenient point, Fig. 4-29.

The minimum end clearance

149

Automotive Engines

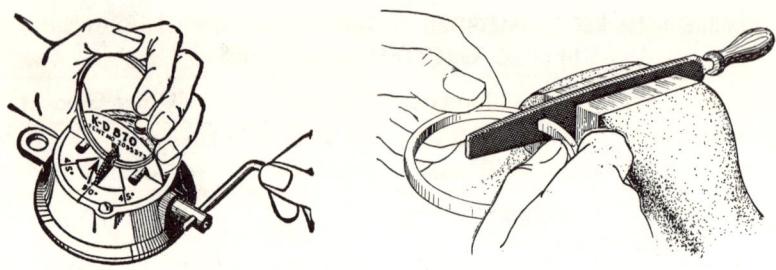

Fig. 4-30. Here are two different ways to adjust ring gap clearance.

should be not less than .001 in. per inch of circumference. However, generally the recommended minimum clearances are slightly higher than this amount. When obtainable, the specifications recommended by the engine manufacturer should be used. In general, the following gap specifications will be found to be satisfactory: up to and including 3 $\frac{1}{2}$ in. bore—minimum gap 0.009 in., 3 $\frac{9}{16}$ to 4 $\frac{3}{8}$ in. bore—minimum gap 0.012 in., 4 $\frac{7}{16}$ to 5 $\frac{1}{4}$ in. bore—minimum gap 0.015. Piston rings having less than the minimum clearances just given may expand sufficiently at operating temperatures to close the gap, causing the rings to scuff or break.

When the clearance is less than the recommended amount, the ring should be removed and filed in a ring filing fixture until the correct clearance is established, Fig. 4-30. When filing rings, keep the ends of the rings square to obtain a joint with uniform clearance. The rings can also be filed with a fine-cut file mounted in a vise, Fig. 4-30. With both ends of the ring held firmly against the file, work the ring back and forth across the surfaces of the file until the proper spacing is obtained. If the gap is $\frac{1}{32}$ in. or more, an oversize ring should be fitted to the cylinder.

Connecting Rods

Eventually, normal wear in the connecting rod bearings will cause the oil clearance space to increase to a point where the bearings throw off an excessive amount of oil. When the oil clearance is doubled, approximately five times as much oil is thrown off as with normal clearance. A clearance four times greater than normal results in a throwoff approximately 25 times greater than normal. The oil thrown off is thrown in a circular spray by the revolving crankshaft. When thrown off in excessive amounts, the piston rings cannot control the oil, resulting in an en-

Pistons, Connecting Rods

gine which pumps or burns oil. Worn bearings will knock, materially shortening the life of the bearing and crankshaft. Insufficient lubrication, excessive heat, overloading, and mechanical abuse also result in rapid deterioration of bearings.

At the small end of the connecting rod, the piston pin secures the piston to the connecting rod. The piston pin must operate within its bushings with a minimum of clearance or the engine will knock.

The piston and connecting rod assembly must be in perfect alignment with the cylinder bores and crankshaft if they are to operate with a minimum amount of friction.

Inspecting Connecting Rods. Connecting rods should be examined to determine the condition of the bore in the connecting rod, the bearing surfaces, and the bolts and nuts that attach the cap to the rod. The piston pin and bushing and the connecting rod bearings and crankpin journal should be measured to determine the clearances that exist between the parts. All oil holes in the connecting rod bearing or piston pin bushing should be examined to see that they are open and free from carbon. Worn or defective parts must be replaced or refitted.

Inspecting Bearing Clearances. Connecting rod bearings that are worn, pitted, scored, corroded, or show signs of fatigue should be replaced. Bearing failure due to fatigue results from the breakdown of the bearing metal after long applications of intermittent and heavy loads at the fairly high temperatures encountered under such conditions. The bearing surface is usually covered with fine cracks that extend through to the backing. Portions of the bearing metal may be dislodged from the bearing, Fig. 4-31. If one or more bearings show such signs of fatigue, all the engine bearings should be replaced. The connecting rod bolts which attach the cap to the connecting rod should be carefully examined and all damaged bolts replaced. Connecting rods employing integral studs should be replaced if the studs are damaged.

On connecting rods with replaceable insert bearings, check the bore of the connecting rod with a telescoping gage and micrometer caliper for an out-of-round condition. Replace the connecting rod if the bore is out-of-round 0.002 in. or more.

Measuring with Feeler Gage Stock. The clearance in the connecting rod bearings can be checked with feeler gage stock. To check the clearance of the bearing in this manner, a piece of 0.0015 in. thickness gage stock approximately ¾ in. long and ¼ in. wide is coated with oil and placed between the bearing and crankpin and parallel

151

Automotive Engines

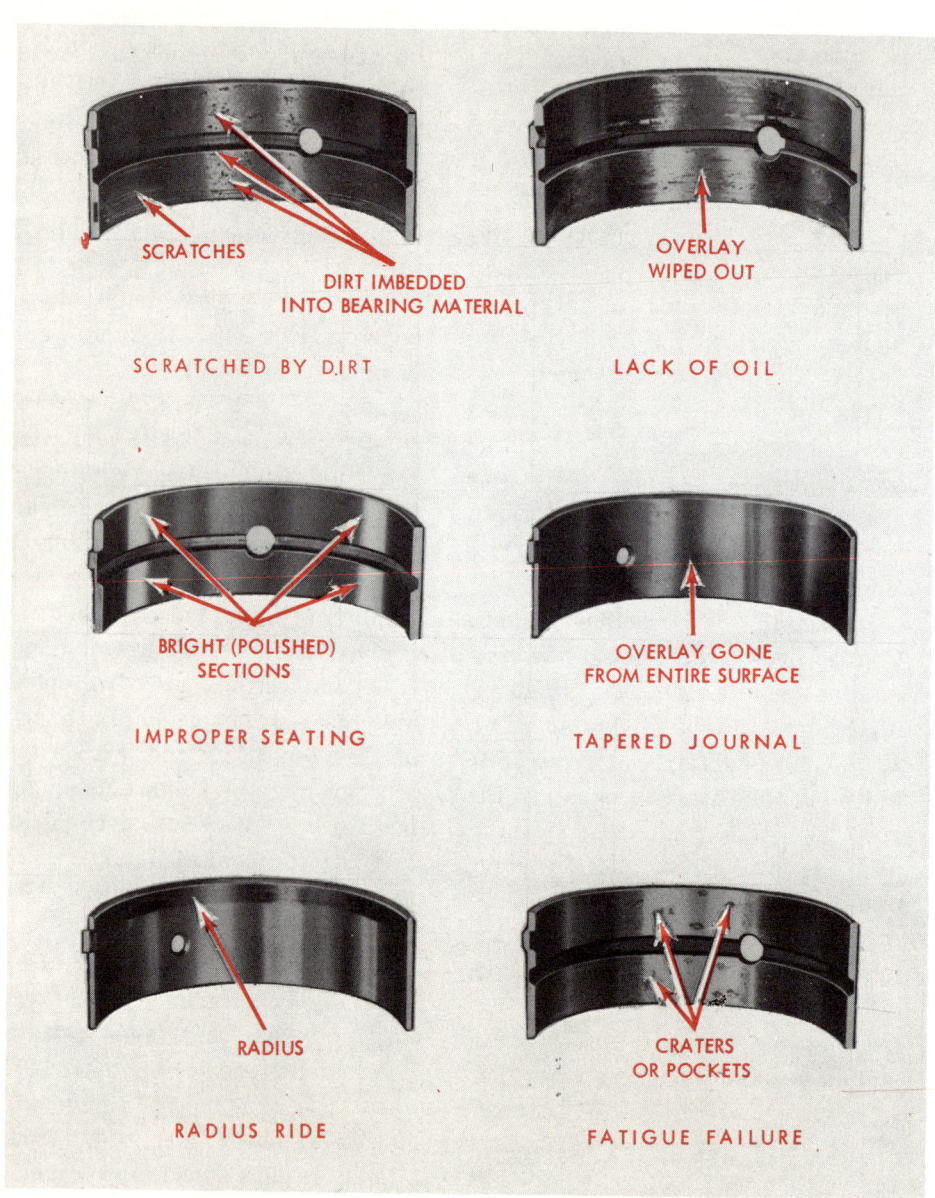

Fig. 4-31. Typical bearing failures. (Ford Div., Ford Motor Co.)

Pistons, Connecting Rods

to the crankshaft. The lower bearing cap is installed and the nuts tightened. If the bearing clearance is correct, there will be a distinctly greater drag felt when the connecting rod is turned a slight distance by hand than is felt without the piece of gage stock. No additional drag indicates that the clearance is excessive. Progressively thicker pieces of feeler gage stock in steps of 0.0005 in. can be tried until one is found that creates a slight drag on the bearing. This gives the approximate clearance of the bearing.

Measuring with Plastigage. Bearing clearances can also be checked with Plastigage, which consists of a thread-like piece of plastic material several thousandths of an inch in diameter and a gage graduated to indicate the bearing clearance in thousandths of an inch, Fig. 4-32. Before checking the clearance, wipe the oil from the bearing because the Plastigage material is soluble in oil.

To check the bearing clearance, a short piece of Plastigage is placed crosswise in the center of the bearing and the bearing tightened to the recommended torque value. Since the Plastigage is larger in diameter than the clearance in the bearing, the Plastigage flattens out. Do not turn the crankshaft with the Plastigage material in the bearing. Remove the bearing cap, and the Plastigage material will be found adhered to

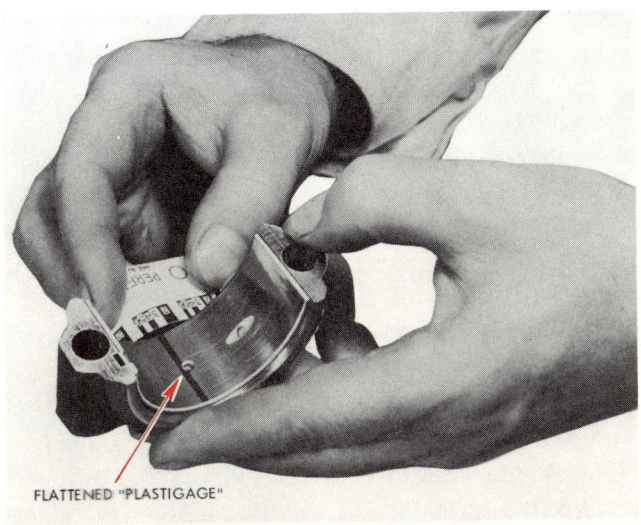

FLATTENED "PLASTIGAGE"

Fig. 4-32. Make sure that Plastigage does not come in contact with oil when checking bearing clearances.

Automotive Engines

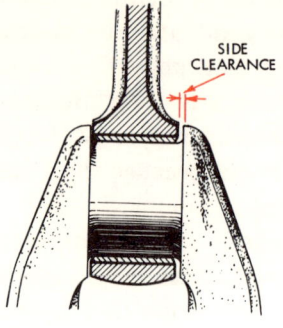

Fig. 4-33. Check connecting rod side clearance with a blade type thickness gage.

the bearing or the crankpin. When checked against the gage provided, the width of the flattened Plastigage indicates the bearing clearance.

Measuring Side Clearance. The side clearance of connecting rods is checked with the connecting rod mounted on the crankpin, Fig. 4-33. Push the connecting rod to one side of the crankpin, and check the side clearance on the opposite side with a thickness gage. On in-line engines the side clearance should be from 0.004 to 0.010 in., and the connecting rod should be replaced if the side clearance exceeds 0.010. On V-type engines with side-by-side connecting rods, the side clearance is from 0.007 to 0.014 in., and if the side clearance exceeds 0.014 in. the connecting rods should be replaced.

Replacing Insert Bearings. Since replaceable type connecting rod bearing inserts are not adjustable, they must be replaced to make adjustments for wear.

The size and condition of the crankpins determine the correct size of replacement rod bearings to be used: measure the crankpins at several points and around their circumference to determine the greatest diameter and the amount of out-of-round and taper, Fig. 4-34. If the out-of-round does not exceed 0.0015 in. and the taper 0.001 in., and the journal surface is free from grooves or ridges, replacement bearings of the correct undersize can be installed in the engine. If the out-of-round or taper exceeds the allowable limits, the crankpins should be reground to a standard undersize and replacement bearings of the correct undersize installed.

If the crankpins are worn 0.001 in. or more but are within the allowable limits of out-of-round and taper, standard undersize bearings of the correct size should be installed if they will establish the desired oil clearance. Replacement insert bearings are available in a

Pistons, Connecting Rods

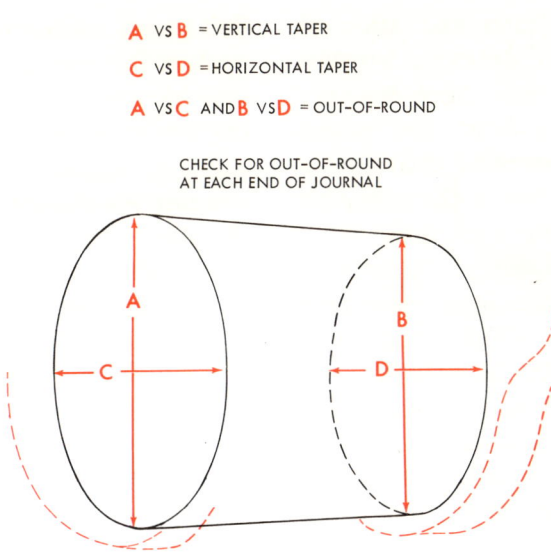

Fig. 4-34. Measuring crankshaft.

TABLE 4-2. RECOMMENDED CONNECTING ROD BEARING OIL CLEARANCES IN INCHES.

Crankpin Diameter (in inches)	Recommended Clearance	Maximum Allowable Clearance (wear Limit)
2 to 2 3/4	0.0005 to 0.0015	0.0035
2 13/16 to 3 1/2	0.0015 to 0.0025	0.005

standard size, in 0.001, 0.002, 0.010, 0.012, 0.020, 0.030, and 0.060 in. undersizes and as semifinished bearings which can be bored to the desired undersize.

When the amount of wear on the crankpins is such that the desired oil clearance cannot be obtained with the available standard undersize bearings, semifinished bearings bored to the correct diameter should be used. To determine the diameter to which semifinished bearings should be bored, the desired oil clearance should be added to the greatest diameter of the crankpin and the bearings bored to that diameter on a connecting rod reboring machine. See Table 4-2.

Piston Pins

Piston pins should be examined

155

Automotive Engines

for their condition and state of wear. Check for clearance between the piston pin and the connecting rod bushing and at the piston bosses. The amount of clearance is designed to be adequate under all engine operating conditions.

When the piston pin is held in the piston by retainers, loose pins can be replaced with oversize pins. In such cases, the holes in the piston bosses and in the connecting rod bushing must be reamed or honed to accommodate the new pin. When the piston pin is held in the connecting rod by friction, the piston and piston pin must both be replaced.

Inspecting and Measuring Piston Pins. The fit of the piston pin can be checked by lightly clamping the connecting rod in a vise, Fig. 4-35.

The piston is moved back and forth against the piston pin to determine whether the piston pin is loose in the piston bosses or in the connecting rod bushing.

After disassembly and thorough cleaning of the parts, the fit of the piston pin in both the piston and connecting rod can be determined with the aid of a telescoping gage and micrometer.

The diameter of the piston pin is measured with a micrometer caliper and should be the same at all points throughout its length. The amount of wear can be readily determined by comparing with the diameter of a new pin of the same size, or by comparing with the narrow, unworn portion of the pin that exists between the piston bosses and the piston pin bushing

Fig. 4-35. Clamp the connecting rod lightly in a vise to check for piston pin looseness. (Paul Lawrence Dunbar Vocational High School, Chicago, Illinois)

Pistons, Connecting Rods

in the small end of the connecting rod. A piston pin which shows signs of wear, has roughened surfaces, or is cracked or broken should be replaced.

The clearance between the piston pin and the piston and the small end of the connecting rod or bushing can be measured with a telescoping gage and micrometer caliper, Fig. 4-36. The hole diameter in the piston and connecting rod end should be measured with the telescoping gage to determine the largest diameter and the gage checked with a micrometer to determine the size. The diameter of the piston pin is determined with a micrometer caliper. The difference in size between the piston pin and the hole in the piston or the connecting rod is the clearance of the piston pin. Pistons and connecting rods having a piston clearance of 0.001 in. or more should have new pins fitted to restore the desired operating clearance.

Fitting Piston Pins. The procedure of fitting piston pins in the piston and connecting rod depends

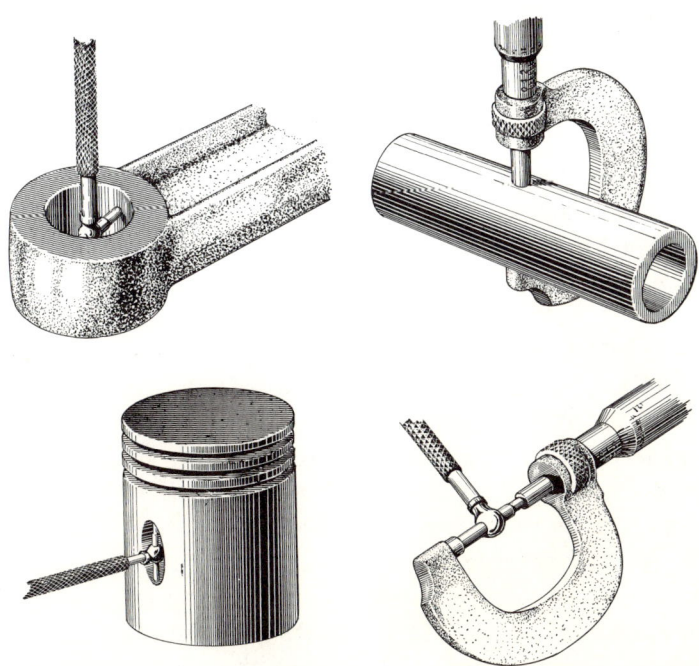

Fig. 4-36. Use a telescoping gage and a micrometer caliper for measuring differences in diameter to determine piston pin clearance.

upon whether the piston pins are to be fitted to old or new pistons. When the old pistons are serviceable and the connecting rod or bushing is worn so that the pin has an excessive clearance, both the connecting rod or bushing and the piston bosses can be reamed or honed to fit an oversize piston pin. Piston bosses can be reamed or honed to fit an oversize piston pin. Piston pins are available in standard sizes and 0.003, 0.005, and 0.010 in. oversize. When the new pistons are being installed in the engine, the connecting rod or bushing must be replaced and/or refitted if the old bushing does not provide the correct fit for a standard size piston pin.

To establish the desired fit between the piston pin and the piston or the diameter in the connecting rod, both the piston and the bushing are either reamed with an expansion reamer or honed with an abrasive stone or fabric abrasive hone.

Reaming. When reaming, the reamer should be clamped in a vise and the parts turned by hand, or the reamer may be mounted in a motor-driven reamer, Fig. 4-37, and the parts held by the operator.

To ream either the connecting rod bushings or the pistons, the reamer is expanded in small steps and the parts reamed until the proper fit has been established. After fitting the first piston pin, the connecting rods or pistons can be reamed quickly by reducing the diameter of the reamer about 0.0005 in. to rough out the bushings or pistons. Then they can be finish reamed.

When reaming connecting rod bushings, care should be taken to keep the reamer in alignment with the hole in the bushing to prevent *bell-mouthing* (reaming the ends of the bushing larger in diameter than the center). Piston bosses should be reamed with a pilot type expansion reamer to assure that the holes in both bosses are reamed in alignment.

Honing. In addition to reaming, piston pins can be fitted to the connecting rod and piston by honing. Fig. 4-38 illustrates a motor-driven honing machine which employs replaceable abrasive stones mounted on a honing head.

To hone either connecting rod bushings or piston bosses, the stones on the honing head are expanded, by means of the graduated dial, to fit with a light drag in the bore of the bushing or piston bosses. Connecting rod bushings are honed by moving the connecting rod back and forth over the stones by hand as the hone revolves until the desired piston pin fit is secured. Some machines are equipped with a connecting rod guide that prevents bell-mouthing of the bushing during honing when the journal end of the rod is held

Pistons, Connecting Rods

Fig. 4-37. Old piston bosses can be reamed to fit oversize piston pins.

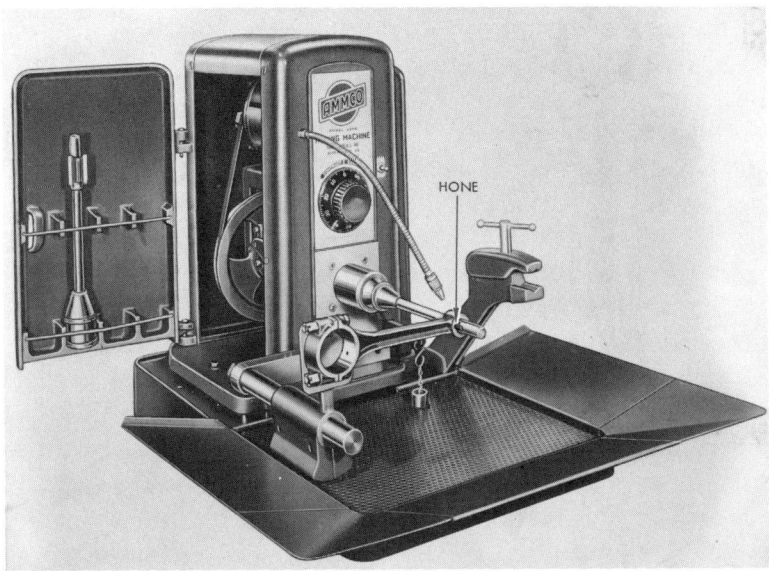

Fig. 4-38. A motor-driven honing machine can also be used to fit piston pins to connecting rods and pistons. (Ammco Tools, Inc.)

Automotive Engines

tightly against the face plate on the guide.

When honing piston bosses, the piston is moved back and forth over the hone through both bosses, the piston being centered by means of a centering cone after the hone passes through the first boss. This permits both holes to be honed in perfect alignment. The operation is repeated until the desired piston pin fit is secured. The graduated dial permits duplication of hole diameters when honing additional connecting rod bushings and pistons.

Final Fitting. The fit of the piston pin in the bushing varies with the type of pin installation in the piston. In the case of the full floating piston pin having retainer rings in aluminum piston pin bosses, the piston pin is usually fitted to a light tap or palm push in the piston with the piston at room temperature. The pin is fitted to a hard thumb or palm push fit in the connecting rod bushing, Fig. 4-39. Manufacturers specifications should always be followed.

Replacing Connecting Rod Bushings. The bushing in the connecting rod must be replaced, in a full floating installation, when new pistons are installed and a standard size piston pin is used.

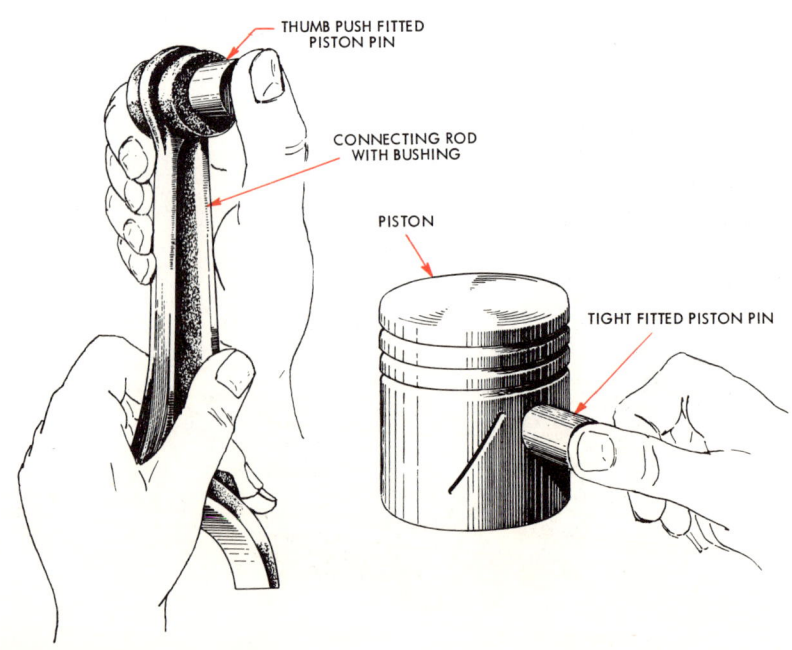

Fig. 4-39. This piston pin is fitted tighter in the piston bosses than in the rod bushing.

Pistons, Connecting Rods

Connecting rod bushings are made of bronze and are of either the rolled or solid type. The bushings are removed by means of a suitable driver or pressed out using an arbor press. New bushings should be pressed into the connecting rod, taking care to align the oil holes correctly. When oil holes must be drilled in the bushing, they should be drilled the same size as the holes in the connecting rod. Rolled bushings with a joint the length of the bushing should be expanded with a suitable burnishing tool to provide a tight fit in the connecting rod before fitting the piston pin. The bushings are either reamed or honed to secure the proper fit of the piston pin in the bushing.

Connecting Rod Alignment

The piston and connecting rod assembly must be in perfect alignment with the cylinder bores and crankshaft if they are to operate with a minimum amount of friction. Since the piston must move in a line at exact right angles to the center line of the crankshaft, the piston pin must be accurately parallel with the crankpin if the piston is to move in the cylinder without twisting or binding.

A bent connecting rod causes the piston to be "cocked" in the cylinder, resulting in an excessive amount of wear on the piston, cylinder walls, piston pin, and connecting rod bearing, Fig. 4-40. The

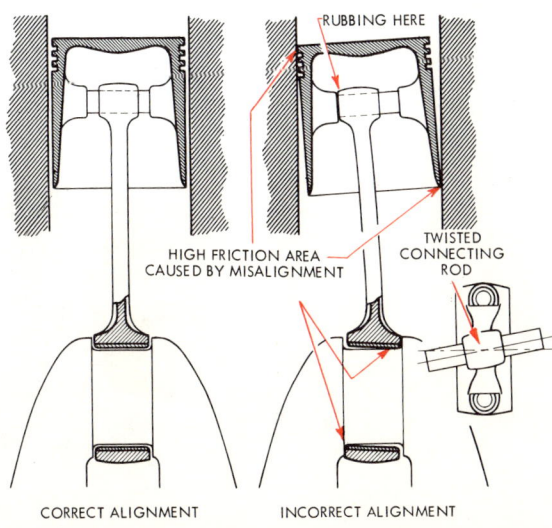

Fig. 4-40. A bent connecting rod can cause misalignment on every bearing surface shown.

Automotive Engines

wear on the pistons occurs at the ring lands on one side of the piston and at the bottom of the piston skirt on the opposite side. Due to the "cocked" position of the piston in the cylinder, the piston rings are prevented from seating properly against the cylinder wall, often resulting in blow-by of gases past the piston rings.

The bent connecting rod also causes uneven wear on the connecting rod bearing and crankpin. The bearing, being "cocked" on the crankpin, develops high friction areas at diagonally opposite edges of the bearing, resulting in rapid wear of the bearing surfaces.

It is extremely doubtful that a connecting rod can twist or bend from the forces imposed during normal engine operation. Rough handling after removal from the engine is the more likely cause of connecting rod misalignment. If some part breaks or seizes during operation, the forces imposed on the rod will be great enough to bend or twist it. Connecting rods must be checked for alignment and straightened, if necessary, before they are reinstalled in the engine.

Connecting rods should be checked carefully for bend and twist in a connecting rod aligning fixture and corrected if necessary, Fig. 4-41. With the piston pin in place, the connecting rod is

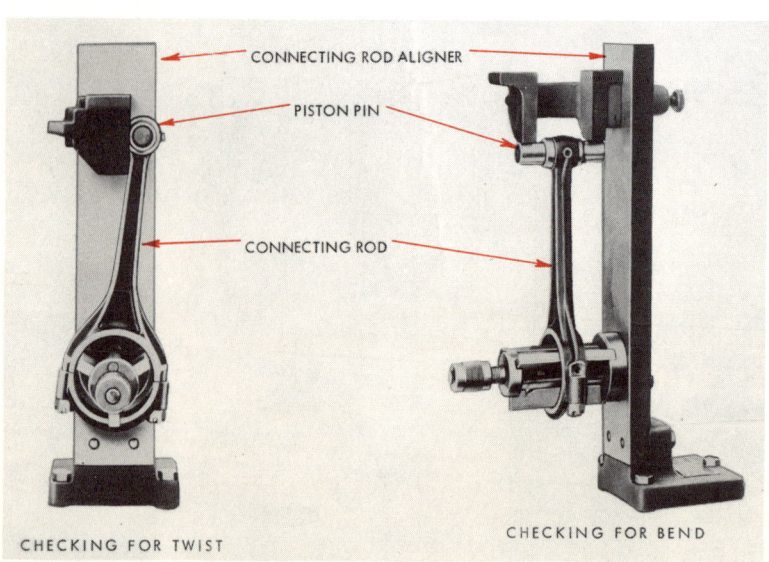

Fig. 4-41. A connecting rod aligning fixture can be used both to check and to correct bent or twisted rods. (Ford Motor Co.)

Pistons, Connecting Rods

clamped securely on the arbor. The amount of twist in the rod can be checked against the side of the machined surface on the aligner. The bottom machined surfaces of the fixture are used to check the rod for bend. If the connecting rod is twisted or bent, it can be straightened with either a bending bar, an adjustable wrench, or special tools furnished with the aligner. Care must be taken not to damage the connecting rod. When checked with a thickness gage, the amount of bend or twist in a rod should not exceed 0.002 in. per 6 in. of length. When straightening a connecting rod, it should first be bent beyond the point desired and then returned to a straight position. It will then retain its position.

Assembly

After the repair operations are completed on the piston pins, piston rings, and connecting rods, the units can be assembled and made ready for installation in the engine. Assembly procedures vary among the different designs of pistons and connecting rods. Because pistons and piston rings are fitted to individual cylinders, they should be assembled to the connecting rod for that cylinder.

Assembling Connecting Rod to Piston

When assembling pistons to connecting rods, take care to see that the two are assembled with both the connecting rod and piston facing in the proper direction for installation in the engine. On pistons with offset piston pins, make certain that the offset is located toward the side recommended by the manufacturer. Generally such pistons are marked to indicate the side of the piston that goes to the front of the engine. Pistons with slots in the skirt should be assembled so that the slots are on the compression thrust side of the engine. Connecting rods usually are marked with cylinder numbers and should be installed so the numbers all face the side of the engine specified by the manufacturer. If the connecting rod has an oil spray hole in the connecting rod bearing, care should be taken that the hole will be located on the proper side when the assembly is installed in the engine.

The piston pin is tapped into place with a mallet or with a push of the hand. The pin must be aligned in the piston or connecting rod so the locking devices can be installed. When the pin is retained in the connecting rod by friction, a special tool must be used to

Automotive Engines

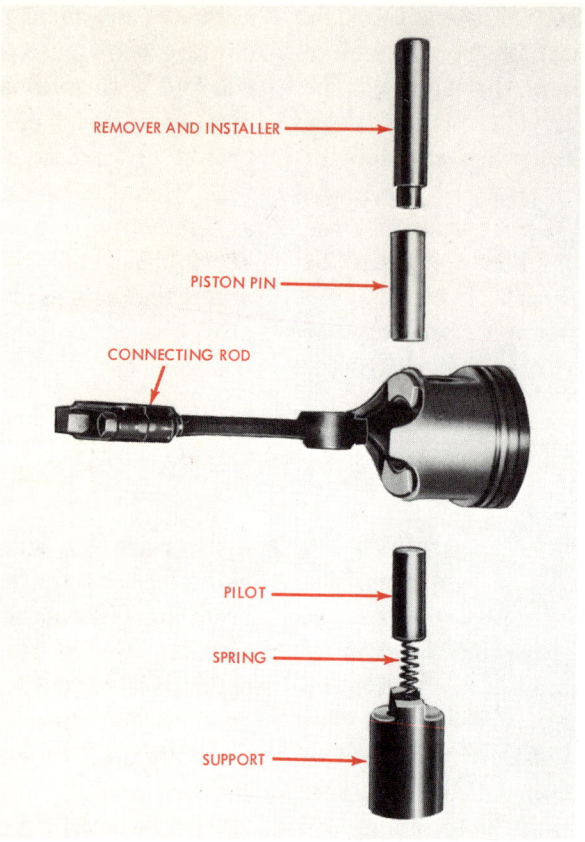

Fig. 4-42. Piston pin removal and installation tool. (Chevrolet Div., General Motors Corp.)

properly insert the piston pin in the piston and connecting rod, Fig. 4-42.

Installing Piston Rings

There are a number of methods of installing piston rings on a piston. It is advisable to use a piston ring expander tool for ring installation, Fig. 4-43. With such a tool there is less possibility of ring distortion or breakage than when other methods are employed. Because the piston rings have been previously fitted to a particular cylinder and piston, they should be installed in their proper order on the proper piston.

To install the rings on a piston, the piston ring is placed in the ring expander and expanded just enough to slip over the piston. When installing the rings, the lowest ring should be placed on the

Pistons, Connecting Rods

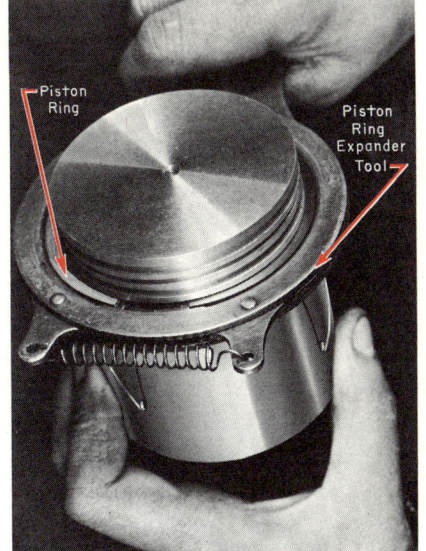

Fig. 4-43. A piston ring expander is the best tool to use when installing piston rings. (Ford Motor Co.)

piston first. The operation is repeated for each piston ring until they are all in place in their respective ring grooves. If the rings are of the one-piece type, space the rings so that the ring gaps on adjacent rings are located on opposite sides of the piston.

When installing new rings, follow closely the ring manufacturer's instructions. Be particularly careful to correctly install grooved, beveled, or tapered rings to ensure good compression and oil control.

With expander type rings, the expander is first placed in the ring groove with the joint toward the compression thrust side of the engine. The outer ring is then placed in the groove over the expander with the gap toward the major or power thrust side of the engine.

Before installing expander type rings, take an accurate count of the parts that make up each ring because an inaccurate count during packing at the factory can sometimes result in more or fewer parts than are necessary.

Installing Piston and Rod in Cylinder

The piston and connecting rod assembly is installed from the top of the cylinder. Take care to install the piston and connecting rod assembly into its proper cylinder and facing in the direction specified by the manufacturer. Improper installation of the assembly can cause a bent connecting rod or a scored cylinder. Connecting rods with oil spray holes must be installed on the correct side of the engine for proper lubrication. The side of the piston designed to take the power thrust must contact the proper side of the cylinder.

Revolve the crankshaft until the journal for the proper cylinder is at the bottom of its stroke and midway between each side of the cylinder block. This position will allow the greatest amount of clearance obtainable when installing the piston and rod assembly. Clean the cylinder walls and lubricate them with engine oil.

Piston Ring Compressor. Lubricate the piston rings and ring grooves. Install a piston ring compressor on the piston and connecting rod assembly. If available, install connecting rod bolt guide sleeves on the connecting rod bolts, Fig. 4-43. Lower the assembly into the cylinder until the ring compressor rests against the top of the engine block. Make sure that the connecting rod (and spray hole, if employed) is facing toward the correct side of the engine. Tighten the ring compressor enough to permit the piston and rings to enter the cylinder. Tap the top of the pis-

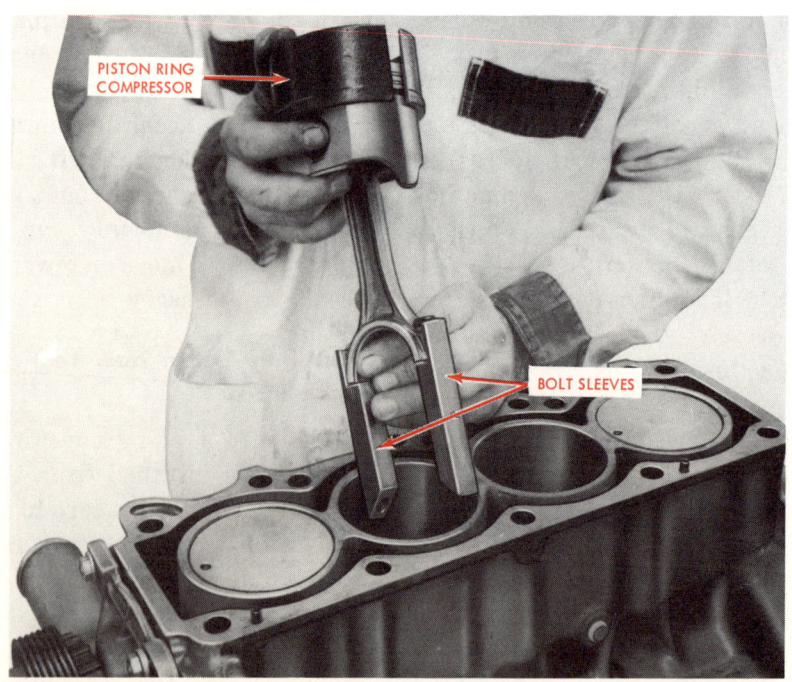

Fig. 4-44. Connecting rod bolt guide sleeves. (Chevrolet Div., General Motors Corp.)

Pistons, Connecting Rods

ton with the handle end of a hammer, Fig. 4-44, until the connecting rod is within one inch of the crankshaft.

Make sure the bore in the connecting rod and bearing cap is clean and dry. Lubricate only the bearing surface (being sure to keep the back of the bearing dry and clean). Place one half of the bearing in the connecting rod and the other half in the bearing cap, making certain that the lips on the inserts fit in the notches in the bearing cap and connecting rod. If the old bearings are being used, make certain that they are installed in their original positions.

Tap on the top of the piston with the hammer handle until the connecting rod is seated on the crankshaft. While doing this, be sure that the threads on the studs in the connecting rod (if bolt guide sleeves are not used) do not scratch the crankshaft journal. Install the bearing cap, making sure that any marks or numbers on the bearing cap and connecting rod are on the same side. Install, but do not completely tighten, the nuts. Install the remaining piston and connecting rod assemblies in the same manner, making certain that all the numbers or marks are on the same side of the engine. Tighten

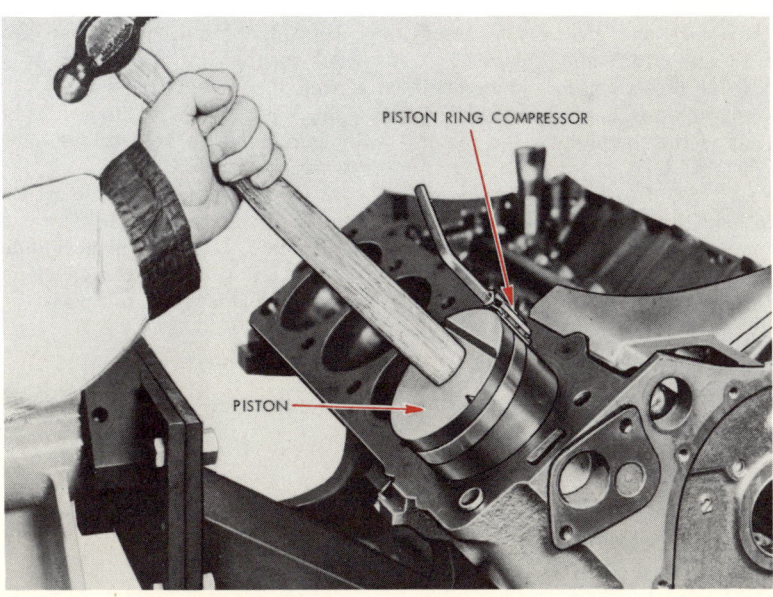

Fig. 4-45. Use a ring compressor when installing the piston and connecting rod assembly in the cylinder bore. (Ford Motor Co.)

the connecting rod nuts to the manufacturer's recommended torque value. If cotter pins or pal nuts are used on the connecting rod bolts, install them.

If the bearings have been properly fitted, it should be possible to move the connecting rod back and forth on the crankpin with one hand.

Checking On Your Knowledge

The following questions give you the opportunity to check up on yourself. If you have read the chapter carefully, you should be able to answer the questions. If you have any difficulty, read the chapter over once more so that you have the information well in mind before you go on with your reading.

DO YOU KNOW

1. What is the purpose of the relief cut into the piston at the piston bosses?

2. Why does the piston require a greater clearance at the head of the piston than at the skirt?

3. What does the electrolytic treatment do to aluminum alloy pistons?

4. In what direction do cam ground pistons expand when heated?

5. What is the purpose of the piston pin?

6. What type of locking device is employed to hold the piston pin in place on engines employing a full-floating type of piston pin?

7. What purpose do the piston rings serve?

8. What would be the effect of excessive ring pressure on the cylinder walls?

9. On three-ring pistons, in which ring groove is the oil control ring usually located?

10. What purpose does the groove or bevel located at the inside or outside corner of a piston ring serve?

11. Why must the connecting rods in an engine all be held to the same close weight limits?

12. How would you use a thickness gage and tension scale to check the clearance of a piston in a cylinder?

13. What would be the effect of insufficient gap clearance in a piston ring?

Cylinder Heads, Valves, and Valve Operating Mechanisms

Chapter **5**

The cylinder head encloses the top of the cylinders, forming the combustion chambers in which the burning of air-fuel mixture takes place. In I-head or valve-in-head engines, the cylinder head contains the valves and valve port openings that lead into the cylinders. In L-head engines, the valves and valve port openings are contained in the cylinder block.

The shape of the combustion chamber in the cylinder head may be flat, spherical, wedge shaped, conical, or in a combination of these shapes.

The valves and valve operating mechanism admit the fuel charge into the cylinders, seal the cylinders to permit compression of the fuel charge, and allow the exhaust gases to be ejected from the cylinders. The valves and valve operating mechanism function under severe conditions which eventually make repairs necessary to maintain engine efficiency and quiet operation. In this chapter the various parts that make up the cylinder head, the valves, and valve operating mechanism are discussed as to their types, construction, and operation. This chapter also covers cleaning, inspection, and repair of the parts comprising the cylinder head and valve assembly.

Cylinder Head Construction

Removable cylinder heads are used on present-day engines. The cylinder head is a one-piece casting that encloses the top of the cylinders forming the combustion chamber. Cylinder heads are made

Automotive Engines

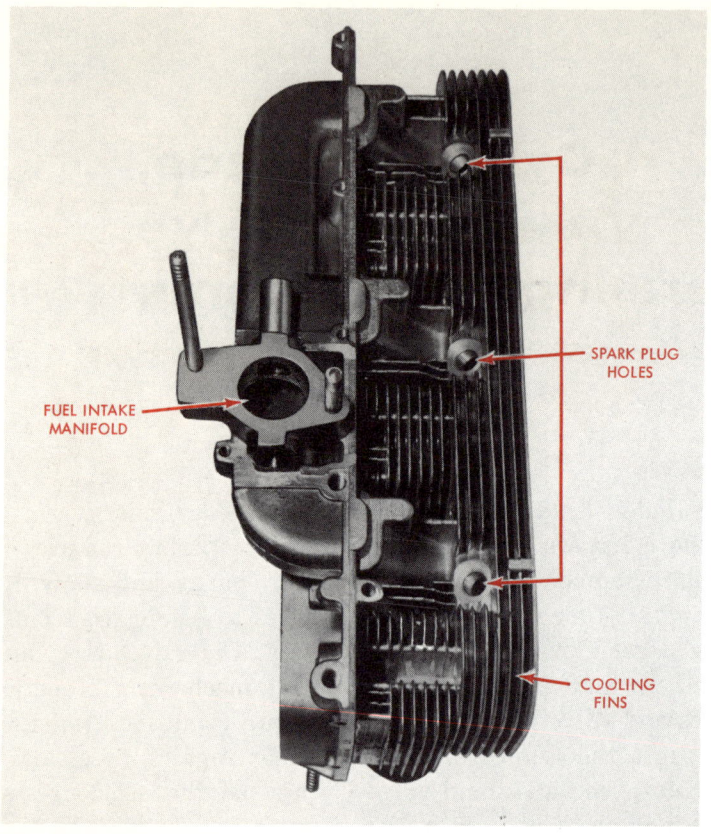

Fig. 5-1. This cylinder head from a horizontally opposed six-cylinder I-head engine is of cast aluminum and the fins and intake manifold are cast integrally with the head. It has wedge shaped combustion chambers and contains the valves for the cylinders. (Chevrolet Motor Div., General Motors Corp.)

of cast gray iron or aluminum. The cylinder head is bolted to the top of the cylinder block and is readily removed to give access to the valves and cylinders for repair.

Air-cooled engines may have individually mounted cylinders. Depending on the design, the cylinder head and cylinder may be removed separately or as a unit after the retaining bolts have been removed.

The cylinder heads for air-cooled engines have fins, Fig. 5-1, which serve to dissipate heat.

In liquid-cooled engines, the cylinder head has passages cast integrally with the head, and the cylinders are entirely surrounded by a liquid coolant, Fig. 5-2. Upward circulation of the coolant is provided for by passageways between the cylinder head and cylinder

Heads, Valve Mechanisms

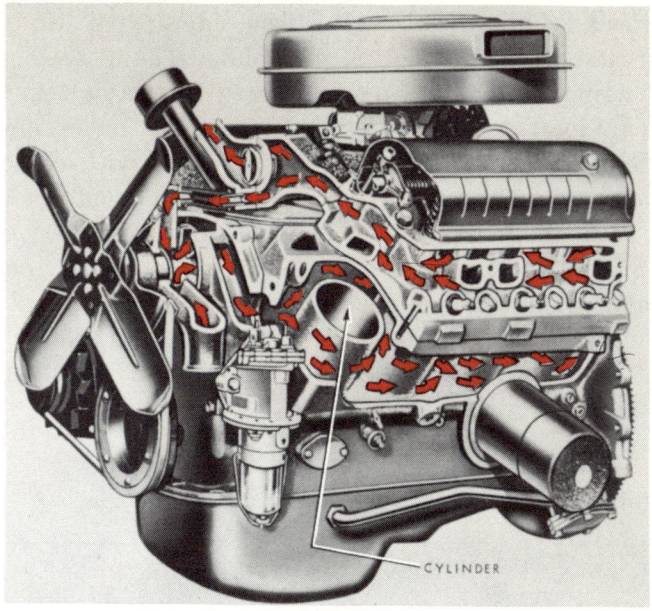

Fig. 5-2. Water passages in the cylinder block and heads of a V-8 engine. The arrows show the direction of water flow. (Lincoln-Mercury Div., Ford Motor Co.)

block. A coolant outlet hose connects the cylinder head to the upper radiator tank.

Present-day engines use an I-head (valve-in-head) arrangement except for one manufacturer that makes available an F-head arrangement whereby the intake valves are in the block and the exhaust valves are in the head. Many of the older model engines used an L-head arrangement.

Fig. 5-3 illustrates a cylinder head used on L-head engines. Fig.

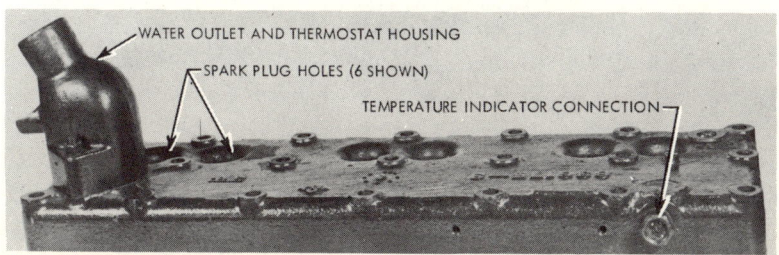

Fig. 5-3. Cylinder head for a six-cylinder L-head engine.

171

Automotive Engines

5-4 illustrates a cylinder head used in I-head (valve-in-head) engines. In I-head engines, the valves and valve ports are located in the cylinder head. Removal of the cylinder head on such engines also removes the valves. Although most cylinder heads are made of cast iron, some engines have aluminum cylinder heads. Aluminum, which has a higher heat conductivity than cast iron, dissipates the heat more rapidly. The F-head will be discussed in a later chapter.

The adoption of high compression ratios, with consequent high pressures, resulted in improvements in combustion chamber design. Combustion chambers in present-day engines are designed to promote turbulence of the fuel charge. The combustion chamber is

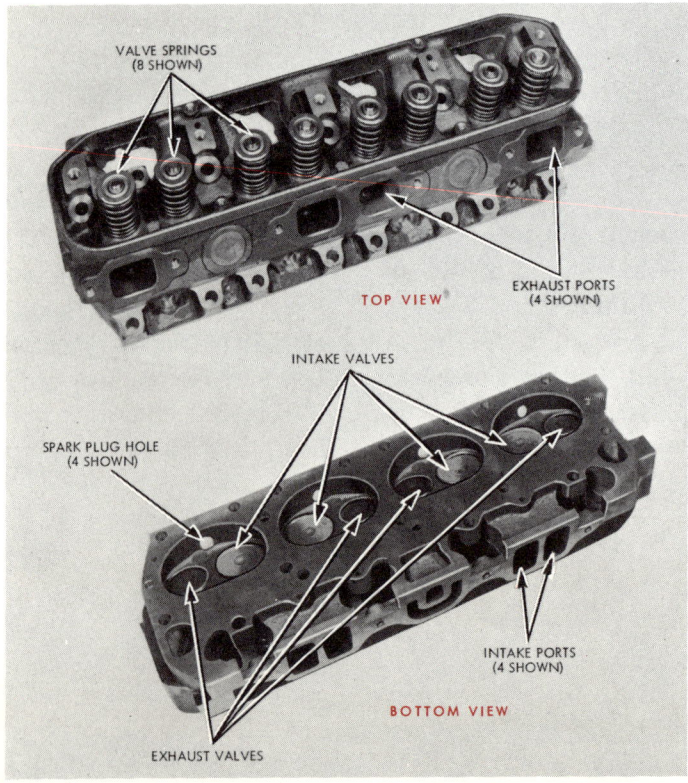

Fig. 5-4. Cylinder head for a V-8 I-head engine. The top view shows the head in its normal operating position. The bottom view shows the cylinder head as it appears when turned over. (Dodge Div., Chrysler Corp.)

Heads, Valve Mechanisms

designed so the flow of the fuel charge into the cylinder and the movement of the piston on the compression stroke cause the fuel charge to swirl. The fuel charge is greatly agitated and compressed into a dense mass at the spark plug gap. This design brings about a more rapid and complete burning of the fuel charge.

Engines presently being manufactured are operating at reduced compression ratios, which allows for the use of non-leaded or low lead content gasoline. This is in preparation for further emission controls in the form of thermal and catalytic converters. The design change has not seriously affected engine power output but has brought about a reduction of emissions.

Gaskets

Cylinder head gaskets may be made of asbestos and covered with steel, copper, or bronze; they may be made of steel wire and covered with asbestos. They are used between the cylinder head and the block in order to make the joint tight against water and pressure. Some auto manufacturers recommend a nonsetting gasket cement to ensure a tight joint.

Fig. 5-5 shows a gasket for a six-cylinder engine. Such gaskets are capable of withstanding the high temperatures developed during engine operation.

The cylinder head gasket has a number of holes in alignment with some of the openings in the cylinder block and head. The holes in the gaskets do not always conform to the water passages but are positioned in such a way and are of the proper size to cause more coolant to circulate around the valves.

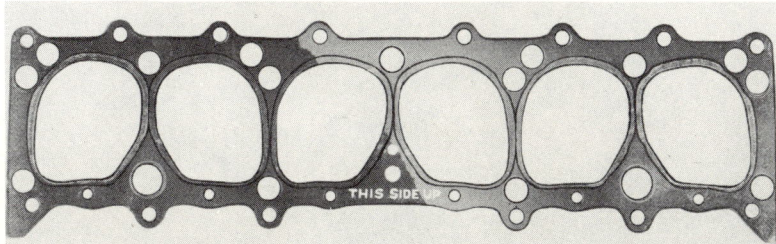

Fig. 5-5. Cylinder head gasket. When replacing cylinder head gaskets, be sure that the new gasket is the same thickness as the old one. If it is not, the compression ratio will be changed (Chevrolet Div., General Motors Corp.)

Automotive Engines

Valves and Valve Operating Mechanisms

In four-stroke-cycle internal combustion gasoline engines, a passage and opening leading into the cylinders must be provided so that the fuel mixture can enter the cylinder on the intake stroke; a similar passage and opening must be provided to permit the exhaust gases to escape from the cylinder on the exhaust stroke. These openings are called valve ports.

The port openings leading into the cylinders are opened and closed at the proper intervals by the valves, which close against a valve seat located in the port opening. Each cylinder must have at least one intake and one exhaust valve.

The valves in each cylinder are opened and closed in their port openings by the valve operating mechanism in proper relation to the position of the piston. Fig. 5-6 illustrates the valve operating mechanism of a typical I-head engine. The valves are opened by the valve lifters, push rods, and rocker arms. The valve lifters are raised

Fig. 5-6. Valves and valve operating mechanism on a V-type I-head engine. (Buick Div., General Motors Corp.)

Heads, Valve Mechanisms

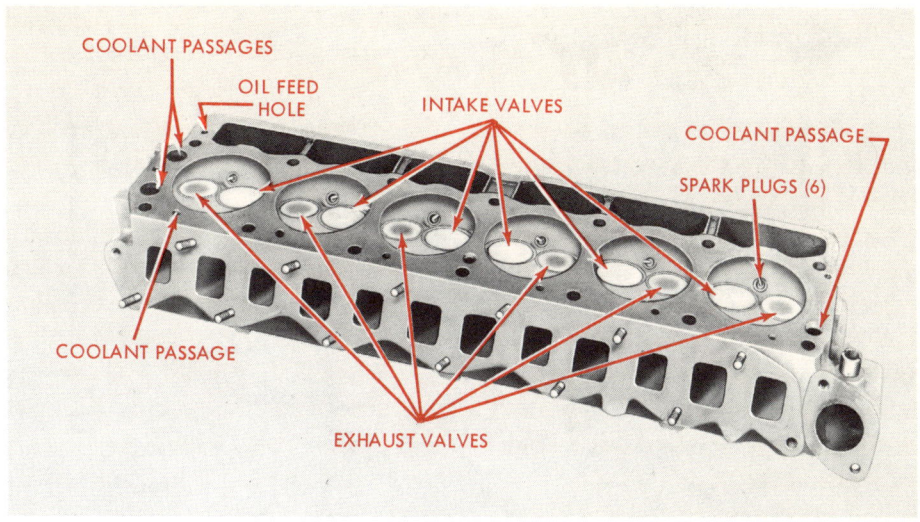

Fig. 5-7. Typical Valve Arrangement. (Plymouth Div., Chrysler Corp.)

by cams on the camshaft. The pressure exerted by the valve spring closes the valves. Although there are some differences in the arrangement of valves and the valve operating mechanism among the various types and designs of four-stroke-cycle engines, they all contain parts which perform similar functions.

Fig. 5-7 is an illustration of a typical valve-in-head arrangement showing the valves, combustion chamber, spark plugs, and the various openings in the cylinder head. Most engines manufactured today are of the overhead valve type. However, a number of engines still in operation have valves located in the block, Fig. 5-9.

Valves

The type of valve most commonly used in four-stroke-cycle engines is known as the poppet or mushroom valve. The poppet valve consists of a valve head and a valve stem, Fig. 5-8. The valve head has a face ground at an angle of 30 to 47 degrees at the outer edge, which closes against the valve seat in the cylinder block or head when the valve is closed. The valve stem has a retainer groove machined in the lower end which receives the split valve locks that hold the valve spring retainer and valve spring in place in the engine, Fig. 5-9.

The valve stems are accurately ground to fit the valve guides in

175

Automotive Engines

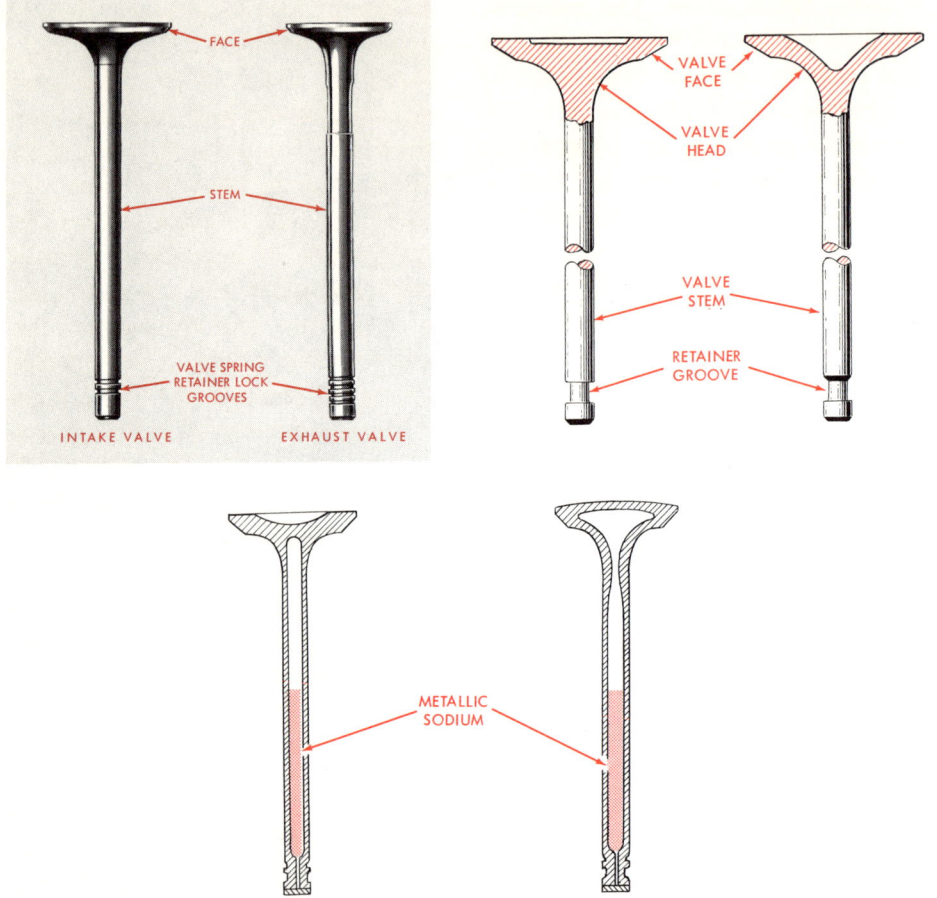

Fig. 5-8. (Top) The heads and lower ends of poppet valves may be of different designs. (Bottom) These valves with hollow stems contain sodium to obtain better heat conductivity for cooling.

which they operate. Intake valves are generally fitted to 0.0015 to 0.0035 in. clearance between the stem and guide. Exhaust valves are fitted to a clearance of 0.0025 to 0.004 in. The valve guide holds the valve in proper position and in alignment with the valve seat in the cylinder block or cylinder head.

The valves used in modern low emission engines must be able to withstand high temperatures during engine operation without warping or distortion. Exhaust valves operate at temperatures as high as 1400°F. Intake valves operate at a much lower temperature because they are cooled by the in-

Heads, Valve Mechanisms

coming fresh gases. The material used in the valve and the seat in the cylinder block or head must be such that a gastight seal can be obtained by grinding, and must resist corrosion and pitting so that a tight seal can be maintained. The valve must be light in weight to keep inertia forces low (resulting from high-speed reciprocating motion). The valves must also have sufficient metal to dissipate the excess heat.

A poppet valve is usually made of one piece of special alloy steel, but some poppet valves are made of two pieces, consisting of an alloy steel head electrically welded to a steel stem. A chromium-nickel alloy steel is often used for intake valves. Exhaust valves are usually made of special heat-resisting alloy steels because of the extremely high temperatures these valves must withstand. On some makes of engines, both the intake and exhaust valves are made of the same material. Some manufacturers use different material in the intake valves at the time the engine is built but supply exhaust valves for use in both exhaust and intake valve replacement.

To obtain better heat conductivity, some valves, Fig. 5-8 (bottom), are made with hollow valve stems. The opening in the valve stem extends well up into the head of the valve and is about half filled with metallic sodium, a much better conductor of heat than steel. Metallic sodium is a solid which turns into a liquid at about 200°F. The liquid sodium absorbs heat from the valve head and dissipates it through the valve stem to the valve guide and cooling system. Such valves are used mainly in some types of automotive engines and air-cooled aircraft engines and are readily identified by the letters SC stamped on the lower part of the valve stem. When sodium-cooled valves are replaced, the old valves should be buried to prevent the possibility of anyone finding and tampering with them. It is dangerous to cut the valve stem open or to throw the valve into a fire. Should the sodium come in contact with air, the person handling the valves is in danger of receiving severe burns.

Valve Seats. The valve seat in the cylinder block or head forms the face of the port opening leading into the combustion chamber of the cylinder, Fig. 5-9. The face of the valve seat is usually ground to an angle corresponding to that on the valve (30 to 47 degrees) to provide a gastight seal against the loss of pressure on the compression and power strokes. In some engines, the face of the valve is ground at a 47-degree angle, and the valve seat at a 45-degree angle, to provide narrow line contact between the valve and the seat.

The valve seats must be able to withstand pitting, corrosion, the

Automotive Engines

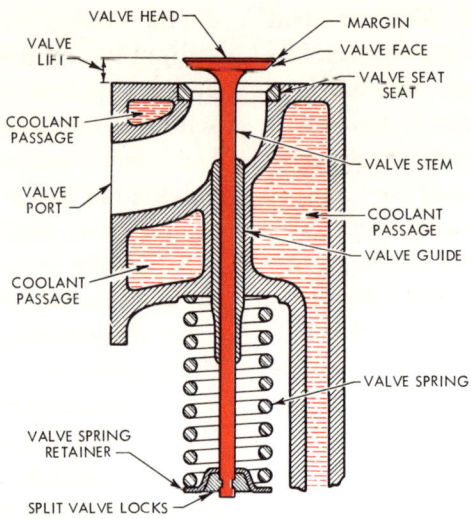

Fig. 5-9. Valve assembly located in cylinder block.

pounding and wear imposed on the seats by the opening and closing of the valves, and the high temperatures imposed by the burning fuel, if they are to maintain a gastight seal over a long period of operation. This is particularly true of the exhaust valve seats, since they are subjected to much higher temperatures than intake valve seats.

Cylinder blocks and cylinder heads are made of aluminum alloy, cast gray iron, or a cast gray iron containing small percentages of chromium, nickel or both. To withstand the conditions under which the valve seats must operate, most engines employ valve seat inserts for the exhaust valves. On such engines the intake valve seats, because they operate at a lower temperature, are machined directly in the cylinder block or head. The valve seat inserts are rings made of either a cast gray iron alloy steel or hardened steel and are harder than the metal of the cylinder block or head, Fig. 5-9. The inserts are pressed or shrunk into a counterbore machined in the exhaust ports, and the valve seat is ground on the insert at the correct angle. Engines with aluminum cylinder heads have hardened steel exhaust and intake valve seat inserts. Valve seat inserts can be replaced when necessary.

Some automotive engines have both the intake and exhaust valve seats machined directly in the cylinder block or head. In such en-

Heads, Valve Mechanisms

gines, the cylinder block or head is usually made of a cast gray iron alloy of a hardness sufficient to withstand the conditions under which the seats must operate.

As the use of no-lead gasoline becomes increasingly common, some manufacturers are, or will be, using an induction hardening process to provide induction hardened valve seats which are capable of withstanding the erosion effect of unleaded gasolines. It has been noted that when lead, which acts as a lubricant, is no longer used, excessive wear or erosion of the exhaust valve seats may take place. Induction hardening eliminates the need for valve seat inserts.

Valve Guides. Poppet valves are held in position and alignment in the cylinder block or cylinder head by valve guides, Fig. 5-9. The valve stem passes through a reamed hole in the valve guide, the stem being accurately ground to fit the valve guide with several thousandths of an inch clearance. To assure proper alignment of the valve face with the valve seat, the reamed hole in the valve guide must be concentric with the valve seat.

Valve guides used in automotive engines are usually made of cast gray iron. On some engines the valve guides consist of a hole bored in the cylinder head, and the valves operate directly in the guide holes. Valve guides that are pressed in can be replaced when worn.

Oil Seals. Because some valve-guide-to-valve-stem clearance must be maintained to provide for expansion, many manufacturers utilize valve stem oil seals to reduce leakage between the valve stem and guide. Seals are commonly used on intake valves to prevent leakage around the intake valve stem which may draw oil vapor from the valve cover into the combustion chamber.

The seal is usually in the form of a cap, Fig. 5-10, which provides a tight seal on the valve stem and at the top of the valve guide. Some valves had a groove cut in the stem in which a neoprene ring was inserted to form a seal between the stem and guide.

Valve Springs. Valve springs close the valves. The valves are opened by the mechanical action of the cams working against the pressure exerted by the valve springs, which close the valves. Valve springs are constructed of high grade spring steel wire. The springs are wound spirally and ground flat at each end to assure an even distribution of pressure. The valve springs are usually given a protective coat of colored paint or clear lacquer to prevent the valve springs from rusting due to accumulation of moisture in the valve compartment. Some valve springs are plated to resist rusting. Automotive engines may employ only one valve spring on each

179

Automotive Engines

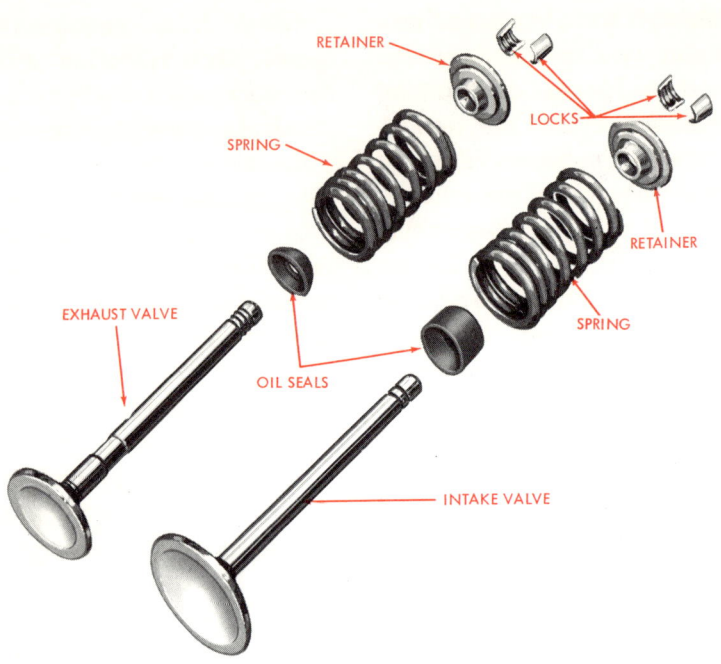

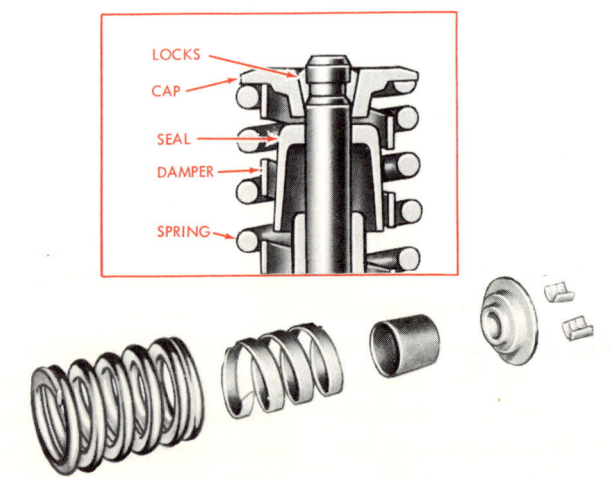

Fig. 5-10. Valve Assemblies—(Top) one spring—(Bottom) two springs.
Top: (Plymouth Div., Chrysler Corp.)
Bottom: (Chevrolet Div., General Motors Corp.)

Heads, Valve Mechanisms

valve, although some makes of engines employ two springs, one inside the other. The use of multiple valve springs permits the use of smaller diameter wire in each spring and assures a more even distribution of pressure around the valve than obtained with single valve springs. Valve springs are held in place by a spring retainer secured to the end of the valve stem. The retainer is held in place by split type wedge collars, Fig. 5-10.

The pressure exerted by the spring or springs must be sufficient to assure that the valve and valve lifter will follow the cam at high engine operating speeds. Weak valve springs exert insufficient pressure to permit the valves and valve lifters to follow the cam, causing the valves to bounce or flutter. Under such conditions the valves do not close at the proper points of the cycle. This affects the flow of air-fuel mixture into the cylinders, the compression, and the temperatures at which the valves operate. Such conditions may cause the engine to miss at high speeds, losing power and economy.

Valves open and close at an increasingly rapid rate as engine speed increases. During such operation, the springs tend to develop periods in which vibration is set up within the valve spring. These vibration periods may develop at several different engine speeds, ranging from medium to high speed. This vibration affects the operation of the engine and may result in valve spring breakage. Through careful valve spring design, manufacturers attempt to locate these vibration periods at infrequently used speeds, or entirely out of the speed range of the engine. Some engines are equipped with special dampers or cups which fit over the valve springs to prevent or reduce the vibration. Many engines employ valve springs with the coils closer together at one end than at the other, reducing spring vibration.

Valve springs that exert an uneven pressure around the circumference of the valve when the valve is being opened and closed tend to "cock" the valves in the valve guide. Such valve springs cause the valve seats, faces, and guides to wear out-of-round and are sometimes responsible for sticking valves.

Valve Rotation. A means of rotating exhaust valves is used in some engines to minimize valve distortion and blow-by. By rotating the valve, a new surface is subjected to the hot gases when combustion occurs. This helps to keep the valve face at a uniform temperature. The turning action also helps to keep carbon from building up on the face and seat.

Several methods are used to bring about valve rotation and

Automotive Engines

they all involve the valve spring retainer. The release type of rotator has a cap which fits over the end of the valve stem and rests on the split valve retainers. The rocker arm contacts the cap rather than the valve stem. When the valve is open, it is free to rotate; the rate of rotation varies depending upon valve movement and vibration.

There are positive rotator caps that rotate at a definite rate because, as pressure is applied to the valve stem, valve spring pressure in the rotator cap causes a seating collar to press against a flexible washer. The washer then presses on small steel balls forcing them to roll down inclined races. This turns the rotator assembly and valve. When pressure is released, the rotator springs force the balls back up the incline.

Valve Cooling. The valves used in modern engines must withstand the high temperatures encountered

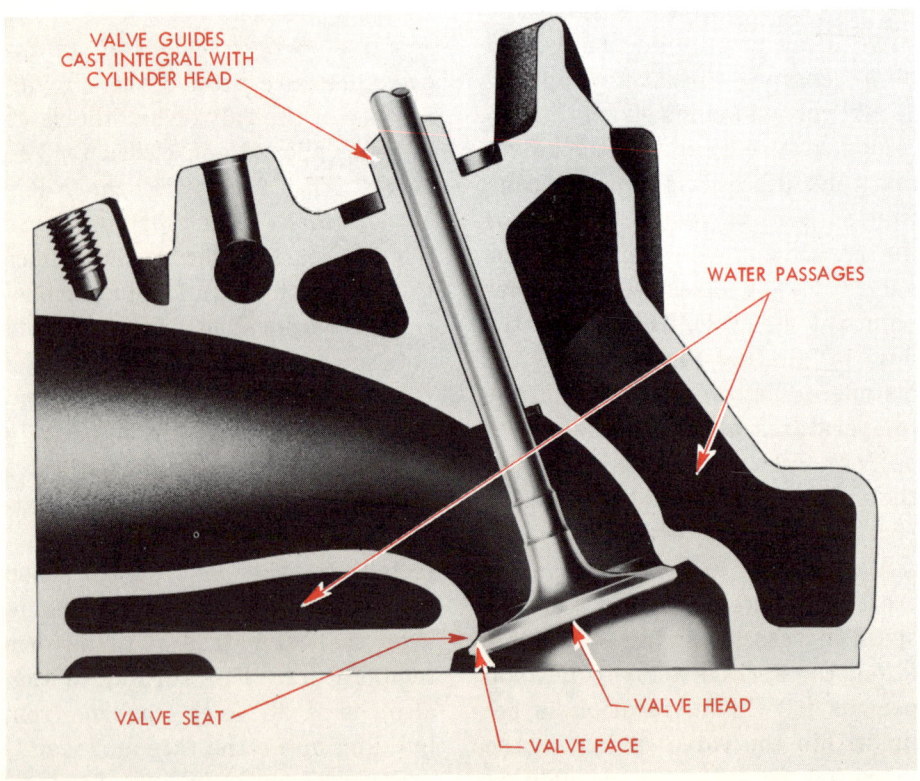

Fig. 5-11. When the valve assembly is located in the cylinder head, coolant circulates around the seat through passages in the head. (Pontiac Div., General Motors Corp.)

Heads, Valve Mechanisms

during engine operation without burning or warping. Exhaust valves operate at temperatures as high as 1400°F. Intake valves operate at a much lower temperature since they are cooled somewhat by the incoming fresh gases. The valves are cooled by the transfer of heat from the valve head to the valve seat, and from the valve stem to the valve guide. Improper seating of the valve on its seat will result in inadequate cooling of the valve. Valve seats are cooled by the circulation of coolant in the cooling system around the valve ports and seats, Fig. 5-11. Passages between the cylinder block and the head assist in cooling by allowing the proper flow of coolant between the block and the head. They also provide temperature balance between both cylinder heads in V-type engines.

Valve Operating Mechanism

While there are some variations in the design and construction of the valve operating mechanisms employed in the various types and makes of engines, they all contain parts which perform similar functions. The parts comprising the valve operating mechanism are the camshaft, timing gears or timing chain and sprockets, valve lifters, pushrods, and rocker arms.

Camshaft. The camshaft has a number of cams along its length that open the valves and hold them open for the correct length of time during the piston stroke, Fig. 5-12. The camshaft is driven by the crankshaft at one-half crankshaft speed. This permits each valve to open and close once every two revolutions of the crankshaft.

The camshaft is usually made in one piece by drop forging or casting. It usually is made of either alloy steels or chilled cast iron. Camshafts are heat treated to resist wear. The shape or *profile* of the cam is carefully determined to open the valve with the proper speed and lift (amount valve is raised off seat) without imposing excessive strains on the moving parts.

The camshaft has an inlet cam

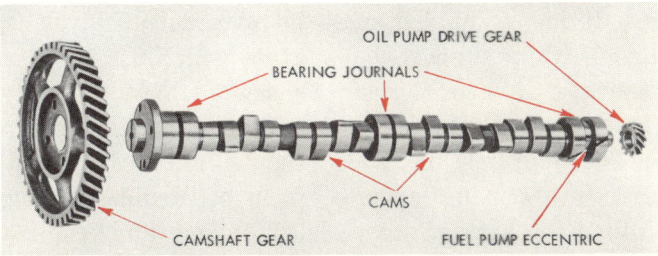

Fig. 5-12. The cams on the camshaft open the valves at the correct moment during the piston stroke. (Ford Motor Co.)

Automotive Engines

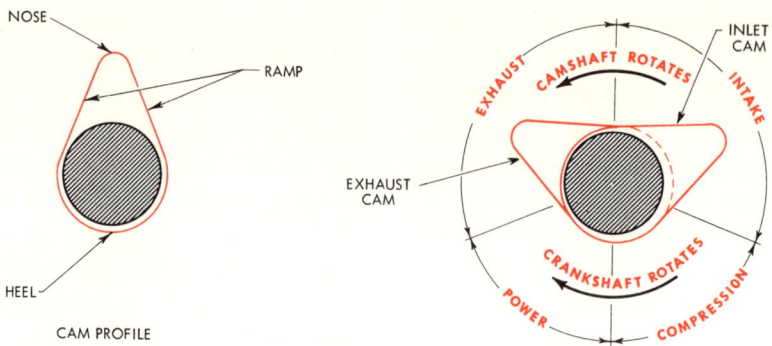

Fig. 5-13. This typical inlet and exhaust cam arrangement shows that the inlet cam actuates the intake valve almost immediately after the exhaust valve has closed.

and an exhaust cam for each cylinder. Fig. 5-13 illustrates a cross section of the camshaft showing the arrangement of the inlet and exhaust cams for one cylinder. The cams for each cylinder are arranged on the camshaft so that all the cylinders complete their cycle of events and produce a power stroke at equal or nearly equal intervals during two revolutions of the crankshaft. The arrangement of the cams on the camshaft and the design of the crankshaft determine the firing order of the cylinders.

The camshaft has a number of bearing journals which support the shaft in bearings in the engine crankcase at several points along its length. The journals on the camshaft usually are made larger in diameter than the highest point on the cams so that the shaft can be assembled in the engine by sliding it through the bearings in the cylinder block. The camshaft drives the distributor through a spiral gear located on the shaft. The oil pump is also driven by the camshaft, through either the same gear that drives the distributor, or a gear mounted at the rear end of the shaft. The camshaft usually operates the fuel pump by means of an eccentric located at some point on the shaft.

Overhead Camshafts. By using an overhead camshaft, a more direct valve action is achieved because pushrods are eliminated. Some modern day vehicles have engines which use an overhead camshaft.

Presently, such engines are of the in-line design and utilize a form of flexible driving belt. The belt is long and requires a tension device to prevent the belt from slipping. (See Fig. 5-25.)

Heads, Valve Mechanisms

Camshaft Drive. The camshaft is driven from the crankshaft by means of timing gears, or a timing belt or chain with sprockets. The timing drive is enclosed in the front end of the engine with a timing case cover which can be removed for inspection and repair.

Gear Driven. Fig. 5-14 illustrates a timing gear type of camshaft drive. The crankshaft gear is pressed on the crankshaft and is prevented from turning on the shaft by means of a key. The large gear is secured to the camshaft with cap screws or is pressed on the shaft and retained in place by a key. The camshaft gear has twice as many gear teeth as the crankshaft gear and, therefore, revolves at one half the speed of the crankshaft.

Since the valves open and close at definite points in relation to the position of the piston, the timing gears must be meshed together properly to assure correct valve timing. The timing gears are marked to assist in their proper assembly. The crankshaft gear gen-

Fig. 5-14. The timing mark on the camshaft gear must match with the mark on the crankshaft gear to assure accurate valve timing. (Chevrolet Div., General Motors Corp.)

erally has a gear tooth marked with a punch mark or an "o," Fig. 5-14. The camshaft gear has a similar mark on a space between two gear teeth.

When the gears are assembled with the marked tooth on the crankshaft gear meshed with the marked space on the camshaft gear, the valves are timed correctly, and the valves will open and close at the proper moment in relation to the position of the piston.

Spiral, or helical cut timing gears are used rather than spur gears because of their quieter operation and less lost motion. Spiral gears have their teeth cut at an angle on the face of the gear, Fig. 5-15. Such gears distribute the load over several gear teeth reducing shock, noise, and wear.

While steel timing gears, or a steel crankshaft gear meshed with an aluminum camshaft gear, have been used in the past, most present-day passenger car engines having a timing gear drive have a molded camshaft gear meshed with a steel crankshaft gear. Molded gears are composed of numerous layers of a canvaslike material impregnated with a resinous substance and formed under heat and pressure. Such gears are strong, long wearing, and extremely quiet in operation. They also permit greater wear between the gear teeth before the gears become noisy.

The timing gears must receive adequate lubrication if they are to operate quietly. On most engines the timing gears are lubricated by a stream of oil directed against the face of the gears by a tube or jet. On some makes of engines the excess oil flowing through the oil pressure relief valve lubricates the timing gears before it returns to the crankcase.

Chain Driven. Most makes of engines employ a timing chain to drive the camshaft. Fig. 5-16 illustrates a typical timing chain drive used on an automotive engine. Two sprockets are employed in this type of design, one keyed to the crank-

Fig. 5-15. Helical gears are more durable and quieter than spur gears.

Heads, Valve Mechanisms

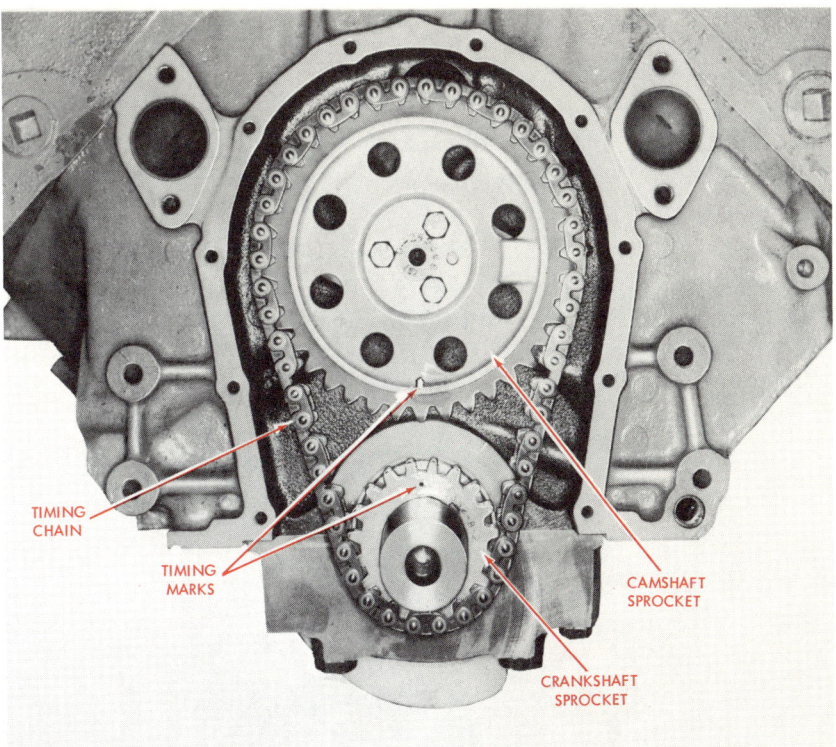

Fig. 5-16. This camshaft drive uses a chain and sprockets rather than gears. (Chevrolet Div., General Motors Corp.)

shaft and the other to the camshaft. The camshaft sprocket has twice as many teeth as the crankshaft sprocket and, as a result, revolves at one half the speed of the crankshaft. An endless timing chain meshing with the teeth on the sprockets drives the camshaft. The chain is kept from slipping off the sprockets by means of guides on each side of the chain or a single guide in the center of the chain. No provisions for adjustment of the timing chain are made in this type of drive. Therefore, the chain must be replaced when it becomes worn.

Timing chains are lubricated by the engine oiling system which throws a stream of oil against the chain through a tube or jet opening or through holes in the crankshaft sprocket.

Belt Driven. Present day overhead camshaft engines employ a synthetic rubber camshaft drive belt, sometimes labeled a timing

Automotive Engines

Fig. 5-17. Overhead camshaft drive train with an auxiliary sprocket. (Ford Div., Ford Motor Co.)

belt. This belt requires no lubrication. The installation shown in Fig. 5-17 utilizes an auxiliary sprocket while the installation in Fig. 5-18 has a direct drive. Both arrangements use a tensioner to prevent belt slippage. Timing alignment marks are found on the sprockets.

Valve Lifters, Pushrods, and Rocker Arms. On L-head engines the motion imparted by the cam is transmitted to the valves by means of valve lifters. Overhead valve or I-head engines use valve lifters, pushrods, and rocker arms to transmit the motion of the cam to the valves.

The rocker arms reverse the lifting action of the cam to open the inverted valves. Engines employing an overhead camshaft may have a rocker arm located between the camshaft and valve stem or a mechanical valve lifter or "tappet" between the camshaft and valve stem.

Heads, Valve Mechanisms

Fig. 5-18. Overhead camshaft drive train. (Chevrolet Div., General Motors Corp.)

Valve Lifters. Fig. 5-19 illustrates the valve operating mechanism of an L-head engine. Mechanical valve lifters with mushroom heads are mounted in guide holes bored in the engine crankcase directly above the camshaft, or may be fitted into brackets that bolt to the side of the engine, the brackets being located in the valve compartment directly above the camshaft. The valve lifter is raised by the action of the cam against the mushroom head of the lifter. The valve lifter is usually located slightly off

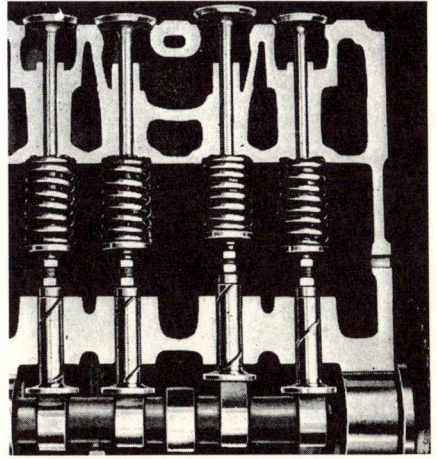

Fig. 5-19. Valve, mechanical valve lifter, and cam arrangement on an L-head engine.

189

Automotive Engines

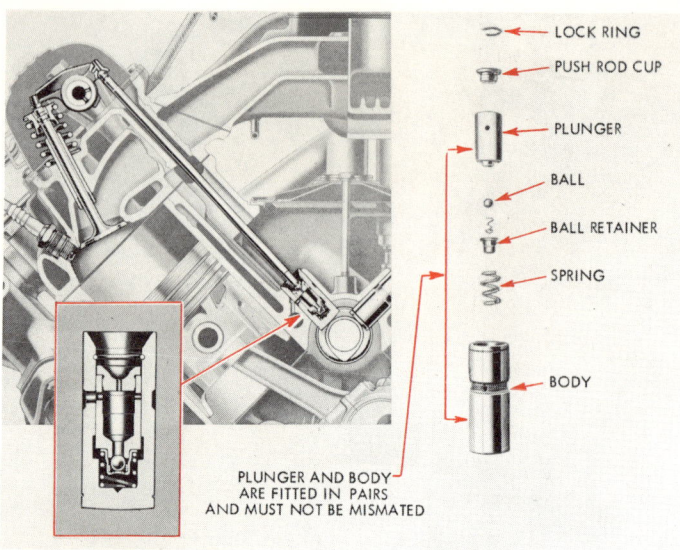

Fig. 5-20. Hydraulic valve lifter in a V-type engine. (Cadillac Motor Car Div., General Motors Corp.)

center in its relation with the cam. During engine operation the off center condition causes the valve lifter to spin or be revolved by the action of the cam, resulting in the wear being distributed over the entire area of the mushroom head of the valve lifter. The upper end of the valve lifter contains an adjusting screw and lock nut which pushes against the valve stem in lifting the valve. The adjusting screw and lock nut are employed to adjust the clearance between the valve lifter and the valve stem. Some adjusting screws do not have a lock nut; the adjusting screw and valve lifter have threads that bind in the valve lifter.

A hydraulic valve lifter employed on both L-head and I-head engines is illustrated in Fig. 5-20. Such valve lifters operate with no clearance between the valve lifter and the valve stem, making clearance adjustments unnecessary.

Pushrods and Rocker Arms. An I-head, V-8 engine valve operating mechanism is shown in Fig. 5-21. The valves are in an inverted position and open downward. Some I-head engines have their valves mounted vertically in the cylinder head, while in others may be at a slight angle. In addition to the valve lifters, I-head engines require two pushrods and two rocker arms to operate the valves for each cylinder. The valve lifters are fitted into guide holes in the engine

Heads, Valve Mechanisms

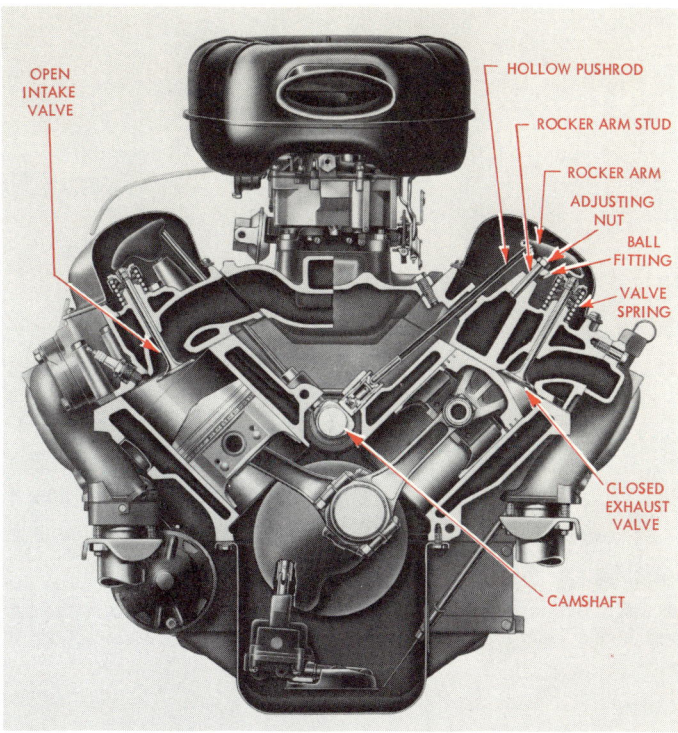

Fig. 5-21. This cross sectioned view of an I-head engine shows the inverted valve positions. The valve operating mechanism uses ball fittings on studs to support the rocker arms. The mechanism is lubricated through hollow pushrods. (Chevrolet Div., General Motors Corp.)

crankcase directly above the camshaft.

On some engines, the rocker arms are supported by a hollow rocker arm shaft running lengthwise to the engine and attached to the cylinder head, Fig. 5-6. On others, the rocker arm is held in place on a rocker arm stud by a ball fitting and adjusting nut, Figs. 5-21 and 5-22.

Pushrods may be solid or tubular. Usually they are made with a ball-shaped lower and upper end to fit the ball-and-socket joints in the rocker arm and valve lifter. On some engines, a half-round socket is formed at the upper end of the pushrod to fit the ball end of the adjusting screw in the rocker arm. The upward motion imparted to the valve lifter by the cam is transmitted by the pushrod to one end of the rocker arm. The other end of the rocker arm is in contact with the valve stem and pushes the valve open. An adjusting screw and lock nut are provided at the

Automotive Engines

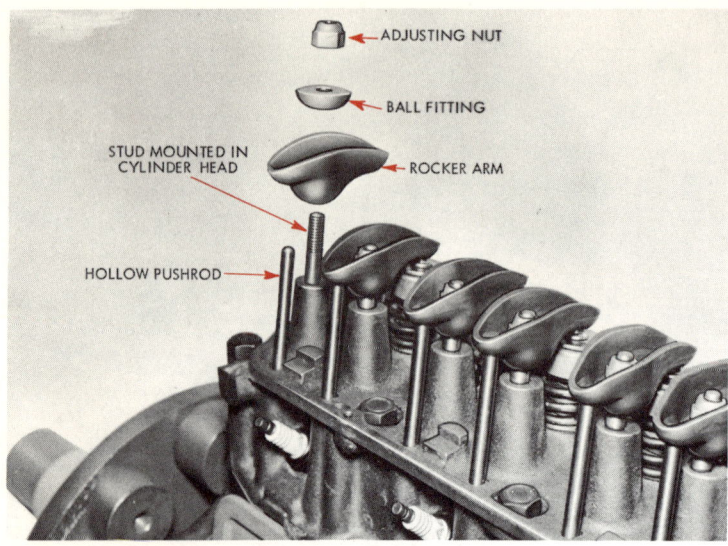

Fig. 5-22. This in-line I-head engine valve operating mechanism uses no rocker arm shaft. A ball fitting supports each rocker arm. An adjusting nut holds the ball fitting on a stud mounted in the cylinder head. (Chevrolet Div., General Motors Corp.)

upper end of the pushrod to adjust the valve clearance.

On some engines, the rocker assembly is pressure lubricated through hollow pushrods. On others, oil is supplied to the rocker arm through the rocker arm support bracket and rocker arm shaft.

On some engines the exhaust valve rocker arms have a drilled passage connected with the rocker arm bushing which supplies oil to the valve ends of the rocker arms to lubricate the exhaust valve stems and guides.

Hydraulic Valve Lifters. Most engines are equipped with silent, self-adjusting, hydraulic valve lifters, Figs. 5-20 and 5-23. The hydraulic unit itself automatically controls the clearance at the valve stem. Fig. 5-23 illustrates the construction of a hydraulic valve lifter. The hydraulic unit is contained in the valve lifter body and consists of a cylinder, plunger, a ball check valve, and a spring. Some hydraulic units use a flat type check valve rather than a ball check valve.

The operation of the valve lifter is shown in Fig. 5-24. Oil under pressure from the engine lubricating system is supplied to the valve lifters through auxiliary oil lines or drilled passages in the engine crankcase and valve lifter guide brackets. This oil flows under

Heads, Valve Mechanisms

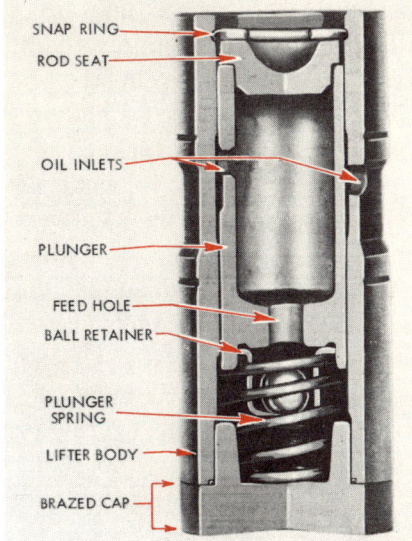

Fig. 5-23. Cross section of a hydraulic valve lifter. (Buick Div., General Motors Corp.)

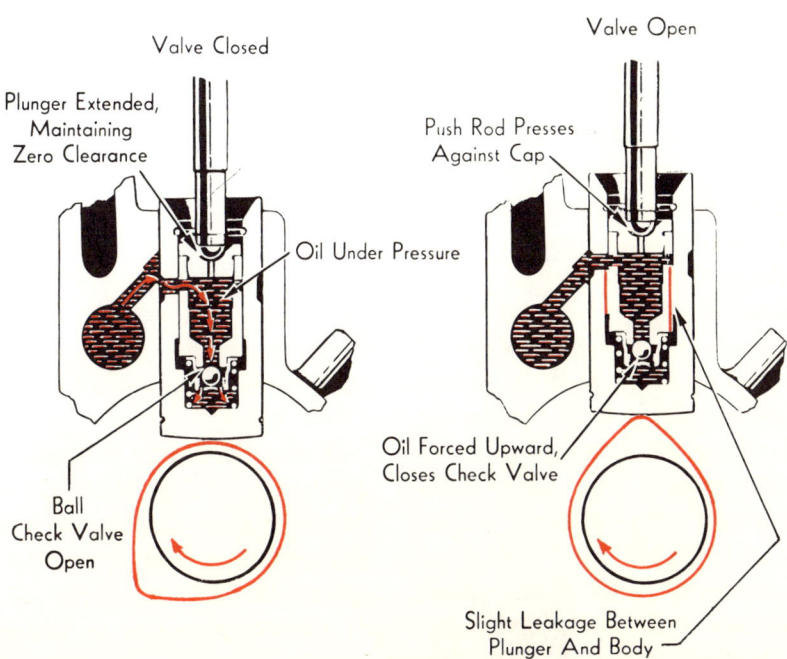

Fig. 5-24. How a hydraulic valve lifter operates. (Cadillac Motor Car Div., General Motors Corp.)

pressure through a hole in the lifter body into the supply chamber each time the hole in the valve lifter body moves past a hole in the valve lifter guide bracket.

With the face of the valve lifter on the heel of the cam, as shown at the left in Fig. 5-24, the plunger spring lifts the hydraulic plunger so the upper end contacts the valve stem, giving zero valve clearance. As the plunger moves upward, increasing the volume of the pressure chamber under the plunger, the ball check valve moves off the seat and the pressure chamber is filled with oil from the supply chamber in the lifter body.

As the camshaft rotates, the cam raises the lifter body, tending to push the plunger into the cylinder. This action increases the pressure in the pressure chamber, forcing the check valve onto its seat. Further rotation of the camshaft moves the valve lifter upward. Since, for all practical purposes, oil can be considered as not being compressible, the confined body of oil in the pressure chamber acts as a

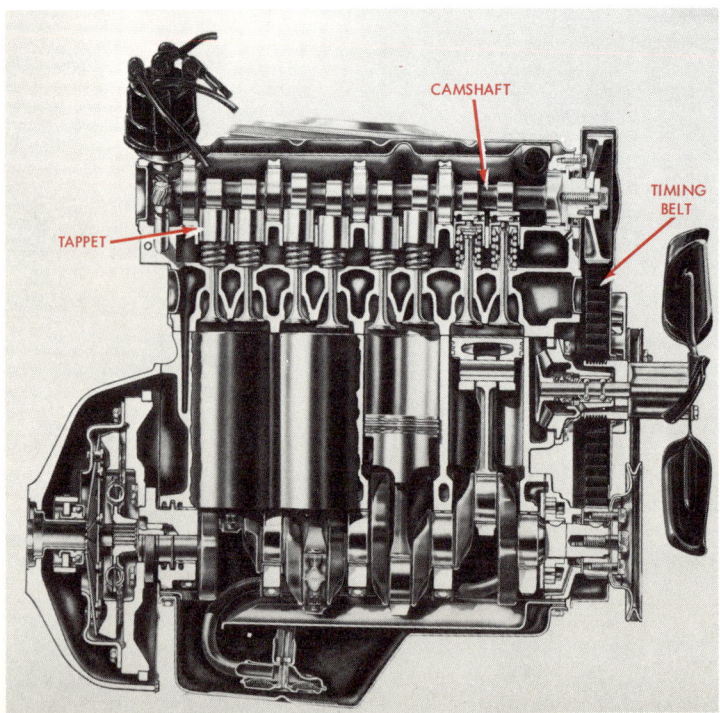

Fig. 5-25. Overhead cam engine. (Chevrolet Div., General Motors Corp.)

Heads, Valve Mechanisms

solid member of the valve-operating mechanism, the valve being lifted on a column of oil.

As long as the valve is off the seat, the load is carried by this column of oil. During this period, a slight leakage of oil from the pressure chamber occurs due to the clearance between the plunger and the cylinder bore. This leakage is necessary to make certain that the valve closes on its seat properly, thus eliminating any clearance between the valve and the seat due to expansion of the valve or lifter assembly. Any excess clearance from any cause is taken up by the plunger spring pushing the plunger upward against the valve stem when the valve is seated. This upward movement of the plunger tends to create a vacuum in the pressure chamber which pulls the ball check valve from its seat, allowing an additional supply of oil to enter the pressure chamber. This cycle is repeated at each revolution of the cam.

An overhead camshaft produces a more direct valve action because pushrods are eliminated. In the engine shown in Fig. 5-25, a simple mechanical valve lifter or "tappet" is installed for adjustment between the camshaft and valve stem in the cylinder head.

Cleaning, Inspection, and Repair of Cylinder Heads

Cylinder heads should be disassembled as completely as possible to permit thorough cleaning, inspection, and repair. The disassembly of cylinder heads varies with their construction. Cylinder heads used on L-head engines require little or no disassembly. Such cylinder heads sometimes have the thermostat located in the water outlet connection. The outlet connection and thermostat should be removed to permit inspection of the water passages in the cylinder head and to permit testing of the thermostat for operation.

Cylinder heads used on I-head engines should have the valves removed from the head. The split valve locks can be removed from the ends of the valves with a valve spring compressor or cylinder head holding fixture designed for the purpose, Fig. 5-26. Remove the valve spring retainers, springs, and valves from the head. The valves to each cylinder should be kept in their proper order so they can be reinstalled in the same location.

Cleaning

When the cylinder head has been disassembled, carbon should be removed from the combustion chambers. This cleaning operation can

Automotive Engines

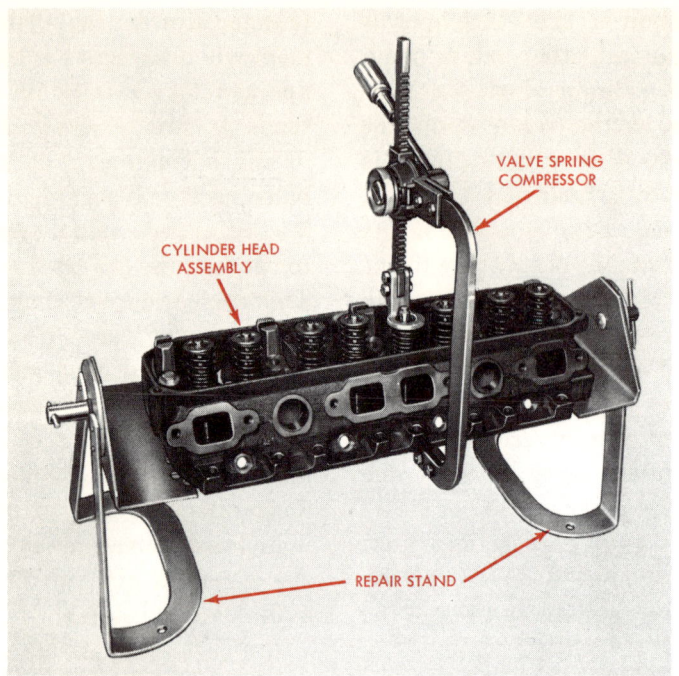

Fig. 5-26. Compressing valve spring. (Plymouth Div., Chrysler Corp.)

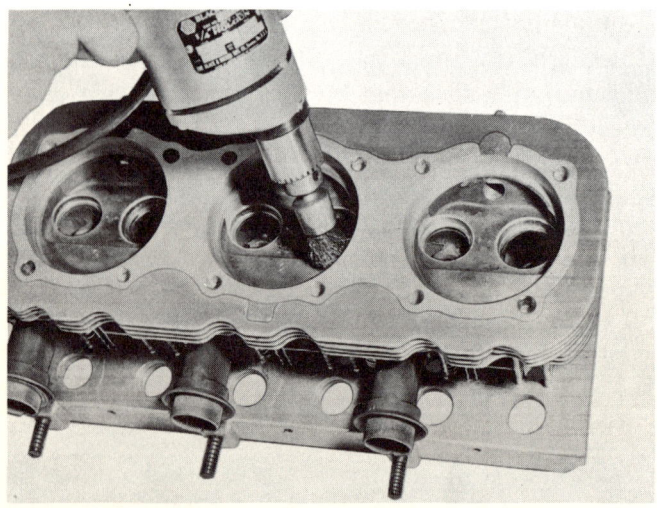

Fig. 5-27. Removing carbon from a combustion chamber with a wire brush. On I-head engines, the valve parts and valve guides must also be cleaned of carbon. (Chevrolet Div., General Motors Corp.)

Heads, Valve Mechanisms

be done either by wire brushing or by scraping as shown in Fig. 5-27. In I-head cylinder heads carbon must also be removed from the valve ports and valve guides. To remove carbon from the inside of valve guides, use a valve guide cleaning tool.

Grease and dirt can be removed from cylinder heads with one of the several types of cleaning solutions. Some types of cleaning solutions are also capable of removing carbon.

Inspection

Cylinder heads are designed to withstand the normal forces imposed during the operation of an engine. Extreme forces produced by overheating, freezing, and improper assembly are usually responsible for much of the damage that occurs to the cylinder head casting. Improper tightening of cylinder head nuts or bolts can cause serious warping of the head.

The cylinder head casting should be carefully inspected to determine its condition. Few repairs are made to such units; the unit generally is replaced when defective. A cracked cylinder head should be replaced. The gasket surface of the head should be checked with a straightedge to determine if the head is warped. A warped head can cause the following:

1. Loss of compression.
2. Loss of oil.
3. Loss of coolant.
4. Ignition misfiring.
5. Oil and gases entering, clogging, and corroding the cooling system.
6. Coolant entering oil supply

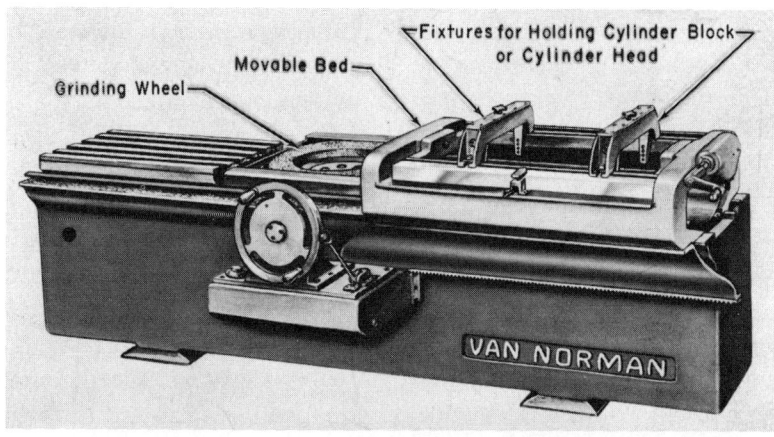

Fig. 5-28. Cylinder block and cylinder head resurfacing machine. A milling machine may be used. (Van Norman Company)

and corroding engine bearings.

Repair

If a head is warped 0.020 in. or more over its full length, it should be resurfaced or replaced. Resurfacing, Fig. 5-28, involves removing metal from the head by grinding or milling in order to produce a perfectly flat mating surface.

When I-head V-type engine heads are resurfaced, the relative positions of the head intake port openings are changed. Therefore, the mating surfaces on the intake manifold must also be milled or ground proportionately so the manifold ports will line up with cylinder head ports.

Damaged threads in the spark plug holes or water temperature gage holes should be restored using a tap of the correct size.

Inspection and Repair of Valves

Wash all parts in a cleaning solvent, and dry immediately after cleaning. Scrape the carbon from the valve heads and stems and the cylinder block and cylinder head. Clean the valves, valve springs, and valve guides. With a valve guide hole cleaner, remove the carbon from the guide hole in one-piece valve guides. When cleaning the valve springs, take care not to use a caustic cleaner or any material that will injure the protective coating on the springs.

The parts comprising the valve and valve operating mechanism must be inspected carefully to determine their condition, size, and the clearances that exist between the parts. This inspection will determine which parts are in serviceable condition and which parts must be replaced. New and serviceable parts, along with careful repair operations, will assure that the valve and valve operating mechanism are restored to a satisfactory operating condition.

Valves having valve stem clearances of 0.005 in. or more for intake valves and 0.006 in. or more for exhaust valves should have the valve or valve guide, or both, replaced unless otherwise specified by the manufacturer.

Inspection

Replace valves that have bent or scored stems. Replace any valves on which the stems are worn 0.002 in. or more. Reface pitted, corroded, or burned valves. Replace valves that are pitted, burned, or warped to the extent that they will not clean up with a light cut of the valve grinding wheel. Replace

Heads, Valve Mechanisms

valves which reface down to a thin edge or margin ($\frac{1}{32}$ in. or less). On engines where valves made of the same alloys are of the same size and are used for both intake and exhaust valves, any new valves to be used should be used as intake valves to keep the intake valve guide clearance to a minimum.

Reface Valves

Valves removed from an engine should be refaced before being reinstalled in the engine. Valves are refaced on a valve refacing machine by clamping the valve in a chuck set at the same angle as the face of the valve (30 or 45 degrees on most valves, 47 degrees on some valves). Light cuts are taken off the face of the valve by means of a grinding wheel as the valve is moved back and forth across the face of the wheel, Fig. 5-29. The valve is refaced properly when all the pits are removed from the face of the valve and the face or seat is concentric with the valve stem.

Fig. 5-29. Valves can be refaced on a valve refacing machine. (Chevrolet Div., General Motors Corp.)

Valve Seats

Valve seats operate under the same operating conditions and high temperatures as the valves and are also subject to wear, corrosion, pitting, and burning. Warped valves and excessive valve guide clearances tend to wear the valve seats out-of-round.

Because they help to cool the valve head when the valve is closed, the valve seats should be maintained at the width specified by the manufacturer. Wide valve seats make it difficult to maintain a tight seal between the valve and seat. Seats which are too narrow provide poor valve head cooling and are easily pounded out of shape by the closing of the valve.

Inspect Valve Seat

Reface any valve seat if there is any indication that the valve has not been seating properly, if the seat is pitted or burned, or if new valve guides have been installed. Replace any valve seat insert that is cracked or is loose in the cylinder block or head. Valve seats which are too wide should be narrowed with the proper angle reamer or grinding wheel.

Reface Valve Seat

Valve seats can be reconditioned to a smooth and true surface concentric with the valve guide hole by means of reamers or valve seat grinders, Fig. 5-30.

A valve seat grinder set consists of a driver, pilots of various sizes to fit the valve guides, a grinding wheel holder, grinding wheels, and a grinding wheel truing fixture. Grinding wheels are available in three grades: soft seat stones for cast-iron valve seats, hard seat stones for high-speed-steel induction hardened seats, or Stellite valve seats, and finishing stones. Sizes range in diameter from $1\frac{1}{2}$ to $3\frac{1}{2}$ in. in steps of $\frac{1}{8}$ in. The grinding wheels should be refaced on the truing fixture each time they are installed on a wheel holder or at any time when the wheel becomes clogged with metal particles.

To reface valve seats, select a pilot of the proper size and anchor it rigidly in the valve guide. Depending upon the type of valve seat, select a soft or hard seat stone slightly larger in diameter than the valve seat and with the same angle as the seat. Install the stone on the grinding wheel holder. After dressing the wheel, install the wheel and holder on the pilot and mesh the driver with the holder. When grinding, the weight of the driver should be held off the grinding wheel. Various methods are employed on the different makes of

Heads, Valve Mechanisms

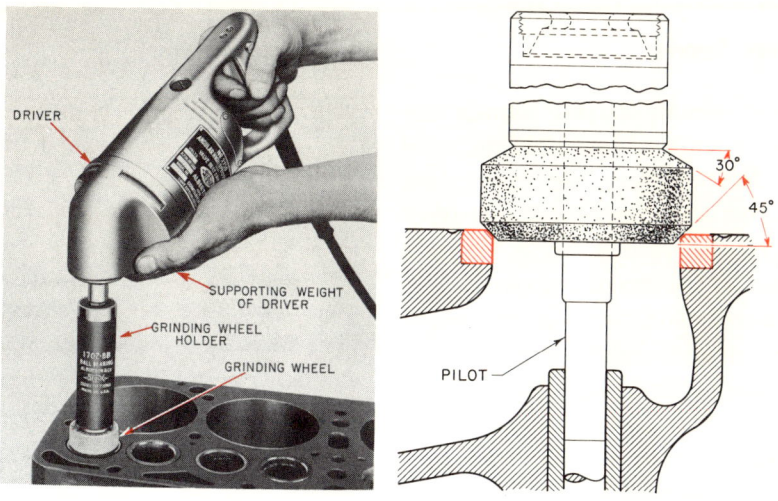

Fig. 5-30. Valve seats can be refinished with a valve seat grinder. (Albertson & Co.)

machines to impart a vibrating motion that causes the grinding wheel to be lifted off the seat momentarily. This permits centrifugal force to clear the wheel of dulling grit, resulting in a good seat finish, faster cutting, and less frequent dressing of the wheel. At no time should pressure be exerted on the wheel because this grooves the wheel and causes it to become clogged rapidly.

Only a few seconds of grinding are necessary to reface an average cast-iron valve seat, while steel and hardened steel inserts may take slightly longer. To obtain a smoother finish, a finishing stone is used to polish the seat. For satisfactory operation, the valve seats should be from $\frac{1}{16}$ to $\frac{3}{32}$ in. wide,

and with the valves in position, the seat should center on the valve face, Fig. 5-31. Valve seats wider than $\frac{3}{32}$ in. should be narrowed. Narrowing is accomplished by removing metal from the bottom of the seat with a 60-degree grinding wheel and from the top of the seat with 15- or 30-degree grinding wheel. By careful use of such wheels, the seats can be narrowed to the desired width and at the same time centered on the face of the valve. When narrowing seats from the top, use a 15-degree wheel for a 30-degree valve seat and a 30-degree wheel for a 45-degree seat. The valve seat insert should be replaced on engines having valve seat inserts, if the narrowing grinding wheels cut into the rolled or peened

Automotive Engines

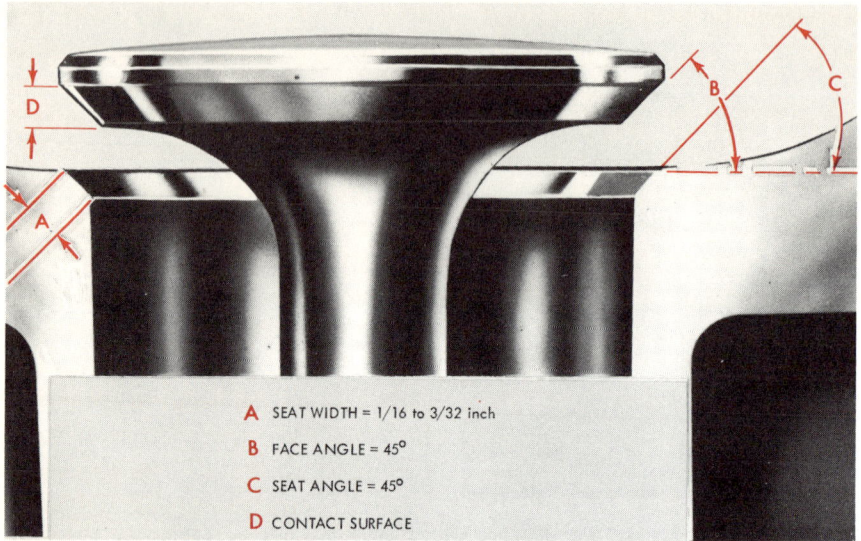

Fig. 5-31. Valve face and seat angle. (Plymouth Div., Chrysler Corp.)

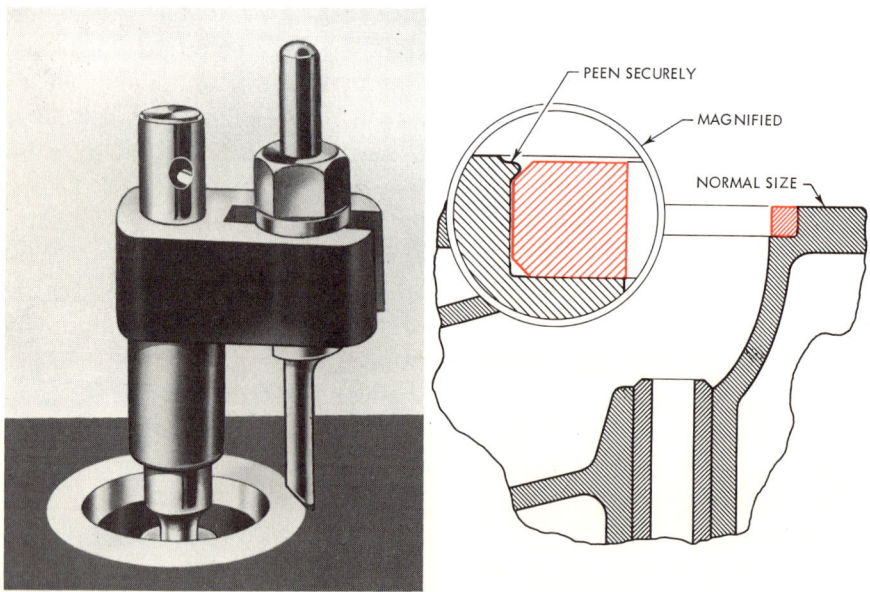

Fig. 5-32. When a valve seat insert is installed, it must be secured by rolling or peening the edge of the counterbore. (Cedar Rapids Engineering Company)

Heads, Valve Mechanisms

surface around the outer edge of the insert.

Replace Valve Seat Insert

Valve seat inserts that are cracked or cannot be refaced properly should be replaced. On such engines, the old inserts can be removed with an insert extracting tool similar to a small pry bar. If such a tool is not available, drill holes slightly smaller than the width of the insert on opposite sides of the insert. Split with a chisel, and pry out the pieces of the insert from the counterbore. Avoid drilling into the counterbore or damaging it with the chisel.

If the counterbore is in good condition, chill a new insert with dry ice for approximately ten minutes and drive it into place so it bottoms on the counterbore. Peen or roll the edge of the counterbore with the tool provided to anchor the insert in the counterbore, Fig. 5-32. Reface the valve seat insert.

When valve seats cast integrally with the cylinder head or cylinder block become too wide or worn so they cannot be refaced properly, they can be replaced with a valve seat insert. Special tools similar to those illustrated in Fig. 5-33 are used to counterbore the cylinder head or block. The insert is installed in the manner described above.

Fig. 5-33. Valve seats cast integrally with the cylinder block can be replaced with valve seat inserts.

Automotive Engines

Valve Springs

The valve springs must close the valve at the right instant at all engine speeds. Valve springs which have too much pressure subject the valve seats to a severe pounding. Broken or weakened valve springs seriously affect engine performance at high speeds. At high engine speeds the valves open and close at such a rapid rate that the broken or weakened springs do not have sufficient time to close the valve. As a result, before the valve has had a chance to close, it is opened again by the next revolution of the cam.

Inspect Valve Springs

Replace the valve springs if they fail to register within ten pounds of the pressure recommended by the manufacturer when compressed to the recommended distance on a spring tester, Fig. 5-34.

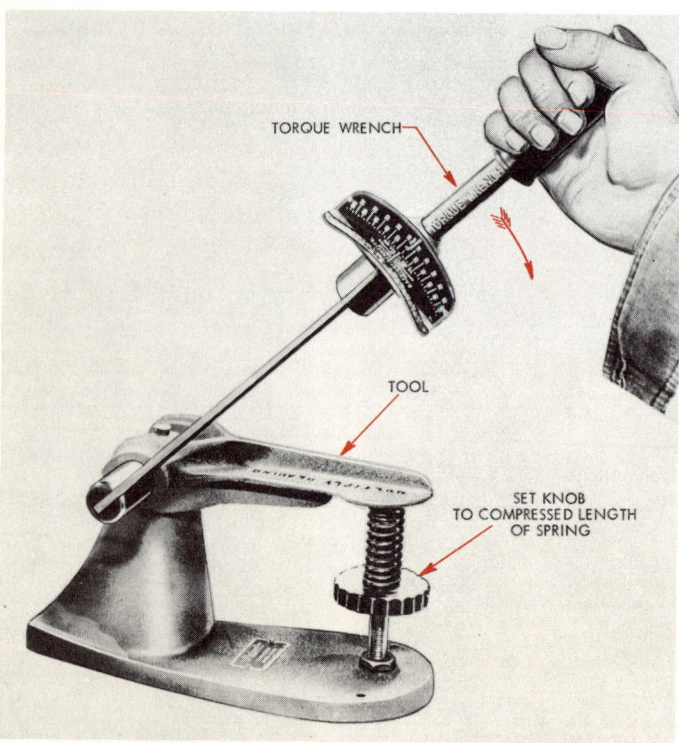

Fig. 5-34. Using a spring tester to check whether or not a valve spring exerts enough pressure to be serviceable. (Mercury-Lincoln Div., Ford Motor Co.)

Heads, Valve Mechanisms

Check each spring for squareness with a steel square and a surface plate, Fig. 5-35. Place the square on the surface plate. Stand each spring on its end on the surface plate and move the spring up to the square. While revolving the spring notice the space between the top of the valve and valve seat during the reconditioning process may cause the valve stem to protrude further above the cylinder head than a valve which has not been reconditioned. This will increase the operating length of the spring, thereby reducing spring tension.

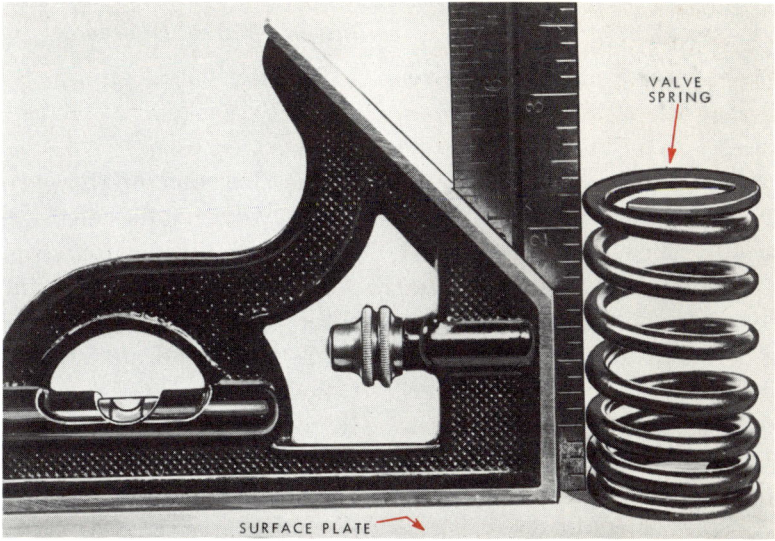

Fig. 5-35. Replace any valve spring that is more than 1/16 in. out of square. (Plymouth Div., Chrysler Corp.)

coil of the spring and the square. Replace any spring that is more than $\frac{1}{16}$ in. out of square. When installing the valve springs in the head be certain that the spring end with the closely wound coils is installed toward the cylinder head.

Removing material from the face After reconditioning valves, always check the installed height of each spring. If the height is excessive, a special washer (these washers are available in different thicknesses) is installed between the cylinder head and end of spring to bring about correct spring tension.

Valve Guides

The opening and closing of the valves subjects the valve guides to wear, increasing the clearance between the valve stem and the valve guide. Valves with an excessive amount of valve stem clearance make it difficult to maintain a gas-tight seal between the valve and seat, because the valve seat and valve head tend to wear out-of-round due to shifting of the valve on the seat when the valve opens or closes. Sometimes excessive valve guide clearances are also responsible for oil consumption. Due to the difference in pressure between the intake valve port and the engine crankcase (vacuum in the intake port and atmospheric pressure in the crankcase), the higher crankcase pressure forces oil past the intake valve stem into the combustion chamber where it is burned.

Most of today's engines utilize oil seals to reduce the amount of oil vapor which may be drawn into the combustion chamber. The seal usually fits around the valve stem and over the top of the valve guide, Fig. 5-10. New seals should be installed whenever the valves are removed.

Inspect Valve Guides

Replace valve guides that are chipped, broken, or have scored guide holes.

The clearance of the valve stem in the valve guide can be checked with a dial indicator, Fig. 5-36. Attach the base of the dial indicator to one of the cylinder block studs on L-head engines or to the cylinder head on I-head engines. Raise the head of the valve $5/16$ in. above the top of the cylinder block or head, and adjust the dial indicator to register the play of the valve stem in the guide. The valve stem

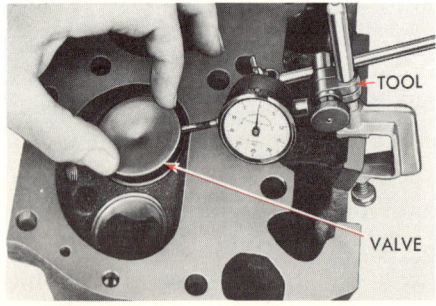

Fig. 5-36. Clearance between the valve stem and valve guide can be checked with a dial indicator. (Plymouth Div., Chrysler Corp.)

Heads, Valve Mechanisms

clearance is one half of the dial indicator reading.

As a general rule, replace any intake valve guides which will permit a clearance of more than 0.005 in. Replace any exhaust valve guides which will permit a clearance of more than 0.006 in. This should be done before valve seats are refaced to ensure that the valve seat will be concentric to the hole in the new valve guide.

Replace Valve Guides

Remove the old valve guides from the cylinder block or head with a properly designed drift or puller. Install the new valve guides with a drift or puller so that the top of the valve guide is the correct distance from the machined surface of the cylinder block or head, according to manufacturers' specifications, Fig. 5-37. Ream the valve guides to establish the clearance recommended by the manufacturer.

When reaming valve guides, a safe general rule to follow for intake valve guides is to allow 0.001 in. clearance for each $3/16$ in. of stem diameter. For exhaust valve guides, allow a clearance of 0.001 in. for each $1/8$ in. of stem diameter. Table 5-1 shows the minimum and maximum valve stem clearances for intake and exhaust valves for several commonly used sizes of valve stems.

To reduce the tendency of the valve to stick at the top of the valve guide due to carbon accumulation

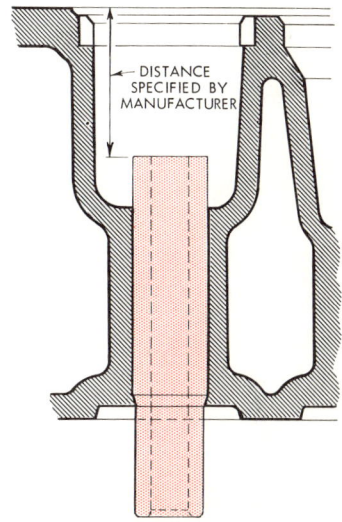

Fig. 5-37. Valve guides must be installed at the correct distance from the machined surface of the cylinder block or head.

TABLE 5-1 VALVE STEM TO VALVE GUIDE CLEARANCES IN INCHES

Nominal Stem Diameter	Intake Valve	Exhaust Valve
$5/16''$	0.0015–0.0035	0.0025–0.0035
$11/32''$	0.0015–0.0035	0.0025–0.004
$3/8''$	0.0015–0.0035	0.0025–0.004

Automotive Engines

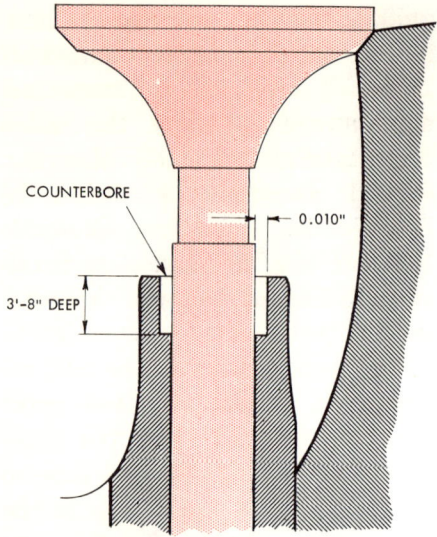

Fig. 5-38. Sometimes exhaust valve guides are counterbored to reduce their tendency to stick.

on the valve stem, some manufacturers recommend that the exhaust valve guides be counterbored, Fig. 5-38. The counterbore is drilled with a drill about 0.020 in. larger in diameter than the valve stem and is drilled approximately $\frac{3}{8}$ in. deep.

Camshaft

Due to improved materials and methods of heat treatment, the camshaft in modern engines seldom needs replacement because of wear unless the engine has been subjected to considerable abuse. Because the camshaft revolves at one-half crankshaft speed, its bearing surface speeds are less than those of the crankshaft, resulting in less wear on the journals and bearings. However, the forces imposed on the camshaft by the opening and closing of the valves tend to wear the camshaft bearings out-of-round. Excessive clearances in the camshaft bearings (0.004 in. or more) result in an excessive amount of oil leaking out of the bearings. This condition must be corrected to remedy low oil pressure.

Inspect Camshaft

Replace a camshaft that has excessively scored or damaged cams,

Heads, Valve Mechanisms

or worn, corroded, scored, or badly discolored bearing journals. Replace a camshaft on which the bearing journals are worn 0.002 in. or more. Replace a camshaft that has visibly worn, broken, or chipped gear teeth on the distributor drive gear. On camshafts having an oil pump drive gear at the rear end of the shaft, the oil pump drive gear should be replaced if it is worn, chipped, or if it has been slipping on the camshaft. Check the camshaft for alignment on V blocks with a dial indicator. If the camshaft is bent more than 0.002 in., the camshaft should be straightened.

Check Camshaft Lobe Lift

The camshaft lobe lift can be checked without removing the camshaft. It should be checked if camshaft lobe wear is suspected. Lobe wear prevents the valve from opening completely. Manufacturer's specifications should be checked for maximum allowable lobe lift loss. In most cases maximum allowable loss is approximately 0.005 in.

To check camshaft lobe lift, remove the rocker arm and make sure the pushrod is in the valve lifter socket. Install a dial gage so that the stem of the gage is on the end of the pushrod and in the same plane as the pushrod movement, Fig. 5-39. Turn the engine over slowly until the cam lobe is at its low point. Set the gage at zero. Turn the engine until the pushrod

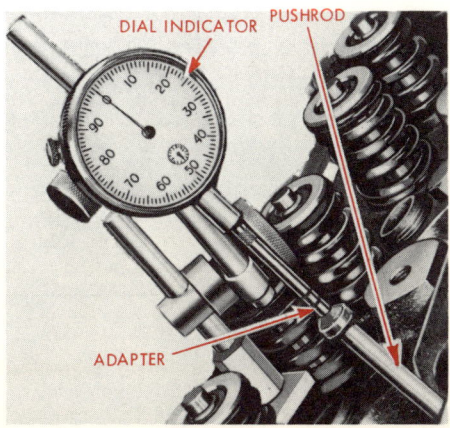

Fig. 5-39. Checking camshaft lobe lift. (Ford Div., Ford Motor Co.)

Automotive Engines

is in the fully raised position. Compare the indicated total lift with specifications, or compare it with the lobe lift of the other lobes. If any lobe does not meet specifications, the camshaft must be replaced.

Inspect Camshaft Bearings

Measure the internal diameter of the bearings at several points with a telescoping gage and micrometer caliper. A comparison of the diameter of the camshaft bearings with the diameters of the camshaft journals gives the amount of clearance in the bearings. To prevent excessive oil consumption, this clearance should not exceed that recommended by the manufacturer. Replace camshaft bearings which are worn 0.002 in. or more. Replace camshaft bearings that are worn, pitted, or scored. (See Appendix C for micrometer instructions.)

Replace Camshaft Bearings

Remove the camshaft bearing from the cylinder block with a puller that draws the bearing out evenly. Install the new camshaft bearings with a replacing tool equipped with a pilot to guide the bearings, Fig. 5-40. When installing the bearings, make certain that the oil passages leading to the bearings are free of sludge and other foreign matter and that the oil hole in the bearings is in line with the hole in the cylinder block. Replacement bearings for some

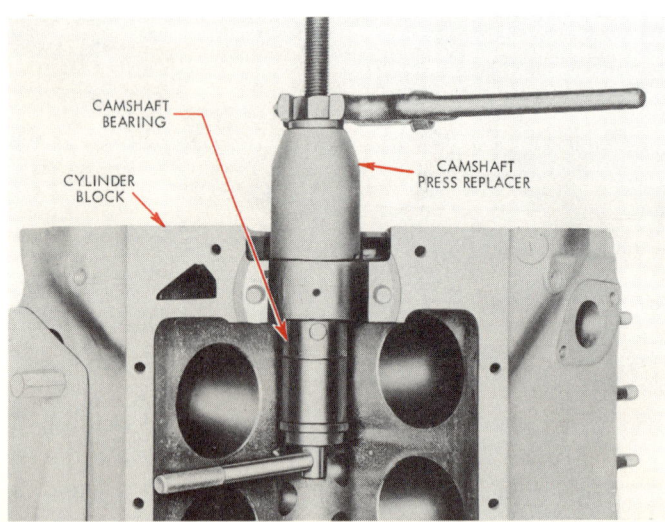

Fig. 5-40. Camshaft bearing replacement requires special tools. (Ford Motor Co.)

makes of engines are supplied in standard and 0.001 and 0.002 in. undersizes to establish the desired clearance. Such bearings do not require reaming. In other makes of engines, undersize bearings must be installed and the bearings line-reamed to establish a clearance of 0.001 to 0.002 in. between the bearings and the camshaft journals.

Timing Gears

Eventually the timing gears may wear to the point where the clearance between the gear teeth becomes excessive. The timing gear teeth are generally fitted to 0.002 to 0.005 in. clearance. Excessive clearances result in the timing gears becoming noisy, producing a humming or knocking sound.

Inspect Timing Gears

Camshaft bearing clearance is a factor that must be taken into consideration in determining gear teeth clearance. Excessive clearance in the camshaft bearings changes the distance between the crankshaft and camshaft center lines, resulting in decreased gear teeth clearances.

Replace the camshaft or crankshaft gears if they are visibly worn, broken, or have chipped teeth. Install a new camshaft gear if the clearance between the gear teeth, when checked with a narrow thickness gage, is 0.010 in. or more, Fig. 5-41. If the clearance with the

Fig. 5-41. Checking timing gear clearance with a narrow thickness gage. (Chevrolet Div., General Motors Corp.)

Automotive Engines

Fig. 5-42. Checking timing gear backlash. (Ford Div., Ford Motor Co.)

new camshaft gear exceeds 0.005 in., replace the crankshaft gear. Excessive clearance between the camshaft gear and crankshaft gear results in excessive *backlash*. Backlash can be checked by using a dial gage. Mount the dial indicator on the cylinder block with the shaft against a camshaft gear tooth, Fig. 5-42. Move the camshaft gear by hand as far as it will go in one direction. Set the dial indicator at zero. Move the gear in the opposite direction. The reading on the gage will indicate the amount of backlash. Check with the manufacturer's specifications. If too much backlash exists, replace the camshaft gear.

Replace Bolt-on Camshaft Gear

Straighten the tabs on the locks or locking ring that secure the cap screws and remove the cap screws and locking ring. Lift the camshaft gear from the camshaft. To install the camshaft gear, place the gear on the camshaft and install the locks or locking ring and cap screws. The holes in the camshaft gear and the camshaft are drilled in such a manner that the gear can be installed only in one position. Tighten the cap screws and bend the tabs to secure them in place.

Replace Press-on Camshaft Gear

On an arbor, press the camshaft gear off the camshaft. Press the new gear on the camshaft. On engines that do not have the gear keyed to the shaft, make certain that the mark on the camshaft is in line with the mark on the camshaft gear within $1/64$ in. On engines employing a thrust plate behind the camshaft gear, make certain that a clearance of 0.001 to 0.003

Heads, Valve Mechanisms

Fig. 5-43. The crankshaft timing gear can usually be removed with a gear puller. (Chevrolet Div., General Motors Corp.)

in. is provided between the thrust plate and the journal. This clearance can be checked with a thickness gage.

Replace Crankshaft Gear

Remove the crankshaft gear with a gear puller, Fig. 5-43, or by pressing the gear off on an arbor press. If the key is damaged, remove the key. To install the crankshaft gear, tap the key into place on the crankshaft and press the gear or sprocket on the crankshaft on an arbor press.

Timing Chain

Over a long period of use, the timing chain and sprockets may become so worn that the chain has an excessive amount of slack. Loose timing chains are often noisy in operation, and, if the wear is great enough, the chain may slip over the sprocket teeth, throwing the valves out of time.

Inspect Timing Chain

With the timing gear cover removed, check the timing chain for wear or stretch by pushing the

Automotive Engines

chain toward the sprockets to draw the opposite side of the chain tight, and then move the slack portion of the chain toward and away from the sprockets. Replace the timing chain when the slack between the sprockets equals one inch or more. Replace the camshaft and crankshaft sprockets if they are worn or have chipped teeth.

Replace Timing Chain

Remove the cap screws that hold the camshaft sprocket to the camshaft and remove the sprocket and timing chain. Replace the camshaft and crankshaft sprockets if the teeth are worn or chipped. Mesh the new chain with the camshaft and crankshaft sprockets and move the camshaft sprocket into position on the camshaft. Align the bolt holes and install the bolts, making certain, at the same time, that the timing sprocket marks are aligned correctly so that the valves will be timed properly.

Timing Belt

The timing belt which takes the

Fig. 5-44. Adjusting timing belt tension. (Chevrolet Div., General Motors Corp.)

Heads, Valve Mechanisms

place of the timing chain on an overhead camshaft installation should be inspected for wear, fraying or cracks. Correct tension is maintained by a spring loaded pulley operating against the outside of the belt. The spring loaded pulley is sometimes labeled as a tensioner. On the installation shown in Fig. 5-18, the belt tensioner is adjusted by loosening the tensioner adjustment bolt, tightening the belt, and then tightening the bolt.

On the installation illustrated in Fig. 5-44, the belt tension is adjusted by using a foot-pound torque wrench and an adapter tool. Drain the cooling system and loosen the water pump. Using the adapter on the torque wrench and the gage hole, Fig. 5-44, apply 15 foot-pounds of torque on the water pump. Then tighten the water pump bolt.

Oil Seal in Timing Gear Cover

Some engines employ a leather or composition oil seal in the timing gear cover to seal the crankshaft against oil leaks. Such oil seals should be soaked in oil for approximately two hours before installation.

To remove the oil seal, place the timing gear cover on a flat sur-

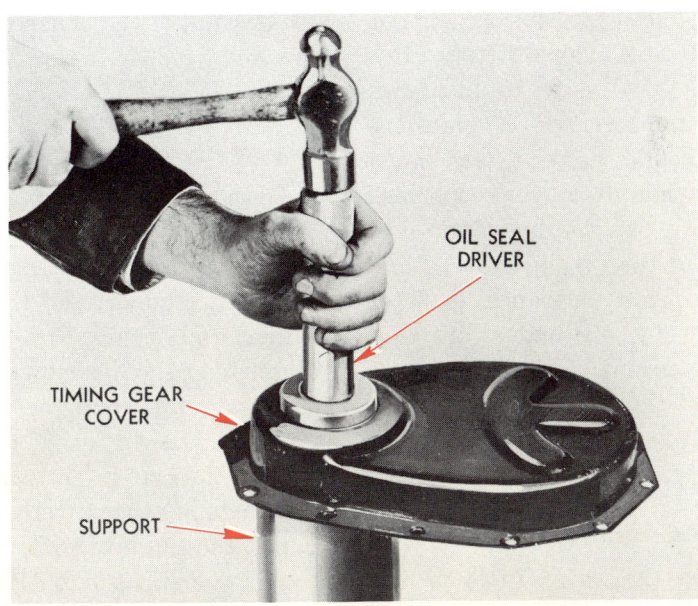

Fig. 5-45. When installing the timing gear cover oil seal, make sure the seal makes even contact with its seat. (Chevrolet Div., General Motors Corp.)

face, and drive the seal out of the cover using a punch and hammer. Keep the seal straight as it moves out of its recess by moving the punch to opposite sides of the seal with each blow of the hammer.

To install the oil seal in the timing gear cover, place the cover on a solid, flat support and place the seal in recess with the free end of the leather or composition seal toward the inside of the cover. Using a driver or flat plate slightly larger than the seal, drive the seal into place in the recess with a few light blows of the hammer, Fig. 5-45. Make certain that the seal bottoms in the recess with an even contact between the seal and its seat.

Valve Lifters

The cam action is transmitted to the valve lifters which open the valves. Since valves operate at high temperatures, they expand. A clearance or *lash* must be provided between the valve lifter and the valve to allow for this expansion. On adjustable valve lifters, this clearance is adjusted by means of a screw and lock nut. Engines using hydraulic valve lifters must have the manufacturer's specified clearance when the hydraulic unit is dry and the piston is at bottom position. This clearance is later taken up by oil under pressure from the engine so that the valves operate without clearance. Excessive valve clearances result in noisy valve operation.

Inspect Adjustable Valve Lifter

Replace the valve lifter if the clearance in the cylinder block or lifter bracket is 0.0035 in. or more or if the bottom surface shows signs of excessive wear, scoring, or pitting, Fig. 5-46. Install a new valve lifter if the threads in the lifter body are damaged or stripped. Replace the adjusting screw or lock nut if the bolt head or nuts are damaged or if the threads are stripped.

Inspect Hydraulic Valve Lifter

Disassemble the valve lifter by removing the lock ring from the lifter body and removing the push-rod seat, plunger, and the ball, retainer, and spring, Fig. 5-47. Keep all parts of the lifter together since the body and plunger are selectively fitted to each other and should not be interchanged with the parts of other lifters. Clean the parts thoroughly with a solvent that loosens varnish. Rinse with kerosene and dry immediately after cleaning.

Heads, Valve Mechanisms

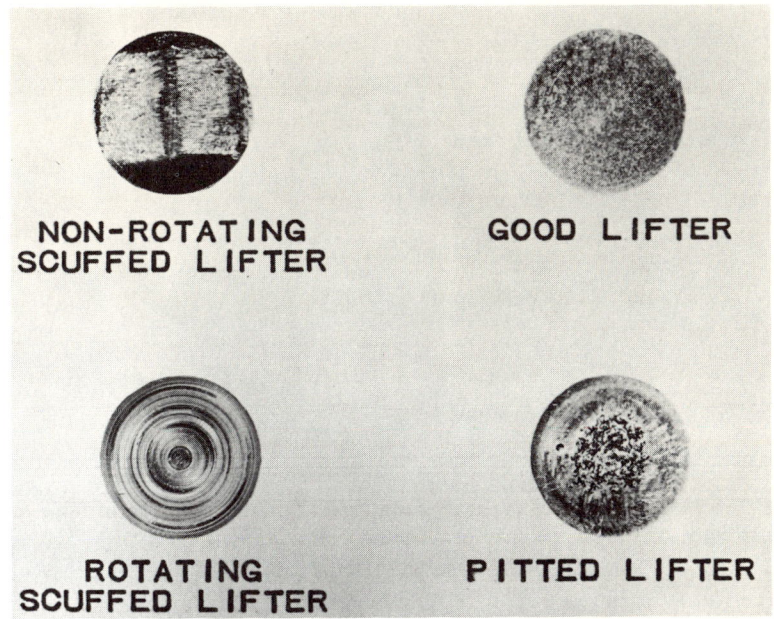

Fig. 5-46. Replace any valve lifters whose bottom surfaces are scuffed or pitted. (Texaco, Inc.)

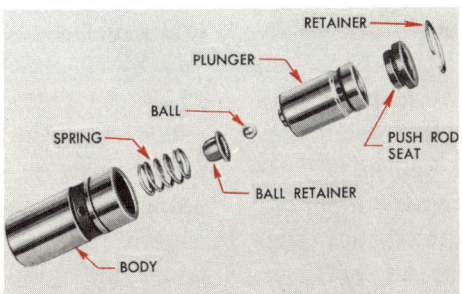

Fig. 5-47. Completely disassemble the hydraulic valve lifter for cleaning and inspection. (Buick Div., General Motors Corp.)

Inspect the inner and outer surfaces of the lifter body for scratches and scoring. Replace the lifter body if either the inner or outer surface is scored or grooved or if the cam contact surface at the lower end is worn, galled, or otherwise damaged. Replace the lifter

217

Automotive Engines

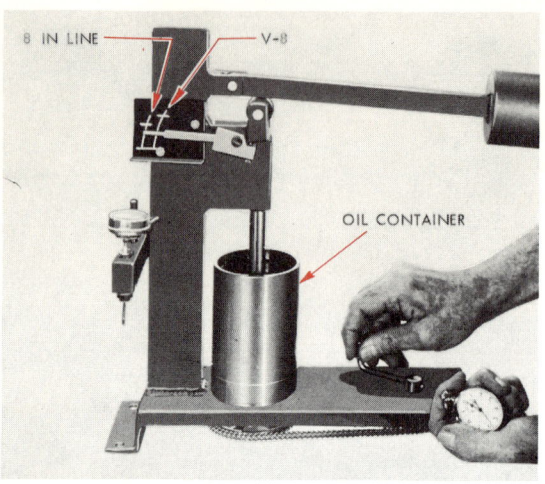

Fig. 5-48. This fixture measures the leak down rate of the hydraulic valve lifter to assure satisfactory lifter operation. (Buick Div., General Motors Corp.)

body if the clearance in the cylinder block is 0.0035 in. or more.

Examine the lifter plunger with a magnifying glass for defects. Replace the lifter if the outer surface of the plunger and the check ball seat are scratched or scored to the extent that the scratches or scores can be felt with a fingernail.

When reassembling the lifter assembly, all parts must be thoroughly clean. Rinse all parts in kerosene, and assemble the parts in the lifter body in their proper order without drying the parts. After assembly, the lifter should be tested to determine if its *leak down rate* is within the limits that will assure satisfactory lifter operation.

Checking leak down rate. The leak down rate is tested in a special fixture provided by the car manufacturer, Fig. 5-48. The lifter assembly is submerged in oil contained in the cup on the test fixture and, by means of a pumping action of the weight arms, all air is expelled from the lifter. The weight arm exerts a pressure on the plunger which causes oil to leak out of the lifter assembly. The leak down rate is indicated by a pointer on a scale mounted on the side of the tester and the leak down rate (time between marks on the scale) should be between 12 to 40 seconds to assure satisfactory lifter operation.

Replace Valve Lifter

To install oversize valve lifters,

Heads, Valve Mechanisms

ream the valve lifter guide holes in the cylinder block or valve lifter brackets to the correct size to establish a clearance of 0.0005 to 0.001 in. To assure perfect alignment when reaming the valve lifter guide holes, use a reamer that has a pilot extending into the hole in the valve guide.

On some engines, the valve lifter guide holes are burnished after reaming to produce a hardened surface. When installing oversize valve lifters on such engines, a burnishing tool of the correct size should be used to size the hole and to restore the original hardened surface.

Pushrods and Rocker Arms

Excess clearance in the pushrod and rocker arm mechanism of overhead-valve engines tends to make the valve mechanism operation noisy. Wear takes place at the ball and socket joints and at the rocker arm bushing and shaft. The contact face on the valve end of the rocker arm becomes pitted at the point of contact with the valve stem, making it impossible to adjust the valve clearance accurately.

Pushrods

Replace any pushrods that are bent or have worn or scored ball or socket joints.

Rocker Arm Assembly

Due to the design of the combustion chamber and the position of the valves in the cylinder head, the rocker arms may be straight or offset to the right or left at a slight angle.

To disassemble, remove the locking device from the end of the shaft. Then remove the rocker arms, support brackets, and springs, Fig. 5-49. To simplify reassembly, place the parts in their proper order on the bench as they are removed from the shaft.

Inspect Rocker Arm. Replace any rocker arm that is bent or the valve contact end if worn. Replace the adjusting screw and lock nut if the threads are stripped or if the ball and socket joint is worn or scored. Replace the rocker arm if the threads in the rocker arm are stripped or otherwise damaged.

Measure the diameter of the bushing with a telescoping gage and micrometer caliper. With a micrometer caliper, measure the diameter of the unworn portion of the rocker arm shaft. Replace the rocker arm if the clearance between the bushing and rocker arm shaft is 0.0045 in. or more.

Inspect Rocker Arm Shaft. Thor-

Automotive Engines

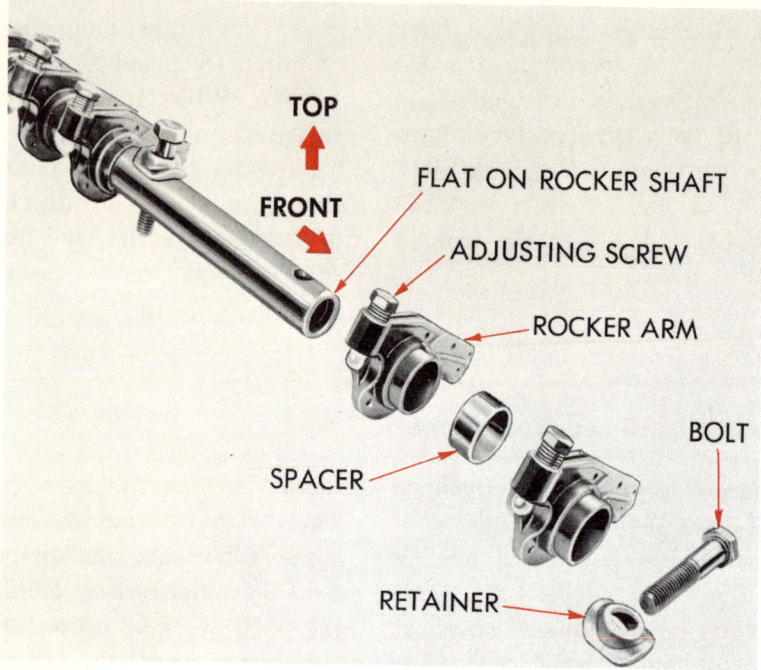

Fig. 5-49. When disassembling rocker arms from their shaft, place the parts on the bench in their proper order. (Plymouth Div., Chrysler Corp.)

oughly clean the rocker arm shaft, making certain that any sediment in the oil passage is removed and that the oil outlet holes leading to the rocker arms are open. Replace the shaft if the rocker arm bearing surfaces are scored. Measure the bearing surfaces with a micrometer caliper and compare the measurement with the diameter of the unworn portion of the shaft. Replace the rocker arm shaft if the bearing surfaces are worn 0.001 in. or more.

Assemble Rocker Arm Assembly. *Rocker arms offset to the right or left at a slight angle are not interchangeable with one another and must be located in their proper position on the rocker arm shaft.*

To assemble the rocker arms on the rocker arm shaft, oil the rocker arm bushings and place the rocker arms, springs, and support brackets on the shaft in their proper order. Make certain that the oil outlet holes in the rocker arm shaft will be at the bottom of the shaft when the assembly is installed on the engine, that the support brackets are properly located for assembly to the engine, and that each rocker arm will line up with the valve it is to operate.

Heads, Valve Mechanisms

Valve Stem Clearance Adjustment

Most present day engines are equipped with hydraulic lifters, which are classified as "no lash" lifters. Hydraulic lifters automatically adjust to take up all clearance between valve stems and rocker arms and also permit the valve to close fully. Some engines equipped with hydraulic lifters have adjustable rocker arms to permit the lifter plunger to be centered and provide for optimum plunger travel as wear occurs.

Mechanical Lifters

Most of the older model engines and a few of the new engines, including the overhead cam engine, use an adjustable mechanical lifter also known as a "tappet". As the engine warms up, the valve stem and other parts of the valve operating mechanism expand. Therefore, a certain amount of clearance must be provided to make sure the valves will close completely regardless of expansion. Too much clearance between the valve stem and rocker arm or tappet will result in a noisy engine; if the clearance is too great, the valve will not open completely.

Any time the valve operating mechanism is removed or disturbed in any way, valve stem clearance must be checked and reset if necessary. The specified amount of valve stem clearance will differ from engine to engine; in some cases the exhaust valve clearance will be greater than the intake valve clearance. Therefore, it is essential that manufacturer's specifications be followed.

The most accurate method of adjusting valve stem clearance is with the engine operating at normal temperature and at slow idle. Insert the recommended size feeler gage blade between the end of the valve stem and rocker arm or tappet. A specified size "go or no-go" gage may be used instead of a feeler gage. If the gage will not go between the valve stem and rocker arm or tappet, loosen the adjusting screw. If too much clearance exists, tighten the adjusting screw, Fig. 5-50. The correct clearance exists when the gage will just slip in between the valve stem and rocker arm or tappet.

Fig. 5-51 illustrates the tappet adjustment used with one type of overhead cam engine. Fig. 5-52 shows the adjustment used on an overhead cam engine having a rocker arm. The adjusting screws on all late model engines are self-locking and do not utilize locknuts.

Some manufacturers give specifications for adjusting the valve stem clearance when the engine is not operating. The engine can be

Automotive Engines

Fig. 5-50. Valve clearance adjustment. (Ford Div., Ford Motor Co.)

Fig. 5-51. Valve lash adjustment on an overhead cam engine. (Chevrolet Div., General Motors Corp.)

Heads, Valve Mechanisms

Fig. 5-52. Checking valve clearance on an overhead cam engine with rocker arms. (Ford Div., Ford Motor Co.)

turned to specified positions to check the clearance of the valve stems.

Hydraulic Lifters

When adjustable rocker arms are used with hydraulic lifters, the valve lash should be adjusted whenever the valve mechanism has been reconditioned. Lash may be adjusted with the engine running or stopped, but the engine must be brought up to operating temperature before making final lifter adjustments. It is generally easier, when hydraulic lifters are used, to get an accurate lash adjustment if the engine is not running.

When adjusting hydraulic lifters with the engine stopped, turn the engine to TDC. This is determined by placing the fingers on the rocker arms of number one cylinder as the engine is turned over and watching the timing marks. If the rocker arms are not moving as the TDC mark on the pulley is coming up, the cylinder will be on top dead center when the mark is lined up with the timing pointer. If the rocker arms are moving, turn the engine one more revolution. At

TDC the following valves can be adjusted:

6 cyl. Exhaust 1,3,5;   Intake 1,2,4.
V-8   Exhaust 1,3,4,8; Intake 1,2,5,7.

Turn the engine over one revolution; now the following valves can be adjusted:

6 cyl. Exhaust 2,4,6;   Intake 3,5,6
V-8   Exhaust 2,5,6,7; Intake 3,4,6,8

To adjust, back out the adjusting nut until lash is felt at the pushrod. Then turn in the adjusting nut until all the lash is removed. Now turn the adjusting nut in one additional turn to center the lifter plunger. (One turn is the required amount for a number of engines. However, always check manufacturer's specifications for the engine being serviced.)

To adjust the hydraulic lifters on an engine while it is running at idle, back off the rocker arm adjusting nut until the rocker arm begins to clatter. Turn the adjusting nut in until the clatter just stops. This is zero lash. Turn the nut in one-fourth turn. Wait 10 seconds for the lifter to adjust itself. Repeat this procedure, turning one-fourth turn and waiting until the required number of turns has been reached (usually one complete turn).

Checking On Your Knowledge

The following questions give you the opportunity to check up on yourself. If you have read the chapter carefully, you should be able to answer the questions. If you have any difficulty, read the chapter over once more so that you have the information well in mind before you go on with your reading.

DO YOU KNOW

1. What is the function of the valves in an internal combustion engine?
2. To what angle is the valve face (usually) ground?
3. To what clearance are the valve stems of intake valves generally fitted? Exhaust valves?
4. What temperature are exhaust valves subjected to during engine operation?
5. How are valves cooled?
6. How does metallic sodium employed in sodium-cooled valves function in cooling the valves?
7. To what angles is the valve face on valve seats generally ground?
8. Where are hardened steel valve seats usually employed?
9. What is the purpose of the valve guide?
10. What is the function of the valve spring?

Heads, Valve Mechanisms

11. What are the effects of valve spring vibration? What methods are employed to reduce or eliminate the effects of valve spring vibration?

12. What provisions are incorporated into the cooling system of some engines to assist in cooling the valves?

13. At what speed does the camshaft revolve in relation to the crankshaft?

14. What methods are employed to drive the camshaft?

15. How many teeth does the camshaft gear have in relation to the crankshaft gear?

16. What advantages do molded timing gears have over steel gears?

17. How is the camshaft drive mechanism lubricated?

18. Why is it desirable to have the valve lifter revolve while the engine is in operation?

19. How does the hydraulic type of valve lifter maintain the valves at zero valve clearance?

20. Why is it important that a slight leakage of oil occurs between the plunger and cylinder of the hydraulic valve lifter when the valve is open?

21. How much wear is permitted in a valve stem before the valve should be replaced?

22. For efficient performance, how wide should a valve seat be after refacing?

23. How do the cylinder heads employed on L-head and I-head engines differ in construction?

24. What is the shape of the combustion chamber formed by the cylinder head?

25. Of what materials are cylinder heads constructed?

26. What provisions are incorporated into the cylinder head to provide for its cooling in liquid-cooled engines?

27. What advantages are claimed for cylinder heads made of aluminum?

28. In what way does turbulence of the air-fuel mixture contained in the cylinder aid combustion?

29. What materials are employed in the construction of cylinder head gaskets?

30. What effect could improper tightening of the cylinder head bolts or nuts have upon the head?

31. What is the permissible amount of warp in a cylinder head before it should be resurfaced or replaced?

Chapter 6

Engine Cooling Systems

This chapter discusses the principles of operation of the several types of cooling systems used to cool internal combustion engines. The construction and operation of the parts that make up the cooling system and methods of inspection and repair also are discussed in this chapter.

Types of Cooling Systems

The temperatures developed within the cylinders during the period of combustion often become as high as 4500°F. A large amount of this heat is absorbed by the cylinder walls, cylinder head, pistons, and valves, bringing about a rise in their temperature. If this absorbed heat is not dissipated, the surfaces of the combustion chambers become red hot, the valves burn and warp and the various parts of the engine expand excessively, resulting in seized pistons and bearings and scored cylinder walls.

Approximately 20 percent of the potential heat contained in the fuel and liberated during combustion passes through the cylinder walls into the cooling system. The cooling system is designed to absorb and dissipate this excess heat to the air stream flowing through the radiator and over the engine, keeping engine temperatures within safe

Engine Cooling Systems

limits. At the same time, the cooling system must maintain within the engine a sufficiently high temperature to assure efficient and economical operation.

The types of engine cooling systems in common use are classified as *air-cooled* and *liquid-cooled*. Air-cooled engines are cooled by the direct flow of air over the cylinder surfaces and head. Liquid-cooled engines are cooled by circulating a liquid through jackets surrounding the cylinders and heads.

Air Cooling Systems

Although air-cooled engines find little use in American-made automotive vehicles (General Motors' Corvair was air-cooled), air cooling is being used on both two- and four-stroke-cycle engines used in some cars of foreign manufacture. It is also used on motorcycles, scooters, airplanes and others, Fig. 6-1.

Air-cooled engines have fins or ribs on the outer surfaces of the cylinders and cylinder heads. The fins are cast integrally with the cylinder and cylinder head and serve to increase the amount of radiation surface presented to the air stream. The heat produced by combustion passes through the walls of the cylinder and cylinder head

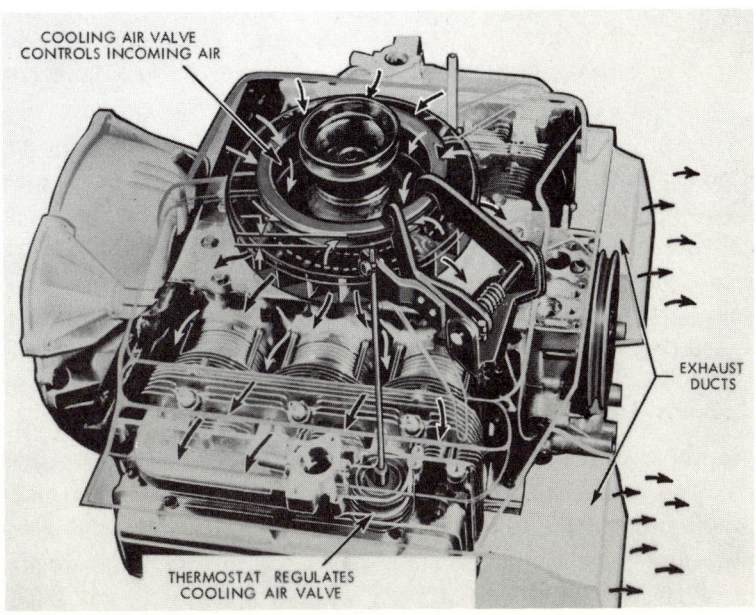

Fig. 6-1. The fins on the cylinders and heads of the air-cooled engine dissipate heat into the air passing over them and out the exhaust ducts. (Chevrolet Div., General Motors Corp.)

to the fins, where it is dissipated into the passing air. Individual cylinders are generally employed to provide ample cooling area.

The air-cooled engine requires the circulation of large volumes of air over and past the fin area. In motorcycles and airplanes, the required amount of air is supplied by the forward motion of the vehicle. When air-cooled engines are used in automobiles, the required volume of air is supplied by a fan or blower sometimes built into the engine flywheel. A cowling or shroud often encloses the engine to control the flow of air over the engine. Baffles are located near or between the cylinders to deflect the air through the fin area and around the rear of the cylinders.

Air-cooled engines operate at a higher temperature than other types of engines. As a result, greater clearances must be provided between the moving parts to allow for their greater expansion. Because of the higher operating temperatures, a heavier grade of lubricating oil is generally used.

Liquid Cooling Systems

In a liquid cooling system, the heat from the cylinders is transferred to a liquid contained in jackets surrounding the cylinders. This liquid then passes through a radiator designed to expose as large an area as possible to the air. Air is circulated over the radiating surface by means of an engine driven fan, and by the forward motion of the vehicle. The heat is carried away by this air stream.

Liquid cooling systems usually permit better temperature control than is possible in air-cooled engines. They are designed to maintain a coolant temperature of about 160°F to 205°F. In automobiles and tractors it is desirable that normal operating temperatures be reached as quickly as possible. In a liquid cooling system, the circulation of the coolant is delayed by means of a thermostatically controlled valve. The coolant is circulated only in the cylinder block and head until the opening temperature of the thermostatic valve is reached. With the thermostatic valve open, the coolant circulates throughout the cylinder block and radiator, maintaining the engine at the normal operating temperature.

Cooling system efficiency is usually rated by the difference in temperature between the coolant and the surrounding air. The temperature of the surrounding air is referred to an *ambient* temperature.

The lower the atmospheric pressure, the lower the boiling point of the coolant. For this reason, cooling systems adequate by a small margin for sea level operation may not be adequate at higher elevations where atmospheric pressure is lower.

Engine Cooling Systems

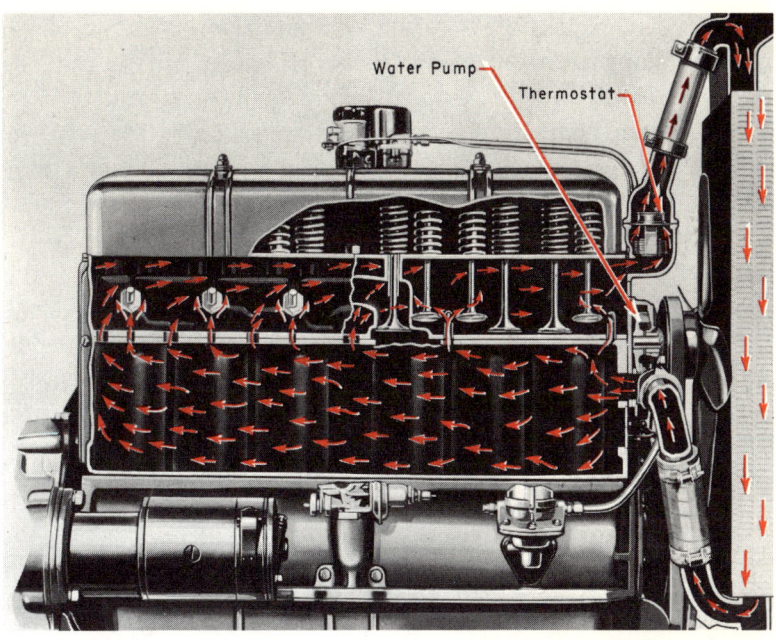

Fig. 6-2. The movement of the coolant through the cooling system. (Chevrolet Motor Div., General Motors Corp.)

A natural thermosiphon action takes place in the cooling system. A cold liquid coolant (water or ethylene glycol) is heavier than a hot coolant. As the solution in the jackets surrounding the cylinders becomes heated, it becomes lighter and rises. The heated solution enters the radiator through the upper connection and, as it is cooled by the air passing through the radiator core, it becomes heavier and settles to the bottom of the radiator core. A water pump is utilized to mechanically assist the thermosiphon action, Fig. 6-2.

Parts of a Liquid Cooling System

The cooling system can be divided into a number of separate parts or divisions that function together to maintain the engine at a normal operating temperature. These divisions of the cooling system are the water jacket, radiator, water pump, fan, baffles, and ther-

229

Automotive Engines

mostat. Some systems use an expansion tank to provide for expansion of the coolant due to heat.

Cooling system components are tailored for the type of equipment installed on the vehicle, as well as the load imposed on the engine. The cooling system for air-conditioned vehicles generally requires a large capacity radiator with a fan shroud, a special water pump, a larger fan, and a thermostatically controlled fan drive. The radiator tank on vehicles with an automatic transmission will usually contain an oil cooler unit to cool the transmission fluid. A trailer towing package is available for some makes of vehicles. This includes a high capacity fan.

Water Jackets

The water jackets are cast as an integral part of the cylinder block and cylinder head and provide passages around the cylinders and valves for the circulation of the coolant, Fig. 6-3. The passages

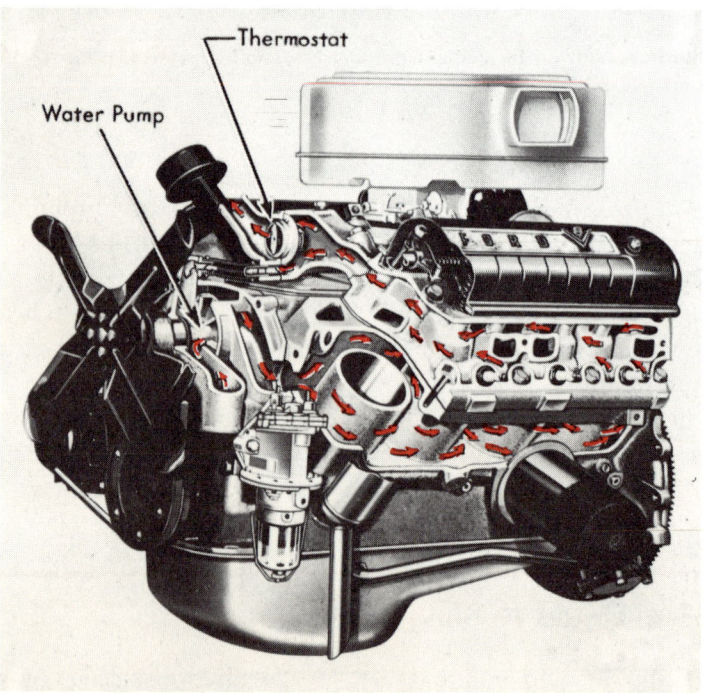

Fig. 6-3. The water jackets on this engine have been partly cut away to show how the coolant circulates to carry heat away from the valve areas, cylinders, and combustion chambers. (Ford Div., Ford Motor Co.)

Engine Cooling Systems

must allow an unrestricted flow of coolant around the cylinders and valves. As the valves and combustion chambers are the points at which maximum temperatures occur, ample cooling must be provided at these points if the engine is to be cooled effectively.

Most engines have full length water jackets that extend to the bottom of the cylinders, Fig. 6-4. This design permits effective cooling of the entire cylinder length. The cylinder block is usually provided with a drain plug at the lowest point in the water jacket so that all the cooling solution can be drained from the jackets. V-type engines usually have one drain plug on each bank of cylinders.

The cylinder block has a cylinder head and gasket attached to its top surface. The cylinder head contains the combustion chamber for each cylinder. To permit coolant circulation between the cylinder block and cylinder head, the mating surfaces of the cylinder block, head, and gasket, are provided with matched openings which connect the water jacket in the block with the passages in the cylinder head. The openings usually differ in size and are located to permit a

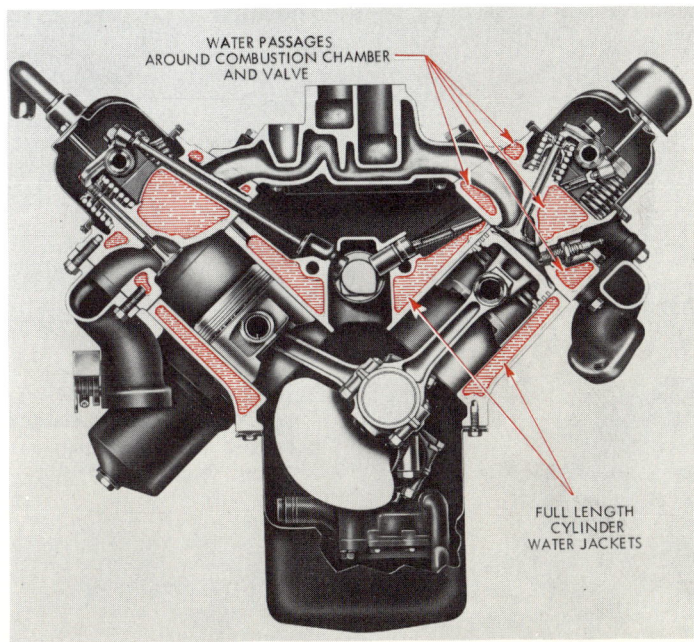

Fig. 6-4. This engine cross section shows how the water jackets extend along the full length of the cylinders to provide ample cooling. (Plymouth Div., Chrysler Corp.)

greater volume of coolant flow on the valve side of the cylinder head or block than on the opposite side. A coolant outlet in the cylinder head connects the cylinder head coolant passages to the upper part of the radiator tank. The cylinder block coolant passages are connected to the lower part of the radiator tank through the coolant inlet opening on the water pump.

Radiator

The purpose of the radiator is to cool the liquid coolant solution received from the engine. The radiator consists of two tanks: an inlet tank, an outlet tank and a core, Fig. 6-5. The two tanks may be located at the top and bottom of the core. This is known as a downflow radiator, or the tanks may be on either side, which is known as a crossflow radiator.

The radiator core divides the coolant into thin streams which flow into the outlet tank. In passing through the core, the solution loses heat, transferring it through the metal tubes and fins of the core to the airstream drawn through the core by the fan. On most vehicles equipped with an automatic transmission, an oil cooler will be located in the lower tank of a downflow radiator and in one of the side tanks of a crossflow radiator.

An overflow tube connected to the filler pipe permits excess cool-

Fig. 6-5. This typical radiator consists of a core with an upper (inlet) and lower (outlet) tank. (McCord Corp.)

Engine Cooling Systems

ant or steam to escape whenever excessive pressure builds up. The overflow tube used on older vehicles not having a pressurized cooling system was located in the upper radiator tank. Some radiators have a baffle plate soldered inside the upper tank above the radiator inlet opening which directs the flow of the coolant toward the radiator core. Others have no baffle plate and the coolant flows directly into the upper tank.

To permit rapid dissipation of heat, the radiator usually is made of copper or brass. Radiators are either tubular or cellular (honeycomb) in construction.

Tubular. The tubular radiator consists of a number of round or flattened tubes, the ends of which are securely soldered in the headers of the inlet and outlet tanks. Radiators are provided with cooling fins which assist in the dissipation of heat. Depending upon the design of the radiator, the cooling fins may be of the continuous type, Fig. 6-6, or may be mounted between the tubes, Fig. 6-7. The fins

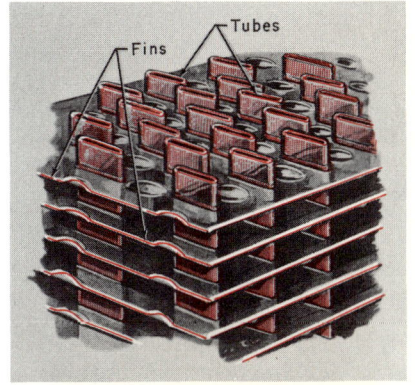

Fig. 6-6. A tubular radiator core with horizontal fins. (McCord Corp.)

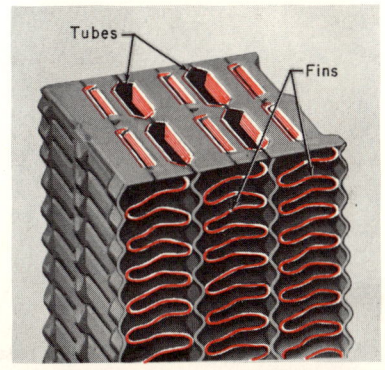

Fig. 6-7. This cellular type radiator core is formed from pressed metal sections. (McCord Corp.)

Automotive Engines

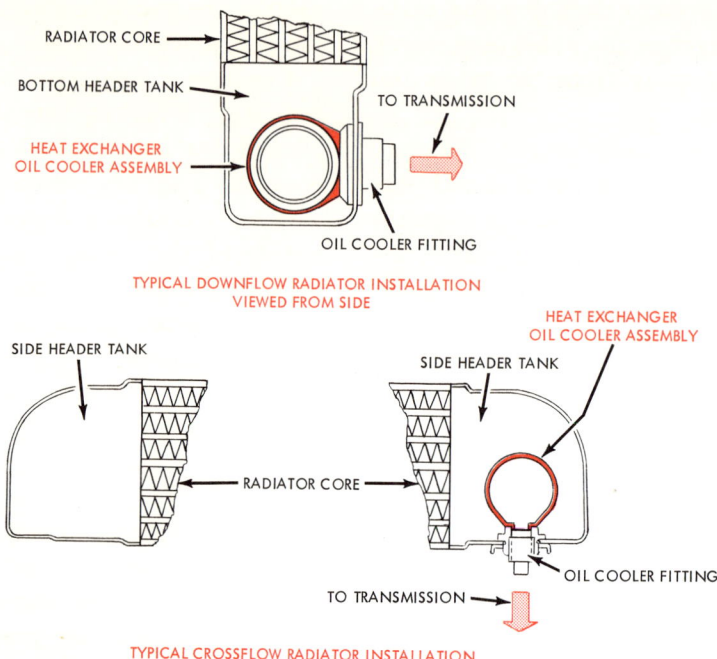

Fig. 6-8. Oil cooler (heat exchanger) for transmission fluid. (Ford Div., Ford Motor Co.)

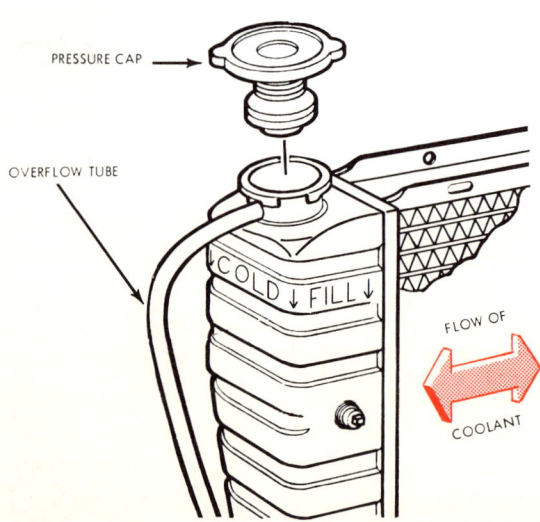

Fig. 6-9. Section of a crossflow radiator. (Ford Div., Ford Motor Co.)

Engine Cooling Systems

are soldered to the tubes and serve to strengthen the tubes and carry the heat away from the tubes and the water.

Cellular. Cellular radiators are constructed of pressed metal sections formed and soldered together to provide a series of straight narrow passages through the core, Fig. 6-7. The passages are open into the inlet and outlet tanks of the radiator. The width of the passages is slightly less than the thickness of the radiator core. Thin copper fins are soldered to the pressed metal sections and serve as conductors to dissipate the heat. Radiators used today may be of the downflow type or of the crossflow type.

Downflow. The downflow radiator has the tubes arranged for a vertical flow of the coolant. Two header tanks, one on the top (inlet) and one on the bottom (outlet), provide for a uniform flow of coolant through the tubes which make up the radiator core. The outlet is connected by a hose to the water pump inlet. The inlet (upper header tank) is connected by a hose to the coolant outlet at the engine, thereby permitting circulation of the coolant through the radiator and engine when the thermostat is open. The bottom header tank installed on most vehicles with an automatic transmission contains a heat exchanger to cool the transmission fluid, Fig. 6-8 (top). The radiator shown in Fig. 6-5 is a downflow type.

Crossflow. The crossflow radiator, Fig. 6-9, has the tubes arranged for horizontal flow of the coolant. The two header tanks, which provide for a uniform distribution of the coolant, are located on opposite sides of the radiator core. If a transmission heat exchanger is used, it will be located in one of the header tanks, Fig. 6-8 (bottom).

Water Pump

Cooling systems employ a centrifugal water pump to maintain circulation. The water pump is centrally mounted at the front of the cylinder block and is driven by a V belt. Most V-type engines employ a single water pump to assure even distribution of coolant to both cylinder blocks. Some of the older V-type engines had two water pumps, one for each bank of cylinders.

The water pump consists of a cast-iron housing with ball bearings in which an impeller shaft revolves. The housing has a water inlet and an outlet opening. Coolant from the bottom of the radiator enters the pump through the inlet opening.

A metal or plastic impeller having two or more blades is mounted on one end of the impeller shaft, and a drive pulley is mounted on the other end of the shaft. Some water pumps have a bolt-on cover

Automotive Engines

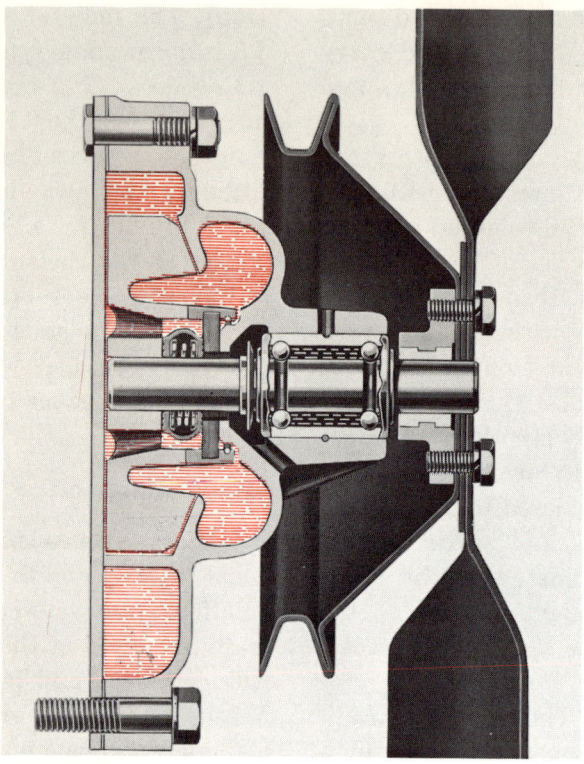

Fig. 6-10. The impeller on this water pump is enclosed by a bolt-on cover. (Plymouth Div., Chrysler Corp.)

to enclose the impeller within the pump housing, Fig. 6-10.

Other pumps use no bolt-on cover, and the impeller remains exposed, Fig. 6-11, until the pump is bolted to the engine block. The cylinder block is provided with a hole to receive the impeller. The impeller is in direct contact with the water in the cylinder water jackets when the pump is installed in the cylinder block.

Seals of various designs are incorporated in the pump to prevent loss of coolant from the system. Water pumps are often designed with bypass openings which permit the circulation of water within the cylinder block and cylinder head only when the engine is cold and the thermostatic valve is closed.

Fan

The purpose of the fan is to draw a rapid stream of air inward through the radiator. The air

Engine Cooling Systems

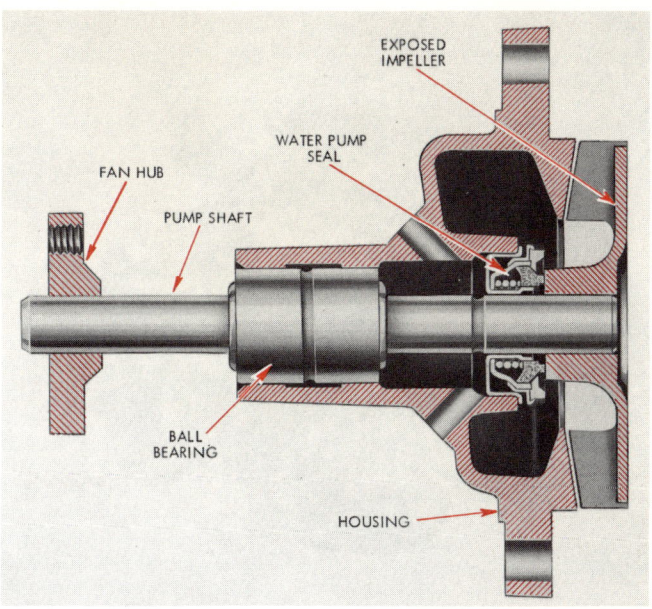

Fig. 6-11. The impeller on this water pump remains exposed until the pump is bolted to the engine block. (Chevrolet Div., General Motors Corp.)

flowing through the radiator helps to dissipate the heat of the coolant flowing through the radiator core. On some rear engine buses the fan is referred to as a "pusher" type fan because it forces air outward through the radiator.

The fan is mounted on the water pump pulley and belt driven by the crankshaft, Fig. 6-12. Some of the older engines had the fan mounted directly on the end of the crankshaft while other engines had the fan mounted on a separate shaft.

The fan may have two, three, four, five, six, or seven blades. Unevenly spaced fan blades are used where, because of the harmonic principle, evenly spaced blades have proven noisy on a particular installation. All fans are driven by a V-type belt. Heavy duty fans may require two belts.

There are no repairs to be made to the fan. If the fan is bent or damaged, it should be replaced. It is essential that the fan assembly remain in proper balance, and proper balance cannot be assured once a fan assembly has been bent or damaged.

Fluid Drive Fan. The power required to drive a fan increases rapidly as the engine speed increases, amounting to several horsepower at high speeds. For

Automotive Engines

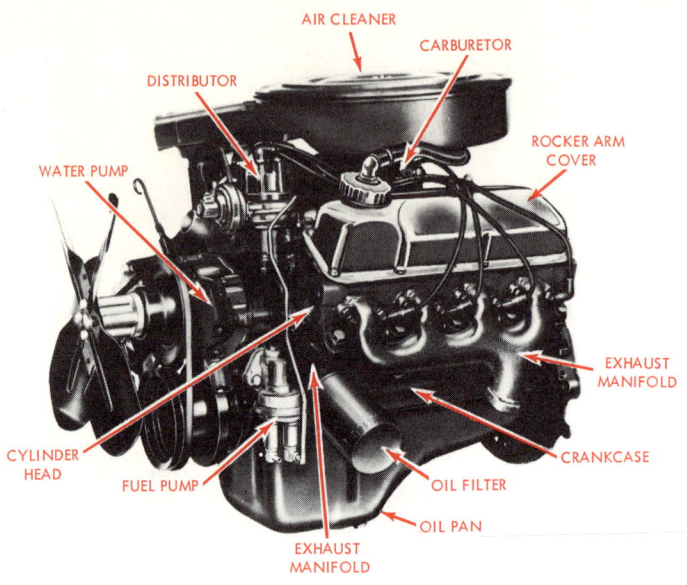

Fig. 6-12. The fan draws air through the radiator to cool the solution flowing through the tubes of the radiator core. (Ford Div., Ford Motor Co.)

this reason, many automobile engines, especially those used in vehicles equipped with air conditioning, will have a type of fluid drive fan, Fig. 6-13. The types of fan assemblies may be referred to as torque control drive fans, variable speed fans, thermal control drive fans, or fans with a drive clutch.

Torque Control Drive Fan. This type of fan has a sealed silicone fluid filled coupling, Fig. 6-14, connecting the fan to the fan pulley. A coupling of this design permits the fan to be driven in a normal manner at low speeds while limiting the fan's top speed to one preset level. This reduces engine load and fan noise at high speed.

The other types of fluid drive fans provide maximum air flow through the radiator when needed but a minimum air flow when less than maximum cooling is required. Using a fan of this type also results in less power loss plus a reduction in fan noise when cooling demands are not at a maximum.

The Variable Speed Fan and the Thermal Control Drive Fan. Both use a fluid drive clutch, and are constructed to modulate between minimum and maximum air flow temperature. This design of fluid

Engine Cooling Systems

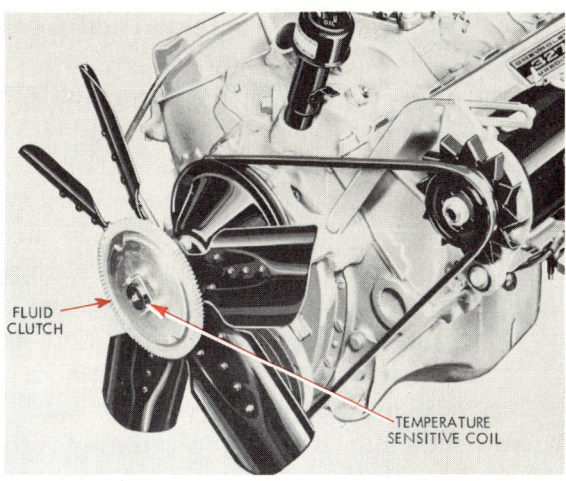

Fig. 6-13. On a fluid drive fan, a temperature sensitive coil controls the flow of silicone liquid in a fluid clutch to vary the speed of the cooling fan. (Chevrolet Div., General Motors Corp.)

Fig. 6-14. Torque control fan drive. (Plymouth Div., Chrysler Corp.)

fan has a silicone base oil-filled coupling connecting the fan blade assembly to the fan drive pulley. Fan speed is regulated by the torque carrying capacity of the fluid. The amount of oil entering the coupling governs the speed at which the fan operates.

The fan drive plate enclosed within the clutch housing is attached directly to the fan drive pulley. The clutch housing and blade assembly are mounted to the input shaft by a sealed bearing and are free to rotate independently of the drive plate and input shaft. The inside chamber of the clutch housing is filled with a fixed amount of silicone base oil.

Centrifugal force caused by the rotation of the clutch plus the pumping action designed into the unit forces the oil around the inner surfaces of the clutch. A small preset clearance between the driving and driven surfaces of the clutch assembly causes the oil forced between the two surfaces to drive the driven unit. The higher the speed the greater the driving force.

A control valve actuated by a temperature-sensitive bimetal coil or strip, Fig. 6-15 and located in the airstream at the front of the clutch unit and near the radiator regulates the amount of oil pumped in or out of the clutch drive area. The air flow temperature acts on

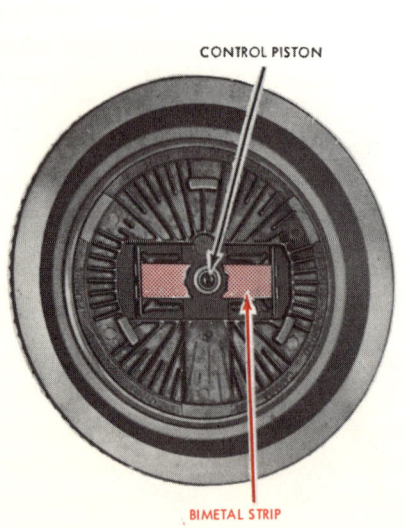 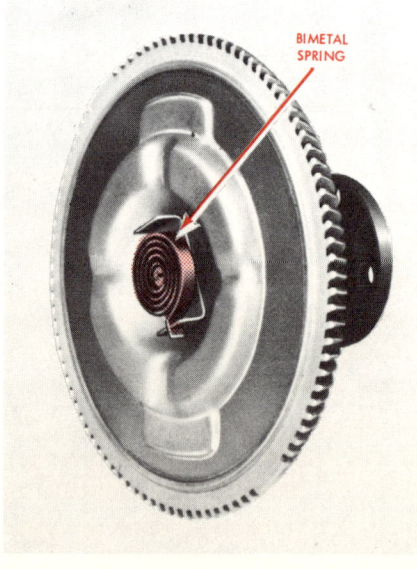

Fig. 6-15. Fluid drive fan assembly with a bimetal strip (left), and with a thermostatic coil spring (right).

Engine Cooling Systems

the coil or strip to determine the fan speed in relation to the drive pulley which, in turn, determines the amount of air drawn through the radiator.

When first starting an engine which has not been operating for a time, near maximum fan noise will be present. Oil will be forced into the close clearance area of the clutch by centrifugal force resulting in the fan being turned at close to pulley speed. As normal operating temperature is reached, the amount of fluid in the close clearance area of the clutch will be regulated by the temperature-sensitive control valve. This determines the fan speed in relation to the drive pulley and the airstream temperature.

After the first start and as long as the air flow around the drive clutch unit does not exceed 150°-180°F, the drive clutch will remain at or near the maximum slippage position. The temperature controlled valve allows a minimum amount of oil to remain in the close clearance (drive) area.

As ambient temperature increases, additional cooling is required. The temperature sensitive coil or strip moves the control valve to the minimum slip position, retaining a maximum amount of oil in the close clearance area resulting in the fan being turned at close to pulley speed.

As cooling requirements change according to engine load, traffic, terrain, etc., the fan will operate within the high and low RPM positions, modulating according to the changes in temperature of the air flow through the radiator.

During high-speed operation, fan drive clutch action will limit the speed of the fan to a predetermined RPM, regardless of ambient temperatures.

Servicing the Fluid Drive Fan. Spin the fan blades by hand. If there is no resistance or if there is very high resistance, further tests should be made.

In the case of engine overheating during idle or slow speed operation, run the engine at approximately 1000 RPM in neutral. If the overheating is not reduced, replace the fluid drive assembly with a unit known to be in good operating condition and test in the same manner. Replace the original unit with a new assembly if the trouble is corrected by the good assembly.

Another method of checking the unit is to operate the engine at a fast idle speed until normal operating temperature is reached. Regardless of temperature, the unit must be operated for at least five minutes before making the test. Stop the engine and immediately turn the fan. If considerable effort is required, the unit is operating satisfactorily. If little effort is required, the unit is not operating properly and should be replaced.

Automotive Engines

Special strobe light and tachometer equipment can be used to check the speed of the fan blades and the speed of the drive pulley at both minimum drive speed and maximum drive speed. Follow the instructions of the equipment manufacturer when making this test.

When it is necessary to remove the fluid drive unit, it will be removed in the same manner as a conventional fan assembly. To prevent the silicone fluid from draining into the fan drive bearing and ruining the grease, do not place the drive unit with the shaft pointing downward. Loss of fluid will make the unit inoperative.

The fluid drive fan unit utilizing a thermostatic bimetal coil spring, Fig. 6-15(right), cannot be disassembled, serviced, or repaired. If the unit does not function properly, replace it.

The fluid drive fan unit utilizing a flat bimetal strip, Fig. 6-15 (left), may be partially disassembled for inspection and freeing up the control valve. Separate the fan from the drive unit. Remove the metal strip by pushing one end of the strip toward the clutch housing so it clears the retaining bracket. Push the strip to one side so the opposite end will spring out of place. Check the movement of the piston control valve. If the piston sticks, clean it with emery cloth. If the bimetal strip is damaged, replace the entire assembly.

When assembling, install the piston control valve so the projection on the end will contact the bimetal strip. Install the strip with the identifying numbers or letters facing the clutch.

Do not dip the clutch assembly in any type of cleaning solvent.

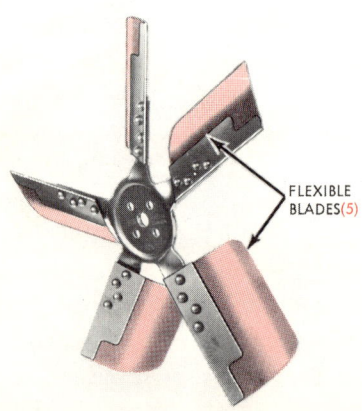

Fig. 6-16. Flexible blade fan. (Ford Div., Ford Motor Co.)

Engine Cooling Systems

Flexible Blade Fan. Some installations utilize a flexible blade fan where extra cooling is required. The fan is part of an integrated cooling system design which includes the radiator, heater, engine, and air conditioner.

The fan consists of a spider stamping with either five or seven blades, Fig. 6-16, to which are riveted flexible blades. Except for the flexible blades, the fan is the same as a conventional fan assembly. As engine speed increases, the blades flatten out, having less pitch and creating less noise, and consuming less power than a conventional fan with a fixed pitch. This fan adjusts itself to engine cooling requirements, to some extent, without a complex fluid drive clutch assembly.

Engine Baffles

The air drawn through the radiator by the fan gives additional cooling as it passes over the surfaces of the engine. The flow of air is directed by the sheet metal parts which form the engine compartment. These parts consist of the hood and baffles attached to the inside of the fenders, Fig. 6-17. On some engines, a shroud on the back of the radiator causes the fan to draw the air through the total area of the radiator instead of just in front of the fan at low speeds.

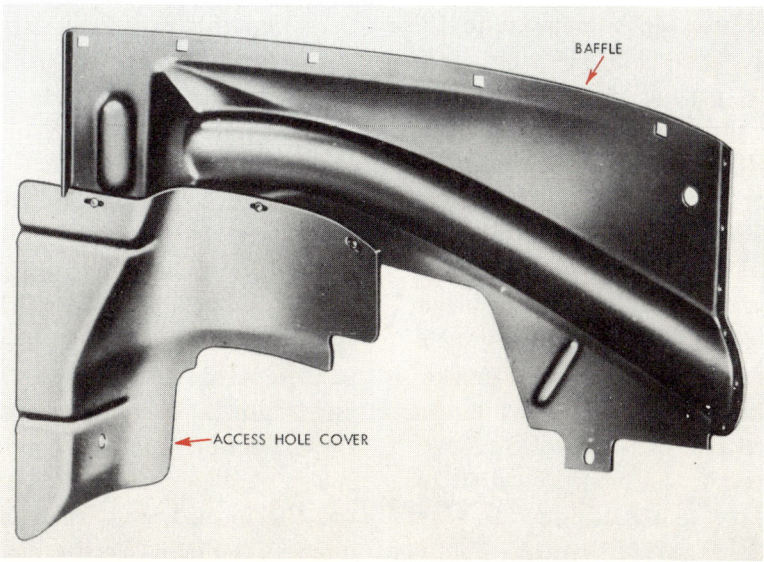

Fig. 6-17. Sheet metal baffles direct the flow of cooling air around the engine. The baffle also forms part of the front wheel housing and protects the engine from water splash.

243

Automotive Engines

Baffles also are used between the grill and the radiator. Such baffles assure that all the air entering the grill passes through the core of the radiator. In addition to directing the flow of air, the baffles keep dirt and stones from entering the engine and radiator compartments.

Thermostats

Normal minimum coolant temperatures in the cooling systems are automatically maintained by a calibrated thermostatic valve that remains closed until the predetermined temperature is reached. The thermostat is usually located in the upper part of the cylinder head or the water manifold leading to the water outlet connection.

The opening and closing of the thermostat is controlled by the temperature of the coolant in the cooling system. During the warmup period, the thermostat is closed, and the water pump circulates the coolant throughout the cylinder block and cylinder head only. When normal operating temperatures are reached, the valve opens and allows coolant to circulate throughout the entire system.

Thermostats are usually marked with the temperature at which the valve starts to open. Standard thermostats commonly used in today's engines are designed to start opening at 177°F to 195°F and should be fully opened at 200°F. Some thermostats have the upper range extended to 205°F. These thermostats are designed only for use with a permanent type antifreeze having an ethylene-glycol base such as Prestone, Zerex, etc. A 160°F thermostat must be used when an alcohol base and water mixture is used as an antifreeze solution.

High temperature thermostats intended for use with permanent antifreeze solutions should not be used with alcohol antifreeze solutions because they will cause overheating with coolant loss and possible engine damage. Due to the so-called "after boil" or rise in temperature of the cooling solution when the engine is stopped or allowed to idle after a high-speed run, low boiling point antifreeze solutions are rapidly vaporized. If the temperature exceeds the boiling point of the solution, violent surging occurs and large quantities of the solution may be forced out of the overflow pipe.

Various types of thermostats have been used. Some had a thin metal bellows attached to a valve which opened or closed as the bellows expanded or contracted due to temperature changes. Others had a bimetal element composed of two different metals bonded together. When cold, the opening in the thermostat was closed by the bimetal element. As the operating temperature increased, the heat applied to the bimetal caused one

Engine Cooling Systems

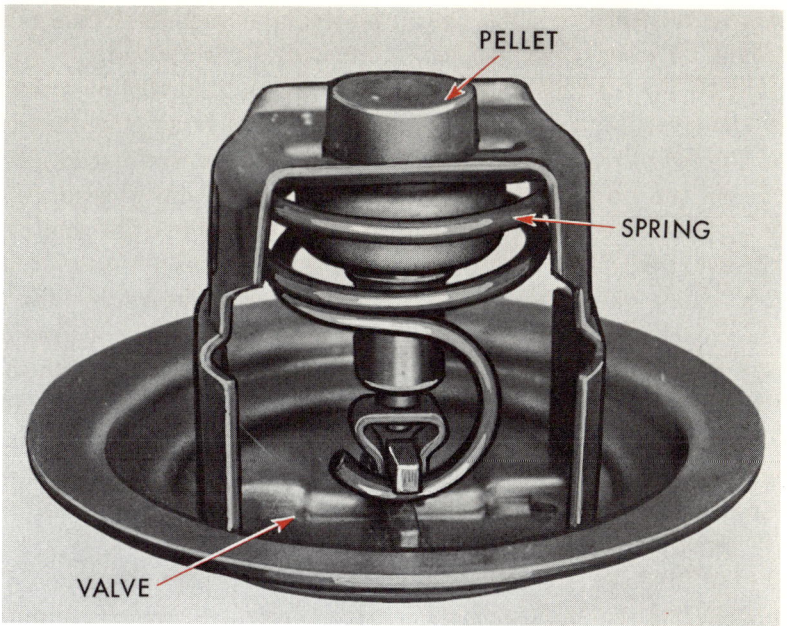

Fig. 6-18. This pellet type thermostat is in the closed position. (Plymouth Div., Chrysler Corp.)

metal to expand more than the other, opening the thermostat.

Most present-day vehicles use a pellet type thermostat to control the flow of coolant throughout the engine, Fig. 6-18. A copper impregnated wax pellet expands when heated and contracts when cooled. The pellet is connected to a valve through a piston. When the pellet is heated it expands, opening the valve and permitting the coolant to circulate through the radiator. As the pellet cools, it contracts and allows the spring to close the valve.

Pressure Type Cooling System

Present automobile engines are designed to operate at much higher temperatures than older model engines. This makes for less exhaust emissions and more engine efficiency. To operate at a higher temperature, the cooling system is pressurized. When a liquid is confined under greater than atmospheric pressure, a higher tempera-

245

ture can be reached before the coolant boils. Pressurized cooling systems make use of this fact by locating the overflow tube in the radiator filler opening and separating it from the radiator header tank by a pressurized filler cap.

The pressurized filler cap contains a pressure relief valve and a vacuum relief valve, Fig. 6-19. The pressure relief valve is held against its seat by a spring. When the pressure within the radiator reaches a predetermined point, the spring is compressed allowing the excessive pressure to be released through the overflow pipe. The vacuum relief valve is also held against its seat by a spring. As the cooling system cools off, a vacuum is created within the system. When the vacuum builds up to a predetermined point, the spring compresses, opening the valve and releasing the vacuum which is present within the system.

A pressurized cooling system increases the boiling point of the coolant by approximately 3°F for each pound of pressure. This means that, when the cooling system is pressurized with a 15 pound pressure cap, the engine can operate at cooling temperatures of up to 257°F with water as the coolant before boiling will occur. Modern cooling systems are pressurized from 12 to 17 psi. Some older model cooling systems operate at only 7 psi.

A pressurized cooling system also increases water pump efficiency by reducing the possibility of cavitation near the pump. "Cavitation" may occur in a vented cooling system if the coolant in the low pressure area near the pump impeller turns to steam causing the

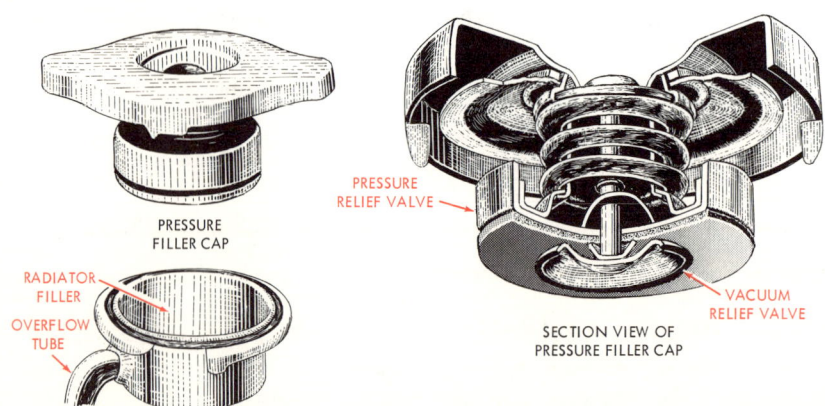

Fig. 6-19. A pressure type radiator cap is used on sealed cooling systems. (Plymonth Div., Chrysler Corp.)

Engine Cooling Systems

impeller blades to spin in the bubbles formed. Cavitation reduces pump efficiency.

When the radiator is hot and the cap is removed or loosened, system pressure drops to atmospheric and, if the coolant operating temperature has been higher than its boiling point, the solution may be lost in the form of steam. Because steam can also form in the engine coolant passages, it can force the coolant upward and out of the radiator and necessitate coolant replacement.

Because many cooling systems operate at temperatures above the boiling point of water, a "permanent" antifreeze solution of water and an ethylene-glycol base product is factory installed in all present-day engines. This provides maximum protection against freezing, overheating (causing "boil-away"), and corrosion. Most manufacturers recommend year around protection of $-20°F$ with a minimum of $0°F$ for satisfactory operation. The solution should be drained at least every two years in order to maintain the necessary rust and corrosion protection in the solution.

The use of an alcohol type of antifreeze is not recommended for today's engines. This solution has a boiling point well below that of water. Therefore, boiling can occur at normal engine operating temperatures forcing the solution out through the overflow pipe. If plain water is used in the cooling system, a rust inhibitor should be added to remove the possibility of rust and corrosion developing in the system.

Antifreeze Solutions

In localities where the temperature does not drop below 32°F, water can be safely used in the cooling system of older model vehicles without a pressurized cooling system. Vehicles with a pressurized system should use a permanent antifreeze the year yound. Where the temperatures drop below 32°F, an antifreeze solution *must* be used that will protect the cooling system at down to the lowest temperatures encountered. A frozen cooling system usually results in a damaged radiator, or a cracked cylinder block or cylinder head.

An antifreeze solution should fulfill certain requirements if the cooling system is to be protected: When mixed with water, it should circulate freely at the lowest operating temperatures. It should retain its antifreeze properties with use. It should not damage the cooling system through corrosive, electrolytic, or solvent action. The cost should be low.

Almost all antifreeze solutions contain a rust inhibitor which tends to prevent the formation of scale and rust in the cooling system. Scale and rust tend to obstruct the flow of coolant through the passages of the system. When such formations are excessive, they can cause overheating and possible engine damage.

Alcohols

Methyl and ethyl alcohol solutions have been used as antifreeze solutions. When mixed in proper proportions with water, they give adequate protection at low temperatures and are not injurious to the cooling system, but they have boiling points that are below, or within the engine operating temperature range of unpressurized cooling systems. As a result, alcohols are lost through evaporation after long engine operating periods. A 160°F thermostat must be used if an alcohol base antifreeze is used. An alcohol base antifreeze *must not* be used in a pressurized cooling system.

Ethylene Glycol

Ethylene glycol is a by-product obtained in the manufacture of artificial gas. In a concentrated solution, it has a boiling point of 330°F. Ethylene glycol is a "permanent" type antifreeze, because it will not boil away or evaporate with use. When mixed in correct proportions with water, it affords complete protection against freezing. It has no odor and will not injure the finish of the automobile. As marketed for antifreeze purposes, ethylene glycol contains a soluble oil corrosion inhibitor, and the solution can be left in the cooling system throughout the year. Manufacturers recommend that the cooling system be drained, flushed with plain water, and refilled with fresh water and ethylene-glycol to provide freezing protection to −20°F every two years.

The cooling system must be carefully serviced to eliminate all leaks before filling. Losses due to leakage must be replaced by adding more antifreeze solution. Any loss of coolant due to evaporation can be replaced by the addition of water.

Cooling System Service

The radiator, cylinder block, and cylinder head must be kept free from leaks and free from rust and scale which might tend to clog the water passages. The water pump must be leakproof and must keep

Engine Cooling Systems

the water circulating in the system. In addition, all hoses must be in good condition so they will not collapse. The connections must be kept tight to prevent leaks. The radiator core must be free of any accumulation of dust or insects to maintain the flow of air through the passages.

Deposits in Cooling System

Over a period of time, the cooling system accumulates rust and scale in the engine water jackets and radiator. If this material is not removed, it will eventually clog the water passages.

The deposits which form in the cooling system come from several sources. One source of deposits is the use of water containing calcium or magnesium salts. These salts leave the solution when exposed to fairly high temperatures and form what is commonly known as water scale.

Rust in the cooling system is caused by oxygen in the water which has a corrosive action on iron and steel. The entrance of air into the cooling system increases the rate at which rust accumulates in the system. Air may enter the cooling system through a leaking water pump seal, or through other leaks in the cooling system.

Air cannot enter sealed cooling systems while the engine is at operating temperature, since the pressure in the cooling system is above atmospheric pressure. In such systems, air can enter the cooling system only after the engine cools off and the pressure returns to less than atmospheric pressure (vacuum). Under this vacuum, air can enter through a leaking water pump seal or through other leaks in the system. Since the overflow pipe enters the radiator above the gasket seal in the pressure type cap, air cannot enter the radiator through the overflow pipe unless the gasket leaks.

Another common cause of corrosion is a loose cylinder head or damaged head gasket. Either of these conditions allows exhaust gases to be blown into the cooling system. As these gases contain strong acids, they tend to cause corrosion in the cooling system. All of these deposits prevent heat transfer. The deposits can eventually become large enough to clog the passages of the radiator, reducing or preventing the circulation of coolant throughout the cooling system. This results in engine overheating, which can cause burned valves, scored pistons and cylinders, or cracked water jackets or cylinder heads, making major engine repairs necessary.

Solutions containing salt, calcium chloride, soda, sugar, honey, or mineral oils such as kerosene or engine oil should never be used in the cooling system. Such solutions will clog the water passages in the cooling system, damage the hose connections, or damage the engine parts by corrosive action.

Cleaning

The cooling system on an operating engine can be cleaned by circulating through the water passages a solution capable of dissolving the rust and scale, draining the solution, and then reverse flushing the radiator and engine with water and compressed air. Care must be taken to follow the manufacturer's instructions with the particular cleaning solution being used.

Chemical Cleaning. To clean the cooling system, the cleaning solution is put into the radiator and the radiator filled with water to about three inches below the top of the overflow pipe. Operate the engine at moderate speeds with engine temperature at approximately 180°F for the length of time recommended in the instructions. At the end of this time, stop the engine and drain the cooling system.

Flushing Radiator. Reverse flushing is accomplished by using air pressure to force water through the system. Disconnect the upper radiator connection from the engine and the lower radiator connection from the water pump. Attach a lead-away hose to the upper radiator connection. Insert the flushing gun into the bottom radiator hose, Fig. 6-20A, and connect the water hose and air hose to the gun. Turn on the water. When the radiator is full, turn on the air in very short blasts, allowing the radiator to fill between blasts of air. Continue this flushing until the water from the lead-away hose runs clear.

In reverse flushing, usually the air pressure supplied to the flushing gun is the normal air line pressure (100 to 125 psi). Since radiators will stand only a limited amount of pressure, care must be taken when applying the air pressure to prevent building up a pressure of more than 20 psi in the radiator.

Flushing Block. Due to variations in water pump design, some manufacturers do not recommend pressure flushing of the water passages in the cylinder block because of possible damage to the water pump seal and seat. Some manufacturers recommend that the cylinder block be pressure flushed in the direction of flow, while others recommend reverse flushing. Always follow the manufacturer's instructions for the particular engine being worked on. Remove the thermostat to avoid damaging it during this operation.

To reverse flush the engine, connect the lead-away hose to the water pump inlet connection and the flushing gun to the water outlet connection on the cylinder head, Fig. 6-20B. Turn on the water.

Engine Cooling Systems

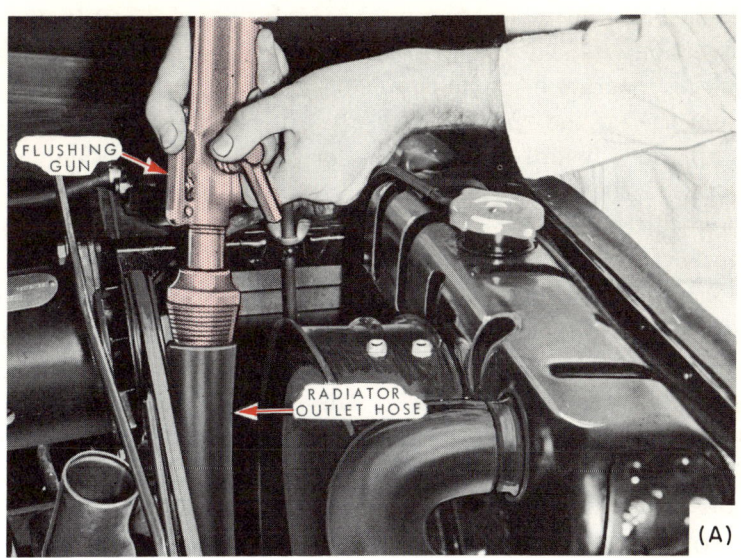

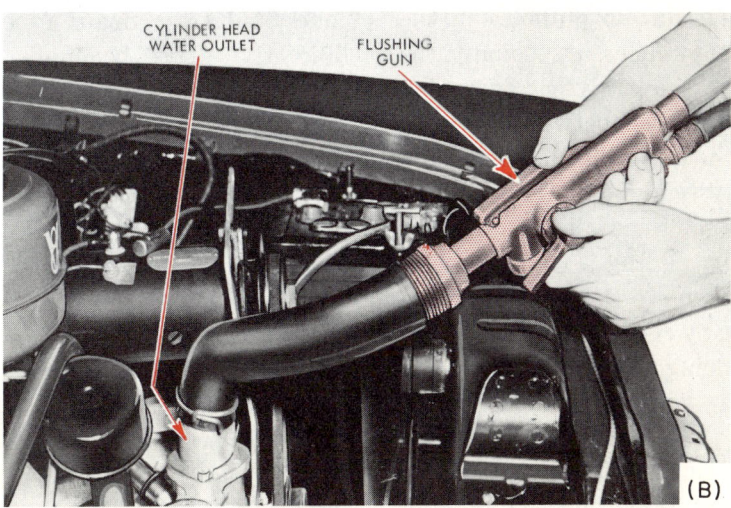

Fig. 6-20. Reverse flushing can be performed on the radiator (top) or on the engine block (bottom). (Plymouth Div., Chrysler Corp.)

When the engine is full, turn on the air in short blasts, until the water from the engine runs clear.

To flush the cylinder block in the direction of flow, attach the lead-away hose to the water outlet connection on the cylinder head and insert the flushing gun in the hose attached to the water pump inlet connection. Repeat the pressure flushing operation until the water from the engine runs clear. Upon completion, install the radiator hoses and thermostat on the engine, and fill the cooling system with solution, as required.

After flushing the cooling system, blow out the dirt and insects that have accumulated in the air passages in the radiator core. Use a compressed air hose at the back of the radiator to reverse the normal direction of air flow.

After reverse flushing, radiators are sometimes found to have small leaks due to pinholes in the core. The pinholes are usually the result of electrolytic corrosion which takes place between the coolant and the dissimilar metals in the cooling system (solder, brass, cast iron, etc.) Such leaks can be stopped by adding a radiator sealing compound to the water or antifreeze, or by removing the radiator and soldering the leaks.

Water Pump

Water pump operation can be checked by operating the engine while squeezing the upper radiator hose. A pressure surge can be felt if the pump is operating. If no surge is felt, make sure the pump vent hole, if there is one, is not obstructed. If it is not, the impeller is not functioning.

Water pump components used on today's engines are not serviced separately. Therefore, in the event of water pump leakage or failure, it will be necessary to replace the complete pump assembly. While some of the older water pumps can be disassembled, it is not advisable to attempt repairs. It is more practical to replace the entire unit.

To remove the water pump, first drain the cooling system. Remove any hoses attached to the pump body. Remove the fan shroud, if so equipped, and loosen the fan pulley and remove all drive belts. Remove the fan blades, spacers, or fluid drive and pulley. To prevent silicone fluid from draining into the fluid fan drive bearings do not place the drive unit with the shaft pointing downward. Remove the bolts attaching the water pump to the engine. Remove the water pump, and discard the used gasket.

To install a new pump, coat a new gasket with a sealer, and install the pump and gasket to the engine. Tighten all bolts to manufacturer's specifications. After the pump has been installed, rotate the shaft by hand to make sure it turns freely.

Install the pulley, blades, and fluid drive unit. Inspect the fan belt, replace the belt if it is worn or if the plies have separated. Install the belt, and tighten to the correct specified tension. Not enough tension will permit slippage while too much tension may

Engine Cooling Systems

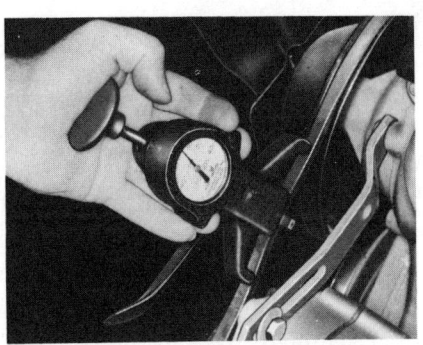

Fig. 6-21. Checking fan belt tension with a tension gage. (Chevrolet Div., General Motors Corp.)

cause rapid wear of the pump bearings and other units drive off the same belt.

Fan belt tension is generally adjusted by loosening the bracket bolt on the alternator and moving the alternator outward to tighten. The tension can be checked with a tension gage as shown in Fig. 6-21. Depending on the manufacturer's specifications, the gage should show a tension of 70 to 140 pounds.

The belt tension can also be checked by applying five pounds of pressure at a point midway between the pulleys; the belt should be deflected one-quarter to three-quarters of an inch depending upon the manufacturer's specifications.

Install the hoses and fill the system with the proper coolant solution. Check for leaks. Install the radiator shroud.

Thermostat

Check the operation of the thermostat by placing it in a pan of hot water which is 25° hotter than the temperature marked on the thermostat. With the thermostat completely under water, the thermostat valve should be fully open.

Repeat the above operation in water which is 10° colder than the temperature marked on the thermostat. Under such conditions, the thermostat valve should be fully closed. Replace the thermostat if it fails to open or close, if the valve does not seat properly, or if the thermostat is damaged.

Radiator

To repair a leaking radiator properly, the radiator should be removed from the vehicle. The radiator should be tested for leaks under a low air pressure (12 to 16 psi) while submerged in water. Leaks should be repaired by soldering. If the radiator shows indications that the water passages are clogged, the condition can usually be corrected by reverse flushing of the radiator core with water and compressed air or by circulating a suitable cleaning solution through the radiator by means of a motor-driven pump.

If the above operation fails to clear the passages, the radiator may have to be disassembled for further cleaning. The radiator is disassembled by unsoldering and removing the inlet and outlet tanks from the core. To clear the passages, a rod of the correct diameter is pushed through each passage while flushing with water. Following this the tanks are installed and resoldered. Replace all collapsed radiator hoses or hoses that have rotted inner linings.

Pressure Test Cooling System

A cooling system that requires frequent addition of water or antifreeze solution to maintain the proper level in the radiator should be thoroughly inspected for leaks. Make the inspection while the engine is cold since rapid evaporation on a hot engine makes it almost impossible to detect a small leak. Rust and dye stains from antifreeze solutions at hose connections are sure indications of a leak. When leaks are not readily apparent, the cooling system should be tested with a pressure tester, Fig. 6-22.

To pressure test the cooling system, fill the radiator to one-half inch below the filler neck. Wipe the filler neck surface clean, and install the pressure tester. Operate the pump on the tester until the pressure on the gage reads 15 psi. A steady pressure gage reading indicates that the cooling system is satisfactory.

If the pressure on the gage drops, examine the radiator core, engine block, water pump, and hose connections for leaks.

If no external leaks are found, remove the tester from the radiator and run the engine until operating temperatures are reached. Re-install the tester and apply a pressure of 15 psi to the cooling system. Increase engine speed to approximately half throttle. A fluctuating gage needle generally indicates a leaking head gasket.

To determine which head gasket leaks on a V-type engine, disconnect the spark plug wires on one bank and operate the engine on the other bank. A fluctuating needle indicates that the gasket on the operating cylinder bank leaks. If the gage needle holds steady, the opposite cylinder bank is the one that leaks.

If the above tests fail to indicate a leak, reconnect the spark plugs and quickly accelerate the engine several times. An excessive amount of water coming out of the tail pipe indicates either a leaking head gasket, a cracked cylinder block, or a cracked cylinder head.

The following method may also be used to check the entire cooling system for leakage.

Engine Cooling Systems

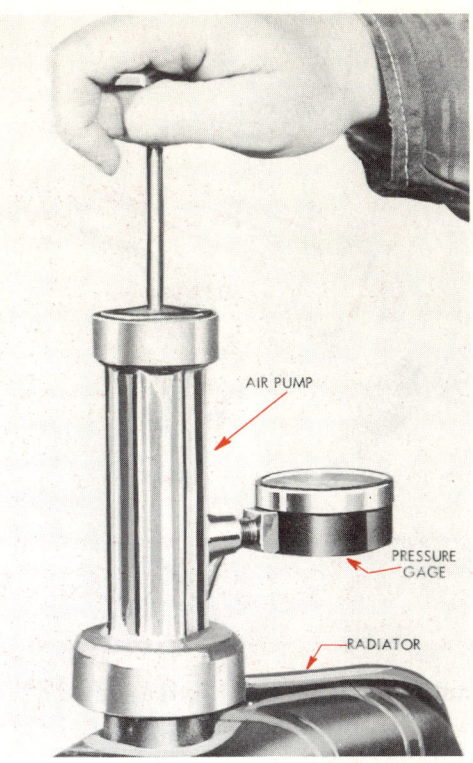

Fig. 6-22. Using a pressure tester to check the cooling system for leaks. (Plymouth Div., Chrysler Corp.)

Shut off the engine, and slowly rotate the radiator cap after first placing a cloth over the cap to avoid the danger of being burned. After the pressure is released, remove the cap. Wet the rubber sealing surface of the cap, and reinstall cap tightly on the radiator.

Disconnect the wire from the engine temperature sending unit, and remove the sending unit. With the cap tightly installed, only a small amount of coolant will escape when the unit is removed. Install an adapter fitting with an air pressure connection on one end in place of the temperature sending unit.

Remove the radiator overflow hose from the clips. Make sure the hose is in good condition and tightly secured to the overflow tube. Insert the bottom end of the hose in a container of water.

Attach the pressure pump and gage to the adapter. Pressurize the system until bubbles appear in the container. Stop pumping. When bubbles no longer appear take a

Automotive Engines

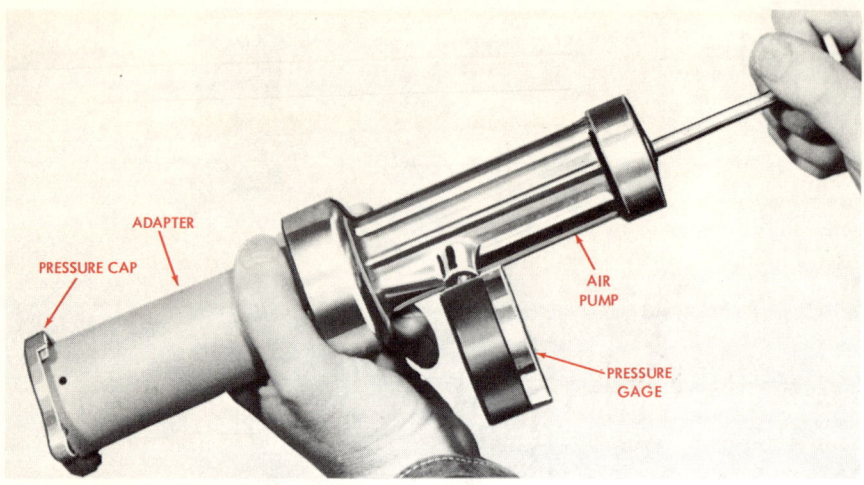

Fig. 6-23. Testing a pressure type radiator cap with a pressure tester. (Plymouth Div., Chrysler Corp.)

pressure gage reading. The reading should agree with the pressure marked on the cap. If the pressure exceeds cap specifications, replace the cap. If bubbles continue below pressure specifications, the cap is leaking and should be replaced.

If the cap pressure is within specifications, observe the gage readings for approximately two minutes. The pressure should not drop. If the pressure drops, check for leaks at any other units of the cooling system.

If no leaks are indicated, release the pressure, remove the adapter, and reinstall the temperature sending unit. Check the coolant, and replace any of the solution which may have been lost.

Never exceed the pressure indicated on the pressure cap while making the above test.

Test Pressure Radiator Cap

On sealed cooling systems, the radiator cap must seat properly on the filler neck to prevent pressure loss at this point.

Pressure type radiator caps are tested with the same tester employed to pressure test the cooling system. To test the radiator cap, install the adaptor and rubber seal on the tester, Fig. 6-23. Dip the radiator cap in water and install on the adaptor. With the pump apply 12 to 15 psi to the cap. If the cap fails to hold pressure within this range, replace the cap. Caps in vehicles with air conditioners should be tested at 15 to 16 psi.

Engine Cooling Systems

Checking On Your Knowledge

The following questions give you the opportunity to check up on yourself. If you have read the chapter carefully, you should be able to answer the questions. If you have any difficulty, read the chapter over once more so that you have the information well in mind before you go on with your reading.

DO YOU KNOW

1. What is the purpose of the fins on the cylinders of an air-cooled engine?
2. What is the normal operating temperature of a liquid-cooled engine?
3. How is circulation of the coolant brought about in thermosiphon types of cooling systems?
4. How is the circulation of coolant brought about in a pump circulating type of cooling system?
5. How does the radiator function in dissipating engine heat?
6. How do cellular radiators differ in construction from tubular radiators?
7. What is the purpose of the bypass employed in the cooling systems of some engines?
8. Why are the fan blades on some engines unevenly spaced?
9. What purpose do the baffles surrounding an engine serve?
10. What is the function of the thermostat in the cooling system?
11. What effect does raising the pressure on the coolant in a cooling system have upon the boiling point of the coolant?
12. What are some of the requirements that antifreeze solutions should meet to be safe for use in an automotive cooling system?
13. What effect does air that enters the cooling system have upon the cooling system?
14. How can you reverse flush an engine block and radiator?
15. How can you pressure test a cooling system?
16. What is the purpose of using a fluid drive fan?
17. How does a fluid fan operate?

Chapter

7 Engine Lubrication

This section discusses the basic principles of lubrication, types of engine lubricating systems, and the parts within a lubricating system. Methods of inspection and repair of the various parts of the lubricating system also are discussed.

Moving engine parts must be lubricated to overcome *friction* (the undesirable resistance to movement due to surfaces in contact). In the engine, friction must be overcome under varying temperatures, pressures, and speeds.

Under microscopic examination, all metals show rough surfaces regardless of how highly they have been polished, Fig. 7-1. If the bearing surfaces are allowed to rub against each other without lubrication, they will develop considerable friction and heat, resulting in excessive wear. This type of friction is termed *solid friction*.

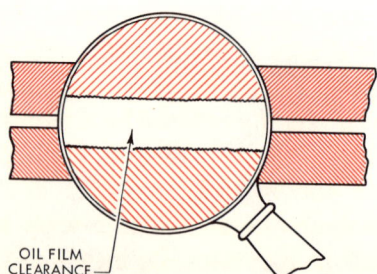

Fig. 7-1. Bearing surfaces appear rough when magnified.

Engine Lubrication

The friction between the moving parts of the engine is decreased by placing a film of oil between the parts so that they ride on the oil film instead of against each other. The bearings and other moving parts of an engine are fitted with clearances to accommodate this film of oil. When the parts are in motion, the oil in the bearing tends to split up into layers, the in-between layers sliding or rolling over each other. The resistance of the oil film to this splitting action results in an internal friction within the oil termed *fluid friction*.

The purpose of lubrication is to substitute fluid friction for solid friction. Since it takes less force to overcome fluid friction than solid friction, the result is less heat and wear between moving parts.

Engine Oils

The oil in the engine has several functions to perform if the engine is to give satisfactory service. The oil must remove heat from the parts it comes in contact with and prevent friction and wear by maintaining an unbroken film of oil between the moving and stationary metal surfaces. The oil must seal the space between the piston and cylinder wall to prevent blow-by of gases. In addition, the oil must clean the metal parts it comes in contact with and hold in suspension any dirt, metal, and carbon particles in the oil.

Adhesion and Cohesion

Oil is employed as an engine lubricant because its *adhesive* qualities (force which causes oil to stick to metals) enable it to cling firmly to metal surfaces. Its *cohesive* properties (force which holds oil together) enable it to hold itself together under a load or pressure that would squeeze out other liquids.

A thin film of oil is made up of a number of layers of molecules. The layer of oil molecules in contact with the metal surfaces is held there by the force of adhesion, while the in-between layers are held to each other by the force of cohesion. Efficient lubrication is obtained when the oil film contains sufficient layers of oil molecules to separate the metal surfaces.

Wedging Action. A shaft rotating within a bearing is lubricated by an oil film maintained by a wedging action, Fig. 7-2. The oil molecules that adhere to the surface of the shaft are carried along with the shaft as it rotates. By means of the

Automotive Engines

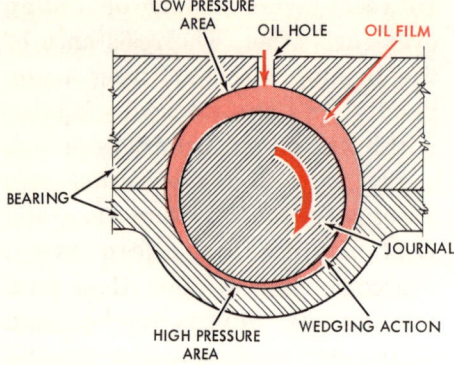

Fig. 7-2. Oil cohesion and journal rotation produce an oil wedging action in the journal bearing.

force of cohesion, this layer of molecules drags along adjacent layers of oil molecules. However, the shaft tends to be forced into the oil film due to its weight and loading conditions. This causes the shaft to assume an eccentric position in relation to the bearing. Due to the rotation of the shaft and the cohesion between the oil molecules, some of the layers of oil are forced or wedged under the shaft. This wedging action lifts the shaft and establishes a film of oil between the bearing surfaces. The wedging action develops considerable pressure in the oil film, creating high and low pressure areas. The oil supplied to the bearing always enters the bearing at the low pressure area.

Factors Determining Grade of Oil Used

Proper lubrication of engine bearing surfaces calls for the use of the thinnest oil that will stay in place and still maintain an oil film between the moving parts under operating conditions without causing excessive oil consumption. The manufacturer considers all of the factors involved when determining the proper grades of oil to use. His recommendations should be carefully followed.

The proper grade of lubricant to use for lubricating bearing surfaces is determined by three factors. These are (1) the rubbing or surface speed of the bearing, (2) the bearing clearance, and (3) the load imposed on the bearing. Various combinations of these factors occur due to the heat generated within the bearings, high or low temperatures outside of the bearings, and the presence of moisture, abrasive dust, and other contaminating substances. High rubbing or surface speeds require the use of an oil with considerable adhesive qualities to

Engine Lubrication

permit the layers of molecules next to the rubbing surfaces to cling to the surfaces.

Bearing Speed and Clearance. The clearance between the journal and its bearing is determined primarily by the speed at which the journal rotates. Journals which revolve at high speed are fitted to less clearance than journals which revolve at slow speeds and, as a result, require the use of lighter oil to maintain an oil film.

Bearing Load. The oil must be able to maintain an oil film in the bearing while the bearing is under a load. The ability of an oil to stay in place in a bearing is determined by the cohesive qualities of the oil and is measured in terms of *viscosity*. Viscosity is a measure of the resistance to flow. Heavy oils have a high viscosity, while thin or light oils have a low viscosity.

Classification of Engine Oils

Oils are classified according to their viscosity numbers (or viscosity indices). Low viscosity numbers, such as SAE 10, indicate lightweight (thin) oils that pour readily. The higher SAE numbers, such as SAE 30 or SAE 40, represent the heavier (thicker) oils.

The letters, SAE, stand for the *Society of Automotive Engineers*. Motor oils used in automotive engines usually range from SAE 5 to SAE 40. The SAE viscosity number indicates whether the oil is light or heavy, but does not indicate other properties or quality factors.

Some oils are designed to combine the easy starting characteristics of the lower viscosity oils with the warm weather operating characteristics of the higher viscosity oils. These are called "multi-viscosity" oils and are rated SAE 5W-20, SAE 10W-30, etc., depending on the viscosity range. Engine oil viscosity recommendations may vary with different manufacturers. Always follow the manufacturer's specifications.

In the absence of specific recommendations, when temperatures range between $-10°F$ and $+32°F$ and a single grade engine oil is to be used, SAE 10W is generally recommended. If a multi-viscosity oil is preferred, SAE 10W-30 or 10W-40 would be used. If temperatures are consistently below $-10°F$, SAE 5W or multi-viscosity SAE 5W-20 is recommended. SAE 5W or 5W-20 oil is not recommended for sustained high-speed driving.

When outside temperatures are consistently above $32°F$, a single grade oil of SAE 30 is usually acceptable or a multi-viscosity oil of 10W-30 or 10W-40 is satisfactory.

In addition to the viscosity numbers, API (*American Petroleum Institute*) grades oil by a certified sequence test method, according to the type of service for which the grade of oil is best suited. The grades are ML, MM, and MS for gasoline or other spark-ignited engines and DG and DS for diesel engines. These oils differ in the additives they contain as well as in other characteristics. Therefore, the same SAE numbered oils may have different service ratings. The oils are graded according to type of service, as follows:

ML: generally suitable for gasoline engines operating under light or moderate conditions.

MM: generally suitable for gasoline engines operating under moderate to severe conditions.

MS: generally suitable for gasoline engines operating under unfavorable or severe conditions.

DG: generally suitable in diesel engines operating under normal service conditions.

DS: generally suitable in diesel engines operating under severe service conditions.

An engine oil performance classification system recently developed jointly by SAE, ASTM (*American Society for Testing Materials*) and API is replacing the former "MS" designation with the designation "SE". Engine oil service classification "SE" describes an oil which provides more protection from high and low temperature engine deposits, wear, rust, and corrosion. It is recommended that an oil with an "SE" designation be used in automobile gasoline engines manufactured after 1968.

Oil Contamination and Sludge Formation

Lubricating oils do not wear out with use. However, the various conditions and temperatures under which the lubricating oil must function cause it to become contaminated. After a period of operation, contamination affects the lubricating value of the oil to such an extent that it becomes unsuitable for further use. Contamination occurs because of oxidation, dilution, water, formation of carbon, lead compounds, metals, dust, and dirt. These contaminants, when mixed with the oil, contribute to the formation of sludge in an engine. A chemical analysis of sludge is given in Table 7-1.

Sludge may be described as a black, brown, or gray deposit having the consistency of soft mud. It is formed in engines as a result of operation at low engine temperatures during starting, warming up, and idling periods.

During cold engine operation, condensed water vapor reaches the crankcase oil, where it emulsifies with the other contaminants usually present in used engine oil to form a pasty mass.

Sludge is decidedly harmful to engine performance. It clogs oil pump intake screens and oil lines, reduces the oil supply, causes bearing failures, and damages other engine parts that depend

Engine Lubrication

TABLE 7-1. ANALYSIS OF SLUDGE DEPOSITS FOUND IN CRANKCASES OF AUTOMOTIVE ENGINES OPERATING UNDER NORMAL DRIVING CONDITIONS

Sludge Composition	As Recieved (Percentage)	Oil-Free (Percentage)
Oil	83.1	....
Water	6.2	36.7
Gasoline diluent	4.7	27.8
Free carbon (fuel soot)	1.6	9.5
Oxidized material	0.8	4.7
Free mineral matter	3.6	21.3
(Chief components: lead, iron)	....	....
(Minor components: aluminum, copper, silica)	....	....

upon pressure lubrication. When sludge is present in an engine, oil filters clog quickly and cease to function. Valves and rings stick when sludge is circulated with the oil. Sludge also clogs oil rings, causing high oil consumption. The source of the products that cause sludge to form are as follows:

Oxidation. Oxidation occurs when a molecule of oxygen from the air attaches itself directly to an original oil molecule to make a more complex compound. A lubricant that is exposed to high temperatures and oxygen will eventually oxidize. The time required for oxidation and the extent to which it occurs depends on the temperature, the extent of exposure to oxygen, the presence of metals which hasten oxidation, and the ability of the lubricant to withstand oxidation.

Of the several products formed by oxidation, the two most objectionable are organic acids and a dark, sticky substance resembling tar. High engine temperatures activate the acids sufficiently to corrode engine parts, particularly the engine bearings. The dark, sticky substance bakes on the engine parts, producing a varnish-like coating that often causes sticking valves and clogged and frozen piston rings.

Oxidation is usually a cumulative process because continued exposure to oxidizing conditions continues the reaction. It is also an accelerating process since the oxidized materials tend to increase the rate at which oxidation occurs. Oxidation occurs at a more rapid rate at high temperatures than at low temperatures.

Dilution. Dilution of the oil in the crankcase is caused by unburned gasoline in the combustion chamber working past the piston rings into the crankcase. Such dilution is common in cold weather operation, particularly if frequent starts and stops are made without allowing the engine to warm up sufficiently to evaporate the gasoline contained in the lubricating oil. Dilution of the lubricating oil lowers its viscosity. If viscosity drops too far, the oil may become too thin, causing excessive wear.

Water. During the combustion of the air-fuel mixture in an internal combustion engine, the oxygen in the air combines with the hydrocarbon structure of the fuel to form water, which is present in the combustion chamber as vapor. Under normal conditions, the major part of this water vapor passes harmlessly out of the exhaust. However, during cold engine operation, much of it condenses on the cold cylinder walls, and part of the water formed is scraped into the crankcase by the piston rings.

Some of this water vapor also reaches the crankcase directly as the result of piston blow-by, where it condenses on the relatively cold sides of the crankcase and oil pan. Under certain conditions, moisture in the air entering the crankcase through the breather will also condense on these relatively cold surfaces. Cooling system leaks may also cause water in the engine crankcase.

One of the most harmful effects of water dilution is the formation of acid. This acid attacks the steel parts and bearings in the engine.

Carbon. The carbon that enters the lubricating oil is a fuel soot similar to lamp black and forms in the combustion chamber in rather large quantities under the rich mixture conditions during starting and warm-up. Incomplete combustion which accompanies cold engine operation also forms carbon. The carbon reaches the crankcase by mixing with the oil that is being returned to the crankcase by the piston rings. Some carbon also reaches the crankcase with the blow-by gases.

Lead Compounds. During the combustion of leaded gasoline, lead compounds are formed. These compounds are carried into the crankcase by mixing with the oil that is scraped off the cylinder walls by the piston rings. Lead is also carried into the crankcase by blow-by gases. Aside from the fact that these compounds are present in sludge that forms in the crankcase, they are not harmful.

Metals. As a result of normal wear, lubricating oil is contaminated by powdered metals in varying amounts. Iron is the most common metal found mixed with the lubricating oil. It originates in the normal wear of such engine parts as piston rings, pistons, and cylinder walls.

At low operating temperatures, water vapor condenses. The con-

Engine Lubrication

densed vapor rusts metal parts and increases wear. The condensed water vapor also combines with combustion gases to form acids which cause corrosion. The accelerated wear and corrosion increase the amount of iron powder in the oil. Where aluminum pistons, copper-lead bearings, and other metals are used, small amounts of these metals will also be found in the oil.

Dust and Dirt. Dust and dirt enter the engine through the carburetor air intake and through the crankcase ventilating system. These contaminants, along with lead salts from leaded fuels and metal particles from engine parts, constitute the source of insoluble mineral matter (matter that cannot be dissolved) that is usually found in sludge.

All quality oils available at the present time contain some form of detergent. Generally the greater amount of detergent the more costly the oil. The detergent additive acts to hold the foreign materials, such as the matter formed by oxidation, carbon, lead compounds, dilution, and other particles in suspension.

Lubricating Systems

Several different types of lubricating systems have been employed to provide efficient lubrication of the internal moving parts of an engine. The various systems supply oil to the moving parts of the engine by splash, by gravity, by pressure feed, or by some combination of these methods. All present day automotive engines utilize a full force feed pressure system whereby oil under pressure is directed to the various moving parts. The splash and circulating pump system, as well as the splash and pressure system, is no longer used in automotive engines.

In the force feed type of oiling system, Fig. 7-3, oil is forced by an oil pump to all main and connecting rod bearings, camshaft bearings, valve lifters, and the timing gears or chain driving the camshaft. In overhead valve engines, the push-rod ball and socket joints and the rocker arm bearings also are lubricated under pressure. Drilled passages in the crankshaft carry the oil from the main bearings to the connecting rod bearings. The cylinder walls, pistons, and piston pins are lubricated by the oil spray thrown off from the connecting rods and crankshaft. Some engines have an oil spray hole drilled in the upper half of the connecting rod bearing. As the crankshaft revolves, this hole aligns itself with

Automotive Engines

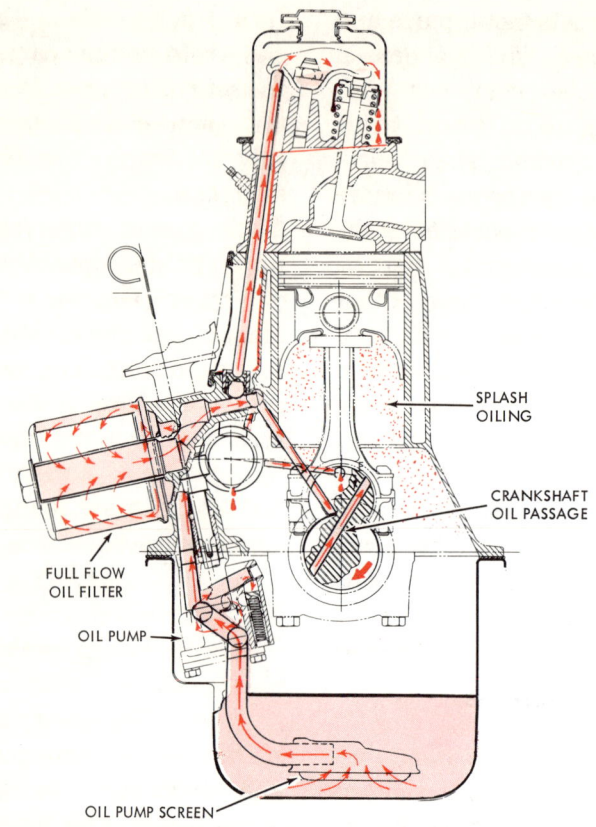

Fig. 7-3. Force feed oil system. (Chevrolet Div., General Motors Corp.)

the oil hole in the crankshaft once every revolution, throwing a spray of oil against the cylinder walls. Some engines had a pressure lubricated piston pin. Oil was forced to the piston pin bushings through a drilled passage in the connecting rod shaft.

All the present-day four-stroke-cycle gasoline and diesel engines are lubricated by a force feed type of lubricating system.

Parts Of An Engine Lubricating System

The main parts of an engine lubricating system are the oil pump, oil strainer, oil pressure regulator, oil pan, and oil filter. Present-day engines employ a system of crankcase ventilation to reduce contami-

Engine Lubrication

nation of the lubricating oil and prevent emissions to the atmosphere.

Oil Pumps

The oil pump circulates oil under pressure through the drilled passages and oil lines to the engine parts which require lubrication. The oil pump is generally located inside the engine crankcase, where it is submerged in the oil. Some may be located outside of the engine crankcase above the oil level. When located outside of the crankcase, drilled passages and oil lines connect the oil pump to the supply of oil in the crankcase. The oil pump is driven by means of a spiral or worm gear on the camshaft.

Oil pumps are classified according to their design as gear pumps, rotor pumps, gear and crescent pumps, or sliding vane type pumps.

Gear Pump. The gear type of oil pump consists of two meshed gears enclosed in a close-fitting housing. A gear type oil pump is shown in Fig. 7-4 (left). The drive gear of the oil pump is securely attached to the shaft which drives the pump, while the other gear acts as an idler gear, revolving on a stub shaft pressed into the housing.

In operation, the two gears revolve in opposite directions. The spaces between the gear teeth form pockets which carry the oil from the inlet side of the pump to the outlet side, where it is discharged, Fig. 7-4 (right). The oil is prevented from returning to the inlet side of the pump by the close fit of the meshed gear teeth and the close fit between the gears and the stationary parts of the pump body.

Rotor Pump. The rotor type oil pump employs an inner and outer

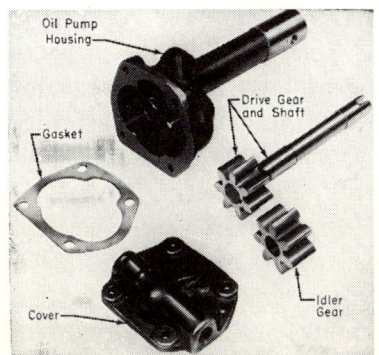
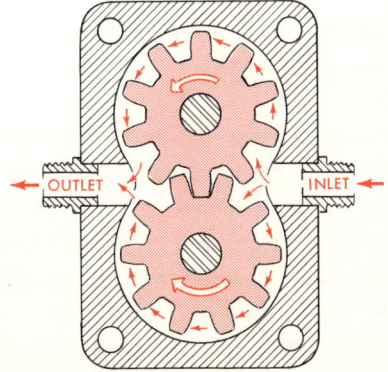

Fig. 7-4. In this disassembled gear type oil pump, the gears function like impellers and force the oil through the outlet and to the engine bearings.

Automotive Engines

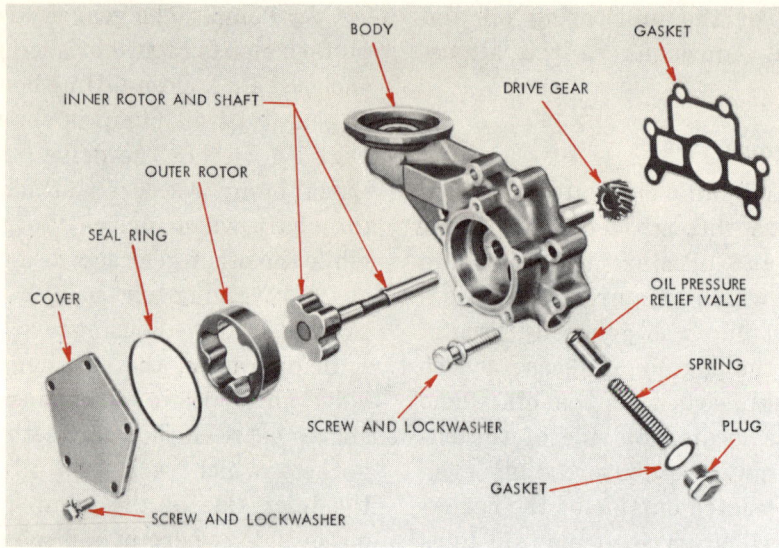

Fig. 7-5. An exploded view of a rotor type oil pump. (Plymouth Div., Chrysler Corp.)

rotor instead of gears in the pump body, Fig. 7-5. The inner rotor has external teeth and is attached to the pump shaft. The outer rotor has internal teeth and fits in the oil pump body. The pump drive shaft is located off-center in the pump body, allowing the internal and external teeth of the two rotors to mesh on one side of the pump body.

When the pump shaft revolves, the inner rotor causes the outer rotor to revolve in the pump body. The revolving rotors form pockets which become filled with oil at the inlet side of the oil pump and discharge at the outlet side. The close fit between the teeth of the two rotors prevents the oil from returning to the intake side of the pump.

Gear and Crescent Pump. The gear and crescent oil pump, Fig. 7-6, is mounted on the front of the engine. The drive gear is mounted directly on the crankshaft. When the drive gear revolves, the driven gear, which is an idler gear, also turns. The crescent remains in a fixed position. The space between the gear teeth and crescent forms a pocket which carries the oil from the inlet side to the discharge side of the pump housing.

When excessive wear occurs between the gears and housing and/or gears and crescent, the entire assembly must be replaced.

Sliding Vane Pump. The sliding vane pump consists of a slotted

Engine Lubrication

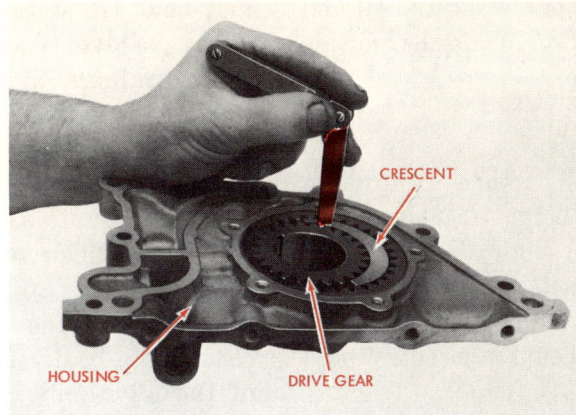

Fig. 7-6. Checking clearance on a disassembled gear and crescent type oil pump. (Chevrolet, Div., General Motors Corp.)

rotor mounted in a housing, Fig. 7-7. Four vanes are mounted in the slots. As the rotor turns, centrifugal force moves the vanes outward against the pump housing. The vanes act in the same manner as

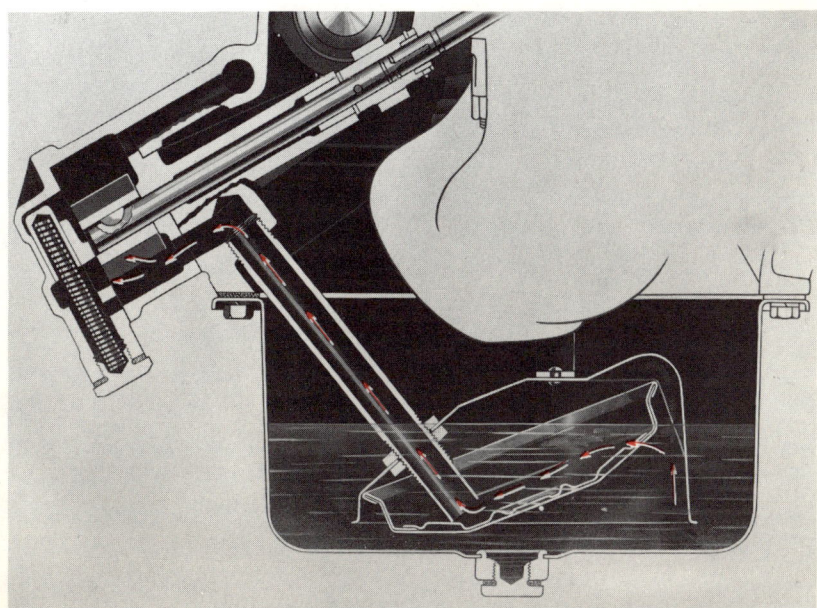

Fig. 7-7. Stationary oil strainer assembly. (Oldsmobile Div., General Motors Corp.)

Automotive Engines

gear teeth in pocketing the oil and forcing it out of the discharge side of the pump.

Oil Strainer

To prevent particles of foreign matter from being circulated with the oil to the engine parts, a fine mesh screen acts as a strainer and is located in the oil pan so all the oil entering the oil pump must pass through it.

The oil strainer may be attached directly to the oil pump or may be connected to the pump by means of an oil suction tube. The strainer may be of the stationary type, Fig. 7-8 or the pivot type, Fig. 7-9. Pivot type strainers are connected so they are free to float near the top of the oil level. A stop prevents the float from moving more than a limited amount. As sediment and foreign particles tend to settle to the bottom of the oil pan, the pivoting action of the strainer causes clean oil to be drawn from the top of the oil supply. If the oil level changes, the oil strainer will follow the top of the oil level, maintaining a constant supply of clean oil to the pump.

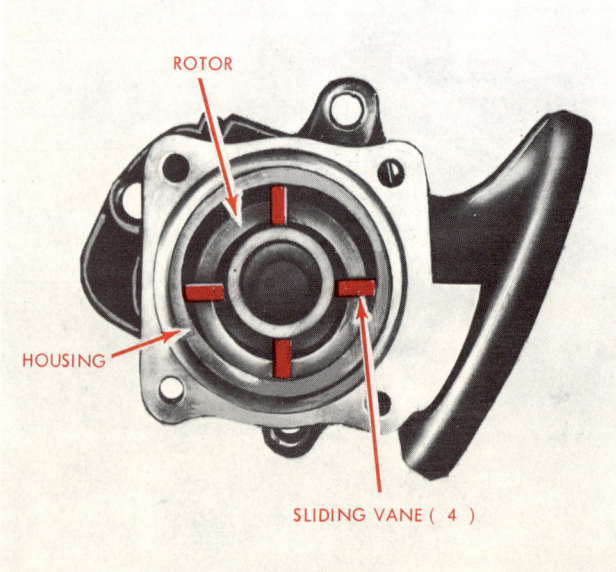

Fig. 7-8. Sliding vane type oil pump (disassembled). (Ford Div., Ford Motor Co.)

Engine Lubrication

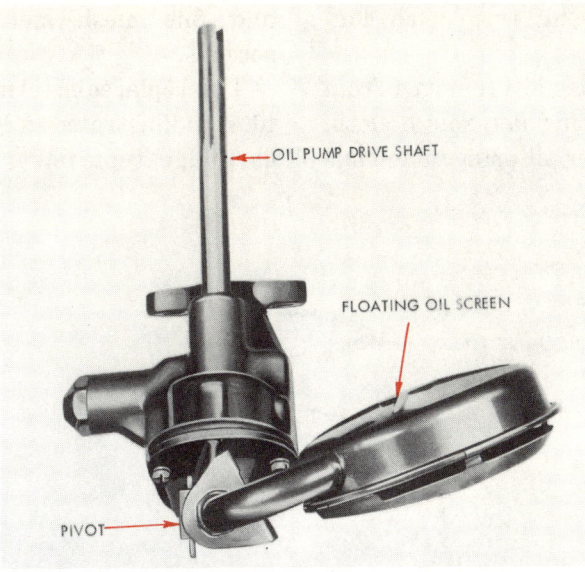

Fig. 7-9. The pivot type oil strainer screen follows the level of the oil. (Buick Div., General Motors Corp.)

Oil Pressure Relief Valve

The oil pump is capable of supplying a greater amount of oil than is required for lubrication of the engine parts. To prevent the oil pressure from becoming excessive at high engine speeds, an oil pressure relief valve is placed in the oil line. The relief valve may be located in the engine crankcase or may be a part of the oil pump. Fig. 7-7 illustrates an oil pressure relief valve.

The oil pressure relief valve consists of a ball or plunger that seats against an opening in the oil line and is held in place by the pressure of a coil spring. No oil flows past the oil pressure relief valve until the oil pressure exceeds the pressure exerted by the spring. When this occurs, the ball or plunger is lifted off the seat, and the excess oil passes through the relief valve returning to the crankcase through a drilled passage. The spring can be changed if it is necessary to vary the pressure.

Oil Filters

During normal engine operation, the lubricating oil tends to become contaminated with carbon, dust, and other impurities. Oil filters are employed on all late model automotive vehicles to remove solid particles from the oil, reducing the wear

Automotive Engines

that would result from such contamination.

Solid particles are removed from the oil by forcing it through cloth, paper, or other filtering materials and fine mesh metal or fabric screens.

The replaceable element type oil filter is illustrated in Fig. 7-10. The cartridge type filter unit is illus-

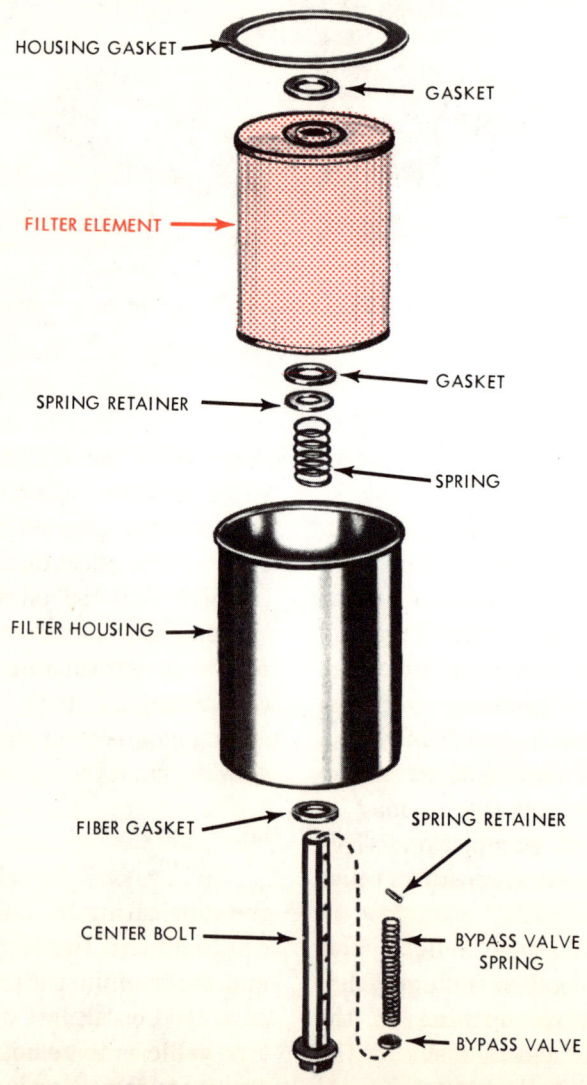

Fig. 7-10. Element type oil filter. (Ford Div., Ford Motor Co.)

Engine Lubrication

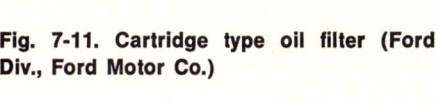

Fig. 7-11. Cartridge type oil filter (Ford Div., Ford Motor Co.)

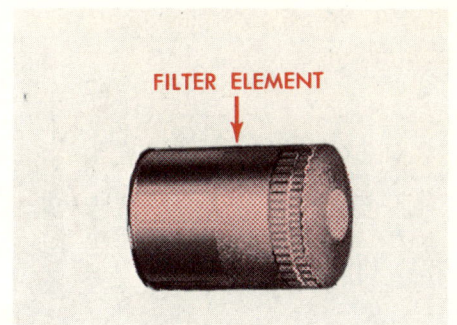

trated in Fig. 7-11. Oil from the engine crankcase enters the filter and flows through the filtering material, trapping the dust, carbon, and other impurities. The filter continues to trap foreign matter until it becomes clogged when it must be replaced.

The cartridge type filter is commonly used on today's engines. It has basically the same filtering characteristics as the element type filter except that the filter element is a permanent part of the housing, Fig. 7-11. The bypass valve will be located in the adapter housing rather than in the center bolt. The entire unit is discarded when the filter is replaced.

Two types of oil filtration systems have been used on automotive vehicles. The most common of these, is the full flow system. The other was the bypass system. Most of the early oil filters were of the bypass type. In this system only a fraction of the oil passed through the filter in a given period of time; most of the oil bypassed the filter. While all the oil eventually passed through the filter, the filtering action was not as great as when a greater amount of oil is constantly passing through the filter. All filters being installed on today's engines are of the full flow type.

The full flow oil filter system is designed to filter all the oil going to the working parts of the engine, Fig. 7-12. In such systems, the oil is picked up by the oil pump and delivered under pressure directly to the filter. The oil flows through the filter to the main oil manifold or gallery, where it is distributed to the working parts of the engine. The main oil pressure relief valve in the system functions only to maintain the oil pressure at a constant value as the engine speed increases, and to return the excess oil to the crankcase.

A second relief valve, functioning as a part of the oil filter, as-

Automotive Engines

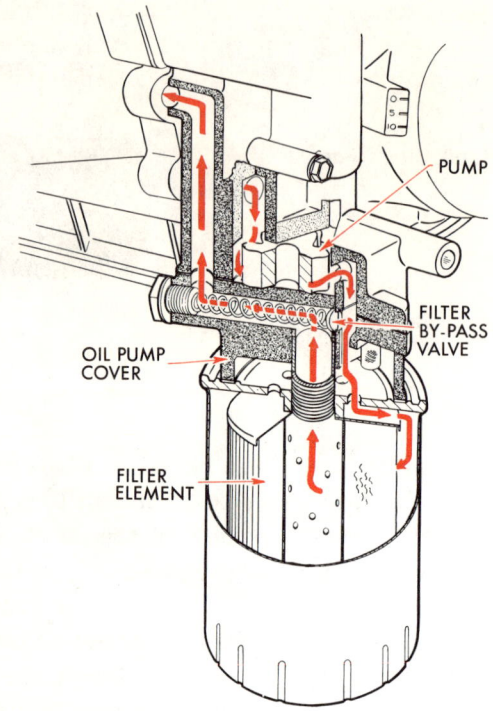

Fig. 7-12 Full flow filtration filters all the oil pumped to the working parts of the engine (Buick Div., General Motors Corp.)

sures an adequate supply of oil to the engine parts in case the filter becomes clogged. When the filter becomes so clogged that oil cannot be forced through it, this valve opens and permits unfiltered oil to pass directly to the oil manifold and engine working parts.

Oil Pan

The oil pan used on automotive engines is made of pressed steel, Fig. 7-13. The oil pan is attached to the engine block by means of cap screws. Gaskets made of cork or of "vellumoid" gasket material are used between the oil pan and crankcase at the sides and ends of the oil pan to provide an oil-tight enclosure. In addition to enclosing the crankshaft and serving as a reservoir for the oil supply, the oil pan serves to cool the lubricant when the engine is in operation.

The oil pan is constructed so that the oil will not surge or flow away from the oil pump when the vehicle is accelerated rapidly or brought to a rapid stop. Such surging would result in an insufficient supply of

Engine Lubrication

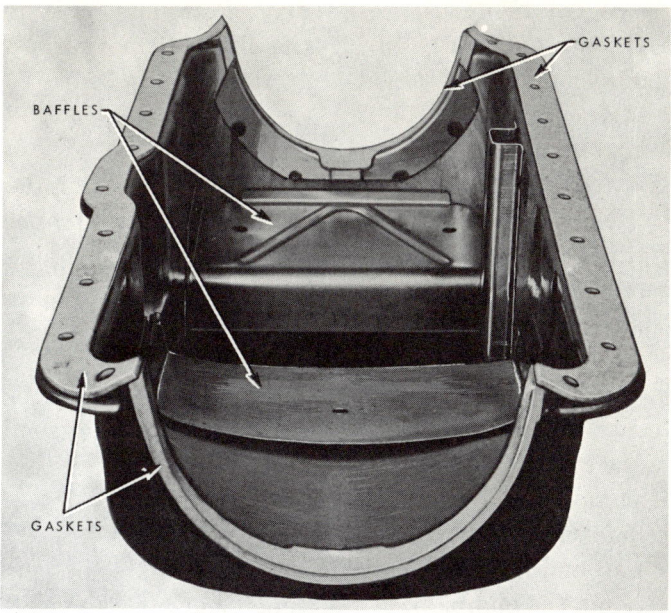

Fig. 7-13. Pressed steel oil pan. One of the functions of the oil pan is to cool the oil during engine operation. (Plymouth Div., Chrysler Corp.)

oil at the pump during the period of acceleration or braking. Sometimes baffle plates attached to the sides of the oil pan are located on one or both sides of the oil pump to prevent such surging.

Crankcase Ventilation

Engines are equipped with crankcase ventilating systems to aid in preventing harmful contamination and dilution of the lubricating oil. Prior to the early 1960's the crankcase was ventilated to the atmosphere. All recent engines utilize a closed ventilating system whereby the vapors developed within the engine are drawn into the combustion chamber where they are burned. The emission control system is discussed in Chaper 8.

Inspection and Repair

The inspection and repair of the oil units must be carefully performed if the engine oiling system is to supply an adequate amount of oil to the moving parts of the engine.

275

Disassembly of Oil Pump

The oil pump may be contained within the engine crankcase, built into the timing chain cover, or attached to the crankcase outside of the engine. Remove the oil pump from the engine.

On oil pumps that have an oil screen attached to the pump, remove the oil screen and screen cover. Remove the cap screws that hold the pump cover to the pump body and remove the cover, Fig. 7-14.

If the oil pump has a built-in oil pressure relief valve, remove the relief valve nut, and lift the spring and plunger from the pump.

Depending upon the type of oil pump being disassembled, remove the oil pump driven gear or the outer rotor from the pump.

On oil pumps that have the oil pump and distributor drive gear attached to the oil pump shaft, drive the pin out of the oil pump drive gear, and press the gear off the shaft. Remove the pump shaft from the pump body.

Cleaning

Clean all parts of the oil pump, oil screen, and oil pressure relief valve thoroughly. Blow out all oil passages in the pump body with compressed air. If the engine is disassembled, clean out all oil passages in the cylinder block. If the engine is not disassembled, clean out all accessible oil passages.

Replacement of Oil Pump

It is possible, in most cases, to repair most oil pumps. But, if wear occurs in one part of the pump, generally the remaining parts, including the housing, will be worn to some extent. Therefore, it is usually advisable to replace the entire unit if some part or parts indicate wear.

Inspect Oil Strainer

Replace a damaged oil screen or strainer assembly. If a screen has collapsed, straighten the screen and the screen supports.

Inspect Oil Pressure Relief Valve

Replace the ball or plunger if the seating surface shows signs of wear. Replace the relief valve spring if the spring is stretched or is weak. If the springs are color coded, replace with a spring of the same color. Install the ball or

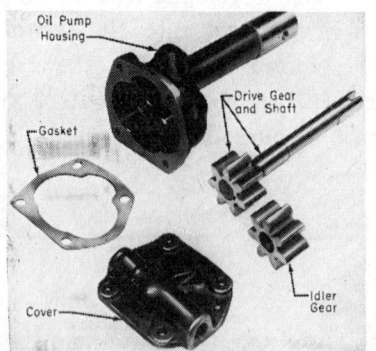

Fig. 7-14. Disassembled gear type oil pump. (Chevrolet Div., General Motors Corp.)

Engine Lubrication

plunger, spring, and adjusting bolt and nut in the cylinder block or oil pump.

Replace Oil Filter

For efficient filtering of the engine oil, the filter should be replaced at the manufacturer's specified time. Manufacturers generally recommend that the oil filter be replaced after about 6,000 miles of service or every six months.

When replacing the cartridge type oil filter, remove the housing by turning the center attaching bolt. It may be necessary to lightly tap the housing after loosening the center bolt so as to break the housing loose from the gasket. Discard the filter element and thoroughly clean the housing in a solvent. Remove the old gasket. Clean the matching surface on the block. Coat a new gasket with oil, and install in the recess in the block. Place the new filter element in the housing, and replace the housing. Tighten the attaching bolt to approximately four foot-pounds using a torque wrench.

The element type filter assembly is a self-contained filtering unit of the disposable type. Remove the filter by turning the entire unit counterclockwise. Clean the surface on the block. Place a light film of oil on the gasket which is attached to the element. Hand tighten the unit on the engine block. Tighten the element approximately one-half turn with a special wrench as shown in Fig. 7-15. When a new filter is installed, an additional quart of oil should be added. Oper-

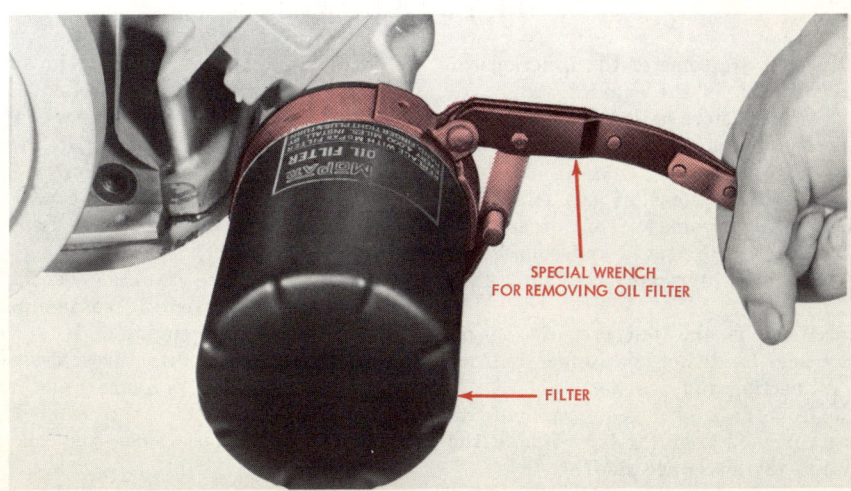

Fig. 7-15. Replacing the element type oil filter. (Plymouth Div., Chrysler Corp.)

ate the engine for approximately five minutes and check for oil leaks.

Service Oil Pan

The location of the oil pan subjects it to damage from obstructions and flying stones that may dent or distort the pan. As some oil pans have little clearance between the oil pan and connecting rods, sometimes such dents or distortion can result in the connecting rods striking the oil pan.

The oil pan should be examined for stripped threads in the drain plug hole, dents, distortion or loose baffles. A badly distorted or dented oil pan or one with stripped threads in the drain plug hole should be replaced. Oil pans with minor dents or loose baffles can be repaired.

A dented oil pan which is not distorted should have the dents hammered out to restore the oil pan to its original shape. Loose baffles can be resoldered to the sides of the pan. Take care to locate them in their original position, Fig. 7-13.

Checking On Your Knowledge

The following questions give you the opportunity to check up on yourself. If you have read the chapter carefully, you should be able to answer the questions. If you have any difficulty, read the chapter over once more so that you have the information well in mind before you go on with your reading.

DO YOU KNOW

1. What are some of the functions of lubricating oil in the engine?
2. What factors determine the proper grade of lubricating oil to use in an engine?
3. What are some of the effects of sludge in the crankcase of an engine?
4. How are the main and connecting rod bearings lubricated in force-feed systems?
5. What is the purpose of the oil spray hole located in the upper half of the connecting rod bearing?
6. How does the gear type of oil pump carry oil from the inlet side of the pump to the discharge side?
7. How is the outer rotor of a rotor type oil pump driven?
8. How is the oil pressure in an engine lubricating system controlled?
9. What controls the amount of oil flowing through the oil filter in the bypass type of oil filtering system?
10. How does the full flow type of oil filtration system differ in operation from the bypass system?
11. How does the crankcase ventilation system aid in preventing contamination and dilution of the engine oil?
12. How do manufactures designate the pressure of oil pressure relief valve springs?
13. What purpose does the oil pan serve?
14. What is the purpose of the baffles located in the oil pan?

Emissions Systems

Chapter **8**

The National Air Quality Standards Act of 1970 states that 90 percent of the pollutants in a passenger vehicle's exhaust, as compared with 1970 models, must be eliminated by 1976.

The automobile engine has been a major contributor to air pollution. It emits harmful invisible hydrocarbons, carbon monoxide, oxides of nitrogen, and lead. Although lead will foul control devices, it is considered a minor pollutant at the present time.

Hydrocarbons are compounds of hydrogen and carbons. Gasoline is made up of many different hydrocarbons. Evaporative losses and exhaust emissions both contain many different hydrocarbons which, when heated by the sun, react photochemically with other gases to form smog.

Carbon Monoxide is a colorless and odorless gas resulting from the combustion of carbon without sufficient air.

Oxides of nitrogen are natural by-products of combustion.

Lead is an additive used in gasoline to reduce engine detonation. A basic problem is that lead in this form fouls pollution control devices.

While it was known that small amounts of the hydrocarbons which make up gasoline are not burned in the combustion process, it was generally thought that these unburned hydrocarbons were emitted only through the exhaust system. Engineers have learned that only 60 percent of a vehicle's unburned hydrocarbons are emitted through the exhaust system while 20 percent escape through the crankcase breather and 20 percent through gasoline evaporation from the fuel tank and carburetor.

The major emissions from an

279

automobile engine without control devices are unburned hydrocarbons, carbon monoxide, and oxides of nitrogen. Of these, unburned hydrocarbons were recognized by engineers as being the major contributors to smog and were selected for emphasis in control. As with most technical advances, progress in controlling these emissions has been made in a series of steps, rather than in a single development.

Emission Controls

The first step in the development of emission control devices was the positive crankcase ventilation (PCV) system. This system, beginning on a nationwide basis with the 1963 models, has substantially reduced the 20 percent of pollutants that were being emitted through the crankcase ventilating system.

The second step dealt with the control of exhaust emissions. Exhaust control systems were installed nationwide on all 1968 model vehicles. This system, along with the PCV system which had been standard equipment, decreased the emissions of hydrocarbons by about 60 percent from the level emitted by an uncontrolled engine.

The third step dealt with evaporative emissions from the fuel tank and carburetor. Beginning in 1972, all vehicle engines had systems to control carburetor and gasoline tank evaporation. As a result, total emissions were reduced by approximately 80 percent compared to 1960 vehicles. The components

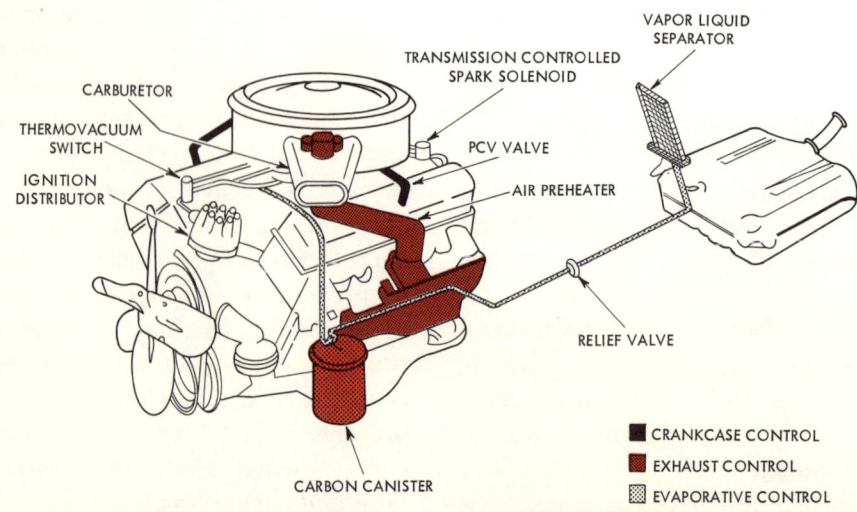

Fig. 8-1. Components of an emission system.

Emissions Systems

which have been added and/or changed to bring about a considerable reduction in automobile engine emissions are shown in Fig. 8-1.

Most engines have been modified to operate on low-lead or unleaded gasoline which, in itself, does not eliminate the air pollution problem but does reduce emissions of hydrocarbons and particulate matter. With the availability of unleaded gasoline, exhaust catalytic converters, exhaust manifold reactors, and exhaust recirculation systems are technically feasible for better emission control. It is also estimated that using unleaded gasoline will double the life of the spark plugs and extend the life of the muffler and tail pipe.

Newly developed components are being combined with present emission reducing units will make it possible to further reduce hydrocarbons by about 95%, carbon monoxide approximately 85% and oxides of nitrogen about 80% compared to 1960 emissions. They will be utilized on many automobile engines within a short time.

In all probability, the following

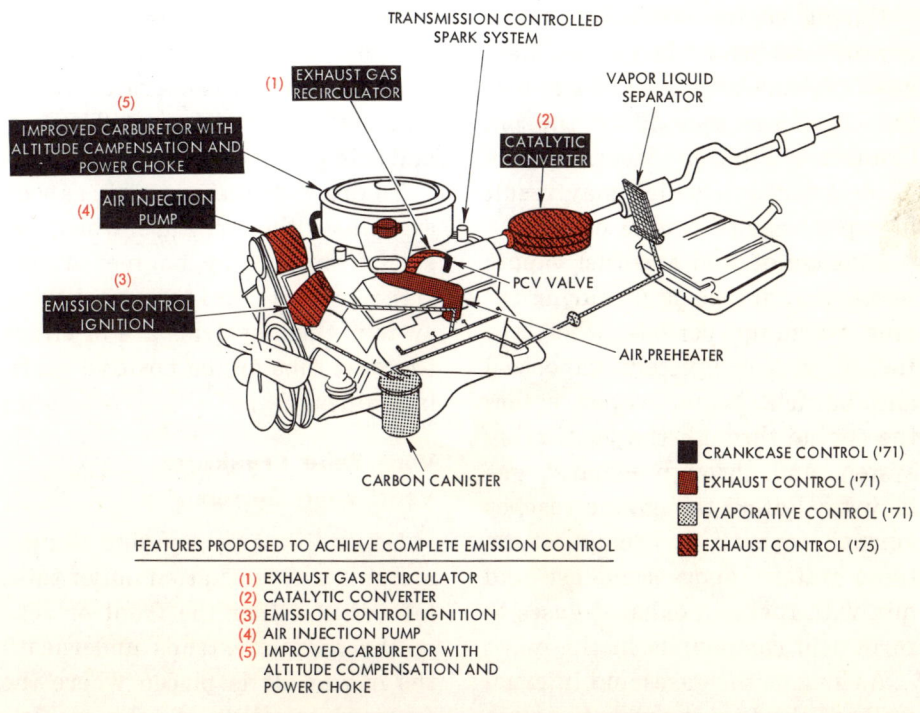

FEATURES PROPOSED TO ACHIEVE COMPLETE EMISSION CONTROL
(1) EXHAUST GAS RECIRCULATOR
(2) CATALYTIC CONVERTER
(3) EMISSION CONTROL IGNITION
(4) AIR INJECTION PUMP
(5) IMPROVED CARBURETOR WITH ALTITUDE COMPENSATION AND POWER CHOKE

Fig. 8-2. Complete emission control system.

units will be adopted in some form or other by some engine manufactures: (a) an improved carburetor with altitude compensator and power choke, and an electric fuel injector all of which are designed to provide a more precise air-fuel ratio, (b) a system which recirculates a small amount of exhaust gas to reduce combustion temperatures and thus reduce the formation of nitrogen oxides. A vital element would be a catalytic converter designed to chemically clean most of the remaining hydrocarbons and carbon monoxide emissions in the exhaust, and to change them into water vapor and carbon dioxide. An air injection pump is necessary in order to supply an adequate amount of air for the catalyst. Fig. 8-2 is a schematic drawing of an emission control system which should achieve the mandated emission restrictions.

Crankcase Ventilation Systems

During engine operation, water is produced inside the engine. Raw gasoline may also seep down into the crankcase and dilute the oil. Crankcase dilution causes engine oil deterioration which may result in rapid wear of engine parts.

Leakage of fuel and fuel vapors into the crankcase occur during engine warm-up periods when the fuel is not completely vaporized and burned. Water vapor enters the engine through the ventilating system and through exhaust gas blow-by. Before the engine reaches normal operating temperature, these water vapors condense and mix with fuel and exhaust gases to form acid compounds in the oil.

As long as the gases and internal walls of the engine are hot enough to keep the water vapor from condensing, no harm will result, but when the engine is operated at low temperatures moisture will collect, and acid compounds will be formed.

To draw off these vapors, as well as relieve the pressure which results from blow-by, engines are designed with a crankcase ventilating system. Such systems are of either the vent tube or the positive ventilation design.

Vent Tube Crankcase Ventilating System

Depending upon engine design, a crankcase ventilation outlet tube, located at either the front or rear of the engine, extends underneath the engine. It is placed where the forward motion of the vehicle

Emissions Systems

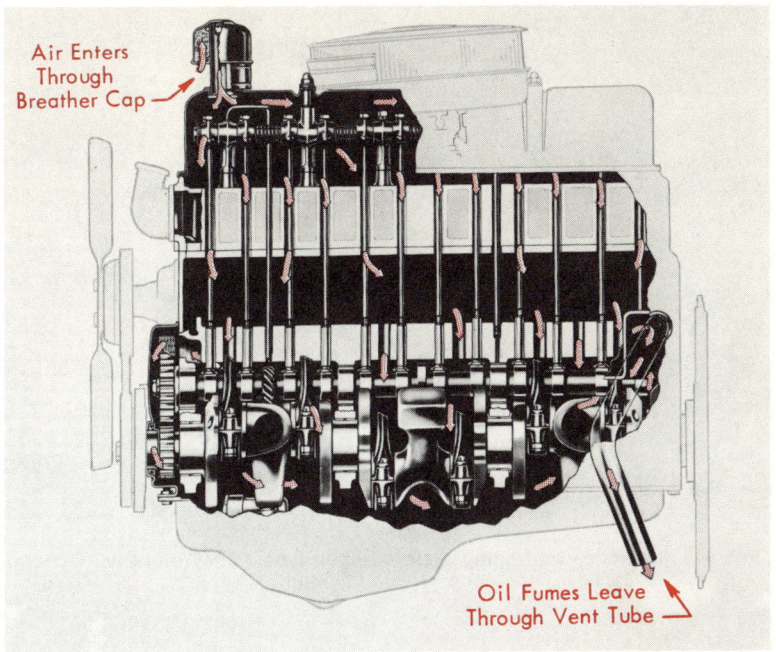

Fig. 8-3. Vent tube type ventilating system. (Ford Div., Ford Motor Co.)

causes a partial vacuum to form at the outlet tube, Fig. 8-3. The vacuum causes air to be drawn into the engine through a filter element of metal wool located in the oil filler cap. As the air passes through the crankcase, it picks up engine fumes and contaminating vapors. The crankshaft imparts a whirling motion to the air which helps direct it into the outlet tube, thus removing the fumes and vapors from the engine.

Positive Crankcase Ventilating Systems

To limit the emission of unburned hydrocarbons into the atmosphere (a factor contributing to smog), a positive crankcase ventilating (PCV) system has been mandated by Federal legislation. This system draws the unburned vapors through the intake manifold to the combustion chambers where they are burned.

There are two types of positive crankcase ventilating systems: the open type and the closed type. The only significant difference between them is in how the fresh air enters the engine. In both systems, the contaminated air is directed into the engine intake manifold and the combustion chambers.

Fig. 8-4 illustrates an open type

Automotive Engines

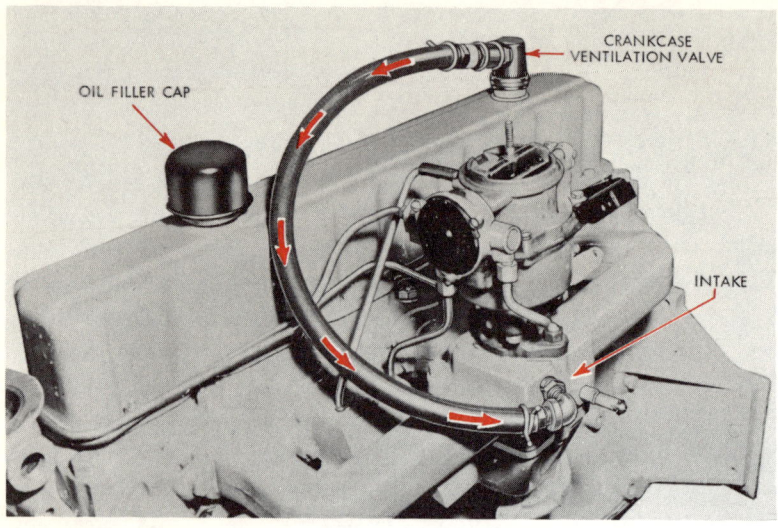

Fig. 8-4. Positive crankcase ventilating system—open type. (Chevrolet Div., General Motors Corp.)

of positive crankcase ventilating system. Fresh air enters the engine through a filter in the oil filler cap. The air then circulates through the valve chamber, engine crankcase, and the chamber containing the timing gears or chain, picking up contaminating fumes and vapors. The rotating action of the crankshaft causes the contaminated air to flow toward the back of the engine and into the rear section of the rocker arm cover, where a spring-loaded regulator valve, (PCV valve) is located. The air passes through the valve and a hose into the intake manifold and the engine cylinders, where it is burned.

The spring-loaded regulator valve (PCV) regulates the amount of air flow to meet changing conditions, Fig. 8-5. When the engine is idling, the intake manifold vacuum is high. The high vacuum overcomes the spring tension and moves the valve to the restricted or low flow position. With the restricted valve opening, there is a minimum of crankcase ventilation. When the engine speed increases, the engine manifold vacuum decreases. The spring now moves the valve to the fully open position, and maximum ventilation results.

The closed type of positive crankcase ventilating system is similar in construction with one exception: the fresh air is picked up at the air cleaner and directed into the engine through a connecting house, Fig. 8-

Emissions Systems

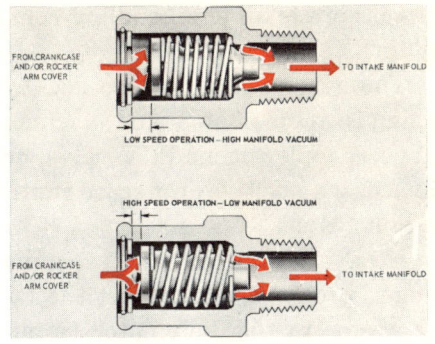

Fig. 8-5. Positive crankcase ventilating system PCV—regulator valve. (Ford Div., Ford Motor Co.)

6, instead of flowing through the oil filler cap. On one installation, the oil filler cap (breather cap) is sealed and connected to the air cleaner by a hose. Thus, the crankcase draws air through the air cleaner and the filler cap. On many late model engines an unvented oil filler cap is used with a tube leading directly from the air cleaner to the rocker arm cover. The PCV valve will be located on the opposite end of the cover on an in-line engine or in the other rocker arm cover for a V-8 engine. A hose is used to connect the PCV valve to the intake manifold.

In order for a closed crankcase ventilation system to obtain maximum reduction of emission, the engine must operate on a lean air-fuel mixture with a retarded ignition timing. With properly adjusted timing, the spark can occur at the peak of the compression

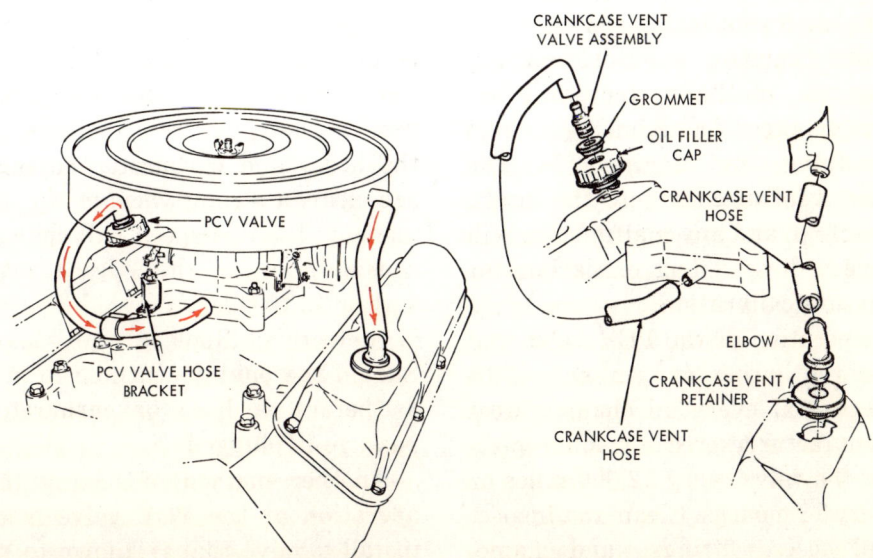

Fig. 8-6. Positive crankcase ventilating system—closed type. (Ford Div., Ford Motor Co.)

285

stroke where a more complete combustion will take place without noticeably affecting engine performance.

If operating properly, the closed crankcase ventilating system will virtually eliminate all crankcase emissions by redirecting the unburned blow-by gases and crankcase vapors back into the combustion chambers instead of venting them into the atmosphere.

For maximum emission reduction, the positive crankcase ventilation system must be clean so it functions properly, and the engine must be at peak operating efficiency.

Testing Positive Crankcase Ventilating System. A malfunctioning closed ventilation system may be indicated by a loping or rough engine idle. Do not disconnect the crankcase ventilating system when making carburetor adjustments. A removal of the system will adversely affect fuel economy, engine breathing, and engine life. The hoses vent directly into the intake manifold, and any malfunction will have a direct effect on carburetor mixture calibration.

Operation of the PCV valve and the ventilating system should be checked at every oil change. Most manufacturers recommend replacing the valve every 12,000 miles or every 12 months. Clean and inspect the hoses, fittings, and flame-arrestor. Check the system any time there is an engine idling complaint.

The system may be checked by using a tachometer and vacuum gage, a replacement PCV valve, or by using a positive crankcase ventilation tester.

If a tachometer and vacuum gage is to be used, connect the tachometer to the distributor terminal in the same manner as when checking idle speed and idle mixture. Connect the vacuum gage to a vacuum outlet on the intake manifold. Set the parking brake, start the engine, and bring it to normal operating temperature. Adjust the idle speed and idle mixture. Pull the PCV out of the rocker arm cover, and place a finger over the end of the valve to block off the flow of air. Check the tachometer reading for engine RPM change. A change of less than 50 RPM indicates a plugged system. To determine where the trouble is located, remove the valve from the hose. If the hoses and carburetor passage are clear, a strong vacuum will be present; the idle speed will change considerably or the engine may stall out. If this occurs, the valve is defective. Replace the valve. Should the engine continue to idle as before, a hose or carburetor passage is plugged.

Another method of testing the operation of the PCV valve is to install a valve that is known to be in good operating order, and com-

Emissions Systems

Fig. 8-7. Crankcase ventilation system tester. (Ford Div., Ford Motor Co.)

pare the engine idle condition with the prior idle condition. If the idle is then satisfactory, replace the valve after making sure all hoses and fittings are in good condition and all passages are clean and clear. If the engine continues to lope and/or run rough after the good valve has been installed and there are no leaks in the hoses or connections and all passageways are open, the ventilating system is not at fault. It will be necessary to check other engine components to locate the cause of the poor idle.

There are positive crankcase ventilation system testers available which are operated by vacuum through the oil filler opening, Fig. 8-7. With the engine at normal operating temperature, one type of tester requires the removal of the oil dip stick and the oil filler cap. Insert a plug tightly into the dipstick hole. Insert the tester adapter tightly in the filler cap opening. The adapter is connected to the tester body by a hose. Turn the selector knob to Number 2. If the engine is equipped with a crankcase ventilating system which has a tube from the air cleaner to the filler cap, remove the tube at the filler cap and plug the tube. With the engine idling, note the color in the tester window:

Green indicates the system is functioning normally.

Green and Yellow indicates the PCV valve or system is partially plugged, the tester hose may be slightly kinked, the selector knob may be improperly set, there is a slight amount of blow-by, or there may be a vacuum leak in the hoses or around the tester plugs.

Yellow indicates that the same problems which caused the green and yellow reading are more pronounced.

Red indicates a completely plugged system or valve, a stuck valve, extreme blow-by, or a plugged or collapsed vent hose.

Yellow and Red indicates the same problems which caused a red color, but the conditions may not be as severe.

There is another type of tester available with which the oil filler cap only is removed and the tester is placed tightly over the opening. If the indicator ball settles in the good (green) area, the system is functioning normally, if the ball settles in the repair (red) area, clean, replace, or repair the malfunctioning unit as required.

Cleaning Positive Crankcase Ventilating System. In both the vent tube and positive open type of crankcase ventilating systems, the filter in the oil filler cap should be cleaned in solvent at each oil change. Remove accumulated deposits in the breather holes. Shake the cap dry and install. Do not dry with compressed air because air pressure may damage the filter element. Do not attempt to clean the positive crankcase ventilating valve (PCV); replace it at the specified mileage intervals or sooner if necessary. Use the correct valve for the particular make and model of engine.

In the case of the closed positive ventilating system, remove the flame arrestor, if so equipped (this unit would be located in the air cleaner), and wash in a solvent. Dry with compressed air.

Clean the hoses, fittings, and tubing in a low-volatility petroleum-base solvent, and dry with compressed air. Clean the fitting in the carburetor spacer or intake manifold with a flexible wire or bottle brush. Be sure all connections and fittings are airtight for proper operation.

Exhaust Emission Control Systems

An exhaust system which will reduce the amount of hydrocarbons and carbon monoxide formed in the combustion chambers by promot-

Emissions Systems

ing more complete combustion greatly reduces the contamination in the exhaust. Reducing the amount of contamination emitted through the exhaust system to an acceptable minimum reduces air pollution.

Basically, there are two types of exhaust emission systems in common use—the controlled combustion system and the air induction (pump) system. Because the temperature of the air entering the carburetor affects the emission output of the engine, a thermostatically controlled air cleaner is generally used in conjunction with the controlled combustion system.

Controlled Combustion Systems

Since limits on the amount of exhaust emission from automobile engines have been mandated by Federal legislation, engine manufacturers are attempting to bring about more complete combustion in all operating ranges.

Combustion efficiency with conventional ignition timing and carburetor calibration will vary with engine speed and load. Emission of exhaust contaminants are a result of combustion efficiency.

The controlled combustion system includes a carburetor that is especially calibrated to provide leaner air-fuel mixtures at idle and low speed operation along with a distributor that is designed to provide retarded ignition timing at engine idle speeds. Carburetors on recently manufactured vehicles are equipped with idle fuel mixture adjustment limiters which prevent a rich idle mixture by preventing the adjusting screw from being turned open too far. Under no circumstances should the limiter caps or stops be mutilated or damaged to make them inoperative. For more information on carburetion and ignition timing, see Chapters 10 and 12.

In addition to the changes in carburetor calibration and distributor timing, some manufacturers have incorporated components in the distributor advance control system to further reduce exhaust emissons, improve combustion efficiency, and retain desirable performance and economy factors.

Some installations utilize a distributor vacuum control valve (thermostatic water temperature switch or temperature operated vacuum bypass) in the cooling system. Others have incorporated a distributor vacuum deceleration valve. Some engines employ a distributor solenoid to retard idle ignition timing. Some manufacturers will use a transmission controlled distributor timing system.

A thermostatically controlled air cleaner (heated air system) is used on most vehicles having the controlled combustion system to effect more complete combustion during engine warm-up.

General Motors Controlled Combustion System (CCS)

The controlled combustion system is used on General Motors products that have no air induction system.

A leaner carburetor calibration requires a retarded ignition idle speed timing. This is accomplished by a vacuum takeoff in the carburetor for the distributor vacuum advance. The takeoff is located just above the throttle plates so there is no vacuum advance at closed throttle but some advance begins when the throttle plates are slightly opened. Initial timing is set at or near TDC (top dead center) and the centrifugal advance does not begin until approximately 1,000 RPM.

Many engines using the controlled combustion system will be equipped with an idle stop solenoid. The purpose of the solenoid is to completely close the throttle when the ignition switch is turned off. Retarded ignition timing and higher operating temperatures tend to cause the engine to "diesel" (continue to run) after the ignition is turned off. This is particularly true of a vehicle with an automatic transmission.

A thermo-vacuum switch may be installed on some engines using this method of controlled combustion. The switch, which is located in the engine cooling system, opens a vacuum to advance timing when the engine temperature rises above normal during idling.

Some vehicles utilizing this system incorporate a transmission controlled vacuum advance to provide better emission control in lower gear ranges. For more information on distributor advance, see Chapter 12.

Ford Improved Exhaust Emission Control System (IMCO)

The improved Exhaust Emission Control System, which is similar to the General Motors Controlled Combustion Systems, improves combustion by reducing contaminants through leaner carburetion and retarded idle timing. The system uses a dual diaphragm distributor advance unit to control ignition timing, Fig. 8-8. For more information on carburetion and ignition timing, see Chapters 10 and 12.

The secondary (inner) diaphragm is connected to the intake manifold. The primary (outer) diaphragm is connected to a vacuum port above the throttle.

At idling, the throttle is closed resulting in high manifold vacuum which actuates the secondary (inner) diaphragm, retarding the timing for improved combustion.

Because the primary (outer) diaphragm is connected to the carburetor above the throttle, vacuum is not present to act on the distrib-

Emissions Systems

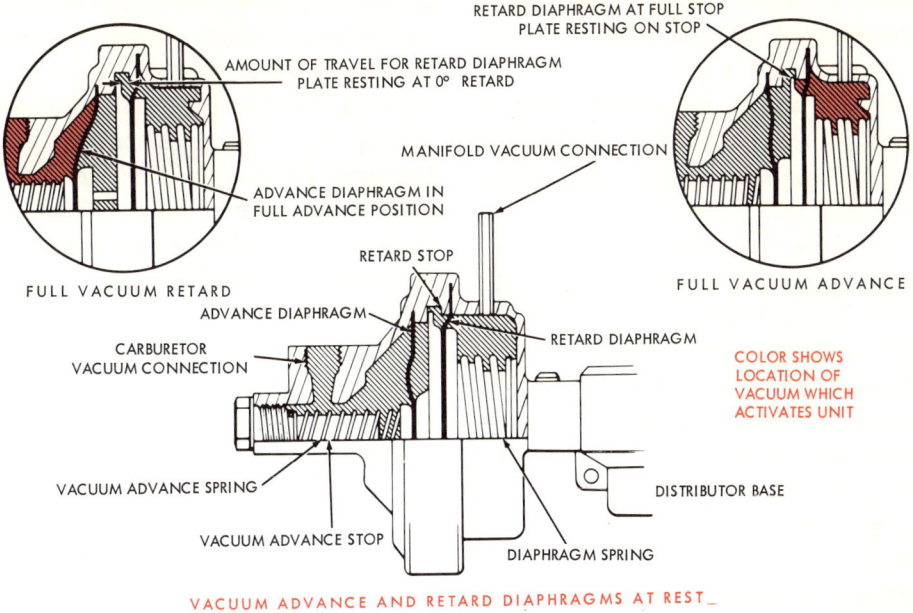

Fig. 8-8. Distributor vacuum advance and retard unit. (Ford Div., Ford Motor Co.)

utor primary vacuum diaphragm until the throttle plates open; then manifold vacuum drops and vacuum above the throttle increases and actuates the primary diaphragm controlling the timing advance in the conventional manner.

Many vehicles employ a distributor vacuum advance control (decelerator) valve along with a thermostatically controlled vacuum switch in this type of installation. A transmission controlled vacuum advance system may also be incorporated.

Chrysler Cleaner Air System (CAS)

The Chrysler Cleaner Air System is similar to the General Motors CCS and the Ford IMCO system.

The carburetor is calibrated to a lean mixture at idle and low speed operation. The distributor is designed to retard timing at idle. A distributor vacuum advance control (decelerator) valve on some models provides advanced timing during deceleration.

Emissions are further reduced at idle because of a lean air-fuel ratio, increased engine speed, and retarded ignition timing. An idle speed solenoid is used on engines having high idle speed so that they do not continue to run or "diesel" after the ignition is turned off.

Certain engines have a solenoid incorporated in the distributor advance mechanism to retard the timing when the throttle is closed. The solenoid is not energized unless the hot idle adjusting screw is against the throttle stop contact. Therefore, the ignition timing is not retarded if the engine is cold.

Distributor Advance Control Units

Each controlled combustion system is designed for a particular make and model of engine. Therefore, a different set of components will be found on each type of engine. Each combination of components is engineered to reduce emissions under varying operating conditions.

The various units which may be found on different engines include a distributor vacuum advance control valve, a temperature operated vacuum bypass valve, a distributor retard solenoid, an idle speed solenoid, and transmission controlled vacuum spark advance systems.

To help reduce emissions upon deceleration, a distributor vacuum advance control (decelerator) valve may be used.

Because the engine tends to overheat when operating at idle with retarded timing, many vehicles will have a temperature operated vacuum bypass valve in the cooling system.

A distributor retard solenoid may be used in the distributor vacuum advance unit to retard timing at idle speeds. An idle speed solenoid may be utilized on some engines to prevent a "dieseling" effect after the ignition switch is turned off. Because engine speeds are high enough to advance ignition timing in lower gear ratios, a system is sometimes used to restrict timing advance through the transmission under certain operating conditions. For more information on distributor advance, see Chapter 12.

Distributor Vacuum Advance Control Valve (Decelerator Valve). Exhaust emissions are reduced at idle speed by lean mixture and a retarded ignition timing. Ignition timing is advanced during deceleration to improve combustion and reduce emissions. A distributor vacuum advance control valve, Fig. 8-9, sometimes referred to as a "decelerator valve," is used on some engines to direct vacuum to the distributor which advances timing upon deceleration. The distributor vacuum advance control valve is connected by vacuum hoses to a port in the carburetor body above the throttle plates, to the intake manifold, and to the distributor vacuum advance unit.

Initial distributor timing is retarded at idle. Because one vacuum port is above the closed throttle plates, at idle speed there is not enough vacuum applied in the distributor advance unit to actuate the diaphragm and advance the timing.

Emissions Systems

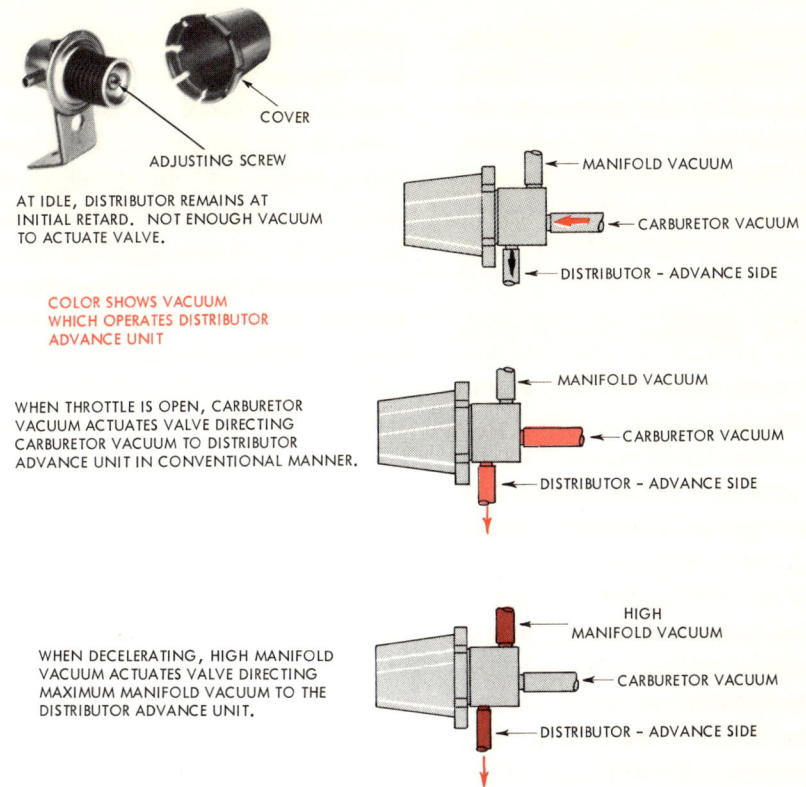

Fig. 8-9. Distributor vacuum advance control valve (decelerator valve). (Ford Div., Ford Motor Co.)

During idle, manifold vacuum acts upon the distributor vacuum advance control valve diaphragm but is not able to overcome diaphragm spring tension. Therefore, the valve is held closed to manifold vacuum and open to carburetor vacuum. When the throttle opens, vacuum from the carburetor operates the distributor advance unit in the conventional manner.

Manifold vacuum reaches its highest point during deceleration and overcomes the advance control valve spring tension directing manifold vacuum to the advance in the distributor. High manifold vacuum causes maximum distributor advance which prevents afterburning and popping back through the carburetor. As soon as the engine returns to a normal idle speed, the distributor vacuum advance unit functions normally.

The distributor vacuum advance control (deceleration) valve normally is used with the dual diaphragm distributor. The primary (outer) diaphragm is connected to the carburetor port above the throt-

293

tle plates which closes off vacuum to the distributor advance control unit. The distributor advance control valve is connected to the intake manifold as well as the distributor primary (outer) diaphragm. The surge of high vacuum occurring in the intake manifold as a result of the sudden throttle closing activates the distributor vacuum advance control valve causing vacuum to be directed to the distributor primary (outer) diaphragm. This action causes maximum timing advance to prevent afterburning and popping back through the carburetor. When the engine returns to normal idle, the valve will return to its original position, and the distributor vacuum advance control will function in a regular fashion.

Distributor Vacuum Advance Control Valve (Decelerator Valve) Test and Adjustment. To adjust the distributor vacuum control valve, connect a tachometer to the engine and set the engine idle speed to specifications. Remove the cover from the distributor vacuum advance control valve exposing the adjusting screw, Fig. 8-9 (upper left).

Slowly turn the adjusting screw counter clockwise without exerting excessive inward pressure. After five but no more than six turns, the engine idle speed should increase to 1,000 RPM. If the speed does not increase after unscrewing the adjustment six turns, push inward on the end of the spring retainer and release. The engine idle speed will increase and remain at approximately 1,000 RPM.

After the valve has been triggered to the fast idle speed, slowly turn the adjusting screw inward (clockwise) until the idle speed drops and remains at the original setting. Turn the adjusting screw in one additional turn.

Increase the engine speed to 2,000 RPM and hold for approximately five seconds; then release the throttle. The engine should return to normal idle within four seconds. Make sure the dashpot is not holding up throttle return. If the throttle return is longer than four seconds, turn the distributor vacuum advance control valve adjusting screw in one quarter turn. Repeat the operation until correct return time is reached. If it takes more than one complete turn of the adjusting screw to reach return time specifications, the valve should be replaced.

Temperature Operated Vacuum Bypass Valve or Ported Vacuum Switch. Because of the possibility of the engine overheating at idle speed with this type of distributor and carburetor calibration, a number of installations will incorporate a temperature operated vacuum bypass valve, Fig. 8-10. This unit may also be referred to as the PVS or Ported Vacuum Switch. The switch is located in the water jacket or the thermostat housing.

Emissions Systems

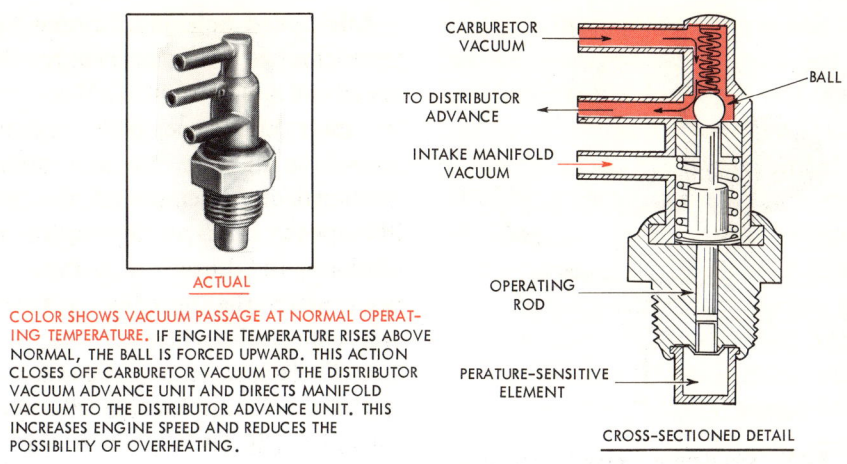

ACTUAL

COLOR SHOWS VACUUM PASSAGE AT NORMAL OPERATING TEMPERATURE. IF ENGINE TEMPERATURE RISES ABOVE NORMAL, THE BALL IS FORCED UPWARD. THIS ACTION CLOSES OFF CARBURETOR VACUUM TO THE DISTRIBUTOR VACUUM ADVANCE UNIT AND DIRECTS MANIFOLD VACUUM TO THE DISTRIBUTOR ADVANCE UNIT. THIS INCREASES ENGINE SPEED AND REDUCES THE POSSIBILITY OF OVERHEATING.

CROSS-SECTIONED DETAIL

Fig. 8-10. Temperature operated vacuum bypass valve or ported vacuum switch. (Ford Div., Ford Motor Co.)

The valve has three ports; one port is connected by a hose to the distributor vacuum advance diaphragm, one port is connected to carburetor vacuum above the throttle plate, and the third port is connected to manifold vacuum. When the coolant temperature rises above normal at idle speed, the valve switches from carburetor vacuum to manifold vacuum, advancing the ignition timing to full vacuum advance. This increases engine speed by 100 RPM or more and reduces the possibility of the engine overheating.

Test Temperature Operated Vacuum Bypass Valve or Ported Vacuum Switch. To test the coolant temperature sensing valve, make certain all vacuum hoses are tight and properly attached. Connect a tachometer and start the engine. Bring the engine to operating temperature and note the engine idle speed. Disconnect the intake manifold vacuum hose leading from the PVS. Fig. 8-10. Plug or clamp the hose and note the engine idle speed. If there is no change in idle speed, the valve is acceptable to this point. If there is a drop of 100 RPM or more, the valve should be replaced.

Check manifold vacuum to make certain it is normal. Verify that the coolant level is correct and that the proper radiator cap is installed.

Cover the radiator so as to induce a high temperature. Run the engine until the red high temperature dashboard light or gage indicates high temperature. If by this

295

Automotive Engines

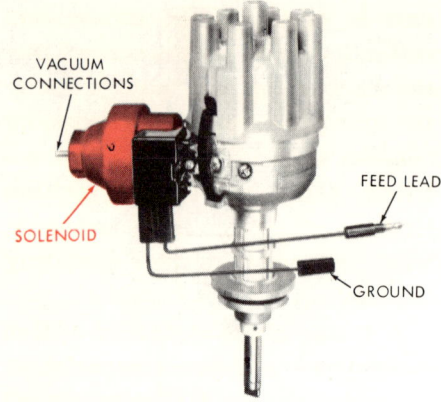

Fig. 8-11. Distributor retard solenoid. (Plymouth Div., Chrysler Corp.)

time the idle speed has increased 100 RPM, the PVS is functioning properly; if not, replace the valve.

Distributor Solenoid. The distributor used on some vehicles with a controlled combustion system will incorporate a solenoid in the vacuum advance control unit, Fig. 8-11. The solenoid serves to retard the ignition timing when the throttle is closed. When the throttle is closed completely, electrical contacts on the throttle stop make contact with the idle adjusting screw. This energizes the distributor solenoid which retards the ignition timing to reduce emissions. With a cold engine or at part throttle, the solenoid will not energize as the hot idle adjusting screw will not be against the throttle stop contacts. Timing must always be set at closed throttle in order for full retard to take place.

Idle Speed Solenoid. Some high performance engines require idle speeds of 800 to 1000 RPM in order to maintain acceptable exhaust emissions during idle and during deceleration. Because of the high idle speeds, the engine may have a tendency to "diesel" (continue running after the ignition is turned off) especially when the engine is hot. To reduce this problem, some engines will employ an idle speed solenoid, Fig. 8-12. When the engine is operating, the idle speed solenoid, which acts as a throttle stop, is energized and holds the throttle at the correct idle speed. When the ignition switch is turned off, the solenoid is de-energized allowing the throttle plates to close more completely, thus preventing the engine from "dieseling."

To adjust the idle speed solenoid, with the engine operating at normal temperature, turn the solenoid

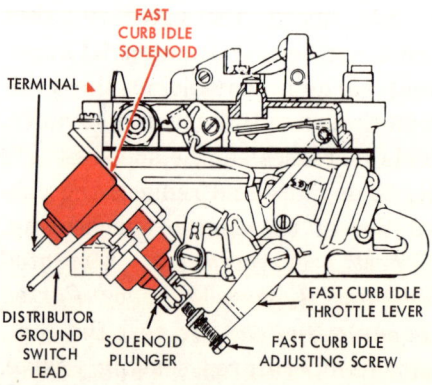

Fig. 8-12. Idle speed solenoid. (Plymouth Div., Chrysler Corp.)

Emissions Systems

adjusting screw to obtain the specified idle speed (approximately 900 RPM in most cases). Adjust the curb idle speed screw until the end of screw just touches the stop on the carburetor throttle body. Back off one full turn to obtain the slow idle curb speed setting.

Manual Transmission Controlled Vacuum Spark Advance System. Under normal operating conditions, exhaust emissions will increase when the vehicle is operated in the lower gear ranges. This is the result of ignition timing advance due to vacuum acting on the diaphragm of the distributor advance unit.

On vehicles equipped with a transmission controlled spark system, the distributor vacuum advance is eliminated when the vehicle is operating in the low forward range of gears.

The components which make up the transmission vacuum advance control system are basically the same as on most vehicles equipped with a manual transmission. Chevrolet also uses the same basic system on some models having an automatic transmission.

In order to keep emissions at a minimum, the distributor vacuum is routed through the vacuum control solenoid. When the vehicle is operated in the lower gear ranges, a grounding switch in the transmission energizes the solenoid. This shuts off vacuum to the distributor and the vacuum advance unit is vented to the atmosphere through a clean air connection into the carburetor air hose. Venting the unit prevents it from becoming vacuum locked in an advanced position. This keeps the ignition timing retarded from what it would be under normal operating conditions.

A temperature controlled switch located in the engine compartment overrides the transmission switch when the ambient temperature is low to provide full vacuum advance in all gear ranges when the engine is cold.

On some installations, a thermostatic water temperature switch provides the signal to energize a normally closed relay. This opens the circuit to the solenoid vacuum switch which provides full vacuum to the advance unit. A temperature controlled vacuum switch installed in the engine cooling system may be used to provide timing advance when the engine temperature becomes too high. Fig. 8-13 illustrates a typical transmission controlled vacuum spark advance switch and wiring diagram.

This valve arrangement has been eliminated on some later models and replaced with a valve which controls only vacuum. The basic function of the transmission controlled vacuum spark advance system is to perform three tasks: to act as a deceleration control (dashpot), to control the vacuum to the

Automotive Engines

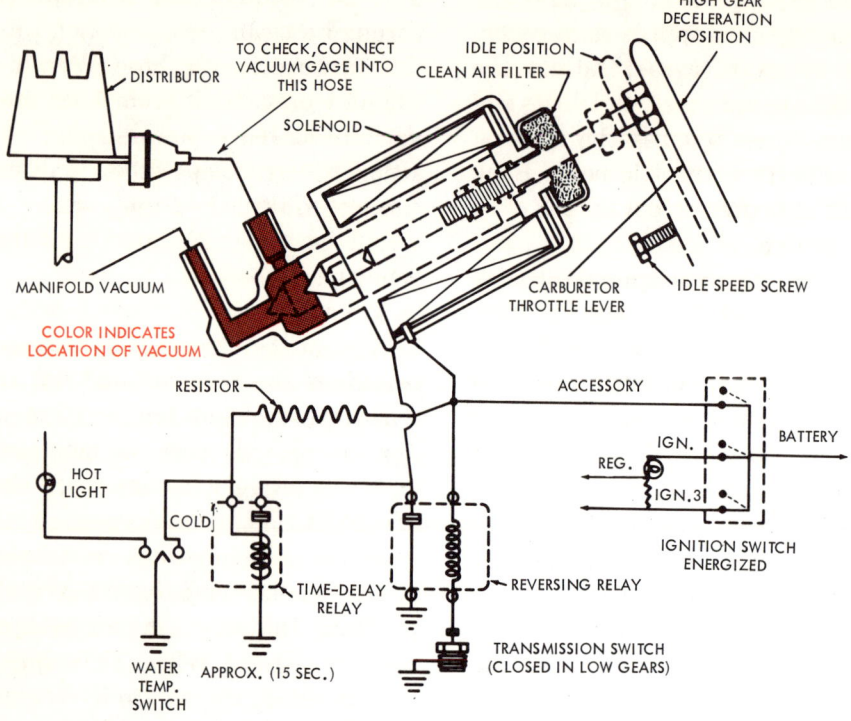

Fig. 8-13. Transmission controlled vacuum spark advance system. (Chevrolet Div., General Motors Corp.)

distributor, and to cause the engine to be turned off without "dieseling." The reversing switch reverses the function of the transmission switch. When the transmission switch is closed (low gear), the reversing relay contact points are open, thereby closing off vacuum to the distributor. When the transmission switch opens, the reversing switch closes, energizing the solenoid and permitting vacuum at the distributor for normal operation. The resistor is connected in parallel to the delay relay.

When the ignition switch is turned on, there is an electrical flow to the ballast resistor or relay through the solenoid coil to the thermal switch. This switch must be closed in order to complete the circuit. If the temperature is below 70°F the switch will be open and the system will be inoperative. Above 70°F the electricity will flow through the thermal switch to the transmission switch. If the transmission is in any gear except direct drive (high), the switch closes thereby completing the circuit to ground. This condition energizes the solenoid vacuum valve, which closes off vacuum to the distributor advance unit and vents the vacuum line. When the transmission is shifted into high gear, the circuit is broken, the vacuum solenoid switch is de-energized, and normal vacuum advance takes place.

Test Manual Transmission Controlled Vacuum Spark Advance System. The system may be checked for correct functioning by connecting a vacuum gage in the hose between the solenoid and distributor. Full vacuum should be present in the gear range as indicated in Fig. 8-13, when the engine is warm and running.

If full vacuum is found in all gears, the following conditions may exist:

1. Transmission switch or wire shorted.
2. Fuse blown.
3. Wire disconnected at solenoid or transmission switch.
4. Transmission switch or solenoid faulty.
5. Temperature override switch energized. Check by disconnecting electrical lead.

If there is no vacuum present in high gear, the following conditions may exist:

1. Clean air hose and distributor vacuum hose reversed at solenoid.
2. Foreign matter in solenoid.
3. Vacuum hose broken or disconnected.
4. Transmission switch or wire grounded.
5. Solenoid plunger return spring broken.

Transmission Controlled Vacuum Spark Advance System Used With An Automatic Transmission. The control systems on vehicles equipped with automatic transmissions use a solenoid valve arrangement to close off and vent vacuum to the distributor advance unit but may utilize a different control system than that used with the manual transmission.

When the Chrysler NOx system is used with an automatic transmission, the engine will utilize a special camshaft and a 185°F thermostat.

This control system is made up of a solenoid vacuum valve, a speed switch, and a control unit assembly, Fig. 8-14. The system is designed to prevent distributor timing advance when the ambient temperature is above 70°F, when vehicle speed is under 30 MPH and upon acceleration. Whenever all three of these conditions exist, the solenoid vacuum valve will be energized, venting the vacuum line from the carburetor and closing off vacuum to the distributor advance unit.

Automotive Engines

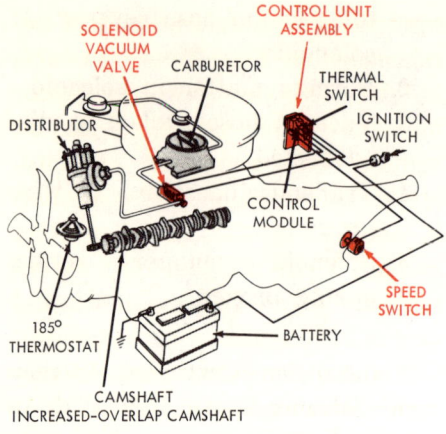

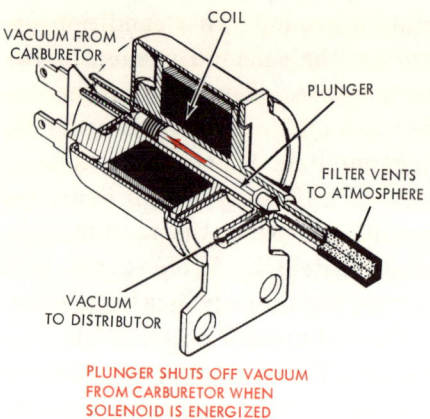

Fig. 8-15. Solenoid vacuum valve. (Plymouth Div., Chrysler Corp.)

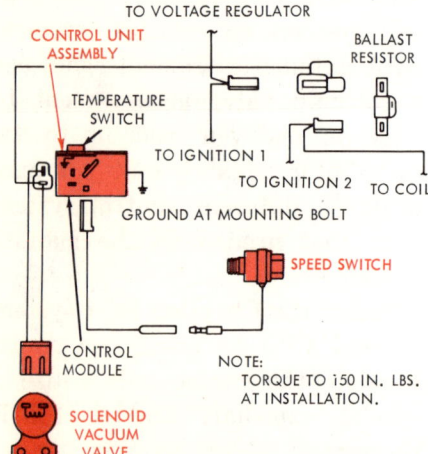

Fig. 8-14. NOx control system on an automatic transmission installation with wiring diagram. (Plymouth Div., Chrysler Corp.)

The solenoid vacuum valve is a simple solenoid with the plunger acting as a valve, Fig. 8-15. One vacuum line is connected to the carburetor port, and the other line is connected to the distributor vacuum advance unit. When the solenoid is de-energized, its spring closes the vent and allows normal vacuum advance. When electrical energy is applied to the solenoid, the valve plunger is drawn to the opposite end of its travel which shuts off vacuum from the carburetor and opens the vent to bleed the system of any vacuum trapped in the distributor vacuum advance chamber.

The speed switch is mounted on the transmission housing in line with the speedometer cable and is, therefore, sensitive to vehicle speed. At speeds above 30 MPH, the switch opens to de-energize the solenoid and permit normal timing advance.

The control unit assembly is mounted on the firewall against the plenum chamber and contains the control module, the thermal switch, and the vacuum switch. The thermal switch senses ambient temper-

Emissions Systems

ature in the plenum chamber. When the ambient temperature is below 70°F, the thermal switch will open the circuit and de-energize the solenoid valve permitting normal vacuum advance. The vacuum switch reacting to manifold vacuum prevents timing advance during acceleration at low speeds.

The unit used to reduce exhaust emissions by control of the distributor timing advance during specific conditions of acceleration and deceleration on Ford Motor products is labeled an electronic distributor modulator. This system is used on vehicles equipped with an automatic transmission. Its operation is similar to the Chrysler NOx system. There are four major components: a speed sensor, a thermal switch, an electronic control amplifier, and a three-way solenoid vacuum valve, Fig. 8-16.

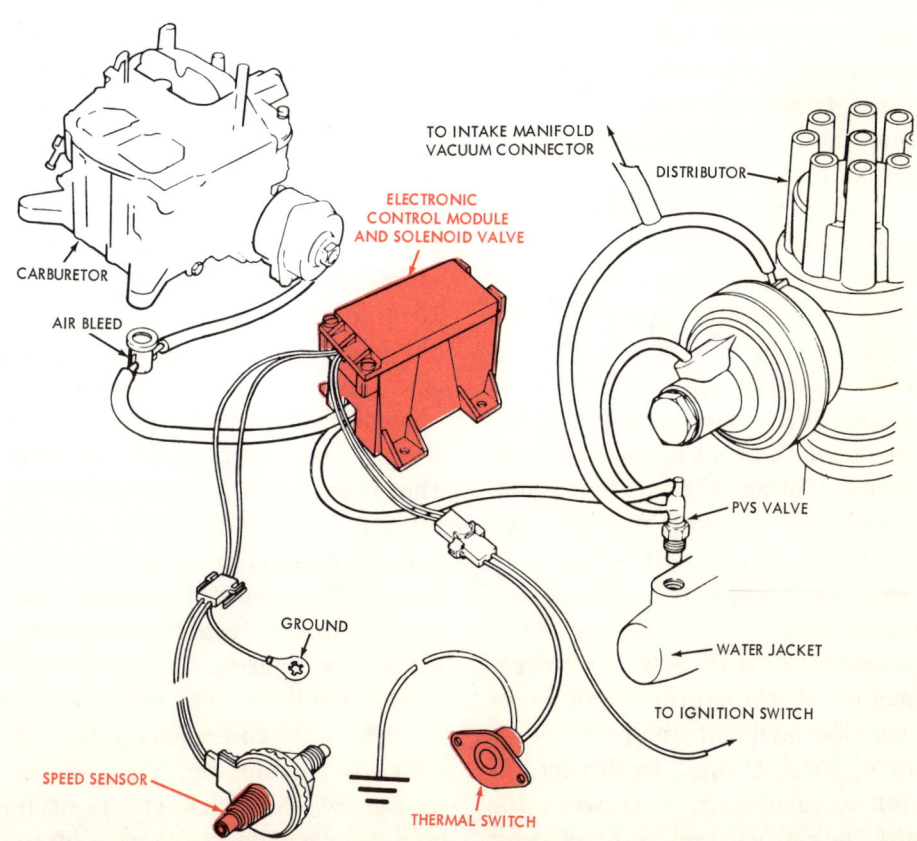

Fig. 8-16. Schematic of the distributor modulator system. (Ford Div., Ford Motor Co.)

The speed sensor is connected to the speedometer drive cable so that it opens the electrical circuit to the vacuum valve at a given speed. The thermal switch is mounted near the door hinge pillar on the outside of the cowl panel. The switch is designed to open the circuit at 58°F to 68°F. The electronic distributor modulator, which is sensitive to manifold vacuum, operates to prevent distributor timing advance below a specific speed when accelerating and to also prevent advance below a specified value on deceleration. Operating speeds will vary with the type of engine. Therefore, it will be necessary to refer to the manufacturer's specifications when checking a unit.

Testing Transmission Controlled Vacuum Spark Advance System Used with an Automatic Transmission. Because temperature, vacuum, and speed requirements will vary according to the differences in makes and models, always check the manufacturer's specifications before testing the various components for malfunctioning. Check all vacuum hoses and connections for leaks. Inspect all electrical connections.

Bring the engine up to normal operating temperature, and make sure the ambient temperature is above 75°F. Using a tee fitting, install a vacuum gage between the distributor vacuum control unit and the solenoid vacuum valve. Raise the rear wheels off the floor. Remove and plug the vacuum line at the vacuum switch on the control unit assembly. Operate the engine at a fast idle, above 850 RPM. The vacuum gage should read "zero." Remove the electrical wire from the ignition switch at the control unit connection. The vacuum gage should read "line vacuum." Connect the wire; the gage should drop to zero. Unplug the vacuum line and connect it to the vacuum switch; then disconnect the wire lead from the control unit to the speed switch. The vacuum gage should now read "line vacuum." Place the transmission in drive range. Rapid acceleration will cause the vacuum gage to drop to zero if the vacuum switch is functioning properly. As engine RPM stabilizes, the vacuum should return to "line vacuum". Reconnect the speed switch lead. Disconnect, and plug the vacuum hose at the solenoid valve. The vacuum gage should now read "zero". Increase the engine speed to above 30 MPH. At approximately 30 MPH the vacuum gage should read "line vacuum". If no solenoid action takes place, the control unit assembly should be replaced.

A simple test can be made to determine if the solenoid vacuum valve is functioning. Turn the ignition switch to the "on" position, and, while holding the case of the solenoid, connect and disconnect one of the electrical connections. If the unit is functioning, you will be able to feel the cycling of the solenoid as the connection is connected and disconnected.

If a separate thermal switch is used, it can be checked by installing a vacuum gage between the distributor vacuum control unit and the solenoid vacuum valve. With the ambient temperature above 75°F, disconnect the electrical line at the thermal switch. If the thermal switch is functioning properly, the vacuum gage will read "normal distributor vacuum."

General Motors Combination Emission Control System (CEC). This system is controlled through the transmission and eliminates distributor vacuum advance in the low forward transmission gear ratios under certain operating conditions. While the basic operating principles are much the same as for the system used on a number of manual transmission installations, additional control features have been incorporated.

The combustion emission control system consists of a solenoid vacuum switch and an idle speed control unit, a transmission switch, a reversing relay, a time-delay relay, a resistor, and a water temperature switch, Fig. 8-13.

When the solenoid vacuum switch is in the non-energized position, vacuum is cut off to the distributor vacuum advance unit and the unit is vented to the atmosphere through a filter located at one end of the solenoid. An air passage is provided by grooves molded in the solenoid spool and clearance between the adjusting screw and the plunger stop.

When the solenoid is energized by grounding the transmission switch, the vacuum port is opened, and the plunger is seated which shuts off the vent. Manifold vacuum is now directed to the distributor advance unit.

The unit is controlled by two switches and a time delay relay. The solenoid is energized in the high forward gears (also reverse gear on the Hydramatic Transmission) by grounding the transmission operated switch. Due to the particular design, a reversing relay is required to reverse the function of the transmission switch.

A thermostatic water temperature switch located in the water jacket is used to override the solenoid transmission switch at temperatures below 82° F.

The time delay relay is incorporated in the circuit to energize the solenoid valve for approximately 15 seconds after the ignition switch is turned on. Full vacuum to the distributor advance unit, regardless of engine temperature, improves the initial drive-away and helps to eliminate engine stall when power is first applied to the drive line. The relay is effective at temperatures above 82°F.

Elimination of engine "dieseling" is achieved by closing the throttle plates tighter, thus resulting in lower curb idle speeds. Lower curb idle speed also results in less transmission creep with an automatic transmission, less noise at idle speed, and less heat rejection resulting in the elimination of the thermal override on most models. To prevent "dieseling" of engines used in vehicles with air conditioning and automatic transmissions which require a faster idle speed, a solid state device is included to allow the air conditioning compressor clutch to become engaged for approximately three seconds after the ignition is turned off. Placing a sudden additional load on the engine causes it to stop sooner, thereby reducing the possibility of "dieseling."

The various components are tested in much the same manner as the units used on vehicles with a manual transmission. Install a vacuum gage in the vacuum hose between the distributor vacuum advance unit and the solenoid vacuum switch. A full vacuum reading should be indicated in the gear range shown in Table 8-1 with the engine warm and running.

Any broken or disconnected electrical connections will prevent the solenoid valve from functioning. Under this condition there will be no distributor vacuum advance and no high gear deceleration throttle position.

If vacuum is present at all times, the transmission switch or wire may be shorted, the fuse may be

TABLE 8-1

		GEAR					
TRANSMISSION	PARK	NEUTRAL	REVERSE	1st.	2nd.	3rd.	4th.
3 SPEED						VAC.	
4 SPEED						VAC.	VAC.
TORQUE DRIVE					VAC.		
POWERGLIDE					VAC.		
TURO HYDRA-MATIC 350			VAC.			VAC.	
TURBO HYDRA-MATIC 400			VAC.			VAC.	

TABLE 8-1 IS AN ILLUSTRATION OF TYPICAL GEAR POSITIONS AND SHIFT RANGES AT WHICH TRANSMISSION CONTROL FOR EMISSION REDUCTION OCCURS ON VEHICLES EQUIPPED WITH THIS TYPE OF DEVICE. REFER TO THE MANUFACTURER'S SPECIFICATIONS FOR EXACT LISTING OF THE VEHICLE BEING SERVICED.

Emissions Systems

blown, a wire may be disconnected, or the temperature override switch may be energized. The temperature switch can be checked by disconnecting the lead.

If there is no vacuum present in high gear ranges, the hoses at the solenoid switch may be reversed, there may be foreign matter in the solenoid, the solenoid may be faulty, a vacuum hose may be broken or disconnected, or the transmission switch or wire may be grounded.

Full vacuum must be present at the distributor advance unit for 15 seconds when starting a warm engine if the time delay switch is functioning properly.

All faulty components must be replaced as a complete unit.

Adjusting Curb Idle and High Gear Deceleration. Curb idle speed provides for greater fuel economy under city traffic conditions because the engine will be operating at a lower RPM than is experienced when the engine is suddenly decelerated.

Note: *If the CEC solenoid valve is used to set engine idle or is adjusted out of limits specified by the manufacturer, a decrease in engine braking may result.* This adjustment needs to be made only after replacement of the vacuum solenoid switch, after a major overhaul has been performed on the carburetor, or after the throttle body has been removed and replaced.

All adjustments to the solenoid valve are made with the valve in the non-energized position. This is assured by removing the electrical lead at the connection. Remove the vacuum hose at the distributor, and plug the end of the hose. The curb idle speed is set to the manufacturer's specifications by turning the carburetor idle speed screw, Fig. 8-13. To set the high gear deceleration throttle position, pull the throttle stop adjusting screw to its most extended position and adjust it to the specified RPM.

Most late model vehicles will have an exhaust emission control sticker in the engine compartment which specifies engine settings.

Thermostatically Controlled Air Cleaners

The thermostatically controlled air cleaner (heated air system) is used on many installations utilizing the controlled combustion system for reduction of exhaust emissions. The system improves carburetor operation and engine warm-up characteristics by keeping the air entering the carburetor at a temperature of at least 100°F. Improper functioning of this system affects the exhaust emission control system and may result in failure to meet Federal emission regulations.

There are two basic types of heated air systems in common use —the thermostatically operated

Automotive Engines

duct and valve assembly and the vacuum and thermostatically operated heated air system. Both types operate on the principle of directing air, which has been heated by the exhaust manifold, into the carburetor air cleaner until such time that the ambient temperature reaches a minimum of 100°F. At this point, the warm engine compartment air is drawn directly through the air cleaner into the air horn of the carburetor.

Thermostatically Controlled Duct and Valve Assembly Air Cleaner. The thermostatically controlled duct and valve assembly heated air system, Fig. 8-17, includes a valve (damper) which is held in a "heat on" position by spring tension when ambient temperature is below 100°F. A thermostat assembly is attached by linkage to the valve. The valve is located between a duct leading directly to the engine compartment and a duct which leads to a heat stove on the exhaust manifold.

When ambient temperature is below 100°F, spring tension keeps the valve closed to the duct leading to the engine compartment. Air is drawn through the duct, past the thermostat, and into the air cleaner. The flow of warm air past the thermostat causes the thermostat to extend the linkage resulting in the valve closing the passage from the heat stove and opening the passageway to the engine compartment. The temperature of the air moving past the thermostat determines the position of the valve.

Some of the thermostatically controlled duct and valve assembly air cleaners installed on particular engines have an auxiliary air inlet valve operated by a vacuum motor, Fig. 8-18. The purpose of the valve is to increase the flow of air into the air cleaner upon sudden acceleration. A spring holds the air inlet valve open when the engine is not operating. As soon as the engine starts, vacuum is directed to the diaphragm of the vacuum motor forcing the air inlet closed. Upon sudden acceleration manifold

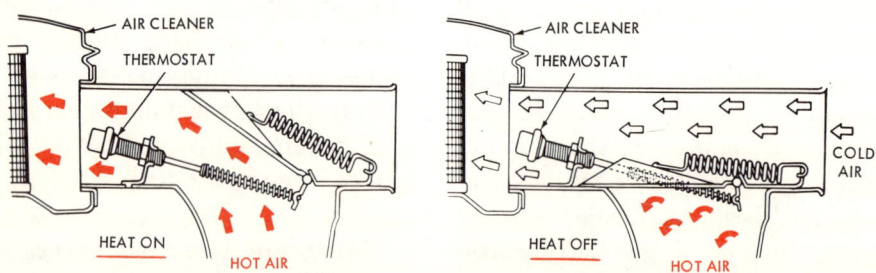

Fig. 8-17. Thermostatically controlled duct and valve assembly air cleaner. (Ford Div., Ford Motor Co.)

Emissions Systems

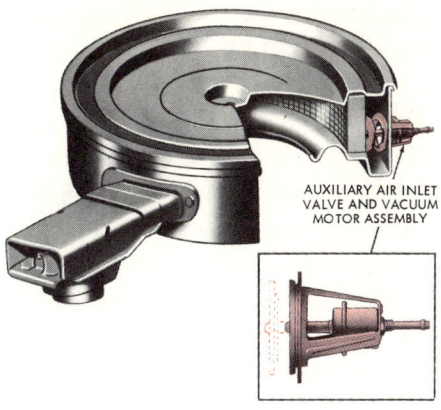

Fig. 8-18. Thermostatically controlled duct and valve assembly with a vacuum motor. (Ford Div., Ford Motor Co.)

vacuum drops and spring tension on the inlet valve causes the valve to open. When engine load is reduced, vacuum will increase resulting in the valve closing again.

Servicing the Thermostatically Controlled Duct and Valve Assembly Air Cleaner. With the assembly installed on the carburetor, the engine cold, and the ambient temperature less than 100°F, the heat damper valve should be in the "heat on" position, Fig. 8-17. If the damper is not in the "heat on" position, check the plate for interference which could cause binding. If the damper can move freely, remove the assembly from the carburetor and immerse the duct assembly in cool water so that the thermostat is covered. Raise the water temperature to 100°F and let

stand for five minutes. The damper should be in the "heat on" position. Increase the water temperature to 135°F and allow it to stabilize for five minutes. The damper valve should move to the "heat off" position. If the assembly does not meet these specifications, the duct and damper valve assembly should be replaced.

On the thermostatically controlled duct and valve assembly with a vacuum motor, in addition to checking the damper valve assembly, the vacuum motor operation must also be checked.

Start the engine; the vacuum motor plate should be fully closed. Disconnect the vacuum hose at the vacuum motor; the plate should be fully open. If the above conditions are not obtained, check the motor rod and plate for alignment and binding. Check the vacuum hose for leaks. There should be a minimum of 15 inches of vacuum in the hose.

Remove the vacuum motor from the air cleaner, and connect it to another source of vacuum. If the motor rod does not move when vacuum is applied, replace the motor.

Vacuum and Thermostatically Controlled Air Cleaner. The vacuum and thermostatically controlled air cleaner system, Fig. 8-19, includes a temperature sensor, a vacuum motor, a control damper (valve) assembly mounted in the air cleaner,

Automotive Engines

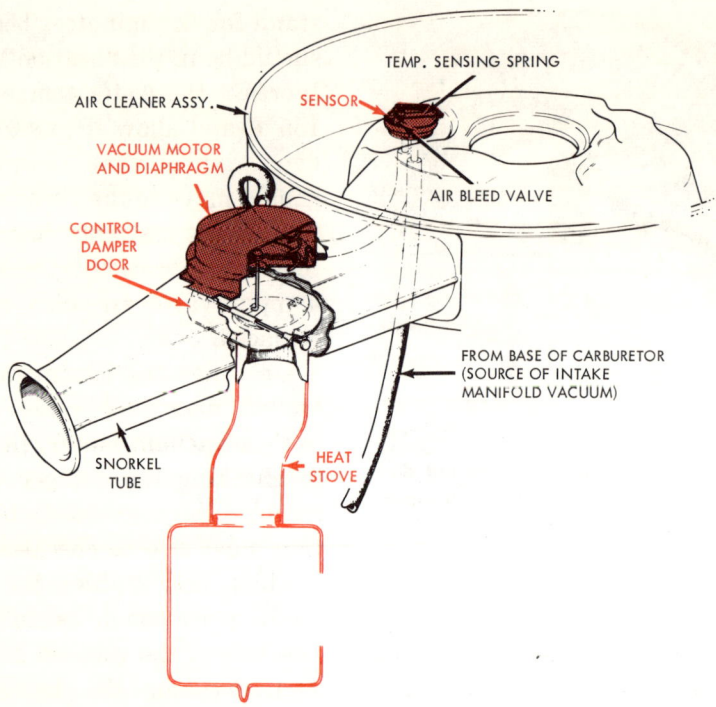

Fig. 8-19. Vacuum and thermostatically controlled air cleaner. (Chevrolet Div., General Motors Corp.)

plus a manifold heat stove with connecting duct and vacuum hoses.

The vacuum motor is controlled by the temperature sensor (thermostat). The vacuum motor operates the air control damper assembly to regulate the hot air flow from the manifold heat stove as well as the engine compartment air flow into the carburetor air cleaner.

When the engine is not running, the control damper assembly is held by diaphragm spring tension in such a position that the passageway from the engine compartment (snorkel tube) is open directly into the air cleaner. Fig. 8-20 illustrates the position of the damper valve assembly under various conditions.

When the engine is started and engine compartment temperature is below 85°F, vacuum will be directed by the temperature sensor unit to the vacuum motor which actuates the damper valve assembly, closing off the snorkel tube opening from the engine compartment air, and opening the passageway to the manifold heat stove.

The modulation of air tempera-

Emissions Systems

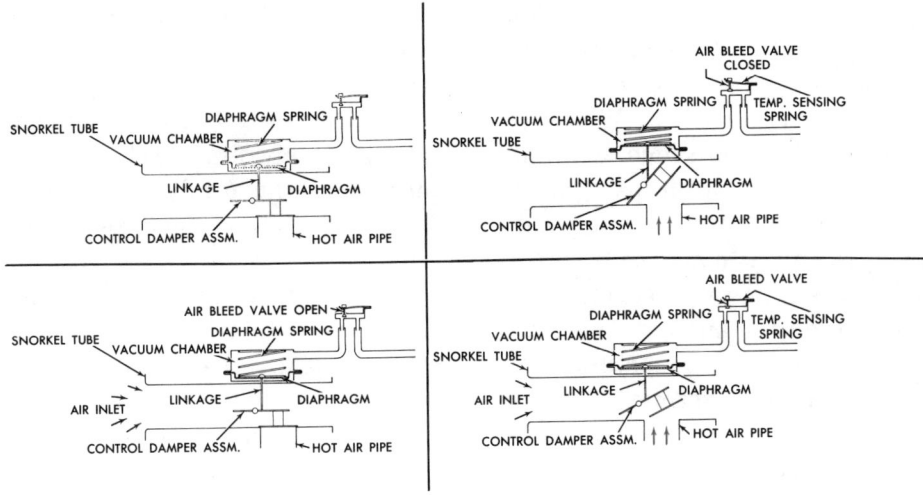

Fig. 8-20. Operation of the vacuum and thermostatically controlled air cleaner. (Chevrolet Div., General Motors Corp.)

ture to the carburetor air horn depends upon intake manifold vacuum, the temperature sensor, and a spring loaded vacuum diaphragm which is connected by linkage to the control damper valve assembly.

A vacuum hose connects one side of the sensor unit to the intake manifold. Another hose connects the other side of the sensor unit to the vacuum chamber of the damper valve assembly diaphragm. The sensor is a bimetal strip attached rigidly on one end which bends according to temperature and controls an air valve on the other end.

The vacuum chamber contains a bellows type diaphragm mounted in a housing with a spring between the diaphragm and the top of the housing. Linkage connects the diaphragm to the damper valve assembly.

When the flow of air past the temperature sensor rises above approximately 85°F, the sensor reacts by starting to close off the vacuum flow to the diaphragm in the motor. With less vacuum reacting on the diaphragm, the diaphragm spring will start to move the control damper to close the passage from the heat stove and open the passage through the snorkel into the air cleaner. By the time the air flow past the temperature sensor has reached 135°F, the heat stove passage should be closed tightly and the snorkel passage should be wide open. Because the vacuum diaphragm is opposed by spring tension, temperature modulating will occur only at road load throttle positions or when manifold vacuum is great enough to overcome spring tension. When the throttle is opened suddenly, intake manifold vacuum drops and the damper valve closes off the hot air passage (if it is not already closed) and opens a direct passage through the snorkel for an free flow of air from the engine compartment.

Some high performance engines use a dual snorkel air cleaner. It performs basically the same as a single snorkel air cleaner at low temperatures and above 135°F, except a heat stove is not attached to the second snorkel. Upon sudden acceleration, which considerably reduces manifold vacuum, both snorkels open to permit an unrestricted flow of air into the air cleaner.

Servicing the Vacuum and Thermostatically Controlled Air Cleaner System. If the engine reaches normal operating temperature as soon as expected, and the cooling system thermostat and exhaust heat control valve are both functioning correctly, check the controlled air system air cleaner.

A visual inspection may detect a malfunction. When the engine is not operating, the damper valve assembly should be positioned so that the passageway through the snorkel is wide open. When ambient temperature is below 85°F, as soon as the engine starts, the damper assembly should close off air flow through the snorkel and open the passageway to the heat stove.

To check the air cleaner damper valve assembly, first check all hoses and connections for fit and leakage. Remove the air cleaner cover and install a thermometer as close to the temperature sensor as possible. The temperature must be below 85°F. Replace the cover. Before starting the engine, observe the position of the damper valve assembly through the snorkel tube. If the damper valve is not open, check for binding of the damper and linkage. Start the engine and operate at idle speed. When the damper valve assembly begins to open, remove the air cleaner cover and check the temperature. It should be between 85°F and 115°F.

If the damper valve does not completely open and close within the above temperature range, check the vacuum motor in the following manner:

1. Shut off the engine, and disconnect the vacuum motor hose at the temperature sensor.
2. Apply at least nine inches of vacuum to the diaphragm assembly through the hose. This can be done by mouth. The damper valves should completely close the snorkel tube when vacuum is applied. If the damper does not fully

Emissions Systems

close, check for a vacuum leak or a bind in the linkage.
3. With vacuum applied, clamp the hose shut. The damper should remain closed. If not, there is a leak in the diaphragm.

If the vacuum motor diaphragm leaks, the vacuum motor must be replaced. This can be done by drilling out the spot welds which fasten the motor to the air cleaner. After replacing the diaphragm assembly, attach the vacuum motor to the air cleaner with short metal screws.

If the vacuum motor is satisfactory, replace the temperature sensor. The temperature sensor is removed by prying up the retaining tabs. Make sure the new sensor unit is installed in the same position as the original assembly.

Air Induction System

An air induction system is used on a number of makes and models of vehicles to induce air into the engine exhaust system near the exhaust ports. Adding air, which contains oxygen, to the hot exhaust gases makes for more complete burning of the gases, thus reducing contamination which would otherwise be emitted from the exhaust system. This helps to reduce air pollution and keep the vehicle operating within the mandated emission standards.

All air induction pump systems function in a similar manner and will consist of the same basic components. Nomenclature of the different units may vary to some degree, but the function will be the same for all makes and models.

The air induction system commonly used consists of a belt-driven air pump with an integral filter arrangement, air injection tubes (one for each cylinder), an air diverter (bypass) valve, check valves (one for in-line engines, two for V-8 engines), air manifold assemblies, and the necessary hoses and tubing to connect the various components, Fig. 8-21.

The air pump filters and compresses air from the engine compartment forcing it through the air manifold, connecting hoses, and injection tubes into the exhaust system in the area of the exhaust valves.

The compressed air pumped into the area near the exhaust ports aids in burning additional amounts of otherwise unburned exhaust gases, thus reducing exhaust contaminations and emissions from the exhaust system.

The diverter valve, sometimes referred to as the bypass valve, is actuated by a sudden increase in manifold vacuum (sudden closing of the throttle) which shuts off injected air to the exhaust port area to prevent backfiring during rich air-fuel mixture periods and particularly upon engine deceleration.

Automotive Engines

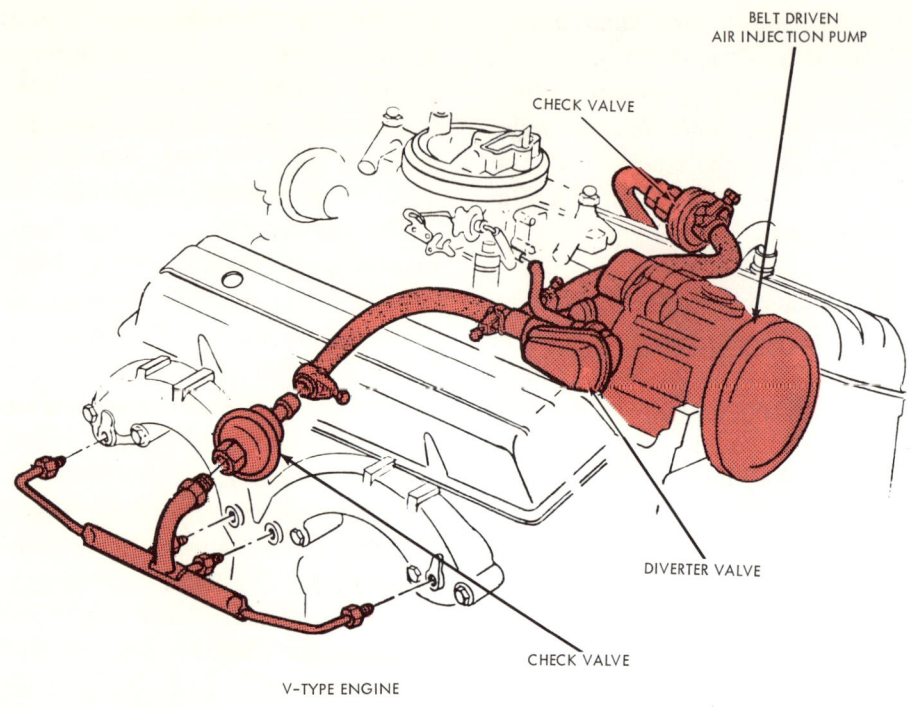

Fig. 8-21. Air induction system. (Chevrolet Div., General Motors Corp.)

On some early systems, when the diverter (bypass valve) was triggered by an increase in manifold vacuum, additional air was supplied in the intake manifold to lean out the air-fuel mixture and prevent backfiring.

On engine "overrun" (rear wheels driving the engine), the total amount of injected air is dumped through a muffler which is generally incorporated in the diverter valve. At high engine speeds, excess air is expelled through the pressure relief valve which is also located in the diverter valve.

The check valve or valves prevent exhaust gases from entering and damaging the air induction system as back pressure is present whenever the engine is running. Fig. 8-22 is a schematic of a typical air induction system.

The carburetor and distributor installed on engines having an air induction system are specifically designed and calibrated for these engines and therefore should not be interchanged or replaced with units not specified for such engines.

A properly maintained and operating air induction system will

Emissions Systems

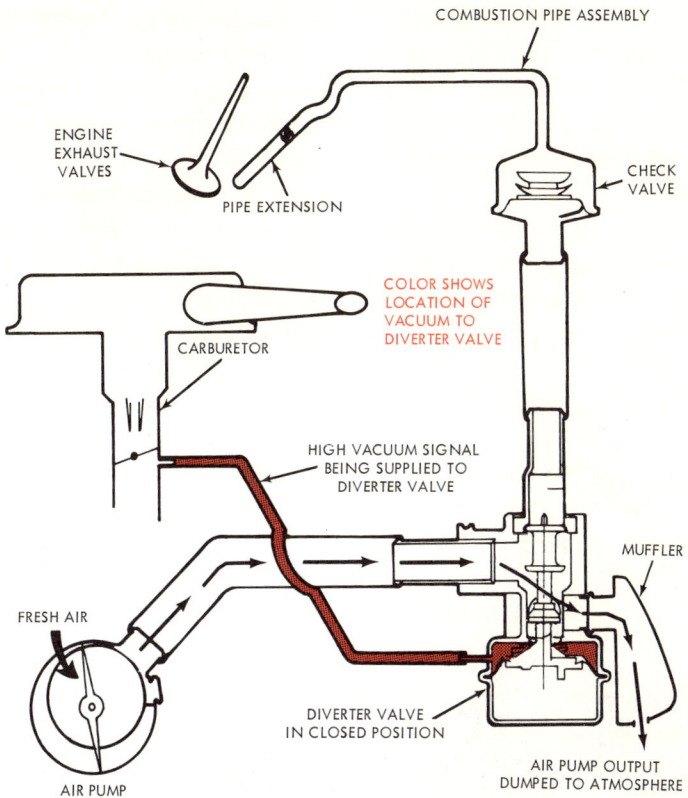

Fig. 8-22. Schematic of an air induction system. (Chevrolet Div., General Motors Corp.)

effectively reduce exhaust emissions. If any component of the air induction system, or any engine unit which operates in conjunction with the system malfunctions, exhaust emissions will be increased.

Because of the interrelationship between exhaust emissions, engine tune-up, crankcase ventilation, air cleaner, and the air induction system, any time engine exhaust emissions increase it is best to make a complete check of all components. A regular periodic engine tune-up should always include the units which affect engine emission.

Maintenance of the Air Induction System. A precise engine tune-up is important to the modern automobile engine with its many advanced designs making it more sensitive and having a decided effect on performance, power, and fuel consumption. Only when units are properly maintained will engine emissions be at a minimum.

Automotive Engines

Therefore, engine tune-up factors should always be checked whenever the air induction system appears to be malfunctioning, especially components which affect air-fuel ratio.

If all of the components affecting air-fuel ratios appear to be functioning effectively, check the various units which make up the air induction system.

Check all hoses and tubing for deterioration and cracks. Check for wear on the hoses or tubing which may be caused by incorrect routing. Check all hose and tubing connections. To aid in detecting leakage, soapy water should be brushed on the hoses, tubes, and connections on the pressure side of the system while the engine is running. The hoses used for this system are made of special materials to withstand high temperature. Therefore, when it is necessary to replace any of the hoses, no other type should be used.

Inspect the drive belt for fraying, cracks, or deterioration, and replace if required. Check the drive belt tension and adjust if below 75 pounds, using a strand tension gage, Fig. 8-23. To replace the belt, loosen the pump mounting bolt and

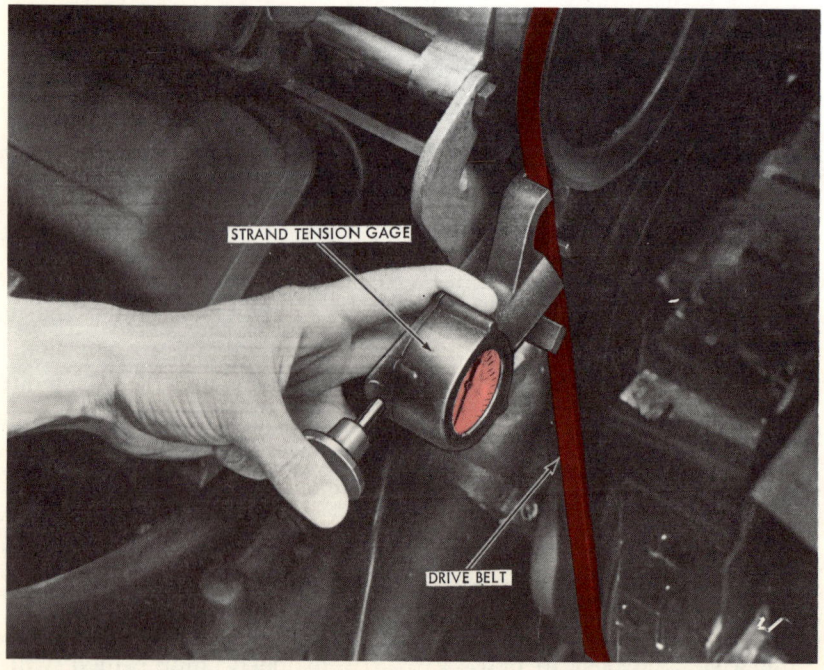

Fig. 8-23. Checking pump belt tension. (Chevrolet Div., General Motors Corp.)

Emissions Systems

pump adjustment bracket bolt. Then move the pump until the belt can be removed. To adjust the belt, move the pump until the belt is tight (70-80 pounds with a used belt, or 120-130 foot pounds with a new belt measured by a strand tension gage). Tighten the adjusting bracket bolt and mounting bolt. Do not pry on the pump housing; distorting the housing will cause extensive damage to the pump.

Some installations incorporate a centrifugal filter located directly behind the drive pulley. To replace the filter, the pulley must be removed. Prevent the pump pulley from turning by compressing the drive belt and then loosen the pulley bolts. Remove the drive belt as previously described. Remove the pulley. Pry loose the outer disc of the filter fan. Pull off the remaining portion of the filter with a pair of pliers, Fig. 8-24. Take care to prevent filter particles from entering the air intake openings. Install a new filter element by drawing it on with the pulley and pulley bolts. Do not attempt to hammer or press the filter into place but draw it into place by alternately torquing the pulley bolts. Make certain that the outer edge of the filter slips into

Fig. 8-24. Removing centrifugal filter. (Ford, Div., Ford Motor Co.)

the housing. A small amount of interference with the housing bore is normal. A new filter may squeal upon initial operation until the outer diameter sealing lip has worn in.

The check valve or valves should be inspected whenever the hoses are disconnected from the valve or whenever check valve failure is suspected. A pump that no longer operates and has indications of exhaust gases in the pump body would indicate a faulty check valve. Blow into the check valve orally (toward the air manifold); then suck back through the valve. Air flow should be in one direction (toward the air manifold). To replace the valve, disconnect the pump outlet hose at the check valve. Remove the check valve from the air manifold being careful not to bend or twist the air manifold.

Before checking the diverter valve (air bypass valve), check the condition and routing of all hoses to the valve, especially the signal line (vacuum line). Disconnect the vacuum hose at the valve, Fig. 8-25. Vacuum must be present in the hose when the engine is running. With the engine operating at a uniform idle speed, there should be no air discharged to the outside from the valve. Manually open and quickly close the throttle manually. A blast of air should be discharged from the diverted air outlet for at

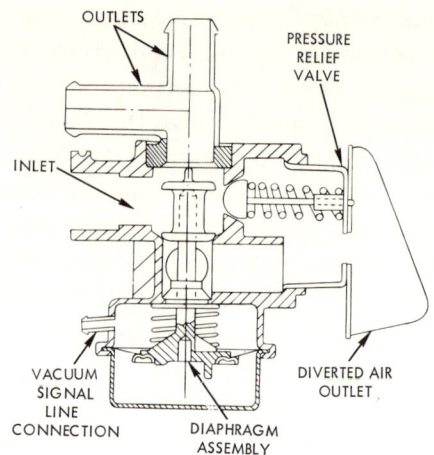

Fig. 8-25. Diverter (air bypass) valve. (Chevrolet Div., General Motors Corp.)

least one second. A defective valve must be replaced.

The only service required for the air injection tubes is to inspect them for carbon deposits and warped or burned tubes whenever the exhaust manifold or cylinder head is removed, exposing the tubes for service. Burned or warped tubes must be replaced. To replace the tubes, first remove the carbon from around the tubes. Then soak them with penetrating oil, and gradually work the tubes out of the manifold or cylinder head.

Two methods can be used to check the operation of the air induction pump. One test requires no equipment while the other involves the use of a fuel pump pressure gage and a special adapter.

Emissions Systems

When test equipment is not used, remove the hose or hoses from the pump. With the engine running, accelerate to approximately 1500 RPM (revolutions per minute) and observe the air flow from the hose or hoses. If the air flow increases as the engine speed is increased, the pump is operating satisfactorily. If the air flow does not increase or is not present, check for proper belt tension. Check for a leaky pressure relief valve. Air may be heard leaking when the engine is operating, if the valve is not functioning properly.

For a more accurate test, assemble a test gage adapter as shown in Fig. 8-26. Install a fuel pump pressure test gage on the adapter. With the engine at normal operating temperature, disconnect the air supply hose or hoses at the air manifold check valves. Close off one hose by inserting a suitable plug in one end and clamping it securely so it will not blow out. Insert the open pipe end of the test adapter in the other air supply hose and clamp securely. Position the adapter so the air blast emitted through the drilled pipe plug will be harmlessly dissipated. Install a tachometer, and bring the engine speed up to 1500 RPM. The air pressure reading should be one pound pressure or more per square inch. If the pressure does not meet minimum requirements, disconnect and plug the air supply hose to the diverter valve. Clamp the plug in place and repeat the test. If the pressure still does not meet requirements, the pump is defective. An air induction pump which does not deliver the necessary pressure must be replaced.

If the pressure relief valve leaks, the diverter valve assembly must be replaced.

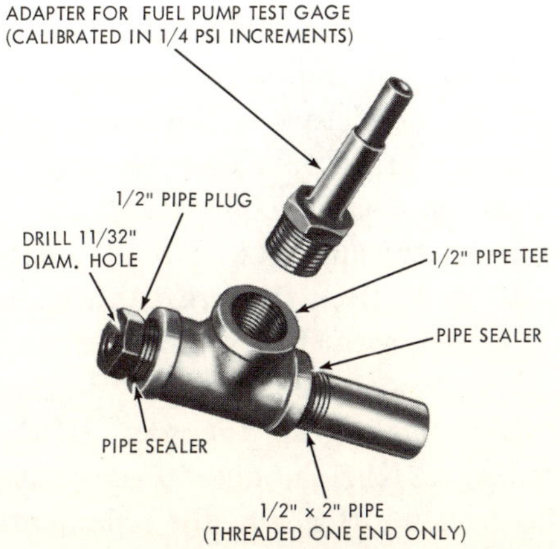

Testing Exhaust Emissions

Incomplete combustion of the air-fuel mixture within the combustion chamber is an important contributing factor toward excessive exhaust emissions. Either a lean mixture or an excessively rich air-fuel mixture can be a factor which results in improper combustion. An exhaust analyzer or an exhaust emission tester, when properly utilized, can indicate improper

Fig. 8-26. Air induction pump test gage adapter. (Ford Div., Ford Motor Co.)

combustion. It does not, however, determine what is causing the problem. The problem may be caused by weak compression, faulty carburetion, imperfect ignition, faulty timing, or a malfunctioning emission system.

The most common combustion analyzer utilizes a Wheatstone bridge which operates on the principle of the thermal conductivity of exhaust gases. Just as different metals have a different rate of conducting heat, so it is with gases. Hydrogen is a better heat conductor than air, and air is a better conductor than carbon dioxide. By measuring the conductivity of the engine exhaust gases, it is possible to determine if the mixture is lean or rich.

The gasoline burned in an engine consists of hydrogen and carbon. The air entering through the carburetor supplies the necessary oxygen to support combustion. During ideal combustion, each atom of carbon will unite with two atoms of oxygen, forming carbon dioxide. Every two atoms of hydrogen will combine with one atom of oxygen, resulting in water. When the mixture is too rich (not enough air), some of the hydrogen does not combine with oxygen. The unchanged hydrogen gas is a good coolant.

When an engine is running rich with an air-fuel ratio of ten or eleven parts of air to one part of fuel, there will be a large amount of unburned hydrogen in the exhaust emission and only a small amount of carbon dioxide. If the engine is running lean, fourteen parts of air to one part of fuel, there will be very little hydrogen but a large amount of carbon dioxide present in the exhaust gas. Because the different gases have a different rate of conductivity, an instrument which measures conductivity can be used to determine if the mixture is rich or lean.

The engine performance tester shown in Fig. 8-27 includes a combustion analyzer which utilizes a Wheatstone bridge circuit. In the circuit, four filaments are provided. Two of the filaments (3 and 4) are sealed in outside air. The other two (1 and 2) are vented to the exhaust collector tube. The four filaments are electrically energized by a power supply. When a voltage is applied to the circuit, a small amount of current will flow through the resistors. When air passes through all the cells, the value of all four resistors is the same, and there will be no meter reading.

When a sample of exhaust gas is drawn through the two filaments (1 and 2), the resistance is changed according to the amount of hydrogen and carbon dioxide which makes up the gas. If the mixture is rich, due to excessive hydrogen it cools the filaments decreasing the resistance. This change is reflected on the meter.

Emissions Systems

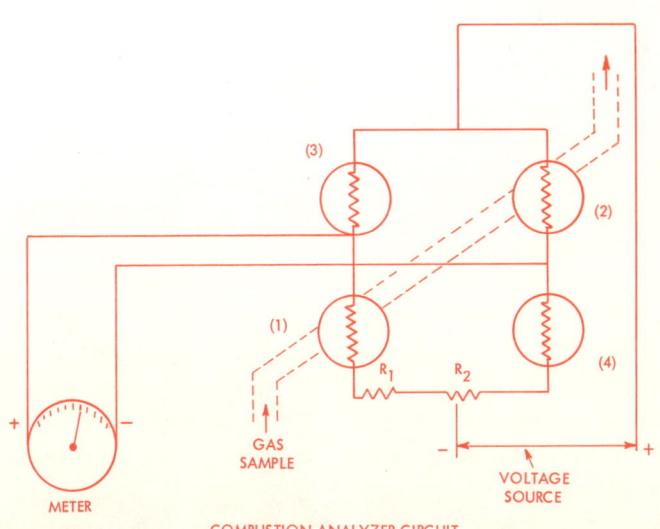

Fig. 8-27. Color shows combustion analyzer and circuit. (Sun Electric Corp.)

Automotive Engines

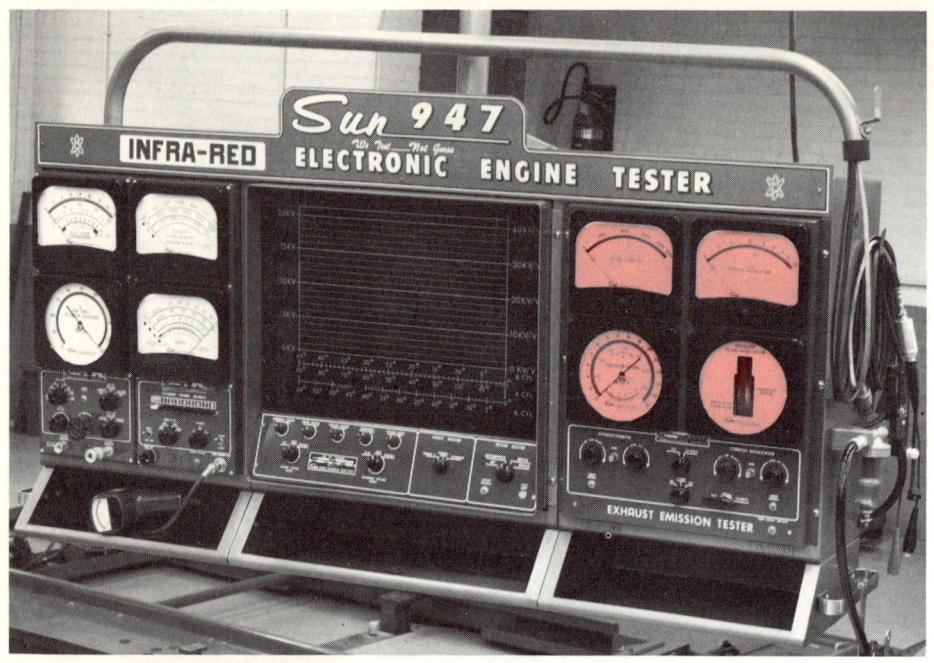

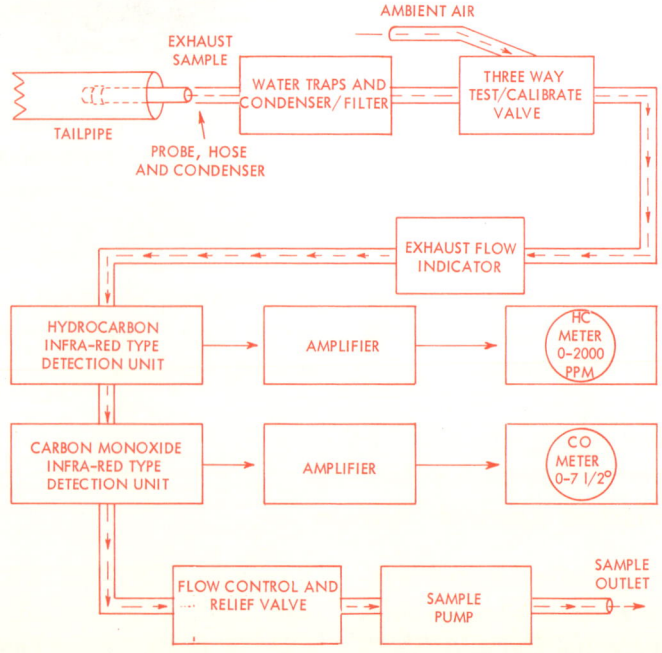

Fig. 8-28. Color shows exhaust emission tester and circuit. (Sun Electric Corp.)

Emissions Systems

If the mixture is lean, a high percentage of carbon dioxide is present, increasing the temperature. Filament resistance is thereby increased, causing the meter to move in the opposite direction from a rich mixture. The meter is calibrated to indicate air-fuel ratio.

A recently developed infra-red exhaust emission tester is being widely used, particularly in inspection stations and diagnosis centers.

The test unit makes the Beckman Instrument's Non-dispersive infra-red technology, for measuring hydrocarbons and carbon monoxide, available for checking automobile engine emissions. The unit is sensitive to N-Hexane hydrocarbons (a portion of gasoline and the by-product of incomplete combustion). Fig. 8-28 shows the tester and the flow of exhaust gases through the unit.

The tester consists of a pump, a condenser, a water trap, a filter, a three-way valve, an exhaust flow indicator, a hydrocarbon infra-red detection unit, a carbon monoxide infra-red detection unit, and the necessary amplifier units.

The exhaust sample is drawn from the exhaust into the tester probe and through the tester by a positive displacement pump. The sample is preconditioned as it passes through the condenser, the water trap, and particulate filter. From the filter the sample passes through the three-way valve, the exhaust flow indicator, and two infra-red units and recording devices. The sample passes through the hydrocarbon infra-red unit where the hydrocarbon is detected. Due to the non-dispersive characteristics of the analyzer, the same sample also passes on into the carbon monoxide infra-red unit where carbon monoxide is detected.

The output signals of both infra-red detection units are fed to their respective meters by solid-state amplifiers.

When using any make or model of tester to analyze exhaust emissions, it is very important that the manufacturer's specifications be carefully followed. The tester must be properly calibrated and the exhaust system must be at normal operating temperature.

Vapor Emission Control System

The vapor emission control system may have various names such as the Evaporative Emission Control System, Vapor Separator, or Vapor Saver System. All, however, will operate in the same manner and be made up of basically the same components.

Automotive Engines

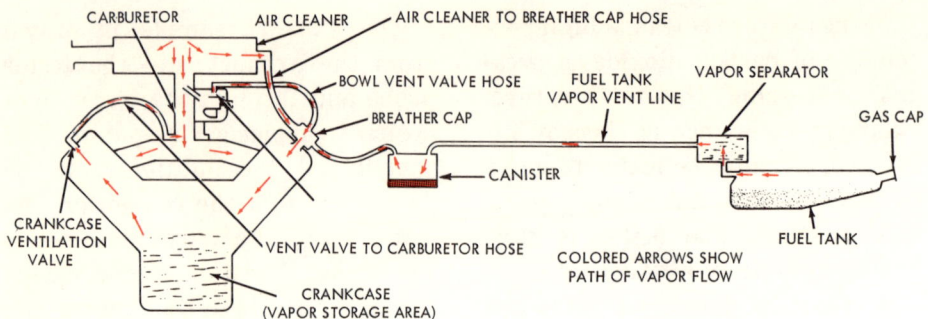

Fig. 8-29. Typical vapor emission control system. (Plymouth Div., Chrysler Corp.)

The system is designed to control fuel vapor emissions that normally vent into the atmosphere from the gasoline tank and carburetor fuel bowl. Instead of allowing the vapors to escape into the atmosphere, they are directed into the combustion chambers where they are burned.

Most systems consist of a fuel tank fill control system which provides expansion space, a vapor-liquid separator device, a pressure-vacuum relief tank fill cap, and a canister filter arrangement to further remove liquid fuel before the vapor enters the engine. Fig. 8-29 illustrates a typical vapor emission control system.

As the system is not vented to the outside, space must be provided at the tank for thermal expansion as well as for vapors to form. On some installations, due to the configuration of the fill pipe and/or internal vent lines within the fill pipe and tank, there will be a 10 to 12 percent air space remaining when the tank is filled to capacity. Other installations may use an over-fill limiter tank inside the regular tank for expansion purposes.

The loss of any fuel or fuel vapor out of the fill pipe is prevented by a sealed fill cap. The pressure-vacuum cap is designed to provide relief after $\frac{1}{4}$ psi of vacuum is reached and when $\frac{1}{2}$ to 1 psi of pressure is reached. (psi = pounds pressure per square inch).

A vapor separator device is used to prevent liquid fuel from entering the vent line leading to the engine. On one installation using a tank that is flat on top, four vent tubes are installed, Fig. 8-30, one in each corner of the tank. The vent lines are connected to a vapor-liquid separator by rubber hoses. Because of differences in height of the vent lines, the tank will always be vented regardless of the angle of the vehicle. One line leads to the crankcase inlet air cleaner.

Emissions Systems

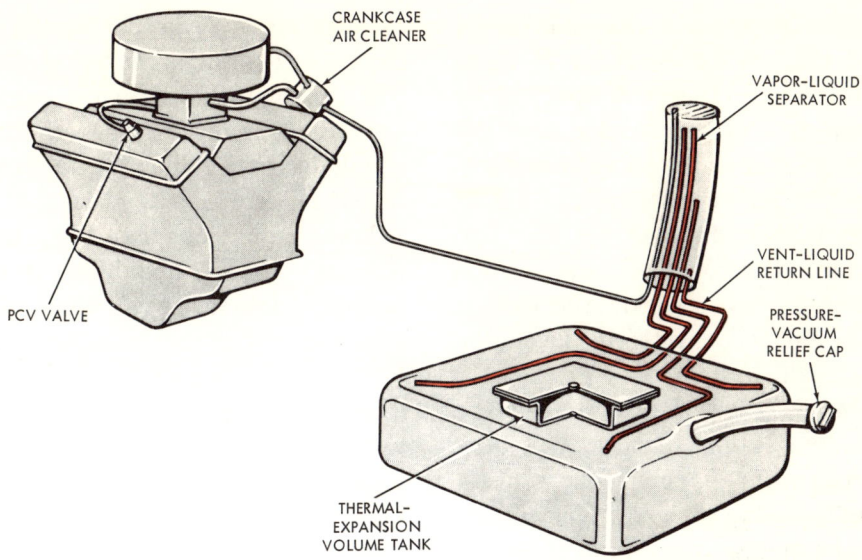

Fig. 8-30. Vapor emission control system with four vent tubes. (Plymouth Div., Chrysler Corp.)

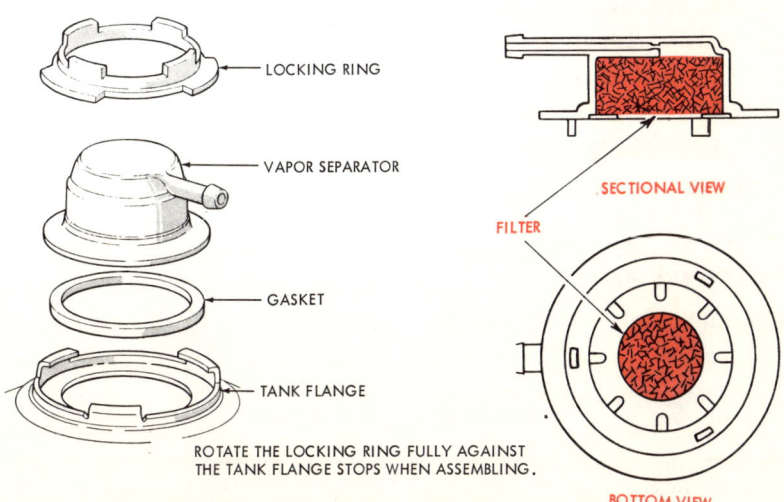

Fig. 8-31. Fuel vapor separator. (Ford Div., Ford Motor Co.)

Other installations will have a vapor-liquid separator unit located in the top of the fuel tank or attached to the outside of the tank. Some separator units will contain a foam material, Fig. 8-31 to act as

323

a baffle in separating the liquid fuel and the vapors. On most of these installations, the vent line will be connected to a canister type of filter located in the engine compartment to further remove any liquid fuel that might get by the fuel vapor separator. The canister will generally have a replaceable carbon filter and is connected to the engine air intake system.

In operation, the vapor from the gasoline tank leaves the tank through the vapor separator assembly to the carbon filter canister in the engine compartment and is then purged through the engine by way of the crankcase or air filter.

The vapor emission control system on some engines will include closed ventilation from the carburetor fuel bowl. These engines will have a hose connecting the carburetor bowl and the crankcase inlet air cleaner.

Maintenance of the Vapor Emission Control System

A minimum amount of maintenance needs to be performed on the vapor emissions control system. The canister located in the engine compartment which uses a filter should have the filter changed every 12,000 miles.

Locating obvious defects such as physical damage and leaks is the biggest diagnosis problem for emission system malfunctions. Any loss of fuel or vapor from the filler cap would indicate an unsatisfactory seal between the cap and filler pipe, plugged passages between the tank and vapor separator unit, a plugged line between the vapor separator and the canister or engine, or a malfunction of the filler cap release valve. Check the cap by placing the cap against the mouth and blowing into the hole in the release valve housing. An immediate release with light blowing or lack of release with hard blowing indicates a defective unit.

The vapor separator unit is replaced as a unit if it is permitting liquid fuel to flow through into the line.

Checking On Your Knowledge

The following questions give you the opportunity to check up on yourself. If you have read the chapter carefully, you should be able to answer the questions.

If you have any difficulty, read the chapter over once more so that you have the information well in mind before you go on with your reading.

Emissions Systems

DO YOU KNOW

1. What are the major air pollutants created by the automobile engine?
2. What are the sources of unburned hydrocarbons caused by the automobile?
3. How does water get into the engine lubricating oil?
4. How does a vent tube crankcase ventilating system operate?
5. Explain the operation of a PCV valve.
6. How is the PCV valve tested for proper operation?
7. What are the two types of exhaust emission control systems in use?
8. What are the different components and factors utilized singularly or in combination to reduce engine emissions?
9. Describe the operation of a dual diaphragm vacuum distributor advance unit.
10. What is the function of the temperature operated bypass valve?
11. How does the distributor retard solenoid operate?
12. How is engine "dieseling" prevented in some engines?
13. Explain how the transmission controlled vacuum spark advance system used with a manual transmission operates and why it is used.
14. How do you check out the transmission controlled vacuum spark advance system used with an automatic transmission?
15. What is the purpose of the thermostatically controlled air cleaner, and how does it operate?
16. How do you check the operation of the thermostatically operated air cleaner having a vacuum motor?
17. What is the purpose of an air induction system?
18. What are the major common components of an air induction system?
19. Why is it important that an engine be tuned properly when checking for excessive emissions?
20. How does a combustion analyzer operate?
21. What components make up the vapor emission control system, and how does it function?

Chapter

9 Fuel and Fuel Systems

The internal combustion automobile engines operates on gasoline mixed with air. Gasoline is a hydrocarbon derived from crude oil. Other hydrocarbons such as alcohol, natural and artificial gas, benzol, propane, and butane have been used successfully in engines designed for gasoline.

To better understand the fuel system, we will explore the nature of the fuels that can be used and what takes place as they are burned in the combustion chamber. The design of the fuel system and the engine are very closely related to the kind of fuel being used.

The automotive fuel system stores liquid fuel and delivers it to the engine cylinders in the form of a vapor mixed with air. The air-fuel mixture must be delivered to the cylinders in varying amounts and proportions of air and fuel to meet the different operating conditions. This chapter discusses automotive fuels and describes the construction and operation of the fuel supply system.

Automotive Fuels

Most internal combustion engines use gasoline as a fuel. Diesel fuel oil and liquified petroleum gas (LPG) are also widely used. Automobile engines are designed to operate on gasoline because of its availability, ease of storage and handling, and high heat value.

Fuel and Fuel Systems

Gasoline

Gasoline is a clear, colorless liquid composed of hydrogen and carbon (hydrocarbon compound) which evaporates readily and burns violently if ignited when exposed to air. Gasoline is a complex compound made by blending several hydrocarbons, each of which contributes certain characteristics to produce a suitable fuel.

Gasoline is derived from petroleum (crude oil). Petroleum is obtained from wells drilled deep into the earth in areas where oil bearing formations are located. Petroleum is an intricate mixture of many compounds that can be separated by refining into many substances called *fractions*.

Refining of Petroleum. It would be impossible in a few pages to describe all of the refining processes used by the petroleum industry to obtain the various fuel and lubricants. The information presented here is intended to give you a general understanding of some of the processes used to obtain engine fuels from petroleum.

The process of refining petroleum or crude oil is accomplished chiefly by some form of distillation. A simple distillation process can be observed by watching a teakettle of boiling water. The vapor emitted through the spout of the kettle is in the form of steam. When the steam contacts a cold surface, it condenses into liquid form. Thus, distillation is the process of deriving gas or vapor from a liquid or solid by heating in a retort or still, and condensing the vapor into a liquid.

Unlike water, petroleum is composed of thousands of different hydrocarbons, each of which has its own boiling point. The light hydrocarbons, such as those in the gasoline range, have quite low boiling points. The heavier materials, such as heavy lubricating oils and tars, have high boiling points. It is the problem of the refiner to separate these different compounds ranging from heavy asphalts, acids, tars, oils, etc., to gasolines, solvents, propane, etc., by the process of evaporation and condensation. The process is much the same as a teakettle and water but the apparatus must be much more complex. A schematic diagram of part of the petroleum refining process is shown in Fig. 9-1.

Essentially, a refiner employs a still, a fractionating tower, and a condenser. Crude oil is placed in a still where heat is applied to vaporize it. The vaporized products then go to the fractionating tower (sometimes referred to as a bubbling tower). The lighter vapors, such as gasoline, rise to the top of the tower where they condense or are withdrawn to a condenser which is operated at a relatively low temperature to convert the vapors to a liquid state. Heavier products, such as kerosene and fuel

Automotive Engines

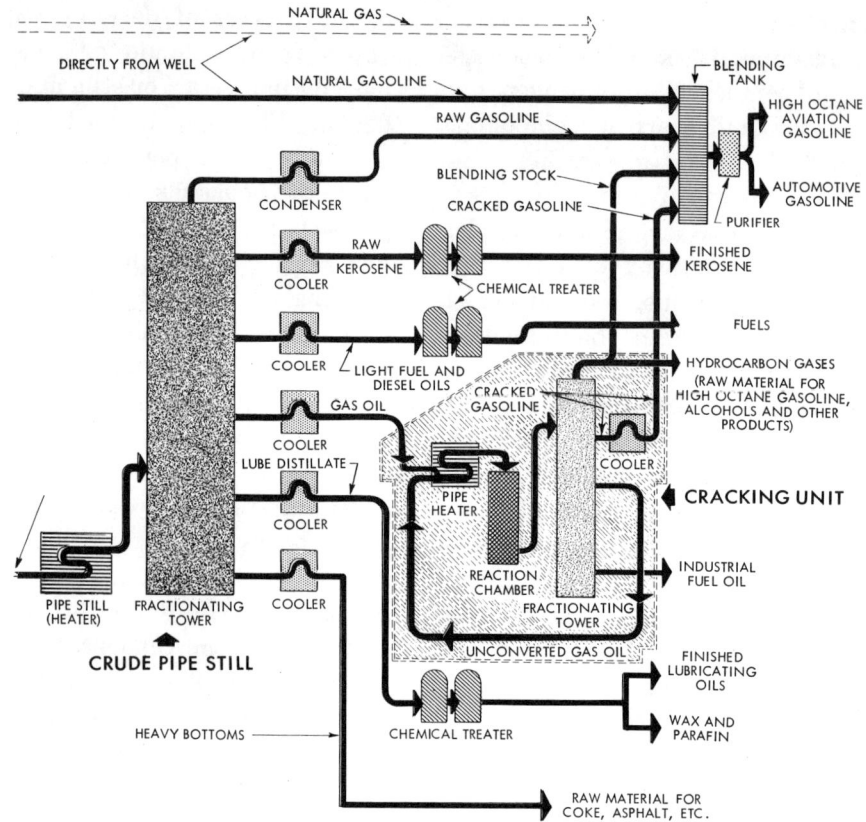

Fig. 9-1. Typical flow chart tracing crude oil from well to finished products. From 100 gallons of crude oil. about 44 gallons of gasoline can be produced by this method. (American Petroleum Institute)

oil, are withdrawn farther down the tower and are also condensed. The heaviest vapors, such as lubricating oils, etc., are taken off near the bottom of the fractionating tower.

When crude oil is subjected to the relatively simple "straight run" process just described, not enough gasoline is obtained to be practical. The gasoline, moreover, is too low in antiknock quality and too high in impurities to be satisfactory for use in modern engines. Over a period of years, the refining industry has overcome these disadvantages by developing many different processes to obtain more gasoline of a higher quality from crude oil. Each refining process rearranges the molecular structure of the oil. The choice of the process depends on the type of crude oil being refined, the antiknock qualities desired, and the cost of operation. Some of the processes being used today are known as thermal cracking, catalytic cracking, reforming, polymerization, and alkylation.

Thermal Cracking. One of the first and most common cracking processes is thermal cracking. In thermal cracking a wide range of charging stock can be used, varying from undesirable heavy gasoline (gas-oil) components to residual oils. With a cracking process it is possible to change more than half of the original crude oil into gasoline. Cracking essentially is the use of high temperature and relatively high pressure which causes a series of chemical changes resulting in the production of a wide range of petroleum products.

Catalytic Cracking. The big difference between thermal and catalytic cracking is in the use of catalysts. A catalyst is a chemical which causes a desired chemical reaction to take place even though it does not take part in the reaction (combine with the solution). Usually the catalyst is recovered and reused. There is a wide variety of catalysts, and new ones are being developed constantly. These include acids, acid treated clays, molybdenum, platinum, nickel, silica, and many other metals. Not only does catalytic cracking accomplish its basic purpose of converting heavy oils, etc., into gasoline components, but the gasoline is usually superior to many others in antiknock quality. The sulfur content will generally be reduced by catalytic cracking.

Reforming. Reforming, like cracking, is available in a variety of processes. Reforming converts low octane and heavy components of gasoline (generally straight run gasolines) into gasolines with higher octane and higher specific gravity. As with most refining operations, a certain volume loss always takes place during the reforming process. However, this is offset to some extent by the improved quality of the gasoline produced.

Thermal Reforming. Thermal reforming is largely a thermal cracking operation using heavy gasoline components as the refining stock. Volatility, specific gravity, and octane ratings of the resulting gasoline are improved.

Catalytic Reforming. Catalytic reforming, like catalytic cracking, rearranges the gasoline molecules to improve the gasoline quality. The reaction takes place in the presence of a catalyst, generally in the form of a precious metal.

Polymerization. Cracking and reforming create a considerable quantity of very light hydrocarbons (butane and propane) which are in vapor form at ordinary temperature and pressure. Usually polymerization is considered to be the combining of two or more of these light hydrocarbons to form a liquid suitable as a quality gasoline component. In recent years, there has also been a considerable increase in the use of LPG (liquified petroleum gas) which is mostly propane and natural gas. This has given these lighter hydrocarbons wider commercial application.

Alkylation. Another refining operation that uses very light hydrocarbons is called alkylation. It is somewhat similar to polymerization in that it takes hydrocarbons which are normally gases and forms them into liquids suitable for use in blending with gasoline. The product of alkylation is called alkylate. Alkylation was once used almost exclusively for the production of aviation gasoline components. At the present time, increasing amounts of alkylate are being used in automotive gasolines.

Combustion of Gasoline

Gasoline plus oxygen is capable of producing tremendous power, however the most efficient gasoline engine can use only a fraction of the power available in the gasoline.

Fuels derived from petroleum contain no oxygen, therefore they must be combined with either oxygen or air in order to burn. Fuels in the gasoline category require approximately fifteen parts of air to one part of fuel by weight to attain complete combustion. The mixing of the fuel and air is accomplished in the carburetor of an automobile engine.

Air-Fuel Mixture. Dry air contains, by weight, approximately 23.2% oxygen, 75.5% nitrogen, and 1.3% of other gases. A large volume of air is necessary to obtain the required amount of oxygen. For complete combustion, a theoretical air-fuel ratio of 15.5 pounds of air to one pound of gasoline would be required as indicated by Table 9-1. The weight of air divided by the weight of gasoline is the air-fuel ratio.

This equation indicates that an engine would theoretically require about 94 pounds of air (9,000 gallons) to burn a gallon of gasoline. Slightly more than a gallon of water (8.9 lbs.) would be produced in the exhaust gases. The nitrogen in the air is not utilized; it remains in the same form after combustion has taken place.

Several factors make it impos-

TABLE 9-1

1 gal. gasoline + air	=	Carbon Dioxide + Water + Nitrogen, etc.
6.2 lbs. + 94 lbs.	=	19.1 lbs. + 8.9 lbs. + 72.2 lbs.

Fuel and Fuel Systems

TABLE 9-2

Operating Conditions	Air-Fuel Ratio
Idling	11-12.5 to 1
Cruising	13.5-17.0 to 1
Full Load	12-13.5 to 1

sible to supply the theoretically correct air-fuel mixture to each cylinder of a multicylinder engine. Actually, the power and performance of an engine are not as satisfactory with the theoretical mixture as they are with a slightly richer mixture. Therefore, carburetors are calibrated to supply a mixture richer than 15 pounds of air per pound of fuel for a full load operation.

As shown in Table 9-2, the best power mixture is quite different from that of the best economy mixture. Usually, gasoline engines will not operate if the mixture is richer than 8 to 1 or leaner than about 17 to 1.

Because the burning of the fuel in the combustion chamber is rarely complete, all the carbon in the fuel is not converted into carbon dioxide. When a shortage of oxygen exists, free carbon and carbon monoxide are formed. Carbon monoxide is a deadly poisonous gas. When more free carbon and carbon monoxide are produced, less heat and power are obtained.

The exhaust system carries out the unburned portion of the fuel from the engine. Most of the hydrogen in the fuel and part of the oxygen combine to form water. In cold weather, the water appears as a vapor in the engine exhaust. All engines are also provided with ventilating systems which dispose of unburned fuels and the by-products of combustion that enter the engine crankcase.

At high altitudes, atmospheric pressure is lower, and air density is less than at sea level. Consequently, the same volume of air weighs less at high altitudes than at sea level. As a result, fewer pounds of air enter an engine at a given speed and throttle opening. This causes the air-fuel mixture to become richer and requires correction if a vehicle is to be operated efficiently at higher than normal altitudes.

Flame Speed. In a four-stroke-cycle engine, the power stroke must furnish enough energy to propel the vehicle and also enough to offset friction, heat, and pumping loss of all four strokes of the cycle. The efficiency and power of an engine are determined by the many parts and characteristics of the engine.

Combustion chamber design, fuel mixture, ignition timing, quality of the spark, compression ratio, valve action, carbon deposits, friction, etc., will all determine the power produced during the power stroke. If all parts of the engine are functioning correctly and normal combustion occurs within the cylinder, the spark plug will ignite the air-fuel mixture and a wave of flame will spread out from the spark plug and move across the combustion chamber burning all the mixture smoothly and evenly until it reaches the other side.

The speed of the flame varies from a possible 20 to over 150 feet per second. The flame speed is determined primarily by the pressure of the fuel mixture, the air-fuel ratio, the turbulence within the chamber, and the combustion chamber design. At wide open throttle, when cylinder pressures are high, the combustion is much more rapid than during low speed cruising or idling condition when cylinder pressures are low.

Pressure Increase. Burning the fuel mixture produces heat causing the gases to expand. Since the burning mixture is confined in the combustion chamber and cannot expand immediately, the heat causes the pressure to increase. As an example, if the initial pressure when the spark plug fires is 160 psi, the final pressure will be almost 600 psi. The pressure increase due to combustion will be about 3½ to 4 times the initial pressure. Each piston of an engine operating at wide open throttle will carry a momentary force of from 3 to 4 tons.

Detonation. If the fuel in the combustion chamber burns too rapidly, the sudden increase in pressure causes the unburned portion of the fuel to ignite, resulting in a violent explosion as the two fronts of burning fuel meet. This secondary explosion, known as detonation, causes a rapping or knocking noise as it imposes sharp blows on the piston. The detonation of gasoline is a phenomenon of combustion to which many names have been given such as "fuel knock," "carbon knock," "spark knock," or "ping." Fig. 9-2 illustrates detonation as well as normal burning within the combustion chamber.

Detonation reduces the force of the primary explosion resulting in a loss of engine power. Detonation also leads to overheating of engine parts such as valves, pistons, and spark plugs. Overheating promotes further detonation which, in severe cases, causes cracked or burned piston heads and shortens the life of the valves and spark plugs.

Detonation can be prevented in many cases by using fuel of higher antiknock quality (octane number). Frequently engines will detonate even though the gasoline is satisfactory. Under these circum-

Fuel and Fuel Systems

The fuel is ignited by the spark plug and starts to burn across the combustion chamber.

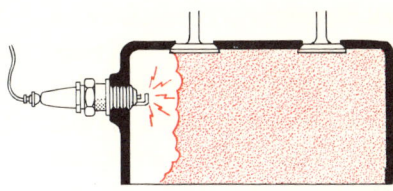

As the fuel burns, the unburned portion is compressed into the far end of the combustion chamber.

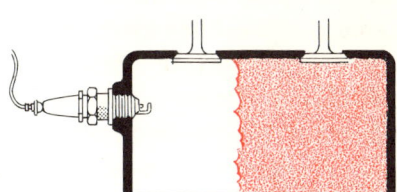

The increased pressure raises the temperature of the unburned fuel.

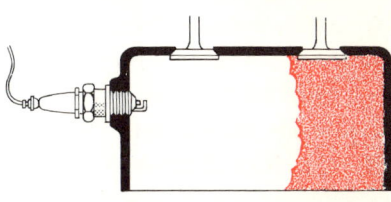

The temperature of gasoline having a low octane rating is increased to such a degree that ignition takes place in the far end of the combustion chamber.

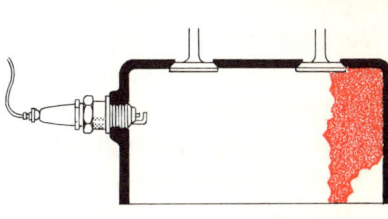

This results in a violent explosion caused by the meeting of the two fronts of burning fuel. This is known as detonation or "knocking".

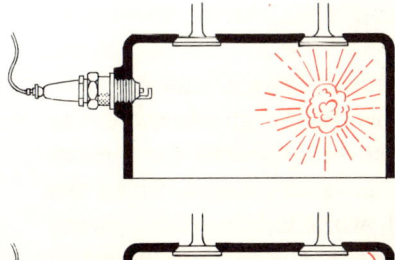

Fuels having an adequate octane rating burn evenly across the combustion chamber without the violent explosion which causes detonation.

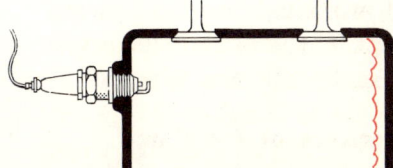

Fig. 9-2. The upper five cross sections show how detonation develops in the combustion chamber. The bottom cross section shows even, detonation-free burning in the combustion chamber.

stances, the cause of the detonation is mechanical and can be corrected by proper maintenance. Mechanical conditions causing detonation may be combustion chamber deposits, cooling system defects, incorrect air-fuel ratio, or improper spark timing and advance.

Preignition. Another type of knocking which occurs in the engine and is sometimes confused with detonation is known as preignition. Preignition occurs whenever the fuel charge is ignited by some means other than the spark plug. Glowing carbon, burning flakes of carbon, hot exhaust valves, or a glowing tip on a spark plug will ignite the fuel charge before the spark plug fires. The knock resulting from preignition is irregular and may occur any time after the fuel charge enters the combustion chamber. Excessive combustion chamber heat, spark plugs with incorrect heat range, and carbon deposits will bring about preignition.

An engine knock can also be caused when the spark occurs at the spark plug before the proper time. This causes combustion pressures to work against the upward movement of the piston, causing a knock usually called a "ping."

Characteristics of Gasoline

Gasoline is blended from a number of different basic hydrocarbons to provide a fuel that permits efficient engine performance under varying conditions. No individual test or combination of tests will predict exactly the performance of a gasoline in a given engine because engines vary considerably even in the same makes and models. Furthermore, there are a great many engine and maintenance factors that affect the performance of gasoline. Certain customary laboratory tests, however, enable the gasoline manufacturers to measure important characteristics which determine the suitability of the gasoline for given applications. Factors which manufacturers take into consideration in the blending process include volatility, harmful chemical and gum content, and octane rating.

Volatility. Volatility is the ability of a fuel to change from a liquid to a vapor. This affects both the starting and operating performance of an engine.

A gasoline that vaporizes readily provides easier starting in cold weather, faster warm up, better fuel distribution to all cylinders, and allows the engine to develop maximum power with efficient operation. A volatile fuel provides quick, smooth acceleration because of its ability to vaporize and burn more completely.

By blending hydrocarbon compounds having different boiling points or volatility, it is possible to vary the volatility of the gasoline. Many manufacturers will increase

Fuel and Fuel Systems

the volatility of their gasoline for winter conditions, particularly in northern climates.

Vapor Lock. When an engine is hot, a gasoline that is highly volatile may vaporize either in the fuel pump or the fuel lines before reaching the manifold. This condition is known as vapor lock. Complete vapor lock will prevent the engine from operating until the fuel and engine have cooled enough to reduce the volume of vapor in the system. Partial vapor lock will reduce top speed and power because it leans out the mixture through reduced gasoline flow. When vapor lock occurs in a fuel system, the pressure of the fuel pump merely compresses the vaporized fuel rather than forcing it into the carburetor. Vapor lock may be prevented to some extent by shielding the fuel pump and fuel lines from the heat of the exhaust and locating the lines as far as possible from the exhaust system. To keep heat away from the carburetor, manufacturers usually equip engines with insulator blocks between the carburetor and intake manifold. If the fuel pump pressure is low and fuel lines are sharply bent or restricted, the system is likely to vapor lock.

Chemicals and Gums in Fuels. In refining and compounding gasoline, every effort is made to minimize harmful chemicals and gum-forming materials.

Sulfur is one of the chemicals often found in small quantities in gasoline. When gasoline with a higher than normal sulfur content is burned in an engine, some of the sulfur enters the engine crankcase where it combines with water to form sulfuric acid. Sulfuric acid is highly corrosive to engine parts. Crankcase ventilation is used to help remove acid forming chemicals from the crankcase.

The gum content of gasoline must be kept to a minimum because the gums tend to form resinous deposits in the carburetor and engine parts. These gums can clog carburetor passages and cause valves and piston rings to stick.

Octane Rating. With modern high compression engines, the antiknock value of the gasoline becomes an extremely important consideration. Engine compression pressures have risen to a point where considerable heat is generated when the fuel charge is compressed. Unless a gasoline is used that has the necessary antiknock value, the high temperature and pressure will result in a secondary explosion known as detonation which is detrimental to engine parts and results in loss of power.

The antiknock value of a gasoline is rated in terms of octane numbers. The octane number of gasoline is a measure of its ability to resist detonation during combustion. The term *octane number* is

Automotive Engines

used widely in the petroleum industry. Yet some confusion exists as to its use and meaning because there are several accepted methods of measuring octane. There are also many factors which influence the knocking tendency of a given gasoline.

Methods of Measuring Octane. In testing laboratories, the octane number of gasoline is measured with a special single cylinder engine which was developed by the Cooperative Fuel Research Committee (CFR). The CFR engine has an unusual feature which allows the compression ratio to be varied while the engine is running.

It is also equipped with a device in the combustion chamber which can record electrically the severity of detonation. This engine has been adopted by both the automotive and oil industries for measuring the detonation characteristics of engine fuels, Fig. 9-3.

The CFR engine is operated on a mixture of iso-octane and heptane, two pure hydrocarbons. Iso-octane is nearly 100% knockless fuel, and heptane is a fuel that will knock under almost any circumstances. The percentage of iso-octane in a mixture of the two hydrocarbons which will give the same results as that obtained by using the gasoline

Fig. 9-3. The CFR engine determines the octane rating of a gasoline through the use of reference fuels. (Ethyl Corp.)

under test is the octane rating or number of the gasoline. Thus, if a mixture of 90% iso-octane and 10% heptane gave the same results in the engine as the gasoline under test, the octane rating of the gasoline would be 90. The higher the octane number, the higher the antiknock quality of the gasoline.

In octane number rating it is obviously impossible to have more than 100% iso-octane in the reference fuel. For gasolines with antiknock qualities above 100 octane the reference fuel becomes iso-octane plus a known amount of tetraethyl lead. As as example, the quality of a certain gasoline rating above 100 octane number might be expressed as "100 + 2.5" indicating that the gasoline has the same octane rating as iso-octane to which 2.5 ml (millilitres) per gallon of tetraethyl lead has been added.

In the early development of the CFR engine, the accepted procedure for establishing octane rating was known as the "Motor Method of Test for Knock Characteristics of Motor Fuels." As new refining processes were developed, gasolines were produced with better road performance than the laboratory numbers would indicate and, as a result, a second method for testing fuels known as the Research Method was adopted. Both of the tests are performed in the same engine but under different standard operating conditions. The Research Method is less severe than the Motor Method. Therefore, most gasolines will have a higher octane number by the Research Method than by the Motor Method.

The difference in octane number ratings by the Motor and Research methods are referred to as the "sensitivity." The sensitivity of a gasoline depends upon the nature of the crude oil and the type of manufacturing processes used. Straight run and natural gasoline, for example, are considered to be insensitive because their Motor and Research octane numbers are about the same value. On the other hand, cracked gasolines are quite sensitive. Some show a sensitivity as high as 15 octane numbers. Gasoline at the average service station has a sensitivity of 6 to 8 octane numbers.

When two fuels have the same Motor octane number the one with the greater Research rating will usually perform better on the road. Conversely, if two fuels have the same Research rating, the least sensitive gasoline will usually be the better. In general, it is felt that Research octane numbers correlate more closely with gasoline performance in engines during low speed than the Motor Method octane numbers which indicate gasoline performance during high engine speed.

Several techniques have been

developed for testing gasolines in vehicles on the road or on laboratory dynamometers which duplicate road conditions. There are also several methods of rating a gasoline in actual vehicles, but in each method the gasoline to be tested is matched with a mixture of iso-octane and heptane.

Gasoline Additives. Like motor oils, gasoline often contains additives or chemicals to improve operating qualities.

Tetraethyl Lead. Most fuels over the years have been treated with tetraethyl lead (TEL) compound to reduce the knocking tendency. These fuels are usually called "ethyl" or premium grade gasolines. They are colored for identification purposes. Gasoline containing TEL is injurious to the human body. *The gasoline vapors should not be breathed, and the gasoline itself should not be brought into contact with the skin.*

Due to the need for reducing engine emissions which contribute to pollution of the atmosphere, automobile engine manufacturers are designing engines and engine components to reduce the lead content requirements for gasolines. Petroleum manufacturers are also changing compounding and refining methods so as to produce the antiknock characteristics in gasolines without the extensive use of tetraethyl lead.

Metal Deactivators. Metal deactivators are often added to prevent gasoline from reacting with metals of the storage container or the fuel tank and system.

Phosphorus Compounds. Phosphorus compounds are widely used to control surface ignition. Metallic deposits from the gasoline combine with combustion chamber deposits causing the material to glow at a lower temperature than it otherwise would. Spark plug misfiring can also be caused by metallic deposits.

Anti-icers. Moisture in the air can cause carburetor icing at certain temperatures. To prevent carburetor icing, some oil companies add anti-icing chemicals such as specially selected and treated alcohols. These act as antifreeze until carburetor temperatures are high enough to prevent icing.

Antioxidant Inhibitors. Antioxidant inhibitors are added to gasoline to prevent the unstable hydrocarbons from absorbing oxygen or from combining with one another to form heavy resinous compounds (gums).

Other Fuels in General Use

Several fuels other than gasoline can be used successfully in internal combustion engines. Certain fuels require special equipment while other fuels can use the same equipment as for gasoline. Diesel fuel, liquified petroleum gas, alcohol, natural or artificial gas, and benzol

Fuel and Fuel Systems

are some of the more common fuels.

Diesel Fuel. Diesel engines burn a fuel oil that is obtained from petroleum during the refining process. The fuel oils are obtained from the heavier oils that remain after gasoline is drawn off. These oils are refined to produce several grades of fuel oil, from light to heavy.

Diesel fuel oils are hydrocarbons with percentages of hydrogen and carbon very nearly the same as those of gasoline, namely 86 per cent hydrogen and small amounts of nitrogen and sulfur. Fuel oils have a higher heat value (measured in British Thermal Units) and economy than gasoline. As a result, Diesel engines have a slightly higher percentage of operating efficiency than gasoline engines and offer some economies in operation. (See the appendix if you would like an explanation of British Thermal Units.)

Liquified Petroleum Gas. Liquified petroleum gas (LPG) in the form of propane or butane is being used in standard gasoline engines equipped with a special fuel system. Liquified petroleum gas is made up of types of hydrocarbons lighter than gasoline. LPG is in a vapor form at ordinary temperatures, because its molecules are very light in weight.

Butane becomes a vapor at temperatures above 32°F, while propane vaporizes at −44°F. Because of the low temperatures at which they vaporize, the fuel is fed into the engine in the form of vapor. When butane is used in cold climates, it must be sent through a heater to be vaporized before it goes into the combustion chamber. Butane is usually mixed with propane so it will vaporize when used at low temperatures.

When LPG is used as an engine fuel, it is stored as a liquid in a pressurized tank. From the tank, the fuel passes through a high pressure regulator which reduces the pressure and sends the fuel to a vaporizer heated by the water in the cooling system. A low pressure regulator takes the place of the carburetor and meters the amount of fuel vapor in proportion to air entering the intake manifold.

Some of the advantages of fuels which are normally gases rather than liquids are their ability to vaporize completely and mix readily with the air. Because the fuel is stored under pressure, there is no need for a fuel pump. A third advantage is that LPG has a high octane rating, making it suitable for use in high compression engines. LPG reduces engine wear for it leaves little or no carbon deposits when it burns. LPG also has the advantage of not going down into the crankcase and diluting the oil because it is in vapor form.

One disadvantage of LPG as an engine fuel is that it must be stored

Automotive Engines

in a relatively heavy pressurized tank and special equipment is required to fill the tank. The availability of LPG is somewhat limited. Therefore, it is not practical in many sections of the country to use LPG as a general automotive fuel.

Alcohol. Alcohol is a liquid fuel and is commonly used in countries where petroleum is not readily available. Alcohol is made from vegetable fiber (wood, sugar cane, etc.). It can be utilized in a standard gasoline fuel system. Alcohol is sometimes added to gasoline as an antiknock agent.

Natural or Artificial Gas. Fuel in the form of natural or artificial gas is often used for the operation of stationary engines, particularly in areas where such fuels are plentiful. Since the fuel is in gaseous form, vaporization is not required. Therefore, it can be introduced directly into the engine combustion chambers by means of a simple mixing valve which adds air to the gas.

Benzol (Benzene). Benzol (benzene) is a by-product of coke ovens. Benzol, a liquid fuel, is sometimes combined with gasoline to increase fuel volatility and to increase its antiknock characteristics.

Components of the Fuel System

The typical automotive fuel system consists of a fuel tank, filter, fuel gage, fuel pump, a carburetor with an air cleaner, an intake manifold, and an exhaust system, Fig. 9-4. Fuel lines connect the tank,

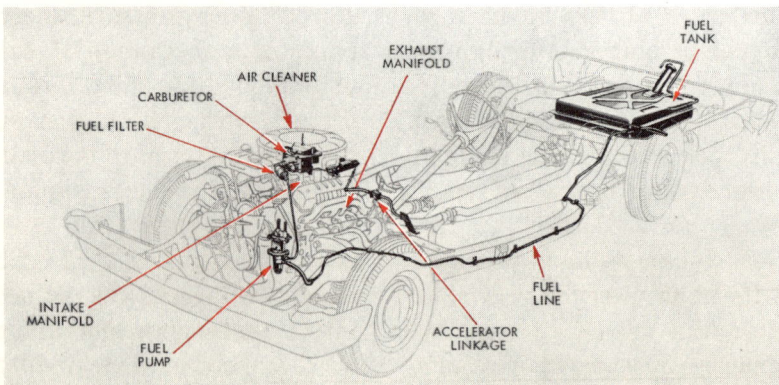

Fig. 9-4. This is how a typical fuel system would appear if the car body were removed. (Ford Div., Ford Motor Co.)

Fuel and Fuel Systems

pump, and the carburetor. An accelerator pedal in the driver's compartment is linked to the carburetor to control the amount of air-fuel mixture entering the engine cylinders.

Fuel Tank

The fuel tank, a container for storing fuel, is usually located at the rear of the vehicle and is attached with metal straps. Baffle plates are attached to the inside of the tank to strengthen the tank and to prevent surging of fuel when the vehicle suddenly stops or goes around a corner.

The tank outlet line draws fuel through a porous filter attached to the outlet line about ¾ in. above the bottom of the tank. As fuel passes through the porous filter, any water in the bottom of the tank, being heavier, gathers in globular form on the surface of the filter and drops back into the tank. Any dirt which may have found its way into the fuel also gathers on the surface of the filter and is washed off by the vigorous motion of the fuel in the tank. Most fuel tanks include a drain plug located in a sump formed in the bottom of the tank.

On vehicles manufactured before 1970—the filler pipe or tank was vented so that the fuel was under atmospheric pressure at all times. It has been mandated by Federal regulations that all currently manufactured passenger vehicles be equipped with fuel evaporative emission systems. A sealed fill cap with a built-in pressure-vacuum relief valve must be used. All gasoline vapors in the fuel tank are routed to the engine where they are burned. This is part of the emission control system and is covered in Chapter 8 entitled Emissions Systems.

Fuel Gage

Automotive vehicles are equipped with an electrically operated fuel gage which consists of a sending unit mounted on the fuel tank and a receiving unit with a calibrated gage mounted on the instrument panel.

Sending Unit. A typical sending unit consists of a float controlled rheostat or variable resistor, Fig. 9-5. This unit is mounted on the fuel tank with the float and float arm extending into the tank. The float always follows the level of the fuel in the tank. The float position determines the amount of electrical resistance within the variable resistor which controls the amount of electricity sent to the receiving unit on the instrument panel.

Receiving Unit. The receiving unit is mounted on the instrument panel and, by the amount of electricity received from the sending unit, indicates, on a calibrated gage, the amount of fuel in the tank.

Automotive Engines

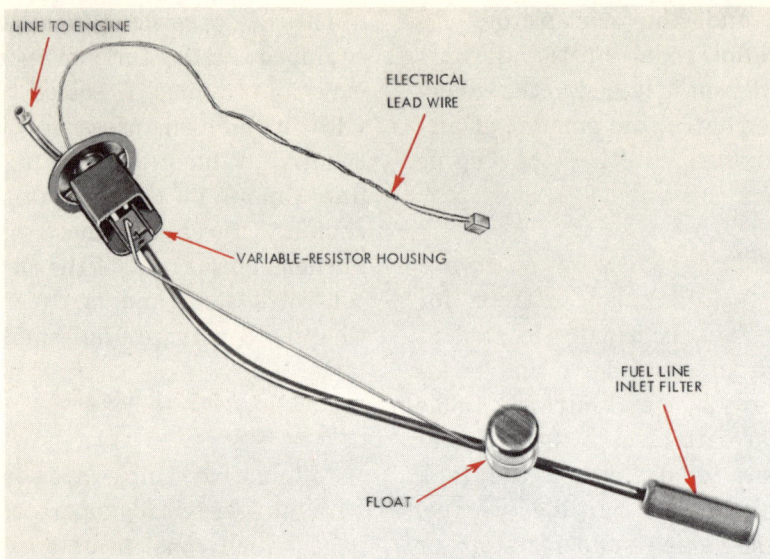

Fig. 9-5. The fuel gage tank unit measures the amount of fuel in the tank and then sends the information to the dash unit. (Plymouth Div., Chrysler Corp.)

Two types of fuel gages are used on automobiles today: a thermostatic type and an electromagnetic type. Both incorporate a sending unit and a receiving unit.

Thermostatic Fuel Gage. The thermostatic fuel gage receiving unit contains a heating coil.

When the fuel tank is low, a grounded sliding contact in the sending unit controlled by the float is near the end of the variable resistance wire and sends only a small amount of current to the heating coil in the receiving unit, Fig. 9-6. The heating coil activates a bimetallic arm which moves the gage pointer to the "E" (empty) position.

When the tank is filled, the float rises with the fuel level and moves the grounded sliding contact toward the beginning of the resistance wire. Thus, electrical resistance decreases, and current flowing to the receiving unit increases. The heating coil in the receiving unit generates more heat and moves the pointer to the "F" (full) position.

The thermostatic type fuel gage uses a voltage regulator to maintain uniform voltage in the fuel gage circuit. This voltage regulator also contains a heating coil which activates a bimetallic arm. When the ignition switch is turned on, the coil heats the bimetallic arm,

342

Fuel and Fuel Systems

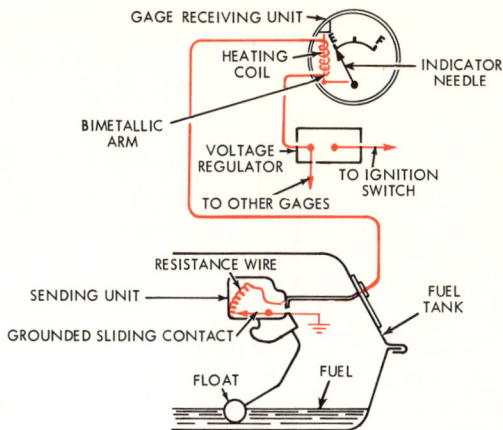

Fig. 9-6. This thermostatic type fuel gage registers "Empty" because the tank sending unit is allowing only a small amount of current to flow to the heating coil in the dash unit. As the tank is filled, the float will move the sliding contact upward along the resistance wire which will allow more current to flow to the coil. The coil will be heated, and the bimetallic arm will bend, moving the needle toward the "Full" position. (Ford Div., Ford Motor Co.)

bending the arm and breaking contacts which disconnects the current supply from the heating coil. When the bimetallic arm cools, it brings the contacts together again. This making and breaking of the contacts maintains a uniform voltage in the thermostatic fuel gage circuit.

Electromagnetic Fuel Gage. The electromagnetic fuel gage contains two electromagnetic field coils in the receiving unit at the dash panel.

One of these two coils is grounded internally. Therefore, when the ignition switch is on, this grounded coil exerts a constant pull on the gage pointer toward the "empty" position, Fig. 9-7.

The other coil in the receiving unit is grounded through the sending unit at the fuel tank. This coil exerts a variable pull on the pointer toward the "full" position. The sending unit contains a variable resistor with a sliding contact which moves as the float moves. The movement induces a strong magnetic field in the receiving coil when the fuel level rises and a weak magnetic field as the level drops. It is this changing magnetic pull which moves the needle on the gage.

Fuel Filters

Fuel filters and/or screens are used at different locations throughout the fuel system for the purpose

343

Automotive Engines

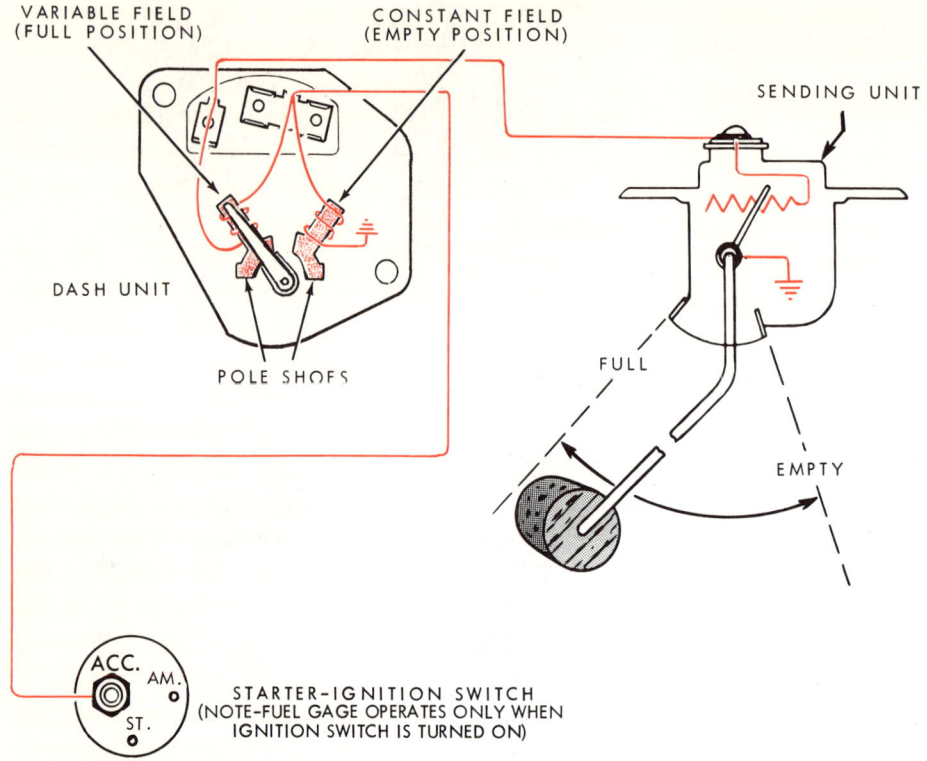

Fig. 9-7. Electromagnetic fuel gage circuit. (Plymouth Div., Chrysler Corp.)

of preventing dirt and water from entering the fuel pump and carburetor. Filters or screens may be located in the fuel tank, fuel line, fuel pump, and/or carburetor.

Some vehicles have a separate filter of either the disk or ceramic type located between the fuel pump and carburetor. Others have a filter located in the fuel line. Many filters are constructed so that they cannot be cleaned and must be replaced if the filter becomes clogged. Some carburetors have a screen located at the inlet of the fuel bowl to filter the fuel just before entering the float bowl.

Fuel Lines

The fuel tank is connected to the fuel pump by metal tubing or synthetic rubber hose. The tubing or hose is usually positioned along the frame side member with metal clips. The carburetor is connected to the fuel pump by means of tubing. A short, flexible line is used between the fuel pump and tank line

Fuel and Fuel Systems

to absorb vibration and to prevent breakage of the line.

Air Cleaner

As previously discussed, for an engine to operate efficiently approximately 15 parts of air must be mixed with one part of gasoline. It has been estimated that as much as 100,000 cubic feet of air (about 4 tons) pass through a carburetor during 1000 miles of driving. Considerable dust particles enter the engine and will cause rapid wear unless the carburetor air intake is equipped with an air cleaner. The air cleaner is mounted on the air horn of the carburetor to trap dirt. The air must pass through the air cleaner before entering the carburetor.

Most air cleaners have a silencing chamber built into the cleaner to reduce the noise caused by the air rushing into the carburetor. The air cleaner also acts as a flame arrester if the engine misfires back through the carburetor.

Three types of air cleaners are used on automotive passenger cars: the oil bath type, the oil-wetted mesh type, and the dry type.

Oil Bath Air Cleaner. The oil bath cleaner is especially good when a vehicle is to be operated in areas where large quantities of sand or abrasive dust are present in the air. The principle employed in the oil bath cleaner is illustrated in Fig. 9-8. Air entering the cleaner moves through the center section and passes over the surface of the oil supply (about one pint) in the reservoir. The air picks up some of the oil and carries it up through the filter material (cactus fiber or metal "wool") in the cleaner body. The oil saturates the cleaner material and drops down into the oil reservoir. As it does so, any parti-

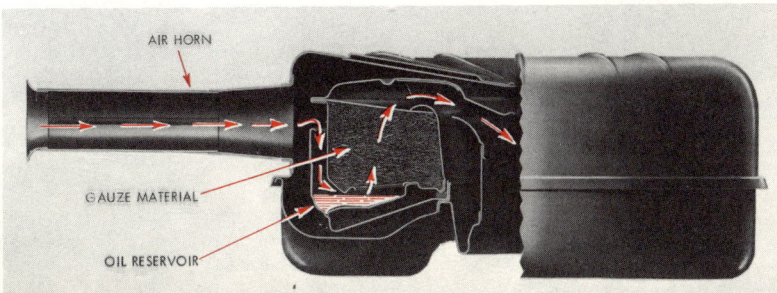

Fig. 9-8. The oil bath air cleaner should be cleaned and renewed periodically. During operation, the air is cleaned by passing through oiled gauze filter material before entering the carburetor. (Chevrolet Div., General Motors Corp.)

345

cles of dirt in the air remain in the oil and also drop into the reservoir. Thus, the gauze cleaning material is being continually washed by an oil bath. The unit should be disassembled, drained and cleaned when dirt accumulates in the bottom of the reservoir to the level of the offset portion.

Oil-Wetted Mesh Air Cleaner. The oil-wetted mesh air cleaner consists of a drum with a ring of nonflammable filter material of fine metal wool, or a flexible reusable polyethane filter element that provides a fine maze that filters out the dust particles. The filter material is wetted with oil before being placed on the carburetor. The oil removes dirt particles from the air that enters the engine. When the mesh becomes clogged with dirt it no longer can properly clean the air unless thoroughly washed and re-oiled. The assembly should be cleaned approximately every 5,000 miles—more often if used in a dusty area.

Dry Type Replaceable Filter Element. Most of today's air cleaners use a replaceable cellulose fiber or paper type of air cleaner element. Air passes through the silencing chamber before passing through the filtering element. After passing through the filter element, the air is deflected into the carburetor. The dirt particles are trapped in the filter element as the air rushes through. This element should be cleaned every 5000 miles by removing the element, cleaning the housing and gently tapping the element to dislodge the dirt. The element should be replaced every 20,000 miles, Fig. 9-9.

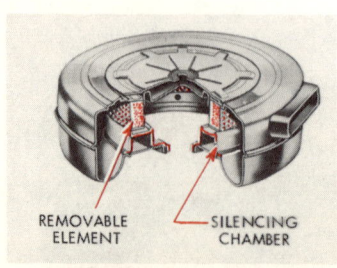 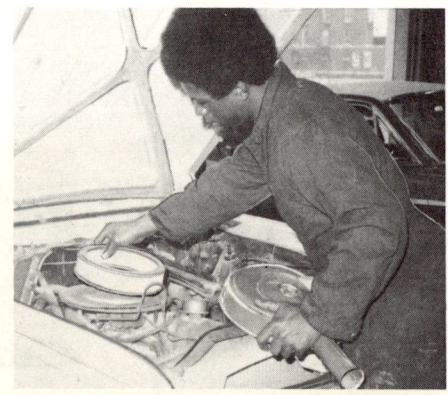

Fig. 9-9. The dry type replaceable filter element should be cleaned every 5,000 miles and replaced every 20,000 miles. (Left: Ford Div., Ford Motor Co., Right: Paul Lawrence Dunbar Vocational High School, Chicago, Illinois)

Fuel and Fuel Systems

Other elements of the same general construction use an oil-wetted paper. This element cannot be cleaned but should be rotated 180° at 12,000 miles and replaced at 24,000 miles.

Some filters which have the crankcase ventilating tube connection attached to the air cleaner have a filter pack located inside where the tube is connected, Fig. 9-10. The filter pack should be cleaned whenever the filter is serviced.

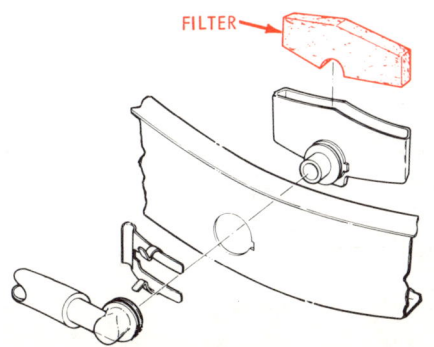

Fig. 9-10. Crankcase ventilation filter pack. (Ford Div., Ford Motor Co.)

One make of vehicle uses a one-piece welded unit air cleaner. Under normal operating conditions, the unit only needs service every 50,000 miles. Then, the entire unit must be replaced.

Ram Air Cleaner. Some engines are equipped with a ram air system which allows outside air to be forced through a hood scoop into the air cleaner during periods of open throttle or heavy load conditions. During normal engine operation, air enters the air cleaner through the conventional duct and valve assembly. A regular dry type filter element is used, Fig. 9-11.

When intake manifold vacuum drops to 4 psi or less, such as when the throttle is wide open or the engine is operating under heavy load, the vacuum motor opens the ram air valve. Opening the valve allows air to be forced into the air cleaner directly from the hood air scoop.

To check the operation of the valve, the valve should be in the wide open position with the engine off or the vacuum hose disconnected. If the valve does not fully open or close, check the valve for binding, vacuum leaks, or a disconnected vacuum line. Check the operation of the motor by applying vacuum directly to the motor. The motor shaft should be in the fully withdrawn position when 7 psi or more of vacuum is applied. Check the hood-to-air-cleaner gasket for all around contact.

Intake Manifold

The intake manifold is basically a series of tubes or passages which are used to carry the air-fuel mixture from the carburetor to the intake valve ports. The number and arrangement of cylinders and the firing order dictate the manifold

Automotive Engines

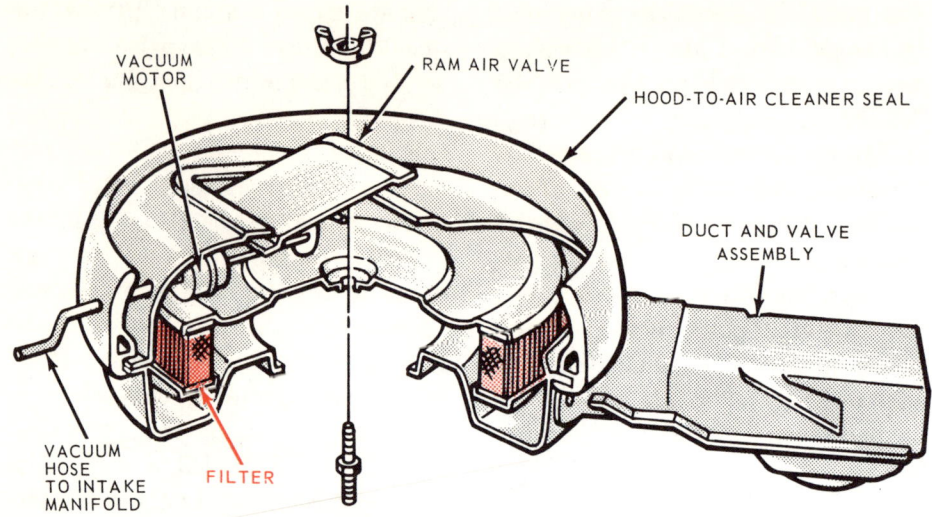

Fig. 9-11. Ram air cleaner. (Ford Div., Ford Motor Co.)

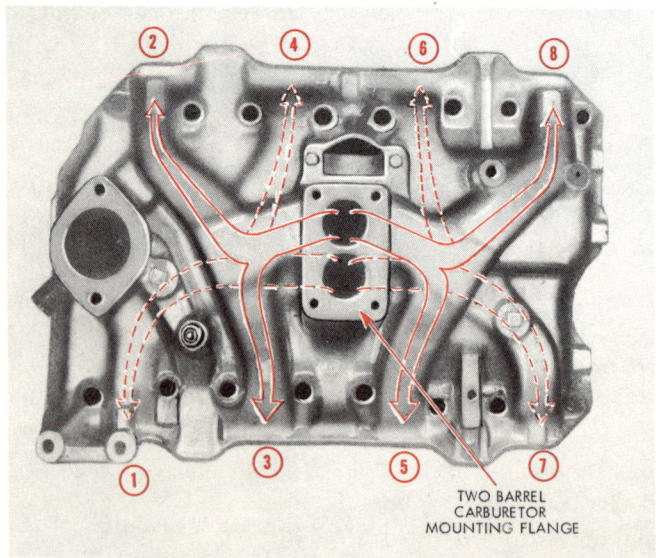

Fig. 9-12. This V-8 intake manifold is designed for a two-barrel carburetor. Each barrel feeds four cylinders. The arrows indicate the air-fuel passageways within the manifold. (Dodge Div., Chrysler Corp.)

design. The intake manifold is located on one side of the cylinder head of an in-line valve-in-head engine and on the side of the cylinder block on an L-head engine. On a V-type eight-cylinder engine, the manifold assembly is mounted in the middle of the V formed by the arrangement of the cylinder banks.

The carburetor body is mounted by studs and nuts to the center of the intake manifold. Passages connect the barrels of the carburetor to the valve intake ports in the engine block. Fig. 9-12 illustrates a V-type eight-cylinder intake manifold on which is mounted a dual (two barrel) carburetor. Each barrel functions to provide air-fuel mixture for four of the cylinders.

Turbocharger

Some engines have used an exhaust driven impeller to improve engine performance. This unit, called a Turbocharger, is located between the carburetor and intake manifold and consists of an exhaust driven turbine wheel attached to a shaft which drives an impeller located between the intake manifold and carburetor.

The purpose of the Turbocharger is to pressurize the air-fuel mixture in the intake manifold. This increases the weight of the mixture, thereby causing the engine to burn more fuel, resulting in additional power.

The hot exhaust gases leaving the exhaust manifold are directed against the turbine wheel, revolving the wheel and impeller shaft at a high rate of speed. The impeller in the compressor portion of the unit, located between the intake manifold and carburetor, draws air-fuel mixture through the carburetor and forces it into the intake manifold under a higher than atmospheric pressure. As the amount of air-fuel mixture available to the cylinder is increased, there will be a greater horsepower output.

Exhaust System

The exhaust system safely conducts poisonous gases from the engine to the atmosphere. The exhaust system consists of the exhaust manifold, a thermostatic heat control valve, an exhaust pipe, muffler, and a tail pipe, Fig. 9-13. On some installations a resonator is located behind the muffler. All V-8 engines have two exhaust manifolds. Although most V-8 engines use a crossover pipe to connect the two manifolds to one exhaust pipe, some have separate exhaust systems for each bank of cylinders, Fig. 9-13. The purpose of two separate exhaust systems is to reduce back pressure by permitting better engine "breathing."

Muffler. The purpose of the muffler is to change the pulsating flow of the exhaust gases to a smooth, quiet flow which will emerge into the outside atmosphere without undue noise. The muffler contains a number of chambers through

Automotive Engines

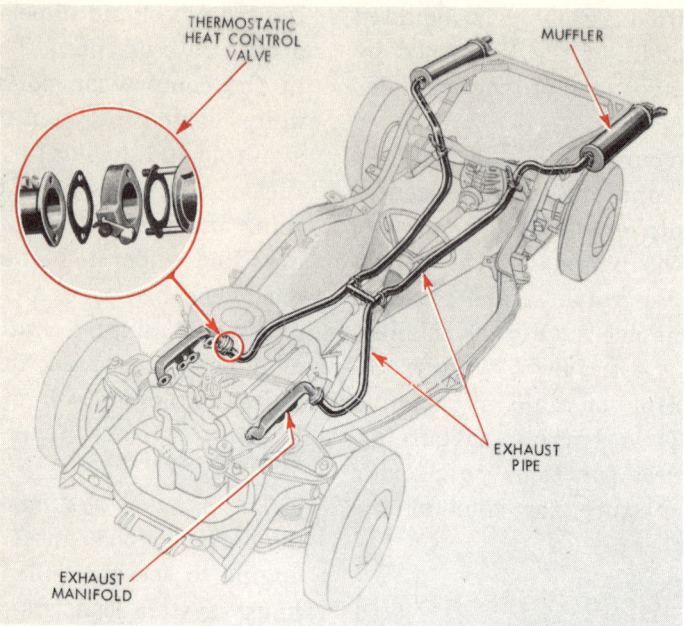

Fig. 9-13. The dual exhaust system is an improvement over single exhaust because it provides more space through which exhaust gases can safely emerge into the atmosphere. The system shown here does not include tail pipes. (Ford Div., Ford Motor Co.)

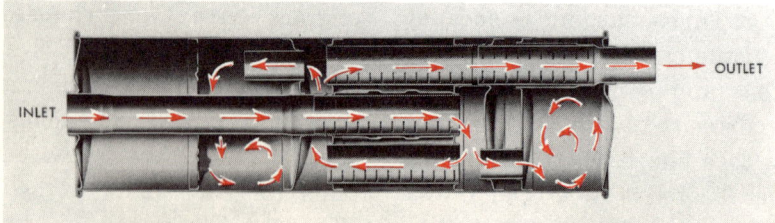

Fig. 9-14. The muffler chambers and passageways serve to quiet the exhaust gases without causing undue back pressure. (Chevrolet Div., General Motors Corp.)

which the gases flow, Fig. 9-14. The size and arrangement of the passages help to reduce exhaust pressure created by the overlapping of the power strokes of the engine. A transversely mounted muffler located between the rear axle housing and rear cross member is used on some vehicles. A muffler of this kind will accommodate either a single or dual exhaust system.

Tail Pipe. Most exhaust systems

Fuel and Fuel Systems

include a tail pipe which conducts gases from the muffler to the atmosphere.

Resonator. A resonator is constructed the same as a muffler, but it contains fewer passages and chambers. Using a resonator permits the use of a muffler which creates less back pressure.

Heat Control Valve. When the intake manifold is cold, the air-fuel mixture does not vaporize thoroughly. A thermostatic heat control valve, Figs. 9-13 and 9-15, is used in most exhaust systems to direct the flow of the hot exhaust gases through a passage in the intake manifold to heat and help vaporize the incoming air-fuel mixture. When the engine warms up, the heat control valve opens and the exhaust gases flow out of the exhaust manifold without going through the passageway or heat chamber in the intake manifold.

V-type Engines. A heat control valve is usually located on one side of the engine only, between the exhaust pipe and manifold, Fig. 9-13. It closes off most of the exhaust flow from this bank at the manifold, forcing the hot exhaust gases to flow through a passage in the intake manifold around the air-fuel passage to the other exhaust manifold, Fig. 9-16. As soon as the engine warms up, the thermostat permits the control valve to open and enables the exhaust to flow freely from both manifolds into the exhaust pipe.

Six-Cylinder In-Line Engines.

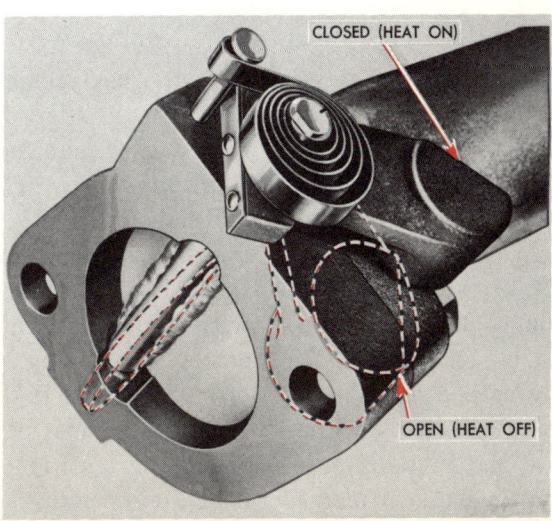

Fig. 9-15. This V-8 engine heat control valve is closed. It will direct exhaust gases through the intake manifold during engine warm-up. (Dodge Div., Chrysler Corp.)

Automotive Engines

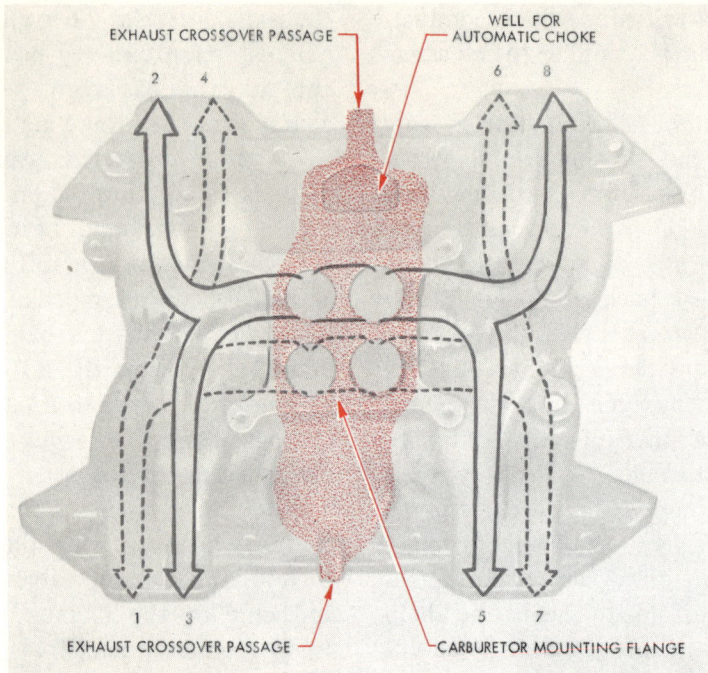

Fig. 9-16. During V-8 engine warm-up, the thermostatic heat control valve remains closed and directs exhaust gases through crossover passages in the intake manifold. The gases heat the manifold to aid fuel vaporization. (Plymouth Div., Chrysler Corp.)

The thermostatic heat control valve used on a six-cylinder engine is usually located in the center of the exhaust manifold below the carburetor and is either built into the exhaust manifold near the exhaust outlet, Fig. 9-17, or is attached between the exhaust manifold and exhaust pipe.

When the engine is cold, the exhaust gases are deflected to the heat chamber of the intake manifold and then to the exhaust manifold. As the thermostatic coil heats, it expands and allows the valve to close the heat chamber permitting exhaust gas to flow directly through the exhaust manifold.

Maintenance. The heat control valve should be checked every 1000 miles. If it is not operating freely, the valve shaft may be lubricated with a special solvent, kerosene, or alcohol containing a small amount of baking soda. If the valve cannot be freed, it must be replaced.

Water Heating. Some engines heat the incoming air-fuel mixture with a carburetor water heater chamber instead of a thermostatic

Fuel and Fuel Systems

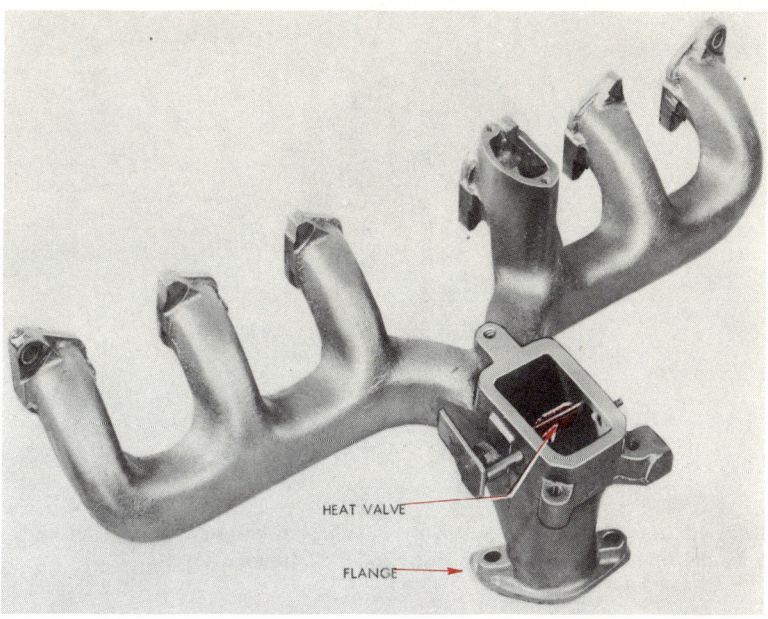

Fig. 9-17. The heat control valve in this six-cylinder in-line engine exhaust manifold is open. It will deflect exhaust gases through the intake manifold heat chamber during engine warm-up. (Dodge Div., Chrysler Corp.)

exhaust gas valve. Hot coolant from the engine circulates through a chamber between the carburetor and intake manifold and heats the incoming air-fuel mixture.

Fuel Pumps

Fuel pumps deliver fuel from the fuel tank to the carburetor. The standard type of fuel pump is mechanically driven by an eccentric on the camshaft. Mechanical fuel pumps have either a single diaphragm for delivering fuel or a second diaphragm that makes it a combination fuel and vacuum booster pump. A few combination pumps are still used today. They use the vacuum section to supplement engine intake manifold vacuum for windshield wiper operation when the vacuum is low.

Several types of electric pumps are available for gasoline engine use. The bellows type and the diaphragm type are similar to the mechanical pump, but they are actuated by an electric solenoid. Another electric fuel pump is the pusher type which uses an electric motor to force fuel out of the tank to the carburetor.

Mechanical Fuel Pump. The principle of operation of all mechani-

353

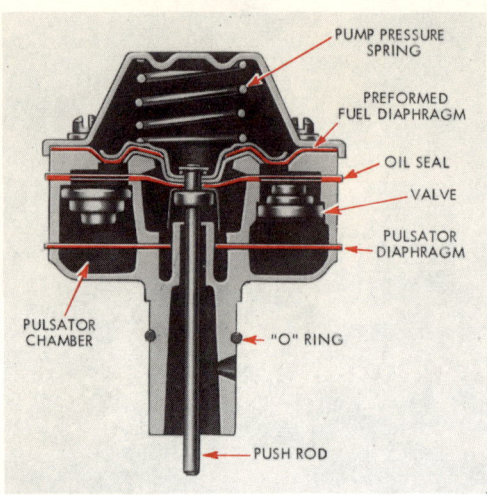

Fig. 9-18. In this mechanical fuel pump, the diaphragm is operated directly by a pushrod actuated by the camshaft. (Chevrolet Div., General Motors Corp.)

cally operated fuel pumps is the same, although there are different models supplied for different types of installations. No rocker arm is used with the pump shown in Fig. 9-18. The diaphragm is operated directly by a pushrod which rides on an eccentric of the camshaft. On some installations, a pushrod may be used between the rocker arm and the camshaft eccentric. In the single diaphragm fuel pump shown in Fig. 9-19 the rocker arm is driven directly off the camshaft.

Diaphragm. In Fig. 9-19, movement of the rocker arm by the camshaft eccentric operates the linkage connected to the diaphragm pull rod. As the diaphragm is pulled upward against spring tension, atmospheric pressure is reduced below the diaphragm. This causes the normal atmospheric pressure (14.7 psi) in the fuel tank to push the fuel out of the tank to the pump. The fuel enters the pump chamber below the diaphragm through the inlet valve. Some pumps incorporate a sediment bowl and screen which filters the fuel before entering the pump diaphragm chamber.

When the camshaft eccentric has revolved a half turn (to the low side), the diaphragm spring exerts pressure downward on the diaphragm, and fuel is forced under a pressure of from $3\frac{1}{2}$ to 5 psi through the outlet valve to the carburetor.

Valves. The inlet and outlet valves used in the fuel pump are

Fuel and Fuel Systems

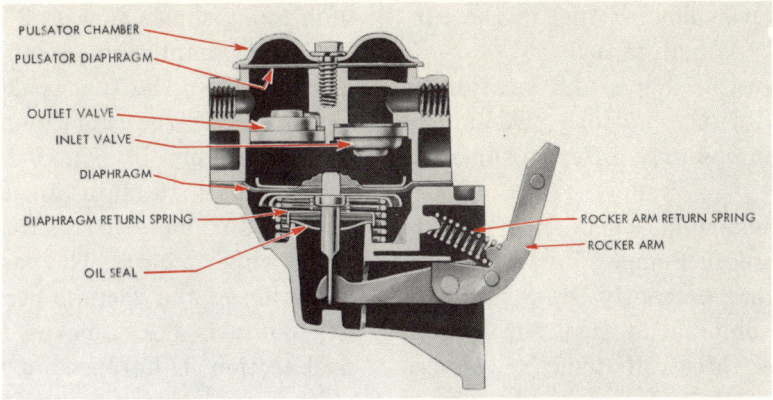

Fig. 9-19. This mechanical fuel pump uses a pulsator diaphragm and chamber but no filter. (Chevrolet Div., General Motors Corp.)

usually identical. However, they are assembled in reverse arrangement, Fig. 9-19, so that when the diaphragm creates a partial vacuum (vacuum stroke) the inlet valve opens to admit gasoline. When the diaphragm spring exerts pressure (pressure stroke) on the diaphragm, the inlet valve closes and the outlet valve opens, allowing gasoline to flow under pressure to the carburetor float bowl.

When the carburetor float bowl is filled to a predetermined level, the float in the bowl closes the carburetor inlet needle valve. Gasoline can then no longer pass through the pump outlet valve, and the pump chamber is filled with fuel, preventing movement of the diaphragm. The diaphragm will remain stationary until the fuel level in the carburetor bowl lowers sufficiently to open the needle valve and allow additional fuel to flow into the bowl. The construction of the rocker arm linkage consists of two or more links which permit the rocker arm to continue its movement without moving the diaphragm.

Rocker Arm Spring. The spring or springs used in connection with the rocker arm linkage keep the rocker arm in constant contact with the pump pushrod, or the eccentric on the engine camshaft, to eliminate noise.

Pulsator Chamber. A pulsator chamber containing a flexible diaphragm is used on many fuel pumps. Because of the surging action of the fuel caused by diaphragm movement, fuel delivery tends to be pulsating or moving in a wave-like fashion. The flexible diaphragm in the pulsating chamber absorbs these pulsations so that

Automotive Engines

more even flow of fuel to the carburetor is maintained.

The size, shape, and location of parts of the various mechanical fuel pumps may differ to some extent.

Combination Fuel and Vacuum Mechanical Pump. Very few engines are presently being equipped with combination fuel and vacuum pumps. Most of today's vehicles use electric windshield wipers which eliminate the need for the combination pump. However, many combination pumps are still in use.

The combination fuel and vacuum pump shown in Fig. 9-20 contains two diaphragms. One moves gasoline from the fuel tank to the carburetor in the same manner as the fuel pump in Fig. 9-19. The other is used to maintain uniform vacuum for operation of the windshield wiper motors. The basic construction of the vacuum section of the pump is the same as for the fuel section. Differences as to size, shape, and location of parts in the combination pump vary as they do in the single diaphragm fuel pump.

Booster Design. The vacuum booster assembly contains the same

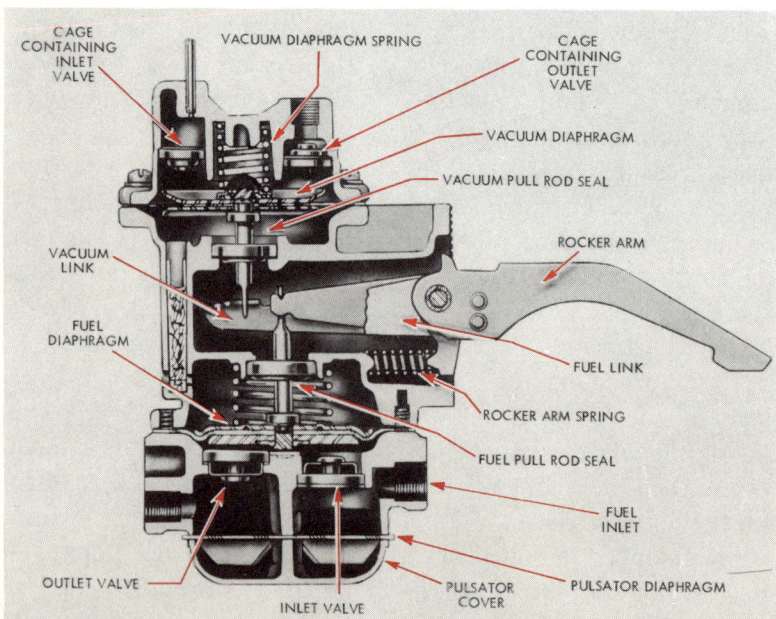

Fig. 9-20. The combination fuel and vacuum mechanical pump includes two diaphragm pumps. The lower diaphragm pumps fuel. The upper diaphragm supplies vacuum for the windshield wiper motors when intake manifold vacuum is low. (Oldsmobile Div., General Motors Corp.)

Fuel and Fuel Systems

parts as the fuel assembly: a diaphragm and link, a connecting link between the rocker arm and diaphragm spring, and a vacuum cover which contains the inlet valve and seat and the outlet valve and seat.

Vacuum Drop. Manifold vacuum varies under different operating conditions. When the throttle is opened for acceleration, manifold vacuum drops. A drop in manifold vacuum slows down windshield wiper operation. The inclusion of a vacuum pump in combination with the fuel pump boosts or supplements manifold vacuum in such instances, providing uniform windshield wiper operation.

Booster Operation. The linkage connecting the rocker arm and diaphragm moves the diaphragm up against spring pressure, causing the vacuum section exhaust valve to open. The air above the diaphragm is then expelled through the outlet valve into the engine intake manifold. Downward movement of the rocker arm linkage permits the compressed diaphragm spring to push the vacuum diaphragm downward. When the diaphragm moves downward, a partial vacuum is created in the chamber above it. This causes the intake valve to open, and atmospheric pressure from the windshield wiper motor enters the chamber. This, in turn, creates a partial vacuum within the wiper motor, acting as a force to operate the wiper motor.

When the windshield wiper is not being used, engine manifold vacuum holds the diaphragm against its actuating spring. The diaphragm cannot, therefore, make a complete stroke.

When the engine manifold vacuum is greater than the partial vacuum created by the pump, both valves in the pump will remain open. Vacuum for operation of the windshield wiper will then be taken directly from the engine intake manifold. When the engine intake manifold vacuum is low, however, the valves will open and close, and a partial vacuum is again created by the movement of the diaphragm. At idle speed the vacuum section should create a minimum of 10 inches of vacuum.

The fuel pump unit is mounted on one end of the pump body, and the vacuum booster unit is mounted on the other end. One rocker arm operates the linkage for both diaphragms. When the fuel link is pulled up, the vacuum link is pushed up. When the fuel diaphragm spring pushes the fuel diaphragm down, the stiff vacuum diaphragm spring pushes the vacuum diaphragm down, creating vacuum.

Electric Fuel Pumps. Electric fuel pumps are used on some heavy duty equipment such as buses and trucks. They also may be used on regular passenger vehicles in place of the mechanical pump or as a

Automotive Engines

stand-by pump for emergency use.

There are three kinds of electric pumps: a *bellows*, a *diaphragm*, and a *pusher* type. The bellows and diaphragm types may be located any place in the fuel line but are generally installed in the engine compartment away from excessive heat. To move more fuel, two pumps may be used in tandem. The pusher type pump is located in the gasoline tank and is generally used on rear engine buses.

Bellows Type. The bellows type electric fuel pump, Fig. 9-21, is connected in the battery circuit. When the ignition key is turned on, the solenoid is energized (receives electrical energy) and the pump starts to operate. This draws the bellows, which is attached to the solenoid, downward. The bellows, in turn, lowers the pressure in the pump chamber, and fuel is drawn in through the inlet valve. The downward movement of the armature breaks the electrical circuit, allowing the drive spring to push the bellows upward, causing fuel to be forced out of the pump chamber and into the carburetor.

The cycle is repeated until the carburetor bowl is filled to the fixed

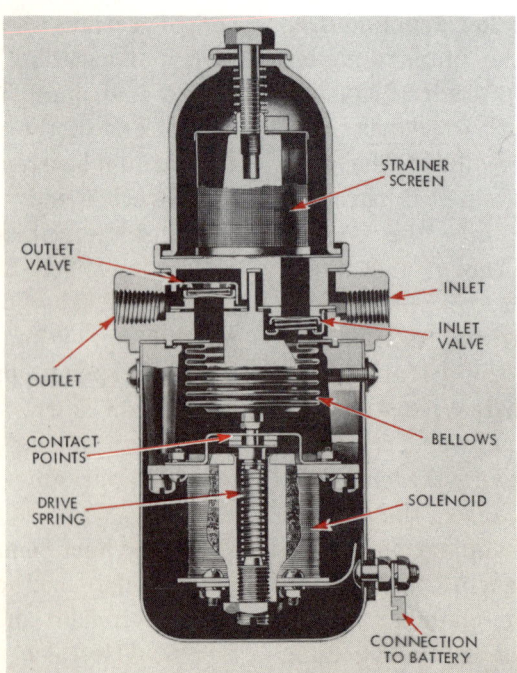

Fig. 9-21. This type of electric fuel pump delivers fuel to the carburetor through a solenoid-actuated bellows.

Fuel and Fuel Systems

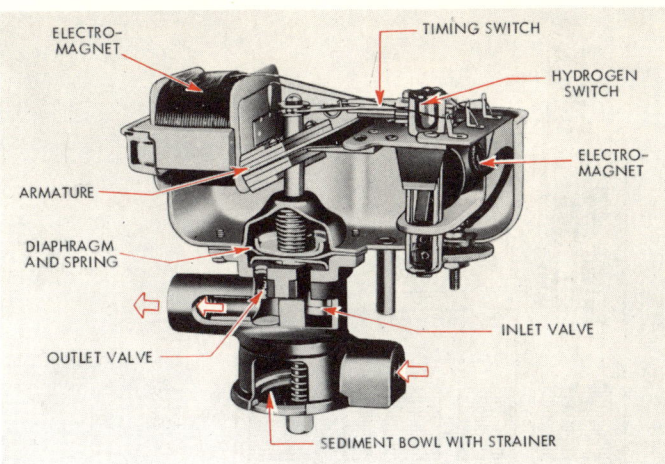

Fig. 9-22. This type of electric fuel pump uses two electromagnets to operate a diaphragm which moves fuel from the tank to the carburetor. (Stewart-Warner Corp.)

level and the float needle valve closes. Back pressure prevents bellows movement and breaks the electrical circuit. Opening and closing of the contact points controls the speed of the pump. The pump operating pressure is from 3.5 to 5 psi.

Diaphragm Type. The diaphragm type, Fig. 9-22, operates in the same manner as the bellows type electric pump. In place of the bellows, a diaphragm is used. As in the case of the bellows type, making and breaking of contact points controls the diaphragm movement which creates pressure to deliver the fuel.

Pusher Type. The pusher type electric fuel pump, Fig. 9-23, pushes fuel from the tank to the carburetor at a pressure of 2.5 to 4 psi. The pump assembly is mounted inside the bottom of the fuel tank. Fuel enters the pump through the filter and flows into the pump throat. When the ignition switch is turned on, the pump circuit is closed. The armature revolves turning the impeller, a rotating wheel which creates a fanning effect, so that the fuel is thrown outward into the voluted housing. Thus, pressure is created which forces fuel through the line to the carburetor. When the float bowl is filled and the float valve closes, the pump returns the fuel to the tank until the float valve again opens. On one type of electric pump located in the fuel tank, the pump is energized when the ignition key is turned to start. After the engine starts, the pump receives current

359

Automotive Engines

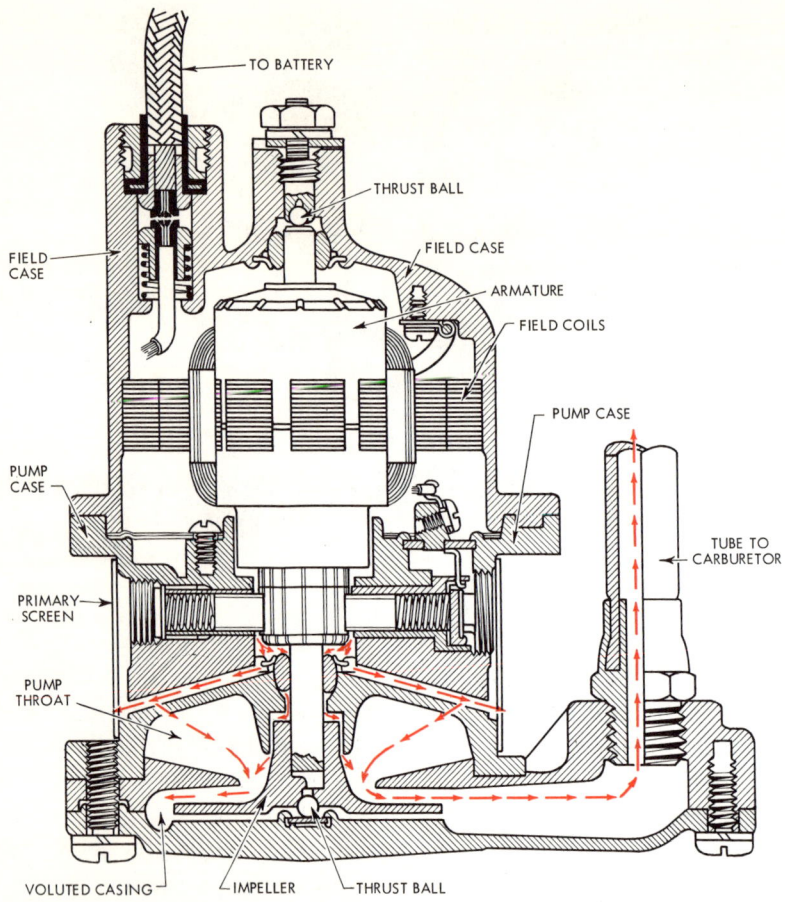

Fig. 9-23. The electric pusher type fuel pump is mounted in the fuel tank. It is commonly used on rear engine buses. (Carter Carburetor Corp.)

through the oil pressure safety switch as long as there is approximately 2 psi of oil pressure. Should pressure drop below 2 psi, the electrical contact is broken and the pump stops.

Checking On Your Knowledge

The following questions give you the opportunity to check up on yourself. If you have read the chapter carefully, you should be able to answer the questions.

Fuel and Fuel Systems

If you have any difficulty, read the chapter over once more so that you have the information well in mind before you go on with your reading.

DO YOU KNOW

1. Describe a simple distillation process.
2. What are the basic principles of the petroleum cracking process?
3. What is the approximate air-fuel ratio necessary for complete combustion?
4. What effect do high altitudes have on the air-fuel ratio?
5. What factors affect the speed of flame travel within the combustion chamber?
6. Describe what takes place when detonation occurs within an engine.
7. What is preignition and how does it differ from detonation?
8. What factors are important in the blending of gasoline?
9. What are some mechanical factors which may contribute to vapor lock?
10. What is the difference between the Research Method and the Motor Method of rating octane, and what method is the most meaningful for today's engine?
11. What are the functions of an air cleaner, and what types are in use?
12. How does a ram air system operate, and what is the reason for such a system?
13. What is the purpose of a muffler, and how does it differ from a resonator?
14. What is a heat control valve, and how does it operate?
15. Trace the flow of fuel in a mechanical fuel pump, and describe the operation of a mechanical fuel pump.
16. What is the purpose of a combination fuel and vacuum pump?

Chapter 10
Carburetors and Carburetion

When gasoline is used as an internal combustion fuel, it must be combined with air to make a combustible mixture. The mixing of air with gasoline in correct proportions to meet engine requirements is known as *carburetion*. The mixing is accomplished by a device known as a *carburetor*. The carburetor meters, atomizes, and distributes the gasoline through the air which is drawn into the engine. It must do these things through a wide range of speeds, loads, and temperature conditions in response to the driver who uses the accelerator to control the amount of fuel flow.

Carburetor Fundamentals

In a four-stroke-cycle engine, gasoline is added to air which flows through the carburetor on the intake stroke of the piston. The intake stroke begins with the piston at the top of the cylinder. This piston position is known as *top dead center* or TDC.

At TDC the exhaust valve is in a closed position and the intake valve is opening. As the piston moves downward in the cylinder, a partial vacuum is created in the cylinder; the atmospheric pressure outside the cylinder then pushes air through the carburetor and gasoline is drawn from the fuel bowl through various circuits of the carburetor. The gasoline is fed into the passing air stream as a fine spray

Carburetors and Carburetion

which causes the gasoline to evaporate very quickly, producing a combustible mixture of gasoline vapor and air which enters the engine cylinder.

The spraying of gasoline into the air stream and the resultant evaporation of the many droplets, turning the air-fuel mixture into a vapor, is known as *atomization*.

The carburetor use three different methods to aid in vaporizing and atomizing the gasoline: (1) A previously mentioned method involves directing hot exhaust gases around the intake manifold at the point where the air-fuel mixture enters the manifold. When gasoline contacts a warm surface, it evaporates more readily than when it contacts a cold surface. (2) Regardless of which circuit in the carburetor is operating, air is bled into each individual circuit as the fuel is forced out, resulting in an atomized mixture of gasoline and air being discharged into the air stream. (3) Located in the carburetor air horn at the point of the main fuel discharge is a constriction known as a *venturi*. Gasoline vaporizes more readily in the partial vacuum created by this venturi.

Fig. 10-1 illustrates a simple carburetor. The carburetor consists of a tube (air horn) with a constriction or narrow section part way down from the top (venturi), a fuel discharge tube or nozzle projecting into the air horn at the venturi, a round disc or valve (throttle) in the lower part of the air horn, and the fuel bowl.

Air enters the air horn and flows through the venturi where a partial vacuum is created. The venturi restricts the opening in the air horn, and as the air passes through, its velocity is increased at the point of restriction. When the air passes through the restricted area into the larger opening of the air horn below the venturi, its velocity is maintained and a partial vacuum (low pressure area) is created in the center of the air stream.

Carburetors are designed so that fuel enters the air stream just below the point of greatest restriction in the venturi. Since the pressure just below the restriction in the venturi is always lower than normal atmospheric pressure, the fuel (under atmospheric pressure) in the carburetor bowl will flow from the main discharge nozzle into the air stream in the form of a fine spray which evaporates and is carried into the combustion chamber. An air-bleed is always connected to the fuel discharge nozzle so that air as well as gasoline is discharged into the air stream.

The throttle valve in the lower part of the air horn may be tilted to control the flow of air-fuel mixture into the combustion chamber. The amount of air-fuel mixture en-

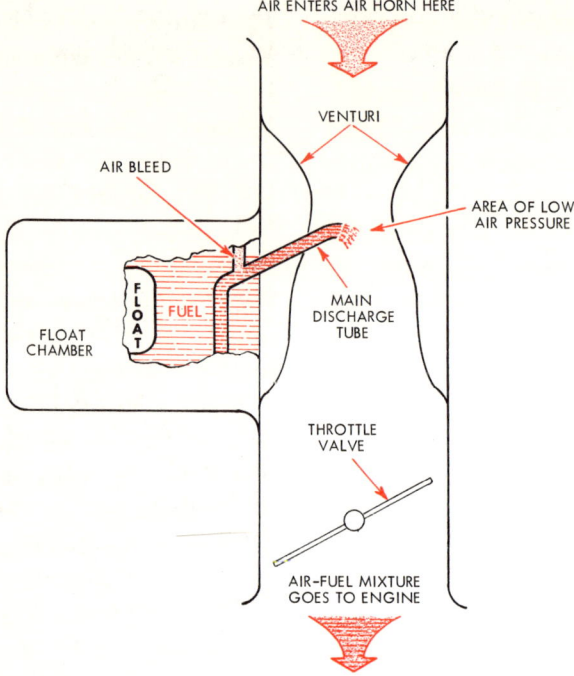

Fig. 10-1. A simple carburetor.

tering the engine is a determining factor in the power the engine develops and the speed at which it operates. When in a horizontal position, the throttle valve shuts off the flow of air-fuel mixture. The throttle valve is linked to a foot-controlled accelerator pedal.

Air-Fuel Mixture Requirements

The carburetor must furnish an air-fuel mixture in varying quantities and proportions so that the engine will deliver maximum performance under all operating conditions; some means must be provided to automatically control the quantities and proportions.

Several systems or circuits are incorporated into the carburetor to furnish an air-fuel mixture that will meet the varying demands of the engine. A fuel reservoir (float bowl), in which a specific quantity of gasoline is maintained by a float actuated valve, supplies fuel to

Carburetors and Carburetion

meet the demands of the following various situations.

Cruising. A mixture of approximately one part gasoline to fifteen or sixteen parts of air, by weight, will give the best performance at cruising speeds. In actual operation, this ideal mixture cannot be maintained. When a vehicle goes up a steep hill, more gasoline must be added to the air stream to keep the vehicle moving. At near wide open throttle, a "richer mixture" is necessary. A power fuel supply system furnishes additional gasoline for high speed or full load operation.

Accelerating. Under sudden acceleration, more gasoline must be added to the air stream to furnish the necessary power to increase the speed of the vehicle. An accelerating pump system momentarily supplies additional fuel whenever engine speed is suddenly increased.

Cold Engine. Gasoline will not vaporize when the carburetor and manifold are cold because gasoline tends to cling to the cold surface and remain liquid. When the engine is cold, a greater proportion of gasoline is needed in the air stream. Therefore, the quantity of air passing through the carburetor must be reduced by means of a choke valve to increase the ratio of gasoline to air. This creates an air-fuel mixture of about nine parts of air to one part of gasoline (by weight). This rich mixture will readily ignite and burn, even under cold weather starting conditions.

Idling. When an engine is running at idle speed, the only work being performed is the overcoming of compression and friction of the moving parts. No external load is being imposed on the engine, and it is running at a constant speed. To meet this need, a separate system, known as the idle system, is built into the carburetor.

A throttle valve is used to control the quantity of air-fuel mixture which can enter the engine cylinders. The throttle valve is connected by linkage to a foot controlled accelerator pedal. As the throttle valve is opened, the other systems begin to function, supplying the proper air-fuel mixture to meet the demands of the engine.

Carburetor Systems

All present-day automotive engines are equipped with a *plain tube* carburetor which is designed to furnish an increasing amount of fuel as the velocity of air entering the carburetor increases.

Automotive Engines

Plain tube carburetors in which the air stream travels downward into the engine are known as *downdraft* carburetors. All standard production automobiles use a downdraft carburetor. Carburetors in which the air stream travels upward into the engine are referred to as *updraft* carburetors. Stationary engines and cab-over-engine trucks utilize carburetors of this type. A carburetor in which air enters through one side of the air horn and fuel mixture leaves the opposite side is referred to as a *side-draft* carburetor. Some stationary engines and multiple carburetor installations on in-line engines use side-draft carburetors.

The single-barrel carburetor is the simplest type of plain tube carburetor. It has one throttle valve which regulates the amount of fuel mixture that can enter the engine intake manifold.

The most common carburetor is the dual, or two-barrel carburetor which has two throttle valves; one barrel feeds the fuel mixture to half the cylinders while the other barrel feeds the remaining cylinders.

Another type is the four-barrel carburetor which basically consists of two dual (two-barrel) carburetors and four throttle valves. The engine normally operates on two barrels. The remaining barrels supply additional fuel mixture for high speed and heavy load operation.

While there is considerable difference in the construction of the various carburetors, the operating principles of all carburetors are the same. Practically all carburetors employ a choke valve, a throttle valve or valves, venturis, an idle system, and an accelerating pump. The information which follows describes the single-barrel carburetor but applies to all carburetors whether they are single-barrel, two-barrel, or four-barrel.

Float System

The float system consists of a fuel bowl (reservoir), a float assembly, and a fuel inlet needle valve and seat assembly. Fuel is delivered through the needle valve and seat to the fuel bowl. The valve is opened and closed by the float which maintains a constant level of fuel in the bowl, Fig. 10-2.

As fuel is used from the bowl, the float lowers permitting fuel from the fuel pump to flow past the needle valve into the bowl. When the incoming fuel reaches a predetermined level, the float closes the needle valve shutting off fuel from the pump. The level of the fuel in the bowl controls the amount of fuel mixed with the air passing through the carburetor. This level must be maintained because the carburetor is calibrated to deliver the proper mixture only when the fuel is at the predetermined level. Too high a float level allows more

Carburetors and Carburetion

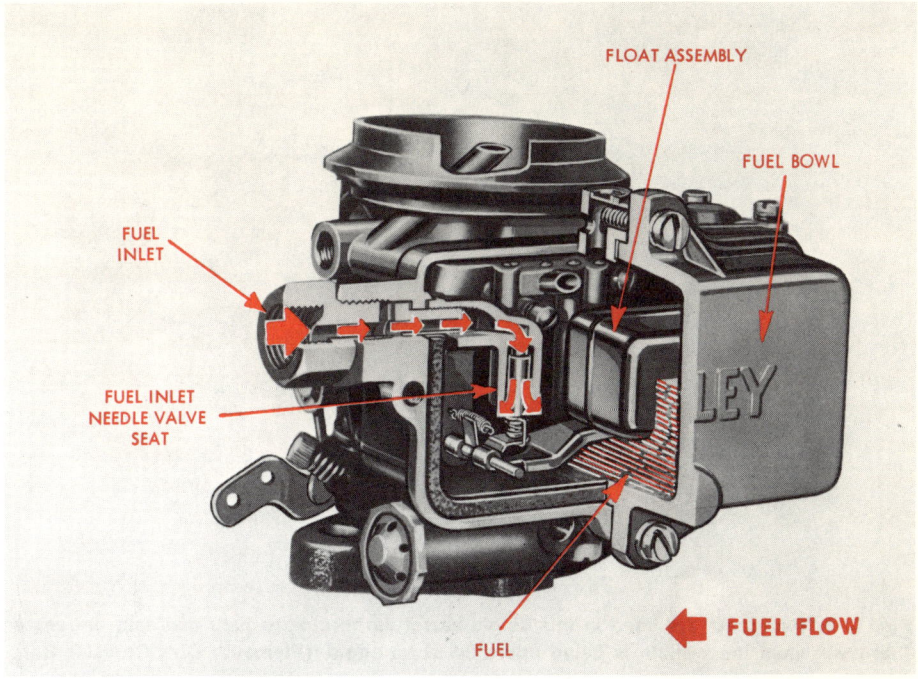

Fig. 10-2. This typical float system controls the amount of fuel mixed with air passing through the carburetor. (Ford Div., Ford Motor Co.)

fuel than necessary to leave the jets causing a richer mixture. Too low a float level results in a leaner mixture because too little fuel leaves the jets. The height of the fuel in the fuel bowl can be changed by bending the tang on the float lever of some floats or by bending the lever itself on other floats. It is also necessary to adjust the amount of float drop and side clearance on some float arrangements.

Floats are made in various shapes and sizes. Some fuel bowls extend around the carburetor and use two connected floats, Fig. 10-3. This design helps to maintain the correct fuel level with the point of fuel discharge when the vehicle is being operated at an angle. Some four-barrel carburetors will use two pairs of floats to control two needle valves in two fuel bowls, Fig. 10-4. The fuel bowls are connected by passages to assure equal fuel levels and air pressures in the two bowls.

Various methods may be used in different carburetors to assure positive response of the needle valve to float movement and to add stability to the float when vibra-

367

Automotive Engines

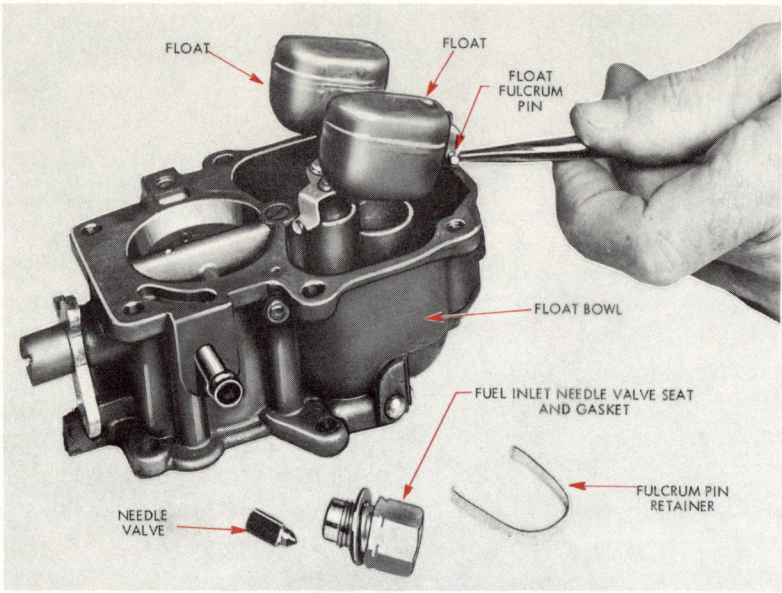

Fig. 10-3. Two floats are used in this single-barrel carburetor to help maintain the correct fuel level when the vehicle is being operated at an angle. (Plymouth Div., Chrysler Corp.)

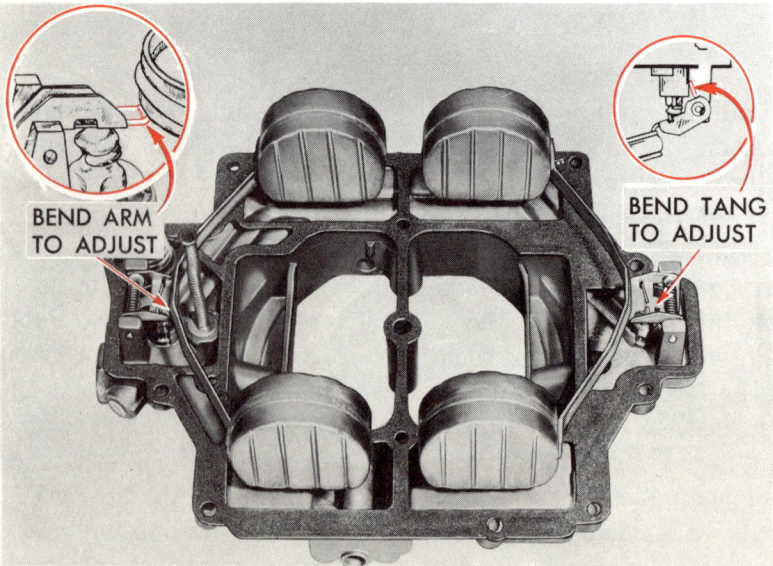

Fig. 10-4. This is a bottom view of a four-barrel carburetor fuel bowl cover. You can see the two pair of floats which control two needle valves in two fuel bowls. (Chevrolet Div., General Motors Corp.)

Carburetors and Carburetion

tions are encountered. On a few installations, a spring and pin inside a hollow inlet needle valve cushions the needle valve against road shock and vibrations. A clip is sometimes attached to the needle valve and float lever, Fig. 10-2. The clip maintains positive fuel inlet needle valve response to the needle valve and float lever. In some cases a low tension spring located between the bottom of the fuel bowl and the bottom of the float gives stability to float action if vibrations occur.

Fuel bowls are vented into the carburetor air horn above the choke valve and below the air cleaner. The vent balances pressure between the fuel in the bowl and the flow of air through the carburetor air horn. The vent will automatically compensate for any air cleaner restriction since the same pressure causing air to flow will also be present in the fuel bowl. Fuel delivered by the main discharge tube is therefore dependent wholly upon venturi vacuum. Any air leaks in the bowl cover gasket will defeat the purpose of the vent.

Idle Fuel Supply System

The idle fuel supply system supplies fuel in the correct amount to operate the engine at idling speeds. The typical idle supply system consists of fuel passages air-bleeds, an adjustable needle valve, and discharge openings, Fig. 10-5.

When the throttle valve is nearly closed, the amount of vacuum present at the main discharge nozzle is not great enough to force fuel out of the nozzle. To enable the engine to operate at low speeds, fuel is drawn into the intake manifold from below the throttle valve through the idle fuel supply system. The degree of throttle opening at idle speed affects the amount of vacuum in the intake manifold and therefore controls the flow of the air-fuel mixture from the main discharge nozzle and the idle fuel supply system.

At idle speed, manifold vacuum acting on the idle passages causes fuel from the float bowl to flow through the main jet, fuel well, and up through a calibrated idle orifice tube or calibrated restriction on its way into the idle passageway. A restriction is incorporated in the idle passage to break up the fuel as it mixes with air drawn through an idle air-bleed located above the level of the fuel in the bowl. When an idle orifice tube is not used to meter the fuel, the restriction performs this function. Often the idle air-bleed also acts as a vent to keep fuel from siphoning through the idle passages at high speeds or when the engine is stopped.

The air-fuel mixture travels down the idle fuel passageways, past the transfer holes or slots in the throttle body, located just above the closed throttle, and is

Automotive Engines

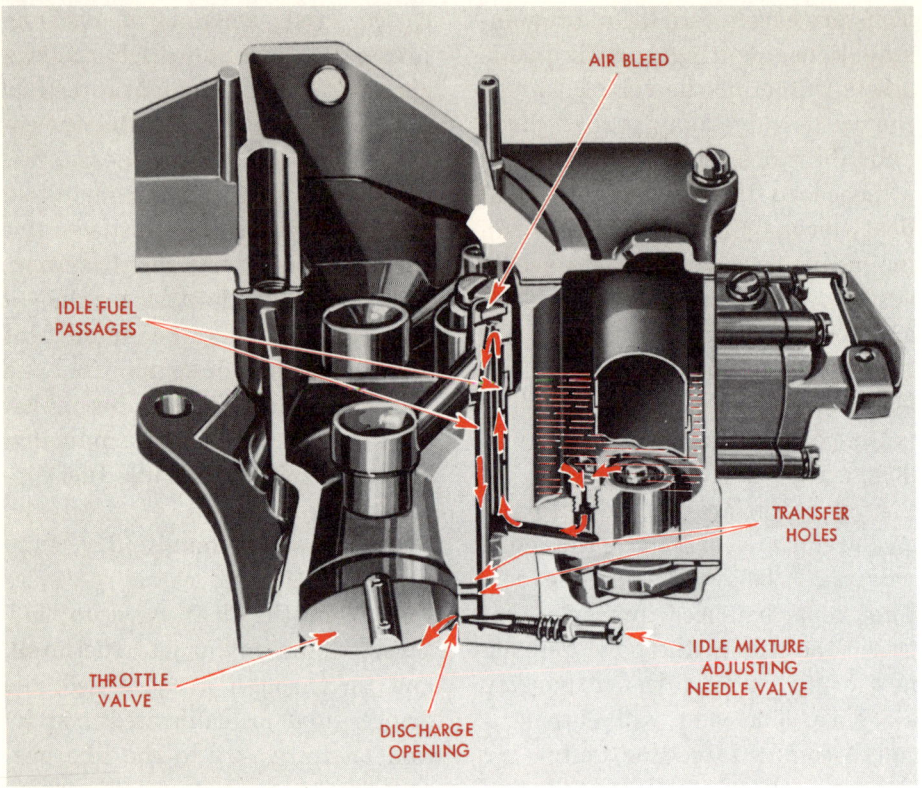

Fig. 10-5. The engine could not operate at low speeds without this idle fuel supply system. The throttle valve is closed. (Ford Div., Ford Motor Co.)

discharged through the idle discharge hole below the closed throttle valve, Fig. 10-5. As the throttle valve is moved past the transfer holes or slots, the holes begin to discharge fuel as they are exposed to manifold vacuum. The transfer holes also act as additional air-bleed when the throttle valve is closed.

The amount of fuel discharged at idle is controlled by an idle adjusting needle seated in the discharge hole. By turning the idle adjusting screw, the amount of air-fuel mixture discharged from the idle port can be varied. Turning the screw in reduces the amount of fuel mixture; turning the screw out increases the amount of fuel mixture.

Any clogging in the idle system results in poor low speed operation. Air leakage through the carburetor

Carburetors and Carburetion

bowl gasket will also cause poor engine idling and low speed operation.

Main Fuel Supply System

The main fuel supply system, which is sometimes referred to as the part-throttle system, supplies most of the fuel used for engine operation. Except when the engine is idling, a metered quantity of fuel proportional to the air velocity is being continually forced into the air stream of the carburetor due to the vacuum created in the air horn by the intake stroke of the piston.

The main fuel supply system generally consists of a main metering jet, main well, a discharge tube or passage, main air-bleed, and fuel discharge nozzle, Fig. 10-6.

The main fuel supply system utilizes a venturi to create additional vacuum in the carburetor air horn. Additional vacuum not only aids vaporization and atomization but also lifts fuel from the float bowl through the main jet, discharge tube, and discharge nozzle into the air stream at a point just below the

Fig. 10-6. This main fuel supply system supplies most of the fuel for the engine at speeds faster than idling. (Ford Div., Ford Motor Co.)

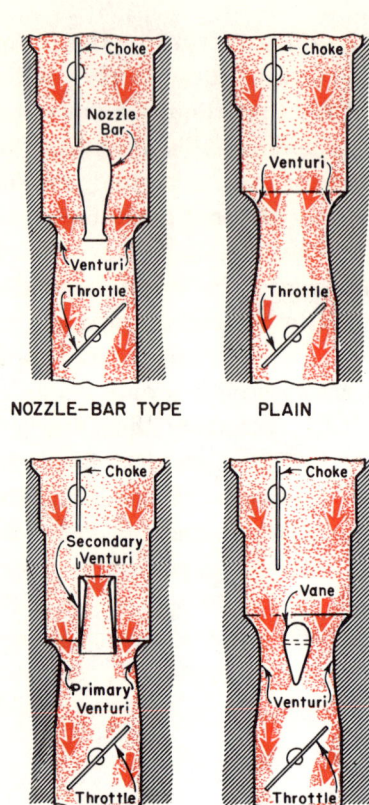

Fig. 10-7. Here are four different types of venturi arrangements. They all create additional vacuum in the carburetor air horn.

ments used in various carburetors.

As the throttle valve is opened, the increased velocity of the air through the venturi creates a partial vacuum in the main discharge nozzle located just below the restriction in the venturi. As the fuel in the carburetor float bowl is subjected to the same air presure as that present in the air horn above the venturi, fuel will flow through the main metering jet and main well, up the discharge tube where it picks up air through the main air-bleed, and out the main discharge nozzle as a mixture of fuel and air. Adding air from the main air-bleed assists in atomizing the fuel before it enters the air stream at the discharge nozzle.

Main Metering Jets. The drilled opening in the main metering jet controls the size of the stream of fuel that can pass through the main fuel supply system. The speed at which the fuel flows, however, is controlled by the velocity of the air in the air stream within the air horn. Main jets are made in various sizes to suit different engines and different types of operations. Atmospheric pressures are lower at higher altitudes, and the size of the so-called standard jets are intended for engine operation in altitudes below 5,000 feet above sea level. At higher altitudes, smaller size jets may be required to maintain the proper air-fuel ratio.

Any foreign matter lodged in the

greatest restriction in the venturi.

Some carburetors use a single venturi tube while others have multiple venturis. When more than one venturi is used, the discharge nozzle is always located at the inside venturi. Nozzle bars or vanes are sometimes inserted in the air stream to increase or change the venturi effect. Fig. 10-7 shows some examples of venturi arrange-

Carburetors and Carburetion

jet or anything which changes the size of the main jet will affect engine operation.

Power Fuel Supply System

To achieve the required mixture when more power is desirable, or when sustained high speed driving is to be maintained, a power fuel supply system is employed to supplement the fuel passing through the main jet. Several methods have been used to provide this additional fuel.

Most power fuel supply systems are vacuum operated and consist of a spring-loaded power valve located in the bottom of the float bowl or a step-up metering rod operating within a main jet.

Power Valve. Some carburetors use a power valve. When engine speed and load conditions are such that additional fuel is needed, the valve opens and permits additional fuel to flow from the float bowl into the main well or passageway. This power valve may be actuated by a piston or a diaphragm.

Actuated by Separate Piston. On installations where a piston is used to actuate the valve, the piston is generally located above the power valve, Fig. 10-8. When the engine is being operated at a constant speed at part throttle, vacuum in the intake manifold is sufficient to hold the piston in an upward position against spring tension. Operating conditions which

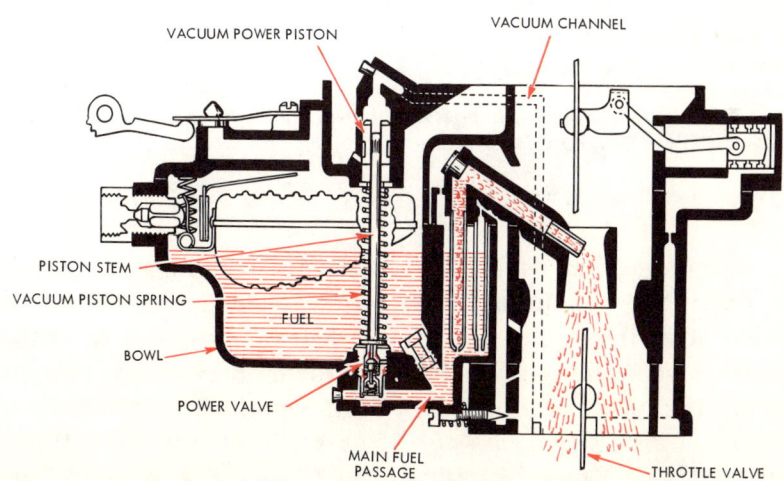

Fig. 10-8. When the throttle valve on this cross sectioned carburetor is open as shown, engine vacuum becomes low and allows the spring to push the stem and piston downward. The stem opens the power valve which allows additional fuel to flow from the fuel bowl into the main fuel passage. (Dodge Div., Chrysler Corp.)

Automotive Engines

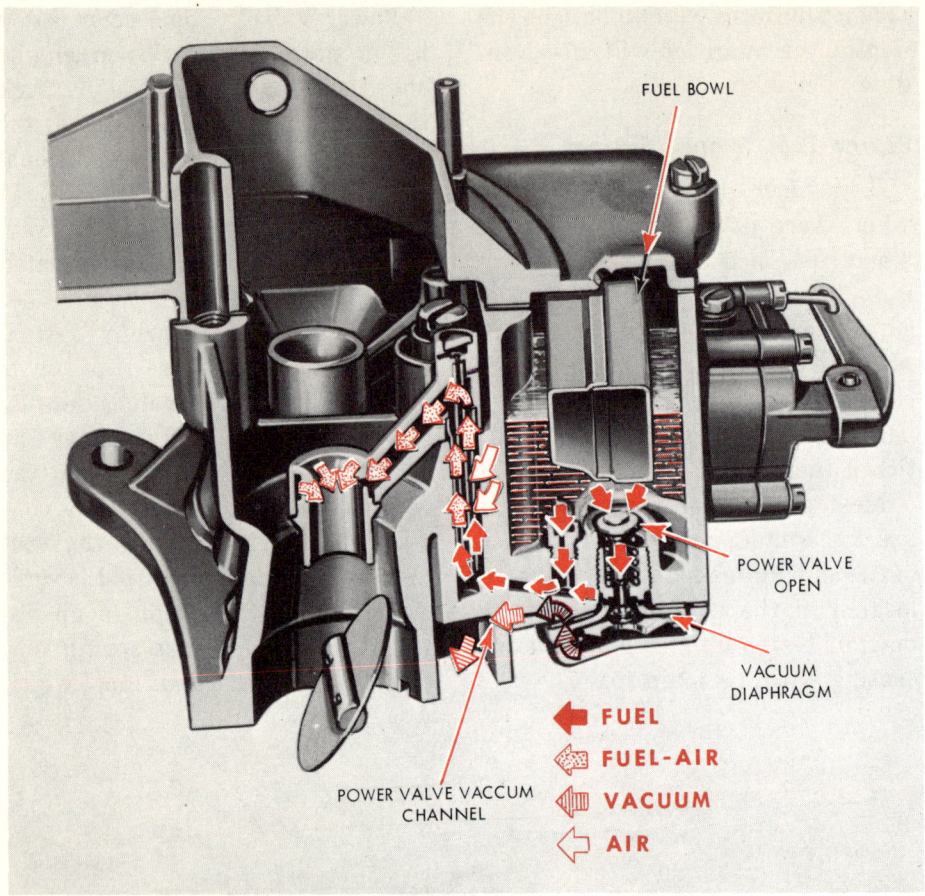

Fig. 10-9. The vacuum diaphragm operated power valve in this carburetor is a self-contained unit. (Ford Div., Ford Motor Co.)

reduce engine vacuum enable the spring below the piston to force the piston stem into contact with the power valve, opening the valve and permitting fuel to flow past the valve seat.

Actuated by Separate Diaphragm. A diaphragm with a spring and stem may be used in the same location as the piston in Fig. 10-10 and may function in the same manner.

Self-Contained Unit. Other diaphragm operated power valves are self-contained units. The complete unit is located in the bottom of the float bowl in Fig. 10-9. The valve is spring-loaded so as to hold the valve off its seat. Intake manifold vacuum is present on the lower

Carburetors and Carburetion

side of the diaphragm when the engine is running. The vacuum holds the power valve closed. Reducing manifold vacuum to approximately 4 to 7 inches by opening the throttle permits the spring to raise the valve off its seat letting additional fuel flow into the main fuel passage.

Step-up Rod Type. A number of carburetors use a step-up rod (metering rod) inserted in the main metering jet, Fig. 10-10, in place of a power valve. The main metering jet is large enough to permit a normal flow of fuel with the rod inserted in the jet. This arrangement increases the flow of fuel through the jet by lifting the rod out of the jet if the rod is of a uniform diameter, or by lifting the rod to a smaller diameter if it has two or more steps of different diameters as in Fig. 10-10. The rod is actuated by a vacuum operated piston located in a cylinder bore along the side of the step-up rod and connected to the top of the rod by a plate or linkage.

Under normal driving conditions when manifold vacuum is high, the manifold vacuum exerts a strong pull on the vacuum piston. This pull holds the piston down keeping the step-up rod in the fuel passage of the main metering jet. A normal

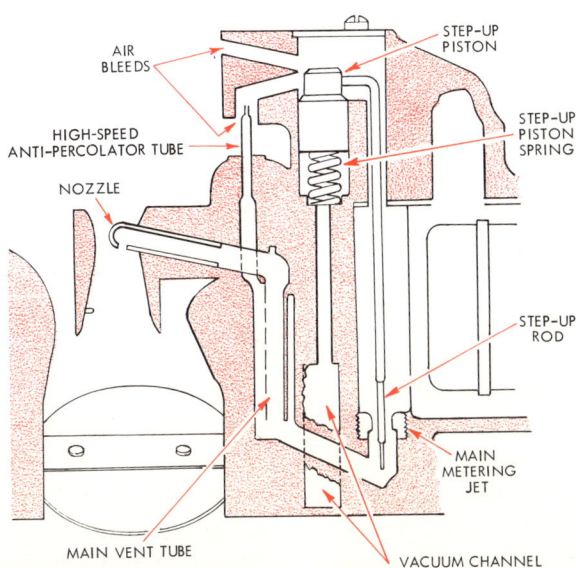

Fig. 10-10. This carburetor is at half throttle where engine vacuum would be high. The vacuum holds the step-up piston and rod down allowing a normal flow of fuel through the main metering jet. Decreased vacuum would allow the spring to push the piston and rod upward and permit additional fuel flow through the jet. (Pontiac Div., General Motors Corp.)

amount of fuel then flows around the rod through the jet into the main passage or well.

When the throttle is opened and manifold vacuum, falls off due to a heavy load, sudden acceleration, or very high engine speed, a spring moves the piston up which in turn moves the step-up rod out of the main metering jet. This positions the smaller diameter or power step of the rod in the jet allowing additional fuel to be metered through the jet.

With the step type step-up rod an arm from the throttle linkage is generally inserted under the step-up rod actuating plate. When the throttle is wide open the step-up rod will be lifted mechanically if vacuum is insufficient to raise the rod. In some of the older carburetors, a step-up rod attached to the throttle linkage is used in the main jet. The throttle moves the rod. When the throttle is wide open, the smallest section of the rod is in the jet allowing the maximum flow of fuel.

Accelerator Pump System

A relatively rich fuel mixture is required for rapid engine acceleration. On sudden acceleration, the velocity of air through the carburetor does not increase immediately. This condition is brought about because of the reduction in manifold vacuum due to sudden throttle opening which floods the manifold with air. The low vacuum causes a lean fuel mixture causing the engine to hesitate and perhaps "sputter." To compensate for the momentary lack of vacuum and the need for a richer mixture, an accelerator pump system is used to provide a rich fuel mixture necessary for smooth operation during rapid acceleration. The accelerator pump is mechanically operated through the throttle linkage.

Plunger Type. In the commonly used plunger type pump system, Fig. 10-11, the pump plunger includes a seal with a spring behind it which maintains pressure on the seal against the walls of the pump cylinder. A spring below the plunger forces the piston upward on the return stroke. The spring above the plunger creates a prolonged fuel discharge.

Fuel from the carburetor float bowl flows into an opening under the pump plunger through a one-way inlet check valve. When the accelerator pedal is depressed suddenly, the plunger is forced downward in the cylinder. The force of the fuel closes the one-way inlet valve. The fuel is forced through the pump discharge passageway, opens the pump outlet valve, and passes through the pump discharge jet, or opening, into the air stream. At the end of the discharge stroke the outlet valve is returned to its seat by the valve spring or the weight of the valve itself and pre-

Carburetors and Carburetion

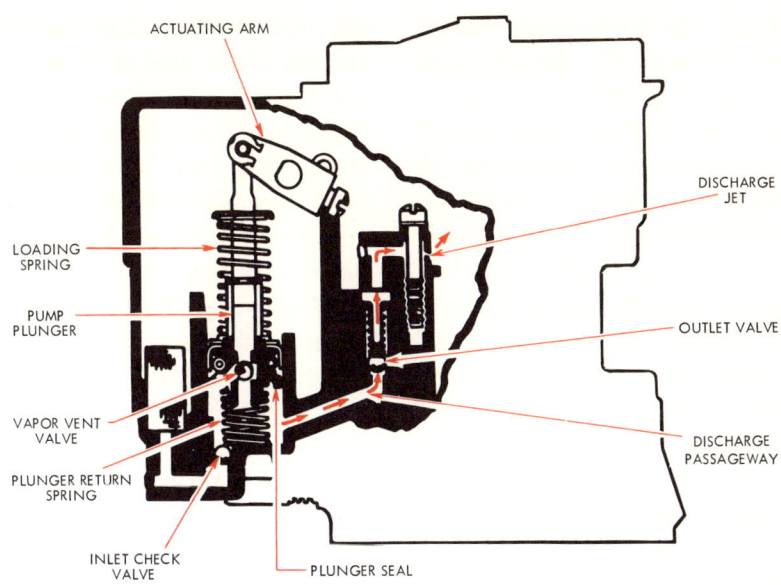

Fig. 10-11. In the plunger type accelerator pump system shown above, the colored arrows show the direction in which the fuel will be forced when the system is brought into operaion. (Oldsmobile Div., General Motors Corp.)

vents air from being drawn into the pump cylinder on the intake stroke. As the pump plunger returns to its original position when the throttle is released, fuel is drawn through the inlet valve into the pump cylinder.

The pump plunger or plunger linkage is spring-loaded in such a manner as to permit the throttle linkage to open the throttle valve much faster than the pump plunger can move downward and force fuel from the cylinder. This is accomplished by using a spring-loaded slotted plunger shaft or linkage, or by holding the plunger on its shaft by springs. This creates a smooth prolonged discharge from the pump.

Some carburetors have a screen in the fuel bowl at the pump inlet valve to prevent foreign matter from entering the pump system.

On one installation the one-way inlet valve, sometimes called a by-pass valve, is located in the pump plunger. As the plunger moves upward, fuel flows through the valve into the cylinder below the plunger. When the plunger is moved downward, the valve closes and fuel is forced out through the outlet valve.

A ball check in the accelerator pump plunger in some pump systems acts as a vapor vent to pre-

377

Automotive Engines

vent fuel vapor pressure from building up below the plunger and forcing fuel out of the discharge opening or jet during extreme heat periods. Downward movement of the piston seats the ball and allows normal operation of the accelerator system.

Diaphragm Type. Instead of a plunger in a cylinder as used in most carburetors, there are some carburetors which use a diaphragm in a chamber, Fig. 10-12. The inlet and outlet valves, the discharge nozzle, and pump linkage function in the same manner as the plunger type of pump. The flexible diaphragm is held in a released position by a spring. When the throttle valve is opened suddenly, a link or pushrod moves the diaphragm, forcing gasoline out of the diaphragm well or chamber through the pump discharge passage and nozzle. The spring returns the diaphragm to its original position when the throttle is released. A prolonged discharge is obtained in the same manner as in the system using a plunger.

Adjustment. On many carburetors, the accelerator pump link-

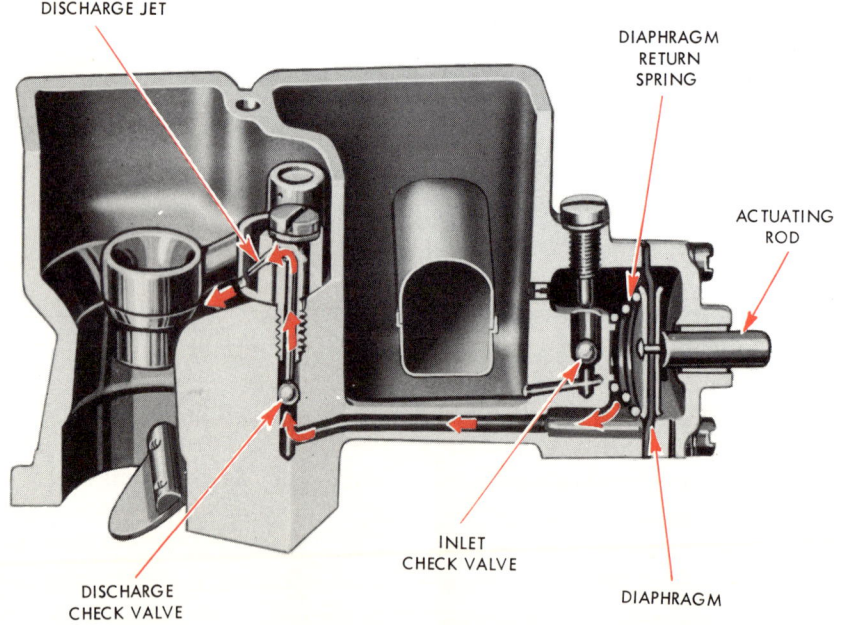

Fig. 10-12. This diaphragm type accelerating pump system is being held in a released position by the diaphragm return spring. The colored arrows show the path of the fuel when the system is actuated. (Ford Div., Ford Motor Co.)

Carburetors and Carburetion

age is constructed so that the length of the pump stroke can be varied according to weather conditions. Holes in the linkage provide a different length of plunger strokes. When three holes are used, the center hole is for average weather. The hole nearest the plunger actuating rod provides a long stroke for extreme cold weather operation. The hole farthest from the plunger actuating rod provides the shortest stroke, usually used during hot weather operation.

Chokes

When an engine uses one carburetor, it must have a choke valve to insure proper starting and driving during cold weather operation. When more than one carburetor is used, only one of the carburetors will employ a choke. The choke consists of a plate type of valve (butterfly) located near the top of the air horn, Fig. 10-13, and is operated manually or automatically. In a few cases, the choke valve is located remotely in an air passage leading to the carburetor air horn.

The purpose of the choke is to restrict the amount of air which can enter the carburetor and at the same time expose the main fuel discharge tube to engine vacuum. This will create a rich mixture.

When an engine is cold, a richer

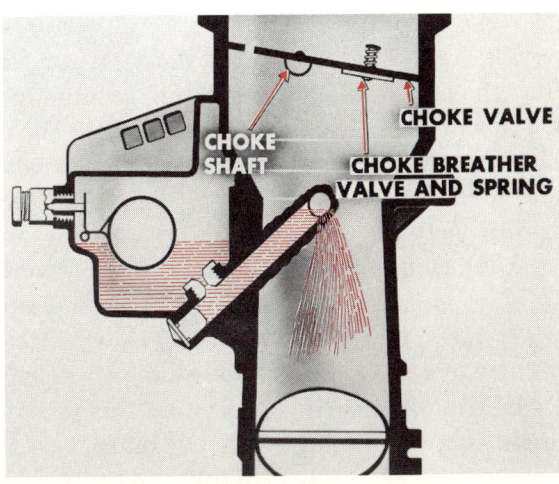

Fig. 10-13. This is a typical choke valve in the closed position. In this position, the choke will cause a rich air-fuel mixture to be drawn into the engine. (Plymouth Div., Chrysler Corp.)

mixture is required for starting, because as the fuel contacts cold metal, it fails to vaporize completely. When the engine is being cranked, air speed is low. Very little vacuum is created to draw fuel from the main discharge tube. By placing a valve in the air horn it is possible to close off most of the flow of outside air. Therefore, the vacuum created by cranking discharges a greater quantity of fuel from the main discharge tube. By varying the amount the choke valve is closed, it is possible to control the richness of the incoming fuel mixture to suit the engine requirements.

Manually Operated Choke. When a manually operated choke valve is used, a choke control button is located on the instrument panel and is connected to the choke shaft control lever by means of a wire or rod. As the choke button is pulled out, the choke valve in the carburetor closes. When the button is in, the choke valve should be wide open. The choke control linkage may be adjusted to maintain the correct relationship between the choke opening and the control button position.

After the engine starts, more air and a leaner mixture are required. To satisfy this condition, which is difficult to do manually, the choke valve is usually mounted off-center on the choke shaft with a spring arrangement on the lever and linkage. It may also be mounted with free play between the lever and actuating mechanism. The choke valve is usually at a slight angle when closed. When the engine starts, the movement of air through the air horn will partially open the off-center choke valve leaning out the mixture. If the engine misfires back through the carburetor, the choke valve can also open to relieve the back pressure. A spring-loaded poppet valve in the choke plate or a spring-loaded section of the plate serves to admit additional air when the engine starts.

Automatic Chokes. When a manually operated choke is used, the driver must control the amount the choke valve is opened or closed. As the engine warms up, failure to properly adjust the choke results in a rich mixture, causing poor performance and excessive fuel consumption. To eliminate such troubles, most carburetors are equipped with an automatic choke control. The automatic choke control regulates the choke valve according to engine manifold temperature.

Two types of automatic choke controls have been used. Both types utilize exhaust manifold temperatures. The electrical type is controlled by electricity and exhaust manifold temperatures, Fig. 10-14. The vacuum type, which is currently used, is controlled by intake manifold vacuum and exhaust manifold temperature.

Carburetors and Carburetion

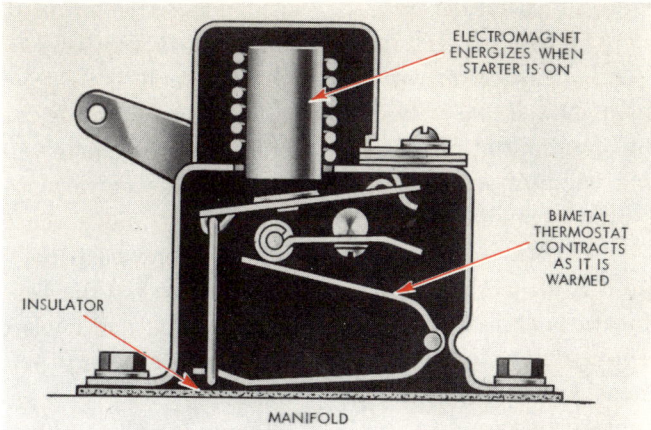

Fig. 10-14. This electrical type automatic choke control unit uses electricity and exhaust manifold heat to control the choke valve. When the control lever moves upward, the choke valve closes. (Plymouth Div., Chrysler Corp.)

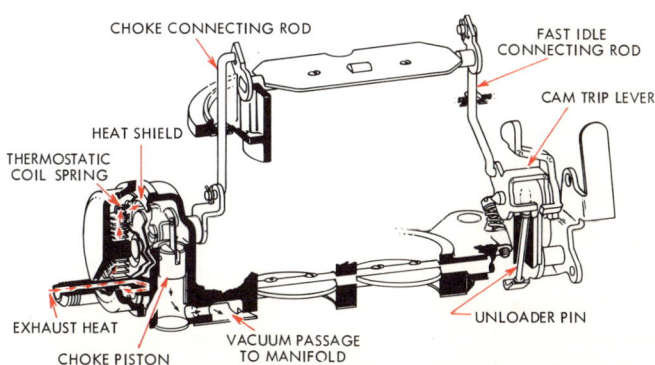

Fig. 10-15. This vacuum type choke control uses exhaust manifold heat and intake manifold vacuum to control the choke valve. Notice that the thermostatic coil spring unit is mounted directly on the carburetor. (Mercury Div., Ford Motor Co.)

The vacuum type choke may be mounted on the exhaust manifold and connected to the choke valve by a link, or it may be an integral part of the carburetor. The choke assembly consists of a vacuum piston, a thermostatic coil, operating linkage, and an adjustable housing or cover, Fig. 10-15. The thermostatic coil consists of two unlike metal strips welded together to form a spiral. The two unlike

381

metals expand at different rates. While the coil is heated, it winds up. As the coil cools, it unwinds. The position of the choke valve is controlled by a combination of intake manifold vacuum, air velocity against the offset choke valve, atmospheric temperature, and exhaust manifold heat.

The thermostatic coil is adjusted to hold the choke valve closed when the engine is cold. As the engine is started, air velocity against the offset choke valve causes it to open slightly against the torque of the thermostatic coil. In addition, intake manifold vacuum is applied to the vacuum piston which tends to pull the choke valve open. The choke valve moves to a position where the torque of the thermostatic coil is balanced against the pull of the vacuum piston and the air velocity against the offset choke valve. This balance regulates the air flow into the carburetor and provides a richer mixture during the warm-up period.

During warm-up, the vacuum piston serves to move the choke valve to compensate for varying engine loads and acceleration. Any load increase or sudden acceleration decreases the vacuum exerted on the choke vacuum piston. This momentarily allows the thermostatic coil to increase choke valve closure to provide a richer mixture for acceleration.

As the engine warms up, heat either radiates or is drawn from the exhaust manifold into the thermostatic coil housing. The heated coil slowly expands, relaxing the tension on the choke valve. Vacuum on the choke valve piston is gradually able to move the choke valve to a full open position.

After the engine is stopped, the thermostatic coil cools off. Its tension increases, and the choke valve closes.

Basically, the construction of all automatic choke controls of this type is the same, but the exhaust heat tube and the intake manifold vacuum passage may be located in different positions. The thermostatic coil cover or housing can be turned to change the tension on the coil, thereby making it possible to adjust the opening or closing tension on the choke valve.

Vacuum type chokes which have the thermostatic bimetal coil recessed into the intake or exhaust manifold are called well or crossover type vacuum chokes, Fig. 10-16.

The thermostatic coil is actuated by exhaust manifold heat. Movement of the coil is transferred to the choke shaft lever by a choke rod. The thermostat unit is calibrated at the factory and cannot be serviced. A vaccum piston located in the air horn and connected to the choke valve maintains a tension on the valve, holding it in the position determined by the thermostatic coil

Carburetors and Carburetion

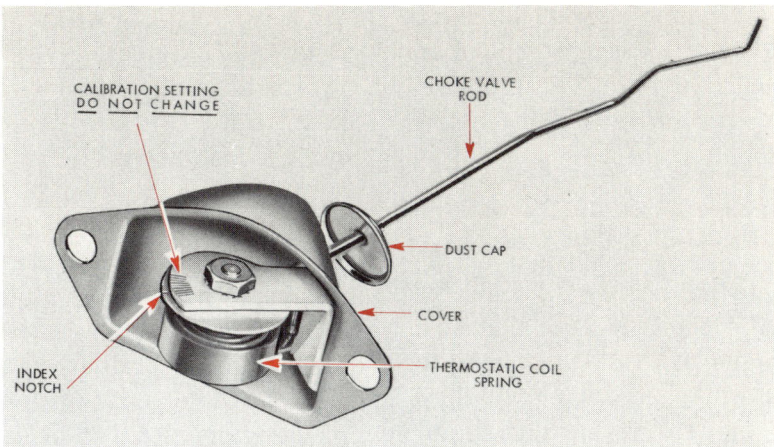

Fig. 10-16. This is a well type thermostatic coil spring unit for a vacuum type automatic choke. It is designed to be mounted to a well or recess in the exhaust manifold instead of directly on the carburetor. (Dodge Div., Chrysler Corp.)

spring. Fig. 10-22 shows a choke vacuum brake which is used on many late model engines that have the automatic choke thermostatic coil located on the manifold. The vacuum brake is used in place of the vacuum piston.

To help reduce engine emissions, some late model engines will use a time modulated choke. These units are designed to open the choke fully after a certain number of seconds of engine operation. During engine warm-up, the amount of choke and the length of time it stays closed has a direct bearing on engine emissions. This more exact timing is brought about by the incorporation of air bleeds, dual vacuum brake units, or silicon fluid cylinders in the choke system.

Auxiliary Carburetor Features

The various carburetor circuits already described are common, in one form or another, to practically all carburetors. There are numerous other features which are incorporated in most carburetors. These include such items as an automatic choke unloader, a fast idle mechanism, an anti-icing feature, an antipercolator vent, an

Automotive Engines

anti-stall dashpot on vehicles using an automatic transmission, and an emission control solenoid on vehicles with an emission control system.

Automatic Choke Unloader

When the engine is cold, the automatic choke is closed. Should the engine fail to start immediately, continued cranking will flood the engine. To prevent flooding or to open the choke valve after the engine has been flooded, generally a rod or link is used to connect the choke valve to the fast idle cam, Fig. 10-17. A tang on the throttle arm will contact an arm or kick lever on the fast idle cam when the accelerator is fully depressed moving the link which partially opens the choke valve.

Fast Idle

When an engine is cold, a faster idle is required to keep the engine running than when the engine is warm. Fast idling is obtained by a fast idle cam arrangement mounted at the throttle shaft and connected by linkage to the choke valve, Fig. 10-18. When the engine is cold, the choke is nearly closed. With the choke closed or partially closed the linkage attached to the choke valve turns the fast idle cam. The idle adjusting screw rests on the high point of the cam and the throttle valve or valves cannot fully close, therefore the engine idles fast. As the engine warms up, the choke valve opens, turning the fast idle cam so that the idle adjusting screw contacts the cam on the low point permitting the engine to idle

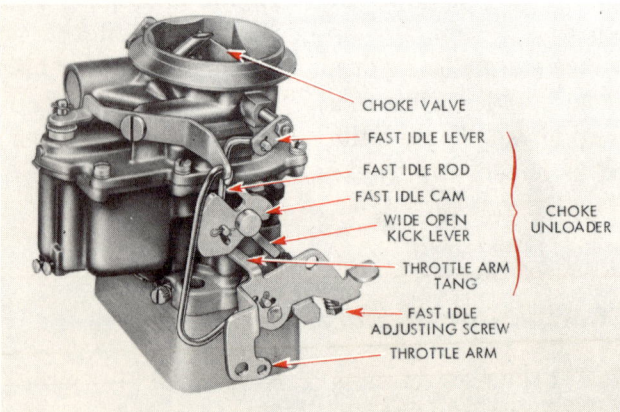

Fig. 10-17. The throttle valves on this carburetor are fully open, and the automatic choke unloader has opened the choke valve. To do so, throttle arm tang actuates the wide open kick lever which pulls the fast idle rod down to open the choke valve. (Dodge Div., Chrysler Corp.)

Carburetors and Carburetion

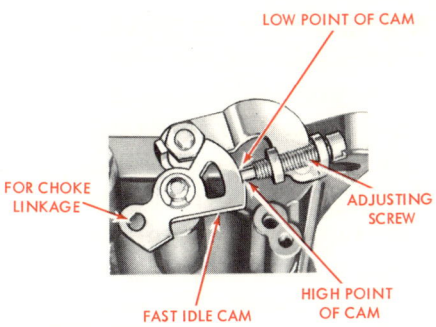

Fig. 10-18. The carburetor idle adjusting screw is resting on the normal idle position of the cam. The engine will operate at a fast idle when the screw rests on the high point of the cam. (Ford Div., Ford Motor Co.)

in a normal manner. The throttle must be opened slightly after the engine is warmed up to permit the cam to return to the low point if a normal idle speed is desired. A fast idle cam is used on both manual and automatic choke installations.

Anti-icing

As gasoline enters the air stream in the carburetor, it turns into a vapor. During vaporization the fuel takes heat from the surrounding air and metal. This effect may be shown by putting a little ether or alcohol in your hand and noting how cold your hand gets as the alcohol or ether evaporates. Blowing on the liquid causes the liquid to evaporate faster and cools your hand more. Under certain humidity and temperature conditions, it is possible for the moisture in the air to condense and freeze on the metal parts and build up enough ice to stall the engine.

To prevent icing, some carburetors have a passageway for hot exhaust gases near the idle ports and throttle ports. When the manifold heat control valve is closed, hot exhaust gases are directed through these passages adding enough heat to prevent icing during the warm-up period. Another type of carburetor has water passages around the throttle valve to circulate water from the cooling system through the carburetor throttle body to aid in carburetor warm-up.

Antipercolator

Heat can cause excess fuel vapor pressure in the carburetor fuel bowl. This vapor pressure can force raw fuel out of the main nozzle causing difficult hot weather starting or rough idling due to a "percolation" effect. Some carburetors reduce this possibility of flooding by incorporating a spring-loaded valve in the fuel bowl. The valve acts as a vent to allow the vapor to escape into the outside air.

The valve is generally located on the top of the carburetor fuel bowl and may or may not be connected to a main air-bleed, Fig. 10-19. The valve is referred to as either an antipercolator valve or a fuel bowl vent. Linkage from the throttle opens the valve when the accelerator is released permitting any vapor which develops in the fuel

Automotive Engines

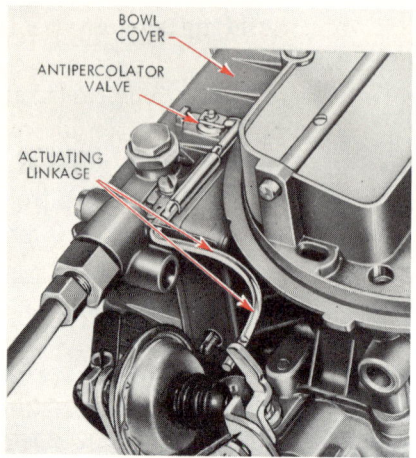

Fig. 10-19. During hot weather or prolonged idling, the anti-percolator valve or fuel bowl vent prevents excess fuel vapor pressure from richening the air-fuel idle mixture. (Ford Div., Ford Motor Co.)

turning the carburetor to an internally balanced condition.

One make of four-barrel carburetor has a thermostatically controlled idle compensator valve, Fig. 10-20, which performs much the same function as an antipercolator valve. A thermostatic valve located on the secondary side of the float bowl allows additional air to enter the primary throttle body under the throttle valves. The additional air drawn into the engine in this manner is sufficient to offset the enriching effects of high temperature and prevents hot idle stalling. With a prolonged hot idle the bimetal strip bends, raises the valve, and uncovers a passageway leading to the underside of the throttle valve. When the underhood temperatures are lowered, the valve closes.

discharge well or float bowl to escape. As soon as the throttle is opened a spring closes the valve, re-

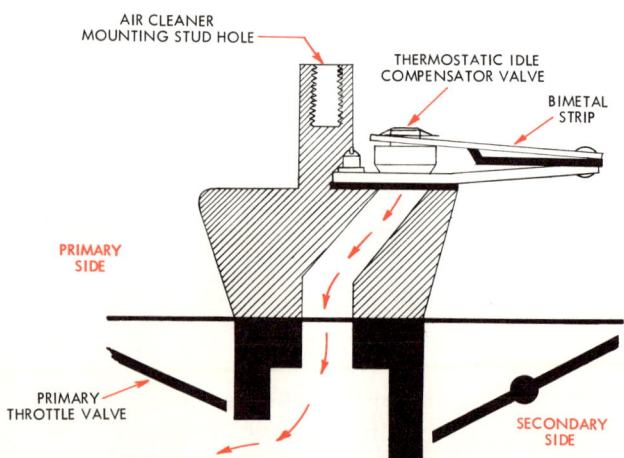

Fig. 10-20. The thermostatically controlled idle compensator valve is allowing additional air to enter under the primary throttle valve to offset the richening effects of high temperature in the fuel bowl. (Buick Div., General Motors Corp.)

Carburetors and Carburetion

Anti-stall Dashpot

The carburetor used on automobiles having an automatic transmission incorporates a throttle return check usually referred to as an *anti-stall dashpot unit*. The anti-stall dashpot is a device which prevents sudden closing of the throttle. Sudden closing of the throttle can cause momentary hesitation or stalling of the engine on a vehicle equipped with a fluid coupling or a torque converter because the rear wheels do not immediately drive the engine when the throttle is suddenly closed.

The most commonly used type of dashpot consists of a spring-loaded diaphragm, mounted on the side of the carburetor ahead of the throttle, which traps air behind it when the throttle is closed, Fig. 10-21. The shaft, which may include an adjusting screw, is moved forward by spring tension when the throttle is opened. When the throttle is closed, a contact arm on the throttle lever moves against the dashpot shaft or adjusting screw. Because the air trapped behind the diaphragm can escape only through a small opening, and spring tension must be overcome, the throttle closing is retarded. The adjusting screw can be turned in or out to regulate the point at which the dashpot is brought into operation, or the entire unit can be moved backward or forward for adjustment.

Combination Emission Control Solenoid

On engines equipped with an emission control system, a combination emission control solenoid is incorporated in the carburetor assembly to provide curb idle speed and high gear deceleration throttle valve adjustment, Fig. 10-22. The combination emission control solenoid is controlled by two switches:

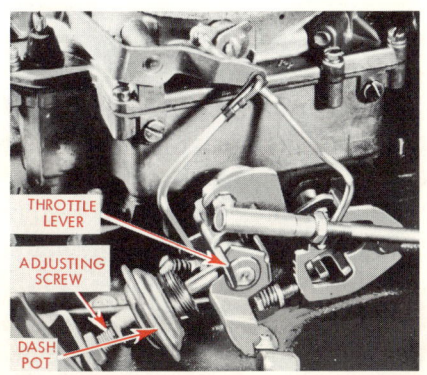

Fig. 10-21. The throttle linkage in this carburetor has just been released abruptly, but the diaphragm type anti-stall dashpot has prevented the throttle lever from closing suddenly and stalling the engine. (Buick Div., General Motors Corp.)

Automotive Engines

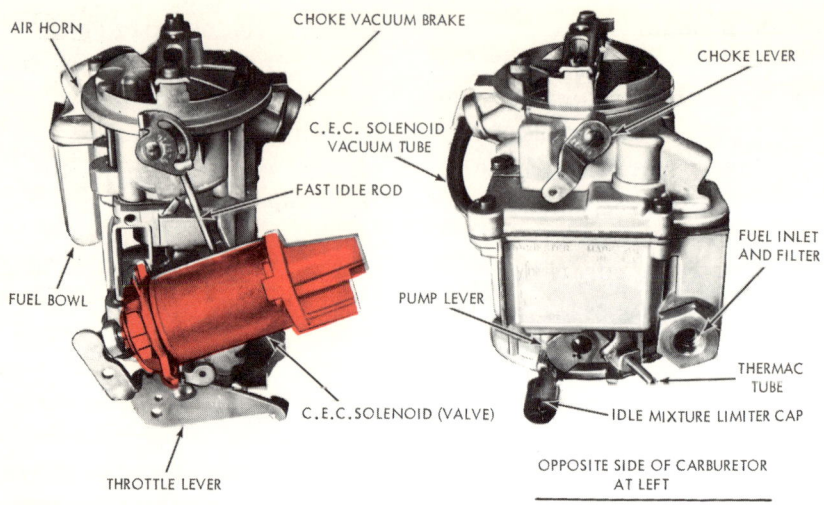

Fig. 10-22. Combination emission control solenoid installed on a carburetor. (Chevrolet Div., General Motors Corp.)

a reversing relay, and a time delay relay. The solenoid is energized in high forward gears and reverse by a transmission switch.

The time delay switch is in the circuit to energize the solenoid for approximately fifteen seconds after the ignition switch is turned on.

This permits full vacuum advance to the distributor, thereby reducing the possibility of cold engine stall.

The solenoid also permits lower curb idle speed for reduced transmission creep and the elimination of "dieseling" when the ignition is turned off.

Multiple Barrel Carburetors

To permit better fuel distribution, multiple barrel carburetors are used on most present-day engines. The use of multiple barrel carburetors with corresponding manifolding gives better fuel mixture distribution. The more evenly the fuel mixture can be distributed to each cylinder the greater will be the efficiency of the engine. Two-barrel and four-barrel carburetors are in common use.

Regardless of the number of barrels used, the operating principles in various systems will be the same. Generally, only one choke, air horn,

Carburetors and Carburetion

and accelerating system is used regardless of the number of barrels involved.

Two-Barrel Carburetors

A two-barrel carburetor, also known as a dual carburetor, is commonly used on all eight-cylinder engines. The two-barrel carburetor intake manifold promotes even air-fuel mixture distribution to the cylinders. There have been a few six-cylinder engines that have used the two-barrel carburetor arrangement.

The two-barrel carburetor intake manifold consists of two sections. Each section supplies air-fuel mixture to one half of the cylinders, Fig. 10-23.

The two-barrel or dual carburetor, in effect, performs the same functions as two single carburetors and uses the same systems as other carburetors, Fig. 10-24. The carburetor has two air-fuel passageways (barrels) which make up the main body of the carburetor, each containing an independent venturi. Two main fuel nozzles carry air-fuel mixture to the individual venturis, and two throttle valves are attached to one throttle shaft. One vacuum power jet allows additional fuel to flow into both main wells.

If step-up rods (metering rods)

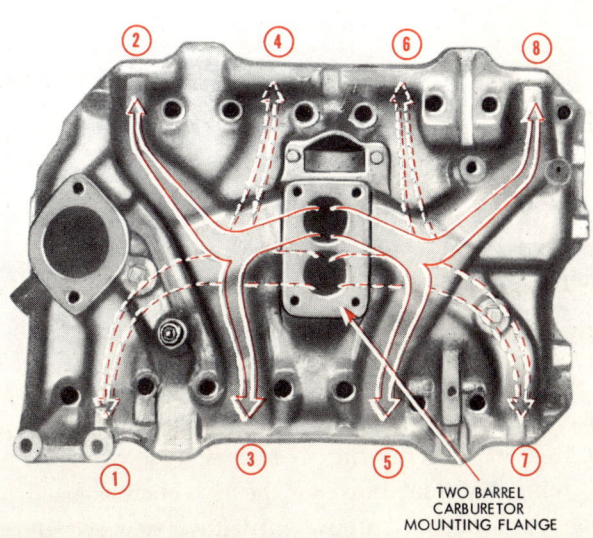

Fig. 10-23. Each section of this two-barrel carburetor intake manifold supplies air-fuel mixture for four of the eight engine cylinders. Each of the two sections draws air-fuel mixture from one barrel of the carburetor. (Dodge Div., Chrysler Corp.)

Automotive Engines

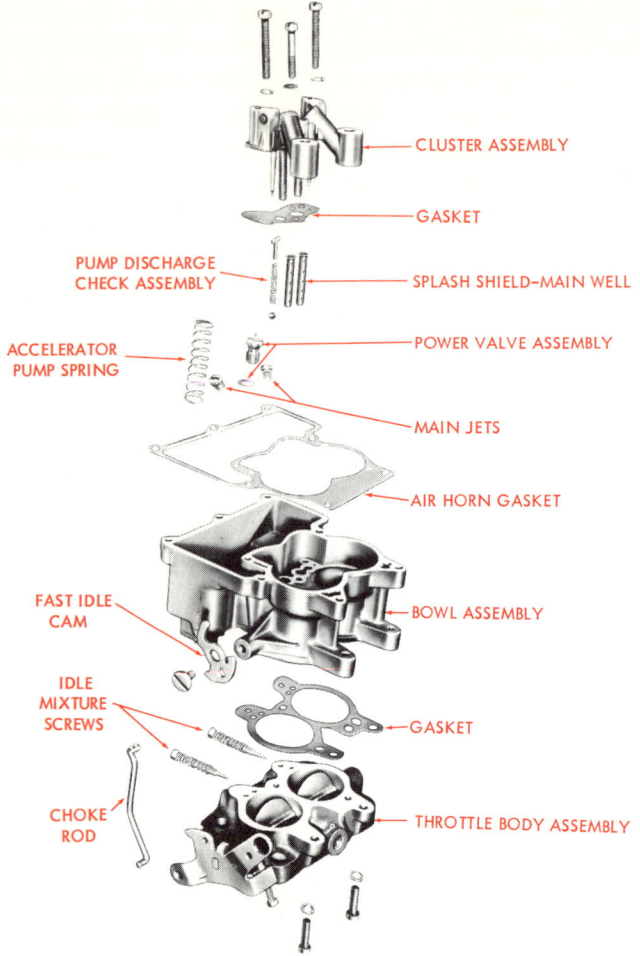

Fig. 10-24. Exploded view of carburetor float bowl and throttle body. (Chevrolet Div., General Motors Corp.)

are used in place of a power jet, one will be located in each of the main metering jets. One float bowl and float system is used, and one accelerator pump system discharges into both barrels. Two separate idle systems are used with individual adjustments for each barrel. One choke valve located in the air horn is used to reduce the air flow to both barrels for cold weather starting. The choke may be manually or automatically operated.

Carburetors and Carburetion

Four-Barrel Carburetors

The four-barrel carburetor, which is used as standard equipment on some V-8 engines and is available as optional equipment on most other V-8 engine installations, consists basically of two dual carburetors built into a single body. One dual section of the carburetor, referred to as the primary side, controls the metering of the air-fuel mixture to the engine under most operating conditions. Fig. 10-25 shows the top view of a typical four-barrel carburetor. When the accelerator is moved toward the wide open throttle position for acceleration or full power operation, the secondary section of the carburetor comes into operation and supplies more air-fuel mixture to the combustion chamber. This combination of operation permits dual carburetion economy at part throttle and improved operation at full throttle. Volumetric efficiency is greatly improved because at full throttle the capacity for air-fuel mixture is doubled. More air-fuel mixture enters the combustion chamber at near wide open throttle and improves high-speed full power performance. (You can find an explanation of volumetric efficiency in Appendix D.)

The four-barrel carburetor intake manifold has four openings at the carburetor mounting. Two

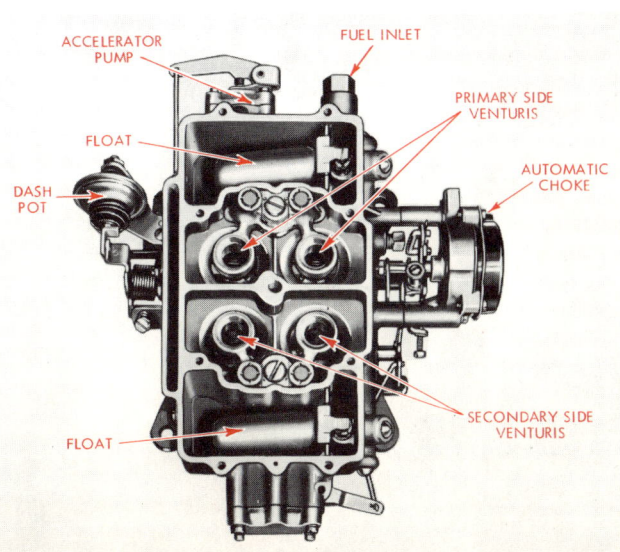

Fig. 10-25. The fuel bowl cover has been removed from this four-barrel carburetor so the two dual sections can be seen. They are viewed from above. (Mercury Div., Ford Motor Co.)

Automotive Engines

openings are for the primary side of the carburetor, and the other two openings are for the secondary side. One opening in the primary side feeds four cylinders, and the other opening in the primary side feeds the remaining four cylinders. The two secondary openings supplement the air-fuel mixture of the primary openings. They are controlled by the throttle plates in the secondary side of the carburetor. Fig. 10-26 illustrates a typical manifold used with a four-barrel carburetor.

The primary side of the carburetor contains all of the previously discussed systems: the float, idle, main, power, accelerator, and choke. They meet the normal engine requirements. The choke used on a four-barrel carburetor usually has a lockout feature which prevents the secondary throttle valves from opening while the choke valve is closed. If the secondary throttle valves opened when the engine was cold and the choke valve closed, the engine would probably stall from too lean a mixture.

The number of systems used in the secondary side of the carbu-

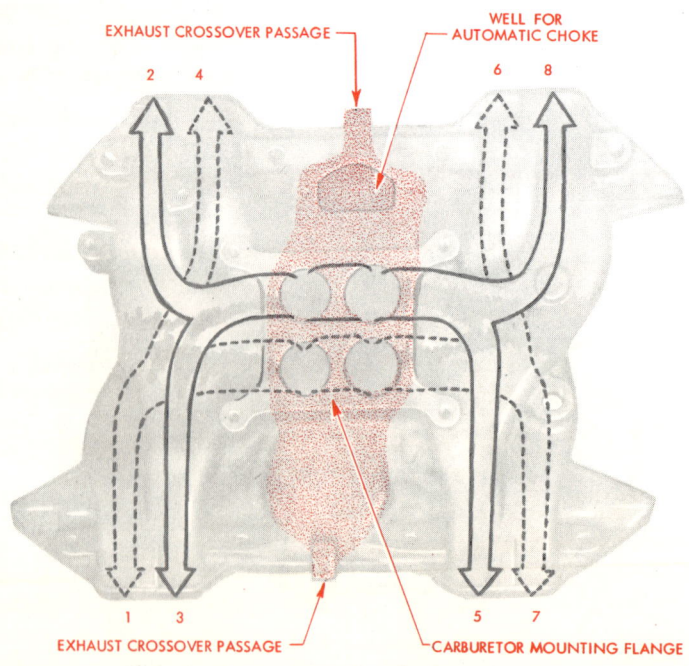

Fig. 10-26. This V-8 engine intake manifold is designed to be used with a four-barrel carburetor. (Plymouth Div., Chrysler Corp.)

Carburetors and Carburetion

retor will vary among the different makes and models of four-barrel carburetors. The minimum number of systems used must include a float system as well as a main system.

Float System. Two sets of floats, generally of the twin type, are used in the four-barrel carburetor. Fig. 10-27 illustrates a typical four-barrel float system. The purpose of the float system is the same as for the single or the two barrel carburetor: to maintain the correct fuel level in the float bowl and discharge tubes. Even though all the fuel enters only one side of the carburetor, the primary and secondary sides usually have their own float systems with separate needle valve assemblies and floats. The float bowls are separated by a partition but both are vented to the air horn and are connected by a fuel balance passage. The fuel level and air pressure are balanced between the two float bowls so as to maintain a uniform fuel level in both bowls.

A number of carburetors have a vapor vent in the float bowl cover. The vent opens as the accelerator pump shaft or linkage returns to the closed throttle position. The open vent permits any vapor which has accumulated in the float bowl to escape, reducing the opportunity for percolation of fuel in the float bowl.

All floats must be properly calibrated and coordinated to function correctly.

Idle System. In the four-barrel carburetor illustrated in Fig. 10-

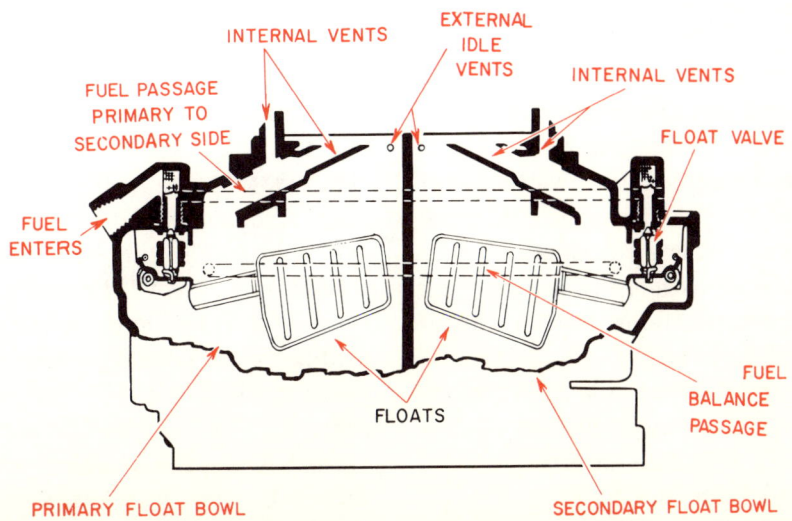

Fig. 10-27. Most four-barrel carburetors have a separate float system for the primary and for the secondary side. (Buick Div., General Motors Corp.)

393

Automotive Engines

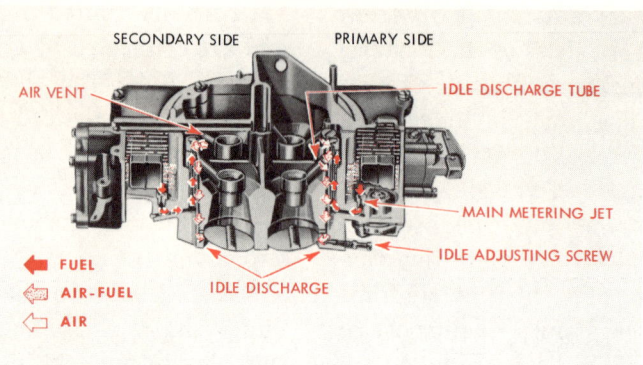

Fig. 10-28. The four-barrel carburetor above has been cross sectioned to show the two idle systems as seen from the side. Only one idle system can be adjusted. (Ford Div., Ford Motor Co.)

28 the idle fuel mixture is discharged into both the primary and secondary barrels. Idle fuel for the primary barrels is drawn from the primary fuel bowl, and idle fuel for the secondary barrels is drawn from the secondary fuel bowl. The fuel enters the main jets and flows through the idle tubes and passages. Then the fuel mixes with air from the idle air-bleeds and is discharged into the primary and secondary barrels. Only a fixed amount of fuel can be discharged into the secondary barrels because no idle mixture adjustment is provided on the secondary side of the carburetor. The primary side of the carburetor does have idle mixture adjusting screws and supplies the remaining idle fuel mixture needed by the engine.

In all four-barrel carburetors, the idle mixture discharge orifices are located above and below the throttle valves, and the air-bleeds are placed above the level of the fuel in the bowls, Fig. 10-28 as they are in a single-barrel carburetor. The idle mixture is adjusted in the same way as in dual or single barrel carburetor.

Other four-barrel carburetors also draw idle fuel from both the primary and secondary fuel bowls, but the idle fuel mixture is discharged into the primary barrels only. About one half of the necessary idle fuel is supplied from the secondary fuel bowl through a fixed system of tubes and passageways leading to the primary barrels. The primary fuel bowl supplies the other half of the idle fuel mixture needed. Only the primary side of the carburetor has idle adjusting screws.

Some four-barrel carburetors

Carburetors and Carburetion

have no idle system whatsoever on the secondary side. Idle mixture adjusting screws are on the primary side.

Main Fuel Supply System. As the throttle valves are opened, more air is forced through the carburetor and more fuel must be supplied by some means other than the idle system to increase engine speed. The primary side of the carburetor supplies this additional fuel through the main fuel supply system to meet engine requirements in the same manner as the single- or two-barrel carburetor. The main fuel supply system in the secondary side of the carburetor is constructed in the same manner as the fuel supply system in the primary side, but it is not brought into operation because the secondary throttle valves remain closed during part throttle operation.

When the primary throttle valves open, air velocity increases in the venturi, creating a vacuum at the main discharge nozzle. Fuel then flows through the main metering jets, into the main wells, and out the discharge nozzles. Fig. 10-29 shows the main fuel supply system of a four-barrel carburetor. Air-bleeds permit air to enter and mix with the fuel as it is forced through the passages so a mixture of air and fuel is discharged at the nozzle. The amount of air-fuel mixture flowing through the venturi depends upon throttle opening. In

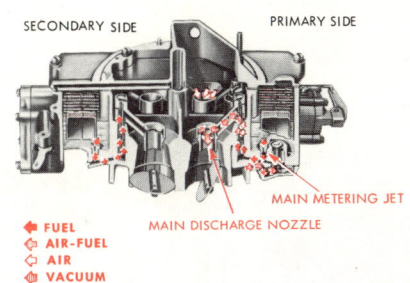

Fig. 10-29. The arrows show the direction of flow in the main fuel supply systems of the four-barrel carburetor above. The secondary throttle valves and main fuel system are not in operation yet because the primary throttle valves are only at part throttle. (Ford Div., Ford Motor Co.)

some carburetors, as throttle opening increases, air velocity increases and an additional air-bleed begins to supply more air. The additional air keeps the air-fuel mixture in the proper ratio while more fuel is being forced into the air stream.

Power Fuel Supply System. To meet the requirements of rapid acceleration or sustained high-speed driving, the four-barrel carburetor employs either a vacuum actuated power jet or step-up rods in the primary side of the carburetor, Fig. 10-30, operating in the same manner as the power fuel supply system used in a single- or two-barrel carburetor. Vacuum, obtained through a vacuum channel opening below the throttle valves, holds the jet or step-up rods closed during normal engine operation.

Automotive Engines

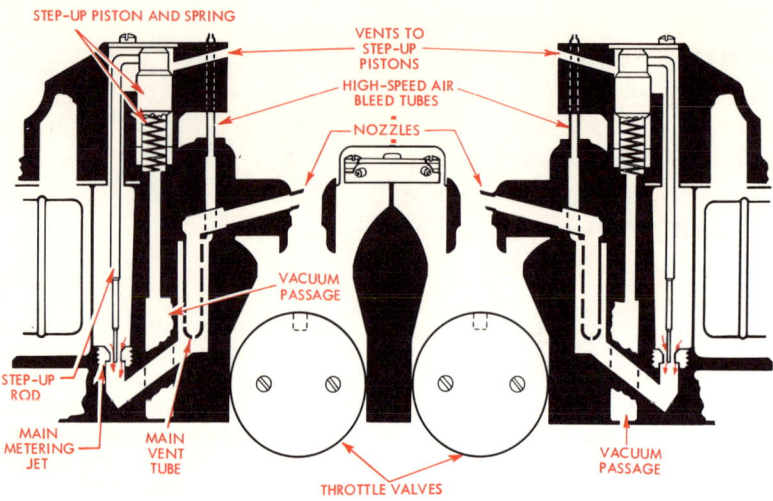

Fig. 10-30. The power fuel supply system in this four-barrel carburetor primary side is in operation because the throttle valves are wide open causing a drop in engine vacuum. (Buick Div., General Motors Corp.)

When the throttle is suddenly opened or is held in a wide open position, engine vacuum drops off, and a spring opens the power jet or raises the step-up rods to permit additional fuel to flow into the main wells supplementing the flow of fuel through the main metering nozzles.

The secondary side of most four-barrel carburetors does not contain a power fuel supply system. If one is used, it operates in the same manner as the power fuel supply system in the primary side. Under load and speed conditions which bring the power fuel supply system into operation, the secondary side of the carburetor is also brought into operation, further supplementing the primary side.

Accelerator Pump System. When the throttle valves on the primary side of the four-barrel carburetor are opened suddenly, manifold vacuum and air velocity decrease quickly, causing the air-fuel supply to lag momentarily. The lag could cause a hesitation in engine operation, but the accelerator pump system suplies the additional fuel required for smooth engine performance during rapid acceleration, Fig. 10-31.

Only one accelerator pump is required in the four-barrel carburetor because the secondary throttle valves remain closed until the engine is at maximum load. The pump used in the primary side is the same type as the pump used in the two-barrel carburetor.

Carburetors and Carburetion

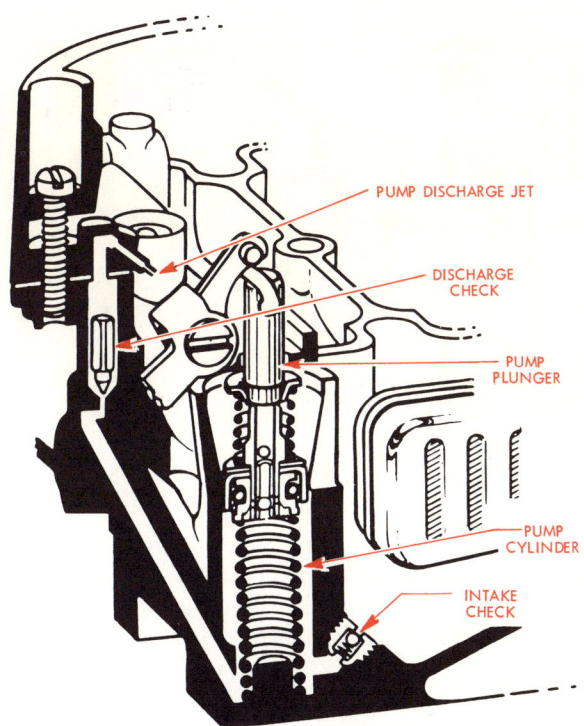

Fig. 10-31. This is a four-barrel carburetor accelerator pump system. It is needed for the primary barrels only. (Buick Div., General Motors Corp.)

Secondary Fuel System. To provide sufficient air-fuel mixture to operate the engine at maximum power (acceleration at high speed), the mixture supplied by the primary side of the carburetor is supplemented by an additional quantity of air-fuel mixture from the secondary side of the carburetor. Different methods are employed to open the throttle valves of the secondary side of the carburetor to furnish manifold vacuum that can force air-fuel mixture from the main discharge nozzles. The secondary throttle valves or the secondary auxiliary throttle valves may be actuated by throttle linkage, venturi vacuum, or air velocity.

Actuated by Linkage. The linkage method, Fig. 10-32 is designed so the secondary throttle valves remain closed until the primary throttle valves are near the wide open position. During the last few remaining degrees of primary throttle valve movent, the linkage opens the secondary throttle valves to a position that corresponds with

397

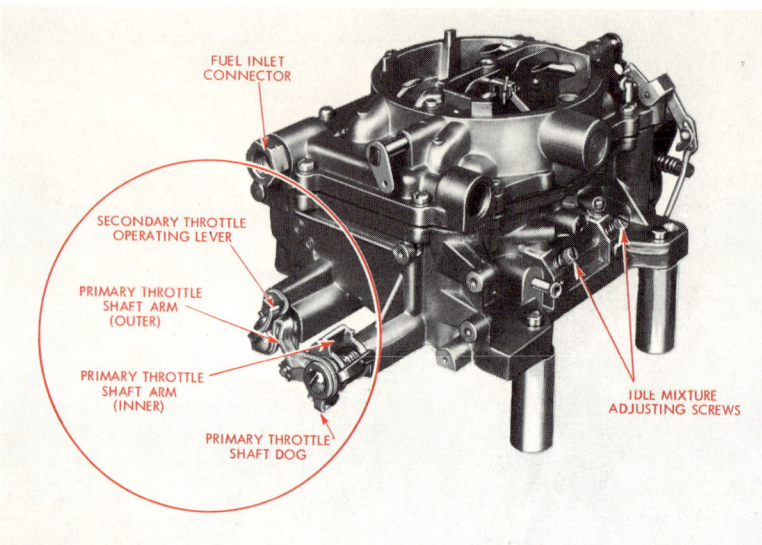

Fig. 10-32. A lever connects the primary and secondary throttle valve shafts of this four-barrel carburetor. The lever will open the secondary throttle valves only during the last few degrees of primary throttle valve travel. (Plymouth Div., Chrysler Corp.)

the primary throttle valve position. The secondary side of the carburetor then operates in the same manner as the primary side.

The connecting linkage must be adjusted very accurately in order to properly coordinate the two sets of throttle valves.

Actuated by Venturi Vacuum. When venturi vacuum actuates secondary throttle valves, vacuum from one of the primary venturis operates a spring-loaded vacuum diaphragm assembly connected by a link to the secondary throttle shaft, Fig. 10-33. A tube extends into one of the primary booster venturis. The vacuum is transmitted through this tube to the secondary

operating diaphragm. As the primary throttle valves are opened, primary venturi vacuum increases. When the vacuum reaches a predetermined value, it begins to act on the secondary system operating diaphragm which starts to open the secondary throttle valves. As the secondary throttle valves begin to open, air-fuel mixture is drawn from the secondary side. The higher the venturi vacuum, the more the throttle valves will open. When decelerating, vacuum in the venturi decreases and the secondary throttle shaft (coupled to the throttle lever) mechanically overcomes any lag in the vacuum system and closes the secondary throttle valves to as-

Carburetors and Carburetion

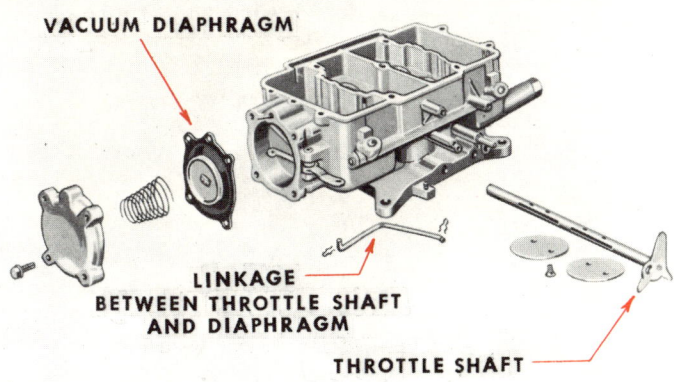

Fig. 10-33. Venturi vacuum controls the secondary throttle valves on this four-barrel carburetor. The vacuum actuates a spring-loaded diaphragm connected to the secondary throttle valve shaft. (Ford Div., Ford Motor Co.)

sure a positive engine deceleration.

Actuated by Carburetor Air Velocity. Another arrangement for bringing the secondary barrels into use is an additional pair of throttle valves located above the regular secondary throttle valves. These are called auxiliary throttle valves, Fig. 10-34, and are operated by air velocity. For high-speed operation, beyond part throttle range, the throttle linkage engages the secondary throttle valves and opens them completely in the remaining few degrees of primary throttle travel in the same manner as linkage controlled secondary throttle valves. The auxiliary throttle valves provide a means of controlling the secondary barrel openings according to air velocity at wide open throttle.

With high air velocity through the carburetor, good metering conditions are present, and fuel is being forced from the main discharge nozzle in correct proportions to create the proper air-fuel ratio. When the secondary throttle valves are open and high air velocity is present, the auxiliary valves are forced open permitting the secondary barrels to function in the normal manner.

Low air velocity reduces metering efficiency. When this condition occurs, the spring tension on the auxiliary valves overcomes the low air velocity and closes the valves. Air which was going through all four barrels now passes through only the primaries. This increases the velocity in the primary barrels, and good metering control extends over a wider range of low speed, wide open throttle operation.

399

Automotive Engines

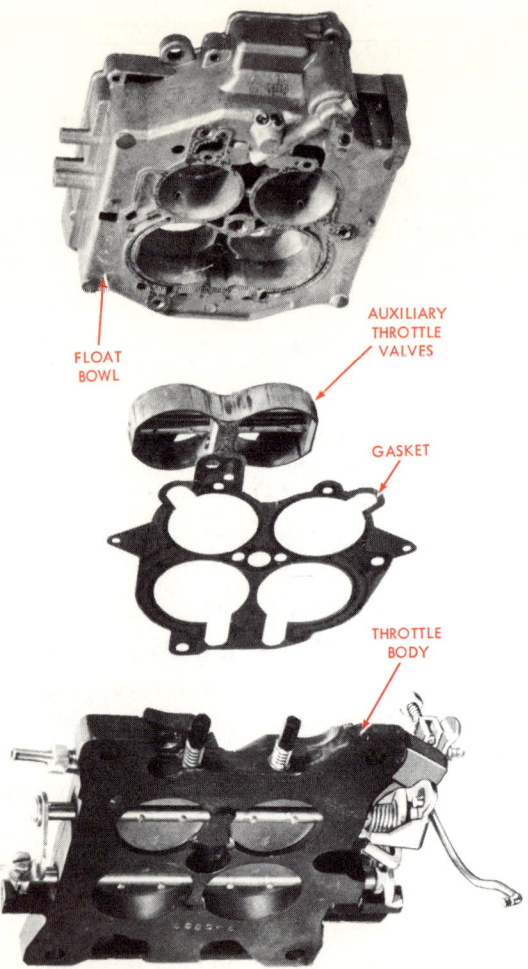

Fig. 10-34. On this disassembled four-barrel carburetor, an auxiliary pair of throttle valves is located above the secondary valves. These auxiliary valves react to air velocities and then control the secondary throttle valves. (Oldsmobile Div., General Motors Corp.)

During the period when the secondary throttle valves are open and air flow is not high enough to open the auxiliary valves, additional fuel is needed for the air which bypasses the auxiliary valves. The additional fuel is supplied by tubes which extend from the mixing channel in the venturi to the low pressure point below the closed auxiliary valves. When the air velocity is high enough to open the auxiliary valves, the tubes no longer feed fuel.

Carburetors and Carburetion

Compound (Multiple) Carburetion

Some manufacturers make available manifolds designed for using more than one carburetor. Two four-barrel carburetors or three two-barrel carburetors may be used on some V-8 engines. Fig. 10-35 illustrates the manifold arrangement used with three two-barrel carburetors. On both types of installations, one carburetor contains all of the regular systems (float, idle, main, power, pump, and choke). This one carburetor supplies all of the air-fuel mixture for idle and part throttle operation. The remaining carburetor or carburetors are brought into use to supplement the primary carburetor for heavy loads and high speed operation. Providing more air-fuel mixture increases torque output at high RPM for improved performance.

Three Two-Barrel Carburetors

When three two-barrel carburetors are used, the center carburetor contains all of the normal systems. The front and rear carburetors contain only the float, main metering, and pump systems.

The throttle valves and accelerator pump in the front and rear carburetors, Fig. 10-36, are actuated by a diaphragm controlled by a vacuum switch mounted on the center carburetor. Vacuum is supplied to the vacuum switch from a vacuum tank reservoir. The throttle shafts on the front and rear carburetors are connected by a com-

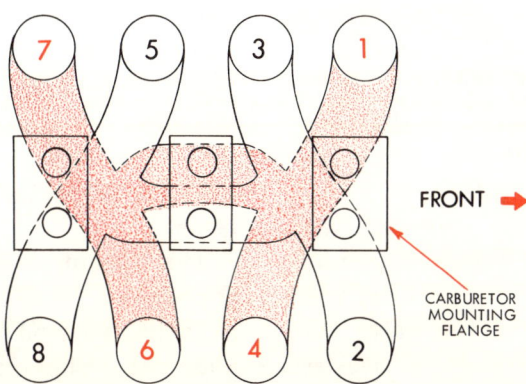

Fig. 10-35. This diagram indicates air-fuel mixture flow in a V-8 engine intake manifold that uses three two-barrel carburetors. It is viewed from above. (Cadillac Div., General Motors Corp.)

Automotive Engines

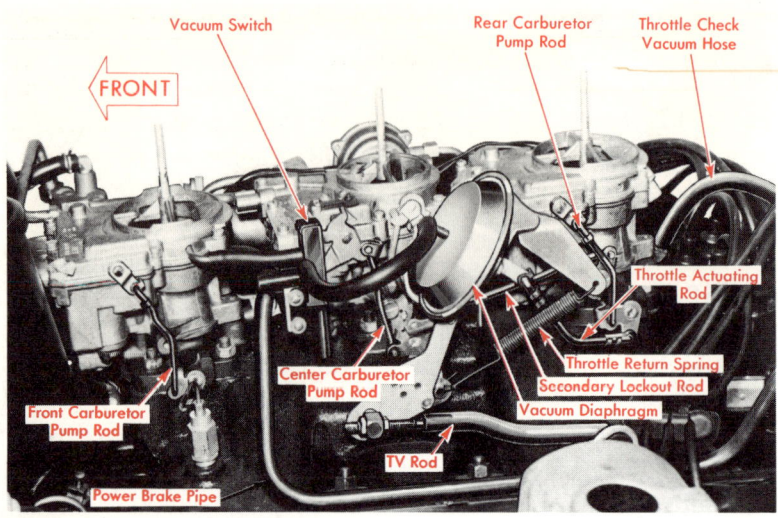

Fig. 10-36. The vacuum switch mounted on the center carburetor controls the throttle valves on the other two carburetors. (Cadillac Div., General Motors Corp.)

mon rod and are actuated by the vacuum diaphragm through the vacuum switch. The TV rod shown in Fig. 10-36 is the Throttle Valve rod to the accelerator pedal. Fig. 10-36 shows the three carburetors and the linkage arrangement. A temperature controlled vacuum valve is located in the water jacket and shuts off all vacuum supplied to the vacuum switch on the center carburetor until the engine is thoroughly warmed up.

During normal operation and acceleration, the center carburetor furnishes all of the air-fuel mixture until the throttle valves are opened approximately 65 degrees. When the throttle valves on the center carburetor reach this point, a tang on the accelerator pump lever actuates the vacuum switch. This applies vacuum from the vacuum tank reservoir to the diaphragm chamber mounted on the rear carburetor which in turn opens the throttle valves in the front and rear carburetors. The accelerator pump is linked to the throttle in the same manner as in a regular carburetor. The air-fuel mixture from the front and rear carburetors now supplements the mixture from the center carburetor.

The vacuum switch closes when the center carburetor throttles close, shutting off the vacuum applied to the diaphragm. Air is then bled through a line from the front carburetor through the vacuum switch to the vacuum diaphragm

Carburetors and Carburetion

Fig. 10-37. The front four-barrel carburetor supplements the rear four-barrel carburetor on this dual manifold. (Chevrolet Div., General Motors Corp.)

allowing the diaphragm to be returned to its normal position by the diaphragm return spring. This closes the throttle valves in the front and rear carburetors.

The throttle linkage must be kept in correct adjustment at all times to properly synchronize carburetor operation. The basic carburetor adjustments will be the same as for a single carburetor installation.

Two Four-Barrel Carburetors

When two four-barrel carburetors are used, both carburetors are constructed much the same as the carburetor used for the single four-barrel installation but the front carburetor does not have a choke valve or a fast idle linkage. Metering calibration and linkage attachment differ to some extent on the dual installation. Fig. 10-37 shows a dual four-barrel carburetor installation. The front carburetor is used to supplement the rear carburetor. The linkage arrangement is set up so the throttle valves in both carburetors are wide open at the same time. The front carburetor throttle valves begin to open when the rear carburetor is at approximately half throttle.

Gasoline Fuel Injection

Fuel injection has been made available in limited quantities for some makes of automobiles. Basically, a fuel injection system con-

403

sists of a pump which delivers liquid gasoline to spray nozzles (injectors). As the liquid fuel is forced through the nozzles, it is broken up into a very fine mist. The nozzles may be located in the intake manifold near the air intake, or close to the intake valve ports. An air meter throttle controls the amount of air entering the intake manifold. Because the fuel is pumped into the manifold, the flow of air is less restricted than when it must pass through a carburetor.

The various venturis, air-bleeds and nozzle arrangements in a conventional carburetor create a certain amount of resistance to the flow of air through the carburetor. The resistance is essential for correct fuel flow and proper atomization. By replacing the carburetor with an air metering device and injecting fuel that is already atomized into the air stream, engine "breathing" (volumetric efficiency) is improved. Most injector systems greatly restrict fuel flow on deceleration, thereby reducing much of the pumping effect which occurs with a regular carburetor and improving fuel economy. (An explanation of volumetric efficiency can be found in Appendix D.)

Superchargers

Although superchargers are sometimes used on racing cars, their use on automotive vehicles is limited.

Most gasoline engines depend upon normal atmospheric pressure (14 psi at sea level) to force the air-fuel mixture into the engine combustion chamber. The purpose of a supercharger is to force the air-fuel mixture into the cylinders under pressure greater than atmospheric pressure.

Checking On Your Knowledge

The following questions give you the opportunity to check up on yourself. If you have read the chapter carefully, you should be able to answer the questions. If you have any difficulty, read the chapter over once more so that you have the information well in mind before you go on with your reading.

Carburetors and Carburetion

DO YOU KNOW

1. Why does air flow through the carburetor?

2. What are the factors involved in the vaporizing and atomizing of gasoline in the carburetor?

3. Describe carburetor venturi action.

4. Under what conditions is it necessary for the carburetor to supply a rich mixture?

5. Why is it important that the proper float level be maintained in the carburetor?

6. Why is it necessary to have a separate idle fuel supply system and how does it operate?

7. What is the significance of the size of the opening in the main metering jet?

8. Why can vacuum be used to operate the power valve?

9. How does a step-up or metering rod operate to supply more fuel?

10. How will an engine operate if the accelerator pump fails?

11. How does a vacuum operated automatic choke operate?

12. What is the fast idle cam and why is it needed?

13. What is carburetor percolation and how would it affect engine operation?

14. Why is an anti-stall dashpot used on some vehicles?

15. Compare a dual carburetor to a single-barrel carburetor.

16. What is the reason for using a four-barrel carburetor?

17. Describe the carburetor action when more than one carburetor is used on the intake manifold.

18. What are the reasons for using gasoline fuel injection?

19. What is the purpose of a supercharger?

Chapter 11

Fuel System and Carburetor Servicing

Trouble in the fuel system units usually causes the engine to fail to start, miss, lose power, accelerate poorly, stall, backfire, burn excessive fuel, etc. This chapter discusses some of the common fuel system troubles and the services or repairs required to restore the units to normal operating condition. The units include the fuel tank, fuel filters, fuel lines, fuel pump, air cleaner, and carburetor.

Repairing a Fuel Tank

Normally, little service is required on a fuel tank unless it has been damaged. A tank which has loose baffles, or is rusted, should be replaced. A leaking tank can sometimes be repaired by soldering. Because passenger car fuel tanks are usually inexpensive, it is advisable to replace a defective tank rather than repair it.

Soldering a fuel tank is a dan- *gerous job. Exercise caution to avoid an explosion. An empty fuel tank will explode as readily as a tank containing fuel.*

When repairing a leaking fuel tank, drain all the fuel and remove the tank and fuel gage sending unit. Flush the tank with water until every trace of gasoline fumes is removed. Fill the tank with water and position it so water will

Fuel System and Carburetor Servicing

not seep out of the section to be repaired. Use a wire brush to clean around the spot to be repaired. Scrape the surface to be soldered until it is clean and bright. Solder the damaged section. Use flux-cored solder or a separate flux and solder.

Do not use a soldering iron when it is red hot. Make sure there is no glowing carbon or oxidation on the tip. Do not hold the iron in any one spot for more than a few seconds at a time.

Drain the water from the tank. Blow compressed air into the tank to remove all traces of moisture. To test the tank for leakage, close all tank openings. Then put soap suds on the repaired area and blow a small amount of air into the tank.

If soap bubbles appear, the tank still leaks.

Carbon tetrachloride may be used in the tank rather than water as a safety measure to avoid a fire or explosion. Make sure the tank is full of carbon tetrachloride fumes before soldering. *Avoid breathing the fumes and avoid prolonged skin contact.*

A fuel tank which cannot be cleaned thoroughly by removing the drain plug should be removed from the vehicle. Remove the fuel gage sending unit and flush the tank with water until all foreign matter is removed. Drain the water from the tank and blow it out thoroughly with compressed air.

Fuel Filter Service

A fuel filter may be located in the fuel tank, in the fuel line, or at the fuel pump.

Fuel Tank Filter

If the built-in fuel tank filter becomes clogged, it can be cleaned without removing the tank as follows:

Disconnect the fuel line at the tank or fuel pump. Remove the drain plug at the bottom of the tank as well as the filler cap. Blow compressed air through the outlet line. Start out with a low pressure. Gradually increase the volume and velocity of the air pressure until the filter is clean. Flush the tank with a small amount of clean gasoline. Then install the drain plug and reconnect the outlet line.

Fuel Filters

Most older model engines used fuel pumps that incorporated a sediment bowl and screen or a filter pack arrangement. The bowl and screen could be removed for cleaning purposes. Whenever the bowl is removed, install a new gasket.

Automotive Engines

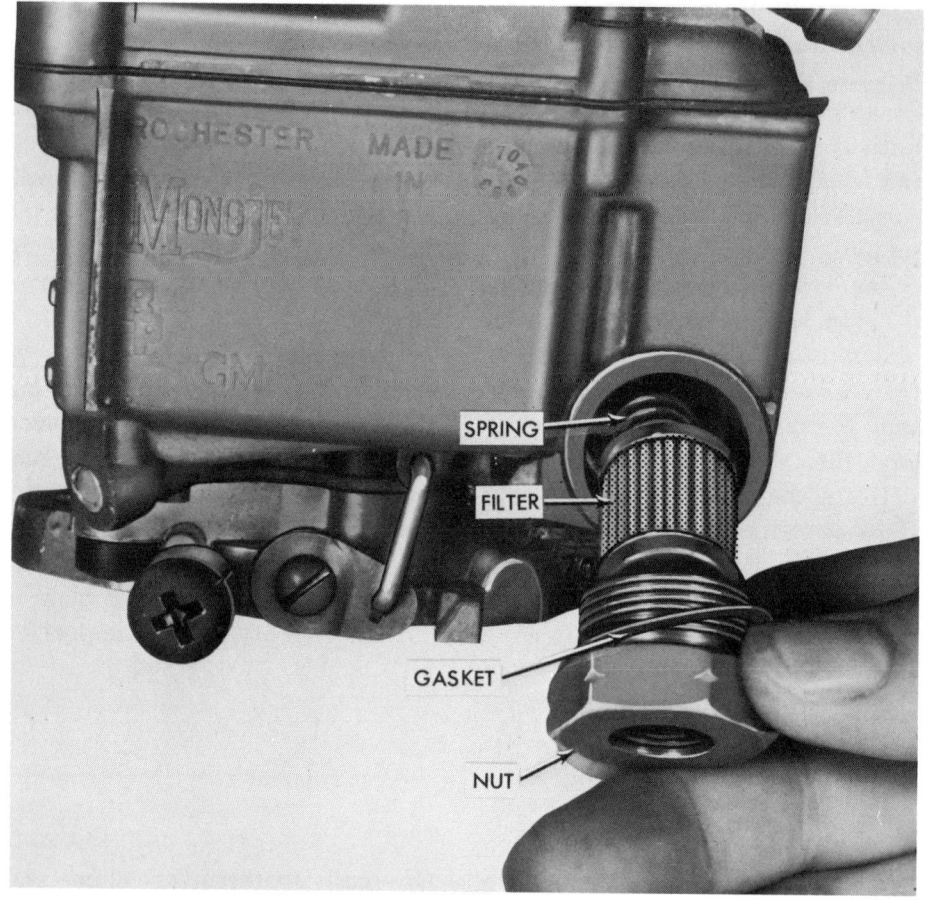

Fig. 11-1. Fuel filter at carburetor inlet. (Chevrolet Div., General Motors Corp.)

On late model vehicles, very few pumps incorporate filters. Filter units are located in the fuel tanks on some vehicles. Many of these are self-cleaning, by the movement of the fuel in the tank.

A number of vehicles use sealed filter units in the fuel line between the pump and carburetor. It is recommended that the unit be replaced at approximately every 24,000 miles.

A number of carburetors have a filter unit located at the inlet to the carburetor float bowl. Some of these are paper elements which should be replaced every 24,000 miles, Fig. 11-1. Other carburetors have a removable screen at the fuel inlet which can be cleaned.

Fuel System and Carburetor Servicing

Repairing and Replacing Fuel Lines

Fuel lines present few problems if they are located properly and handled correctly. Fuel lines can crack and leak if they are kinked or bent unnecessarily. Too sharp a bend also creates a restriction to fuel flow. When loosening a coupling having two fittings, use two wrenches to prevent twisting the line. Make sure the wrenches are of the correct size to prevent damage to the coupling or fittings.

Replacing Line

When a fuel line needs to be replaced, install the new line in the same position as the old. The location of the original line was selected to protect it against flying stones and to support it adequately at various points along the frame or body.

Repairing Line

A small break in a fuel line can be repaired if a new line is not available. Cut out the damaged piece and slide one sleeve on each end of the line. Fasten the fittings together with a connector, Fig. 11-2.

A flared type of fitting may be used in place of a compression fitting if desired. Cut out the damaged part of the line. Cut the ends straight and smooth. Any nicks, scratches, or roughness at the end of the tube will result in a poor joint and leakage. Slip the nuts onto the ends of the tubes. Then

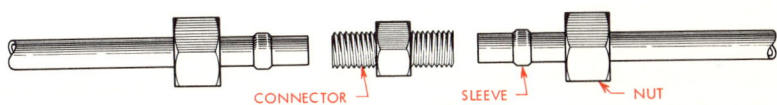

Fig. 11-2. A compression type fuel line fitting does not require special tools for insulation.

Fig. 11-3. Special flaring tools are needed to install a flared fuel line fitting. A flared fitting resists vibration better than a compression fitting.

flare the ends of the tubes with a flaring tool. Using a double flare will give more strength than a single flare. Insert a connector between the two fittings and fasten the nuts to the connector, Fig. 11-3.

Fuel Pump Troubleshooting

If a fuel pump is suspected of not operating, simply remove the fuel line at the carburetor, disconnect the high voltage lead, and crank the engine. If the fuel pump is operating, fuel will spurt from the line when the engine is cranked. Before replacing a fuel pump always make sure the fuel lines and filter are clear.

Two tests may be used to determine if a fuel pump is delivering the correct amount of fuel: the pressure test and the capacity test.

Pressure Test

To check fuel pump pressure, remove the fuel line at the carburetor and install a pressure gage. With the engine running at idle speed, the pump should deliver approximately 4 to 7 pounds pressure. The engine should run for a few seconds on the fuel in the carburetor bowl with the fuel line disconnected. Too low a pressure results in gasoline starvation causing poor engine performance. Too high a fuel pump pressure causes excessive fuel consumption and fouled spark plugs.

Capacity Test

To make a fuel pump capacity test, disconnect the fuel line at the carburetor bowl. With the engine running at idle speed, the pump should deliver approximately one pint of fuel in 30 seconds.

Checking a Combination Fuel and Vacuum Pump

The fuel section of a combination pump is checked in the same manner as a single fuel pump.

A faulty vacuum section may be indicated by irregular operation of the windshield wiper motor. When the engine is under load, the wiper action slows down.

A cracked or porous vacuum diaphragm can sometimes cause excessive oil consumption because manifold vacuum may draw oil spray from the crankcase through the cracked diaphragm into the intake manifold and engine cylinders where it is burned.

To check the vacuum section, disconnect the intake manifold vacuum line from the pump or manifold. Connect a vacuum gage in the line to the windshield wiper

Fuel System and Carburetor Servicing

motor. With the engine running at idle speed, the pump should create approximately 10 inches of vacuum.

Fuel Pump Inspection and Repair

It is standard practice to exchange a faulty fuel or combination fuel and vacuum pump for a new or rebuilt pump. While the older model fuel pumps could be completely disassembled and the parts replaced, it is not considered practical to attempt to overhaul a single diaphragm fuel pump. Many fuel pumps are now permanently sealed and cannot be repaired.

Before installing the pump, it is good practice to crank the engine so that the nose of the camshaft

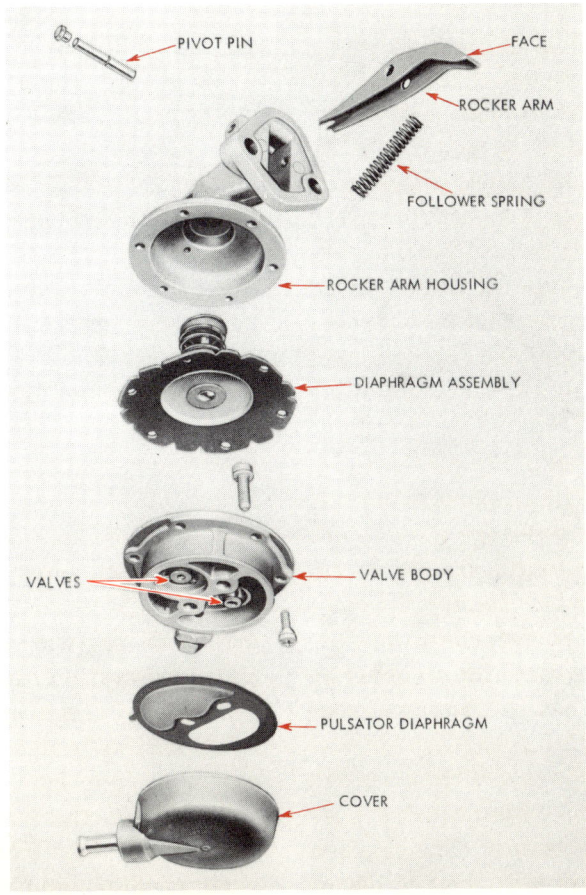

Fig. 11-4. This fuel pump has been disassembled completely except for the valves. The valves must be pried out if they are to be replaced. (Plymouth Div., Chrysler Corp.)

eccentric does not interfere with the fuel pump rocker arm when the pump is installed. This will place the least amount of tension on the rocker arm, thereby easing the installation of the pump.

It is possible to overhaul and rebuild a pump without the use of special tools. If the fuel pump is to be rebuilt, consult the manufacturer's shop manual for the specific procedures and make sure it is possible to obtain a rebuilding kit before overhauling the defective pump.

Before disassembling a fuel pump, inspect it to determine the extent of disassembly and repair necessary. If the pump has been operating satisfactorily but leaks gasoline through the pump body, only the diaphragm assembly needs replacing. In the case of a combination pump, only the malfunctioning section needs repair.

Inspect the linkage carefully for wear and lost motion. Any wear on the contact face of the arm or play in the links or pins will result in lost motion. When the face of the arm is not worn and no play or wear is evident in the linkage when moving the mechanism by hand, it need not be disassembled unless the linkage must be removed to permit removal of other parts or prevent damage to other parts during removal.

Two different repair kits are available for some fuel pumps: a diaphragm repair kit containing valves, gaskets, and diaphragm, and a fuel pump parts kit containing practically all of the replaceable parts of the pump. The extent of disassembly and type of kit needed is determined by the repairs necessary. Fig. 11-4 illustrates a disassembled fuel pump.

Air Cleaner Service

At regular periods the air cleaner on the carburetor should be removed so that the filter element can be serviced.

Oil Bath Type

Service this type of cleaner when dirt accumulates in the bottom of the reservoir to the level of the offset portion. Disassemble the unit, drain the oil, wash all parts in a cleaning solution, and clean with a lintless rag and compressed air. Then fill with new oil when reassembling.

Oil-wetted Mesh Type

Disassemble and wash the parts in a cleaning solution. Dry with a rag and compressed air. Dip the

Fuel System and Carburetor Servicing

filter mesh element in oil and let the surplus oil drain off. Reassemble the air cleaner.

Dry Type

The element can be cleaned by tapping it against a hard surface. Clean the air cleaner body and cover in cleaning solvent and wipe dry. Do not immerse the filter element in a cleaner or blow out with compressed air. It is recommended that this type of filter element be replaced at approximately every 20,000 miles.

Fuel System Troubleshooting

A properly functioning carburetor delivers the correct air-fuel ratio for all operating conditions. When a carburetor fails to function properly, a thorough cleaning, replacement of all worn parts, and correct adjustment should permit the carburetor to function again in a normal manner.

Any change in carburetion generally comes about gradually due to an accumulation of dirt, moisture, or an air leak. Therefore, any sudden malfunction in engine operation will generally be found in some unit other than the carburetor. Check the ignition system and compression before condemning carburetion. Ordinarily, carburetors require very little service other than adjustment.

Preliminary Tests

When troubleshooting for engine malfunctioning, first check the strength of the spark from the end of the spark plug wires (see Chapter 13) and also measure the compression with a compression tester. Then set the ignition timing and clean and gap the spark plugs. This procedure will uncover any trouble in the engine mechanism or the ignition system. Usually, when the trouble is not found by this operation, the fuel system is at fault.

Symptoms

Trouble in the fuel system can cause a wide variety of engine malfunctions. Faulty fuel system operation can cause poor idling, hard starting when the engine is warm, failure to start unless primed, and slow engine warm-up. Improper carburetion can result in excessive fuel consumption, lack of power, poor acceleration, or poor high-speed performance. Improper carburetion can also cause too rich a mixture resulting in black exhaust, engine stalling on warm-up, engine backfiring, and engine stalling after high-speed driving. The engine may also miss on varying cylinders.

Fuel Not Reaching the Engine. When an engine starts, but fails to keep running, or if when running normally it suddenly stops, the trouble is usually due to lack of fuel in the carburetor. First, check to make sure there is enough fuel in the tank; a faulty fuel gage can indicate fuel when the tank is too low or empty. The trouble might also be due to insufficient vacuum created in the fuel pump because of air leakage in the fuel system. A clogged fuel line or filter, a stuck carburetor float, frozen water in the system, or vapor lock can each prevent fuel from entering the carburetor. Carburetor icing can prevent fuel from leaving the carburetor. In any case, fuel is prevented from reaching the engine.

Insufficient Vacuum Due to Air Leakage. Although the fuel pump pushes fuel to the carburetor, it is atmospheric pressure exerted on the surface of the fuel in the fuel tank that forces the fuel up to the pump. Leakage at any point that will permit air to enter the intake side of the pump or the fuel line destroys vacuum so that fuel will not be forced to the pump. The most common point of air leakage is in the flexible fuel hose usually located at the point where the fuel line leaves the frame and connects to the pump. Inspect this hose first if fuel is not reaching the pump.

Vapor Lock. When a hot engine is stopped, particularly with a highly volatile fuel, heat from the engine may vaporize the fuel in the lines or pump. This is commonly known as *vapor lock* and can also occur on the road under maximum load conditions in hot weather. Restarting is usually no problem if the vapor lock did not exist prior to stopping because the fuel in the carburetor is still liquid. However, as soon as this fuel is used up, no more fuel will flow to the carburetor until the vapor lock is relieved. Allowing the engine to sit for awhile or pouring cold water over the fuel pump and lines will often permit starting. Insulating and shielding the fuel lines and fuel pump will aid in reducing the possibility of vapor lock.

Carburetor Icing. When atmospheric temperature is slightly above freezing and the humidity is high, the drop in temperature inside the carburetor due to venturi action can cause the moisture in the air to form ice which may shut off the air-fuel mixture. Usually, if the engine is allowed to sit for a few moments, the heat from the engine will melt the ice and the engine can be started. Many of today's gasolines are treated with an "anti-icer" to prevent this condition from occurring.

Frozen Water in Fuel System.

Fuel System and Carburetor Servicing

In freezing weather, water in the fuel pump can freeze and prevent the pump from operating, or water anywhere in the lines or in the gas tank can freeze and thus shut off fuel. In each case the fuel in the carburetor float bowl, still there from previous operation, will permit the engine to start. However, since no more fuel is flowing into the carburetor, the engine stops as soon as this fuel is used up. Since the engine will run only a very few minutes, usually not enough heat is developed to melt the ice and the engine will not start again.

Carburetor Floods. In addition to an unevenly running engine, usually a strong odor of gasoline is present when the carburetor is flooding. If the carburetor is flooding due to overchoking or fuel percolation, open the throttle wide, and crank the engine to exhaust the rich gases.

Percolation. On an engine where the carburetor is insufficiently insulated from the heat of the engine, the carburetor becomes heated when the engine is stopped and the circulation of air around it is cut off. When the carburetor is hot, vaporized bubbles form in the discharge tubes and passages. These bubbles rise in the tubes, pushing the liquid fuel with them into the carburetor venturi in the same manner as the bubbles in a coffee percolator raise the water in the percolator. Most modern carburetors have an antipercolator valve (or vent) or a bleeder opening in the discharge tube to relieve this vapor and prevent percolation. When percolation does take place, the liquid fuel spills into the manifold, and the engine is flooded. A hot engine will usually vaporize this liquid fuel before the engine cools but, in the meantime, the engine is flooded and may not restart.

If the engine will not start and percolation is suspected, hold the throttle wide open, using care to guard against excess manipulation of the accelerator pump, and crank the engine to exhaust the rich mixture in the cylinders.

To determine if percolation exists, with the engine hot, stop the engine, remove the air cleaner, and look into the carburetor air horn. If fuel is percolating, the fuel nozzle will be discharging raw fuel into the carburetor venturi as the bubbles rise in the discharge nozzle tube.

Carburetor flooding is usually the result of faulty choke action, high fuel pump pressure, high float level, a stuck float needle valve, or a leaking float valve in the carburetor.

Faulty Choke Action. To check choke action, remove the air cleaner, and observe if the carburetor choke valve opens freely. If the choke action is faulty, make the necessary adjustments or repairs.

Test the fuel pump pressure with the engine running at idle speed. If the fuel pump pressure is too high replace the fuel pump.

Stuck Float Valves. Sometimes foreign matter will lodge between the float needle valve and seat. Tapping the carburetor float chamber with a screw driver handle may dislodge the dirt and allow the carburetor to function properly. If this does not correct the trouble, remove and disassemble the carburetor. Clean all parts. Examine the float for a leak, and check the float needle valve and seat for wear or corrosion. Make repairs as required, and set the float level.

Fuel Mixture Too Rich. If the exhaust color (or exhaust gas analyzer) indicates the mixture is too rich at low speeds at which the carburetor is adjustable (idle range), adjust the carburetor. In many instances, however, the too rich mixture will be caused by something not influenced by the normal adjustments.

When too rich a fuel mixture is encountered, the cause of the trouble usually will be that the fuel level in the carburetor float bowl is too high, or that something is mechanically wrong within the carburetor.

Fuel Level. High fuel level can be the result of an improperly adjusted float, a faulty float valve and seat, or high fuel pump pressure. The float is designed to maintain the correct fuel level at a specific fuel pump pressure. A pressure several pounds greater than this amount will result in a high fuel level and a consequently richer fuel mixture. A leaking float valve would give the same results. In most cases replacing the float valve and seat and properly adjusting the float level will correct the trouble. It is unusual for a fuel pump to develop higher pressure than it is normally supposed to develop.

Mechanical Faults. Larger than standard carburetor jets in the carburetor will result in a richer mixture. Jet size can be checked against specification numbers or with a drill rod of the specified diameter given in thousandths of an inch.

A leaking power jet will permit extra fuel to be discharged into the carburetor air stream when the engine is not under full load. Improperly adjusted step rods will also have the same effect.

Faulty choke operation whereby the choke is not fully opening as soon as it should, will result in a rich fuel mixture.

Any restriction to the incoming air, as would be caused by a dirty or clogged air cleaner, will cause a rich fuel mixture. A felt silencer pad is sometimes employed in air cleaners. If wetted, this pad may sag, restricting the incoming air.

Fuel System and Carburetor Servicing

Any restriction in the various airbleeds in the carburetor can also cause a mixture richer than normal.

An improperly adjusted accelerator pump stroke will cause too much fuel to be pumped into the carburetor air stream each time the accelerator pedal is depressed.

Carburetors designed to operate at sea level will produce a rich fuel mixture at high elevations. The reverse is also true; carburetors designed to operate at high elevations will produce a lean mixture at lower elevations.

Fuel Mixture Too Lean. Some of the conditions that cause fuel to be completely shut off can account for a reduction in the amount of fuel without shutting it off completely. This reduction can cause an air-fuel mixture that is too lean.

Idling. Adjust the idle fuel mixture and idle speed. This adjustment is effective only in the idle range.

Fuel Lines. Make sure the fuel lines are not clogged and not leaking and that the fuel tank vent is open and unrestricted. Remove the flexible line at the intake side of the fuel pump, and replace it if there is any indication of leakage or stoppage. Remove the fuel tank cap and blow compressed air back through the fuel line to remove any obstruction.

Fuel Pump. Test the fuel pump pressure. If the pressure is not normal, repair or replace the fuel pump.

Engine Vacuum. Test the engine vacuum by connecting a vacuum gage to the vacuum line from the intake manifold, Fig. 11-5. If the vacuum is low, it may be due to leakage. Tighten the intake manifold cap screws or nuts. Check for leaks at the vacuum lines to the windshield wiper, distributor, power brakes, etc. Check manifold gaskets and the carburetor gasket.

Remove, clean, and adjust the carburetor if other conditions are normal.

Excessive Fuel Consumption. Many times it is difficult to isolate malfunctions without considerable checking, particularly in the case of excessive fuel consumption. Numerous conditions, other than carburetion, cause excessive fuel consumption such as a weak spark at the spark plugs, inaccurate ignition timing, a restricted exhaust system, a slipping clutch, excessive friction due to dragging brakes, low tire pressure, improper wheel alignment, too heavy a lubricant in the engine, transmission or differential assembly, tight engine, etc.

Driving habits also have a great deal to do with excessive fuel consumption. Such things as racing the engine, long periods of idling, "jack rabbit" starts, start and stop driving, etc., all have an adverse

Automotive Engines

Fig. 11-5. If this normal engine is operated at sea level, the gage will register between 17 and 20 on the vacuum scale. (Chevrolet Div., General Motors Corp.)

effect on gasoline mileage. High-speed driving requires more fuel per mile. A vehicle that gets 20 miles per gallon at 30 miles per hour may get as little as 15 miles per gallon at 60 miles per hour and at 80 miles per hour may get less than 10 miles per gallon. A vehicle driven at high speeds consistently uses considerably more fuel than a vehicle driven at moderate speeds.

Test Procedure. Sometimes it is necessary to make an accurate measurement of fuel consumption. Probably the best and easiest method of making such a test is to use a fuel mileage tester. The most common type is a $\frac{1}{10}$ gallon container which mounts in a convenient place above the carburetor where it can be observed by the operator. Using such an arrangement makes it possible to observe differences in fuel consumption according to driving habits, load, speed, and acceleration and to make an accurate accounting of the gasoline used and mileage obtained.

Fuel System and Carburetor Servicing

Diagnosing Carburetor Troubles

Before attempting carburetor repairs always make sure the carburetor is at fault. In some cases carburetor troubles can be corrected by merely making adjustments without disassembling the unit. By determining what carburetor system is at fault, trouble can be spotted more readily when the unit is disassembled. The extent of disassembly often will be determined by the malfunction.

A number of quick checks, requiring no special equipment, can be made which may give an indication as to whether a particular internal carburetor system is at fault or not.

Idling

If the engine does not idle evenly and smoothly, the idle system may be at fault. If the engine speed does not increase evenly as the throttle is gradually opened and then evens out when speed is increased above the idle range, the idle system could be faulty.

Float Level

Sometimes too high a float level can be detected by removing the air cleaner and observing the fuel discharge nozzle with the engine running at a slow idle speed. If the nozzle is wet or discharging fuel at idle, the float level is too high.

Accelerator Pump

The discharge characteristics of the accelerator pump can be checked by removing the air cleaner and depressing the accelerator pedal quickly while watching the pump discharge jet or jets in the air horn. The discharge should continue for some time after the throttle valve reaches the wide open position. This check must be performed with the engine stopped. For safety purposes, never look into a carburetor while the engine is being cranked or accelerated. A backfire could occur and result in serious facial burns.

Power Fuel System

The high speed system (power valve) in a carburetor can best be checked by using a chassis dynamometer. As engine speed is increased under load, near wide open throttle, a slight surge will be noticed when the power valve comes into operation.

Using Test Gages

A vacuum gage and a combustion analyzer, sometimes called an exhaust gas analyzer, will give an accurate indication of carburetion if the compression and ignition systems are in good operating condition and adjustment.

Vacuum Gage. A reading of intake manifold vacuum is a valuable indication of engine efficiency. An intake manifold vacuum reading is used in three different ways: as a preliminary test before any corrections are made, as a final test after corrections have been made to prove their effectiveness, and to adjust the carburetor.

Normal Vacuum. For all three uses, connect the vacuum gage to the windshield wiper connection on the intake manifold or remove a plug in the intake manifold and install an adapter to which is attached the vacuum gage hose, Fig. 11-5. Taken at idle speed, an intake manifold vacuum reading that is normal and steady is a fair indication that the engine has little, if anything, wrong in its operation. With the engine idling, normal vacuum reading is between 17 and 20 inches at sea level.

Faulty Vacuum. Faulty carburetor operation is indicated by a slow oscillation of the vacuum gage needle or by an irregular drop from a normal reading. If the idle mixture adjustment will not bring the vacuum reading up to normal, the carburetor is faulty. Always remember that anything that affects the efficiency of the engine will also affect the vacuum reading.

Combustion Analyzer. A combustion analysis, like an intake manifold vacuum test, is a measure of engine efficiency at the speed and load at which it is operating at the time of the test. It must be remembered that readings of rich or lean do not necessarily mean faulty carburetion.

Normal Combustion. If combustion is normal, a definite percentage of the exhaust gases will be carbon dioxide. The combustion analyzer, or exhaust gas analyzer as it is sometimes called, indicates when the exhaust gas is unbalanced (contains more or less carbon dioxide than normal) denoting poor combustion.

Poor Combustion. Poor combustion can be caused not only by faulty carburetion, but also by faulty compression, defective ignition, or ignition occurring either too early or too late. If you fail to keep this in mind, and attempt to diagnose trouble from an exhaust analysis alone, you will be in error since the reading does not provide enough information to make a diagnosis. In other words, corrections must be made to the ignition system and compression before diagnosing carburetor troubles.

The gasoline burned in the engine is made up of hydrogen and carbon. The air taken in at the carburetor supplies oxygen. During normal combustion, each carbon atom unites with two oxygen atoms forming carbon dioxide. Each two hydrogen atoms combine with one oxygen atom forming water.

Fuel System and Carburetor Servicing

When the mixture is rich (not enough air) the combustion is not normal and some of the hydrogen does not combine with oxygen. This pure hydrogen is a good coolant.

Various combustion analyzers are on the market but most are of the Wheatstone bridge type. This instrument works on the principle of thermal heat conductivity of gases. Just as some solid materials, like steel and brass are a much better conductor of heat than wood or cloth, so is hydrogen a better conductor of heat than air. Air, in turn, is a better conductor of heat than carbon dioxide. The temperature of the gases when passing over a filament in the bridge that is carrying an electrical current affects the resistance of the filament and reduces or increases the amount of current flowing.

If an engine is running rich, with an air-fuel ratio of ten or eleven parts of air to one part of fuel, there will be a large amount of hydrogen present in the exhaust gas and only a small amount of carbon dioxide. If the engine is running lean, sixteen parts of air to one part of fuel for example, there will be very little hydrogen, but a large amount of carbon dioxide present in the exhaust gas.

With a rich mixture resulting in a lot of hydrogen the filament is cooled and decreases the electrical resistance. This in turn increases the electrical flow to the meter causing the meter to indicate "rich." If the fuel mixture is lean, the high percentage of carbon dioxide heats the filament, thereby increasing electrical resistance and reducing electrical flow. This causes the meter to read in the opposite direction, or toward the lean side.

Carburetor Service

A few precautions should be remembered when servicing carburetors. Dirt is one of the worst enemies of proper carburetion. Keep all parts clean. *Gasoline vapor is very explosive. Be extremely careful and keep all open flames and sparks away from gasoline vapors.* Always use the correct size wrenches and screwdrivers on carburetor parts.

Most carburetors can be overhauled with ordinary tools if a reasonable amount of care is exercised. Some carburetors, however, require special jet pullers and gages to permit complete disassembly and to make correct adjust-

Automotive Engines

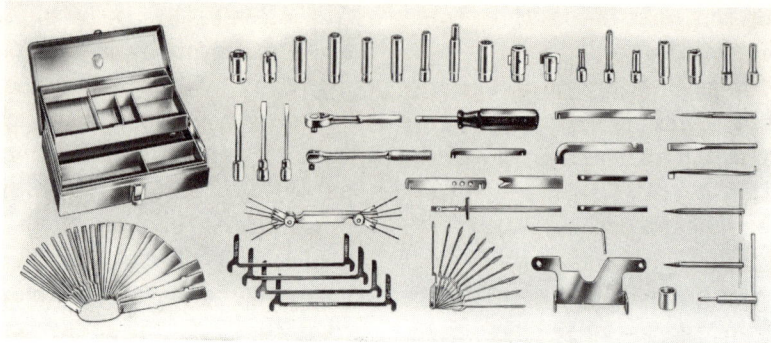

Fig. 11-6. There are many carburetor tools and gages. (Snap-on Tools Corp.)

ments. Proper tools used correctly will prevent marring and distorting the parts during assembly and disassembly. Marring or distorting any metered opening such as a jet, air-bleed, nozzle, etc., will affect carburetor efficiency. Fig. 11-6 illustrates some of the common tools and gages used in carburetor servicing.

Use new gaskets throughout the carburetor when assembling to make certain that joints are tight. In many cases, the proper height of a nozzle or valve will depend upon the gasket.

Most carburetor troubles are the result of deposits of foreign matter in the carburetor. Complete cleaning usually is the only service work necessary.

Cleaning

Numerous cleaning solutions are available which are made especially for cleaning carburetor parts. In the absence of a special cleaner, alcohol, lacquer thinner, gasoline, or kerosene may be used, but be careful because there is always danger when using these inflammable materials. They require much more hand work than when a special carburetor cleaner is used. The type of cleaner used is usually governed by the volume of carburetor work being done because special carburetor cleaners are expensive but can be used several times. The cleaning procedure must remove all dirt and grease plus all sediment, gum, and corrosion found in the carburetor. Leather parts, nonmetallic diaphragms, and gaskets should never be cleaned in anything but gasoline.

Soak all castings and metal parts in the cleaning solution long enough to soften and loosen all foreign matter. Place the parts to be cleaned in a metal basket and sus-

Fuel System and Carburetor Servicing

pend the basket in the cleaning solution to keep the parts out of the sediment in the bottom of the cleaning container. Agitate the parts in the solution to do a more thorough job of cleaning. After the parts have soaked a sufficient length of time, scrub the remaining foreign matter with a stiff bristle brush. Do not use a buffing wheel, wire brush, file, or any sharp instrument. Rinse the parts in hot water to remove all traces of the cleaning solution.

After cleaning, blow out all passageways, jets, and tubes, and dry all the parts with compressed air. Do not wipe parts with a cloth, because the cloth may leave particles of lint which could cause trouble. Wire should not be used to clean jets, tubes, or passageways, because the wire may enlarge the openings. Hand-held standard size drills of the correct diameter generally can be used for cleaning and measuring jets if necessary.

Carburetor Repair

The amount of service work to be performed on a carburetor generally depends on its period and type of service. Shops specializing in carburetor rebuilding may completely disassemble the carburetor to the extent of removing throttle and choke valves and shafts and most of the rivets and plugs. On the other hand, many service establishments, as a part of their tune-up procedure, remove the carburetor bowl cover or air horn, check the float level and any pistons, plungers, tubes, or jets that are accessible, and blow out any foreign material. Also determine if carburetor repair is necessary.

Always consult the manufacturer's shop manual for exact procedure and specifications.

When a carburetor needs to be repaired it should be disassembled into major subassemblies for inspection. Perhaps the best method to use in disassembling a carburetor is to use a separate pan or tray for each system. Time can usually be saved by this method, and the possibility of improper assembly is largely eliminated. The separation of the carburetor into major assemblies, Fig. 11-7, makes the jets, passageways, and tubes accessible for cleaning, inspection and removal. If inspection of the subassemblies reveals that cleaning is the only service work necessary, clean the carburetor, reassemble, and adjust it.

Carburetor gasket kits and carburetor repair kits are available

Automotive Engines

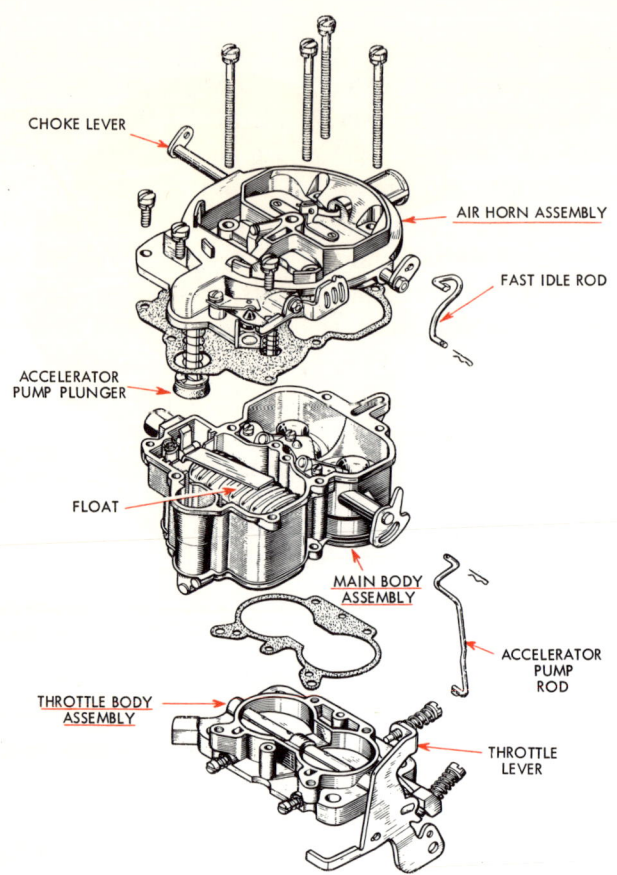

Fig. 11-7. Separate the carburetor into its major assemblies to make it accessible for servicing or repair. (Dodge Div., Chrysler Corp.)

for most carburetors. Every time a carburetor is disassembled, the old gaskets should be discarded and new ones installed. Carburetor repair kits consist of replacements for all parts which are normally subject to wear or are likely to be damaged during disassembly. When several parts of the carburetor indicate need for replacement, it may be advisable to obtain a repair kit for the specific carburetor being worked on and install all of the parts in the kit.

Separating Into Subassemblies

Before disassembling the carburetor into subassemblies, scrape away all the dirt and grease from the outside of the carburetor to prevent any foreign matter from getting inside the carburetor.

Fuel System and Carburetor Servicing

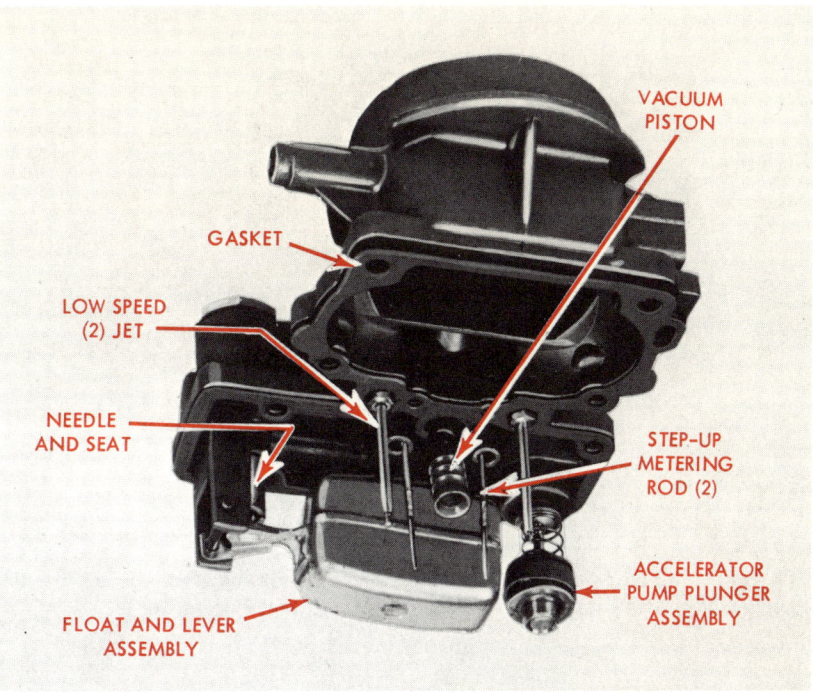

Fig. 11-8. This air horn assembly has been lifted for inspection from a two-barrel carburetor. (Buick Div., General Motors Corp.)

On most carburetors, one or several rods or levers are used to actuate the accelerator pump, choke, or throttle. This linkage must be removed or at least disconnected at one end before the carburetor can be separated into subassemblies. Usually the method of removal is obvious and may require removal of hairpin-like clips and retaining screws or disengaging spring-loaded ball sockets.

After the linkage has been removed, the carburetor can be carefully separated into subassemblies. A number of variations will occur in the different carburetors. Some will separate into two assemblies while others will separate into three units. The way in which the carburetor separates is usually obvious. Fig. 11-8 illustrates the parts of an air horn assembly used on one type of two-barrel carburetor. Step-up rods (metering rods) are used in this carburetor to increase the fuel flow for full throttle operation. The float mechanism is part of the air horn assembly. Fig. 11-9 illustrates the main body assembly parts for the same carburetor.

425

Automotive Engines

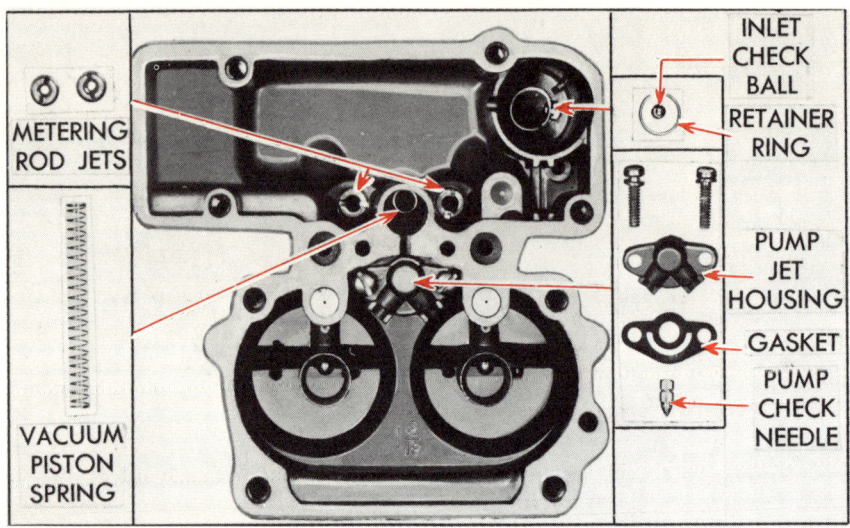

Fig. 11-9. This carburetor main body assembly is being viewed from above. The air horn assembly, Fig. 11-8, has been removed. (Buick Div., General Motors Corp.)

Regardless of which subassembly contains the various parts, the service work performed on each part will be the same.

Air Horn Assembly. The air horn assembly consists of the choke valve and shaft and some arrangement for actuating and positioning the choke valve. Some carburetors have the float mechanism attached to the air horn, Fig. 11-8.

If no wear or play is apparent in the choke shaft or choke valve, it is not necessary to remove them. Any movement up and down between the choke shaft and air horn body indicates wear and calls for replacement of the shaft. If a new shaft does not remove the play between the shaft and the housing, the air horn must be replaced. Close the choke valve and hold the assembly against the light. If light shows between the edge of the valve and air horn, the valve is not closing properly and repairs are needed.

Replace the choke valve if the poppet valve spring is weak or broken, or if the plate is damaged. If any part of the air horn assembly is cracked, or is warped or nicked enough to permit leakage at any gasket surface, it must be replaced.

Replacing Choke Valve. To replace the choke valve, remove the screws which hold the valve to the shaft, and remove the shaft and valve. If the choke valve screws are

Fuel System and Carburetor Servicing

peened over, file the ends of the screws so they can be removed.

When assembling the choke valve to the shaft, make sure the chamfered edge of the valve is on the same side of the shaft as when removed. Start the screws; then close the choke valve tight in the air horn so the valve will center itself as the screws are tightened.

Stake in place the screws which hold the choke valve to the shaft. Connect any spring which may be used on the choke shaft or linkage.

Replacing Throttle Valve. The throttle valve and shaft are replaced in the same manner as the choke valve and shaft. Any play found between the throttle shaft and the carburetor body will necessitate replacement.

Float Mechanism. The method of removal and installation of the float mechanism is generally obvious regardless of whether the float mechanism is attached to the air horn or located in the main carburetor body.

Shake the float to check for leakage. If it leaks, there will probably be gasoline inside the float and it must be replaced. The needle valve must move freely inside the seat. Check the float needle valve and seat for wear. If a ridge or groove is present on the seating surface of either the needle valve or its seat, both should be replaced. The needle valve and seat can be replaced only in matched sets. Every time the seat is removed, a new gasket should be installed to ensure correct float action. After the needle valve and seat and the float are installed, the float must be properly adjusted.

Cleaning and Assembly

Thoroughly clean all castings and parts in an approved carburetor cleaner and blow out all openings with compressed air. Check all parts for wear, particularly the metering rods (step-up rods) and jets if used. Ordinarily very little wear takes place in the carburetor. Therefore very few parts should need replacement other than gaskets, the accelerator pump plunger and the diaphragm type power jet.

After cleaning, carefully assemble the various subassemblies. Then assemble the subassemblies to one another except for the air horn. The float level must be checked and set before completing the final assembly. Use new gaskets throughout the carburetor when assembling it to make certain that tight joints will result. In some cases, the proper height of a nozzle or valve will depend upon the gaskets.

After completing assembly, it is usually advisable to install the carburetor on the engine and make the needed linkage adjustments. After making the linkage and choke adjustments, start the engine and make the final adjustments.

Carburetor Adjustments

Proper adjustment is most essential for correct carburetor operation. Because of the variations in linkages, design, and equipment used with different carburetors, the number and manner of adjustments differ considerably. Therefore, the information presented will be general. Consult the manufacturer's shop manual for the exact procedures and specifications. The adjustments which are common to all carburetors are the idle speed and idle mixture adjustment, choke adjustment, and the float adjustment.

Other adjustments which may be found on the different carburetors are the metering rod linkage, dash pot, accelerator pump stroke, antipercolator or vapor vent adjustment, fast idle cam, choke unloader, throttle linkage, secondary throttle linkage and the secondary throttle lockout adjustment.

Idle Speed and Idle Mixture Adjustments

The two adjustments most commonly made on a carburetor are the idle speed adjustment and the idle fuel mixture adjustment. When making these adjustments, a tachometer and a vacuum gage can be used to advantage. The engine should be running at normal operating temperature.

Adjusting the Idle Speed. Idle speed is established by adjusting the throttle stop screw. If possible, use a tachometer when setting the idle speed. The idle speed adjustment usually has to be made at least twice each time the carburetor is adjusted—before and after the idle mixture adjustment is made. When making this final idle speed adjustment on a vehicle equipped with an automatic transmission, follow the manufacturer's recommendations for idle speed, otherwise the vehicle may "creep." On vehicles without an automatic transmission, the normal idle speed is generally 450 to 500 RPM. Fig. 11-10 shows the location of the idle speed adjustment screw on a typical carburetor.

Always consult manufacturer's specifications when adjusting idle speed. The type of emission control system used has a bearing on idle speed setting. Some specifications require that the automatic transmission be placed in drive range. On some vehicles having air conditioning, the idle speed is adjusted with the air conditioning operating.

Adjusting the Idle Mixture. Fig. 11-11 illustrates the location of the

Fuel System and Carburetor Servicing

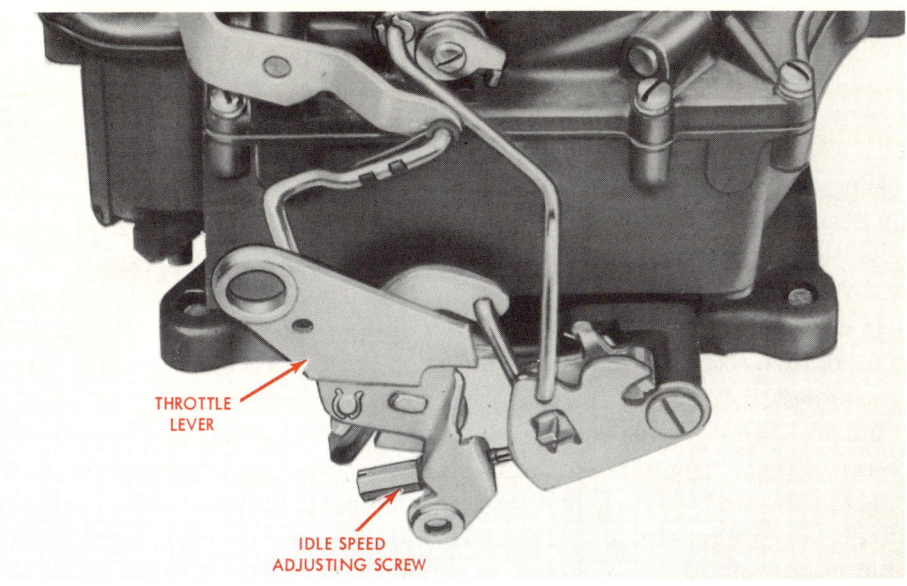

Fig. 11-10. The idle speed should be adjusted before and after the idle mixture is adjusted. (Chevrolet Div., General Motors Corp.)

Fig. 11-11. Each idle mixture screw on this four-barrel carburetor is adjusted in the same manner as on a single-barrel carburetor. (Chevrolet Div., General Motors Corp.)

idle mixture adjusting screws on a four-barrel carburetor. When a vacuum gage is used, turn the idle mixture adjusting screw in or out until the highest steady vacuum reading is obtained. The vacuum gage should be connected to the tube leading from the intake manifold.

If a tachometer is used, turn the idle mixture screw in or out until the highest tachometer reading is obtained with the idle speed adjustment remaining in a fixed position. One lead of the tachometer is attached to the distributor primary connection, and the other lead is connected to ground.

When no gages are available, turn the mixture screw in until the engine begins to miss. Turn the screw out until the engine begins to "roll." Then turn the screw back in until the engine runs most smoothly.

On two- or four-barrel carburetors, Fig. 11-11, adjust the mixture on one side of the carburetor and then on the other side in the same manner as when adjusting a single-barrel carburetor. Both idle mixture screws should be turned out about the same amount. Then reset the idle speed to specifications.

On late model vehicles, which have an emission control system, a limiter is incorporated on the idle mixture screw, Fig. 11-12. The purpose of the limiter is to prevent changing the adjustment to the point where it will affect engine emissions. Do not remove or force the adjustment beyond the established limits.

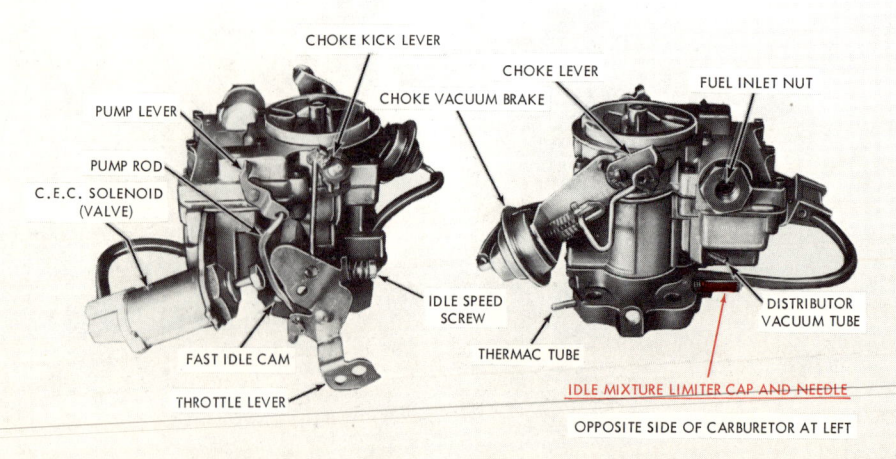

Fig. 11-12. Idle mixture control limiter on an emission controlled carburetor. (Chevrolet Div., General Motors Corp.)

Fuel System and Carburetor Servicing

When a carburetor is overhauled, new replacement caps will be included in the carburetor repair kit for carburetors used on vehicles having an emission control system. The new caps should be installed after the carburetor has been adjusted for proper idle mixture emission levels. It is illegal to tamper with or purposely upset emission devices.

Automatic Choke Adjustment

Two types of automatic chokes are employed on engines today. The thermostatic coil spring type, which is installed in a well in the manifold, uses a separate vacuum brake mounted on the carburetor to regulate the choke valve against thermostatic tension. The self-contained choke unit with the thermostatic spring and vacuum piston are in one assembly. The thermostatic spring is mounted in the cover and is adjusted by turning the cover, Fig. 11-13.

Adjusting Vacuum Operated Automatic Choke

Remove the air cleaner. Hold the throttle partially open, and move the choke valve to make sure it operates freely. If the valve sticks when closed, loosen the screws which hold the valve to the choke shaft and permit the valve to center itself. Tighten the choke plate screws.

With the carburetor at room temperature and the throttle partly open, loosen the choke cover retaining screws. Rotate the choke cover against the thermostatic coil spring tension until the choke valve just closes. Tighten the cover retaining screws. In most cases, the index mark will line up with the specified point on the choke housing, Fig. 11-13. Replace the air cleaner.

Manufacturers recommend the choke be set according to specifications (generally the center index mark on the housing). This setting will be satisfactory for most operating conditions. If the engine stalls or hesitates on acceleration during warmup, the choke setting may be tailored richer or leaner to meet particular engine requirements. Never set the choke more

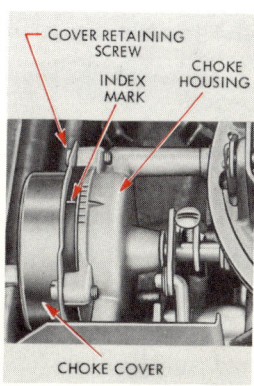

Fig. 11-13. After this vacuum-operated automatic choke has been adjusted, usually the index mark on the cover will line up with the specified point on the choke housing. (Ford Div., Ford Motor Co.)

431

Automotive Engines

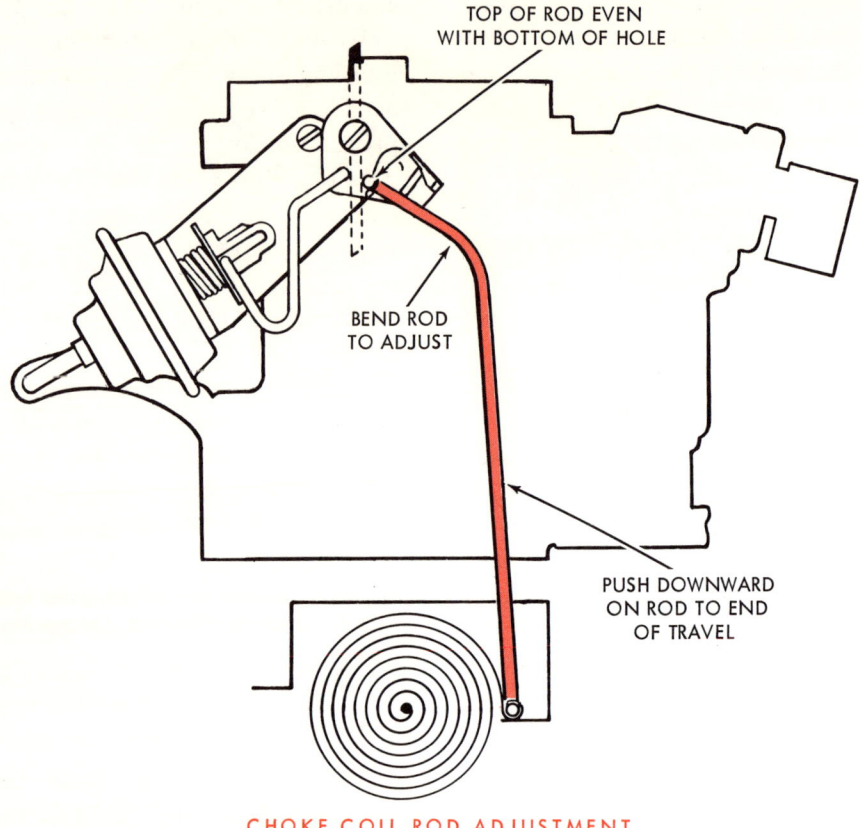

CHOKE COIL ROD ADJUSTMENT

Fig. 11-14. Adjusting choke valve rod. (Chevrolet Div., General Motors Corp.)

than two notches in either direction of the specified setting.

To adjust the automatic choke having the thermostatic spring mounted in a well in the manifold, pull the choke valve control rod downward until it stops (bottoms). The choke valve should be fully closed. If the valve is not completely closed or closes too soon, bend the control rod to obtain the proper setting, Fig. 11-14.

Float Level Adjustment

Different specifications are used to establish correct float level in the various carburetors. The manufacturer's shop manual must be consulted for correct specifications and exact procedure for measuring and setting of float level which controls fuel level. Fuel level in the carburetor bowl is extremely important. Too high a fuel level results in a rich mixture while too

Fuel System and Carburetor Servicing

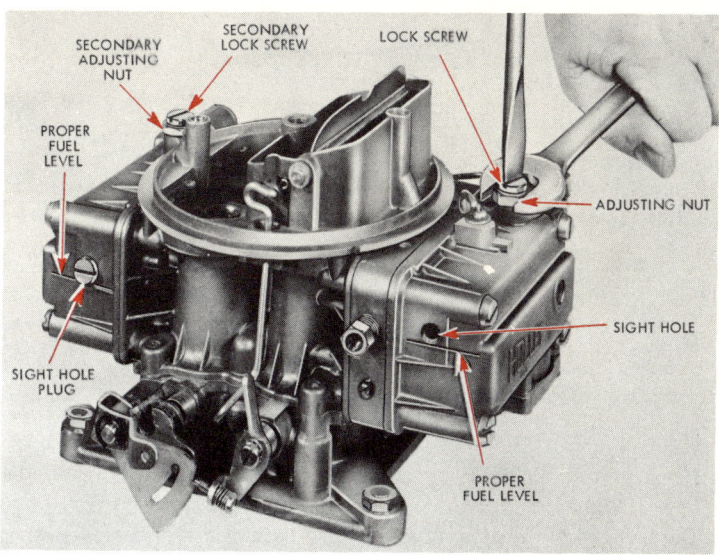

Fig. 11-15. The float level on this carburetor is adjusted by turning the adjusting nut until fuel barely dribbles out of the sight hole. Then the lock screw is tightened. (Dodge Div., Chrysler Corp.)

low a fuel level results in a lean mixture.

On some carburetors, fuel level specifications call for a measurement from the top surface of the float bowl to the surface of the fuel. In these carburetors, run the engine for a few minutes. Then remove the float bowl cover and measure the fuel level. On some automobiles, the engine can be run with the float bowl cover removed.

Some carburetors, Fig. 11-15, are provided with a tapped hole and a plug to permit checking the fuel level. With the vehicle level and the engine idling, remove this plug. The fuel should just dribble out of the sight hole. Reset the float level if the fuel level is too high or too low. On some carburetors of this type, a float adjusting nut is located on the top of the float bowl.

With a wrench and screw driver, loosen the lock screw, and turn the adjusting nut up or down until the fuel barely dribbles out of the sight hole. After the correct level has been obtained, tighten the lock screw while holding the adjusting nut with a wrench. Reinstall the sight plug and tighten securely.

A carburetor in which the float is mounted on the float bowl cover is checked by measuring the posi-

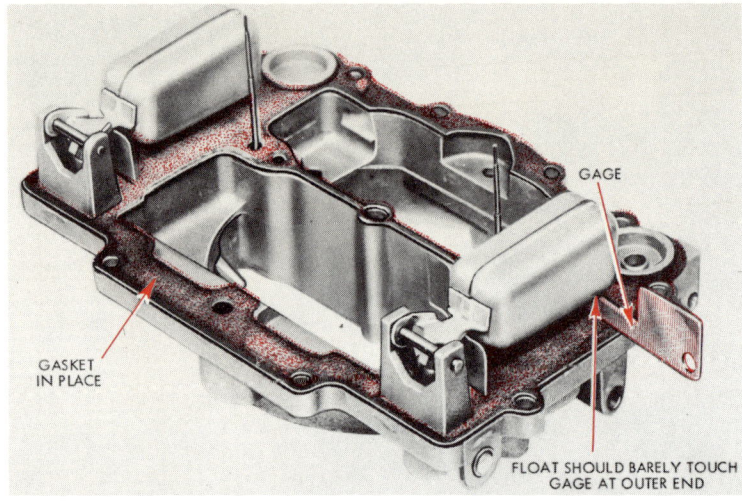

Fig. 11-16. The level of the float on this air horn assembly is adjusted by changing the distance between the top of the float bowl cover. (Cadillac Div., General Motors Corp.)

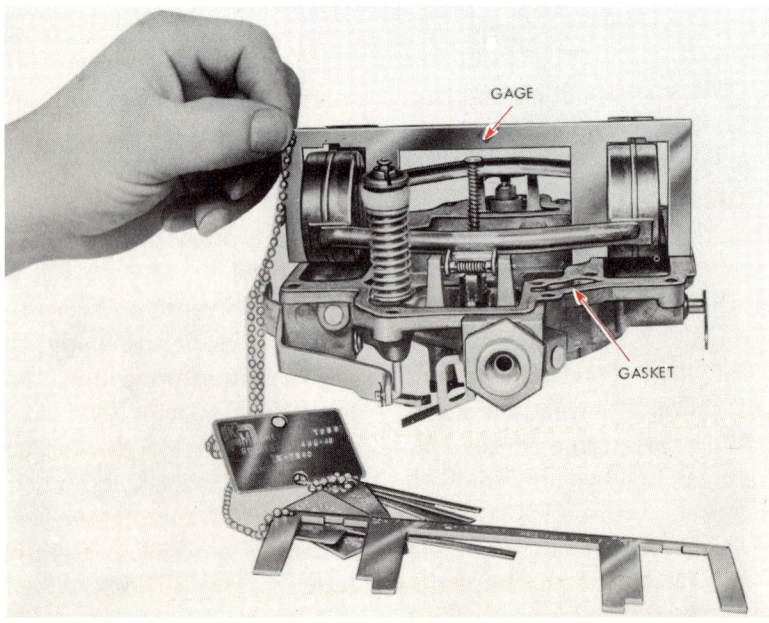

Fig. 11-17. A gage can be used to set these dual floats and to check their alignment. (Chevrolet Div., General Motors Corp.)

Fuel System and Carburetor Servicing

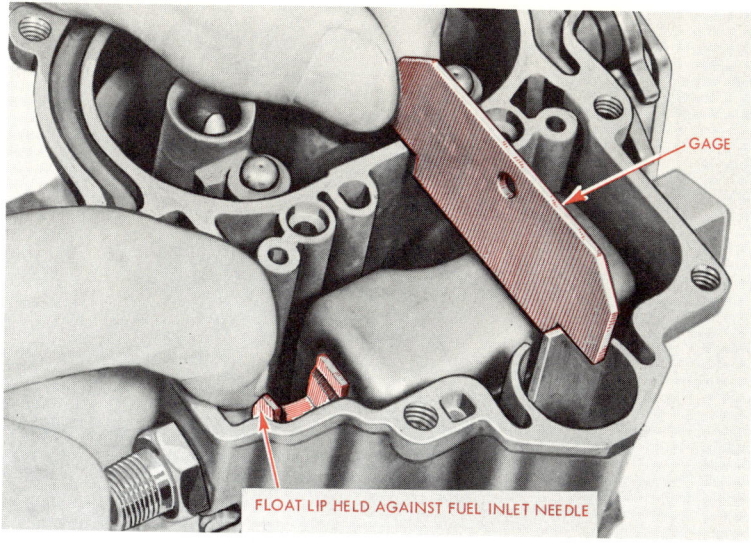

Fig. 11-18. To check the float level in this carburetor, measure the distance between the top of the float and the top of the float bowl. (Dodge Div., Chrysler Corp.)

tion of the float with regard to the float bowl cover. Fig. 11-16 shows one method of checking the distance between the bowl cover and top of the float. When dual floats are used, both floats are checked and set in the same manner. Fig. 11-17 illustrates another method of checking the level of floats mounted on the fuel bowl cover. These dual floats are checked for alignment as well as for correct level. All floats must be aligned so they do not come in contact with the sides of the float bowl.

In some carburetors, the float level is checked by measuring the distance from the top of the float bowl to the top of the float, Fig. 11-18. Generally, the measurement is taken with the gasket removed and the float valve closed.

Float Drop. On a few carburetors, it is necessary to check and adjust the float drop, Fig. 11-19. This measurement is taken with the float valve open. Usually a tab located next to the float valve can be bent to change the float drop setting. After the float drop setting is made, the float level must be checked and set.

Regardless of whether the specification is for fuel level or for float position, the adjustment consists of changing the float position. Float position can be changed by bending the tab on the float arm

435

Automotive Engines

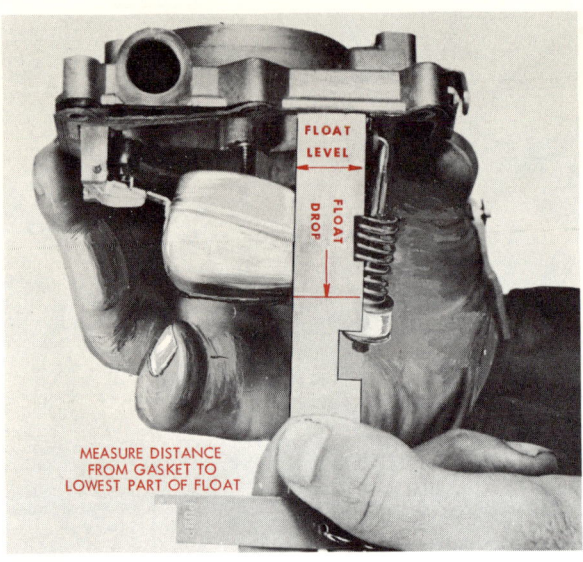

Fig. 11-19. Float drop is checked by measuring the distance between the top of the float bowl cover and the bottom of the float in its lowest position. (Oldsmobile Div., General Motors Corp.)

or bending the float arm itself. Remember that the float must move freely on its pivot and not contact the sides of the float bowl. When dual floats are used, both floats must be set to exactly the same specifications.

Throttle Linkage Adjustment

Due to wear or bending of the throttle to accelerator pedal linkage, it may be necessary to adjust the length of the throttle linkage. The throttle linkage must be adjusted to permit full throttle travel to wide open throttle operation and the throttle must fully close when the accelerator pedal is released. A threaded swivel is generally used on the throttle end of the throttle link, Fig. 11-20. Disconnect the linkage from the throttle arm and, while holding the throttle valve wide open and the accelerator pedal fully depressed, turn the swivel until it freely enters the hole in the throttle valve arm. If no adjustment is used, bend the rod until it will freely enter the hole in the throttle valve arm. The linkage must always move freely without binding.

Accelerator Pump Adjustment

Correct accelerator pump movement is essential for proper engine operation when the accelerator is suddenly depressed.

Fuel System and Carburetor Servicing

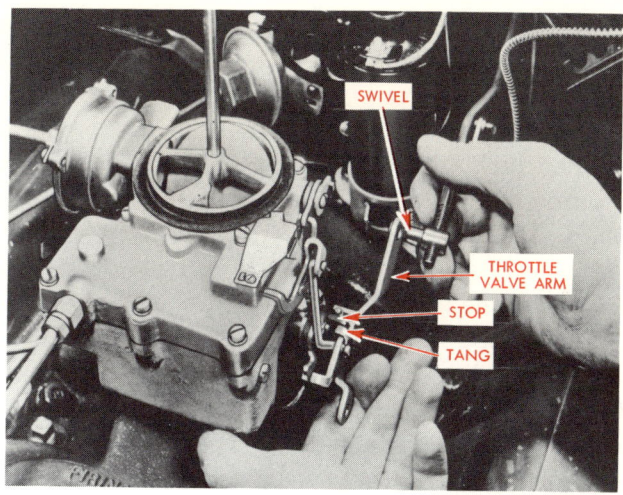

Fig. 11-20. Adjusting throttle linkage. (Chevrolet Div., General Motors Corp.)

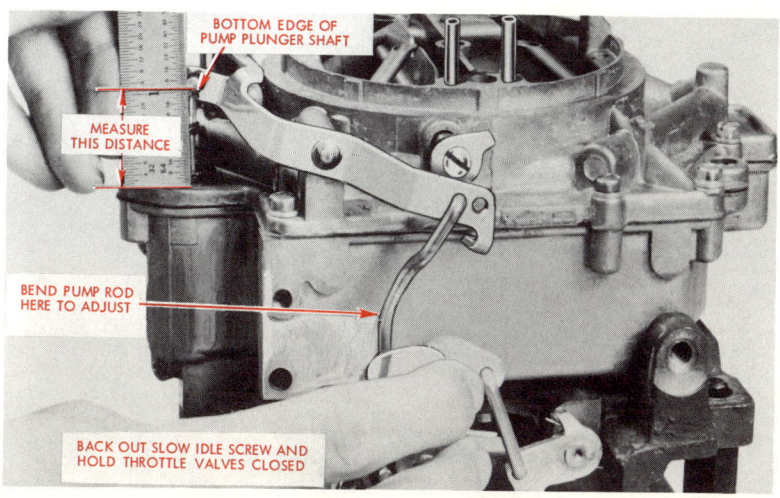

Fig. 11-21. On some carburetors, the accelerator pump is adjusted by bending the pump rod. (Oldsmobile Div., General Motors Corp.)

Adjusting Linkage. When the pump actuating arm has more than one hole for the pump linkage, the pump stroke can be changed to meet specific climatic conditions. For extremely hot weather opera-

437

tion, the link should be placed in the hole which gives as short a stroke as possible. For extremely cold weather operation, place the link in the hole which gives the longest stroke. For most operating conditions, place the link in the center hole.

Bending Linkage. When only one linkage hole is used, the stroke of the pump is changed by bending the pump operating link. With the throttle valve closed and the idle speed adjusting screw backed out, measure the distance from the top of the carburetor float bowl cover to a prescribed point on the pump plunger shaft as indicated by specifications, Fig. 11-21. Bend the pump linkage to obtain the correct distance.

Metering Rod Adjustment

If metering rods are used, they must be properly adjusted in relation to wide open throttle. Although they are vacuum operated, a small tab operated by throttle linkage must lift the metering rods at wide open throttle if vacuum conditions are such that the metering rods are not lifted.

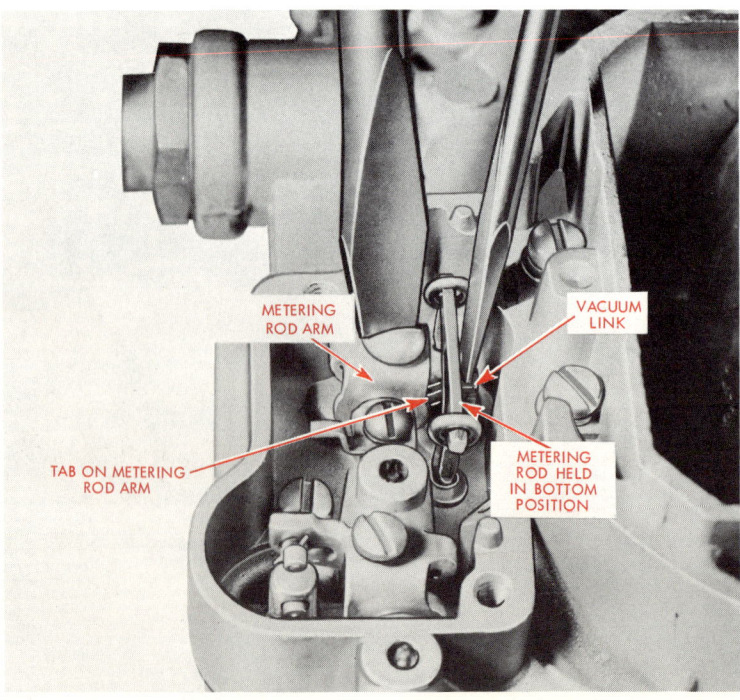

Fig. 11-22. When adjusting the metering rods, tighten the set screw when the tab on the metering rod arm contacts the vacuum link. (Chevrolet Div., General Motors Corp.)

Fuel System and Carburetor Servicing

To check and set the metering rods, back out the idle speed adjustment screw until the throttle valves close completely. Loosen the screw in the metering rod arm. Press down on the metering rod vacuum link until the rods just bottom, Fig. 11-22. While holding the metering rods down and with the throttle valves closed, rotate the metering rod arm until the small tab lightly contacts the vacuum link. Lock the arm in this position by tightening the set screw.

Dash Pot (Throttle Return Check) Adjustment

When an automatic transmission is used, a carburetor *dash pot* is used to prevent the engine from stalling when the throttle is suddenly closed.

With the engine running at normal operating temperature, open the throttle to clear the fast idle cam and rotate the cam to its extreme fast position and allow the throttle to close against the fast idle cam, Fig. 11-23. Turn the dash pot or dash pot adjusting screw until the plunger just contacts the throttle lever. With the transmission in "Drive" and the brakes applied, accelerate suddenly. Then release the throttle immediately. If the engine stalls from the rapid throttle closing, move the dash pot operating plunger forward about one-half turn until the engine no longer stalls. If the throttle does not close rapidly enough, move the

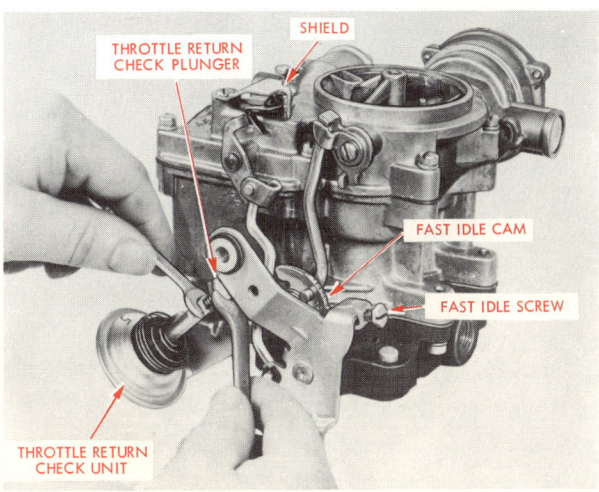

Fig. 11-23. When an automatic transmission is used, a throttle return check unit ("dash pot") on the carburetor will prevent the engine from stalling when the throttle is closed suddenly. (Chevrolet Div., General Motors Corp.)

439

Automotive Engines

plunger backward until the engine does not idle too fast, yet does not stall. If proper adjustment cannot be obtained, replace the dash pot unit.

Vapor Vent Opening (Antipercolator) Adjustment

The linkage from the throttle arm to the fuel bowl vapor vent valve can be adjusted, in most cases, by bending the linkage so the vent valve will be open a specified amount when the throttle plates are closed.

With the throttle in normal idle position, check the amount the vapor vent valve is open, Fig. 11-24. Bend the linkage between the throttle arm and the vent operating arm to obtain the correct setting according to specifications.

Fast Idle Speed Adjustment

When the choke valve is closed, it moves a rod linked to the fast idle cam. The cam turns and prevents the throttle from closing to normal idle speed. Some design variations occur, but the principle remains the same. The engine must speed up enough to keep running when cold with the choke closed or partially closed, but it must return to normal idle speed when the choke is wide open. This is ac-

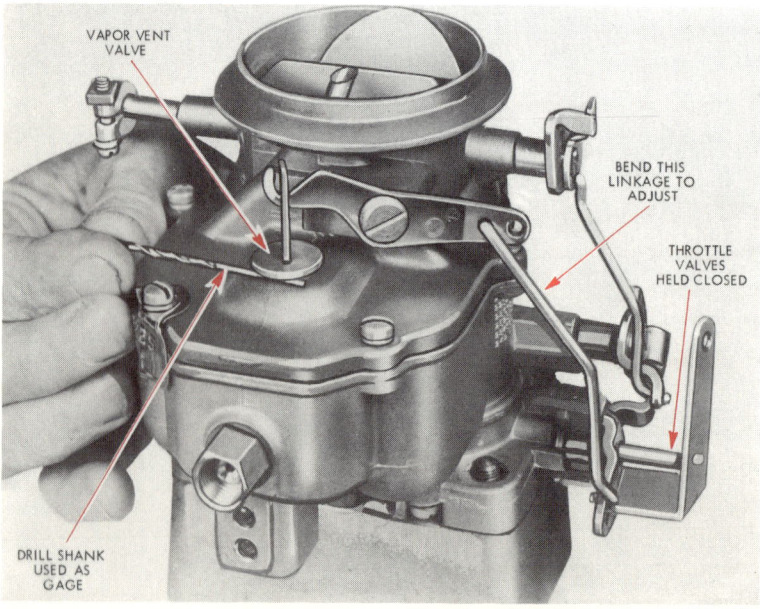

Fig. 11-24. The vapor vent valve must be open a specified amount when the throttle is in idling position. (Plymouth Div., Chrysler Corp.)

Fuel System and Carburetor Servicing

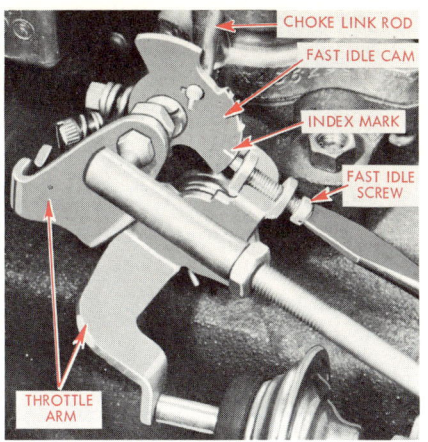

Fig. 11-25. When adjusting the fast idle speed, the index mark on the fast idle cam should line up with the center of the fast idle screw. (Buick Div., General Motors Corp.)

complished through the fast idle cam actuated by a rod linked to an arm on the choke valve.

With Index Mark. On one type of adjustment, open the throttle and close the choke valve. The fast idle cam should rotate and align the index mark with the center of the fast idle screw, Fig. 11-25. Bend the outer lever lug mounted on the choke shaft to bring the mark into the correct position. Turn the fast idle screw to obtain an engine speed of 1500 RPM with the fast idle screw lined up with the index mark and the engine at normal operating temperature.

Without Index Mark. On another type of adjustment when an index mark is not used, adjust the engine to normal operating idle speed. Turn the fast idle adjusting screw in until it just contacts the lowest (bottom) step on the fast idle cam. Back off the fast idle speed screw $\frac{1}{4}$ to $\frac{1}{2}$ turns from the lowest step on the fast idle cam.

Gage. Some fast idle adjustment procedures require a special gage which is inserted between the choke valve and air horn. If necessary, the linkage is bent to properly line up the correct fast idle step on the cam or the index mark with the fast idle screw. The fast idle screw is turned to just contact the idle cam.

Choke Unloader Adjustment

When an automatic choke is used and the engine is cold, a linkage between the choke and throttle should open the choke a given amount when the throttle is fully depressed. If the engine becomes flooded during cold starting, the choke is opened by fully depressing the accelerator pedal to clean out excessive fuel in the intake manifold.

With the engine cold, check the unloader adjustment by holding the throttle open. The unloader projection on the throttle lever contacts the unloader lug on the fast idle cam and partially opens the choke valve. In most cases a gage is inserted between the choke valve and carburetor bore, Fig. 11-26.

441

Automotive Engines

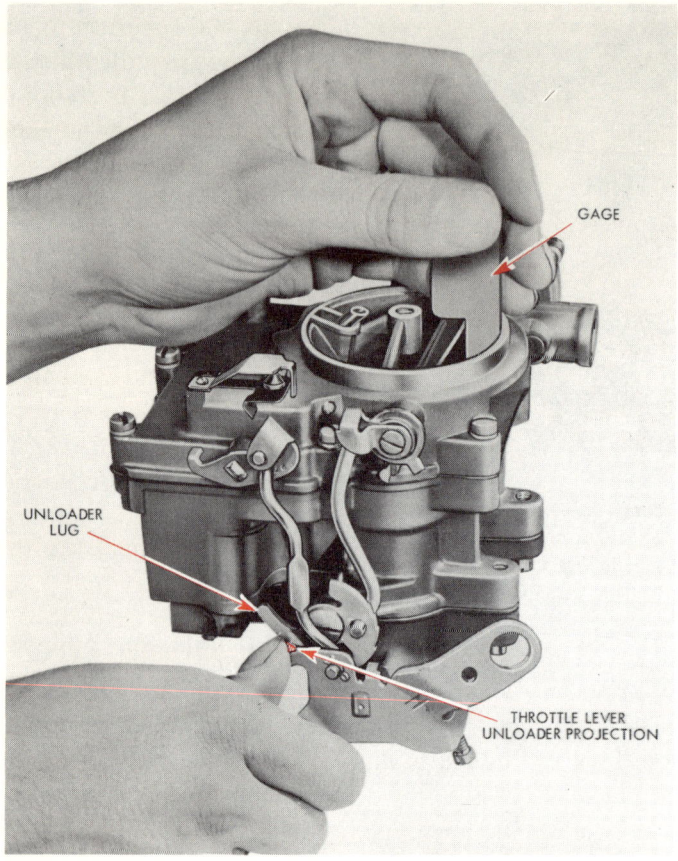

Fig. 11-26. The choke unloader must open the choke valve a specific amount when the throttle is fully open. (Chevrolet Div., General Motors Corp.)

If the choke valve does not open the correct amount, bend the unloader projection on the throttle lever until the gage slides freely between the choke valve and the carburetor bore.

Secondary Throttle Adjustment

The secondary throttle valves on four-barrel carburetors remain closed at idling and cruising speeds. They are brought into operation only when the primary throttle valves approach the wide open position. They open fully when the primary throttle valves are in wide open position. Numerous arrangements are used to correlate the operation of the two sets of throttle valves. In most cases,

Fuel System and Carburetor Servicing

a cam and linkage setup controls secondary throttle valve opening. One make of carburetor employs venturi vacuum to operate the secondary throttles. In addition to the throttle actuating mechanism, a lockout lever is incorporated to ensure that the secondary throttle valves remain closed when the choke valve is closed or partially closed.

Due to differences in construction of mechanisms for actuating the secondary throttle valves, no specific information can be given that would apply to all carburetors. They are usually adjusted by bending a throttle actuating rod or a tang or lug on a lever. Always consult the manufacturer's shop manual to obtain specifications and adjustment procedures for the carburetor being worked on.

Checking On Your Knowledge

The following questions give you the opportunity to check up on yourself. If you have read the chapter carefully, you should be able to answer the questions. If you have any difficulty, read the chapter over once more so that you have the information well in mind before you go on with your reading.

DO YOU KNOW

1. What tests can be made to check fuel pump operation, and how are the tests made?
2. How do you check a combination fuel and vacuum pump?
3. What is the correct procedure for installing a fuel pump?
4. What are some of the indications of fuel system malfunctions?
5. What will cause a carburetor to flood?
6. What are some of the causes of too rich a mixture?
7. What effects do driving habits have on fuel consumption?
8. How can you make an accurate check of fuel consumption?
9. What should generally be checked before servicing the carburetor?
10. What is the most common cause of carburetor troubles?
11. What equipment should be used when making adjustments to the fuel system?
12. What are the two most common carburetor adjustments?
13. What is the procedure for adjusting the vacuum operated automatic choke?
14. Do you know what the various types of float level adjustments are?
15. What is the usual accelerator pump linkage setting?
16. What is the throttle position when

443

the metering rod adjustment is checked?

17. When should the vapor vent valve be open?

18. At what throttle position, approximately, should the secondard throttle of a four-barrel carburetor open?

19. What is the purpose of the idle mixture limiter?

Ignition Systems

Chapter **12**

Internal-combustion engine operation depends upon the burning and expansion of an air-fuel mixture within each engine cylinder. The air-fuel mixture cannot burn and expand unless it is ignited. The automotive ignition system produces an electrical spark which ignites the air-fuel mixture within the engine cylinders. Most vehicles use a conventional battery-coil type of ignition system.

The ignition system has the job of taking 12 volts (or less) supplied by the storage battery or the electrical charging system and increasing it to the 5,000 to 25,000 volts required to jump a spark across the spark plug electrodes located in the combustion chamber. A typical ignition system must produce about 12,000 sparks for each mile a vehicle is driven. About 200 sparks per second must be produced in a vehicle traveling 60 miles per hour. To realize what a tremendous job the ignition system has to perform, it must be understood that each spark is the result of a complete cycle of events that transforms low voltage into high voltage and then delivers the high voltage to the proper spark plug at the right time.

The Conventional Battery-Coil Ignition System

The battery-coil ignition system is the type most widely used at the present time. As the name "battery-coil" suggests, a battery and a coil are the main parts of the system. The battery supplies electrical current to the coil which is part of the ignition system. The coil, as we shall see later on, is a type of electrical transformer which changes low-voltage electricity into high-voltage electricity. Thus, the battery-coil system uses

445

Automotive Engines

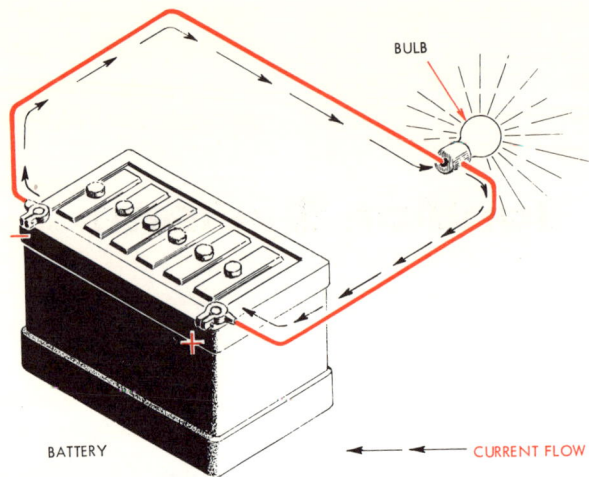

Fig. 12-1. If storage battery terminals are connected by a wire, electrical current will flow from the negative to the positive terminal. If a light bulb is connected in the circuit, the current flow will cause the bulb filament to glow.

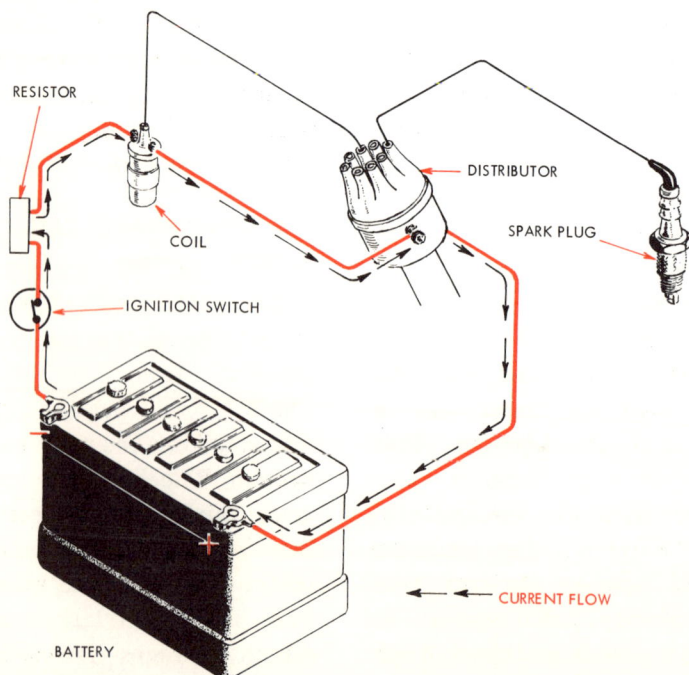

Fig. 12-2. If an ignition system is connected to a storage battery, current can flow through the system from the negative to the positive battery terminal.

Ignition Systems

electrical current to produce an ignition spark.

Current Flow and the Battery. The automobile battery produces electrical current through a chemical reaction. If we connect the two terminals of a battery with a wire, electrons will flow through the wire from the negative terminal to the positive terminal, Fig. 12-1. Electrons are negatively charged particles of electricity. The electron flow, known as current, will be in the same direction all the time. If a light bulb is connected in the circuit, the flow of current will cause the bulb to glow. If we connect an ignition system circuit to the battery, current can also flow from negative to positive through the ignition system, Fig. 12-2.

The first section of this chapter describes circuits and components of the conventional battery-coil ignition system. The second section of the chapter covers transistorized battery-coil systems. Transistorized systems are similar to conventional battery-coil systems. If the mechanic thoroughly understands conventional ignition systems, he can more easily understand transistorized ignition operation.

The Primary Circuit and the Secondary Circuit

Every battery-coil ignition system contains a primary circuit and a secondary circuit. The two separate and distinct circuits work together to develop a high-voltage electrical current and then deliver it to the combustion chamber where the voltage can jump a spark across the spark plug electrodes at the right time.

This section of the chapter contains four parts. The first two parts will describe the main circuits of the ignition system. The third part will describe the individual construction and operation of the components which make up the main ignition circuits. The last part of this section explains battery-coil ignition operation as a whole—how the ignition components all work together as a team to produce an electrical spark.

The Primary Circuit

The primary circuit receives low-voltage electrical current from the battery. The low-voltage current within the primary circuit is known as the primary current. The primary current flows to a primary winding of wire within a transformer known as an *ignition coil*. The primary circuit switches

447

Automotive Engines

its low-voltage current on and off in the primary winding.

The Secondary Circuit

The on-off switching of low-voltage current in the primary winding induces an intermittent high-voltage current in a secondary winding located close to the primary winding within the ignition coil.

The secondary winding within the ignition coil is part of the secondary ignition circuit. The high voltage produced in the secondary winding is known as the secondary voltage. The secondary ignition circuit distributes the secondary voltage to each engine cylinder to produce a timed spark which ignites the air-fuel mixture within the combustion chamber.

Components of the Ignition System

The ignition system components can be grouped under the circuits in which they operate (also see Fig. 12-11, page 459):

Primary Circuit

ignition switch
resistance unit or resistor wire in the circuit
primary winding in the ignition coil
distributor contact points
capacitor
low-voltage wiring

Secondary Circuit

secondary winding in ignition coil
coil-to-distributor high-voltage cable
distributor rotor
distributor cap
ignition cables
spark plugs

Each of the components performs a specific function in its circuit. The ignition coil and the distributor each serve both circuits.

Ignition Switch. When the ignition switch, Fig. 12-2, is turned on, it allows a low-voltage current to flow from the vehicle's storage battery or electrical charging system into the primary ignition circuit so that the engine can be started and operated. When the switch is turned off, the engine stops.

Ignition Coil. The coil is a pulse type of transformer that transforms or steps up the low voltage to the high voltage necessary to jump a spark across the gap at each spark plug.

The ignition coil, Fig. 12-3, is composed of a primary winding having about 200 turns of a relatively heavy wire, and a secondary winding of as many as 20,000 turns of a very fine wire wound in insulated layers. The windings concentrate magnetic lines of force during operation by being wound over a soft iron core and enclosed within a soft iron shell. The soft iron core is composed of thin strips of iron.

Present-day coils usually have the primary over the secondary

Ignition Systems

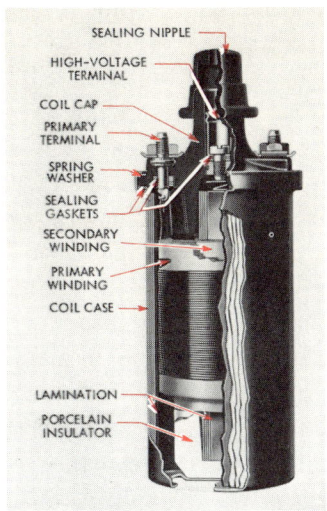

Fig. 12-3. Cutaway view of a typical ignition coil. (Delco-Remy Div., General Motors Corp.)

coil, Fig. 12-2. This is known as the outside primary type.

The coil assembly is built into a metal case with a coil cap made of molded unsulating material which contains both primary and secondary terminals. The coils are generally oil-filled and are hermetically sealed (airtight). The oil permits a rapid heat dissipation, provides greater insulation, and reduces the possibility of insulation failures.

Action of the Coil. When the ignition switch is turned on and the contact points in the distributor are closed, current flows through the primary ignition coil winding. This current flow produces a magnetic field around both coil windings.

If the flow abruptly stops, the primary circuit is sharply broken and, as the lines of magnetic force collapse, the magnetic field cuts through the coil. This action causes a high voltage to be induced in every turn of both the primary and the secondary windings. In the primary winding, the voltage may reach a value as high as 250 volts. In the secondary winding, the voltage could go as high as 25,000 volts because the secondary winding may contain up to 100 times as many turns of wire as the primary. This voltage is usually somewhere between 4,000 and 18,000 volts. The actual voltage depends on such factors as engine compression, operating speed, air-fuel ratios, width of spark plug gap, and the spark plug heat range.

Ignition Coil Resistance Unit. On vehicles with a 12-volt battery, the ignition system has a resistance in the primary circuit connecting the ignition switch with the primary coil winding, Fig. 12-2. On the early 12-volt systems, the resistance was in the form of a separate unit. Most of today's ignition systems use a calibrated resistor wire.

The purpose of the resistance is to limit to a safe maximum the amount of primary current flowing through the coil and distributor contacts. The resistance protects the contact points at low engine speeds when the points are closed for longer intervals.

449

Automotive Engines

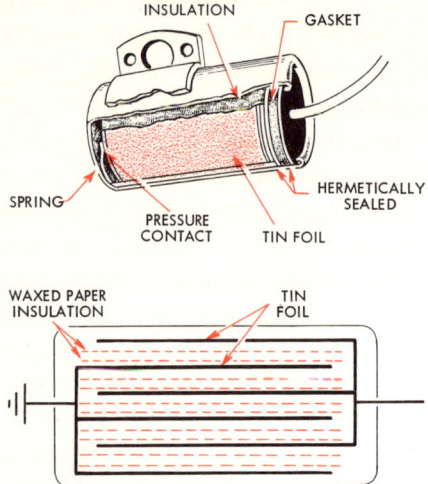

Fig. 12-4. Cutaway view of a capacitor (top) and a diagram of capacitor construction (bottom).

If current in excess of the calibrated amount flows through the circuit, the resistor becomes hot. The heat increases the value of the resistance and thus reduces the current in the circuit. It also protects the ignition coil against excessive build-up of the primary current when the ignition switch is left on with the engine at rest and the contact points closed.

The resistance is bypassed during cranking, thus connecting the ignition coil directly to the battery. The direct connection permits maximum starting performance at low temperatures. The resistance is bypassed by means of a special terminal on the ignition switch or starting motor solenoid switch which is connected directly to the coil. This bypass makes full battery voltage available to the coil and keeps the ignition voltage as high as possible during cranking.

Capacitor. The ignition capacitor is made up of two or more long sheets of tin foil separated from each other by an insulator in the form of a waxed paper, Fig. 12-4. The unit is rolled into a cylinder and sealed in a small metal container. One sheet or plate of foil is connected to the metal case, and the other to a terminal wire projecting through the insulated cover on the case and connected to the fixed distributor point. Electricity cannot pass through the capacitor as there is no direct connection between the plates.

Purposes of the Capacitor. The capacitor serves two purposes. It prevents excessive sparking at the breaker points when they open and speeds up the collapse of the magnetic field in the ignition coil. The capacitor was formerly known as the condenser.

When current is flowing in the primary circuit, the distributor contact points are opened and the primary circuit is broken. If it were not for the capacitor, the current flowing through the primary coil winding would continue to surge across the points as they separate. The energy in the coil (stored momentarily in the form of a magnetic field) would be consumed in this arc. Not only would

Ignition Systems

the contact points be burned but normal ignition performance would be impaired.

Action of the Capacitor. The capacitor prevents arcing at the contact points by providing an alternate path for the current to flow, thus bringing the primary current to a quick, controlled stop. The magnetic field, produced and sustained by current flow in the primary coil winding, is able to collapse quickly due to capacitor action.

Ignition Distributor. The ignition distributor, Fig. 12-5, performs two major functions in the ignition system.

First, its breaker or contact points act as a switch to open and

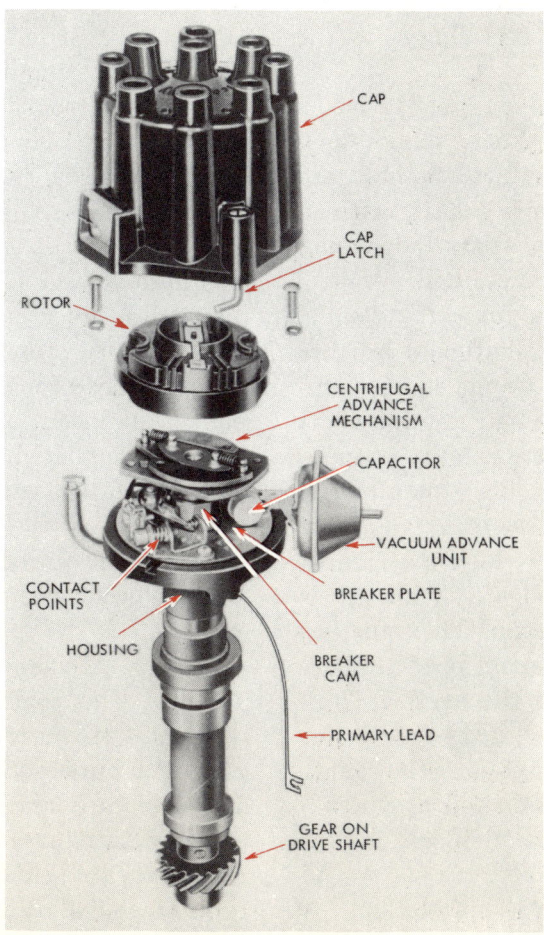

Fig. 12-5. An exploded view of an ignition distributor. It performs two major functions in the ignition system. (Oldsmobile Div., General Motors Corp.)

close the primary ignition circuit. When the points are closed, current flows through the ignition coil and builds up a magnetic field. When the points are opened, current through the coil is stopped and the magnetic field collapses, creating a high-voltage current.

Secondly, the distributor distributes the high voltage current from the coil to the upper cylinder at the proper time to ignite the compressed air-fuel charge in the cylinder.

The distributor consists of a housing, a breaker plate upon which the contact points are mounted, a drive shaft with a breaker cam, a spark advancing mechanism, a rotor, and a cap.

Distributor Contact Points. The distributor shaft and breaker cam are driven by the engine camshaft at one-half crank-shaft speed. As the cam rotates, it opens and closes the contact points. The number of degrees of breaker cam rotation during which the contact points remain closed is known as the "dwell" period. The cam has the same number of lobes as there are cylinders in the engine. Thus, in one revolution of the distributor cam (two revolutions of the crankshaft) the ignition coil produces a spark for each cylinder in the engine.

Distributor Rotor and Cap. A rotor made of insulating material is mounted so that it rotates with the distributor cam. A distributor cap, also made of insulating materials, is provided with a center terminal and a terminal for each cylinder. The distributor cap fits on the distributor so that its center terminal is in constant contact with a metal contact strip on top of the rotor. A high-voltage wire in the secondary circuit connects the center distributor cap terminal with the ignition coil.

As the distributor shaft turns, the rotor distributes the high-voltage current from the ignition coil to the spark plugs at the proper time in accordance with the firing order of the engine.

Spark Advance Mechanisms. The high-voltage current from the distributor must produce a spark to ignite the fuel charge at all speed and load conditions. The timing of ignition and combustion must be regulated to produce the desired power with a minimum consumption of fuel. When ignition timing is advanced, the spark is made to occur earlier in the engine cycle.

Factors Determining Ignition Timing. The combustion rate of the fuel, the engine speed and degree of compression, and the power developed are among the factors which determine ignition timing. Fuels vary in their rate of burning. Ignition should occur at an instant which allows complete burning of the fuel. The engine speed deter-

Ignition Systems

mines the period of time over which the power stroke will occur. Therefore, ignition should be timed to match the engine speed.

Idling. When the engine is idling, the spark is usually timed to occur in the cylinder just before the piston reaches top dead center. At low engine speeds, this gives the fuel mixture sufficient time to burn completely, and it permits the total pressure developed to be applied to the piston as it starts downward on the power stroke.

At higher engine speeds, however, there is a shorter time interval available for the mixture to ignite, burn, and deliver its power to the piston. Therefore, if full power is to be obtained, the ignition system must distribute the high-voltage current to the spark plugs earlier in the engine cycle by advancing the spark.

Part Throttle. During part-throttle operation, when maximum power is not demanded, compression pressures are lower and the rate of combustion is slower. Therefore, timing must be advanced for better combustion.

Full Throttle at Low Speeds. During full or wide-open throttle at low speeds, when maximum power is demanded, a maximum fuel charge enters the cylinder so that higher compression takes place. The combustion rate is faster than during part-throttle operation at the same engine speed. Since less combustion time is required to produce maximum power, the ignition is advanced a smaller amount.

High Engine Speeds. As the engine approaches maximum speeds at full throttle, the timing must also be advanced. The timing during acceleration, however, is not advanced as far as at part-throttle operation. At maximum speeds, the throttle is fully open, but the time available for the power stroke to take place is reduced to a point where it is no longer possible to fill the cylinder with a full charge of air-fuel mixture. Compression is low because there is less mixture to compress. The rate of combustion is slower. Therefore, maximum timing advance is reached at this point.

Types of Spark Advance Mechanisms. Most distributors are constructed with both a centrifugal type advance mechanism and a vacuum controlled advance mechanism. Some distributors use only vacuum advance, employing both manifold vacuum and carburetor venturi vacuum.

Centrifugal Advance. In many present-day distributors, the centrifugal advance mechanism is located above the circuit breaker cam inside the rotor. The centrifugal type, Fig. 12-6, consists of an advance cam as part of the distributor shaft, a pair of advance weights, two springs, and a weight

Automotive Engines

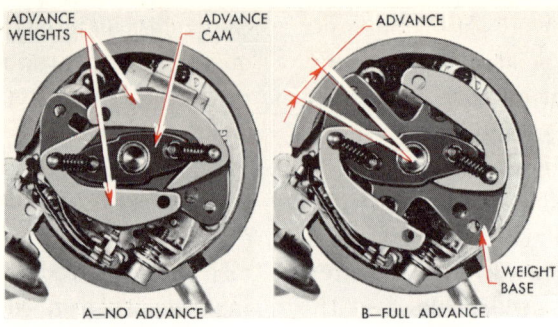

Fig. 12-6. A centrifugal advance mechanism viewed from the top of the distributor. In the full advance position, the weights have moved outward and rotated the weight base ahead of its original position. (Buick Div., General Motors Corp.)

base (or weight-carrying) plate which is assembled to the distributor cam. At idle speeds, the springs hold the advance weights, Fig. 12-6A, so that there is no spark advance and the spark occurs in the cylinders according to the initial manual setting of the distributor. As the engine speed increases, centrifugal force causes the weights to gradually move outward against the spring tension, Fig. 12-6B. Due to this motion, the arms on the weights push against the advance cam, thus rotating the weight base plate and the distributor cam ahead of its original position on the distributor shaft. In so doing, the spark is advanced and the distributor cam lobes open and close the contact points earlier in the compression stroke.

Vacuum Advance. Under part-throttle operation, there is a high vacuum in the intake manifold. As a result, a smaller amount of air-fuel mixture enters the cylinder. This mixture is less highly compressed and thus burns at a slower rate. Under such conditions, an additional spark advance beyond that already provided by the centrifugal advance mechanism will increase fuel economy.

The vacuum-advance unit consists of an airtight, spring-loaded diaphragm linked either to the

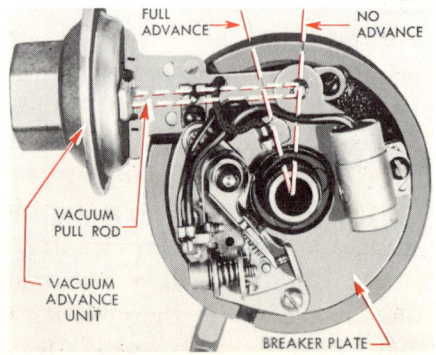

Fig. 12-7. The vacuum advance unit pull rod moves the breaker plate to automatically advance and retard the spark. (Buick Div., General Motors Corp.)

Ignition Systems

distributor breaker plate or to the housing, Fig. 12-7. The airtight side of the diaphragm is connected by means of tubing to the carburetor air horn. This opening is on the atmospheric side of the throttle valve when the throttle is in idling position. During idle, no vacuum is imposed on the diaphragm, so the spring holds the distributor or breaker plate in the retarded position.

When the throttle valve is opened slightly, the vacuum at the opening is sufficient to cause the diaphragm to compress the spring and to rotate the breaker plate or distributor against the rotation of the breaker cam. This movement enables the contact points to open earlier on the compression stroke. The amount of throttle opening and the engine load determine the amount of intake manifold vacuum and therefore, the amount of spark advance.

On some engines, the vacuum unit is connected directly to the intake manifold. With the engine idling, the high manifold vacuum results in full vacuum advance. When the throttle is opened for acceleration, or when the engine is under heavy load, manifold vacuum drops and the spring moves the breaker plate or distributor to the retarded position. As engine speed increases, the manifold vacuum increases, advancing the spark.

There is usually some centrifugal advance beginning at engine crankshaft speeds of 900 RPM and above. The centrifugal advance will increase as engine crankshaft RPM increases. Vacuum advance will be added to the existing centrifugal advance depending upon throttle opening. Thus, at part throttle operation, both mechanical and vacuum advance are present. At wide-open throttle position, there is usually no vacuum advance. The total ignition advance for any engine is the sum of centrifugal advance and vacuum advance.

To reduce emissions, most of the vacuum units used on present distributors reach maximum advance at lower engine speeds than on previous models. For further details see Chapter Eight (Emissions Systems) for distributor modulator operation under the section entitled "Transmission Controlled Spark Advance System Used with an Automatic Transmission".

A number of engines equipped with emissions systems use a dual-diaphragm vacuum advance mechanism to aid in reducing engine emissions at idle speeds. The outer (primary) diaphragm utilizes carburetor vacuum to advance timing while the inner (secondary) diaphragm utilizes intake manifold vacuum to provide additional timing retard at closed throttle, Fig. 12-8.

Automotive Engines

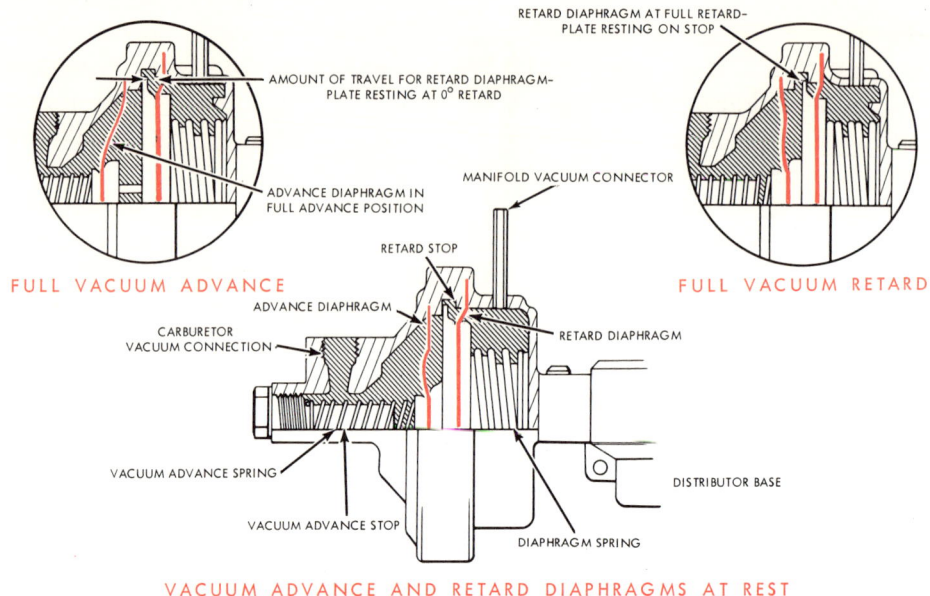

Fig. 12-8. Dual diaphragm vacuum advance mechanism. (Ford Div., Ford Motor Co.)

The outer diaphragm is connected to the movable breaker plate in the same manner as in the conventional distributor. As vacuum increases, the diaphragm moves the plate in the opposite direction from cam rotation, thereby advancing the timing. During idle or deceleration, the throttle valve is closed, and vacuum is closed off to the primary diaphragm. This permits diaphragm spring tension to return the breaker plate to full retard.

At idle, manifold vacuum is directed to the inner diaphragm. This moves the breaker plate in the direction of distributor rotation, which further retards the timing. Automatically retarding the timing at idle, beyond the basic timing setting, aids in keeping engine emissions at a minimum.

Spark Plugs. The spark plug, Fig. 12-9, provides a spark gap inside the engine cylinder. When the engine is operating, the high-voltage current produced by the ignition coil arcs across the gap and creates a spark that ignites the air-fuel mixture in the cylinder. The number of cylinders in an engine determines the number of spark plugs used.

Construction. The spark plug consists of three main parts: 1) a threaded metal shell with a ground electrode which is screwed into holes in the cylinder head, 2) a porcelain insulator, and 3) the

Ignition Systems

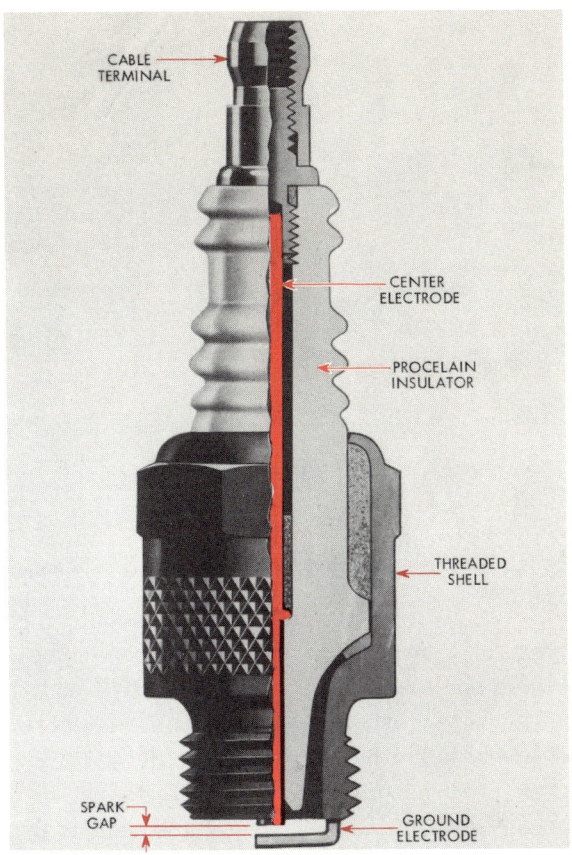

Fig. 12-9. Cutaway view of a spark plug. The electrodes provide the gap for the ignition spark.

high-voltage or center electrode. Some spark plugs contain a special resistor built into the center electrode to eliminate radio and television interference. The electrodes are made of nickel or nickel alloy to withstand the high temperatures encountered. Spark plugs are usually adjusted to provide a gap of 0.025 in. to 0.040 in. between the electrodes. The spark plugs are assembled by means of gaskets and cement to provide a tight seal between the shell and the insulator.

Factors Affecting Spark Plug Operation. Spark plugs are designed to meet a wide variety of engine requirements, Fig. 12-10. Engine load and speed, air-fuel ratio, temperature, and type of fuel affect spark plug operation.

Spark plugs are classified according to a heat rating as "cold" or "hot," depending upon the

457

Automotive Engines

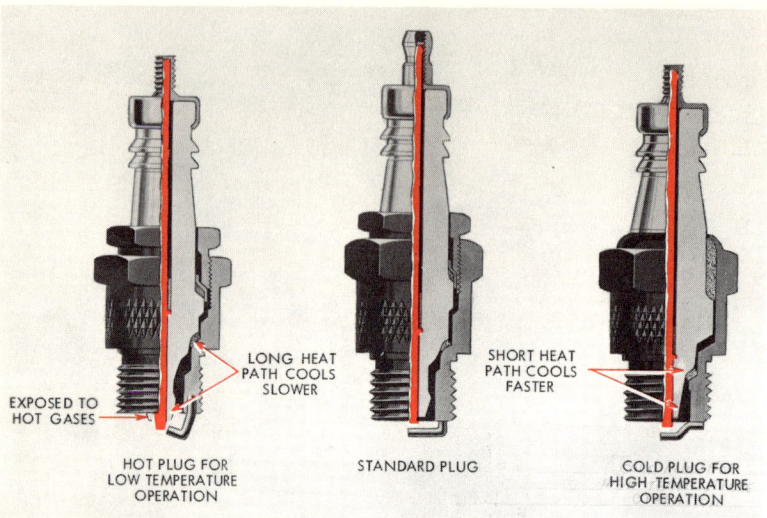

Fig. 12-10. There is a specific spark plug design for each type of engine operation.

length of the porcelain insulator within the spark plug shell. "Cold" plugs are generally used in heavy-load, high-speed operation where high temperatures are encountered. Lower-speed, intermittent loading, and colder operating conditions require a "hotter" plug.

Certain additives in fuels, such as tetraethyl lead which is introduced into gasoline to change its combustion rate, will affect spark plug operating. When tetraethyl lead is used, oxides of lead will form at certain ratios and temperatures. At extreme temperatures, the oxides will be deposited on the porcelain insulator within the shell. Some conditions produce reverse effects where oxides are reduced and lead is deposited on the insulator. These deposits of oxides or lead can foul the plug. Fouling can cause misfiring and sometimes complete failure by shorting the plugs, preventing proper spark action. Fouling, shorting, and misfiring can be minimized by using plugs designed for the particular engine and operating conditions.

Operation of the Conventional Ignition System

You have studied each part of the ignition system and how each part functions *as a unit*. Now you will see how the parts work to-

Ignition Systems

gether as a team to produce the high-voltage spark in the combustion chamber.

Operation of the Primary Circuit

When the ignition switch is turned to the "start" position, Fig. 12-11, a connection is made between the battery and the positive terminal of the ignition coil at the same instant that the starting motor begins to crank the engine. The completion of this circuit bypasses the resistance in the primary circuit, making the full battery voltage available to the coil during cranking. Once the engine starts, moving the ignition switch to the "on" position connects the resistance coil or resistor wire into the coil circuit, thus limiting to a safe maximum the amount of primary current flowing through the coil and contact points.

When the contact points in the distributor are closed, Fig. 12-12, the battery, generator, or alternator current flows through the primary winding of the ignition coil and through the contact points to ground. The flow of current through the primary windings of the coil creates a magnetic field around the coil windings, storing potential electrical energy in the coil.

When the distributor cam causes the contact points to separate, Fig.

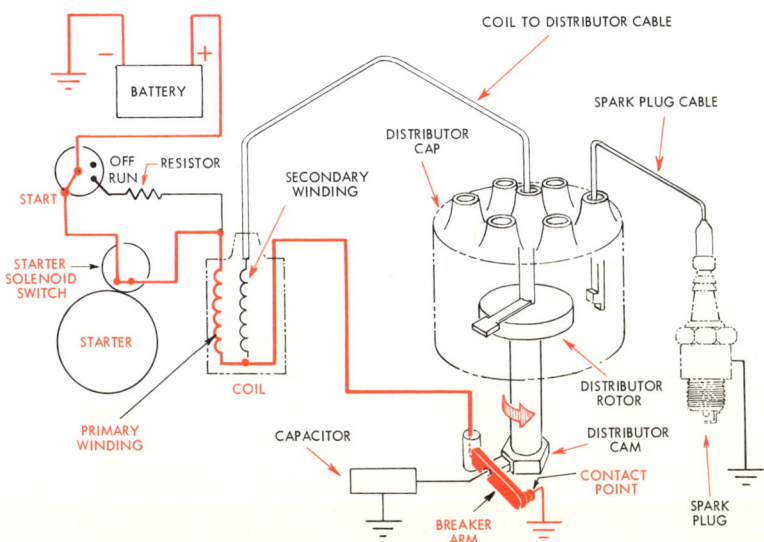

Fig. 12-11. Current flow in the primary ignition circuit during engine starting. The colored portions denote current flow. While the ignition switch is in "start" position, current flows to the starter for cranking. Current bypasses the ignition resistor and flows directly from the starter and through the primary ignition circuit.

459

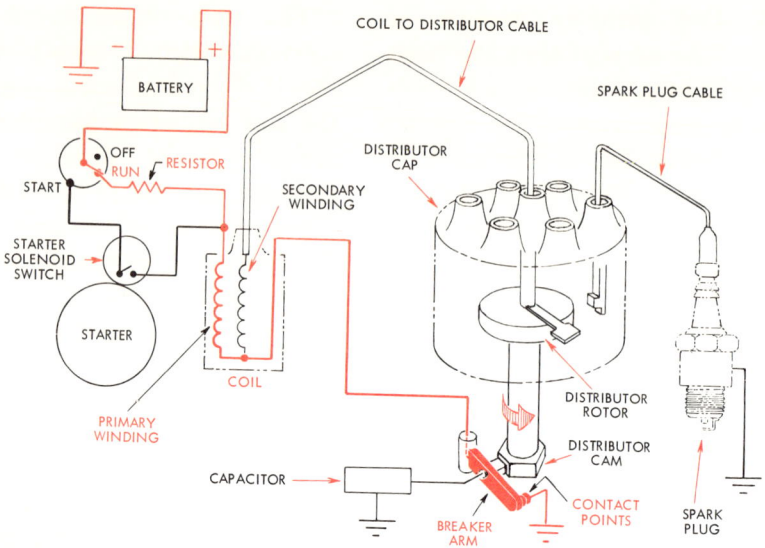

Fig. 12-12. Current flow in the primary ignition circuit while the engine is running. The ignition switch is in "run" position. Current now flows through the ignition resistor and then through the primary circuit and back to ground through the closed ignition contact points. Magnetic lines of force are built up in the ignition coil.

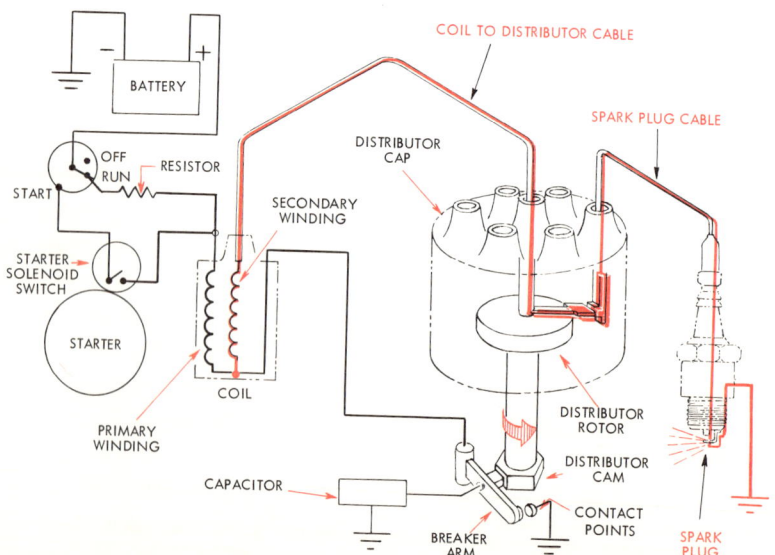

Fig. 12-13. Current flow in the secondary ignition circuit while the engine is running. The distributor cam opens the contact points, interrupting the flow of current in the primary circuit. The magnetic lines of force in the coil break down and induce a surge of high-voltage current in the secondary coil winding. The high-voltage surge travels to the distributor and through the rotor and spark plug cable to the spark plug. At the spark plug, the high-voltage current produces a spark by jumping the gap to the ground electrode.

Ignition Systems

12-13, the primary circuit is broken. The current that has been flowing through the coil windings tends to surge across the opened contact points but is absorbed by the capacitor. This action brings the primary current flow to a quick, controlled stop.

Operation of the Secondary Circuit

The extremely rapid change in the strength of the magnetic field, brought about when the primary circuit was broken, causes a high voltage to be induced in both the primary and secondary windings of the ignition coil.

The high-voltage surge in the secondary circuit travels through the high-voltage cable connecting the coil secondary winding to the center of the distributor cap, through the rotor to the distributor cap segment in line with the rotor, from where it is conducted to the proper spark plug by the spark plug cables. The high voltage jumps the gap between the spark plug electrodes producing the spark required to ignite the air-fuel mixture in the engine cylinder.

The above sequence of action occurs each time the distributor cam opens the contact points.

Transistorized Battery-Coil Ignition Systems

Over the years the many improvements made on automotive engines have resulted in improved engine performance and higher engine RPM's. These changes have brought about a need for higher voltage to the spark plugs to provide an adequate spark at the higher speeds.

To provide the higher voltages, some manufacturers used a dual contact point distributor to increase the "dwell" (coil build-up time). Now all manufacturers have adopted a 12-volt electrical system to provide a higher voltage output at the spark plugs. Even with these changes, (because of the nature of the ignition system) there is still a voltage fall-off at high speeds, which may be as much as 50%.

One method which would provide higher secondary voltage is to increase the current flow in the primary side of the ignition system. However, this increases the load on the ignition contacts which are already operating at the limit of their current-carrying ability. The stronger the current, the greater the pitting, (metal trans-

Automotive Engines

fer between contacts) and the shorter the contact life.

To overcome some of the problems inherent in the modern ignition system some manufacturers have developed a transistorized ignition system. The actual construction of the different makes will vary to some extent but the underlying principles are the same for all systems.

Transistor Fundamentals

A transistor has the ability to switch large amounts of current without the use of moving parts. This ability gives the transistor its advantage in ignition systems, because it can be used to switch currents as much as 30 times larger than the amount required to trigger it. The distributor contact points can handle the small triggering current without strain while a much higher secondary current increases the ignition spark in the combustion chamber.

Basic Materials. Transistors are made of materials called *semiconductors* which have properties that place them as intermediate types between good conductors and good insulators. The most common material in use for automotive transistors and diodes is *germanium* which is a borderline insulator with very few free electrons. (The fewer free electrons a material contains, the less electricity it will conduct.) For use in transistors, an element must be added to change the number of electrons and make the material a semiconductor.

Current flow in a semiconductor results from either an excess or a deficiency of electrons in the material; the added element determines which direction the material is to conduct. When the element *antimony* is added to germanium, it becomes a semiconductor with an excess of electrons and is called an "N" or negative type material. If *boron* is added to germanium, the material will have a deficiency of electrons and will be known as "P" or positive type material.

A transistor is made up of three

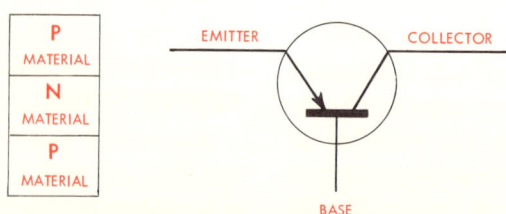

Fig. 12-14. PNP transistor structure.

Ignition Systems

small sections of "P" and "N" materials joined together and enclosed in a container, Fig. 12-14. If two sections are "N" material and one section is "P" material, it is known as an "NPN" transistor. If it is made up of two sections of "P" material and one section of "N" material, it is known as a "PNP" transistor. It is the PNP type of transistor that is generally used in automotive ignition systems.

Diodes. When only two sections of material, one of P-material and the other of N-material are joined together, they form a *diode,* also used in the ignition system, Fig. 12-15. The diode acts as a voltage-actuated relay to protect the transistor from excess voltage. The diode holds down to a negligible value back and forth oscillations of current in the primary circuit.

Parts of the Transistor. The input and the output resistance of a transistor varies with the manner in which it is connected into the circuit. The characteristics of the transistor will depend upon the

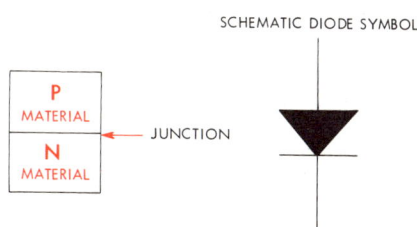

Fig. 12-15. Diode structure.

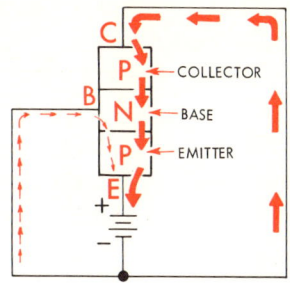

Fig. 12-16. Transistor connected to a source of current (battery). Colored arrows are used to show direction and relative strength of current flow in the circuit.

method of connection. The names attached to the three different parts of the transistor are: the *Emitter,* the *Base,* and the *Collector.*

From a single source, current will flow simultaneously through the E-B or emitter-base circuit and the E-C, emitter-collector, circuit, Fig. 12-16. It is also known that the base current is only a fraction of the collector current yet the collector current cannot exist without the base current. An interruption of the small current flow in the base circuit produces a corresponding interruption of a large flow of current in the collector circuit. This means that the base current triggers the collector circuit.

Transistors in the Primary Ignition Circuit

To utilize the transistor in an ignition system, it is connected as illustrated in Fig. 12-17. The base is connected to the ignition contact

463

Automotive Engines

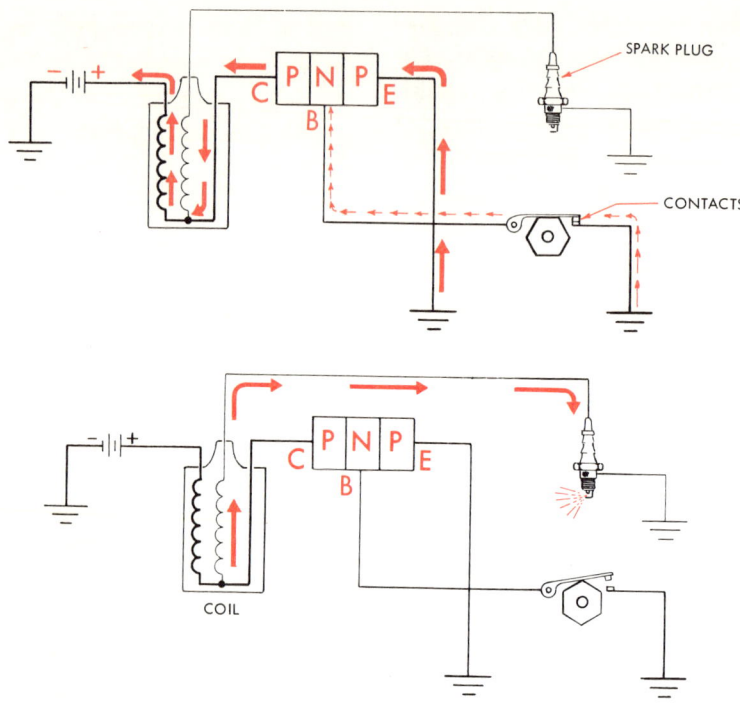

Fig. 12-17. Simplified diagram showing use of the transistor in an operating ignition system.

points. The collector is connected to the primary winding of the ignition coil. The emitter is grounded.

The major advantage of a transistorized ignition system is that the contact points carry only about $1/15$ the amount of the current that the conventional ignition contacts transmit. This small amount of current triggers the transistor which is capable of carrying as much as 30 times the triggering current. This is considerably more current than would be practical with conventional contacts in the regular ignition system. The small amount of current flowing through the contacts practically eliminates all contact arcing and oxidation thereby prolonging contact point life considerably and keeping contact resistance at a minimum. The additional current flowing through the transistor into the primary of the coil reduces the voltage fall-off at high speeds. There is also practically an instantaneous current build-up when the contacts close due to the increased current flow. In some systems, a special low-resistance coil is used which also builds up faster than the conventional coil.

At low speeds the transistor-

Ignition Systems

ized system furnishes only slightly more voltage than the conventional system. However, at approximately 4,000 RPM, the transistorized system may supply as much as 50% or more voltage from the secondary system than the conventional ignition system.

Types of Transistorized Ignition Systems

Each manufacturer will have a somewhat different arrangement for the use of transistors in the ignition system. Some are more complex than others. In every case the end results are the same: prolonged ignition contact and spark plug life and gap settings remaining fixed for a longer period of time. There is also a greater voltage delivered to the spark plugs at high speed compared to the conventional system. Transistorized systems are a comparatively recent development. Therefore, numerous changes and improvements are being made as time goes on and additional manufacturers enter the field.

Simple Transistorized System

One of the simplest systems is composed of a distributor, a special coil for rapid build-up, a resistance unit, a transistor and the necessary diode and resistors for protection of the unit. The capacitor is eliminated from the circuit completely. The transistor, diode, and resistors are sealed in a "heat sink." The heat sink is a finned aluminum casting which must be exchanged as a unit if failure occurs in any one component.

More Complex System

A more complex transistorized ignition system consists of a heat sink, transistor, zener diode, ignition capacitor, toroid, safety capacitor, resistors, tach block, fuse, cold start relay, and a distributor.

Heat Sink. The heat sink houses the transistor, diode, ignition capacitor, toroid, base-emitter resistor and safety capacitor. The heat sink is generally located as far away from sources of heat as possible because both the transistor and diode have limitations which necessitate the rapid dissipation of heat. An ambient temperature of approximately 170° is about maximum for efficient performance. Fig. 12-18 illustrates a heat sink with the various components.

Transistor. The transistor located in the heat sink is of the PNP type. It is designed for a base current of one ampere, a collector cur-

465

Automotive Engines

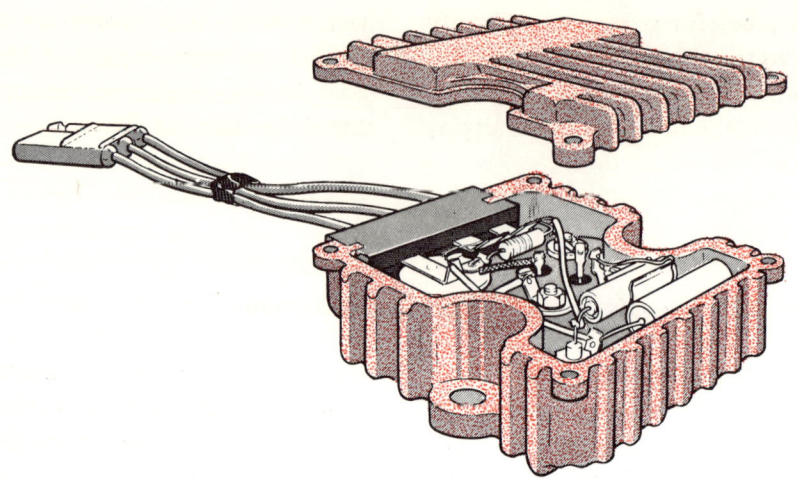

Fig. 12-18. Heat sink assembly. (Ford Div., Ford Motor Co.)

rent of 12 amperes, a base to emitter voltage of one volt maximum and a collector to emitter potential of 0.75 volts maximum. In such transistors, the base sandwiched between the two P sections is composed of very thin N-material having a metal ring around its outer circumference, Fig. 12-19. This results in a shorter distance between the emitter and collector than the emitter and base.

Diode. A zener diode acts as a voltage actuated protection relay whenever the voltage reaches a predetermined value. A diode is a one-way switch allowing electricity to flow in one direction only, but if the voltage becomes too great it breaks down and passes a reverse bias current. This does not harm a zener diode as this is the function it was designed for.

Ignition Capacitor. The igni-

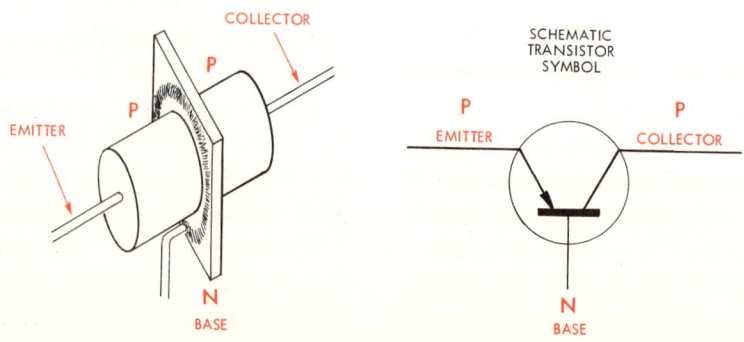

Fig. 12-19. Transistor construction.

Ignition Systems

tion capacitor serves the same purpose as it does in a conventional ignition system, but it must carry a higher current load and have a greater capacity. Because it is a part of the collector circuit, it has no effect on the ignition contacts which are part of the base circuit.

Toroid. The toroid, a block and coil assembly, serves to stop the collector current (coil current) at the instant of the initial opening of the contacts.

Safety Capacitor. The capacitor is simply a safety device used to prevent transistor damage if someone should open the battery circuit when the engine is running.

Base-Emitter Resistor. The resistor in the base-to-emitter toroid circuit controls the path of the current in the emitter-base circuit. It prevents current from bypassing the base-to-emitter section of the transistor when the contacts are closed and the transistor is in operation.

Resistors. A base resistor located between the transistor and coil is similar to the conventional ignition system resistor wire. It limits the current flow to the transistor.

Tach Block. The collector and emitter resistors limit voltage and current flow in their respective circuits.

A tach block is included in the

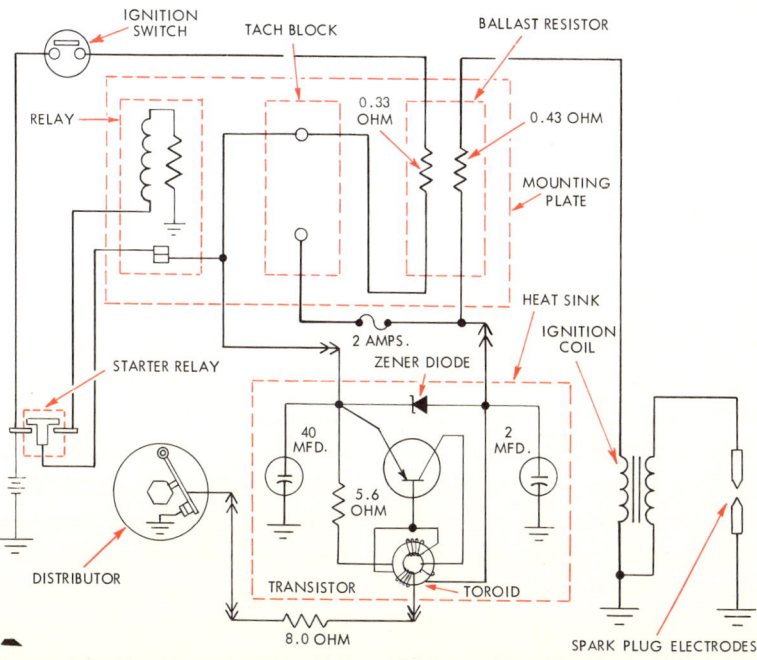

Fig. 12-20. Schematic wiring diagram of a transistorized ignition system. (Ford Div., Ford Motor Co.)

circuit of this system for the purpose of attaching test instruments. A two-ampere fuse also located in the collector-to-tach lead is to prevent the transistor from being damaged by the hooking up of external devices other than the proper test equipment.

Cold Start Relay. A cold start relay is incorporated in the circuit at the starter relay interrupting the battery-to-coil lead. The relay will bypass the ignition resistor and make available additional battery current to the ignition circuit if the current to the ignition circuit drops below a predetermined value while cranking the engine.

Distributor and Contact Points. Because ignition contact life is much longer in a transistorized ignition system, the distributor cam is highly polished to reduce rubbing block wear and maintain proper contact setting over a longer period of time. Fig. 12-20 illustrates the wiring diagram for this system.

Magnetic Pulse Distributor

Another system, which utilizes many of the same components with the exception of the addition of two more transistors (one a triggering transistor and another a switching transistor) uses a magnetic pulse distributor. This distributor resembles the standard distributor in most respects except that the breaker plate and contact assembly

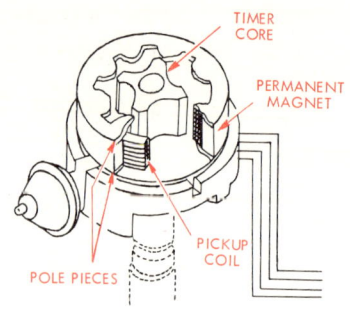

Fig. 12-21. This magnetic pulse distributor for transistorized ignition systems does not use a breaker plate or contact points. (Delco-Remy Div., General Motors Corp.)

has been eliminated. In its place is a rotating iron timer core and a magnetic pickup assembly, Fig. 12-21. The magnetic pickup assembly consists of a permanent magnet, two pole pieces and a pickup coil. The pole pieces have precisely shaped internal teeth—one for each cylinder. The timer core which is attached to the distributor shaft has a number of equally spaced vanes, 4 for an 8-cylinder engine, 3 for a 6-cylinder engine.

As the vanes of the iron timer core on the distributor shaft pass through the magnetic field created by the permanent magnet on the internal teeth, a magnetic field alternately builds up and collapses. Each time a vane passes a tooth an electric current is developed. Each voltage pulse is conducted to the transistor control unit where it turns on the triggering transistor and causes it to turn off the switching transistor.

Ignition Systems

Checking On Your Knowledge

The following questions give you the opportunity to check up on yourself. If you have read the chapter carefully, you should be able to answer the questions. If you have any difficulty, read the chapter over once more so that you have the information well in mind before you go on with your reading.

DO YOU KNOW

1. What function does the storage battery serve in the ignition system?
2. In what way does the primary coil winding differ from the secondary windings?
3. What is the purpose of hermetically sealing the coil parts in oil?
4. Describe each component of the conventional ignition system and how each component operates.
5. What is the purpose of the primary coil winding?
6. Describe the construction of a capacitor.
7. What is the purpose of the ignition coil resistance unit or resistance wire in the primary ignition circuit?
8. Explain the action of a capacitor.
9. What is the purpose of the ignition contact points?
10. What is the function of the rotor and distributor cap?
11. What are some of the factors that determine ignition timing?
12. Describe how the centrifugal advance unit operates.
13. Describe how the vacuum advance unit operates.
14. What is meant by a "cold" or a "hot" spark plug?
15. What factors affect the operation of spark plugs?
16. Discuss the operation of the primary and secondary circuit in a conventional ignition system.
17. What basic materials are typically used to construct a PNP transistor?
18. What ability does a transistor have which makes it useful in an ignition system?
19. What is a semiconductor?
20. What is the purpose of a diode in a transistorized ignition system?

Chapter 13
Ignition System Service

Ignition failures and normal lowering of ignition system efficiency are probably the most common automobile troubles. A complete engine tune-up should be performed at 15,000-mile intervals to maintain peak performance and economy and prevent ignition failures. When an engine loses power, misfires, or does not run, check the ignition system first to make sure all units are in good working condition.

Use test equipment to do a proper and scientific job of ignition tune-up. Even a minimum amount of equipment can help to locate ignition system troubles and make necessary repairs.

Ignition Troubles

Ignition trouble occurs in two forms: the engine fails to start; or it shows signs of steady or intermittent miss, hard starting, power loss, spark knock, or overheating.

Failure to start may result from the loss of electrical energy in either the primary or the secondary circuit. Ignition failures may also be caused by improper adjustments or improper operation of some specific unit. Fig. 13-1 shows a typical ignition system.

Primary Circuit

Trouble in the primary circuit that causes failure to run or missing may be caused by a discharged

Ignition System Service

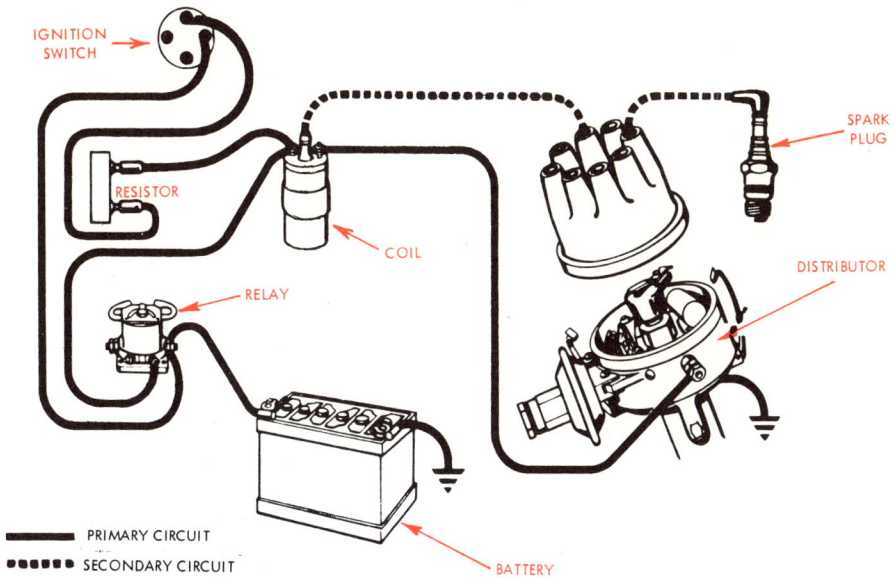

Fig. 13-1. A typical 12-volt ignition system showing the units which must be checked if the engine does not start or run properly.

battery, poor connections or a short circuit, burned or improperly adjusted contact points, defective ignition switch, defective resistance unit (12-volt system), defective primary circuit in the ignition coil, or a defective capacitor.

Secondary Circuit

Loss of high-voltage electrical current in the secondary circuit can prevent engine operation. The loss may be caused by current leaking to ground at the coil cap, at the distributor, the rotor, or from the high-voltage cables and their connections. Leakage can be caused by defective insulation which permits grounding on adjacent metal parts. High-voltage current can sometimes burn a path through insulation, particularly when the insulation becomes old or worn. Leakage to ground can be caused by moisture in the dirt and dust that adheres to ignition parts. In humid weather, spark plugs with dirty insulators may become wet enough to permit the high-voltage current to jump to ground across the damp surface of the insulator, preventing starting. Spark plugs with fouled or incorrectly gapped electrodes or with broken insulators can cause an engine miss. Loss of power may also be caused by im-

471

Automotive Engines

properly set timing or a defective spark advance mechanism.

Because numerous units may cause these conditions, make a complete checkup of the ignition system when trouble occurs.

Ignition Troubleshooting

Most engine troubleshooting procedures start with tests that either establish the ignition system as the source of trouble or free the ignition system from further consideration. Before testing the ignition system, make sure the battery has enough charge to operate the cranking motor freely and that the fuel is reaching the carburetor.

When making ignition tests, avoid electric shocks by holding only the insulated portions of high-voltage cables. Avoid shorts by not laying tools on top of the battery. Avoid electrical burns by not wearing rings on the fingers.

No Spark at the Spark Plug Cables (Engine Does Not Run)

Push all spark plug cables firmly into sockets in the distributor cap. Also make sure they are making positive contact at the spark plugs. To establish the fact that there is no spark at the spark plug cables, turn the ignition switch on and hold the end of one spark plug cable ¼ in. away from the cylinder head (good ground) while cranking. Repeat this at each spark plug cable.

If no spark is present at the ends of any of the cables, the next step is to free from consideration as large a part of the system as possible.

Inspect the coil-to-distributor high-voltage cable to see if the insulation is worn through or damaged at any point near metal. See that the terminals are fastened securely to the cable. Replace the cable if it is defective. Make sure the terminals are seated in the distributor cap and coil terminal socket. Be sure the coil-to-distributor primary wire makes good contact at both ends and is not grounded.

The next step is to bypass the circuit from the battery to the coil. Connect one wire of a 0-10 ammeter to the battery post that is not grounded, and the other ammeter wire to the battery terminal of the ignition coil, Fig. 13-2. This bypasses the ignition switch, ammeter or indicator light, resistor unit, and most of the primary circuit.

Ignition System Service

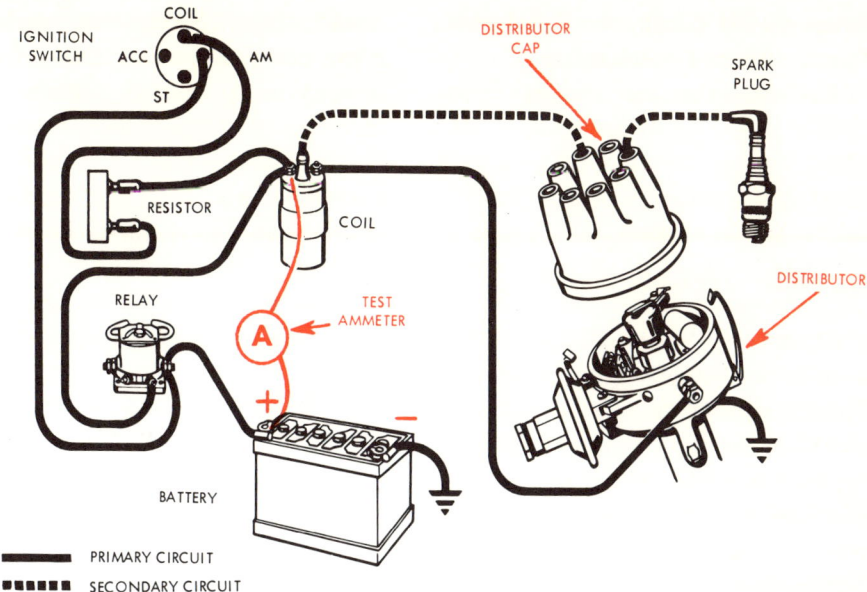

Fig. 13-2. An ammeter can be used to check the ignition system section between the battery and the coil. (Ford Div., Ford Motor Co.)

If the engine will now start and run, the trouble is in the primary circuit between the battery and ignition coil. Check the condition of wires and other units in the circuit.

If the engine will not start and the ammeter reads zero when the engine is cranked, the trouble is in the primary circuit from the battery terminal of the coil to the grounded side of the distributor contact points. Ground the capacitor's insulated terminal. If the ammeter still reads zero, make sure the primary wire from the coil to the distributor is not broken and the terminals are making good contact. If the primary wire is good and there is still no current, replace the coil.

If the ammeter shows a reading when the capacitor is grounded, there is trouble in the contact points or the primary circuit wire to the contact point arm assembly. Clean, replace, or adjust the points, or repair the primary circuit wire.

If the engine still will not start after checking the contact points, the trouble is either in the capacitor or in the secondary circuit. Test the capacitor before you replace it.

If the engine still will not start, remove the high-voltage cable from the coil and replace with a high-voltage jumper cable. Hold the other end of the jumper cable ¼ in.

from some metal of the engine. Crank the engine with the starting motor. Observe the quality of the spark. If the spark is weak or absent, replace the ignition coil. A good spark should jump at least ¼ in. to ground when the engine is cranked.

If the spark is good and the engine still will not start, the trouble is a grounded secondary circuit in the distributor rotor or cap. Check the rotor for carbon tracks, cracks, or poor center contact. Inspect the distributor cap for cracks and corroded terminals. Replace any defective parts.

Satisfactory Spark From Some But Not All Spark Plug Cables

Test the spark from the end of each spark plug cable at idle speed. A spark that fails to jump at least ¼ in. regularly is considered weak. The fact that a satisfactory spark is obtained from some spark plug cables means that the primary circuit, including the contact points, the capacitor, and the coil are satisfactory. Also, the rotor, as well as the coil-to-distributor high-voltage circuit can be eliminated from further consideration.

Check the spark plug cables. Make sure wire is making contact with metal terminals. Cables with a carbon core instead of wire, may have a gap in the carbon core which causes a resistance which interferes with high-voltage current flow. Replace them if the insulation is damaged. Make sure that the spark plug cable terminals and terminal sockets are free from corrosion, and that the cables are firmly seated in the distributor cap.

Check the distributor cap for burned terminals or cracks. Replace all faulty parts.

Intermittent Spark at All Spark Plug Cables

An intermittent spark is one which does not consistently jump the gap. This is generally due to trouble in the primary circuit. The fact that the spark is normal between "misses" means that the trouble is probably not in the secondary circuit except when the secondary spark jumps to ground or to another wire.

Make sure all connections are clean and tight. Adjust or replace the contact points. Test the coil and the capacitor.

Weak Spark at All Spark Plug Cables

A weak spark at all the spark plug cables can only be due to trouble in some unit or units that have an equal effect on all the spark plug cables. The entire primary circuit, including the contact points, has such an effect. So does the high-voltage wire from the coil to distributor. A weak secondary circuit in the ignition coil will

Ignition System Service

similarly weaken the spark. It is possible for all the high-voltage cables leading from the distributor cap or the cap itself to leak; however, this is generally considered unlikely. A poor contact between the rotor and the distributor cap may weaken the spark.

Make sure all terminals and connections in the primary circuit are clean and tight. Check the distributor contact point spacing. Improper spacing may affect the build-up time of the ignition coil and weaken the voltage output.

Badly burned and pitted points create a resistance to current which also weakens the spark. Test coil and capacitor for correct output.

Checking Voltage Drop in the Primary Circuit. Loose or dirty connections and broken strands in stranded wire will increase the resistance to the current flow in the primary circuit and will cause a "voltage drop" below the required value. Any voltage drop in the primary circuit causes the voltage of the current flowing through the

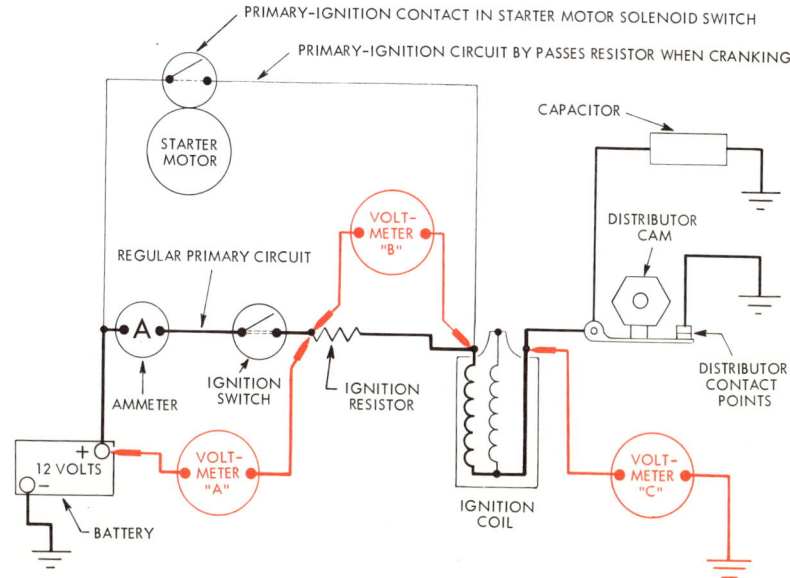

VOLTMETER "A" READING = 0.2 VOLTS WITH IGNITION SWITCH AND DISTRIBUTOR POINTS CLOSED

VOLTMETER "B" READING = 6.5 VOLTS MAX. 5.5 VOLTS MIN.—ENGINE HOT, IGNITION SWITCH AND END DISTRIBUTOR POINTS CLOSED

VOLTMETER "C" READING = 0.1 VOLTS WITH IGNITION SWITCH AND DISTRIBUTOR POINTS CLOSED

Fig. 13-3. Primary circuit voltage drop schematic diagram. When checking voltage drop, remember that a high resistance in any one portion of the ignition circuit will cause an abnormally low voltage reading when checking other portions of the circuit. The defective portion of the circuit, however, will give an abnormally high reading.

primary windings of the ignition coil to be lower than normal, reduces the voltage output of the coil, and thus causes weak spark at all of the plugs.

All terminals and connections in the ignition primary circuit must be clean and tight to insure that the voltage in that circuit does not decrease and drop below the voltage specified to produce a satisfactory spark at the spark plugs.

Voltage drop can be checked by connecting a voltmeter at certain points in the ignition primary circuit to measure the actual voltage in those portions of the circuit as shown in Fig. 13-3. The voltage readings obtained are checked against the voltage readings provided by the vehicle manufacturer for those parts of the circuit. Voltage readings higher than those set as standard by the manufacturer indicate a high resistance in the portion of the circuit being tested and should be corrected by cleaning and tightening connections or by replacing any damaged wires or components.

Figure 13-3 shows a voltmeter connected at three different locations. Only one meter is necessary. No connections need to be disconnected. The prods on the voltmeter lead wires are tightly pressed against the terminals indicated and the meter is read. The voltage readings shown in the caption below the illustration are typical of the voltage values specified by the manufacturer against which you check the readings you obtain.

Ignition Service

Many units in the ignition system should be tested with special equipment to determine if they are functioning properly. Distributor adjustment, for example, often requires special equipment. Proper timing must also be set by means of special equipment. Gages are needed to check the spark plug gap. When using test equipment, you should always follow the directions for making connections. Failure to do so may give incorrect readings or even ruin the equipment. Comply with the automobile manufacturer's specifications regarding each unit and any necessary adjustments.

Coil and Capacitor

In the case of a coil or a capacitor, it is impractical to make any repairs. Therefore, the unit must be replaced if defective. In many

Ignition System Service

cases it is essential that a coil tester be used. The coil may function properly under certain circumstances, and yet fail under others. The same situation may exist with a capacitor. An internal breakdown may occur only under certain load conditions.

Coil Test. A coil is tested for resistance and continuity of the primary and secondary windings. Some coils will perform satisfactorily when cold but break down when warm. Hence, a coil should always be warm before testing. Some testers check the output voltage, while others check the current reading in milliamperes of the spark as well. Generally the voltage and the current are checked against the readings of a "master" coil.

Capacitor Test. Capacitor testers as a rule give three types of readings—capacitance in microfarads, leakage, and series resistance. Since a capacitor is relatively low in cost, it is generally a good idea to replace it when in doubt if you do not have the means of measuring its capacitance.

Spark Plugs

The spark plugs should be cleaned and adjusted regularly. Regardless of how good a spark is developed in the ignition system, if the spark plug is unsatisfactory, maximum efficiency cannot be obtained.

Spark plug electrodes should be cleaned with a sandblast type of spark plug cleaner. Remove the spark plug from the engine. Clean the threads on the base of the plug with a wire brush. Make sure the insulator above the base is clean and free from oil. Sandblast the spark plug. Use the sandblast only long enough to clean the plug. Prolonged operation will erode the insulator. Blow out all grit after sandblasting. File the end of the center electrode with a point file until clean and flat. Adjust the spark plug gap to manufacturer's specifications by bending the outer (ground) electrode, Fig. 13-4. Use new spark plug gaskets when reinstalling the spark plugs. Some plugs have a tapered seat and do not use a gasket. Make sure the tapered mating surfaces are clean.

Spark plug testers determine the sparking efficiency of a cleaned

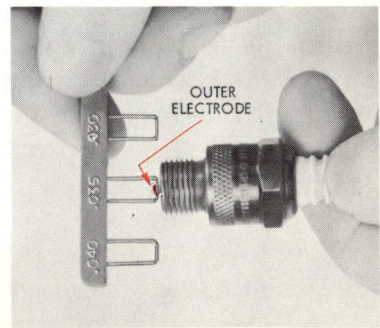

Fig. 13-4. Check spark plug gap with a wire type gage. The gap can be adjusted by bending the outer (ground) electrode. (American Motors Corp.)

477

and regapped spark plug by comparing it with the performance of a new spark plug of the same type under compression conditions similar to those in the engine cylinder. The cleaned plug is screwed into an opening in a sealed chamber. A window and mirror arrangement makes both the new and the cleaned plug electrodes visible. The chamber is put under air pressure (simulating cylinder compression). By pushing a button, high-voltage current is sent first through the new plug, then through the cleaned plug. The window and mirror arrangement permits comparison of the sparks produced. Some testers are provided with a meter which indicates the efficiency of the sparking action.

When installing new spark plugs, be sure to install plugs of the correct heat range. Another important factor when replacing spark plugs is the length of the spark plug threads. The length is known as the "reach" of the plug. Plugs must have the proper reach. If the threads extend too far into the combustion chamber, they can become glowing hot and cause preignition.

Distributors

The condition of the contact point matching surfaces is very important to proper functioning of the ignition system. Oxidation on the contact surfaces increases resistance, as do misalignment and burned or pitted contact points. The matching surfaces can be cleaned by filing with a clean point file, but it is generally better to replace the points if any pitted or burned surface is found.

Contact point spacing is also important. They must be kept within the specifications. Whenever new contact points are installed or the old points cleaned with a file, the spacing must be checked and adjusted.

To adjust the contact points on most distributors, crank the engine so the distributor cam rotates until the rubbing block is on the high point of the distributor cam lobe. Loosen the stationary contact plate lock screw, and set the contact gap to specifications with a feeler gage. Tighten the lock screw and then recheck the gap.

Equipment for checking the contact point dwell is commonly used while the distributor is mounted in a distributor tester, Fig. 13-5. A dwell meter indicates the length of time the contact points are closed and is calibrated in terms of the dwell or cam angle. This reading is directly related to the contact point gap, and any change in contact point gap setting will change the dwell angle reading.

On distributors having a window in the distributor cap, the dwell angle is set with the engine running or with the distributor

Ignition System Service

Fig. 13-5. Checking vacuum spark advance characteristics in a distributor tester. The tester will also check centrifugal spark advance and cam dwell or angle.

mounted in a distributor tester. Raise the window in the distributor cap. Insert the head of a hex wrench on that of the adjusting screw, Fig. 13-6. Turn the screw until the correct dwell angle is obtained. If a dwell meter is not available, turn the adjusting screw clockwise until the engine begins to miss, then reverse it one half turn.

When installing new contact points, you should make sure they are properly aligned, as in Fig. 13-7. Align the points by bending the stationary contact support.

Make sure the contact arm moves freely on the pivot post. Check the contact arm spring tension, Fig. 13-8. If the tension is too great, rapid wear of the rubbing block and cam will result. If the tension is too little, the rubbing block will not follow the contour of the cam at high speeds. The tension can be changed by bending the contact point movable arm spring.

Check the cam surface for roughness. Place a small amount of high temperature lubricant on the cam surface to reduce rubbing block wear.

479

Automotive Engines

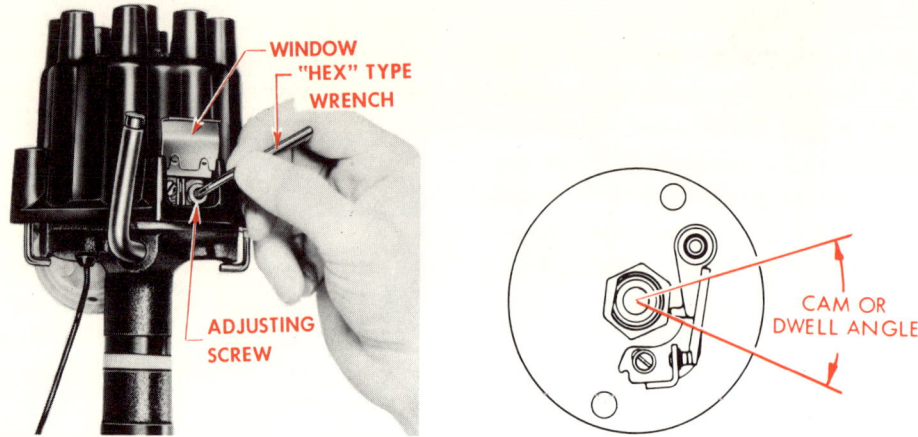

Fig. 13-6. Setting dwell angle (left). Right view shows the angle measurement. (Chevrolet Div., General Motors Corp.)

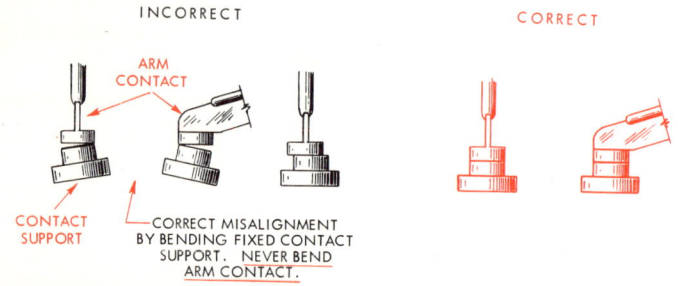

Fig. 13-7. Ignition contact arm alignment. (Chevrolet Div., General Motors Corp.)

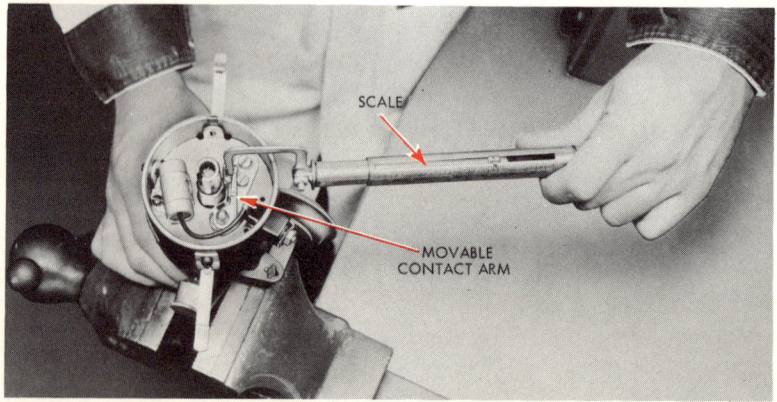

Fig. 13-8. Checking ignition contact arm spring tension with a spring scale. (Chevrolet Div., General Motors Corp.)

Ignition System Service

Distributor Advance Mechanisms

All distributors are provided with some means of advancing the ignition timing under certain load and speed conditions. Most distributors have a centrifugal as well as a vacuum advance mechanism. A correct advance pattern is necessary for efficient engine operation.

Centrifugal Advance. To check and set the advance when the distributor is removed from the engine, a distributor tester is necessary. Mount the distributor in the tester. At specified speeds, the centrifugal advance mechanism should advance the spark timing a specific amount. Change the spring tension on the distributor advance weight by bending the spring hangers to change the advance pattern.

Vacuum Advance. Distributor testers also have devices capable of developing sufficient vacuum to test the operation of the vacuum advance unit. With the distributor mounted on the machine and in operation, a specified amount of vacuum should advance the spark a specific number of degrees. Change the diaphragm spring tension by adding or subtracting washers to correct the advance pattern.

A timing advance tester is available which can be used to check vacuum advance as well as distributor centrifugal advance while the engine is operating. When initial timing is checked with a timing advance tester, timing advance mechanisms can also be checked.

Ignition Timing

Correct ignition timing is essential for maximum engine efficiency. Timing which is too advanced causes detonation; timing which is too retarded causes lack of power and overheating.

A timing light or a timing advance tester is used to properly set ignition timing. Timing marks on most engines are found on the vibration damper or pulley with a pointer located on the timing chain cover. On some older engines the timing marks are found on the flywheel. A small opening with a pointer is located on the front side of the flywheel cover.

Place a chalk mark on the specified number of degrees of advance. The timing light is always connected to No. 1 spark plug and the battery, if of the battery-powered type. The vacuum line or lines connected to the distributor vacuum

Automotive Engines

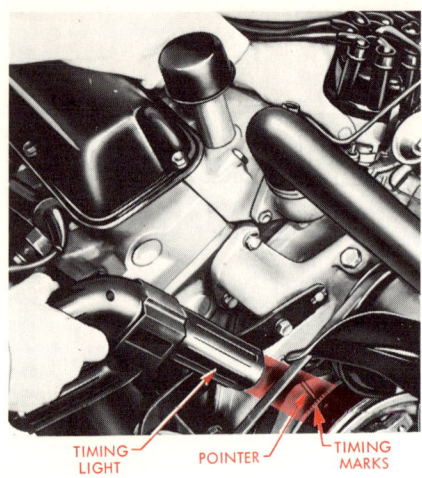

Fig. 13-9. Setting ignition timing. (Ford Div., Ford Motor Co.)

advance unit must be disconnected and plugged on the engine side before setting initial timing. Always set the timing after the contact point gap or dwell has been set to specifications. Make sure the engine is idling or very near to the specified idle speed. Many times timing is set incorrectly because the engine was not idling at the hot idle specifications.

Start the engine and operate at a slow idle. Aim the timing light directly at the timing mark pointer. The timing flash should occur at the instant the chalk mark directly faces the pointer, Fig. 13-9. If not, loosen the distributor clamp bolt and rotate the distributor clockwise or counterclockwise until the correct setting is obtained. Tighten the distributor clamp bolt. As engine speed is increased, the timing light should indicate a gradual spark advance if the advance mechanism is operating.

Initial Timing

If the distributor has been removed and the exact position of the rotor shaft is not known when reinstalling, turn the crankshaft to top dead center for No. 1 cylinder. Top dead center can be found by first removing No. 1 spark plug. Place a thumb over the spark plug hole. Be sure to keep fingers out of the spark plug holes. Slowly turn the crankshaft until compression can be felt against the thumb. Continue turning the crankshaft until the TDC timing mark lines up with the timing mark pointer.

Install the distributor on the engine with the rotor pointing toward the No. 1 spark plug cable when the distributor cap is in

Ignition System Service

place. Rotate the distributor until the points are just ready to open. The engine is now ready to fire No. 1 cylinder. If the spark plug cables have been removed, install them in correct firing order in the direction of rotor rotation.

The timing should be reset by using a timing light after the engine is started.

Checking On Your Knowledge

The following questions give you the opportunity to check up on yourself. If you have read the chapter carefully, you should be able to answer the questions. If you have any difficulty, read the chapter over once more so that you have the information well in mind before you go on with your reading.

DO YOU KNOW

1. Why is it logical that a tune-up operation be performed on an engine every 15,000 miles?

2. How can you determine if failure of the vehicle to start is due to trouble in the ignition system?

3. What distance should a normal spark jump from the end of the spark plug wire to ground?

4. What type of test is used to determine if a connection is loose or dirty?

5. Why should the spark plug electrodes be filed?

6. Why is it important that the ignition contact points be properly aligned?

7. What is the importance of having the ignition contact points properly spaced?

8. How do you check and set contact gap spacing when the engine is not running?

9. How would you adjust the contact points when the engine is running?

10. How do you change the advance pattern setting of the centrifugal advance mechanism?

11. What are the characteristics of an engine when the ignition timing is advanced too much? retarded too much?

12. How is the initial timing set when the engine is running?

Appendix A
English and Metric Measuring Systems

Two major systems of measurement are in use throughout the world: the English system and the metric system. The English system of measurement is the accepted standard of measurement used by American and British industry. In this system, the inch, the foot (12 inches), and the yard (36 inches) are the common units of linear measurement. These units may be further divided into smaller units by means of decimals or fractions.

The metric system, used in many countries, is based entirely upon multiples of ten. The units used in the metric system are divisions of, or multiples of, the meter. The meter is 39.37 inches in length. The millimeter is 0.03937 inches in length.

The automotive mechanic should be familiar with both systems so that he can service foreign-made vehicles with specifications given in metric measurement.

Common Fractional Divisions

The fractional divisions of an inch are obtained by dividing the inch into equal parts. The common divisions are halves, quarters, eighths, sixteenths, thirty-seconds, and sixty-fourths, Fig. A-1. The divisions are commonly expressed as one-half inch, one-quarter inch, one-eighth inch, one-sixteenth inch, one-thirty-second inch, and one-sixty-fourth inch.

Decimal Divisions

In the decimal system, the inch is divided into tenths, hundredths, thousandths, and ten-thousandths. Thus, $\frac{1}{2}$ inch is equal to five hun-

English and Metric Measuring Systems

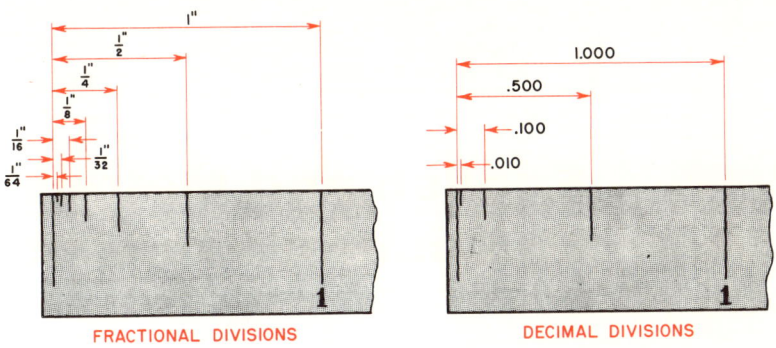

Fig. A-1. Fractional and decimal systems of dividing the inch.

dred one-thousandths, Fig. A-1, and is written as 0.500; ⅛ is equal to one hundred twenty-five one-thousandths and is written as 0.125. Decimal equivalent charts, such as illustrated in Table A-1, simplify the conversion of common equivalents.

The cumbersomeness of the English system of measurement has, to an extent, been reduced by manufacturers who have substituted decimal equivalents for fractions of inches. Table A-1 shows the decimal equivalent of various fractional portions of one inch as well as the equivalent millimeter.

Conversion Tables

Distance, area, weight, and liquid and dry measures each have two ways of being expressed. Also, heat and temperature each have two ways of being expressed. The English system is in most cases more cumbersome, and for this reason most scientists and engineers use the metric system in establishing formulas or in expounding their theories.

The mechanic can convert English measurements to metric and metric, to English by using the following instructions and Tables A-2 and A-3.

Table A-2 lists factors for converting units from metric to English, while Table A-3 lists factors for converting from English to metric units.

To convert a quantity from *metric* to *English* units:

1. Multiply by the factor shown in Table A-2.
2. Round off the result to the precision required.

To convert a quantity from *English* to *metric* units:

1. If the English measurement is expressed in fractional form,

Automotive Engines

TABLE A-1 DECIMAL EQUIVALENTS

Inches in Fractions	Equivalent Inches in Decimals	Equivalent in Millimeters
1/64	0.015625	.39675
1/32	0.03125	.79350
3/64	0.046875	1.19025
1/16	0.0625	1.587
5/64	0.078125	1.98375
3/32	0.90375	2.38050
7/64	0.109375	2.77725
1/8	0.125	3.175
9/64	0.140625	3.57175
5/32	0.15625	3.96850
11/64	0.171875	4.36525
3/16	0.1875	4.762
13/64	0.203125	5.15875
7/32	0.21875	5.5555
15/64	0.234375	5.95225
1/4	0.250	6.350
17/64	0.265625	6.74675
9/32	0.28125	7.14350
19/64	0.296875	7.54025
5/16	0.3125	7.937
21/64	0.328125	8.33375
11/32	0.34375	8.73050
23/64	0.359375	9.12725
3/8	0.375	9.525
25/64	0.390625	9.92175
13/32	0.40625	10.3185
27/64	0.421875	10.71525
7/16	0.4375	11.112
29/64	0.453125	11.50875
15/32	0.46875	11.9055
31/64	0.484375	12.30225
1/2	0.500	12.700
33/64	0.515625	12.09675
17/32	0.53125	13.49350
35/64	0.546875	13.89025
9/16	0.5625	14.287
37/64	0.578125	14.68375
19/32	0.59375	15.0805
39/64	0.609375	15.47725
5/8	0.625	15.875
41/64	0.640625	16.27175
21/32	0.65625	16.6685
43/64	0.671875	17.06525
11/16	0.6875	17.462
45/64	0.703125	17.85875
23/32	0.71875	18.2555
47/64	0.734375	18.65225
3/4	0.750	19.050
49/64	0.765625	19.44675
25/32	0.78125	19.8435
51/64	0.796875	20.24025
13/16	0.8125	20.637
53/64	0.828125	21.03375
27/32	0.84375	21.43050
55/64	0.859375	21.82725
7/8	0.875	22.225
57/64	0.890625	22.62175
29/32	0.90625	23.01850
59/64	0.921875	23.41525
15/16	0.9375	23.812
61/64	0.953125	24.20875
31/32	0.96875	24.6055
63/64	0.984375	25.00225

English and Metric Measuring Systems

TABLE A-2 CONVERSION OF METRIC TO ENGLISH UNITS

LENGTHS:		WEIGHTS:	
1 MILLIMETER (MM)	= 0.03937 IN.	1 GRAM (G)	= 0.03527 OZ (AVDP)
1 CENTIMETER (CM)	= 0.3937 IN.	1 KILOGRAM (KG)	= 2.205 LBS
1 METER (M)	= 3.281 FT OR 1.0937 YDS	1 METRIC TON	= 2205 LBS
1 KILOMETER (KM)	= 0.6214 MILES	LIQUID MEASUREMENTS:	
AREAS:		1 CU CENTIMETER (CC)	= 0.06102 CU IN.
1 SQ MILLIMETER	= 0.00155 SQ IN.	1 LITER (= 1000 CC)	= 1.057 QUARTS OR 2.113 PINTS OR 61.02 CU INS.
1 SQ CENTIMETER	= 0.155 SQ IN.	POWER MEASUREMENTS:	
1 SQ METER	= 10.76 SQ FT OR 1.196 SQ YDS	1 KILOWATT (KW)	= 1.341 HORSEPOWER
VOLUMES:		TEMPERATURE MEASUREMENTS:	
1 CU CENTIMETER	= 0.06102 CU IN.	TO CONVERT DEGREES CENTIGRADE TO DEGREES FARENHEIT, USE THE FOLLOWING FORMULA: DEG F = (DEG C X 9/5) + 32	
1 CU METER	= 35.31 CU FT OR 1.308 CU YDS		

SOME IMPORTANT FEATURES OF THE CGS SYSTEM ARE:
1 CC OF PURE WATER = 1 GRAM. PURE WATER FREEZES AT 0 DEGREES C AND BOILS AT 100 DEGREES C.

TABLE A-3 CONVERSION OF ENGLISH TO METRIC UNITS

LENGTHS:		WEIGHTS:	
1 INCH	= 2.540 CENTIMETERS	1 OUNCE (AVDP)	= 28.35 GRAMS
1 FOOT	= 30.48 CENTIMETERS	1 POUND	= 453.6 GRAMS OR 0.4536 KILOGRAM
1 YARD	= 91.44 CENTIMETERS OR 0.9144 METERS	1 (SHORT) TON	= 907.2 KILOGRAMS
1 MILE	= 1.609 KILOMETERS	LIQUID MEASUREMENTS:	
AREAS:		1 (FLUID) OUNCE	= 0.02957 LITER OR 28.35 GRAMS
1 SQ IN.	= 6.452 SQ CENTIMETERS	1 PINT	= 473.2 CU CENTIMETERS
1 SQ FT	= 929.0 SQ CENTIMETERS OR 0.0929 SQ METER	1 QUART	= 0.9463 LITER
1 SQ YD	= 0.8361 SQ METER	1 (US) GALLON	= 3785 CU CENTIMETERS OR 3.785 LITERS
VOLUMES:		POWER MEASUREMENTS:	
1 CU IN.	= 16.39 CU CENTIMETERS	1 HORSEPOWER	= 0.7457 KILOWATT
1 CU FT	= 0.02832 CU METER	TEMPERATURE MEASUREMENTS:	
1 CU YD	= 0.7646 CU METER	TO CONVERT DEGREES FARENHEIT TO DEGREES CENTIGRADE, USE THE FOLLOWING FORMULA: DEG C = (DEG F X 5/9) -32	

TABLE A-4 CONVERSION TABLE - TEMPERATURE

Degrees Fahrenheit		Degrees Centigrade
−459.4°	absolute zero	−273°
409		250
373		225
328		200
283		175
238		150
211		125
148		100
103		75
58		50
32		25.6
0.4		18
+ 32	water freezes	0
77		+ 25
98.6	body temperature	37
122		50
167		75
212	water boils	100
257		125
302		150
347		175
392		200
437		225
482		250
527		275
572		300

To convert from degrees Centigrade to Fahrenheit, use the following equation: $F = \frac{9}{5} C + 32$

To convert from degrees Fahrenheit to Centigrade, use the following equation: $C = \frac{5}{9}(F-32)$

change this to an equivalent decimal form (Table A-1).
2. Multiply this quantity by the factor shown in Table A-3.
3. Round off the result to the precision required.

Relatively small measurements, such as 17.3 cm, are generally expressed in equivalent millimeter form. In this example the measurement would be read as 173 mm.

Heat Units. The English and metric systems employ different units for measuring heat.

In the English system, the unit of heat measurement is the British Thermal Unit or BTU. The BTU represents the quantity of heat required to raise the temperature of one pound of water one degree Fahrenheit.

In the metric system, the unit used for the measurement of heat is the calorie. A calorie is the amount of heat necessary to increase the temperature of one gram of water by one degree Centigrade.

1 BTU = 0.252 kilogram calorie
1 BTU = 252.0 calories
1 kilogram calorie = 3.968 BTU
1 calorie = 0.003968 BTU

Table A-4 can be used to compare Fahrenheit to Centigrade.

Angular Measurements

Appendix

The standard unit of angular measurement is the degree, or $\frac{1}{360}$ of a complete circle. In order to obtain more accurate measurements, the degree is divided into 60 minutes and each minute into 60 seconds. Degrees are designated by (°), minutes by ('), and seconds by ("). Thus an angle of 45 degrees, 30 minutes, 12 seconds is written as 45° 30′ 12″. Fig. B-1 illustrates a circle divided into degrees, each of the smallest divisions being one degree.

On automotive engines, the valve timing and ignition timing specifications are usually given in degrees, and the flywheel or vibration damper often have degree marks stamped at the proper location to permit accurate ignition timing.

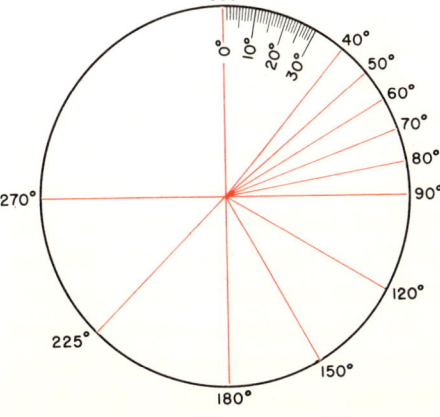

Fig. B-1. A circle shown with divisions for angular measurement.

Appendix C

Micrometers

The micrometer is a precision measuring tool capable of making measurements accurately to one-thousandth (0.001) of an inch, Fig. C-1 (top). The mechanic uses the micrometer chiefly for measuring the size of engine parts so that the amount of wear and clearance can be determined. The temperature of the parts being measured should be approximately 70° F if accurate comparative readings are to be obtained.

The skilled mechanic often uses the sense of sight to estimate measurements finer than the graduations on the tool he is using. For example, on the ordinary micrometer caliper graduated to measure in thousandths of an inch, it is possible to subdivide the 0.001 in. graduations on the thimble into fractions such as ½, ¼, etc.

How to Use the Micrometer Caliper

When measuring, a micrometer should be held lightly in the hand so that the fingers are used to make the necessary adjustments. The sense of touch is greatly reduced if the tool is grasped too firmly.

The part to be measured is placed between the anvil and the spindle, and the thimble is turned until the spindle tightens slightly on the part being measured. The size of the part is read from the graduations on the hub (sometimes called "sleeve") and the thimble.

One turn of the thimble moves the spindle in or out only $\frac{1}{40}$, or 0.025 in. The hub of the micrometer caliper is graduated and has a reference line running through the graduations. Each division on the hub represents one turn of the

Micrometers

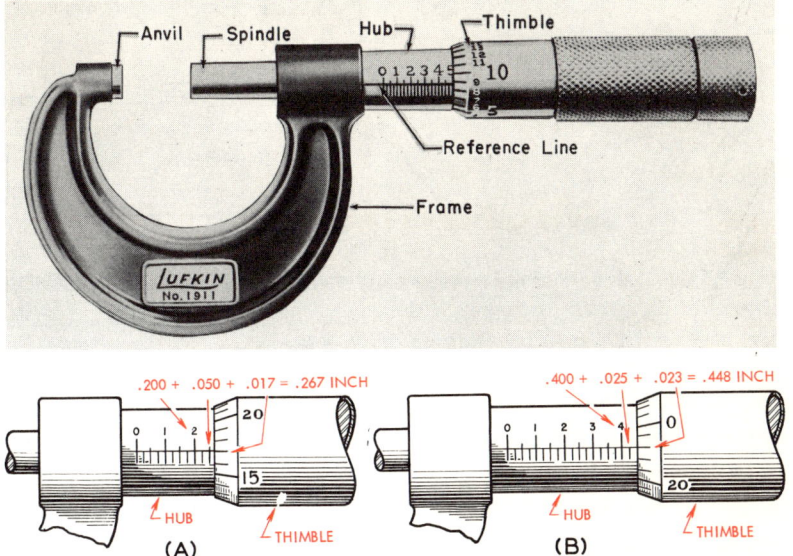

Fig. C-1. A micrometer caliper (top) with some sample readings (bottom).

thimble, or 0.025 in. Every fourth line on the hub is numbered and represents one-tenth of an inch. Thus the numbers 1, 2, 3, etc., indicate 100, 200, and 300 one-thousandths of an inch.

The micrometer caliper is read by noting the figure visible farthest to the right on the hub. This figure indicates the number of hundred one-thousandths of an inch. Add to this the amount represented by the visible graduations beyond this figure (obtained by multiplying the number of graduations by 0.025 inch), and the number of divisions on the bevel edge of the thimble at the reference line. Thus, the micrometer caliper reading in Fig. C-1A is 0.200 + 0.050 + 0.017 = 0.267 in.; in Fig. C-1B the reading is 0.400 + 0.025 + 0.023 = 0.448 in.

One-inch micrometer calipers have an adjustable measuring range of only one inch. Measurements of more than one inch are made with micrometer calipers capable of measuring from one to two inches, two to three inches, three to four inches, etc. One type of micrometer caliper in use has only a single frame with removable anvils. This micrometer caliper set includes several anvils, each anvil differing in length by one inch. By installing anvils of different lengths in the micrometer caliper frame, measurements varying from zero to five inches can be obtained.

Automotive Engines

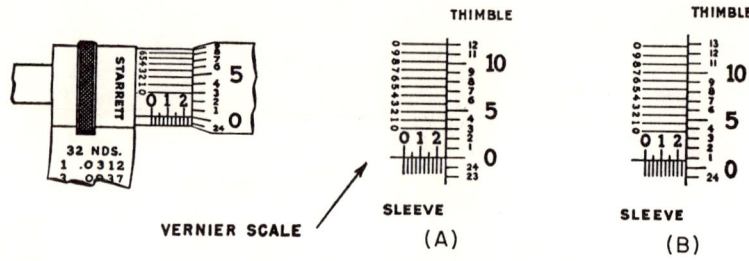

Fig. C-2. Vernier micrometer caliper scale. (L. S. Starret Co.)

Vernier Scale. Vernier micrometer calipers enable the mechanic to measure accurately to one ten-thousandth of an inch (0.0001). The vernier micrometer caliper is similar in construction to other micrometer calipers with the exception that it has a vernier scale consisting of ten divisions marked on the sleeve (or "hub") of the micrometer caliper, Fig. C-2. The ten vernier divisions on the sleeve occupy the same space as nine divisions on the bevel edge of the thimble. Thus the difference between the width of one of the ten vernier spaces on the sleeve and one of the spaces on the thimble is one-tenth of one of the spaces on the thimble. Since each space on the thimble is equal to one-thousandth of an inch (0.001), one-tenth of the space is one ten-thousandth of an inch (0.0001).

In making measurements with a vernier micrometer caliper, first read to thousandths as with a regular micrometer caliper. Then see which of the vernier markings coincides with a line on the thimble. Add to the previous reading the number of ten-thousandths indicated by the vernier line on the sleeve that coincides with the line on the thimble. In Fig. C-2A, the zero on the thimble coincides with the reference line on the sleeve, and the vernier zero line on the sleeve coincides with a line on the thimble. Thus the reading is an even 0.2500 in. In Fig. C-2B, the zero line on the thimble has been moved beyond the reference line on the sleeve and indicates a reading greater than 0.2500 in. but less than 0.2510 in. Examination of the vernier scale shows that the seventh vernier line on the sleeve coincides with a line on the thimble, giving a true micrometer reading of 0.2507 in.

Engine Power Measurements

Appendix

Piston Displacement

Piston displacement refers to the amount of space through which the top surface of the piston passes when the piston moves from bottom dead center to top dead center, Fig. D-1. The total piston displacement of an engine is the displacement of one cylinder multiplied by the number of cylinders, and can be found mathematically if the bore, stroke, and number of cylinders are known.

EXAMPLE:

(a) Divide the size of the bore (diameter of the cylinder) by 2 to determine the radius of the cylinder.

(b) Square the radius (multiply it by itself).

(c) Multiply the square of the radius by *pi* (3.1416) to determine

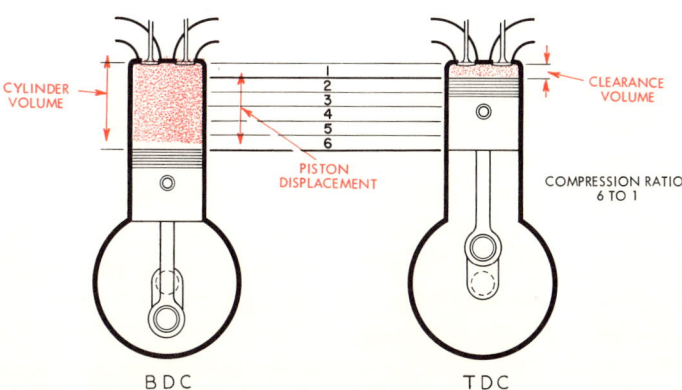

Fig. D-1. Relationship between piston displacement, compression ratio, and cylinder volume.

the area of the cylinder cross section.

(d) Multiply this product (area) by the length of the stroke.

(e) Multiply this product by the number of cylinders.

This could be shown simply by the following equation:

$$R^2 \times \pi = \text{area. Area} \times \text{stroke} \times \text{cylinders} = \text{displacement.}$$

This would be read as radius squared times *pi* times the stroke times the number of cylinders equals displacement.

To find the displacement of a V-8 engine having 4.001″ bore, 3.25″ stroke, the problem would appear as:

$$\left(\frac{4.001}{2}\right)^2 = 4.002'' \times 3.1416 \times 3.250'' \times 8$$
$$= 327 \text{ cubic inches}$$

The fractions of an inch have been dropped in the above answer.

Other things being equal, the greater the piston displacement the more air-fuel mixture can be taken into the cylinders, so that more power is possible.

Compression Ratio

The compression ratio of an engine is the ratio of the total volume of the cylinder with the piston at bottom dead center (piston displacement plus clearance volume) to the volume of the combustion chamber when the piston is at top dead center (clearance volume). Fig. D-1 illustrates the relationship between piston displacement, clearance volume, and compression ratio. Compression ratio may also be expressed as the total volume of the cylinder divided by the clearance volume.

EXAMPLE: To find the compression ratio of an engine, divide the total volume of a cylinder by its clearance volume.

This could be shown simply by the following equation:

$$\frac{\text{total volume}}{\text{clearance volume}} = \text{compression ratio}$$

To find the compression ratio of a V-8 engine with each piston displacing 40.86 cubic inches and with a clearance volume of 3.99 cubic inches, we would proceed as follows:

$$40.86 + 3.99 = 44.85$$
$$= \text{total cylinder volume}$$

then

$$\frac{44.85}{3.99} = 11.24.$$

Therefore, 11.24 to 1 is the compression ratio.

An increase in the compression ratio results in a higher degree of compression. Combustion occurs at a faster rate because the molecules of the fuel mixture are more closely packed together and the space through which the flame must travel is small. However, compression ratios are limited by the design of the engine, the ignition qualities of the fuels available, detonating or knocking factors, and the availability of high-octane fuels. In gasoline engines, compres-

Engine Power Measurements

sion ratios seldom exceed a ratio of 11.5 to 1. In Diesel engines, compression ratios are as high as 20 to 1.

Horsepower

The horsepower of an engine is measured by the rate at which it can do work. One horsepower is equivalent to lifting 33,000 pounds per foot in a minute.

The horsepower developed by an engine depends upon the pressure exerted on the pistons by the expanding gases and the rate at which the power impulses are applied to the crankshaft.

The horsepower that an engine develops can be measured by several methods.

SAE Horsepower. A simple formula approved by the Society of Automotive Engineers for determining horsepower is sometimes used for licensing purposes. Although the formula does not give an accurate indication of the actual horsepower developed, it does provide a simple method of comparing engines according to their displacement.

$$\text{Horsepower} = \frac{(\text{bore of cylinder})^2 \times \text{number of cylinders}}{2.5}$$

EXAMPLE: To find the horsepower of a V-8 engine for licensing purposes with a bore of 4.001 in., you would proceed as follows:

Bore = 4.001 in.

$$\text{Horsepower} = \frac{(4.001)^2 \times 8}{2.5} = 51.2$$

Note that this formula does not consider factors such as length of stroke, RPM, etc.

Brake Horsepower. The brake horsepower of an engine is the actual horsepower delivered by the crankshaft and can be measured by means of an electric dynamometer, Fig. D-2. Tests are performed on an electric dynamometer using only essential engine driven equipment. The fan, air cleaner, alternator, and exhaust system are removed. The term "brake horsepower" (gross horsepower) has been used over the years by the

Fig. D-2. An engine undergoing an electric dynamometer test. (Chrysler Corp.)

various manufacturers to indicate maximum engine capability.

Electric Dynamometer. The dynamometer is actually an electric generator which produces current when driven by the engine whose horsepower is being tested. The output of the generator is a measure of the horsepower the engine is developing while undergoing the test, Fig. D-2. The current developed may be absorbed through suitable resistances or may be used for lighting and other uses. The output produced by the generator is known as the electric horsepower and is always less than the horsepower of the engine that drives it, due to friction in the generator and other losses. Knowing the efficiency of the generator, the electric horsepower of the generator can readily be converted into actual brake horsepower developed by the engine.

Net Horsepower. The present trend is to list the "net" or "as-installed" horsepower rating which represents the actual performance of the engine in an automobile with the fan, air cleaner, exhaust system, alternator, etc., installed and functioning.

Hydraulic Dynamometer. A "drive-on" type of hydraulic dynamometer is used in many service establishments to check engine efficiency, vehicle performance, and road horsepower without removing the engine. Engine output is measured through driven rollers.

The rear wheels of the vehicle are driven onto a roller assembly, usually located in the floor. Engine torque is applied to the wheels which revolve the rollers. The rollers are connected to a power absorption unit. The absorption unit dissipates power by controlling a flow of water within a rotor and stator assembly. Resistance (load) is created according to the flow of water through the assembly.

Often the roller assemblies are connected to large electric motors which can be used to drive the wheels for the purposes of testing brakes and the dynamic stability of the vehicle.

Indicated Horsepower. The rate at which work is done by the expanding gases in pushing the piston downward is known as the indicated horsepower. The indicated horsepower of an engine is used purely for experimental and laboratory purposes.

The pressures acting on a piston during the power or working stroke are not uniform throughout the stroke. Since the burning of the fuel charge is almost instantaneous, it results in high pressures at the top of the stroke and decreasing pressures as the piston moves downward. Through a device attached to the engine, the actual pressures in the engine cylinder at all points of the cycle are

Engine Power Measurements

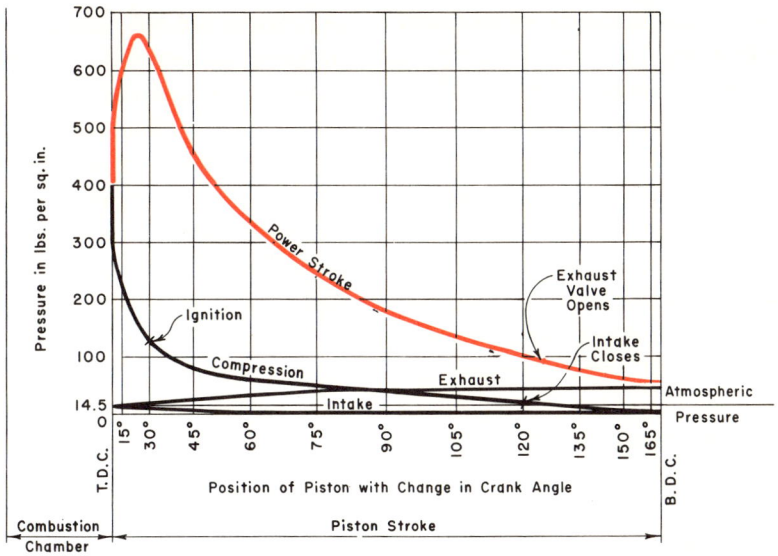

Fig. D-3. An indicator diagram showing the varying pressures within a cylinder during the different piston strokes. The diagram is used to determine an average or mean effective pressure which is used to find the indicated horsepower of an engine.

recorded on an indicator card, Fig. D-3. From the data on the card an average or mean effective pressure within the cylinder is determined.

The mean effective pressure is the average of the pressures exerted on the piston during the power stroke minus the average of opposing pressures encountered on the intake, compression, and exhaust strokes. If the mean effective pressure could be substituted for the actual varying pressures in a cylinder, it would produce the same amount of work.

Indicated horsepower can be determined by means of the following formula:

$$\text{Indicated Horsepower} = \frac{\text{PLANK}}{33{,}000}$$

The letters in the formula stand for the following:

P = mean effective pressure in pounds per sq. in.
L = length of stroke in feet
A = area of cylinder cross section in sq. in.
N = number of power strokes per minute, or $\left(\frac{\text{RPM}}{2}\right)$
K = number of cylinders

The indicated horsepower of an engine is always higher than the actual brake horsepower developed by the engine as it does not take into consideration the power necessary to overcome the friction of the engine. The indicated horsepower is obtained by adding the friction losses to the brake horsepower.

Engine Torque

The pressure developed in the cylinders by the combustion of the fuel charge exerts a pushing force on the piston. This force is transmitted to the crankshaft by the connecting rod. This pressure or power impulse acts through the crank arm to develop a torque or turning force at the crankshaft. The amount of torque developed depends upon the pressure exerted on the pistons and the length of the crank arm. Torque is measured in pounds-feet. Thus, a pushing force of one pound exerted a distance of one foot from the center of a shaft exerts a torque of one pound-foot.

A torque curve is shown in Fig. D-4. The torque developed by this particular engine increases as the engine speed increases up to approximately 2200 RPM, and then decreases as the engine speed continues to increase. The RPM at which the maximum torque is ob-

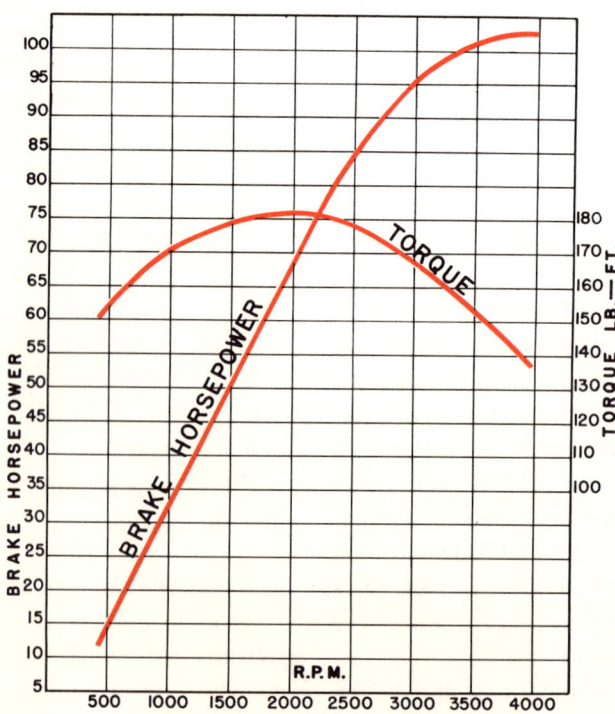

Fig. D-4. The relationship between torque, RPM, and horsepower during the operation of a particular engine.

Engine Power Measurements

tained is determined by engine design. The increase in the torque developed is due to the throttle valve opening and permitting a greater amount of fuel charge to enter the cylinders. As the engine speed increases, less torque or pushing effort is exerted on the pistons because less fuel charge can enter the cylinders at high engine speed.

Engine Efficiency

The efficiency of any engine is determined by the relationship between the results obtained and the energy expended to produce such results. While we think of the modern internal-combustion engine as being an efficient mechanism, actually its efficiency in some respects is quite low. Efficiency is commonly measured as (1) mechanical efficiency, (2) thermal or heat efficiency, and (3) volumetric efficiency.

Mechanical Efficiency. The mechanical efficiency of an engine is the ratio of the power actually delivered by the crankshaft (brake horsepower) to the power developed within the cylinders of the engine (indicated horsepower) at the same RPM. The power delivered at the crankshaft is always less than that developed within the cylinders, because some of the power is expended in overcoming the friction of the moving engine parts.

The mechanical efficiency of an engine can be found by the following formula:

$$\text{Mechanical Efficiency} = \frac{\text{brake horsepower}}{\text{indicated horsepower}}$$

The mechanical efficiency of an internal-combustion engine is approximately 90 percent.

Thermal Efficiency. The thermal or heat efficiency of an engine is

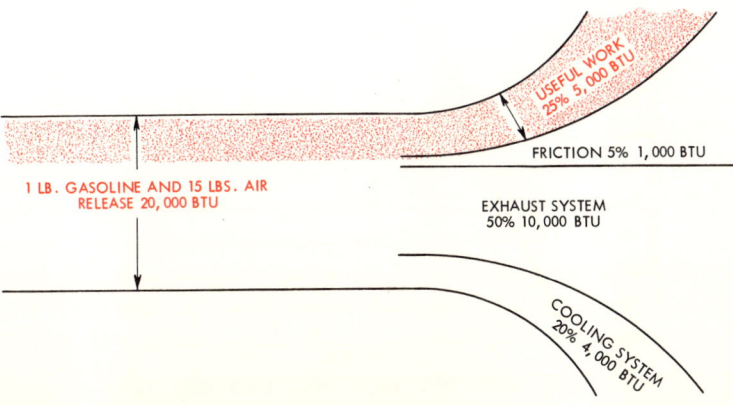

Fig. D-5. Heat loss and utilization in a typical gasoline engine. A BTU is a British Thermal Unit. (See Appendix A.)

the ratio of work done to the energy contained in the fuel. Thermal efficiency is expressed as a percentage and can be computed as follows:

$$\text{Thermal Efficiency} = \frac{\text{brake horsepower} \times 33{,}000}{\text{wt. of fuel used per min.} \times \text{heat value} \times .778}$$

If an engine could convert all the heat developed by the combustion of fuel in the cylinders into useful work, its thermal efficiency would be 100 percent. Actually, the thermal efficiency of modern engines is about 25 percent. Fig. D-5 illustrates a heat-balance diagram showing where the heat energy in gasoline goes.

The cooling system dissipates about 20 percent of the heat energy developed in the engine. Approximately 50 percent is lost through the exhaust system. Losses in overcoming friction account for about 5 percent of the total, leaving a balance of about 25 percent that is actually converted into useful work.

Volumetric Efficiency. The volumetric efficiency of an engine is the ratio of the air-fuel mixture that enters the cylinders compared to the total piston displacement of the engine. The volumetric efficiency of engines is expressed in terms of percentages and can be computed as follows:

$$\text{Volumetric Efficiency} = \frac{\text{vol. of charge at atm. temp. and pressure}}{\text{piston displacement}}$$

It must be realized that a given mass (weight) of air-fuel mixture occupies different volumes under different conditions of atmospheric pressure and temperature. In determining volumetric efficiency, a comparison must be made with the volume the mass of air-fuel charge would occupy under particular conditions, such as standard atmospheric pressure and temperature.

The volumetric efficiency of modern internal-combustion engines is usually less than 100 percent.

Index

A

Accelerator pump, carburetor, 376-379, 419
 adjustment, 436-438
Accuracy, cylinder finishing, 80
Acid
 battery, 10, 15
 compounds in oil, 282
 sulfuric, 335
Additives, gasoline, 338
Adhesion, oil, 259-260
Adjustable valve lifter, 216
Adjustments, carburetor, 428-443
 fan belt, 253
 timing belt, 215
 valve lifter, 221-224
 valve stem, 198
Advance, ignition distributor, 290, 293, 452-456, 481
Agent, wetting, 38
Air-bleed, carburetor, 369-370
Air cleaner, 345-347
 thermostatically controlled, 305-311
Air cooling, engine, 74, 170, 227-228
Air-fuel mixture, 49, 68, 169, 282, 326, 330-331, 364-365, 445
Air horn, carburetor, 363, 426-427
Air induction system, 311-317
Alcohol, 247, 248, 326, 340
Alignment
 connecting rod, 161-163
 piston and connecting rod, 151
Alloy steel piston pins, 126
Altitude compensator, 282
Aluminum, 79
 alloy pistons, 123-124
 camshaft gear, 186
 cast, 76
 cylinder block, 85
 cylinder head, 172
Ambient temperature, 228, 241
Analyzer, combustion, 420-421
Angular measurement, 489
Anodic treatment, piston, 124
Antifreeze solutions, 247-248
Antifriction metals, 93
Anti-icers, 338
Anti-icing, carburetor, 385
Antioxidant inhibitors, 338
Anti-percolator, carburetor, 338-386
 adjustment, 440
Arbor press, 108
Arrestor, flame, 286
Artificial gas, 326, 340
Assembly of
 carburetor, 427
 connecting rod to piston, 163-164
 piston to connecting rod, 163-168
 rocker arms, 220
Atmosphere, 44
Automatic choke, 380-383
 adjustment 430, 431

B

Babbitt, 138
Backlash, camshaft gear, 212
Baffles
 engine compartment cooling, 243-245
 gas tank, 341

Balance, flywheel, 95
Base-emitter resistor, 467
Battery, 10
Battery acid, 10, 15
BDC (bottom dead center), 51, 52, 53, 54
Bearing
  camshaft, 184, 210-211
  crankpin, 154-155
  "crush", 139
  engine, 48
  main, 85
  thrust, 86
Bell-mouthing, connecting rod, 158
Belt driven camshaft, 60, 184, 187-188
Belt, fan, 237
  adjusting tension, 253
Belt, timing, 187-188
  adjustment, 215
Bent connecting rod, 161-162
Benzol, 326
Beveled piston rings, 165
Bimetal, coil and/or strip, 240, 242
Blade type thickness gage, 32
Block, cylinder, 45, 75-85
  flushing, 250
Blower, flywheel, 228
Blower, Roots type, 73
Boiling point, coolant, 228
Bolt-on camshaft gear, replacing, 212
Bolts, 33
Booster, fuel pump, 357
Boring, cylinder, 80
Boss, piston, 46
  offset, 121

Bottom dead center (BCD), 51, 52, 53, 54
Bowl, fuel, 366
Box wrenches, 23-24
Brake horsepower, 495-496
British Thermal Units (BTU), 339, 488
BTU, (see above)
Burning, valves, 226
Burns, treatment of, 14
Bushing, connecting rod, 137
  replacing, 160-161
Bushing, piston pin, 137
Butane, 326, 339
Bypass, water pump, 236

C

Caliper, micrometer, 29-31, 490-492
Cam profile, 183
Camshaft, 48, 60, 79, 83, 85, 183-188, 208
  bearings, 210-211
  belt driven, 60
  chain driven, 60
  lobe lift, 209-210
  replacing bolt-on gear, 212
Canister, vapor emission, 324
Capacitor, ignition, 450-451, 466-467, 476-477
Capacity test, fuel pump, 410
Cap, distributor, 452
Cap, radiator, 9
Carbon
  dioxide, 331
  in oil, 264
  knock, 332
  monoxide, 331

Carburetors, 8
  compound type, 401-403
  flooding, 415-416
  fundamentals, 362
  multiple, 401-403
  systems, 365-383
CAS (Cleaner Air System), 291
Cast aluminum, 76
Cast gray iron, 97
Casting, cylinder block, 76-79
Cast-iron cylinder head, 172
Cast main bearings, 115
Catalyst, 329
Catalytic converter, 173-281
CCS (Controlled Combustion System), 290
CEC (Combustion Emission Control System), 303-304
Cellular type, radiator, 235
Centrifugal advance, ignition, 453-454
CFR (Cooperative Fuel Research Committee) 336
Chain driven camshaft, 60, 186-187
Chain, timing, 186, 187, 213-214
Chamber, combustion, 169
Cheek, thrust, 94
Chemicals, 9
  in fuel, 335
Chisels, 19
Choke, 379-383
  adjustment, 430-431
  automatic, 380-383
  faulty action, 415-416
  unloader adjustment, 441-442

Index

Chromium, 76
Circuit
  primary, 447-448, 459-461
  secondary, 448, 461
Cleaner Air System (CAS), 291-292
Cleaning
  carburetor, 422-423, 427
  cooling system, 250-252
  crankshaft, 106
  cylinder block, 99
  cylinder bores, 106
  emulsion, 39-40
  oil pump, 276
  parts, 37-42
  piston and connecting rod, 141-142
  solutions, 38-39
  solvent, 40-42
  steam, 37-38
  water pressure, 38-40, 42
Cleanliness, 14
Clearance
  camshaft gear, 212
  connecting rod, 139, 150-155
  cylinder and piston, 145-147
  main bearing, 94-95
  piston, 123, 124-125
  rocker arm shaft, 219
  thrust surface on piston, 125
  valve stem, 198, 221-224
"Cling", oil and grease, 39
Clutch, 85
  throwout lever, 117
  thrust load, 94
"Cocked", piston, 161-162
Cohesion, oil, 259-260
Coil, ignition, 448-449, 476-477
Cold start relay, 468
Collapsed piston skirt, 144-145
Collar, thrust, 94
Combination Emission Control System (CEC), 303-304
Combustion, 45
  analyzer, 420-421
  chamber, 169
  gasoline, 330
  spontaneous, 10
Combustor, turbine, 69
Components
  fuel system, 340-360
  ignition system, 448-458
Compound carburetion, 401-403
Compression, Diesel engine, 71-72
Compression piston rings, 126-135
Compression ratio, 494-495
Compression stroke, 51, 52, 53, 54, 82
  in Wankel engine, 67-68
Compressor, piston ring, 166
Compressor, turbine, 69
Concentric piston rings, 128
Conductivity, heat, 76
Connecting rod, 46, 47, 79, 85
  assembling to piston, 163-164
  assembly, 127
  bearing materials, 137-139
  bearings, 87, 136-139
  bushing replacement, 160-161
  bushings, 137
  construction, 135-137
  deflection, 135
  inspection, 151
  installation, 136-137
  out-of-round, 151
  reboring, 155
  side clearance, 95
  straightening, 163
Construction
  connecting rod, 135-137
  cylinder block, 75-85
  cylinder head, 169-173
Contact points, ignition, 468
Contamination, oil, 262-265
Control amplifier, electronic, 301
Controlled Combustion System (CCS) 289-290
Control valve, heat, 351-353
Conversions, English to metric, 485-488
Conversions, metric to English, 485-488
Conversion tables, 485-488
  fraction-decimal, 486
Converter, catalytic, thermal, 173
Cooling
  air, 74
  engine, 79
  fins, 79
  liquid, 74
  methods, 74, 226-229
  valve, 182-183
Cooling system
  cleaning, 250-252
  deposits, 249-250
  parts of, 229-245
  pressure type, 245-247
  types, 226-229
Cooperative Fuel Re-

search Committee (CFR), 336
Core
  radiator, 232
  sand, 79
Corrosion, in cooling system, 249
Cotter pins, 34
Counterbalances, crankshaft, 86, 93
Counterbore, valve seat, 203
Counterweights, crankshaft, 86, 93
Cowling, 228
Cracked valve seat, 200
Crankarm, 46, 86
  arrangement, 64-65
Crankcase, 48, 83
Crankpins, 85-86
  bearing sizes, 154-155
  fillet, 139
  out-of-round, 154
Crankshaft, 46, 48, 79, 83, 85-93
  balance, 92, 93
  cleaning, 106
  counterweights, 86
  endplay, 94
  flange dowels, 95
  gear, replacing, 213
  heat treating, 86
  in-line, 56-57
  insert main bearing, 95, 110
  machining, 86
  oil passages, 86
  reground, 95
  thrust cheek or collar, 94
  Wankel engine, 66-67
Crankshaft types
  four-cyclinder in-line, 87
  six-cylinder in-line, 87-88
  V-type eight cylinder, 90, 91, 92
  V-type six cylinder, 89, 90
Crossflow radiator, 232, 235
Crude oil, 327
"Crush", bearing, 139
Cutting tools, 25-26
Cylinder, 43
Cylinder and piston clearance, 145-147
Cylinder block, 45
  aluminum, 85
  heat treating, 79
  lower, 83, 84
  machining, 79
  material, 76
  seasoning, 79
  V-type, 79
Cylinder heads, 195-198
  construction, 169-173
  gasket, 173
Cylinders, engine, 49, 52, 53
  arrangement, 55-58
  dry sleeve, 81
  finishing, 80
  individual castings, 79
  installing piston and rod in, 165-168
  liner, 79
  lubrication, 137
  numbering, 92
  number of, 55-58
  out-of-round, 80
  taper, 80, 100-102
  wear, 82-83, 102
  wet sleeve, 81

D

Dashpot, anti-stall, 297
  adjustment, 439-440
Dead center
  bottom (BDC), 54
  top (TDC), 54
Deceleration valve, 289, 291, 292-294
Decimal divisions, 484-485
Deflection
  connecting rod, 135
  crankshaft, 93
Degrees, in angular measurement, 489
Deposits in cooling system, 249-250
Design
  connecting rod, 135-137
  crankshaft, 87
  engine, 55-74
  piston, 120-123
Detonation, 332-334
Diagnosis of carburetor troubles, 419-421
Dial indicator, 108, 206
Diaphragm, fuel pump, 354
Dies, 19-20
Diesel engine, 70-74
  fuel, 339
  fuel injection, 73
  two-stroke cycle, 73-74
"Dieseling", 291, 296, 304
Differences in engine operation, 61-69
Dilution, oil, 263-264
Diode, zener, 466
Dirt in oil, 265
Disassembly, oil pump, 276
Disassembly, piston and connecting rod, 140-141
Displacement, piston, 493-495
Disposable oil filter, 277
Distillation, 327
Distortion, ring, 164
Distributor, ignition,

Index

451-452, 478-481
advance solenoid, 293
advance unit, dual diaphragm, 290
magnetic pulse, 468-469
modulator, 301
retard solenoid, 296
transmission controlled timing, 289
vacuum control valve, 289
vacuum deceleration valve, 289
Diverter valve, 311, 316
Divisions
  decimal, 484-485
  fractional, 484
Double-cut files, 26
Dowels, crankshaft flange, 95
  insert main bearing, 95
Downdraft carburetor, 366
Downflow radiator, 235
Drills, 24-25
Drill sizes, 25
Drive train, 46
Drop, voltage, checking, 475-476
Dry type cylinder sleeves, 81, 82
Dual diaphragm distributor advance unit, 290
Dust in oil, 265
Dynamic crankshaft balance, 93
Dynamometer, electric, 496
  hydraulic, 496

E

Efficiency
  engine, 499-500
  mechanical, 499
  thermal, 499-500
  volumetric, 500
Eight-cylinder engine, 85
  firing order, 65
  in-line engine, 56
  V-type crankarm arrangement, 65
Electric
  dynamometer, 496
  tools, 13
Electrolytic
  action, 40-41
  piston treatment, 124
Electromagnetic fuel gage, 343
Electronic
  control amplifier, 301
  distributor modulator, 301
Element, filter, 283
Emissions
  exhaust tester, 321
  need for controls, 280-282
  reduction, 173
Emulsion cleaning, 39-40
En bloc casting, 76
End clearance
  piston ring, 148, 149, 150
  thrust bearing, 94
Energy, kinetic, 45
Engine
  block material, 76
  cooling, 79
  design differences, 55-74
  Diesel, 70-74
  efficiency, 499-500
  fuels, 69-70
  horsepower, 495-498
  oils, 259-265
  operation differences, 61-69
  power measurements, 493-500
  torque, 498-499
  turbine, 68-69
Engine bearings, 46
English to metric conversions, 485-488
Ethylene glycol, 229, 248
Evaporative Emission Control System, 321
Exhaust, 9
  port, Diesel, 94
  stroke, 50, 52, 53, 54, 67-68
  stroke in Wankel engine, 67-68
  system, 349-353
Exhaust emission tester, 317-321
Exhaust manifold, 49
Expander
  tool, piston ring, 141
  type piston ring, 133-134, 165
Expanding process, piston, 146
Expansion
  gases in cylinder, 43-45
  reamer, 25-26
Extinguishers, fire, 10
Extractors, screw, 21

F

Face, valve, 175
Fan
  belt, 8
  belt tension, 253
  engine cooling, 236-237
  flexible blade, 243
  fluid drive, 237
  pusher type, 237
  service, 241

505

thermal control drive, 238-241
torque control drive, 238
variable speed, 238-241
Fastening devices, 14, 32-36
bolts, 33
cotter pins, 34
keys, 36
lock washers, 34-35
nuts, 33
screws, 33-34
snap rings, 36
splines, 36
studs, 33
Fast idle, carburetor, 384-385
adjustment, 440-441
Feeler gage, inspecting rod clearance with, 151, 153
F-head engine, 171
four-cylinder, in-line, 62
valve arrangement, 60, 62
Files, 26-27
Filler cap, pressurized, 246
Fillet, crankpin, 139
Filter, fuel, 343-344
service, 407-408
Filter, oil, 271-274, 277
filler cap, 283-288
replacement, 277-278
Finishing, cylinder, 80
Fins, cooling, 79
Fire, 9
extinguishers, 10
Firing order, 64-66, 87
eight-cylinder, 65
four-cylinder, 64
six-cylinder, 64
First aid, 14
Fitting

main bearings, 95
piston pins, 157-161
Flame
arrestor, 286
speed, 331-332
Flammable liquids, 10
Float carburetor, 366-369, 393, 427
adjustment, 432-436
stuck float valve, 416
Flooding, carburetor, 415-416
Fluid
coupling replacement, 116
drive fan, 237, 241-243
hydraulic, 11
Flushing
block, 250
radiator, 250, 253-254
Flywheel, 85
damage, 116
timing marks, 95-96
weight, 95
Force feed, oil system, 265
Ford Improved Exhaust Emission Control System (IMCO), 290-291
Foreman, shop, 4
Four-barrel carburetors, 391-401, 403
Four-cylinder engine, 62, 56, 85
crankarm arrangement, 64
crankshaft, 87
F-head, 62
firing order, 64
Four-piece piston rings, 134-135
Four-stroke cycle, 50, 52, 53, 54, 55
compared to two-stroke, 61-64

Diesel engine, 71-73
Fractional divisions, 484
Fractions, petroleum, 327
Friction
fluid, 259
solid, 258
Fuel
knock, 332
tank, 341
tank repair, 406-407
Fuel injection
diesel, 73
gasoline, 403-404
Fuel injector, 282
Fuel lines, 8, 344-345
repair, 409-410
Fuel pump
booster, 357
diaphragm, 354
electric, 357-358
mechanical, 353-356
pusher type, 353
vacuum and mechanical, 357
valves, 355
Fuels, engine, 69-70, 326-340
Full throttle ignition operation, 453
Fumes, 11

G

Gage
"feeler", 151
fuel, 341-343
pressure, 255-256
telescoping, 30-31
thickness, 32, 143, 145-146, 148, 151, 154
vacuum, 286
Gap spacing, piston ring, 165
Gases, 43-45

Index

artificial, 340
natural, 340
Gaskets, cylinder head, 173
Gasket surface, head, 197
Gasoline, 9
  additives, 338
  characteristics of, 334-338
  tank, 9
Gear and crescent oil pump, 268-270
Gear, camshaft, press-on, replacing, 212-213
Gear, crankshaft, replacing, 213
Gear driven camshaft, 185-186
Gears, timing, 211-213
Gear type oil pump, 267
General Motors Controlled Combustion System (CCS), 290
Goggles, 13, 19, 28
Graphite, 76
Gray iron, 76, 79
Grinder, valve seat, 200
Grinding, 80
Grooved piston rings, 165
Grooves, piston ring, 142
  remachining, 147-148
  worn, 143-144
Guide, valve, 175-176, 179, 206-208
  cleaning, 198
Gums in engine and fuel, 335

H

Hacksaw, 21-22
Hammers, 15-16

Head, cylinder, 195-198
  damage, 197
  warped, 197-198
Head, piston, 120
Heat
  conductivity, 76
  control valve, 351-353
  exchanger, automatic transmission, 235
  piston, 121
  sink, 465-467
  treating, crankshaft, 86
  treating, cylinder block, 79
Helical, timing gears, 186
Heptane, 337
High-speed ignition operation, 453
High-voltage, ignition, 8
Honing, 80
  connecting rod, 159-160
  cylinder, 146
Hood
  safety measure, 9
  scoop, 347
Horizontally opposed engine, 58, 59
Horsepower measurements, engine
  brake, 495-496
  indicated, 496-498
  net, 496
  SAE (Society of Automotive Engineers), 495
Hydraulic
  dynamometer, 496
  fluid, 11
  valve lifter, 192-195
  valve lifter adjustment, 221-223
Hydramatic transmission, 303

Hydrocarbons, 279, 281, 283, 326, 329

I

Icing, carburetor, 414
Idling
  adjusting screw, 370
  fuel mixture adjustment, 428-429
  fuel supply, 369-371, 393-395, 419
  ignition timing, 453
  speed adjustment, 428
  speed solenoid, 296
Ignition
  battery-coil, 445-447
  components, 448-458
  high-voltage, 8
  service, 476-481
  timing procedure, 481-483
  timing factors, 452-453
  timing marks, 95-96
  transistorized, 458-461
  transistorized battery-coil system, 461-465
  trouble-shooting, 472-476
I-head
  engine, 77, 78, 171, 172, 174
  valve arrangement, 59, 60
IMCO (Improved Exhaust Emission Control System), 290
Impact tool, 28
Impact wrench, 28
Impeller, water pump, 235

507

Indicated Horsepower, 496-498
Individual cylinders, 79, 228
Inertia forces, piston, 119
Infra-red tester, 321
Inhibitors, antioxidant, 338
Initial timing, ignition, 483
Injection, fuel, 73
Injector, fuel, 282
Inlet tank, radiator, 232
In-line engine, 56, 57, 85
  crankarm arrangement, 64-65
  four-cylinder, 62, 64
  six-cylinder, 56, 57, 65
Insert main bearing, replaceable, 95
  installing, 110
Insert, valve seat, replacing, 203
Inside micrometer, 30
Inspection
  connecting rod, 151
  oil pressure relief valve, 276-277
  oil pump, 275-278
  piston and connecting rod, 142-163
  piston pin, 156-157
  rocker arm, 219
  rocker arm shaft, 219-220
Installation
  piston and rod in cylinder, 165-168
  piston ring, 130-132, 164-165
Intake
  manifold, 49, 343-349
  port, Diesel, 73
  stroke, 50, 51, 52, 53, 54, 67-68
  stroke in Wankel engine, 67-88
Internal combustion, 45
Iron, gray, 76
Iso-octane, 337

J

Jacket, water, 79, 230-232
Jacking, 12
Jaws, vise, 27
Journal, bearing, 46

K

Keys, 36
Kinetic energy, 45
Knock, carbon, 332
Knock, fuel, 332
Knock, spark, 332
"Knurlizing", piston, 146-147

L

Lands, piston ring, machining, 125
Lathe, 108
Lead
  compounds, in oil, 264
  in gasoline, 173
  tetraethyl, 11
Lean fuel mixture, 417
L-head engine, 77-78, 169, 171
  valve arrangement, 58-59
Lift, hydraulic, 12
Lifter, valve, 49, 60, 77, 174, 216-224
  hydraulic, 217-218, 223-224
  mechanical, 221-223
Light, strobe, 242
Line-boring main bearing saddles, 110
Liner, cylinder, 79
Lines:
  fuel, 8, 344-345
  oil, 83
Liquid-cooled engines, 170
Liquid cooling, 74
  systems, 228-229
Liquified petroleum gas, 339
Liquids, flammable, 10
Lobe lift, camshaft, 209-211
Locks, valve, 175
Lock washers, 34-35
Lower cylinder block, 83-85
Low-speed ignition operation, 453
LPG (Liquified Petroleum Gas), 339
Lubricants, 10
Lubrication
  cylinder wall, 137
  oil spray, 265
  piston pin, 137
  timing gear, 186

M

Machining
  crankshaft, 86
  cylinder block, 79-80
  piston ring lands, 125
Magnetic pulse distributor, 468-469
Main bearings, 85, 90
  cast, 115
  design for thrust load, 94
  insert type, 95
  materials, 95
  sizes, 114-115
Main fuel supply, carburetor, 371-373, 395
Main metering jets, 372

Index

Maintenance, vapor emission control system, 321-322
Mallets, 15
Manifolds, 9
  intake and exhaust, 49
Manual choke, 380
Marks, timing gear, 185-186
Materials
  camshaft, 183
  connecting rod, 137
  connecting rod bearing, 137-139
  cylinder block, 76
  head gasket, 173
  main bearing, 95
  piston, 123-125
  piston ring, 126
  thermostat, 244
  valve, 177
Measurement, angular, 489
Measuring
  connecting rod side clearance, 154
  crankshaft journals, 109
  out-of-round cylinder, 102
  piston pin, 156-157
  piston ring clearance, 148
Measuring tools
  dial indicator, 31
  micrometer caliper, 29-31, 490-492
  steel rule, 28
  telescoping gage, 30-31
  thickness gage, 32
Mechanical
  efficiency, 499
  fuel pump, 353-356
  vacuum fuel pump, 357

valve lifter and adjustment, 221-223
Mechanism, valve operating, 183-195
Metal deactivators, 338
Metals
  antifriction, 93
  in oil, 264, 265
Metering jets, carburetor, 372
Metering rod adjustment, 438-439
Methods of cooling, 74
Metric to English conversions, 485-488
Micrometer caliper, 29-31, 490-492
Milling, cylinder head, 198
Minutes, in angular measurement, 489
Misalignment, connecting rod, causes of, 162
Modulator, distributor, electronic, 301
Molded camshaft gear, 186
Molecules, 43
Molybdenum, 76
Motor method of octane rating, 337
Muffler, 349-350
Multiple barrel carburetors, 388-400
Multiple carburetion, 401-403
Mushroom valve, 175

N

Narrow valve seats, 200
Natural gas, 326, 340
Needle valve, 366, 368
Net Horsepower, 496
N-Hexane, 321
Nickel, 76

Nitrogen, 330
NO_x system, 299
Notches, piston, 120
Nuts, 33

O

Octane
  number, 335
  rating, 335-338
Off-center, valve lifter, 189-190
Offset
  connecting rod bearing, 136-137
  piston boss, 121
Oil
  classification of, 261-262
  engine, 10, 259-265
  factors in, 260-262
  pressure relief valve, 276
  pressurized, 87
  silicone base, 240
Oil clearance, connecting rod bearing, 139
Oil control, piston rings, 128
Oil filter
  disposable, replacing, 277
  types, 271-274
Oil holes
  connecting rod, 151
  piston pin, 151
Oil lines, 83
Oil pan service, 278
Oil passages, crankshaft, 86
Oil pump, 83, 267-271
Oil seal
  timing gear cover, 215-216
  valve, 179-181

Oil spray lubrication, 265
Oil strainer, inspection, 276
Open-end wrenches, 23
Operating mechanism, valve, 183-195
Opposed
 cylinders, 58, 59
 engine, 58, 59
 engine crankshaft, 92
 six-cylinder engine, 85
Outlet tank, radiator, 232
Out-of-round
 connecting rod, 151
 crankpin, 154
 crankshaft journal, 95
 cylinder, 80, 82, 102
 valve seats, 200
Overhead camshaft, 184
Oversize piston rings, 148
Oxidation, oil, 263
Oxides of nitrogen, 279-280, 281
Oxygen in coolant, 249

P

Paints, 11
Pan, oil, 274-275
 service, 278
Parallel surfaces, cylinder block, 80
Particulate matter, 281
Parts, cleaning, 37-42
Part-throttle ignition operation, 453
Passages, water, 183
PCV (Postive Crankcase Ventilation), 280

"peening" piston, 146
Petroleum gas, liquified, 339
Phosphorous compounds, 338
Pilot bearing, clutch, 116, 117
"Ping", 332
Pinned piston ring, 128
Pin, piston, 46, 155-161
 alloy steel, 126
 methods of retaining, 126, 127
 sizes, 158
Pins, cotter, 34
Piston, 45, 46, 49, 52, 53, 79, 85, 119-125
 aluminum alloy, 123, 124
 and connecting rod assembly, 127, 163-164
 and cylinder clearance, 123, 124-125, 145-147
 boss, 46
 displacement, 493-495
 expanding process, 146
 head, 120
 inspection and repair, 142-148
 "knurlizing", 146-147
 materials, 123-124
 notches, 120
 ribs, 120-121
 scoring, 128
 scuffing, 128, 143
 seized, 226
 skirts, 122-123, 144-145
 thrust, 82, 121, 122
 types of, 124, 125
Piston pin, 46, 126, 127, 155-161
 alloy steel, 126
 bushing, 137

 fitting, 157-160
 lubrication, 137
 removal, 141
 retainers, 126, 127
Piston ring, 126-135, 148-150
 compressor tool, 166
 compression type, 130-132
 concentric, 128
 distortion, 164
 end clearance, 148 149, 150
 expander tool, 141
 gap, 128, 150
 grooves, 142-144
 installation, 132, 164-165
 machining lands, 125
 materials, 126
 oil control, 128, 132-135
 pinned, 128
 plated, 126-127
 pressure, 83, 129
 remachining grooves, 147-148
 removal, 140-141
 segmented, 124
 side clearance, 148
 sizes, 148
 staggered gap, 128
 unit pressure, 130
Pitch, thread, 34
Plain tube, carburetor, 365
Plastigage, 112, 153-154
Plated piston rings, 126-127
Pliers, 16
Plugs, spark, 456-458, 477-478
Points, ignition contact, 468
Poppet valve, 175
Port, Diesel exhaust, 74
Ported vacuum switch

Index

(PVS), 294, 295-296
Port, valve, 169, 174
Positive Crankcase Ventilation, (PCV), 280, 283-288
Power
 choke, 282
 equipment, 13
 fuel supply, carburetor, 373-376, 395-396, 419
 impulses at flywheel, 95
 measurements, engine, 493-500
 overlap, 87, 91, 92
 stroke, 50, 52, 53, 54, 67-68, 82
 stroke in Wankel engine, 67-68
 tools, 27-28
 valve, carburetor, 373-375, 419
Press, arbor, 108
Press-on camshaft gear, replacing, 212-213
Pressure
 atmospheric, 43-45, 51
 gage, 255-256
 increase in cylinder, 332
 oiling of crankshaft, 86, 87
 piston ring, 83, 129
 relief valve, oil, 271, 276-277
 type of cooling system, 245-247
Pressure test
 cooling system, 254-256
 fuel pump, 410
Primary ignition circuit, 447-448, 459-461, 470
 transistors in, 463-465
Profile, cam, 183
Propane, 326, 339
Pulsator, fuel pump chamber, 355-356
Pump, oil, 83, 267-271
 gear and crescent type, 268-270
 gear type, 267
 rotor type, 267-268
Pump, water, 252-253, 235-236
 installation and removal, 252
Punches, 16-18
Pusher
 type of fan, 237
 type of fuel pump, 353
Pushrods, 60, 190-192, 219
PVS (Ported Vacuum Switch), 294, 295-296

R

Radial loads, engine, 93-94
Radiator, 9, 232-235, 253-254
 cap, 9, 246, 256
 flushing, 250, 253-254
 tank, 171
Ram air intake, 347
Ratio, compression, 494-495
Reamers
 expansion and solid type, 25-26
 cylinder ridge, 103
Reaming
 connecting rod, 158
 cylinder ridge, 103
Reboring
 connecting rod, 155
 cylinder, 102-103
Receiving unit, fuel gage, 341-342
Refacing valves and valve seats, 199-200
Refrigerant-12, 11
Regrinding crankshaft journals, 109
Relay, cold start, 468
Remachining ring grooves, 147-148
Removable cylinder head, 85
Removal
 piston pin, 141
 piston ring, 140-141
Repair
 carburetor, 423-427
 connecting rod, 163
 fuel pump, 411-412
 fuel tank, 406-407
 oil pump, 275-278
 piston and connecting rod, 142-163
Replaceable insert bearing, 95
Replacement
 connecting rod bushing, 160-161
 oil filter, 277-278
 oil pump, 276
 valve guide, 207
 valve lifter, 216
Research method of octane rating, 337
Resistance unit, ignition coil, 449-450
Resistor, base-emitter, 467
Resonator, 351
Resurfacing cylinder block, 100
Retainers, piston pin, 126
Rheostat, 341

511

Ribs, piston, 120-121
Rich fuel mixture, 416-417
Ridge, cylinder, 83
  removing with ridge reamer, 103
Ring gear, 97
  damage to, 116
Ring, piston (see "piston ring")
Ring, snap, 36
Road tests, 11
Rocker arms, 60, 190-192
  assembling and assembly, 219-220
  inspection, 219-220
  shaft and springs, 355
Rod, connecting, 46, 47, 150-155
  alignment, 161-163
  bearing sizes, 154-155
Roots type blower, 73
Rotating combustion engine, 66-68
Rotation, valve, 181-182
Rotator, valve, 182
Rotor, distributor, 452
Rotor, in Wankel engine, 66-68
Rule, steel, 28

S

SAE
  horsepower rating, 495
  oil viscosity numbers, 261
Safety, 6-14
  battery acid, 10, 15
  capacitor, 450-451, 467
  carburetor, 8
  chemicals, 9
  cleaning solutions, 41

  electrical tools, 13
  exhausts, 9
  fan and belt, 8
  files, 27
  fire, 9
  fire extinguishers, 10
  first aid, 14
  flammable liquids, 10
  fuel lines, 8
  fumes, 11
  gasoline, 9
  gas tank, 9
  goggles, 13, 19, 28
  hammers, 15
  heavy lifting, 12
  hydraulic fluid, 11
  hydraulic lift, 12
  ignition high-voltage, 8
  jacking, 12
  lubricants, 10
  manifolds, 9
  oil, 10
  paints, 11
  power equipment, 13
  radiator, 9
  refrigerant-12, 11
  road test, 11
  shields, 13
  shoes, 13
  smoking, 10, 11
  solvents, 11
  tetraethyl lead, 11
  tools, 13
  welding, 10
Salts in coolant, 249
Sand cores, 79
Scale, vernier, 492
Scoop, hood, 347
Scoring, piston, 128, 142, 143
Screwdrivers, 16-17
Screw, idle adjusting, 370
Screws, 33-34
Scuffing, piston, 128, 142, 143

Seals, oil, valve, 179-181
Seasoning, cylinder block, 79
Seat, valve, 177-179, 183, 200-203
Secondary
  fuel system, 397-400
  ignition circuit, 448, 461, 471-472
  throttle adjustment, 442-443
Seconds in angular measurement, 489
Segmented piston ring, 124
Seized piston, 226
Sending unit, fuel gage, 341-343
Sensitivity, gasoline, 337
Sensor, speed, 301, 302
Separate casting, block, 77
Series, thread, 34
Service Manager, duties of, 5
Servicing
  air cleaner, 412-413
  carburetor, 421-423
  cooling system, 248-256
  fuel filter, 407-408
  oil pan, 278
Shields, safety, 13
Shoes, safety, 13
Shop Foreman, opportunities for, 4
Shop safety, 6-14
Shroud, radiator, 228, 230, 253
Side-by-side connecting rods, 136
Side clearance
  connecting rod, 95, 139, 154
  connecting rod bearing, 139

Index

piston ring, 148
Side-draft, carburetor, 366
Silicone base oil, 240
Single cut files, 26
Sink, heat, 467
Six-cylinder engine, 52, 53, 85
  firing order, 64
  in-line crankshaft, 65, 87-89
  in-line engine, 56-57
  V-type engine, 58
Sizes
  drill, 25
  main bearing, 114-115
  piston pin, 158
  rod bearing, 154-155
  thread, 34
Skirt, piston, 122-123, 142, 144-145
Slap, piston, 121
Sleeves, cylinder, 80-82
  dry type, 81, 82
  wet type, 81
Sludge, oil, 262-265
Smoking, 10, 11
Snap ring, 36
Socket wrenches, 24
Sodium in valve stem, 177
Solenoid
  distributor, 293, 296
  emission control, 387-388
  idle speed, 296-297
  vacuum valve, 299, 301
Solid friction, 259
Solid type reamers, 25-26
Solution
  alcohols, 248
  antifreeze, 247-248
  cleaning, 38-39
  ethylene glycol, 248

Solvents, 11
  cleaning, 40-42, 242
Spark knock, 332
Spark plugs, 456-458, 477-478
Specialty Mechanic, opportunities for, 4
Speed of camshaft, 185, 187
Speed sensor, 301, 302
Splines, 36
Split-skirt piston, 125, 146
Spontaneous combustion, 10
Spray emulsion cleaning, 39
Spring
  rocker arm, 355
  valve, 179-181, 204-205
Spring expander piston rings, 133-134
Sprocket, camshaft, 186
Starting motor, 83
Static crankshaft balance, 92, 93
Steam cleaning, 37-38
Steel rule, 28
Stem, valve
  clearance adjustment, 221-224
  hollow, 177
Step-up rod, carburetor, 375-376
Sticking valve guide, 207-208
Straightening connecting rod, 163
Strainer, oil, 270, 276
Strobe light, 242
Strokes, number of in a cycle, 61-64, 73-74
Studs, 33
Sulfur, 335
Sulfuric acid, 335
Supercharger, 404

Switch
  ignition, 448
  thermal, 301, 302
  thermostatic water temperature, 297
Systems, carburetor, 365-383, 393-396

T

Tables
  air-fuel ratio, 330
  air-fuel ratio under varying conditions, 331
  sludge deposits in crankcase, 263
  connecting rod bearing oil clearances, 155
  decimals-to-inches measurement conversions, 486
  metric-to-English measurement conversions, 487
  piston ring side clearance, 149
  valve stem and guide clearance, 201
Tachometer, 286
Tail pipe, 350-351
Tang, throttle arm, 384
Tank
  fuel, 341
  radiator, 171
Tank cleaning, 39-40
  emulsion type, 39-40
  solvent type, 41
Taper
  crankpin, 154
  crankshaft journal, 95
  cylinder, 80, 82, 100-102
  measuring cylinder for, 100-101

piston ring, 165
Tappet, 195, 221
Taps, 19
TDC (top dead center), 50, 54, 362
Telescoping gage, 30-31
Temperature
  ambient, 228
  of exhaust valve, 183
  of thermostat, 244
Testing
  carburetor, 419
  exhaust emissions, 317-321
  infra-red, 321
  positive crankcase ventilation, 286-288
  pressure cooling system, 245-247
  pressure type radiator cap, 256
  road, 11
  valve spring, 204
Tetraethyl lead, 338
Thermal
  converters, 173
  efficiency, 499-500
  switch, 301, 302
Thermal control drive fan, 238-241
Thermosiphon action, 228-229
Thermostat, 195, 244-245, 253
Thermostatic
  fuel gage, 342-343
  water temperature switch, 297
Thermo-vacuum switch, 290
Thickness gage, 32, 143, 145-146, 148, 151, 154
  blade type, 32
  inspecting connecting rod side clearance

    with, 153-154
  wire type, 32
Threads
  pitch, 34
  series, 34
  sizes, 34
Throttle
  adjustment, secondary, 442-443
  linkage adjustment, 436
  valve, 363-364, 365
Throwout lever, clutch, 117
Thrust
  bearing, 86
  bearing end clearance, 94
  crankshaft, 86
  load, clutch, 94
  main bearing and design, 94
  piston, 82, 121-122
  surface, piston clearance, 125
Timing
  belt, 187-188, 214-215
  chain, 186-187, 213-214
  gear cover oil seal, 215-216
  gears and inspection of, 211-213
  ignition, 481-482
  marks for valves, 95-96, 186
  marks on vibration damper, 97
Tools, 13, 14-32
  box wrenches, 23-24
  chisels, 19
  cutting, 25-26
  dies, 19-20
  drills, 24
  files, 26-27
  hacksaws, 21-22
  hammer, 15

  hand, 14
  impact, 28
  inside micrometer, 30
  mallets, 15
  measuring, 14, 28-32
  micrometer caliper, 29-31, 490-492
  open-end wrenches, 23
  plier, 16
  power, 14, 27-28
  punches, 16-18
  reamers, 25-26
  screwdrivers, 16-17
  screw extractors, 21
  socket wrenches, 24
  steel rule, 28
  taps, 19
  telescoping gage, 30-31
  thickness gage, 32
  torque wrenches, 24
  vise, 19, 27
  wrenches, 22-24
Top dead center (TDC), 50, 54, 121
Toroid, 467
Torque
  engine, 498-499
  value for tightening rod bearing cap, 138
  wrench, 24, 215
Torque control drive, 238
Torsional crankshaft vibration, 93
Transistor fundamentals, 462-463, 465-468
Transistorized ignition system, 458-461, 465
Transmission controlled distributor timing system, 289
Troubleshooting

Index

fuel system, 413-418
ignition system, 472-476
T-slot piston, 125, 146
Turbine compressor, 69
Turbine engine, 68-69
Turbocharger, 349
Tubular type, radiator, 232-235
Turbulence, fuel charge, 172
Twin-rotor rotating combustion (Wankel) engine, 67-68
Two-barrel carburetors, 389-390, 401-403
Two-piece piston rings, 133
Two-rotor Wankel engine, 67-68
Two-stroke cycle
compared to four-stroke cycle, 61-64
Diesel engine, 73-74

U

UNC thread, 34
Undercut piston at boss, 121
UNF thread, 34
Unit pressure, piston ring, 129-130
Unleaded gasoline, 281
Unloader, choke, automatic, 384
adjustment, 441-442
Updraft carburetor, 366
U-slot piston, 125-146

V

Vacuum
bypass valve, 294-296
gage, 286-420
ignition advance, 454-456
switch, ported, 294, 295-296
take-off, carburetor, 290
valve, solenoid, 299
Vacuum and mechanical fuel pump, 357
Valve
decelerator, 291, 292-294
diverter, 311, 316
fuel pump, 354-355
needle, 366, 368
vacuum, solenoid, 299
Valve arrangement, 58-62
F-head, 60, 62
I-head, 59, 60
L-head, 58, 59
valve-in-head, 58
Valve-in-head engine, 58, 171
Valve lifters, 49, 60, 216-129
adjustable, 216
guides, 77, 79
hydraulic, 190, 192-195
mechanical, 189, 195
replacing, 216
Valve operating mechanism, 47, 79, 183-195
Valve seat, 77, 200-203
loose, narrow, or wide, 200
Valves, intake and exhaust, 48, 50, 52, 53
burned, 226
cooling, 182-183
face angle, 175
guides, 206-207
refacing, 199
springs, 204-205
timing marks on flywheel, 95-96
warped, 226

Valve stem clearance adjustment, 221-224
with hydraulic lifters, 223-224
with mechanical lifters, 221-223
Vapor
canister, 324
emission control system, 321-324
lock, 335, 414
saver system, 321
separator, 321
Variable speed fan, 238-241
V-blocks, checking chankshaft with, 108
V-8 crankarm arrangement, 65
Ventilation system, crankcase, 275, 282-288
vent tube type, 282-283
Venturi, 363
Vernier scale, 492
Vibration
damper, 98, 99
torsional 97, 98
period, 93
Vise, 19, 27
Voltage drop and checking of, 475-476
Volumetric efficiency, 500
V-type engine, 56-58, 85
crankarm arrangement, 65
cylinder blocks, 79
eight-cylinder crankshafts, 90-92
eight-cylinder engine, 85
six-cylinder crankshafts, 89-90

515

six-cylinder engine, 58

W

Wankel engine, 66-68
Warped cylinder head, 197-198
Warping of valves, 226
Washers, lock, 34-35
Water
  frozen in fuel system, 414-415
  jacket, 70, 230-232
  passages, 183
  pressure cleaning, 38, 39, 40, 42
Water pump, 235-236, 252-253
  installation, 252
  removal, 252
Wear
  connecting rod, 151
  crankshaft journal, 95
  cylinder, 82, 83, 102
  piston ring grooves, 143-144
  timing chain, 213-214
Welding, 10
Wetting agent, 38
Wet type cylinder sleeve, 81
Wide valve seats, 200
Wire type thickness gage, 32
Worn piston ring grooves, 143-144
Wrenches, 22-24
  box, 24
  impact, 28
  open-end, 23
  socket, 24
  torque, 24
Wrist pin, 126

Z

Zener diode, 466

Harmony High School Library
R. R. #1 Westover, Pa.